Java

Object Oriented Programming in

Vol-1

V.K. Jain
BE, M.TECH, FIE FIETE, MISHRAE
CHARTERED ENGINEER
&
HEMLATA

CYBER TECH PUBLICATIONS
4230/1, First Floor, Ansari Road, Darya Ganj
New Delhi 110002 Ph. : 3244078

JAVA OBJECT ORINTED PROGRAMMING

First Edition 2026

Published by :
Parikshit Rawat for Cyber Tech Publication
4230/1, Ansari Road, Daryaganj,
New Delhi-110 002

Printed at :
Tanwar Printers, Maujpur, Delhi-110053. Ph.: 2195710

FROM AUTHOR'S DESK

Java is a network-oriented programming language invented by Sun Microsystems that is specifically designed for writing programs that can be safely downloaded to your computer through the Internet and immediately run without fear of viruses or other harm to your computer or files. Using small Java programs (called "Applets"), Web pages can include functions such as animations, calculators, and other fancy tricks.

You can expect to see a huge variety of features added to the Web using Java, since you can write a Java program to do almost anything a regular computer program can do, and then include that Java program in a Web page. Therfore learning Java is a must for all students. Java is a need and craze in present day programming environment and is straight forward in the sense that no previous experience is required.

A vast amount of curriculum exists at different levels. Contents have been included in such a manner that needs of almost are available syllabee are fulfilled.

Department of electronics and Computer Society of India together has done a great service to nation by way of accrediting the courses and thus prescribing the syllabi for different levels. This book has been written exactly as per syllabus of DOEACC syllabus for "A" level Examination.Keeping in view the diversified syllabus prescribed by DOEACC every possible efforts have been made to present entire textware in concised form and allout effrts had been made by the author to present the contents commensurate with latest available knowledge on this subjectware. The authors have tried to make the textware as simple as possible.The book is full of Examples and illustrations including real life examples.

The various facaades of computer science are changing its attributes with such a fast speed that its very difficult to keep track of latest development and its a great task to get aware with the latest happenings in the field. Therefore in presenting the state-of-the art textware, immense help had been sought by the authors from various literature forms who in turn expresses his gratitude to the authors of the works from where information has been derived.

We are to acknowledge with great sense of gratitude to Mrs. Heera Jain, Consultant Engineer Amitabh Bajaj BE and Naveena Bajaj M.Sc., Anurag Jain Director NICT (Vikas Marg Branch) and Shree TP Gupta of Compographic for the great help provided in manuscripting and in preperation of the figures etc.

Any suugestions in direction of improving the textware may be forwarded at following address and shall be highly welcome and acknowledged.

Ms. Hemlata
B.A.
Java Programmer
24.3.2001

Er. V.K.Jain
B.E., M.Tech, FIE, FIETE
MISHRAE
Chartered Engineer
11 LF Tansen Marg, N. Delhi.
Tel. 3316697, 3711906

Contents

1

Introduction to Java

1.1 Java

Java is a programming language for Internet (World Wide Web) and intranet applications from the JavaSoft division of Sun. Java was modeled after C++, and Java programs can be called from within HTML documents or launched stand alone. The first Web browsers to run Java applications were Sun's HotJava and Netscape's Navigator 2.0. Java was designed to run in small amounts of memory and provides its own memory management.

Java (with a capital J) is a high-level, third generation programming language, like C, Fortran, Smalltalk, Perl, and many others. You can use Java to write computer applications that crunch numbers, process words, play games, store data or do any of the thousands of other things computer software can do.

Java was originally developed in 1991 as a language for embedded applications such as those used in set-top boxes and other consumer-oriented devices. It became the fuel to ignite a revolution in thinking when Sun transitioned it to the Web in 1994. Unlike HTML, which is a document display format that has been matched up with a variety of interfaces and plug-ins, Java is a full-blown programming language like C and C++. It allows for the creation of sophisticated client/server applications to be developed for the Web and for intranets.

Java, formerly known as oak, is an object-oriented programming language developed by Sun. It shares many superficial similarities with C, C++, and Objective C (for instance for loops have the same syntax in all four languages); but it is not based on any of those languages, nor have efforts been made to make it compatible with them.

Java is sometimes referred to as C++ ++ —. The language was originally created because C++ proved inadequate for certain tasks. Since the designers were not burdened with compatibility with existing languages, they were able to learn from the experience and mistakes of previous object-oriented languages. They added a few things C++ doesn't have like garbage collection and multithreading; and they threw away C++ features that had proven to be better in theory than in practice like multiple inheritance and operator overloading. (There's still argument over whether they made the right choices. I tend to think they were correct to throw out operator overloading and probably correct to throw out multiple inheritance. For now let's just say that neither choice is likely to be reviewed soon.)

Even more importantly Java was designed from the ground up to allow for secure execution of code across a network, even when the source of that code was untrusted and possibly malicious. This required the elimination of more features of C and C++. Most notably there are no pointers in Java. Java programs cannot (at least in theory) access arbitrary addresses in memory.

Furthermore Java was designed not only to be cross-platform in source form like C, but also in compiled binary form. Since this is frankly impossible across processor architectures, Java is compiled to an intermediate byte-code which is interpreted on the fly by the Java interpreter. Thus to port Java programs to a new platform all that is needed is a port of the interpreter and a few native code libraries.

Finally Java was designed to make it a lot easier to write bug free code. Shipping C code has, on average, one bug per 55 lines of code. About half of these bugs are related to memory allocation and deallocation. Thus Java has a number of features to make bugs less common:

- Strong Typing
- No unsafe constructs
- The language is small so its easy to become fluent.
- The language is easy to read and write. Obfuscated Java isn't nearly as common as obfuscated C.
- There are no undefined or architecture dependent constructs.
- Java is object oriented so reuse is easy.
- Java has concurrency.

1.1.1 Where did Java come from?

In the late 1970's Bill Joy thought about doing a language that would merge the best features of MESA and C. However other projects (like cofounding Sun) intervened. In the late 1980's he got Sun's engineers started on a complete revision of the UNIX operating system that involved merging SunOS4.x with AT&T's SYSVR4.

In 1989 Joy sold his Sun stock, invested heavily in Microsoft and moved out of mainstream Sun to Aspen, Colorado. By the early 90's Bill was getting tired of huge programs. He decided that he wanted to be able to write a 10,000 line program that made a difference. In late 1990 Bill wrote a paper called Further which outlined his pitch to Sun engineers that they should produce an object environment based on C++. Today Joy freely admits that C++ was too complicated and wasn't up to the job.

Around this time James Gosling (of emacs fame) had been working for several months on an SGML editor called "Imagination" using C++. The Oak language (now Java) grew out of Gosling's frustration with C++ on his "Imagination" project.

Patrick Naughton, then of Sun, now vice-president of technology at StarWave, started the Green Project on December 5th, 1990. Naughton defined the project as an effort to "do fewer things better". That December he recruited Gosling and Mike Sheridan to help start the project. Joy showed them his Further paper, and work began on graphics and user interface issues for several months in C.

In April of 1991 the Green Project (Naughton, Gosling and Sheridan) settled on smart consumer electronics as the delivery platform, and Gosling started working in earnest on Oak. Gosling wrote the original compiler in C; and Naughton, Gosling and Sheridan wrote the runtime-interpreter, also in C. Oak was running its first programs in August of 1991. Joy got his first demos of the system that winter, when Gosling and Naughton went skiing at Joy's place in Aspen.

By the fall of 1992 "*7", a cross between a PDA and a remote control, was ready This was demoed to Scott McNealy, Sun's president, in October. He was blown away. Following that the Green Project was set up as First Person Inc., a wholly owned Sun subsidiary.

In early 1993 the Green team heard about a Time-Warner request for proposal for a settop box operating system. First Person quickly shifted focus from smart consumer electronics (which was proving to be more hype than reality) to the set-top box OS market, and placed a bid with Time-Warner.

Fortuitously, Sun lost the bid. The Time-Warner project went nowhere, the same place it probably would have gone if Sun had won the bid. First Person continued work on settop boxes until early 1994, when it concluded that like smart consumer electronics settop boxes were more hype than reality.

Without a market to be seen First Person was rolled back into Sun in 1994. However around this time it was realized that the requirements for smart consumer electronics and settop box software (small, platform independent secure reliable code) were the same requirements for the nascent web.

For a third time the project was redirected, this time at the web. A prototype browser called WebRunner was written by Patrick Naughton in one weekend of inspired hacking. After additional work by Naughton and Jonathan Payne this browser became HotJava. The rest, as they say, is history.

Information in this section is primarily based on the first hand accounts of Bill Joy and Patrick Naughton (which don't always agree). No doubt other people have still different memories of what occurred. If you've got any more first hand information about what went on in the Green project I'd like to hear from you.

World Wide Web uses Java but not necessarily. Java is a programming language. When work began on what has become Java, the World Wide Web was just getting started at CERN; and Mosaic wasn't even a glint in Marc Andreesen's eye. The original use of the Java language (settop boxes) required security and the ability to execute code from untrusted hosts. It turns out these are virtually the same requirements for allowing people to download and run programs from the Web. No other language has the built-in security of Java. The key here is the security features. The object-oriented nature of Java is secondary, and mainly reflects the preferences and prejudices of the developers who set out to write a secure language. The C-like syntax of the language is even less crucial.

1.2 Java Was Designed to be Interpreted

Java programs are downloaded into the user's machine and run by the Java interpreter. In a client/server Web application, the server software may be written in a compiled language for highest speed since it serves multiple users.

Java is an interpreted language that uses an intermediate language. The source code of a Java program is compiled into "byte code," which cannot be run by itself. The byte code must be converted into machine code at runtime. Upon finding a Java applet, the Web browser switches to its Java interpreter (Java Virtual Machine) which translates the byte code into machine code and runs it. This means Java programs are not dependent on any specific hardware and will run in any computer with the Java Virtual Machine. On the server side, Java programs can also be compiled into machine language for fastest performance, but they lose their hardware independence as a result.

Like other programming languages, Java is royalty free to developers for writing applications. However, the Java Virtual Machine, which executes Java applications, is licensed to the companies that incorporate it in their browsers and servers.Java is a full-blown and difficult programming language not intended for the casual programmer and certainly not the end user. JavaScript, on the other hand, is a script language from Netscape that is somewhat easier to use, but not as powerful. JavaScript uses the HTML page as its user interface, whereas Java can display a completely customized interface like C and C++.

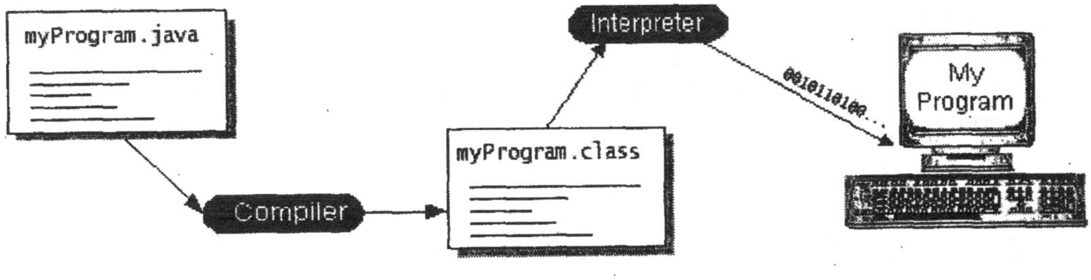

Fig. 1.1 : Java Compilation and Interpretation

1.3 Java as Multimedia Environment : An Overview

Once the domain of code jockeys only, Java is now accessible to Web developers who don't like to hand code, thanks to several multimedia authoring programs. These programs let you create common Java applets with point-and-click ease.

Of course, Java is only one of several options developers have for building interactivity into pages. These same tasks could be accomplished by writing JavaScript code, or could be handled in any of several proprietary solutions.

Let us review two Java authoring programs, Lotus' JavaBeans and Interleaf's Jamba, as well as Macromedia's Director, to see how they handled a few simple multimedia tasks, such as buttons that activate on rollover or on mouse click, ticker tapes, and animations.

Some of Java's advantages are it runs on most modern browsers (anything from Netscape or Microsoft 3.0 or better) without a plug-in. Everything a user needs to run a Java applet comes with the download, which means applets can be delivered enterprisewide, regardless of platform.

Among Java's many uses is creating multimedia events. A common example of an event is a mouse click, which can trigger an action. Click on a graphic, and a sound plays. A more sophisticated event could be a timer that waits a few moments after a page is loaded, then plays an animation, then loads a different page.

Java multimedia programs are written to appeal not only to programmers, but also to users who don't necessarily want to know how an object is built, just how it can work. Most offer prebuilt Java objects and samples, and many offer wizards to make creating Java as easy as a point and click.

Lotus BeanMachine, Interleaf Jamba, and Macromedia Director all let you create various multimedia objects and save them as Java. Director, which is more commonly associated with creating Shockwave animations, differs from the other two programs in that it's a high-end all-purpose tool for creating sophisticated multimedia titles that can be delivered to a variety of media, including the Web.

Using these tools, we'll give you an idea how easy it is to create some common objects such as interactive events, rollovers, and ticker tapes. We'll also touch on how complex you can get when using a program such as Director to create multimedia Web titles.

1.4 A Simple Program

The computer age is here to stay. Households and businesses all over the world use computers in one way or another because computers help individuals and businesses perform a wide range of tasks with speed, accuracy, and efficiency. Computers can perform all kinds of tasks ranging from running an animated 3D graphics application with background sound to calculating the number of vacation days you have coming to handling the payroll for a Fortune 500 company.

When you want a computer to perform tasks, you write a program. A program is a sequence of instructions that define tasks for the computer to execute. This lesson explains how to write, compile, and run a simple program written in the JavaTM language (Java program) that tells your computer to print a one-line string of text on the console.

But before you can write and compile programs, you need to understand what the Java platform is, and set your computer up to run the programs.

1.4.1 A Word About the Java Platform

The Java platform consists of the Java application programming interfaces (APIs) and the Java1 virtual machine (JVM). Java APIs are libraries of compiled code that you can use in your programs.

They let you add ready-made and customizable functionality to save you programming time.

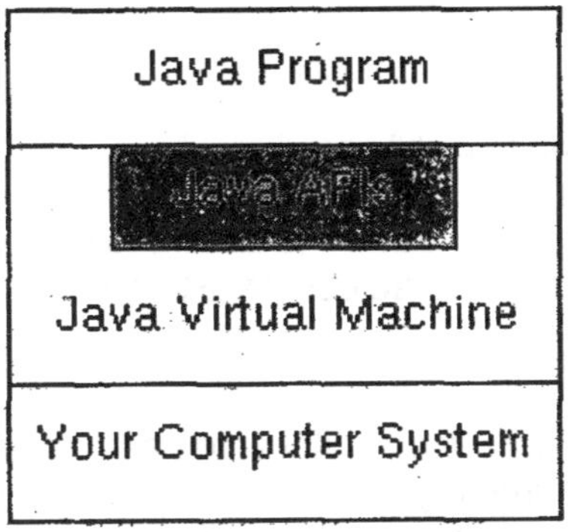

The simple program in this lesson uses a Java API to print a line of text to the console. The console printing capability is provided in the API ready for you to use; you supply the text to be printed.

Java programs are run (or interpreted) by another program called the Java VM. If you are familiar with Visual Basic or another interpreted language, this concept is probably familiar to you. Rather than running directly on the native operating system, the program is interpreted by the Java VM for the native operating system. This means that any computer system with the Java VM installed can run Java programs regardless of the computer system on which the applications were originally developed.

For example, a Java program developed on a Personal Computer (PC) with the Windows NT operating system should run equally well without modification on a Sun Ultra workstation with the Solaris operating system, and vice versa.

1.4.2 Setting Up Your Computer

Before you can write and run the simple Java program in this lesson, you need to install the Java platform on your computer system.

The Java platform is available free of charge from the java.sun.com web site..You can choose between the Javar 2 Platform software for Windows 95/98/NT or for Solaris. The download page contains the information you need to install and configure the Java platform for writing and running Java programs.

Note: Make sure you have the Java platform installed and configured for your system before you try to write and run the simple program presented next.

1.4.3 Writing a Program

The easiest way to write a simple program is with a text editor. So, using the text editor of your choice, create a text file with the following text, and be sure to name the text file ExampleProgram.java. Java programs are case sensitive, so if you type the code in yourself, pay particular attention to the capitalization.

Example 1.1

```
//A Simple Example
class ExamProgram
{
    public static void main(String[] args){
    System.out.println("Thank you for simple Program");
```

```
}
}
```

Another

```
The Hello World Application
class HelloWorld {
    public static void main (String args[]) {
    System.out.println("Hello World!");
}
}
```

Enter above exactly it is written herewith capitalwards as capital and smallcase letters in small as Java is case sensitive. Make a directory by name temp at C:\ prompt and save this file by name ExamProgram.java in this directory. The sequence of commands shall be as shown below:

```
C:\temp>set path = c:\jdk1.2\bin;

C:\temp>javac ExamProgram.java

C:\temp>java ExamProgram
Thankyou for simple program
```

Fig. 1.2 : Command entries at C:\ prompt for compiling and executing a simple Java Program

Hello World is very close to the simplest program imaginable. When you successfully compile and run it, it prints the words "Hello World!" on your display. Although it doesn't teach very much programming, it gives you a chance to learn the mechanics of typing and compiling code. The goal of this program is not to learn how to print words to the terminal. It's to learn how to type, save and compile a program. This is often a non-trivial procedure, and there are a lot of things that can go wrong even if your source code is correct.

To write the code you need a text editor. You can use any text editor like Notepad, Brief, emacs or vi. Personally I use BBEdit on the Mac and TextPad on Windows.

You should not use a word processor like Microsoft Word or WordPerfect since these save their files in a proprietary format and not in pure ASCII text. If you absolutely must use one of these, be sure to tell it to save your files as pure text. Generally this will require using Save As... rather than Save. If you have an integrated development environment like Symantec's Cafe or Natural Intelligence's Roaster, that will include a text editor you can use to edit Java source code. It will probably change your words various colors and styles for no apparent reason. Don't worry about this yet. As long as the text is correct you'll be fine.

When you've chosen your text editor, type or copy the above program into a new file. For now type it exactly as it appears here. Like C and unlike Fortran, Java is case sensitive so System.out.println is not the same as system.out.println. CLASS is not the same as class, and so on.

However, white space is not significant except inside string literals. The exact number of spaces or tabs you use doesn't matter.

Save this code in a file called HelloWorld.java. Use exactly that name including case. Congratulations! You've written your first Java program.

1.4.4 Saving Files on Windows

Some Windows text editors including Notepad add a three letter ".txt" extension to all the files they save without telling you. Thus you can unexpectedly end up with a file called "HelloWorld.java.txt."

This is wrong and will not compile. If your editor has this problem, you should get a better editor. However in the meantime enclose the filename in double quotes in the Save dialog box to make editor save the file with exactly the name you want.

1.4.5 Compiling and Running Hello World

To make sure your Java environment is correctly configured, bring up a command-line prompt and type

```
javac nofile.java
```

If your computer responds with

```
error: Can't read: nofile.java
```

you're ready to begin. If, on the other hand, it responds

```
javac: Command not found
```

or something similar, then you need make sure you have the Java environment properly installed and your PATH configured.

Assuming that Java is properly installed on your system there are three steps to creating a Java program:

- writing the code
- compiling the code
- running the code

Under Unix, compiling and running the code looks like this:

```
% javac HelloWorld.java
% java HelloWorld
Hello World
%
```

Under Windows, it's similar. You just do this in a DOS shell.

```
C:> javac HelloWorld.java
C:> java HelloWorld
Hello World
C:>
```

Notice that you use the .java extension when compiling a file, but you do not use the .class extension when running a file.

On the Mac, you compile files by dragging and dropping them onto the compiler.

for loops

```
class Count {
    public static void main (String args[]) {
    int i;
    for (i = 0; i < 50; i=i+1) {
    System.out.println(i);
    }
}
}
```

Example.

Variable declaration inside for loop.

```
class Count {
public static void main (String args[]) {
for (int i = 0; i < 50; i = i+1) {
System.out.println(i);
}
}
}
```

1.4.6 Compiling the Program

A program has to be converted to a form the Java VM can understand so any computer with a Java VM can interpret and run the program. Compiling a Java program means taking the programmer-readable text in your program file (also called source code) and converting it to bytecodes, which are platform-independent instructions for the Java VM.

The Java compiler is invoked at the command line on Unix and DOS shell operating systems as follows:

```
javac ExampleProgram.java
```

Note: Part of the configuration process for setting up the Java platform is setting the class path. The class path can be set using either the -classpath option with the javac compiler command and java interpreter command, or by setting the CLASSPATH environment variable. You need to set the class path to point to the directory where the ExampleProgram class is so the compiler and interpreter commands can find it. See Java 2 SDK Tools for more information.

1.4.7 Interpreting and Running the Program

Once your program successfully compiles into Java bytecodes, you can interpret and run applications on any Java VM, or interpret and run applets in any Web browser with a Java VM built in such as Netscape or Internet Explorer. Interpreting and running a Java program means invoking the Java VM byte code interpreter, which converts the Java byte codes to platform-dependent machine codes so your computer can understand and run the program.

The Java interpreter is invoked at the command line on Unix and DOS shell operating systems as follows:

```
java ExampleProgram
```

At the command line on your screen , you should see:

```
I'm a Simple Program
```

1.5 Code Comments

Code comments are placed in source files to describe what is happening in the code to someone who might be reading the file, to comment-out lines of code to isolate the source of a problem for debugging purposes, or to generate API documentation. To these ends, the Java language supports three kinds of comments: double slashes, C-style, and doc comments.

1.5.1 Double Slashes

Double slashes (//) are used in the C++ programming language, and tell the compiler to treat everything from the slashes to the end of the line as text.

Example 1.2

//A Very Simple Example

```
    class ExampleProgram {
    public static void main(String[] args){
    System.out.println("I'm a Simple Program");
    }
}
```

1.5.2 C-Style Comments

The second is the traditional C-style comment that was inherited by C++. These comments begin with a /* and continue, possibly across many lines, until a */. Note that many programmers will begin each line of a continued comment with a *, so you'll often see:

```
This is
A comment that continues
Across lines
/
```

Remember, however, that everything inside the /* and */ is ignored so it's no different to say:

/* This is a comment that continues across lines */

The second form of comment comes from C++. It is the single-line comment, which starts at a // and continues until the end of the line. This type of comment is convenient and commonly used because it's easy. You don't need to hunt on the keyboard to find / and then * (you just press the same key twice), and you don't need to close the comment. So you will often see:

```
// this is a one-line comment
```

Instead of double slashes, you can use C-style comments (/* */) to enclose one or more lines of code to be treated as text.

- These are C-style comments

```
*/
    class ExampleProgram {
    public static void main(String[] args){
    System.out.println("I'm a Simple Program");
    }
}
```

1.5.3 Doc Comments

To generate documentation for your program, use the doc comments (/** */) to enclose lines of text for the javadoc tool to find. The javadoc tool locates the doc comments embedded in source files and uses those comments to generate API documentation.

Example 1.3

```
/** This class displays a text string at
*  the console.
*/
class ExampleProgram
{
public static void main(String[] args)
{
System.out.println("I'm a Simple Program");
}
}
```

With one simple class, there is no reason to generate API documentation. API documentation makes sense when you have an application made up of a number of complex classes that need documentation. The tool generates HTML files (Web pages) that describe the class structures and contain the text enclosed by doc comments. The javadoc Home Page has more information on the javadoc command and its output.

1.6 API Documentation

The Java platform installation includes API Documentation, which describes the APIs available for you to use in your programs. The files are stored in a doc directory beneath the directory where you installed the platform. For example, if the platform is installed in /usr/local/java/jdk1.2, the API Documentation is in /usr/local/java/jdk1.2/doc/api.

1.7 Java Program Development With Class

To create Java applications, we will follow these steps:

1. Create a class diagram in With Class.
2. Generate Java code from the class diagram using a script, e.g. JAVBASIC.SCT.
3. Open the generated Java code in a Java Editor
4. Compile the generated code from the Java Editor using the Sun Java Development Kit
5. Execute the Java code from the Java Development Kit (JDK) or an HTML Web page.
6. After modifying the Java code in Java Editor, reverse engineer the code in With Class to create a reversed class diagram.

1.8 Creating Another JAVA Program

To create your first Java program, launch your Java Editor. Configure the editor to be able to find the Java Compiler, e.g. C:\Java\Bin\javac.exe. Enter the following code in the editor.

Example 1.4

```
class Hello
{
    public static void main ( String args[])
    {
    System.out.println ("Hello World");
}
}
```

Then select the File - Save Document to save the Java file, e.g. hello.java. To compile the file, select Run -Compile Document menu item or click on the Compile icon. In the Dick Chase Java Editor shown below, click the coffee cup icon in the upper toolbar to compile. To execute the program, select Run and enter c:\java\bin\java hello.

1.9 Using With Class to Create a Class Diagram and Generate Java Code

To create your first Java program in With Class, launch With Class and set the Utilities - Preferences to Java. Create the class diagram, counter.omt. Select the class icon or Draw - Class. Place the class on the diagram. Enter the class name Counter. Enter the attribute currentValue. Enter the operation names Increment, Decrement, and GetValue. To generate Java code select Utilities - Generate Code per File. Select Java. If neceasary, select Browse to find the script file javbasic.sct. To view the generated code counter.java, select File - Edit File and open counter.java. Then open the Java editor and open counter.java. Compile counter.java in the Java Editor to create counter.class.

Then run the program from the Java Editor. Alternatively, run the program from the DOS command prompt with the command java counter.

Once you have created the class diagram, double click on the class to bring up the Class Form shown below. In the Class Form, click on the Spec Button to update the class specification shown below. The Counter class is a normal class. It is not an abstract or final class. It is not an interface. To indicate packages or classes to be imported select the Include Button to enter a package or class to be imported, e.g. java.util.*.

On the Class Form, double click on the attribute to bring up the Attribute Specification. Enter the Attribute Type, e.g. int, Attribute Visibility, e.g. private, and the Attribute Initial Value, e.g. 0.

Click on the Code button to bring up the Code Form shown below. Enter Java code for the Increment Operation, e.g. currentValue = currentValue + 1; Later, if you update this code in your Java Editor, you can import the updated code by selecting the Import Java button.

1.10 Creating Your First Java Program with a Java Editor and the Java Development Kit (JDK)

You can create a Java development environment by downloading Java tools from various Web sites. You can download the With Class CASE tool demo version from www.microgold.com. You may download a Java editor by searching for Java Editor. One Java Editor is Dick Chase's Java Editor that can be downloaded from Compuserve in the file javaedit.zip. Another Java Editor is Java Maker by Hee Chang Choi at hcchoi@khgw.info.samsung.co.kr in the file javamake.zip. Another Java Editor is Symantec Caf Lite that can be downloaded from www.symantec.com. You may download the Java Development Kit (JDK) from java.sun.com in the file jdk-1_0_.exe. When you execute the file jdk-1_0_.exe several directories, e.g. c:\java and c:\java\bin are created. You must update your autoexec.bat files with these entries:

```
SET PATH=C:\JAVA;C:\JAVA\BIN;
C:\JAVA\INCLUDE;C:\JAVA\LIB
SET CLASSPATH=.;C:\JAVA\LIB
```

If you get "Cannot Open File" or "Cannot Find File" error messages, you may need to change the CLASSPATH statement so that the JDK can find your files, e.g. SET CLASSPATH=C:\JAVAPROG;C:\JAVA\LIB or SET CLASSPATH=C:\JAVA\LIB\Classes.zip. Do not unzip Classes.zip since the JDK directly uses this file. It is also necessary to have a Windows compression program like WinZip (wnzip.zip) that understands long file names and four character suffixes like program1.java. It is helpful to place DOSKEY in your autoexec.bat file since you may use the DOS command line to compile and execute java programs, e.g. java hello.

1.11 Java Lexical Issues

There are several other issues you must understand before seeing your first Java program.

1.11.1 Name Visibility

A problem in any programming language is the control of names. If you use a name in one module of the program, and another programmer uses the same name in another module, how do you distinguish one name from another and prevent the two names from "clashing"? In C this is a particular problem because a program is often an unmanageable sea of names. C++ classes (on which Java classes are based) nest functions within classes so they cannot clash with function names nested within other classes. However, C++ still allowed global data and global functions, so clashing was still possible. To solve this problem, C++ introduced namespaces using additional keywords.

Java was able to avoid all of this by taking a fresh approach. To produce an unambiguous name for a library, the specifier used is not unlike an Internet domain name. In fact, the Java creators want you to use your Internet domain name in reverse since those are guaranteed to be unique. Since my domain name is BruceEckel.com, my utility library of foibles would be named com.bruceeckel.utility.foibles. After your reversed domain name, the dots are intended to represent subdirectories.

In Java 1.0 and Java 1.1 the domain extension com, edu, org, net, etc., was capitalized by convention, so the library would appear: COM.bruceeckel.utility.foibles. Partway through the development of Java 1.2, however, it was discovered that this caused problems and so now the entire package name is lowercase.

This mechanism in Java means that all of your files automatically live in their own namespaces, and each class within a file automatically has a unique identifier. (Class names within a file must be unique, of course.) So you do not need to learn special language features to solve this problem - the language takes care of it for you.

1.11.2 Using other Components

Whenever you want to use a predefined class in your program, the compiler must know how to locate it. Of course, the class might already exist in the same source code file that it's being called from. In that case, you simply use the class - even if the class doesn't get defined until later in the file. Java eliminates the "forward referencing" problem so you don't need to think about it.

What about a class that exists in some other file? You might think that the compiler should be smart enough to simply go and find it, but there is a problem. Imagine that you want to use a class of a particular name, but the definition for that class exists in more than one file. Or worse, imagine that you're writing a program, and as you're building it you add a new class to your library that conflicts with the name of an existing class.

To solve this problem, you must eliminate all potential ambiguities. This is accomplished by telling the Java compiler exactly what classes you want using the import keyword. import tells the compiler to bring in a package, which is a library of classes. (In other languages, a library could consist of functions and data as well as classes, but remember that all code in Java must be written inside a class.)

Most of the time you'll be using components from the standard Java libraries that come with your compiler. With these, you don't need to worry about long, reversed domain names; you just say, for example:

```
import java.util.Vector;
```

to tell the compiler that you want to use Java's Vector class. However, util contains a number of classes and you might want to use several of them without declaring them all explicitly. This is easily accomplished by using ' *' to indicate a wildcard:

```
import java.util.*;
```

It is more common to import a collection of classes in this manner than to import classes individually.

1.12 Comment Documentation

One of the thoughtful parts of the Java language is that the designers didn't consider writing code to be the only important activity - they also thought about documenting it. Possibly the biggest problem with documenting code has been maintaining that documentation. If the documentation and the code are separate, it becomes a hassle to change the documentation every time you change the code. The solution seems simple: link the code to the documentation. The easiest way to do this is to put everything in the same file. To complete the picture, however, you need a special comment syntax to mark special documentation and a tool to extract those comments and put them in a useful form. This is what Java has done.

1.12.1 Javdoc

The tool to extract the comments is called javadoc. It uses some of the technology from the Java compiler to look for special comment tags you put in your programs. It not only extracts the information marked by these tags, but it also pulls out the class name or method name that adjoins the comment. This way you can get away with the minimal amount of work to generate decent program documentation.

The output of javadoc is an HTML file that you can view with your Web browser. This tool allows you to create and maintain a single source file and automatically generate useful documentation. Because of javadoc we have a standard for creating documentation, and it's easy enough that we can expect or even demand documentation with all Java libraries. First time readers may ignore the section 1.12.2 hereafter.

1.12.2 Syntax

All of the javadoc commands occur only within /** comments. The comments end with */ as usual. There are two primary ways to use javadoc: embed HTML, or use "doc tags." Doc tags are commands that start with a ` @' and are placed at the beginning of a comment line. (A leading ` *', however, is ignored.)

There are three "types" of comment documentation, which correspond to the element the comment precedes: class, variable, or method. That is, a class comment appears right before the definition of a class; a variable comment appears right in front of the definition of a variable and a method comment appears right in front of the definition of a method. As a simple example:

```
/** A class comment */
public class docTest
{
/** A variable comment */
public int i;
/** A method comment */
public void f() {}
}
```

Note that javadoc will process comment documentation for only public and protected members. Comments for private and "friendly" members are ignored and you'll see no output. (You can use the -private flag to include private members as well.) This makes sense, since only public and protected members are available outside the file, which is the client programmer's perspective. However, all class comments are included in the output.

The output for the above code is an HTML file that has the same standard format as all the rest of the Java documentation, so users will be comfortable with the format and can easily navigate your classes. It's worth entering the above code, sending it through javadoc and viewing the resulting HTML file to see the results.

Embedded HTML

Javadoc passes HTML commands through to the generated HTML document. This allows you full use of HTML; however, the primary motive is to let you format code, such as:

```
/**
* <pre>
* System.out.println(new Date());
* </pre>
*/
```

You can also use HTML just as you would in any other Web document to format the regular text in your descriptions:

```
/**
* You can <em>even</em> insert a list:
* <ol>
* <li> Item one
* <li> Item two
* <li> Item three
* </ol>
*/
```

Note that within the documentation comment, asterisks at the beginning of a line are thrown away by javadoc, along with leading spaces. Javadoc reformats everything so that it conforms to the standard documentation appearance. Don't use headings such as <h1> or <hr> as embedded HTML because javadoc inserts its own headings and yours will interfere with them.

All types of comment documentation - class, variable, and method - can support embedded HTML.

@see: referring to other classes

All three types of comment documentation can contain @see tags, which allow you to refer to the documentation in other classes. Javadoc will generate HTML with the @see tags hyperlinked to the other documentation. The forms are:

@see classname
@see fully-qualified-classname
@see fully-qualified-classname#method-name

1.12.3 Documentation Example

Here is the first Java program again, this time with documentation comments added:

Example 1.4

```
//: Property.java
import java.util.*;
/** The first Thinking in Java example program.
* Lists system information on current machine.
* @author Bruce Eckel
* @author http://www.BruceEckel.com
* @version 1.0
*/
public class Property
{
/** Sole entry point to class & application
* @param args array of string arguments
* @return No return value
* @exception exceptions No exceptions thrown
```

```
*/
public static void main(String[] args)
{
System.out.println(new Date());
Properties p = System.getProperties();
p.list(System.out);
System.out.println("— Memory Usage:");
Runtime rt = Runtime.getRuntime();
System.out.println("Total Memory = "
+ rt.totalMemory()
+ " Free Memory = "
+ rt.freeMemory());
}
} ///:~
The first line:
//: Property.java
```

uses my own technique of putting a ' :' as a special marker for the comment line containing the source file name. The last line also finishes with a comment, and this one indicates the end of the source code listing, which allows it to be automatically extracted from the text of the book and checked with a compiler. This is described in detail in Chapter 17.

1.13 Coding Style

The unofficial standard in Java is to capitalize the first letter of a class name. If the class name consists of several words, they are run together (that is, you don't use underscores to separate the names) and the first letter of each embedded word is capitalized, such as:

```
class AllTheColorsOfTheRainbow { // ...
```

For almost everything else: methods, fields (member variables) and object handle names, the accepted style is just as it is for classes except that the first letter of the identifier is lower case. For example:

```
class AllTheColorsOfTheRainbow
{
int anIntegerRepresentingColors;
void changeTheHueOfTheColor(int newHue)
{
// ...
}
// ...
}
```

Of course, you should remember that the user must also type all these long names, and be merciful.

1.14 Merits of Using Java

At the lowest level the advantage of Java to the web is that it provides a secure, cross-platform way for code to be executed. At a somewhat higher level Java adds several features to existing web sites:

1.14.1 Java is Simple

Java was designed to make it much easier to write bug free code. According to Sun's Bill Joy, shipping C code has, on average, one bug per 55 lines of code. The most important part of helping programmers write bug-free code is keeping the language simple.

Java has the bare bones functionality needed to implement its rich feature set. It does not add lots of syntactic sugar or unnecessary features. Despite its simplicity Java has considerably more functionality than C, primarily because of the large class library.

Because Java is simple, it is easy to read and write. Obfuscated Java isn't nearly as common as obfuscated C. There aren't a lot of special cases or tricks that will confuse beginners.

About half of the bugs in C and C++ programs are related to memory allocation and deallocation. Therefore the second important addition Java makes to providing bug-free code is automatic memory allocation and deallocation. The C library memory allocation functions malloc() and free() are gone as are C++'s destructors.

Java is an excellent teaching language, and an excellent choice with which to learn programming. The language is small so it's easy to become fluent. The language is interpreted so the compile-run-link cycle is much shorter. The runtime environment provides automatic memory allocation and garbage collection so there's less for the programmer to think about. Java is object-oriented unlike Basic so the beginning programmer doesn't have to unlearn bad programming habits when moving into real world projects. Finally, it's very difficult (if not quite impossible) to write a Java program that will crash your system, something that you can't say about any other language.

1.14.2 Java is Object-Oriented

Object oriented programming is the catch phrase of computer programming in the 1990's. Although object oriented programming has been around in one form or another since the Simula language was invented in the 1960's, it's really begun to take hold in modern GUI environments like Windows, Motif and the Mac. In object-oriented programs data is represented by objects. Objects have two sections, fields (instance variables) and methods. Fields tell you what an object is. Methods tell you what an object does. These fields and methods are closely tied to the object's real world characteristics and behavior. When a program is run messages are passed back and forth between objects. When an object receives a message it responds accordingly as defined by its methods.

Object oriented programming is alleged to have a number of advantages including:

- Simpler, easier to read programs
- More efficient reuse of code
- Faster time to market
- More robust, error-free code

In practice object-oriented programs have been just as slow, expensive and buggy as traditional non-object-oriented programs. In large part this is because the most popular object-oriented language is C++. C++ is a complex, difficult language that shares all the obfuscation of C while sharing none of C's efficiencies. It is possible in practice to write clean, easy-to-read Java code. In C++ this is almost unheard of outside of programming textbooks.

1.14.3 Java is Platform Independent

Java was designed to not only be cross-platform in source form like C, but also in compiled binary form. Since this is frankly impossible across processor architectures Java is compiled to an intermediate form called byte-code. A Java program never really executes natively on the host machine. Rather a special native program called the Java interpreter reads the byte code and executes the corresponding native machine instructions. Thus to port Java programs to a new platform all that is needed is to port the interpreter and some of the library routines. Even the compiler is written in Java.

The byte codes are precisely defined, and remain the same on all platforms.

The second important part of making Java cross-platform is the elimination of undefined or architecture dependent constructs. Integers are always four bytes long, and floating point variables follow the IEEE 754 standard for computer arithmetic exactly. You don't have to worry that the meaning of an integer is going to change if you move from a Pentium to a PowerPC. In Java everything is guaranteed.

However the virtual machine itself and some parts of the class library must be written in native code. These are not always as easy or as quick to port as pure Java programs. This is why for example, there's not yet a version of Java 1.1 for the Mac.

1.14.4 Java is Safe

Java was designed from the ground up to allow for secure execution of code across a network, even when the source of that code was untrusted and possibly malicious.

This required the elimination of many features of C and C++. Most notably there are no pointers in Java. Java programs cannot access arbitrary addresses in memory. All memory access is handled behind the scenes by the (presumably) trusted runtime environment. Furthermore Java has strong typing. Variables must be declared, and variables do not change types when you aren't looking. Casts are strictly limited to casts between types that make sense. Thus you can cast an int to a long or a byte to a short but not a long to a boolean or an int to a String.

Java implements a robust exception handling mechanism to deal with both expected and unexpected errors. The worst that an applet can do to a host system is bring down the runtime environment. It cannot bring down the entire system.

Most importantly Java applets can be executed in an environment that prohibits them from introducing viruses, deleting or modifying files, or otherwise destroying data and crashing the host computer. A Java enabled web browser checks the byte codes of an applet to verify that it doesn't do anything nasty before it will run the applet.

However the biggest security problem is not hackers. It's not viruses. It's not even insiders erasing their hard drives and quitting your company to go to work for your competitors. No, the biggest security issue in computing today is bugs. Regular, ordinary, non-malicious unintended bugs are responsible for more data loss and lost productivity than all other factors combined. Java, by making it easier to write bug-free code, substantially improves the security of all kinds of programs.

1.14.5 Java is High Performance

Java byte codes can be compiled on the fly to code that rivals C++ in speed using a "just-in-time compiler." Several companies are also working on native-machine-architecture compilers for Java. These will produce executable code that does not require a separate interpreter, and that is indistinguishable in speed from C++.

While you'll never get that last ounce of speed out of a Java program that you might be able to wring from C or Fortran, the results will be suitable for all but the most demanding applications.

As of January, 1997, the fastest VM, Microsoft's, is about 80% as fast as C++; which is itself only a few percent slower than C or Fortran. (Since January speeds of several VMs including Sun's and Microsoft's have improved but I don't have accurate figures.)

It is certainly possible to write large programs in Java. The HotJava browser, the Java Workshop integrated development environment and the javac compiler are large programs that are written entirely in Java.

1.14.6 Java is Multi-Threaded

Java is inherently multi-threaded. A single Java program can have many different threads executing independently and continuously. Three Java applets on the same page can run together with each getting equal time from the CPU with very little extra effort on the part of the programmer.

This makes Java very responsive to user input. It also helps to contribute to Java's robustness and provides a mechanism whereby the Java environment can ensure that a malicious applet doesn't steal all of the host's CPU cycles.

Unfortunately multithreading is so tightly integrated with Java, that it makes Java rather difficult to port to architectures like Windows 3.1 or the PowerMac that don't natively support preemptive multi-threading.

There is a cost associated with multi-threading. Multi-threading is to Java what pointer arithmetic is to C, that is, a source of devilishly hard to find bugs. Nonetheless, in simple programs it's possible to leave multi-threading alone and normally be OK.

1.14.7 Java is Dynamic(ly linked)

Java does not have an explicit link phase. Java source code is divided into .java files, roughly one per each class in your program. The compiler compiles these into .class files containing byte code. Each .java file generally produces exactly one .class file.

(There are a few exceptions we'll discuss later in the semester, non-public classes and inner classes).

The compiler searches the current directory and directories specified in the CLASSPATH environment variable to find other classes explicitly referenced by name in each source code file. If the file you're compiling depends on other, non-compiled files the compiler will try to find them and compile them as well. The compiler is quite smart, and can handle circular dependencies as well as methods that are used before they're declared. It also can determine whether a source code file has changed since the last time it was compiled.

More importantly, classes that were unknown to a program when it was compiled can still be loaded into it at runtime. For example, a web browser can load applets of differing classes that it's never seen before without recompilation.

Furthermore, Java .class files tend to be quite small, a few kilobytes at most. It is not necessary to link in large runtime libraries to produce a (non-native) executable. Instead the necessary classes are loaded from the user's CLASSPATH.

1.14.8 Java is Garbage Collected

You do not need to explicitly allocate or deallocate memory in Java. Memory is allocated as needed, both on the stack and the heap, and reclaimed by the garbage collector when it is no longer needed. There's no malloc(), free(), or destructor methods.

There are constructors and these do allocate memory on the heap, but this is transparent to the programmer.

1.14.9 Arbitrary Graphics

Java lets the server draw pictures in a window on the client. In theory this allows a web page to do anything a regular program can do by drawing in a window.

1.14.10 Arbitrary Data Types

In practice rather than using graphics primitives to create your desired web page you'd use a graphics program to draw the page and then write a program that could read and display the file formats of that program. Java lets you write content handlers that display any particular data format. This way you can download your data and your data display program rather than downloading a bitmapped snapshot of the display. People are already using this to add sound and animation to web pages. Rather than having to download a file and spawn an external viewer, the viewer is included with the data; and the data is displayed right on the page.

1.14.11 Less Load On The Server

CPU intensive cgi-bin scripts place a large load on a server, particularly at busy sites. With Java you can off-load the calculations to the client's PC. I've written an applet that calculates all possible ram configurations for a given Mac model. However on models with many memory slots the sheer number of permutations can tie up even a fast machine for several hours. Publishing this as a cgi-bin would bring my server to its knees, but by publishing it as a Java applet I can distribute the load across all the machines that want to run it.

1.14.12 More User Interaction

Finally Java allows for more interaction with the user. Java not only allows you to paint arbitrary data on the screen. It also allows you to collect input from the user in the form of mouse clicks, keystrokes and the like. This lets you put almost any application on your web page that doesn't require disk access.

1.15 Java Demerits

1. Java does not support multiple inheritance. Superclasses of a class are indicated with the extends keyword rather than with a :. Methods must be defined inside the class to which they belong. They may not be declared inside the class and defined outside the class as is common in C++.
2. Most Java virtual machines use an inefficient, mark and sweep garbage collector.

1.16 What Platforms does Java run on?

Sun has made a Java Development Kit <http://www.javasoft. com/products/jdk/1.1/index.html> (JDK) available for Sparc and X86 Solaris, Windows NT and Windows 95 Intel. The JDK is free, and most third party ports are based on this.

Sun also published a 1.0.2 JDK for MacOS 7.5 on PowerMacs and 68030 (25 MHz and faster) and 68040 Macs. However it's dropped development for Macs in favor of Apple's own Macintosh Runtime for Java <http://applejava.apple.com/> (MRJ) which is a better option for Mac users. Currently MRJ supports Java 1.0. Java 1.1 support is promised soon.

1.17 C++ and Java

Java is in fact a much easier language to learn than C++. A little further out in left field, it isn't even necessary to know Java to write Java programs. Intermetrics is beta testing an ADA-95 to Java byte code compiler. Other such cross-compilers are probably possible including ANSI Fortran-77, COBOL, and Basic. However the one most people probably want, a C/C++ to Java byte code compiler, is probably not possible due to Java's lack of pointers.

Compared to other programming languages, Java is most similar to C. However although Java shares much of C's syntax, it is not C. Knowing how to program in C or, better yet, C++, will certainly help you to learn Java more quickly, but you don't need to know C to learn Java. Unlike C++ Java is not a superset of C. A Java compiler won't compile C code, and most large C programs need to be changed substantially before they can become Java programs.

What's most special about Java in relation to other programming languages is that it lets you write special programs called applets that can be downloaded from the Internet and played safely within a web browser. Traditional computer programs have far too much access to your system to be downloaded and executed willy-nilly. Although you generally trust the maintainers of various ftp archives and bulletin boards to do basic virus checking and not to post destructive software, a lot still slips through the cracks. Even more dangerous software would be promulgated if any web page you visited could run programs on your system. You have no way of checking these programs for bugs or for out-and-out malicious behavior before downloading and running them.

Java solves this problem by severely restricting what an applet can do. A Java applet cannot write to your hard disk without your permission. It cannot write to arbitrary addresses in memory and thereby introduce a virus into your computer. It should not crash your system.

1.18 Difference Between Javascript and Java

Java and JavaScript are about as closely related as the Trump Taj Mahal in Atlantic City is to the Taj Mahal in India. In other words Java and JavaScript both have the word Java in their names. JavaScript is a programming language from Netscape which is incorporated in their browsers. It is superficially similar to Java in the same way C is similar to Java but differs in all important respects.

Two classes of language features have been removed from C++ to make it Java. These are those language features which make C++ unsafe and those which make it hard to read.

Features removed that make Java easier to read and understand than C++ include #define, typedef, operator overloading, enum, unions and structs.

The main feature removed to make Java safer and more robust than C++ is pointer arithmetic.

Other features removed include global variables, standalone functions (everything is a method), friend functions (Everything in a package is a friend of everything else in the package.) and non-virtual functions.

A number of features have been added to Java to make it safer including true arrays with bounds checking, garbage collection, concurrency, interfaces (from Objective C) and packages. There is no need to explicitly allocate or free memory in Java.

1.19 JAVA Programming Environment

1.19.1 Control Statements

Java contains if, else, for, while, do while and switch statements. The syntax is identical to C's. However all condition tests must return boolean values. Since non-boolean assignment statements and arithmetic statements do not return a boolean value, some of the more obfuscated condition tests in C are prohibited.

1.19.2 Command Line Arguments

Command line arguments are like C's except that argv has become a string array commonly called args and args[0] is the first command line argument, not the name of the program. The other arguments are all shifted one to the left from where they'd be in C or C++.

Example 1.5 Print statements

```
class PrintArgs
{
```

```
    public static void main (String args[])
    {
    for (int i = 0; i < args.length; i++)
    {
    System.out.println(args[i]);
    }
}
}
% java PrintArgs Hello there!
Hello
there!
```

System.out.println() prints its arguments followed by a platform dependent line separator (carriage return (ASCII 13, \r) and a linefeed (ASCII 10, \n) on Windows, linefeed on Unix, carriage return on the Mac) System.err.println() prints on standard err instead.

You can concatenate arguments to println() with a plus sign (+), e.g.

```
System.out.println("There are"+ args.length+"command line arguments");
```

Using print() instead of println() does not break the line. For example,

```
System.out.print("There are ");
System.out.print(args.length);
System.out.print(" command line arguments");
System.out.println();
```

System.out.println() breaks the line and flushes the output. In general nothing will actually appear on the screen until there's a line break character.

Example of Command line arguments

```
class printArgs {
    public static void main (String args[]) {
    for (int i = 0; i < args.length; i++) {
    System.out.println(args[i]);
    }
}
}
```

The name of the class is not included in the argument list

Command line arguments are passed in an array of Strings. The first array component is the zeroth.

For example, consider this invocation:

```
% java printArgs Hello There
args[0] is the string "Hello". args[1] is the string "There".
args.length is 2.
```

All command line arguments are passed as String values, never as numbers. Later you'll learn how to convert Strings to numbers.

1.19.3 White Space

White space consists mostly of the space character that you produce by hitting the space bar on your keyboard and that is commonly used to separate words in sentences. There are four other white space characters in Java, the horizontal tab, the form feed, the carriage return, and the linefeed. Depending on your platform, when you hit the return or enter key, you get either a carriage return (the

Mac), a linefeed (Unix) or both (DOS, Windows, VMS). This produces a hard line break in the source code text.

Outside of String literals Java treats all white space and runs of white space (more than one white space character in immediate succession) the same. It's used to separate tokens, and one space is as good as seven spaces, a tab and two carriage returns. Exactly which white space characters you use is primarily a result of what's convenient for human beings reading the code. The compiler doesn't care.

Inside String and character literals the only white space permitted is the space character. Carriage returns, tabs, line feeds and form feeds must be inserted with special escape sequences like \r, \t, \f, and \n. You cannot break a String across a line like this:

```
String poem = "Mary had a little lamb
whose fleece was white as snow
and everywhere that Mary went
the lamb was sure to go.";
Instead you must use \n and the string concatenation operator, +,
like this:
String poem = "Mary had a little lamb\n" +
"whose fleece was white as snow\n" +
"and everywhere that Mary went\n" +
"the lamb was sure to go.";
```

Note that you can break a statement across multiple lines, you just can't break a String literal.

Also note that \n only works on Unix. You should probably use System.getProperty("line.separator") instead to return the proper line separator string for the platform your program is running on.

Java does not have all the escape sequences C has. Besides those already mentioned it has only \b for backspace, \\ for the backslash character itself.

There are also \u escapes that let you include any Unicode character.

1.19.4 Literals

Literals are pieces of Java source code that mean exactly what they say. For instance "Hello World!" is a String literal and its meaning is the words Hello World!

The string "Hello World!" looks like it's several things; but to the compiler it's just one thing, a String. This is similar to how an expression like 1,987,234 may be seven digits and two commas but is really just one number.

The double quote marks tell you this is a string literal. A string is an ordered collection of characters (letters, digits, punctuation marks, etc.). Although the String may have meaning to a human being reading the code, the computer sees it as no more than a particular set of letters in a particular order. It has no concept of the meaning of the characters. For instance it does not know that "two" + "two" is "four." In fact the computer thinks that "two" + "two" is "twotwo"

The quote marks show where the string begins and ends. However the quote marks themselves are not a part of the string. The value of this string is Hello World!, not "Hello World!" You can change the output of the program by changing Hello World to some other line of text.

A string in a Java program has no concept of italics, bold face, font family or other formatting. It cares only about the characters that compose it. Even if you're using an editor like NisusWriter that lets you format text files, "Hello World!" is identical to "Hello World!" as far as Java is concerned.

char literals are similar to string literals except they're enclosed in single quotes and must have exactly one character. For example 'c' is a char literal that means the letter c.

true and false are boolean literals that mean true and false.

Numbers can also be literals. 34 is an int literal and it means the number thirty-four. 1.5 is a double literal. 45.6, 76.4E8 (76.4 times 10 to the 8th power) and -32.0 are also double literals.

34L is a long literal and it means the number thirty-four. 1.5F is a float literal. 45.6f, 76.4E8F and -32.0F are also float literals.

1.19.5 Identifiers in Java

Identifiers are the names of variables, methods, classes, packages and interfaces. Unlike literals they are not the things themselves, just ways of referring to them. In the HelloWorld program, HelloWorld, String, args, main and System.out.println are identifiers.

Identifiers must be composed of letters, numbers, the underscore _ and the dollar sign $. Identifiers may only begin with a letter, the underscore or a dollar sign.

Each variable has a name by which it is identified in the program. It's a good idea to give your variables mnemonic names that are closely related to the values they hold. Variable names can include any alphabetic character or digit and the underscore _. The main restriction on the names you can give your variables is that they cannot contain any white space. You cannot begin a variable name with a number. It is important to note that as in C but not as in Fortran or Basic, all variable names are case-sensitive. MyVariable is not the same as myVariable. There is no limit to the length of a Java variable name. The following are legal variable names:

```
MyVariable
myvariable
MYVARIABLE
x
i
_myvariable
$myvariable
_9pins
andros
a?d???
OReilly
This_is_an_insanely_long_variable_name_that_just_keeps_going_and_
going_and_going_and_well_you_get_the_idea_The_line_breaks_arent_
really_part_of_the_variable_name_Its_just_that_this_variable_name_
is_so_ridiculously_long_that_it_won't_fit_on_the_page_I_cant_
imagine_why_you_would_need_such_a_long_variable_name_but_if_you_
do_you_can_have_it
```

The following are not legal variable names.

```
My Variable // Contains a space
9pins // Begins with a digit
a+c // The plus sign is not an alphanumeric character
testing1-2-3 // The hyphen is not an alphanumeric character
O'Reilly // Apostrophe is not an alphanumeric character
OReilly_&_Associates // ampersand is not an alphanumeric character
```

Tip: How to Begin a Variable Name with a Number

If you want to begin a variable name with a digit, prefix the name you'd like to have (e.g. 8ball) with an underscore, e.g. _8ball. You can also use the underscore to act like a space in long variable names.

1.19.6 Keywords

Keywords are identifiers like public, static and class that have a special meaning inside Java source code and outside of comments and Strings. Four keywords are used in Hello World, public, static, void and class.

Keywords are reserved for their intended use and cannot be used by the programmer for variable or method names.

There are fifty reserved keywords in Java 1.1. The forty-eight that are actually used in are listed below. Don't worry if the purposes of the keywords seem a little opaque at this point. They will all be explained in much greater detail later.

Keywords Used in Java 1.1

Keyword	Purpose
`abstract`	declares that a class or method is abstract
`boolean`	declares a boolean variable or return type
`break`	prematurely exits a loop
`byte`	declares a byte variable or return type
`case`	one case in a switch statement
`catch`	handle an exception
`char`	declares a character variable or return type class signals the beginning of a class definition
`continue`	prematurely return to the beginning of a loop default default action for a switch statement
`do`	begins a do while loop
`double`	declares a double variable or return type
`else`	signals the code to be executed if an if statement is not true
`extends`	specifies the class which this class is a subclass of
`final`	declares that a class may not be subclassed or that a field or method may not be overridden
`finally`	declares a block of code guaranteed to be executed
`float`	declares a floating point variable or return type
`for`	begins a for loop
`if`	execute statements if the condition is true
`implements`	declares that this class implements the given interface
`import`	permit access to a class or group of classes in a package
`instanceof`	tests whether an object is an instanceof a class
`int`	declares an integer variable or return type
`interface`	signals the beginning of an interface definition
`long`	declares a long integer variable or return type
`native`	declares that a method is implemented in native code
`new`	allocates a new object
`package`	defines the package in which this source code file belongs
`private`	declares a method or member variable to be private

continued...

`protected`	declares a class, method or member variable to be pro tected
`public`	declares a class, method or member variable to be public
`return`	returns a value from a method
`short`	declares a short integer variable or return type
`static`	declares that a field or a method belongs to a class rather than an object
`super`	a reference to the parent of the current object
`switch`	tests for the truth of various possible cases
`synchronized`	Indicates that a section of code is not thread-safe
`this`	a reference to the current object
`throw`	throw an exception
`throws`	declares the exceptions thrown by a method
`transient`	This field should not be serialized
`try`	attempt an operation that may throw an exception
`void`	declare that a method does not return a value
`volatile`	Warns the compiler that a variable changes asynchronously
`while`	begins a while loop

Two other keywords, const and goto, are reserved by Java but are not actually implemented. This allows compilers to produce better error messages if these common C++ keywords are improperly used in a Java program.

true and false appear to be missing from this list. In fact, they are not keywords but rather boolean literals. You still can't use them as a variable name though.

1.19.7 Separators in Java

Separators help define the structure of your program. The separators used in HelloWorld are parentheses, ( ), braces, { }, the period, ., and the semicolon, ;. The table lists the five Java separators (eight if you count opening and closing separators as two).

Separator	Purpose
( )	Encloses arguments in method definitions and calling; ad justs precedence in arithmetic expressions; surrounds cast types and delimits test expressions in flow control state ments
{ }	defines blocks of code and automatically initializes arrays
[ ]	declares array types and dereferences array values
;	terminates statements
,	separates successive identifiers in variable declarations; chains statements in the test, expression of a for loop
.	Selects a field or method from an object; separates pack age names from sub-package and class names

1.19.8 Unicode

Java uses the Unicode character set. Unicode is a two-byte character code set that has characters representing almost all characters in almost all human alphabets and writing systems around the world including English, Arabic, Chinese and more.

Unfortunately many operating systems and web browsers do not handle Unicode. For the most part

Java will properly handle the input of non-Unicode characters. The first 128 characters in the Unicode character set are identical to the common ASCII character set. The second 128 characters are identical to the upper 128 characters of the ISO Latin-1 extended ASCII character set. It's the next 65,280 characters that present problems.

You can refer to a particular Unicode character by using the escape sequence \u followed by a four digit hexadecimal number. For example

`\u00AE`	)	The copyright symbol
`\u0022`	"	The double quote
`\u00BD`	1/2	The fraction 1/2
`\u0394`	?	The capital Greek letter delta
`\u00F8`	x	A little o with a slash through it

You can even use the full Unicode character sequence to name your variables. However chances are your text editor doesn't handle more than basic ASCII very well. You can use Unicode escape sequences instead like this

```
String Mj\u00F8lner = "Hammer of Thor";
```

but frankly this is way more trouble than it's worth.

1.19.9 Java Flow Control

The if statement in Java

All but the most trivial computer programs need to make decisions. They test a condition and operate differently based on the outcome of the test. This is quite common in real life. For instance you stick your hand out the window to test if it's raining. If it is raining then you take an umbrella with you. If it isn't raining then you don't.

All programming languages have some form of an if statement that tests conditions. In the previous code you should have tested whether there actually were command line arguments before you tried to use them.

1.20 The Java Class Library

Java contains an extensive library of pre-written classes you can use in your programs. These classes are divided into groups called packages.

The Java 1.1 packages

```
package java.applet
package java.awt
package java.awt.datatransfer
package java.awt.event
package java.awt.image
package java.awt.peer
package java.beans
package java.io
package java.lang
package java.lang.reflect
package java.math
package java.net
package java.rmi
package java.rmi.dgc
```

```
package java.rmi.registry
package java.rmi.server
package java.security
package java.security.acl
package java.security.interfaces
package java.sql
package java.text
package java.util
package java.util.zip
```

Each package defines a number of classes, interfaces, exceptions, and errors.

Packages can be split into sub-packages. for example, the java.lang package has a sub-package called java.lang.reflect. These are really completely different packages. A class in a sub-package has no more access to a class in the parent package (or vice versa) than it would to a class in a completely different package.

1.20.1 The java.net package

Each package defines a number of classes, interfaces, exceptions, and errors. For example, the java.net package contains these, interfaces, classes, and exceptions:

Interfaces in java.net

- ContentHandlerFactory
- FileNameMap
- SocketImplFactory
- URLStreamHandlerFactory
- Classes in java.net
- ContentHandler
- DatagramPacket
- DatagramSocket
- DatagramSocketImpl
- HttpURLConnection
- InetAddress
- MulticastSocket
- ServerSocket
- Socket
- SocketImpl
- URL
- URLConnection
- URLEncoder
- URLStreamHandler
- Exceptions in java.net
- BindException
- ConnectException
- MalformedURLException
- NoRouteToHostException
- ProtocolException
- SocketException
- UnknownHostException
- UnknownServiceException

1.20.2 Documentation for the Class Library

Javasoft provides a large amount of documentation for the classes, interface's and exceptions in the class library. If you've installed the JDK on your own PC, you'll find this in your JDK directory in docs/api/packages.html You can load that file into a web browser, and peruse the entire library.

If you have not installed the JDK, you can find it online at

`<http://java.sun.com/products/jdk/1.1/docs/api/packages.html>`

Bookmark this URL now!

Reading the documentation for a class in the class library

For example, let's suppose you want to use the URL class in the java.net package. By reading the documentation for the class you discover that it has the following public methods and constructors:

```
public URL(String protocol, String host, int port, String file)
throws MalformedURLException
public URL(String protocol, String host, String file) throws
MalformedURLException
public URL(String spec) throws MalformedURLException
public URL(URL context, String spec) throws MalformedURLException
public int getPort()
public String getFile()
public String getProtocol()
public String getHost()
public String getRef()
public boolean equals(Object obj)
public int hashCode()
public boolean sameFile(URL other)
public String toString()
public URLConnection openConnection() throws IOException
public final InputStream openStream() throws IOException
public static synchronized void
setURLStreamHandlerFactory(URLStreamHandlerFactory factory)
```

You use this class just like you'd use any other class with these methods that happens to be named java.net.URL.

1.20.3 Using a Class from the Class Library

You use the java.net.URL class just like you'd use any other class with these methods that happens to be named java.net.URL.

For example,

Example 1.6

```
public class URLSplitter {
public static void main(String[] args) {
for (int i = 0; i < args.length; i++) {
try {
java.net.URL u = new java.net.URL(args[i]);
System.out.println("Protocol: " + u.getProtocol());
System.out.println("Host: " + u.getHost());
```

```
System.out.println("Port: " + u.getPort());
System.out.println("File: " + u.getFile());
System.out.println("Ref: " + u.getRef());
}
catch (java.net.MalformedURLException e) {
System.err.println(args[i] + " is not a valid URL");
}
}
}
}
```

Here's the output:

```
% java SplitURL http://www.poly.edu
Protocol: http
Host: www.poly.edu
Port: -1
File: /
Ref: null
```

EXERCISES

1. *Following the first example in this chapter, create a "Hello, World" program that simply prints out that statement. You need only a single method in your class (the "main" one that gets executed when the program starts). Remember to make it static and to put the argument list in, even though you don't use the argument list. Compile the program with javac and run it using java.*
2. *Write a program that prints three arguments taken from the command line.*
3. *Find the code for the second version of Property.java, which is the simple comment documentation example. Execute javadoc on the file and view the results with your Web browser.*

Take the program in Exercise 1 and add comment documentation to it. Extract this comment documentation into an HTML file using javadoc and view it with your Web browser.

2

Data Types Variable and Arrays

2.1 Data Types

The following table lists, by keyword, all of the primitive data types supported by Java, their sizes and formats, and a brief description of each. The MaxVariables program declares one variable of each primitive type.

The Java programming language has two categories of data types: primitive and reference. Table 2.1 shows all of the primitive data types:

Table 2.1 Data Types in Java

Keyword	Description	Size/Format
(1) Primitive	(integers)	byte Byte-length integer 8-bit two's complement short Short integer 16-bit two's comple ment int Integer 32-bit two's complement long Long inte ger 64-bit two's complement
	(real numbers)	float Single-precision floating point 32-bit IEEE 754 double Double-precision floating point 64-bit IEEE 754
	(other types)	char A single character 16-bit Unicode character boolean A boolean value (true or false) true or false
(2) Reference types are arrays, or names of classes or interfaces.		

The variable declaration also implicitly sets the variable's scope, and you may optionally provide an initial value for the variable within its declaration. The value of a final variable may not change after it's initialized.

Java's primitive data types are very similar to those of C. (The boolean type has been added.) However the implementation of the data types has been substantially cleaned up in several ways.

Where C and C++ leave a number of issues to be machine and compiler dependent (for instance the size of an int) Java specifies everything.

Java prevents casting between arbitrary variables. Only casts between numeric variables and between sub and superclasses of the same object are allowed.

- **boolean**

Booleans are named after George Boole, a nineteenth century logician. Each boolean variable has one of two values, true or false. These are not the same as the Strings "true" and "false". They are not the same as any numeric value like 1 or 0. They are simply true and false. Booleans are not numbers; they are not Strings. They are simply booleans.

Boolean variables are declared just like any other variable.

```
boolean test1 = true;
boolean test2 = false;
```

Note that true and false are reserved words in Java. These are called the Boolean literals. They are case sensitive. True with a capital T is not the same as true with a little t. The same is true of False and false.

Size is 1-bit. May take on the values true and false only.

true and false are defined constants of the language and are not the same as True and False, TRUE and FALSE, zero and nonzero, 1 and 0 or any other numeric value. Booleans may not be cast into any other type of variable nor may any other variable be cast into a boolean.

- **byte**

1 signed byte (two's complement). Covers values from -128 to 127.

- **short**

2 bytes signed (two's complement), -32,768 to 32,767

- **int**

4 bytes, signed (two's complement). -2,147,483,648 to 2,147,483,647. Like all numeric types ints may be cast into other numeric types (byte, short, long, float, double). When lossy casts are done (e.g. int to byte) the conversion is done modulo the length of the smaller type.

- **long**

8 bytes signed (two's complement). Ranges from -9,223,372,036,854,775,808 to +9,223,372,036,854,775,807.

- **float**

4 bytes, IEEE 754. Covers a range from 1.40129846432481707e-45 to 2.40282346638528860e+38 (positive or negative).

Like all numeric types floats may be cast into other numeric types (byte, short, long, int, double). When lossy casts to integer types are done (e.g. float to short) the fractional part is truncated and the conversion is done modulo the length of the smaller type.

- **double**

8 bytes IEEE 754. Covers a range from 4.94065645841246544e-324d to 1.79769313486231570e + 308d (positive or negative).

char

- **2 unsigned bytes, Unicode.**

Chars are not the same as bytes, ints, shorts or Strings.

sizeof isn't necessary in Java because all sizes are precisely defined. i.e. an int is always 4 bytes. This may not seem to be adequate when dealing with objects that aren't base data types. However even if you did know the size of a particular object, you couldn't do anything with it anyway. You cannot convert an arbitrary object into bytes and back again.

Strings are a reference or object type, that is a instances of the class java.lang.String. They are not null terminated and are not the same as an array of chars.

You can put a literal primitive value directly in your code. For example, if you need to assign the value 4 to an integer variable you can write this:

```
int anInt = 4;
```

The digit 4 is a literal integer value. Here are some examples of literal values of various primitive types:

Examples of Literal Values and Their Data Types

Literal Data Type

```
178 int
8864L long
37.266 double
37.266D double
87.363F float
26.77e3 double
'c' char
true boolean
false boolean
```

Generally speaking, a series of digits with no decimal point is typed as an integer. You can specify a long integer by putting an 'L' or 'l' after the number. 'L' is preferred as it cannot be confused with the digit '1'. A series of digits with a decimal point is of type double. You can specify a float by putting an 'f' or 'F' after the number. A literal character value is any single Unicode character between single quote marks. The two boolean literals are simply true and false.

Arrays, classes, and interfaces are reference types. The value of a reference type variable, in contrast to that of a primitive type, is a reference to (an address of) the value or set of values represented by the variable.

A reference is called a pointer, or a memory address in other languages. The Java programming language does not support the explicit use of addresses like other languages do. You use the variable's name instead.

2.2 The Char Data Type in Java

A char is a single character, that is a letter, a digit, a punctuation mark, a tab, a space or something similar. A char literal is a single one character enclosed in single quote marks like this

```
char myCharacter = 'g';
```

Some characters are hard to type. For these Java provides escape sequences. This is a backslash followed by an alphanumeric code. For instance '\n' is the newline character. '\t' is the tab character. '\\' is the backslash itself. The following escape sequences are defined:

`\b`	backspace
`\t`	tab
`\n`	linefeed
`\f`	formfeed
`\r`	carriage return
`\"`	double quote, "

```
\'          single quote, '
\\          backslash, \
```

The double quote escape sequence is used mainly inside strings where it would otherwise terminate the string. For instance

```
System.out.println("And then Jim said, \"Who's at the door?\"");
```

It isn't necessary to escape the double quote inside single quotes. The following line is legal in Java

```
char doublequote = '"';
```

However there are only seven kinds of literals, and one of those is not a primitive data type:

- **boolean: true or false**

```
int: 89, -945, 37865
long: 89L, -945L, 5123567876L
float: 89.5f, -32.5f,
double: 89.5, -32.5, 87.6E45
char: 'c', '9', 't'
String: "This is a string literal"
```

There are no short or byte literals.

Strings are a reference or object type, not a primitive type. However the Java compiler has special support for strings so this sometimes appears not to be the case.

2.3 Variables

A variable is an item of data named by an identifier. An object stores its state in variables.

You must explicitly provide a name and a type for each variable you want to use in your program. The variable's name must be a legal identifier —an unlimited series of Unicode characters that begins with a letter. You use the variable name to refer to the data that the variable contains. The variable's type determines what values it can hold and what operations can be performed on it. To give a variable a type and a name, you write a variable declaration, which generally looks like this: type name

In addition to the name and type that you explicitly give a variable, a variable has scope. The section of code where the variable's simple name can be used is the variable's scope. The variable's scope is determined implicitly by the location of the variable declaration, that is, where the declaration appears in relation to other code elements.

The following sections elaborate on the various aspects of variables, including data types, names, scope, initialization, and final variables. The MaxVariablesDemo program uses two items with which you might not yet be familiar and are not covered in this section: several constants named MAX_VALUE and an if-else statement. Each MAX_VALUE constant is defined in one of the number classes provided by the Java platform and is the largest value that can be assigned to a variable of that numeric type.

All variables in the Java language must have a data type. A variable's data type determines the values that the variable can contain and the operations that can be performed on it. For example, in the MaxVariables program, the declaration int largestInteger declares that largestInteger is an integer (int). Integers can contain only integral values (both positive and negative). You can perform arithmetic operations, such as addition, on integer variables. The Java programming language has two major categories of data

A variable of primitive type contains a single value of the appropriate size and format for its type: a number, character, or boolean value. For example, the value of an int is an integer, the value of a char is a 16-bit Unicode character, and so on. Arrays, classes, and interfaces are reference types. The value of a reference type variable, in contrast to that of a primitive type, is a reference to the actual value or set of values represented by the variable. A reference is called a pointer or a memory address in other languages. A reference is like your friend's address: The address is not your friend, but it's a way to reach your friend. A reference type variable is not the array or object itself but rather a way to reach it.

Following listing gives the glimpse of data types

Example 2.1

```
class Variables
{
    public static void main (String args[])
    {
        boolean b = true;
        int low = 1;
        long high = 76L;
        long middle = 74;
        float pi = 2.1415292f;
        double e = 2.71828;
        String s = "Hello World!";
    }
}
```

All numeric variables in Java are signed.

sizeof isn't necessary in Java because all sizes are precisely defined. For instance, an int is always 4 bytes. This may not seem to be adequate when dealing with objects that aren't base data types. However even if you did know the size of a particular object, you couldn't do anything with it anyway. You cannot convert an arbitrary object into bytes and back again.

The MaxVariablesDemo program, shown below, declares eight variables of different types within its main method. The variable declarations are red:

```
public class MaxVariablesDemo
{
public static void main(String args[])
{
// integers
byte largestByte = Byte.MAX_VALUE;
short largestShort = Short.MAX_VALUE;
int largestInteger = Integer.MAX_VALUE;
long largestLong = Long.MAX_VALUE;
// real numbers
float largestFloat = Float.MAX_VALUE;
double largestDouble = Double.MAX_VALUE;
// other primitive types
char aChar = 'S';
boolean aBoolean = true;
```

```
// display them all
System.out.println("The largest byte value is " + largestByte);
System.out.println("The largest short value is " + largestShort);
System.out.println("The largest integer value is " + largestInteger);
System.out.println("The largest long value is " + largestLong);


System.out.println("The largest float value is " + largestFloat);
System.out.println("The largest double value is " + largestDouble);


if (Character.isUpperCase(aChar)) {
System.out.println("The character " + aChar + " is upper case.");
} else {
System.out.println("The character " + aChar + "is lower case.");
}
System.out.println("The value of aBoolean is" + aBoolean);
}
}
```

The output from this program is:

```
The largest byte value is 127
The largest short value is 32767
The largest integer value is 2147483647
The largest long value is 9223372036854775807
The largest float value is 2.40282e+38
The largest double value is 1.79769e+308
The character S is upper case.
The value of aBoolean is true
```

2.4 Final Variables

You can declare a variable in any scope to be final, including parameters to methods and constructors. The value of a final variable cannot change after it has been initialized.

To declare a final variable, use the final keyword in the variable declaration before the type:

```
final int aFinalVar = 0;
```

The previous statement declares a final variable and initializes it, all at once. Subsequent attempts to assign a value to aFinalVar result in a compiler error. You may, if necessary, defer initialization of a final local variable. Simply declare the local variable and initialize it later, like this:

```
final int blankfinal;
. . .
blankfinal = 0;
```

A final local variable that has been declared but not yet initialized is called a blank final. Again, once a final local variable has been initialized it cannot be set and any later attempts to assign a value to blankfinal result in a compile-time error.

2.5 Variable Initialization

Local variables and member variables can be initialized with an assignment statement when they're declared. The data type of both of the assignment operator's operands must match. The MaxVariables program provides initial values for all of its local variables when they are declared. The variable declarations from that program is shown below with the initialization code in red:

```
// integers
byte largestByte = Byte.MAX_VALUE;
short largestShort = Short.MAX_VALUE;
int largestInteger = Integer.MAX_VALUE;
long largestLong = Long.MAX_VALUE;
// real numbers
float largestFloat = Float.MAX_VALUE;
double largestDouble = Double.MAX_VALUE;
// other primitive types
char aChar = 'S';
boolean aBoolean = true;
```

Method parameters and exception-handler parameters cannot be initialized in this way. The value for a parameter is set by the caller.

2.6 Variable Names

A program refers to a variable's value by its name. For example, when the MaxVariables program displays the value of the largestByte variable, it simply uses the name largestByte.

In Java, the following must hold true for a variable name:

It must be a legal Java identifier comprised of a series of Unicode characters. Unicode is a character-coding system designed to support text written in diverse human languages. It allows for the codification of up to 65,536 characters, currently 34,168 have been assigned. This allows you to use characters in your Java programs from various alphabets, such as Japanese, Greek, Cyrillic, and Hebrew. This is important so that programmers can write code that is meaningful in their native languages. It must not be a keyword, a boolean literal (true or false), or the reserved word null. It must be unique within its scope.

By Convention: Variable names begin with a lowercase letter and class names begin with an uppercase letter. If a variable name consists of more than one word, such as isVisible, the words are joined together and each word after the first begins with an uppercase letter. Rule #3 implies that variables may have the same name as another variable whose declaration appears in a different scope. This is true. In addition, in some situations, a variable may share names with another variable which is declared in a nested scope. Scope is covered in the next section.

Purity Tip: In other languages, the format and size of primitive data types may depend on the platform on which a program is running. In contrast, the Java language specifies the size and format of its primitive data types. Hence, you don't have to worry about system-dependencies.

2.7 Scope of a Variable

A variable's scope is the region of a program within which the variable can be referred to by its simple name. Secondarily, scope also determines when the system creates and destroys memory for the variable. Scope is distinct from visibility, which applies only to member variables and determines whether the variable can be used from outside of the class within which it is declared. Visibility is set with an access modifier.

The location of the variable declaration within your program establishes its scope and places it into one of these four categories:

- member variable
- local variable
- method parameter
- exception-handler parameter

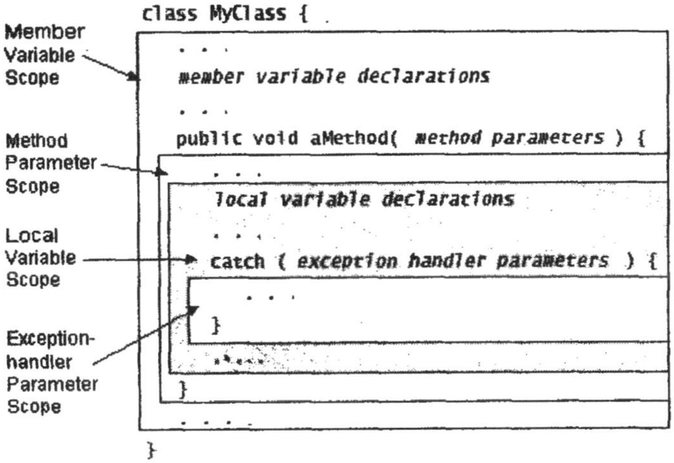

Fig 2.1

A member variable is a member of a class or an object. It is declared within a class but outside of any method or constructor. A member variable's scope is the entire declaration of the class. However, the declaration of a member needs to appear before it is used when the use is in a member initialization expression. For information about declaring member variables, refer to Declaring Member Variables in the next lesson.

You declare local variables within a block of code. In general, the scope of a local variable extends from its declaration to the end of the code block in which it was declared. In MaxVariablesDemo, all of the variables declared within the main method are local variables. The scope of each variable in that program extends from the declaration of the variable to the end of the main method —indicated by the first right curly bracket } in the program code.

Parameters are formal arguments to methods or constructors and are used to pass values into methods and constructors. The scope of a parameter is the entire method or constructor for which it is a parameter.

Exception-handler parameters are similar to parameters but are arguments to an exception handler rather than to a method or a constructor. The scope of an exception-handler parameter is the code block between { and } that follow a catch statement. Handling Errors with Exceptions talks about using exceptions to handle errors and shows you how to write an exception handler that has a parameter.

Consider the following code sample:

```
if (...)
{
int i = 17;
...
}
System.out.println("The value of i = " + i); // error
```

The final line won't compile because the local variable i is out of scope. The scope of i is the block of code between the { and }. The i variable does not exist anymore after the closing }. Either the variable declaration needs to be moved outside of the if statement block, or the println method call needs to be moved into the if statement block.

The location of a variable declaration implicitly sets the variable's scope, which determines what section of code may refer to the variable by its simple name. There are four categories of scope: member variable scope, local variable scope, parameter scope, and exception-handler parameter scope.

You can provide an initial value for a variable within its declaration by using the assignment operator (=).

You can declare a variable as final. The value of a final variable cannot change after it's been initialized.

Common pitfalls when using operators

One of the pitfalls when using operators is trying to get away without parentheses when you are even the least bit uncertain about how an expression will evaluate. This is still true in Java.

An extremely common error in C and C++ looks like this:

```
while(x = y) {
// ....
}
```

The programmer was trying to test for equivalence (==) rather than do an assignment. In C and C++ the result of this assignment will always be true if y is nonzero, and you'll probably get an infinite loop. In Java, the result of this expression is not a boolean, and the compiler expects a boolean and won't convert from an int, so it will conveniently give you a compile-time error and catch the problem before you ever try to run the program. So the pitfall never happens in Java. (The only time you won't get a compile-time error is when x and y are boolean, in which case x = y is a legal expression, and in the above case, probably an error.)

A similar problem in C and C++ is using bitwise AND and OR instead of logical. Bitwise AND and OR use one of the characters (& or |) while logical AND and OR use two (&& and ||). Just as with = and ==, it's easy to type just one character instead of two. In Java, the compiler again prevents this because it won't let you cavalierly use one type where it doesn't belong.

2.8 Casting Operators

The word cast is used in the sense of "casting into a mold." Java will automatically change one type of data into another when appropriate. For instance, if you assign an integral value to a floating-point variable, the compiler will automatically convert the int to a float. Casting allows you to make this type conversion explicit, or to force it when it wouldn't normally happen.

To perform a cast, put the desired data type (including all modifiers) inside parentheses to the left of any value. Here's an example:

```
void casts()
{
int i = 200;
long l = (long)i;
long l2 = (long)200;
}
```

As you can see, it's possible to perform a cast on a numeric value as well as on a variable. In both casts shown here, however, the cast is superfluous, since the compiler will automatically promote an int value to a long when necessary. You can still put a cast in to make a point or to make your code more clear. In other situations, a cast is essential just to get the code to compile.

In C and C++, casting can cause some headaches. In Java, casting is safe, with the exception that when you perform a so-called narrowing conversion (that is, when you go from a data type that can hold more information to one that doesn't hold as much) you run the risk of losing information. Here the compiler forces you to do a cast, in effect saying "this can be a dangerous thing to do - if you want me to do it anyway you must make the cast explicit." With a widening conversion an explicit cast is not needed because the new type will more than hold the information from the old type so that no information is ever lost.

Java allows you to cast any primitive type to any other primitive type, except for boolean, which doesn't allow any casting at all. Class types do not allow casting. To convert one to the other there must be special methods. (String is a special case, and you'll find out later in the book that objects can be cast within a family of types; an Oak can be cast to a Tree and vice-versa, but not to a foreign type such as a Rock.)

2.9 Literals

Ordinarily when you insert a literal value into a program the compiler knows exactly what type to make it. Sometimes, however, the type is ambiguous. When this happens you must guide the compiler by adding some extra information in the form of characters associated with the literal value. The following code shows these characters:

Example 2.2

```
//: Literals.java
class Literals
{
char c = 0xffff; // max char hex value
byte b = 0x7f; // max byte hex value
short s = 0x7fff; // max short hex value
int i1 = 0x2f; // Hexadecimal (lowercase)
int i2 = 0X2F; // Hexadecimal (uppercase)
int i3 = 0177; // Octal (leading zero)
// Hex and Oct also work with long.
long n1 = 200L; // long suffix
long n2 = 200l; // long suffix
long n3 = 200;
//! long l6(200); // not allowed
float f1 = 1;
float f2 = 1F; // float suffix
float f3 = 1f; // float suffix
float f4 = 1e-45f; // 10 to the power
float f5 = 1e+9f; // float suffix
double d1 = 1d; // double suffix
double d2 = 1D; // double suffix
double d3 = 47e47d; // 10 to the power
} ///:~
```

Hexadecimal (base 16), which works with all the integral data types, is denoted by a leading 0x or 0X followed by 0-9 and a-f either in upper or lower case. If you try to initialize a variable with a value bigger than it can hold (regardless of the numerical form of the value), the compiler will give you an error message. Notice in the above code the maximum possible hexadecimal values for char, byte, and short. If you exceed these, the compiler will automatically make the value an int and tell you that you need a narrowing cast for the assignment. You'll know you've stepped over the line.

Octal (base 8) is denoted by a leading zero in the number and digits from 0-7. There is no literal representation for binary numbers in C, C++ or Java.

A trailing character after a literal value establishes its type. Upper or lowercase L means long, upper or lowercase F means float and upper or lowercase D means double.

Exponents use a notation that I've always found rather dismaying: 1.39 e-47f . In science and engineering, 'e' refers to the base of natural logarithms, approximately 2.718. (A more precise double value is available in Java as Math.E.) This is used in exponentiation expressions such as 1.39 x e - 47, which means 1.39 x 2.718 -47. However, when FORTRAN was invented they decided that e would naturally mean "ten to the power," which is an odd decision because FORTRAN was designed for science and engineering and one would think its designers would be sensitive about introducing such an ambiguity. [16] At any rate, this custom was followed in C, C++ and now Java. So if you're used to thinking in terms of e as the base of natural logarithms, you must do a mental translation when you see an expression such as 1.39 e-47f in Java; it means 1.39 x 10 -47.

Note that you don't need to use the trailing character when the compiler can figure out the appropriate type. With

```
long n3 = 200;
```

there's no ambiguity, so an L after the 200 would be superfluous. However, with

```
float f4 = 1e-47f; // 10 to the power
```

the compiler normally takes exponential numbers as doubles, so without the trailing f it will give you an error telling you that you must use a cast to convert double to float.

2.10 Promotion

You'll discover that if you perform any mathematical or bitwise operations on primitive data types that are smaller than an int (that is, char, byte, or short), those values will be promoted to int before performing the operations, and the resulting value will be of type int. So if you want to assign back into the smaller type, you must use a cast. (And, since you're assigning back into a smaller type, you might be losing information.) In general, the largest data type in an expression is the one that determines the size of the result of that expression; if you multiply a float and a double, the result will be double; if you add an int and a long, the result will be long.

Java has no "sizeof"

In C and C++, the sizeof( ) operator satisfies a specific need: it tells you the number of bytes allocated for data items. The most compelling need for sizeof( ) in C and C++ is portability. Different data types might be different sizes on different machines, so the programmer must find out how big those types are when performing operations that are sensitive to size. For example, one computer might store integers in 32 bits, whereas another might store integers as 16 bits. Programs could store larger values in integers on the first machine. As you might imagine, portability is a huge headache for C and C++ programmers.

Java does not need a sizeof( ) operator for this purpose because all the data types are the same size on all machines. You do not need to think about portability on this level - it is designed into the language.

2.11 Precedence revisited

Upon hearing me complain about the complexity of remembering operator precedence during one of my seminars, a student suggested a mnemonic that is simultaneously a commentary: "Ulcer Addicts Really Like C A lot."

Mnemonic	Operator type	Operators
Ulcer	Unary	+ - ++ - [[rest...]]
Addicts	Arithmetic (and shift)	* / % + - << >>
Really	Relational	> < >= <= == !=
Like	Logical (and bitwise)	&& || & | ^
C	Conditional (ternary)	A > B ? X : Y
A Lot	Assignment	= (and compound assignment like *=)

Of course, with the shift and bitwise operators distributed around the table it is not a perfect mnemonic, but for non-bit operations it works.

A Compendium of Operators

The following example shows which primitive data types can be used with particular operators. Basically, it is the same example repeated over and over, but using different primitive data types. The file will compile without error because the lines that would cause errors are commented out with a //!.

Example 2.3

```
//: AllOps.java
// Tests all the operators on all the
// primitive data types to show which
// ones are accepted by the Java compiler.


class AllOps {
// To accept the results of a boolean test:
void f(boolean b) {}
void boolTest(boolean x, boolean y) {
// Arithmetic operators:
//! x = x * y;
//! x = x / y;
//! x = x % y;
//! x = x + y;
//! x = x - y;
//! x++;
//! x—;
//! x = +y;
//! x = -y;
// Relational and logical:
//! f(x > y);
```

```
//! f(x >= y);
//! f(x < y);
//! f(x <= y);
f(x == y);
f(x != y);
f(!y);
x = x && y;
x = x || y;
// Bitwise operators:
//! x = ~y;
x = x & y;
x = x | y;
x = x ^ y;
//! x = x << 1;
//! x = x >> 1;
//! x = x >>> 1;
// Compound assignment:
//! x += y;
//! x -= y;
//! x *= y;
//! x /= y;
//! x %= y;
//! x <<= 1;
//! x >>= 1;
//! x >>>= 1;
x &= y;
x ^= y;
x |= y;
// Casting:
//! char c = (char)x;
//! byte B = (byte)x;
//! short s = (short)x;
//! int i = (int)x;
//! long l = (long)x;
//! float f = (float)x;
//! double d = (double)x;
}
void charTest(char x, char y) {
// Arithmetic operators:
x = (char)(x * y);
x = (char)(x / y);
x = (char)(x % y);
x = (char)(x + y);
x = (char)(x - y);
x++;
x—;
x = (char)+y;
x = (char)-y;
```

```
// Relational and logical:
f(x > y);
f(x >= y);
f(x < y);
f(x <= y);
f(x == y);
f(x != y);
//! f(!x);
//! f(x && y);
//! f(x || y);
// Bitwise operators:
x= (char)~y;
x = (char)(x & y);
x  = (char)(x | y);
x = (char)(x ^ y);
x = (char)(x << 1);
x = (char)(x >> 1);
x = (char)(x >>> 1);
// Compound assignment:
x += y;
x -= y;
x *= y;
x /= y;
x %= y;
x <<= 1;
x >>= 1;
x >>>= 1;
x &= y;
x ^= y;
x |= y;
// Casting:
//! boolean b = (boolean)x;
byte B = (byte)x;
short s = (short)x;
int i = (int)x;
long l = (long)x;
float f = (float)x;
double d = (double)x;
}
void byteTest(byte x, byte y) {
// Arithmetic operators:
x = (byte)(x* y);
x = (byte)(x / y);
x = (byte)(x % y);
x = (byte)(x + y);
x = (byte)(x - y);
x++;
x-;
```

```
x = (byte)+ y;
x = (byte)- y;
// Relational and logical:
f(x > y);
f(x >= y);
f(x < y);
f(x <= y);
f(x == y);
f(x != y);
//! f(!x);
//! f(x && y);
//! f(x || y);
// Bitwise operators:
x = (byte)~y;
x = (byte)(x & y);
x = (byte)(x | y);
x = (byte)(x ^ y);
x = (byte)(x << 1);
x = (byte)(x >> 1);
x = (byte)(x >>> 1);
// Compound assignment:
x += y;
x -= y;
x *= y;
x /= y;
x %= y;
x <<= 1;
x >>= 1;
x >>>= 1;
x &= y;
x ^= y;
x |= y;
// Casting:
//! boolean b = (boolean)x;
char c = (char)x;
short s = (short)x;
int i = (int)x;
long l = (long)x;
float f = (float)x;
double d = (double)x;
}
void shortTest(short x, short y) {
// Arithmetic operators:
x = (short)(x * y);
x = (short)(x / y);
x = (short)(x % y);
x = (short)(x + y);
x = (short)(x - y);
```

```
x++;
x--;
x = (short)+y;
x = (short)-y;
// Relational and logical:
f(x > y);
f(x >= y);
f(x < y);
f(x <= y);
f(x == y);
f(x != y);
//! f(!x);
//! f(x && y);
//! f(x || y);
// Bitwise operators:
x = (short)~y;
x = (short)(x & y);
x = (short)(x | y);
x = (short)(x ^ y);
x = (short)(x << 1);
x = (short)(x >> 1);
x = (short)(x >>> 1);
// Compound assignment:
x += y;
x -= y;
x *= y;
x /= y;
x %= y;
x <<= 1;
x >>= 1;
x >>>= 1;
x &= y;
x ^= y;
x |= y;
// Casting:
//! boolean b = (boolean)x;
char c = (char)x;
byte B = (byte)x;
int i = (int)x;
long l = (long)x;
float f = (float)x;
double d = (double)x;
}
void intTest(int x, int y) {
// Arithmetic operators:
x = x * y;
x = x / y;
x = x % y;
```

```
x = x + y;
x = x - y;
x++;
x—;
x = +y;
x = -y;
// Relational and logical:
f(x > y);
f(x >= y);
f(x < y);
f(x <= y);
f(x == y);
f(x != y);
//! f(!x);
//! f(x && y);
//! f(x || y);
// Bitwise operators:
x = ~y;
x = x & y;
x = x | y;
x = x ^ y;
x = x << 1;
x = x >> 1;
x = x >>> 1;
// Compound assignment:
x += y;
x -= y;
x *= y;
x /= y;
x %= y;
x <<= 1;
x >>= 1;
x >>>= 1;
x &= y;
x ^= y;
x |= y;
// Casting:
//! boolean b = (boolean)x;
char c = (char)x;
byte B = (byte)x;
short s = (short)x;
long l = (long)x;
float f = (float)x;
double d = (double)x;
}
void longTest(long x, long y) {
// Arithmetic operators:
x = x * y;
```

```
x = x / y;
x = x % y;
x = x + y;
x = x - y;
x++;
x—;
x = +y;
x = -y;
// Relational and logical:
f(x > y);
f(x >= y);
f(x < y);
f(x <= y);
f(x == y);
f(x != y);
//! f(!x);
//! f(x && y);
//! f(x || y);
// Bitwise operators:
x = ~y;
x = x & y;
x = x | y;
x = x ^ y;
x = x << 1;
x = x >> 1;
x = x >>> 1;
// Compound assignment:
x += y;
x -= y;
x *= y;
x /= y;
x %= y;
x <<= 1;
x >>= 1;
x >>>= 1;
x &= y;
x ^= y;
x |= y;
// Casting:
//! boolean b = (boolean)x;
char c = (char)x;
byte B = (byte)x;
short s = (short)x;
int i = (int)x;
float f = (float)x;
double d = (double)x;
}
void floatTest(float x, float y) {
// Arithmetic operators:
```

```
x = x * y;
x = x / y;
x = x % y;
x = x + y;
x = x - y;
x++;
x--;
x = +y;
x = -y;
// Relational and logical:
f(x > y);
f(x >= y);
f(x < y);
f(x <= y);
f(x == y);
f(x != y);
//! f(!x);
//! f(x && y);
//! f(x || y);
// Bitwise operators:
//! x = ~y;
//! x = x & y;
//! x = x | y;
//! x = x ^ y;
//! x = x << 1;
//! x = x >> 1;
//! x = x >>> 1;
// Compound assignment:
x += y;
x -= y;
x *= y;
x /= y;
x %= y;
//! x <<= 1;
//! x >>= 1;
//! x >>>= 1;
//! x &= y;
//! x ^= y;
//! x |= y;
// Casting:
//! boolean b = (boolean)x;
char c = (char)x;
byte B = (byte)x;
short s = (short)x;
int i = (int)x;
long l = (long)x;
double d = (double)x;
}
void doubleTest(double x, double y) {
// Arithmetic operators:
```

```
x = x * y;
x = x / y;
x = x % y;
x = x + y;
x = x - y;
x++;
x--;
x = +y;
x = -y;
// Relational and logical:
f(x > y);
f(x >= y);
f(x < y);
f(x <= y);
f(x == y);
f(x != y);
//! f(!x);
//! f(x && y);
//! f(x || y);
// Bitwise operators:
//! x = ~y;
//! x = x & y;
//! x = x | y;
//! x = x ^ y;
//! x = x << 1;
//! x = x >> 1;
//! x = x >>> 1;
// Compound assignment:
x += y;
x -= y;
x *= y;
x /= y;
x %= y;
//! x <<= 1;
//! x >>= 1;
//! x >>>= 1;
//! x &= y;
//! x ^= y;
//! x |= y;
// Casting:
//! boolean b = (boolean)x;
char c = (char)x;
byte B = (byte)x;
short s = (short)x;
int i = (int)x;
long l = (long)x;
float f = (float)x;
}
} ///:~
```

Note that boolean is quite limited. You can assign to it the values true and false, and you can test it for truth or falsehood, but you cannot add booleans or perform any other type of operation on them.

In char, byte, and short you can see the effect of promotion with the arithmetic operators. Each arithmetic operation on any of those types results in an int result, which must be explicitly cast back to the original type (a narrowing conversion that might lose information) to assign back to that type. With int values, however, you do not need to cast, because everything is already an int. Don't be lulled into thinking everything is safe, though. If you multiply two ints that are big enough, you'll overflow the result. The following example demonstrates this:

Example 2.4

```
//: Overflow.java
// Surprise! Java lets you overflow.
public class Overflow {
public static void main(String[] args) {
int big = 0x7fffffff; // max int value
prt("big = " + big);
int bigger = big * 4;
prt("bigger = " + bigger);
}
static void prt(String s) {
System.out.println(s);
}
} ///:~
```

The output of this is:

big = 2147483647
bigger = -4

and you get no errors or warnings from the compiler, and no exceptions at run-time. Java is good, but it's not that good.

Compound assignments do not require casts for char, byte, or short, even though they are performing promotions that have the same results as the direct arithmetic operations. On the other hand, the lack of the cast certainly simplifies the code.

You can see that, with the exception of boolean, any primitive type can be cast to any other primitive type. Again, you must be aware of the effect of a narrowing conversion when casting to a smaller type, otherwise you might unknowingly lose information during the cast.

2.12 Java Operators

An operator is a symbol that operates on one or more arguments to produce a result. The Hello World program is so simple it doesn't use any operators, but almost all other programs you write will.

An operator performs a function on either one, two, or three operands. An operators that requires one operand is called a unary operator. For example, ++ is a unary operator that increments the value of its operand by 1. An operator that requires two operands is a binary operators. For example, = is a binary operator that assigns the value from its right-hand operand to its left-hand operand. And finally a ternary operator is one that requires three operands. The Java programming language has one ternary operator, ?:, which is a short-hand if-else statement. The unary operators support either prefix or postfix notation. Prefix notation means that the operator appears before its operand:

```
operator op
```

Postfix notation means that the operator appears after its operand:

```
op operator
```

All of the binary operators use infix notation, which means that the operator appears between its operands:

```
op1 operator op2
```

The ternary operator is also infix; each component of the operator appears between operands:

```
expr ? op1 : op2
```

In addition to performing the operation, an operator also returns a value. The return value and its type depends on the operator and the type of its operands. For example, the arithmetic operators, which perform basic arithmetic operations such as addition and subtraction, return numbers—the result of the arithmetic operation. The data type returned by the arithmetic operators depends on the type of its operands: If you add two integers, you get an integer back. An operation is said to evaluate to its result. It's useful to divide the operators into these categories:

Table 2.2 Operators in Java

<table>
<tr><th>Operator</th><th>Purpose</th></tr>
<tr><td>+</td><td>addition of numbers, concatenation of Strings</td></tr>
<tr><td>+=</td><td>add and assign numbers, concatenate and assign Strings</td></tr>
<tr><td>-</td><td>subtraction</td></tr>
<tr><td>-=</td><td>subtract and assign</td></tr>
<tr><td>*</td><td>multiplication</td></tr>
<tr><td>*=</td><td>multiply and assign</td></tr>
<tr><td>/</td><td>division</td></tr>
<tr><td>/=</td><td>divide and assign</td></tr>
<tr><td>|</td><td>bitwise OR</td></tr>
<tr><td>|=</td><td>bitwise OR and assign</td></tr>
<tr><td>^</td><td>bitwise XOR</td></tr>
<tr><td>^=</td><td>bitwise XOR and assign</td></tr>
<tr><td>&</td><td>bitwise AND</td></tr>
<tr><td>&=</td><td>bitwise AND and assign</td></tr>
<tr><td>%</td><td>take remainder</td></tr>
<tr><td>%=</td><td>take remainder and assign</td></tr>
<tr><td>></td><td>greater than</td></tr>
<tr><td>>=</td><td>greater than or equal to</td></tr>
<tr><td><</td><td>less than</td></tr>
<tr><td><=</td><td>less than or equal to</td></tr>
<tr><td>!</td><td>boolean NOT</td></tr>
<tr><td>!=</td><td>not equal to</td></tr>
<tr><td>++</td><td>increment by one</td></tr>
<tr><td>—</td><td>decrement by one</td></tr>
<tr><td>>></td><td>shift bits right with sign extension</td></tr>
<tr><td>>>=</td><td>shift bits right with sign extension and assign</td></tr>
<tr><td><<</td><td>shift bits left</td></tr>
<tr><td><<=</td><td>shift bits left and assign</td></tr>
<tr><td>>>></td><td>unsigned bit shift right</td></tr>
<tr><td>>>>=</td><td>unsigned bit shift right and assign</td></tr>
<tr><td>&&</td><td>boolean AND</td></tr>
<tr><td>||</td><td>boolean OR</td></tr>
<tr><td>==</td><td>boolean equals</td></tr>
<tr><td>=</td><td>assignment</td></tr>
<tr><td>~</td><td>bitwise NOT</td></tr>
<tr><td>?:</td><td>conditional</td></tr>
</table>

2.13 Mathemetical (Arithmetical) Operators

The Java language supports various arithmetic operators for all floating-point and integer numbers. These include + (addition), - (subtraction), * (multiplication), / (division), and % (modulo). For example, you can use this Java code to add two numbers:

```
addThis + toThis
```

Or you can use the following Java code to compute the remainder that results from dividing divideThis by byThis:

```
divideThis % byThis
```

This table summarizes Java's binary arithmetic operations:

Operator	Use Description
+	op1 + op2 Adds op1 and op2
-	op1 - op2 Subtracts op2 from op1
*	op1 * op2 Multiplies op1 by op2
/ op1 / op2	Divides op1 by op2
% op1 % op2	Computes the remainder of dividing op1 by op2

Note: The Java language extends the definition of the + operator to include string concatenation. You'll see more about this in Arrays and Strings.

The + and - operators have unary versions that perform the following operations:

Operator	Use Description
+	+op Promotes op to int if it's a byte, short, or char
-	-op Arithmetically negates op

2.13.1 Unary Minus and Plus Operators

The unary minus (-) and unary plus (+) are the same operators as binary minus and plus. The compiler figures out which use is intended by the way you write the expression. For instance, the statement

```
x = -a;
```

has an obvious meaning. The compiler is able to figure out:

```
x = a * -b;
```

but the reader might get confused, so it is more clear to say:

```
x = a * (-b);
```

The unary minus produces the negative of the value. Unary plus provides symmetry with unary minus, although it doesn't do much.

2.13.2 Auto Increment and Decrement

Java, like C, is full of shortcuts. Shortcuts can make code much easier to type, and either easier or harder to read.

There also are two short cut arithmetic operators, ++ which increments its operand by 1, and — which decrements its operand by 1. Either ++ or — can appear before (prefix) or after (postfix) its operand. The prefix version, ++op/—op, evaluates to the value of the operand after the increment/decrement operation. The postfix version, op++/op—, evaluates the value of the operand before the increment/decrement operation.

Two of the nicer shortcuts are the increment and decrement operators (often referred to as the auto-increment and auto-decrement operators). The decrement operator is — and means "decrease by one unit." The increment operator is ++ and means "increase by one unit." If A is an int, for example, the expression ++A is equivalent to (A = A + 1). Increment and decrement operators produce the value of the variable as a result.

There are two versions of each type of operator, often called the prefix and postfix versions. Pre-increment means the ++ operator appears before the variable or expression, and post-increment means the ++ operator appears after the variable or expression. Similarly, pre-decrement means the — operator appears before the variable or expression, and post-decrement means the — operator appears after the variable or expression. For pre-increment and pre-decrement, (i.e., ++A or —A), the operation is performed and the value is produced. For post-increment and post-decrement (i.e. A++ or A—), the value is produced, then the operation is performed. As an example:

Example 2.5

```
//: AutoInc.java
// Demonstrates the ++ and — operators
public class AutoInc {
public static void main(String[] args) {
int i = 1;
prt("i : " + i);
prt("++i : " + ++i); // Pre-increment
prt("i++ : " + i++); // Post-increment
prt("i : " + i);
prt("—i : " + —i); // Pre-decrement
prt("i— : " + i—); // Post-decrement
prt("i : " + i);
}
static void prt(String s) {
System.out.println(s);
}
} ///:~
```

The output for this program is:

```
i : 1
++i : 2
i++ : 2
i : 3
—i : 2
i— : 2
i : 1
```

You can see that for the prefix form you get the value after the operation has been performed, but with the postfix form you get the value before the operation is performed. These are the only operators (other than those involving assignment) that have side effects. (That is, they change the operand rather than using just its value.)

The increment operator is one explanation for the name C++, implying "one step beyond C." In an early Java speech, Bill Joy (one of the creators), said that "Java=C++—" (C plus plus minus minus), suggesting that Java is C++ with the unnecessary hard parts removed and therefore a much simpler language. As you progress in this book you'll see that many parts are simpler, and yet Java isn't that much easier than C++.

Example 2.6 Recall the Sort program.

```
public class Sort {
public static void main(String[] args) {
int[] arrayOfInts = { 32, 87, 3, 589, 12, 1076,
2000, 8, 622, 127 };
for (int i = arrayOfInts.length; —i >= 0; ) {
for (int j = 0; j < i; j++) {
if (arrayOfInts[j] > arrayOfInts[j+1]) {
int temp = arrayOfInts[j];
arrayOfInts[j] = arrayOfInts[j+1];
arrayOfInts[j+1] = temp;
}
}
}
for (int i = 0; i < arrayOfInts.length; i++) {
System.out.print(arrayOfInts[i] + " ");
}
System.out.println();
}
}
```

Let's look at how the Sort program uses — to control the outer of its two nested sorting loops. Here's the statement that controls the outer loop:

```
for (int i = arrayOfInts.length; —i >= 0; ) {
    ...
}
```

The return value of the operation —i is compared to 0 to determine whether to terminate the loop. Using the prefix version of — means that the last iteration of this loop occurs when i is equal to 0. If we changed the code to use the postfix version of —, the last iteration of this loop occurs when i is equal to -1, which is incorrect for this program. The other two loops in the program use the the postfix version of ++. In both cases, the version used doesn't really matter because the value returned by the operator isn't used for anything. The short cut increment/decrement operators are summarized in the following table:

Operator		Use Description
++	op++	Increments op by 1; evaluates to the value of op before it was incremented
++	++op	Increments op by 1; evaluates to the value of op after it was incremented
–	op–	Decrements op by 1; evaluates to the value of op before it was decremented
–	–op	Decrements op by 1; evaluates to the value of op after it was decremented

The basic mathematical operators are the same as the ones available in most programming languages: addition (+), subtraction (-), division (/), multiplication (*) and modulus (%, produces the remainder from integer division). Integer division truncates, rather than rounds, the result.

Java also uses a shorthand notation to perform an operation and an assignment at the same time.

This is denoted by an operator followed by an equal sign, and is consistent with all the operators in the language (whenever it makes sense). For example, to add 4 to the variable x and assign the result to x, use: x += 4; .

This example shows the use of the mathematical operators:

Example 2.7

```
//: MathOps.java
// Demonstrates the mathematical operators
import java.util.*;

public class MathOps
{
// Create a shorthand to save typing:
static void prt(String s)
{
System.out.println(s);
}
// shorthand to print a string and an int:
static void pInt(String s, int i)
{
prt(s + " = " + i);
}
// shorthand to print a string and a float:
static void pFlt(String s, float f)
{
prt(s + " = " + f);
}
public static void main(String[] args)
{
// Create a random number generator,
// seeds with current time by default:
Random rand = new Random();
int i, j, k;
// '%' limits maximum value to 99:
j = rand.nextInt() % 100;
k = rand.nextInt() % 100;
pInt("j",j);  pInt("k",k);
i = j + k; pInt("j + k", i);
i = j - k; pInt("j - k", i);
i = k / j; pInt("k / j", i);
i = k * j; pInt("k * j", i);
i = k % j; pInt("k % j", i);
j %= k; pInt("j %= k", j);
// Floating-point number tests:
float u,v,w;  // applies to doubles, too
v = rand.nextFloat();
w = rand.nextFloat();
pFlt("v", v); pFlt("w", w);
```

```
u = v + w; pFlt("v + w", u);
u = v - w; pFlt("v - w", u);
u = v * w; pFlt("v * w", u);
u = v / w; pFlt("v / w", u);
// the following also works for
// char, byte, short, int, long,
// and double:
u += v; pFlt("u += v", u);
u -= v; pFlt("u -= v", u);
u *= v; pFlt("u *= v", u);
u /= v; pFlt("u /= v", u);
}
} ///:~
```

The first thing you will see are some shorthand methods for printing: the prt( ) method prints a String, the pInt( ) prints a String followed by an int and the pFlt( ) prints a String followed by a float..Of course, they all ultimately end up using System.out.println( ).

To generate numbers, the program first creates a Random object. Because no arguments are passed during creation, Java uses the current time as a seed for the random number generator. The program generates a number of different types of random numbers with the Random object simply by calling different methods: nextInt( ), nextLong( ), nextFloat( ) or nextDouble( ) .

The modulus operator, when used with the result of the random number generator, limits the result to an upper bound of the operand minus one (99 in this case).

2.15 Relational Operators

Relational operators generate a boolean result. They evaluate the relationship between the values ot the operands. A relational expression produces true if the relationship is true, and false if the relationship is untrue. The relational operators are less than (<), greater than (>), less than or equal to (<=), greater than or equal to (>=), equivalent (==) and not equivalent (!=). Equivalence and nonequivalence works with all built-in data types, but the other comparisons won't work with type boolean.

Java has six relational operators that compare two numbers and return a boolean value. The relational operators are <, >, <=, >=, ==, and !=.

x < y	Less than	True if x is less than y,	otherwise false.
x > y	Greater than	True if x is greater than y,	otherwise false.
x <= y	Less than or equal to	True if x is less than or equal to y,	otherwise false.
x >= y	Greater than or equal to	True if x is greater than or equal to y,	otherwise false.
x == y	Equal	True if x equals y,	otherwise false.
x != y	Not Equal	True if x is not equal to y,	otherwise false.

Here are some code snippets showing the relational operators.

```
boolean test1 = 1 < 2;  // True. One is less that two.
boolean test2 = 1 > 2;  // False. One is not greater than two.
boolean test3 = 2.5 != 1;  // True. One does not equal 2.5
boolean test4 = 17*2.5 >= 67.0 - 42; //True. 59.5 is greater than 5
boolean test5 = 9.8*54 <= 654; // True. 529.2 is less than 654
boolean test6 = 6*4 == 3*8; // True. 24 equals 24
boolean test7 = 6*4 <= 3*8; // True. 24 is less than or equal to 24
boolean test8 = 6*4 < 3*8; // False. 24 is not less than 24
```

This, however, is an unusual use of booleans. Almost all use of booleans in practice comes in conditional statements and loop tests. You've already seen several examples of this. Earlier you saw this

```
if (args.length > 0) {
System.out.println("Hello" + args[0]);
}
args.length > 0 is a boolean value. In other words it is either true
or it is false. You could write
boolean test = args.length > 0;
if (test) {
System.out.println("Hello" + args[0]);
}
```

instead. However in simple situations like this the original approach is customary.

Similarly the condition test in a while loop is a boolean. When you write

while (i < args.length) {

i < args.length is a boolean.

2.15.1 Relational Operator Precedence

Whenever a new operator is introduced you have to ask yourself where it fits in the precedence tree. If you look back at the example in the last section, you'll notice that it was implicitly assumed that the arithmetic was done before the comparison. Otherwise, for instance

```
boolean test8 = 6*4 < 3*8; // False. 24 is not less than 24
```

4 < 3 returns false which would then be multiplied by six and eight which would generate a compile time error because you can't multiply booleans. Relational operators are evaluated after arithmetic operators and before the assignment operator. == and != have slightly lower precedences than <, >, <= and >=. Here's the revised order:

`*, /, %`	Do all multiplications, divisions and remainders from left to right.
`+, -`	Next do additions and subtractions from left to right.
`<, >, >=, <=`	Then any comparisons for relative size.
`==, !=`	Then do any comparisons for equality and inequality
`=`	Finally assign the right-hand side to the left-hand side

For example,

```
boolean b1 = 7 > 3 == true;
boolean b2 = true == 7 > 3;

b = 7 > 3;
```

2.15.2 Testing Objects for Equality

<, >, <= and >= can only be used with numbers and characters. They cannot be used with Strings, booleans, arrays or other compound types since there's no well-defined notion of order for these objects. Is true greater than false? Is "My only regret is that I have but one life to give for my country" greater than "I have a dream"?

Equality is a little easier to test however. true is equal to true and true is not equal to false. Similarly "My only regret is that I have but one life to give for my country" is not equal to "I have a dream." However you might be surprised if you ran this program:

Example 2.8

```
class JackAndJill {
public static void main(String args[]) {
String s1 = new String("Jack went up the hill.");
String s2 = new String("Jack went up the hill.");

if ( s1 == s2 ) {
System.out.println("The strings are the same.");
}

else if ( s1 != s2 ) {
System.out.println("The strings are not the same.");
}
}
}
```

The result is

```
The strings are not the same.
```

2.15.3 Testing for Equality with equals()

That's not what you expected. To compare strings or any other kind of object you need to use the equals(Object o) method from java.lang.String. Below is a corrected version that works as expected. The reasons for this odd behavior go fairly deep into Java and the nature of object data types like strings.

Example 2.9

```
class JackAndJill {
public static void main(String args[]) {
String s1 = new String("Jack went up the hill.");
String s2 = new String("Jack went up the hill.");

if ( s1.equals(s2) ) {
System.out.println("The strings are the same.");
}
else {
System.out.println("The strings are not the same.");
}
}
}
```

2.15.4 Testing object equivalence

The relational operators == and != also work with all objects, but their meaning often confuses the first-time Java programmer. Here's an example:

Example 2.10

```
//: Equivalence.java
public class Equivalence
{
public static void main(String[] args)
```

```
{
Integer n1 = new Integer(47);
Integer n2 = new Integer(47);
System.out.println(n1 == n2);
System.out.println(n1 != n2);
}
} ///:~
```

The expression System.out.println(n1 == n2) will print out the result of the boolean comparison within it. Surely the output should be true and then false, since both Integer objects are the same. But while the contents of the objects are the same, the handles are not the same and the operators == and != compare object handles. So the output is actually false and then true. Naturally, this surprises people at first.

What if you want to compare the actual contents of an object for equivalence? You must use the special method equals( ) that exists for all objects (not primitives, which work fine with == and !=). Here's how it's used:

Example 2.11

```
//: EqualsMethod.java
public class EqualsMethod
{
public static void main(String[] args)
{
Integer n1 = new Integer(47);
Integer n2 = new Integer(47);
System.out.println(n1.equals(n2));
}
} ///:~
```

The result will be true, as you would expect. Ah, but it's not as simple as that. If you create your own class, like this:

```
//: EqualsMethod2.java
class Value
{
int i;
}
public class EqualsMethod2
{
public static void main(String[] args)
{
Value v1 = new Value();
Value v2 = new Value();
v1.i = v2.i = 100;
System.out.println(v1.equals(v2));
}
} ///:~
```

you're back to square one: the result is false. This is because the default behavior of equals( ) is to compare handles. So unless you override equals( ) in your new class you won't get the desired behavior. Unfortunately, you won't learn about overriding until Chapter 7, but being aware of the way equals( ) behaves might save you some grief in the meantime.

Most of the Java library classes implement equals( ) so that it compares the contents of objects instead of their handles.

2.16 Relational and Conditional Operators

A relational operator compares two values and determines the relationship between them. For example, != returns true if the two operands are unequal. This table summarizes Java's relational operators:

Operator	Use Returns true if
> op1 > op2 op1	is greater than op2
>= op1 >= op2 op1	is greater than or equal to op2
< op1 < op2 op1	is less than op2
<= op1 <= op2 op1	is less than or equal to op2
== op1 == op2 op1	and op2 are equal
!= op1 != op2 op1	and op2 are not equal

Relational operators often are used with the conditional operators to construct more complex decision-making expressions. One such operator is &&, which performs the boolean and operation. For example, you can use two different relational operators along with && to determine if both relationships are true. The following line of code uses this technique to determine if an array index is between two boundaries. It determines if the index is both greater than 0 and less than NUM_ENTRIES (which is a previously defined constant value):

```
0 < index && index < NUM_ENTRIES
```

Note that in some instances, the second operand to a conditional operator may not be evaluated. Consider this code segment:

```
(numChars < LIMIT) && (...)
```

The && operator will return true only if both operands are true. So, if numChars is greater than LIMIT, the left-hand operand for && is false and the return value of && can be determined without evaluating the right-hand operand. In such a case, Java will not evaluate the right-hand operand. This has important implications if the right-hand operand has side effects such as reading from a stream, updating a value, or making a calculation. The operator & is similar to && if both of its operands are of boolean type. However, & always evaluates both of its operands and returns true if both are true. Likewise, I is similar to II if both of its operands are boolean. This operator always evalutes both of its operands and returns false if they are both false.

Java supports five binary and one unary conditional operators, shown in the following table:

Operator Use Returns true if

```
&&  op1 && op2  op1 and op2 are both true, conditionally evaluates
op2
||  op1 || op2  either op1 or op2 is true, conditionally evaluates
op2
!  ! op  op is false
&  op1 & op2  op1 and op2 are both true, always evaluates op1 and op2
```

```
|  op1 | op2  either op1 or op2 is true, always evaluates op1 and op2
^  op1 ^ op2  if op1 and op2 are different—that is if one or the other
of the operands is true but not both
```

2.17 Logical Operators in Java

The relational operators you've learned so far (<, <=, >, >=, !=) are sufficient when you only need to check one condition. However what if a particular action is to be taken only if several conditions are true? You can use a sequence of if statements to test the conditions, as follows:

```
if (x == 2) {
if (y != 2) {
System.out.println("Both conditions are true.");
}
}
```

This, however, is hard to write and harder to read. It only gets worse as you add more conditions. Fortunately, Java provides an easy way to handle multiple conditions: the logic operators. There are three logic operators, &&, || and !.

&& is logical and. && combines two boolean values and returns a boolean which is true if and only if both of its operands are true. For instance

```
boolean b;
b = 3 > 2 && 5 < 7; // b is true
b = 2 > 3 && 5 < 7; // b is now false
```

|| is logical or. || combines two boolean variables or expressions and returns a result that is true if either or both of its operands are true. For instance

```
boolean b;
b = 3 > 2 || 5 < 7; // b is true
b = 2 > 3 || 5 < 7; // b is still true
b = 2 > 3 || 5 > 7; // now b is false
```

The last logic operator is ! which means not. It reverses the value of a boolean expression. Thus if b is true !b is false. If b is false !b is true.

```
boolean b;
b = !(3 > 2); // b is false
b = !(2 > 3); // b is true
```

These operators allow you to test multiple conditions more easily. For instance the previous example can now be written as

```
if (x == 2 && y != 2)
{
System.out.println("Both conditions are true.");
}
```

That's a lot clearer.

2.17.1 The Order of Evaluation of Logic Operators

When Java sees a && operator or a ||, the expression on the left side of the operator is evaluated first. For example, consider the following:

```
boolean b, c, d;
b = !(3 > 2); // b is false
c = !(2 > 3); // c is true
d = b && c; // d is false
```

When Java evaluates the expression d = b && c;, it first checks whether b is true. Here b is false, so b && c must be false regardless of whether c is or is not true, so Java doesn't bother checking the value of c.

On the other hand when faced with an || Java short circuits the evaluation as soon as it encounters a true value since the resulting expression must be true. This short circuit evaluation is less important in Java than in C because in Java the operands of && and || must be booleans which are unlikely to have side effects that depend on whether or not they are evaluated. Still it's possible to force them. For instance consider this code.

```
boolean b = (n == 0) || (m/n > 2);
```

Even if n is zero this line will never cause a division by zero, because the left hand side is always evaluated first. If n is zero then the left hand side is true and there's no need to evaluate the right hand side. Mathematically this makes sense because m/0 is in some sense infinite which is greater than two.

This isn't a perfect solution though because m may be 0 or it may be negative. If m is negative and n is zero then m/n is negative infinity which is less than two. And if m is also zero, then m/n is very undefined.

The proper solution at this point depends on your problem. Since real world quantities aren't infinite, when infinities start popping up in your programs, nine times out of ten it's a sign that you've lost too much precision. The remaining times are generally signals that you've left out some small factor in your physical model that would remove the infinity.

Therefore if there's a real chance your program will have a divide by zero error think carefully about what it means and how you should respond to it. If, upon reflection, you decide that what you really want to know is whether m/n is finite and greater than zero you should use a line like this

boolean b = (n != 0) && (m/n > 0);

2.17.2 Avoiding Short Circuits

If you want all of your boolean expressions evaluated regardless of the truth value of each, then you can use & and | instead of && and ||. However make sure you use these only on boolean expressions. Unlike && and ||, & and | also have a meaning for numeric types which is completely different from their meaning for booleans.

2.17.3 Precedence

Finally let's add the &&, ||, &, | and ? operators to the precedence table

Table 2.5 Precedence

*, /, %	Multiplicative operators
+, -	Additive operators
<, >, >=, <=	Relational operators
==, !=	Then do any comparisons for equality and
inequal	ity
	& Bitwise and
	| Bitwise or
	&& Logical and
||	Logical or
? :	Conditional operator
=	Assignment operator

2.17.4 Bitwise Operators

The bitwise operators allow you to manipulate individual bits in an integral primitive data type. Bitwise operators perform boolean algebra on the corresponding bits in the two arguments to produce the result.

The bitwise operators come from C's low-level orientation; you were often manipulating hardware directly and had to set the bits in hardware registers. Java was originally designed to be embedded in TV set-top boxes, so this low-level orientation still made sense. However, you probably won't use the bitwise operators much.

The bitwise AND operator (&) produces a one in the output bit if both input bits are one; otherwise it produces a zero. The bitwise OR operator (|) produces a one in the output bit if either input bit is a one and produces a zero only if both input bits are zero. The bitwise, EXCLUSIVE OR, or XOR (^), produces a one in the output bit if one or the other input bit is a one, but not both. The bitwise NOT (~, also called the ones complement operator) is a unary operator; it takes only one argument. (All other bitwise operators are binary operators.) Bitwise NOT produces the opposite of the input bit - a one if the input bit is zero, a zero if the input bit is one.

The bitwise operators and logical operators use the same characters, so it is helpful to have a mnemonic device to help you remember the meanings: since bits are "small," there is only one character in the bitwise operators.

Bitwise operators can be combined with the = sign to unite the operation and assignment: &=, |= and ^= are all legitimate. (Since ~ is a unary operator it cannot be combined with the = sign.)

The boolean type is treated as a one-bit value so it is somewhat different. You can perform a bitwise AND, OR and XOR, but you can't perform a bitwise NOT (presumably to prevent confusion with the logical NOT). For booleans the bitwise operators have the same effect as the logical operators except that they do not short circuit. Also, the bitwise operators on booleans gives you a XOR logical operator that is not included under the list of "logical" operators. You're prevented from using booleans in shift expressions, which is described next.

2.17.5 Shift and Logical Operators

A shift operator allows you to perform bit manipulation on data. The shift operators also manipulate bits. They can be used solely with primitive, integral types. The left-shift operator (<<) produces the operand to the left of the operator shifted to the left by the number of bits specified after the operator (inserting zeroes at the lower-order bits). The signed right-shift operator (>>) produces the operand to the left of the operator shifted to the right by the number of bits specified after the operator. The signed right shift >> uses sign extension : if the value is positive, zeroes are inserted at the higher-order bits; if the value is negative, ones are inserted at the higher-order bits. Java has also added the unsigned right shift >>>, which uses zero extension : regardless of the sign, zeroes are inserted at the higher-order bits. This operator does not exist in C or C++.

This table summarizes the shift operators available in the Java programming language.

Operator	Use Operation
`>>   op1 >> op2`	shift bits of op1 right by distance op2
`<<   op1 << op2`	shift bits of op1 left by distance op2
`>>>   op1 >>> op2`	shift bits of op1 right by distance op2 (unsigned)

Each shift operator shifts the bits of the left-hand operand over by the number of positions indicated by the right-hand operand. The shift occurs in the direction indicated by the operator itself. For example, the following statement shifts the bits of the integer 13 to the right by one position:

```
13 >> 1;
```

The binary representation of the number 13 is 1101. The result of the shift operation is 1101 shifted to the right by one position—110 or 6 in decimal. Note that the bit farthest to the right falls off the end into the bit bucket. The Java programming language also provides these four operators that perform logical functions on their operands:

Operator	Use	Operation
&	`op1 & op2`	bitwise and
|	`op1 | op2`	bitwise or
^	`op1 ^ op2`	bitwise xor
~	`~op2`	bitwise complement

The & operation performs the logical "and" function on each parallel pair of bits in each operand. The "and" function sets the resulting bit to 1 if both operands are 1, as shown in this table:

op1	op2	Result
0	0	0
0	1	0
1	0	0
1	1	1

Suppose you were to "and" the values 12 and 13:

```
12 & 13
```

The result of this operation is 12. Why? Well, the binary representation of 12 is 1100, and the binary representation of 13 is 1101. The "and" function sets the resulting bit to 1 if both operand bits are 1, otherwise, the resulting bit is 0. So, if you line up the two operands and perform the "and" function, you can see that the two high-order bits (the two bits farthest to the left of each number) of each operand are 1. Thus the resulting bit in the result is also 1. The low-order bits evaluate to 0 because either one or both bits in the operands are 0:

```
1101
& 1100
1100
```

The I operator performs the inclusive or operation and ^ performs the exclusive or operation. Inclusive or means that if either of the two bits are 1 then the result is 1. The following table shows the results of your inclusive or operations:

op1	op2	Result
0	0	0
0	1	1
1	0	1
1	1	1

Exclusive or means that if the two operand bits are different the result is 1, otherwise the result is 0. The following table shows the results of your exclusive or operation.

op1	op2	Result
0	0	0
0	1	1
1	0	1
1	1	0

And finally, the complement operator inverts the value of each bit of the operand: if the operand bit is 1 the result is 0 and if the operand bit is 0 the result is 1. Among other things, bitwise manipulations are useful for managing sets of boolean flags. Suppose for example, that you had several boolean flags in your program that indicated the state of various components in your program: is it visible, is it draggable, and so on. Rather than define a separate boolean variable to hold each flag, you could define a single variable, flags, for all of them. Each bit within flags would represent the current state of one of the flags. You would then use bit manipulations to set and get each flag.

First, set up constants that indicated the various flags for your program. These flags should each be a different power of two to ensure that the "on" bit doesn't overlap with another flag. Define a variable, flags, whose bits would be set according to the current state of each flag. The following code sample initializes flags to 0 which means that all flags are false (none of the bits are set).

```
static final int VISIBLE = 1;
static final int DRAGGABLE = 2;
static final int SELECTABLE = 4;
static final int EDITABLE = 8;
int flags = 0;
```

To set the "visible" flag when something became visible you would use this statement:

```
flags = flags | VISIBLE;
To test for visibility, you could then write:
if ((flags & VISIBLE) == VISIBLE)
{
...
}
```

If you shift a char, byte, or short, it will be promoted to int before the shift takes place, and the result will be an int. Only the five low-order bits of the right-hand side will be used. This prevents you from shifting more than the number of bits in an int. If you're operating on a long, long will be the result. Only the six low-order bits of the right-hand side will be used so you can't shift more than the number of bits in a long. There is a problem, however, with the unsigned right shift. If you use it with byte or short you might not get the correct results. (It's broken in Java 1.0 and Java 1.1.) These are promoted to int and right shifted, but the zero extension does not occur, so you get -1 in those cases. The following example can be used to test your implementation:

```
//: URShift.java
// Test of unsigned right shift

public class URShift {
public static void main(String[] args)
{
int i = -1;
i >>>= 10;
System.out.println(i);
long l = -1;
l >>>= 10;
System.out.println(l);
short s = -1;
s >>>= 10;
System.out.println(s);
```

```
byte b = -1;
b >>>= 10;
System.out.println(b);
}
} ///:~
```

Shifts can be combined with the equal sign (<<= or >>= or >>>=). The lvalue is replaced by the lvalue shifted by the rvalue. s

Here's an example that demonstrates the use of all the operators involving bits:

```
//: BitManipulation.java
// Using the bitwise operators
import java.util.*;
public class BitManipulation ]
{
public static void main(String[] args)
{
Random rand = new Random();
int i = rand.nextInt();
int j = rand.nextInt();
pBinInt("-1", -1);
pBinInt("+1", +1);
int maxpos = 2147483647;
pBinInt("maxpos", maxpos);
int maxneg = -2147483648;
pBinInt("maxneg", maxneg);
pBinInt("i", i);
pBinInt("~i", ~i);
pBinInt("-i", -i);
pBinInt("j", j);
pBinInt("i & j", i & j);
pBinInt("i | j", i | j);
pBinInt("i ^ j", i ^ j);
pBinInt("i << 5", i << 5);
pBinInt("i >> 5", i >> 5);
pBinInt("(~i) >> 5", (~i) >> 5);
pBinInt("i >>> 5", i >>> 5);
pBinInt("(~i) >>> 5", (~i) >>> 5);
long l = rand.nextLong();
long m = rand.nextLong();
pBinLong("-1L", -1L);
pBinLong("+1L", +1L);
long ll = 9223372036854775807L;
pBinLong("maxpos", ll);
long lln = -9223372036854775808L;
pBinLong("maxneg", lln);
pBinLong("l", l);
pBinLong("~l", ~l);
```

```
pBinLong("-1", -1);
pBinLong("m", m);
pBinLong("l & m", l & m);
pBinLong("l | m", l | m);
pBinLong("l ^ m", l ^ m);
pBinLong("l << 5", l << 5);
pBinLong("l >> 5", l >> 5);
pBinLong("(~l) >> 5", (~l) >> 5);
pBinLong("l >>> 5", l >>> 5);
pBinLong("(~l) >>> 5", (~l) >>> 5);
}
static void pBinInt(String s, int i)
{
System.out.println(
s + ", int: " + i + ", binary: ");
System.out.print("   ");
for(int j = 31; j >=0; j—)
if(((1 << j) &  i) != 0)
System.out.print("1");
else
System.out.print("0");
System.out.println();
}
static void pBinLong(String s, long l)
{
System.out.println(
s + ", long: " + l + ", binary: ");
System.out.print("   ");
for(int i = 63; i >=0; i—)
if(((1L << i) & l) != 0)
System.out.print("1");
else
System.out.print("0");
System.out.println();
}
} ///:~
```

The two methods at the end, pBinInt( ) and pBinLong( ) take an int or a long, respectively, and print it out in binary format along with a descriptive string. You can ignore the implementation of these for now.

You'll note the use of System.out.print( ) instead of System.out.println( ). The print( ) method does not put out a new line, so it allows you to output a line in pieces.

As well as demonstrating the effect of all the bitwise operators for int and long, this example also shows the minimum, maximum, +1 and -1 values for int and long so you can see what they look like. Note that the high bit represents the sign: 0 means positive and 1 means negative. The output for the int portion looks like this:

```
-1, int: -1, binary:
11111111111111111111111111111111
```

```
+1, int: 1, binary:
00000000000000000000000000000001
maxpos, int: 2147483647, binary:
01111111111111111111111111111111
maxneg, int: -2147483648, binary:
10000000000000000000000000000000
i, int: 59081716, binary:
00000011100001011000001111110100
~i, int: -59081717, binary:
11111100011110100111110000001011
-i, int: -59081716, binary:
11111100011110100111110000001100
j, int: 198850956, binary:
00001011110110100011100110001100
i & j, int: 58720644, binary:
00000011100000000000000110000100
i | j, int: 199212028, binary:
00001011110111111011101111111100
i ^ j, int: 140491384, binary:
00001000010111111011101001111000
i << 5, int: 1890614912, binary:
01110000101100000111111010000000
i >> 5, int: 1846303, binary:
00000000000111000010110000011111
(~i) >> 5, int: -1846304, binary:
11111111111000111101001111100000
i >>> 5, int: 1846303, binary:
00000000000111000010110000011111
(~i) >>> 5, int: 132371424, binary:
00000111111000111101001111100000
```

The binary representation of the numbers is referred to as signed two's complement .

2.18 Assignment Operators

You use the basic assignment operator, =, to assign one value to another. The MaxVariables program uses = to initialize all of its local variables:

```
// integers
byte largestByte = Byte.MAX_VALUE;
short largestShort = Short.MAX_VALUE;
int largestInteger = Integer.MAX_VALUE;
long largestLong = Long.MAX_VALUE;
// real numbers
float largestFloat = Float.MAX_VALUE;
double largestDouble = Double.MAX_VALUE;
// other primitive types
char aChar = 'S';
boolean aBoolean = true;
```

Java also provides several short cut assignment operators that allow you to perform an arithmetic, logical, or bitwise operation and an assignment operation all with one operator. Suppose you wanted to add a number to a variable and assign the result back into the variable, like this:

```
i = i + 2;
You can shorten this statement using the short cut operator +=.
i += 2;
```

The two previous lines of code are equivalent.

This table lists the shortcut assignment operators and their lengthy equivalents:

<table>
<tr><th>Operator</th><th>Use Equivalent to</th></tr>
<tr><td>+=</td><td>op1 += op2 op1 = op1 + op2</td></tr>
<tr><td>-=</td><td>op1 -= op2 op1 = op1 - op2</td></tr>
<tr><td>*=</td><td>op1 *= op2 op1 = op1 * op2</td></tr>
<tr><td>/=</td><td>op1 /= op2 op1 = op1 / op2</td></tr>
<tr><td>%=</td><td>op1 %= op2 op1 = op1 % op2</td></tr>
<tr><td>&=</td><td>op1 &= op2 op1 = op1 & op2</td></tr>
<tr><td>|=</td><td>op1 |= op2 op1 = op1 | op2</td></tr>
<tr><td>^=</td><td>op1 ^= op2 op1 = op1 ^ op2</td></tr>
<tr><td><<=</td><td>op1 <<= op2 op1 = op1 << op2</td></tr>
<tr><td>>>=</td><td>op1 >>= op2 op1 = op1 >> op2</td></tr>
<tr><td>>>>=</td><td>op1 >>>= op2 op1 = op1 >>> op2</td></tr>
</table>

2.19 Operator Precedence in Java

It's possible to combine multiple arithmetic expressions in one statement. For instance the following line adds the numbers one through five:

```
int m = 1 + 2 + 3 + 4 + 5;
```

A slightly more interesting example: the following program calculates the energy equivalent of an electron using Einstein's famous formula E = mc2.

```
class mc2
{
public static void main (String args[])
{
double mass = 9.1096E-25;
double c = 2.998E8;
double E = mass * c * c;
System.out.println(E);
}
}
```

Here's the output:

```
% javac mc2.java
% java mc2
8.18771e-08
%
```

This is all very obvious. However if you use different operators on the same line it's not always clear what the result will be. For instance consider the following code fragment:

```
int n = 1 - 2 * 3 - 4 + 5;
```

Is n equal to -2? You might think so if you just calculate from left to right. However if you compile this in a program and print out the result you'll find that Java thinks n is equal to -4. Java got that number because it performs all multiplications before it performs any additions or subtractions. If you like you can think of the calculation Java did as being:

```
int n = 1 - (2 * 3) - 4 + 5;
```

This is an issue of order of evaluation. Within the limited number of operators you've learned so far here is how Java calculates:

`*, /, %`	Do all multiplications, divisions and remainders from left to right.
`+, -`	Do additions and subtractions from left to right.
`=`	Assign the right-hand side to the left-hand side

2.20 Miscellaneous Operators

2.20.1 The ? : operator in Java

The value of a variable often depends on whether a particular boolean expression is or is not true and on nothing else. For instance one common operation is setting the value of a variable to the maximum of two quantities. In Java you might write

```
if (a > b)
{
max = a;
}
else
{
max = b;
}
```

Setting a single variable to one of two states based on a single condition is such a common use of if-else that a shortcut has been devised for it, the conditional operator, ?:. Using the conditional operator you can rewrite the above example in a single line like this:

max = (a > b) ? a : b;

(a > b) ? a : b; is an expression which returns one of two values, a or b. The condition, (a > b), is tested. If it is true the first value, a, is returned. If it is false, the second value, b, is returned. Whichever value is returned is dependent on the conditional test, a > b. The condition can be any expression which returns a boolean value.

The conditional operator only works for assigning a value to a variable, using a value in a method invocation, or in some other way that indicates the type of its second and third arguments.

For example, consider the following

```
if (name.equals("Rumplestiltskin"))
s
{
System.out.println("Give back child");
}
```

```
else
{
System.out.println("laugh");
}
```

This may not be written like this:

```
name.equals("Rumplestiltskin") ?
System.out.println("Give back child"); :
System.out.println("Give back child");;
```

First of all, both the second and third arguments are void. Secondly, no assignment is present to indicate the type that is expected for the second and third arguments (though you know void must be wrong).

The first argument to the conditional operator must have or return boolean type and the second and third arguments must return values compatible with the value the entire expression can be expected to return. You can never use a void method as an argument to the ? : operator.

The conditional operator only works for assigning a value to a variable, using a value in a method invocation, or in some other way that indicates the type of its second and third arguments.

For example, consider the following

```
if (name.equals("Rumplestiltskin"))
{
System.out.println("Give back child");
}
else {
System.out.println("laugh");
}
```

This may not be written like this:

```
name.equals("Rumplestiltskin") ?
System.out.println("Give back child"); :
System.out.println("Give back child");;
```

First of all, both the second and third arguments are void. Secondly, no assignment is present to indicate the type that is expected for the second and third arguments (though you know void must be wrong).

The first argument to the conditional operator must have or return boolean type and the second and third arguments must return values compatible with the value the entire expression can be expected to return. You can never use a void method as an argument to the ? : operator.

2.20.2 The Comma Operator

The comma is used in C and C++ not only as a separator in function argument lists, but also as an operator for sequential evaluation. The sole place that the comma operator is used in Java is in for loops, which will be described later in this chapter.

2.20.3 String Operator +

There's one special usage of an operator in Java: the + operator can be used to concatenate strings, as you've already seen. It seems a natural use of the + even though it doesn't fit with the traditional way that + is used. This capability seemed like a good idea in C++, so operator overloading was added to C++ to allow the C++ programmer to add meanings to almost any operator. Unfortunately, operator overloading combined with some of the other restrictions in C++ turns out to be a fairly complicated feature for programmers to design into their classes. Although operator overloading would have been much simpler to implement in Java than it was in C++, this feature was still considered too complex, so Java programmers cannot implement their own overloaded operators as C++ programmers can.

The use of the String + has some interesting behavior. If an expression begins with a String, then all operands that follow must be Strings:

```
int x = 0, y = 1, z = 2;
String sString = "x, y, z ";
System.out.println(sString + x + y + z);
```

Here, the Java compiler will convert x, y, and z into their String representations instead of adding them together first. However, if you say:

```
System.out.println(x + sString);
```

earlier versions of Java will signal an error. (Later versions, however, will turn x into a String.) So if you're putting together a String (using an earlier version of Java) with addition, make sure the first element is a String (or a quoted sequence of characters, which the compiler recognizes as a String).

2.20.4 Common pitfalls when using operators

One of the pitfalls when using operators is trying to get away without parentheses when you are even the least bit uncertain about how an expression will evaluate. This is still true in Java.

An extremely common error in C and C++ looks like this:

```
while(x = y)
{
// ....
}
```

The programmer was trying to test for equivalence (==) rather than do an assignment. In C and C++ the result of this assignment will always be true if y is nonzero, and you'll probably get an infinite loop. In Java, the result of this expression is not a boolean, and the compiler expects a boolean and won't convert from an int, so it will conveniently give you a compile-time error and catch the problem before you ever try to run the program. So the pitfall never happens in Java. (The only time you won't get a compile-time error is when x and y are boolean, in which case x = y is a legal expression, and in the above case, probably an error.)

A similar problem in C and C++ is using bitwise AND and OR instead of logical. Bitwise AND and OR use one of the characters (& or |) while logical AND and OR use two (&& and ||). Just as with = and ==, it's easy to type just one character instead of two. In Java, the compiler again prevents this because it won't let you cavalierly use one type where it doesn't belong.

2.20.5 Casting Operators

The word cast is used in the sense of "casting into a mold." Java will automatically change one type of data into another when appropriate. For instance, if you assign an integral value to a floating-point variable, the compiler will automatically convert the int to a float. Casting allows you to make this type conversion explicit, or to force it when it wouldn't normally happen.

To perform a cast, put the desired data type (including all modifiers) inside parentheses to the left of any value. Here's an example:

```
void casts()
{
    int i = 200;
    long l = (long)i;
    long l2 = (long)200;
}
```

As you can see, it's possible to perform a cast on a numeric value as well as on a variable. In both casts shown here, however, the cast is superfluous, since the compiler will automatically promote an int value to a long when necessary. You can still put a cast in to make a point or to make your code more clear. In other situations, a cast is essential just to get the code to compile.

In C and C++, casting can cause some headaches. In Java, casting is safe, with the exception that when you perform a so-called narrowing conversion (that is, when you go from a data type that can hold more information to one that doesn't hold as much) you run the risk of losing information. Here the compiler forces you to do a cast, in effect saying "this can be a dangerous thing to do - if you want me to do it anyway you must make the cast explicit." With a widening conversion an explicit cast is not needed because the new type will more than hold the information from the old type so that no information is ever lost.

Java allows you to cast any primitive type to any other primitive type, except for boolean, which doesn't allow any casting at all. Class types do not allow casting. To convert one to the other there must be special methods. (String is a special case, and you'll find out later in the book that objects can be cast within a family of types; an Oak can be cast to a Tree and vice-versa, but not to a foreign type such as a Rock.)

2.20.6 Ternary Operator

The Java programming language supports one ternary operator—the ?: operator. This operator is a conditional operator and is short-hand for an if-else statement:

```
op1 ? op2 : op3
```

The ?: operator returns op2 if op1 is true or returns op3 if op1 is false.

2.20.7 A compendium of operators

The following example shows which primitive data types can be used with particular operators. Basically, it is the same example repeated over and over, but using different primitive data types. The file will compile without error because the lines that would cause errors are commented out with a //!.

```
//: AllOps.java
// Tests all the operators on all the
// primitive data types to show which
// ones are accepted by the Java compiler.
class AllOps
{
// To accept the results of a boolean test:
void f(boolean b) {}
void boolTest(boolean x, boolean y)
{
// Arithmetic operators:
//! x = x * y;
```

```
//! x = x / y;
//! x = x % y;
//! x = x + y;
//! x = x - y;
//! x++;
//! x--;
//! x = +y;
//! x = -y;
// Relational and logical:
//! f(x > y);
//! f(x >= y);
//! f(x < y);
//! f(x <= y);
f(x == y);
f(x != y);
f(!y);
x = x && y;
x = x || y;
// Bitwise operators:
//! x = ~y;
x = x & y;
x = x | y;
x = x ^ y;
//! x = x << 1;
//! x = x >> 1;
//! x = x >>> 1;
// Compound assignment:
//! x += y;
//! x -= y;
//! x *= y;
//! x /= y;
//! x %= y;
//! x <<= 1;
//! x >>= 1;
//! x >>>= 1;
x &= y;
x ^= y;
x |= y;
// Casting:
//! char c = (char)x;
//! byte B = (byte)x;
//! short s = (short)x;
//! int i = (int)x;
//! long l = (long)x;
//! float f = (float)x;
//! double d = (double)x;
}
void charTest(char x, char y)
```

```
{
// Arithmetic operators:
x = (char)(x * y);
x = (char)(x / y);
x = (char)(x % y);
x = (char)(x + y);
x = (char)(x - y);
x++;
x—;
x = (char)+y;
x = (char)-y;
// Relational and logical:
f(x > y);
f(x >= y);
f(x < y);
f(x <= y);
f(x == y);
f(x != y);
//! f(!x);
//! f(x && y);
//! f(x || y);
// Bitwise operators:
x= (char)~y;
x = (char)(x & y);
x  = (char)(x | y);
x = (char)(x ^ y);
x = (char)(x << 1);
x = (char)(x >> 1);
x = (char)(x >>> 1);
// Compound assignment:
x += y;
x -= y;
x *= y;
x /= y;
x %= y;
x <<= 1;
x >>= 1;
x >>>= 1;
x &= y;
x ^= y;
x |= y;
// Casting:
//! boolean b = (boolean)x;
byte B = (byte)x;
short s = (short)x;
int i = (int)x;
long l = (long)x;
float f = (float)x;
```

```
double d = (double)x;
}
void byteTest(byte x, byte y)
{
// Arithmetic operators:
x = (byte)(x* y);
x = (byte)(x / y);
x = (byte)(x % y);
x = (byte)(x + y);
x = (byte)(x - y);
x++;
x--;
x = (byte)+ y;
x = (byte)- y;
// Relational and logical:
f(x > y);
f(x >= y);
f(x < y);
f(x <= y);
f(x == y);
f(x != y);
//! f(!x);
//! f(x && y);
//! f(x || y);
// Bitwise operators:
x = (byte)~y;
x = (byte)(x & y);
x = (byte)(x | y);
x = (byte)(x ^ y);
x = (byte)(x << 1);
x = (byte)(x >> 1);
x = (byte)(x >>> 1);
// Compound assignment:
x += y;
x -= y;
x *= y;
x /= y;
x %= y;
x <<= 1;
x >>= 1;
x >>>= 1;
x &= y;
x ^= y;
x |= y;
// Casting:
//! boolean b = (boolean)x;
char c = (char)x;
short s = (short)x;
```

```
int i = (int)x;
long l = (long)x;
float f = (float)x;
double d = (double)x;
}
void shortTest(short x, short y)
{
// Arithmetic operators:
x = (short)(x * y);
x = (short)(x / y);
x = (short)(x % y);
x = (short)(x + y);
x = (short)(x - y);
x++;
x--;
x = (short)+y;
x = (short)-y;
// Relational and logical:
f(x > y);
f(x >= y);
f(x < y);
f(x <= y);
f(x == y);
f(x != y);
//! f(!x);
//! f(x && y);
//! f(x || y);
// Bitwise operators:
x = (short)~y;
x = (short)(x & y);
x = (short)(x | y);
x = (short)(x ^ y);
x = (short)(x << 1);
x = (short)(x >> 1);
x = (short)(x >>> 1);
// Compound assignment:
x += y;
x -= y;
x *= y;
x /= y;
x %= y;
x <<= 1;
x >>= 1;
x >>>= 1;
x &= y;
x ^= y;
x |= y;
// Casting:
```

```
//! boolean b = (boolean)x;
char c = (char)x;
byte B = (byte)x;
int i = (int)x;
long l = (long)x;
float f = (float)x;
double d = (double)x;
}
void intTest(int x, int y)
{
// Arithmetic operators:
x = x * y;
x = x / y;
x = x % y;
x = x + y;
x = x - y;
x++;
x—;
x = +y;
x = -y;
// Relational and logical:
f(x > y);
f(x >= y);
f(x < y);
f(x <= y);
f(x == y);
f(x != y);
//! f(!x);
//! f(x && y);
//! f(x || y);
// Bitwise operators:
x = ~y;
x = x & y;
x = x | y;
x = x ^ y;
x = x << 1;
x = x >> 1;
x = x >>> 1;
// Compound assignment:
x += y;
x -= y;
x *= y;
x /= y;
x %= y;
x <<= 1;
x >>= 1;
x >>>= 1;
x &= y;
```

```
x ^= y;
x |= y;
// Casting:
//! boolean b = (boolean)x;
char c = (char)x;
byte B = (byte)x;
short s = (short)x;
long l = (long)x;
float f = (float)x;
double d = (double)x;
}
void longTest(long x, long y)
{
// Arithmetic operators:
x = x * y;
x = x / y;
x = x % y;
x = x + y;
x = x - y;
x++;
x—;
x = +y;
x = -y;
// Relational and logical:
f(x > y);
f(x >= y);
f(x < y);
f(x <= y);
f(x == y);
f(x != y);
//! f(!x);
//! f(x && y);
//! f(x || y);
// Bitwise operators:
x = ~y;
x = x & y;
x = x | y;
x = x ^ y;
x = x << 1;
x = x >> 1;
x = x >>> 1;
// Compound assignment:
x += y;
x -= y;
x *= y;
x /= y;
x %= y;
x <<= 1;
```

```
x >>= 1;
x >>>= 1;
x &= y;
x ^= y;
x |= y;
// Casting:
//! boolean b = (boolean)x;
char c = (char)x;
byte B = (byte)x;
short s = (short)x;
int i = (int)x;
float f = (float)x;
double d = (double)x;
}
void floatTest(float x, float y)
{
// Arithmetic operators:
x = x * y;
x = x / y;
x = x % y;
x = x + y;
x = x - y;
x++;
x--;
x = +y;
x = -y;
// Relational and logical:
f(x > y);
f(x >= y);
f(x < y);
f(x <= y);
f(x == y);
f(x != y);
//! f(!x);
//! f(x && y);
//! f(x || y);
// Bitwise operators:
//! x = ~y;
//! x = x & y;
//! x = x | y;
//! x = x ^ y;
//! x = x << 1;
//! x = x >> 1;
//! x = x >>> 1;
// Compound assignment:
x += y;
x -= y;
x *= y;
```

```
x /= y;
x %= y;
//! x <<= 1;
//! x >>= 1;
//! x >>>= 1;
//! x &= y;
//! x ^= y;
//! x |= y;
// Casting:
//! boolean b = (boolean)x;
char c = (char)x;
byte B = (byte)x;
short s = (short)x;
int i = (int)x;
long l = (long)x;
double d = (double)x;
}
void doubleTest(double x, double y)
{
// Arithmetic operators:
x = x * y;
x = x / y;
x = x % y;
x = x + y;
x = x - y;
x++;
x—;
x = +y;
x = -y;
// Relational and logical:
f(x > y);
f(x >= y);
f(x < y);
f(x <= y);
f(x == y);
f(x != y);
//! f(!x);
//! f(x && y);
//! f(x || y);
// Bitwise operators:
//! x = ~y;
//! x = x & y;
//! x = x | y;
//! x = x ^ y;
//! x = x << 1;
//! x = x >> 1;
//! x = x >>> 1;
// Compound assignment:
```

```
x += y;
x -= y;
x *= y;
x /= y;
x %= y;
//! x <<= 1;
//! x >>= 1;
//! x >>>= 1;
//! x &= y;
//! x ^= y;
//! x |= y;
// Casting:
//! boolean b = (boolean)x;
char c = (char)x;
byte B = (byte)x;
short s = (short)x;
int i = (int)x;
long l = (long)x;
float f = (float)x;
}
} ///:~
```

Note that boolean is quite limited. You can assign to it the values true and false, and you can test it for truth or falsehood, but you cannot add booleans or perform any other type of operation on them.

In char, byte, and short you can see the effect of promotion with the arithmetic operators. Each arithmetic operation on any of those types results in an int result, which must be explicitly cast back to the original type (a narrowing conversion that might lose information) to assign back to that type. With int values, however, you do not need to cast, because everything is already an int. Don't be lulled into thinking everything is safe, though. If you multiply two ints that are big enough, you'll overflow the result. The following example demonstrates this:

Example 2.13

```
//: Overflow.java
// Surprise! Java lets you overflow.

public class Overflow
{
public static void main(String[] args)
{
int big = 0x7fffffff; // max int value
prt("big = " + big);
int bigger = big * 4;
prt("bigger = " + bigger);
}
static void prt(String s)
{
System.out.println(s);
}
} ///:~
```

The output of this is:

```
big = 2147483647
bigger = -4
```

and you get no errors or warnings from the compiler, and no exceptions at run-time. Java is good, but it's not that good.

Compound assignments do not require casts for char, byte, or short, even though they are performing promotions that have the same results as the direct arithmetic operations. On the other hand, the lack of the cast certainly simplifies the code.

You can see that, with the exception of boolean, any primitive type can be cast to any other primitive type. Again, you must be aware of the effect of a narrowing conversion when casting to a smaller type, otherwise you might unknowingly lose information during the cast.

2.21 Parentheses in Java

Sometimes the default order of evaluation isn't what you want. For instance, the formula to change a Fahrenheit temperature to a Celsius temperature is C = (5/9) (F - 32) where C is degrees Celsius and F is degrees Fahrenheit. You must subtract 32 from the Fahrenheit temperature before you multiply by 5/9, not after. You can use parentheses to adjust the order much as they are used in the above formula. The next program prints a table showing the conversions from Fahrenheit and Celsius between zero and three hundred degrees Fahrenheit every twenty degrees.

Example 2.14

```
// Print a Fahrenheit to Celsius table
class FahrToCelsius  {
public static void main (String args[])
{
double fahr, celsius;
double lower, upper, step;
// lower limit of temperature table
lower = 0.0;
// upper limit of temperature table
upper = 300.0;
// step size
step  = 20.0;
fahr = lower;
while (fahr <= upper) {
celsius = (5.0 / 9.0) * (fahr-32.0);
System.out.println(fahr + " " + celsius);
fahr = fahr + step;
}
}
}
```

As usual here's the output:

```
% javac FahrToCelsius.java
% java FahrToCelsius
0 -17.7778
20 -6.66667
```

```
40 4.44444
60 15.5556
80 26.6667
100 37.7778
120 48.8889
140 60
160 71.1111
180 82.2222
200 92.3333
220 104.444
240 115.556
260 126.667
280 137.778
300 148.889
%
```

This program is a little more involved than the previous examples. Mostly it's stuff you've seen before though so a line by line analysis isn't necessary. The line to be concerned with is

celsius = (5.0 / 9.0) * (fahr-32.0);

This is a virtual translation of the formula C = (5/9)(F - 32) with the single change that a * was added because Java does not implicitly multiply items in parentheses. The parentheses are used just as they are in regular algebra, to adjust the precedence of terms in a formula. In fact the precedence of operations that use the basic arithmetic operators (+, -, *, /) is exactly the same as you learned in high school algebra.

Remember, you can always use parentheses to change the order of evaluation. Everything inside the parentheses will be calculated before anything outside of the parentheses is calculated. If you're in doubt it never hurts to put in extra parentheses to clear up the order in which terms will be evaluated.

2.22 Mixing Data Types

Order can make a differenc when data types are mixed. For example,

```
1 / 2 * 2.5 = 0.0
2.5 * 1 / 2 = 1.75
2.5 / 2 = 1.75
```

You cannot assume that the usual mathematical laws of commutativity apply when mixing data types, especially integer and floating point types.

```
1.0 / 2 * 2.5 = 1.75
2.5 * 1.0 / 2 = 1.75
1 / 2.0 * 2.5 = 1.75
2.5 * 1.0 / 2.0 = 1.75
```

As well as combining different operations, you can mix and match different numeric data types on the same line. The program below uses both ints and doubles, for example.

Example 2.15

```
class IntAndDouble
{
public static void main (String args[])
```

```
{
int i = 10;
double x = 2.5;
double k;
System.out.println("i is " + i);
System.out.println("x is " + x);
k = i + x;
System.out.println("i + x is " + k);
k = i * x;
System.out.println("i * x is " + k);
k = i - x;
System.out.println("i - x is " + k);
k = x - i;
System.out.println("x - i is " + k);
k = i / x;
System.out.println("i / x is " + k);
k = x / i;
System.out.println("x / i is " + k);
}
}
```

This program produces the following output:

```
% java IntAndDouble
i is 10
x is 2.5
i + x is 12.5
i * x is 25
i - x is 7.5
x - i is -7.5
i / x is 4
x / i is 0.25
%
```

2.23 Arithmetic Promotion and Binary Operations

An int divided by an int is an int, and a double divided by a double is a double, but what about an int divided by a double or a double divided by an int? When doing arithmetic on unlike types Java tends to widen the types involved so as to avoid losing information. After all 3 * 54.2E18 will be a perfectly valid double but much too big for any int.

The basic rule is that if either of the variables in a binary operation (addition, multiplication, subtraction, addition, remainder) are doubles then Java treats both values as doubles. If neither value is a double but one is a float, then Java treats both values as floats. If neither is a float or a double but one is a long, then Java treats both values as longs. Finally if there are no doubles, floats or longs, then Java treats both values as an int, even if there aren't any ints in the equation. Therefore the result will be a double, float, long or int depending on the types of the arguments.

2.24 Arithmetic Promotion, Assignments, and Casting

In an assignment statement, i.e. if there's an equals sign, Java compares the type of the left hand side to the final type of the right hand side. It won't change the type of the left hand side, but it will check to make sure that the value it has (double, float, int or long) on the right hand side can fit in the type on the left hand side. Anything can fit in a double. Anything except a double can fit in a float. Any integral type can fit in a long, but a float or a double can't, and ints, shorts, and bytes can fit inside ints. If the right hand side can fit inside the left hand side, the assignment takes place with no further ado.

Assigning long values to int variables or double values to float variables can be equally troublesome. In fact it's so troublesome the compiler won't let you do it unless you tell it you really mean it with a cast. When it's necessary to force a value into a particular type, use a cast. To cast a variable or a literal or an expression to a different data type just precede it with the type in parentheses. For instance:

```
int i = (int) 9.0/4.0;
```

A cast lets the compiler know that you're serious about the conversion you plan to make.

When a value is cast down before assignment, series of operations takes place to chop the right hand side down to size. For a conversion between a floating point number and an int or a long, the fractional part of the floating point number is truncated (rounded toward zero). This produces an integer. If the integer is small enough to fit in the left hand side, the assignment is completed. On the other hand if the number is too large, then the integer is set to the largest possible value of its type. If the floating point number is too small the integer is set to the smallest possible value of its type.

This can be a nasty bug in your code. It can also be hard to find since everything may work perfectly 99 times out of a hundred and only on rare occasions will the rounding become a problem. However when it does there will be no warning or error message. You need to be very careful when assigning floating point values to integer types.

2.25 Converting Strings to Numbers

When processing user input it is often necessary to convert a String that the user enters into an int. The syntax is straightforward. It requires using the static Integer.valueOf(String s) and intValue() methods from the java.lang.Integer class. To convert the String "22" into the int 22 you would write

```
int i = Integer.valueOf("22").intValue();
Doubles, floats and longs are converted similarly. To convert a
String like "22" into the long value 22 you would write
long l = Long.valueOf("22").longValue();
To convert "22.5" into a float or a double you would write:
double x = Double.valueOf("22.5").doubleValue();
float y = Float.valueOf("22.5").floatValue();
```

The various valueOf() methods are relatively intelligent and can handle plus and minus signs, exponents, and most other common number formats. However if you pass one something completely non-numeric like "pretty in pink," it will throw a NumberFormatException. You haven't learned how to handle exceptions yet, so try to avoid passing theses methods non-numeric data.

You can now rewrite the E = mc2 program to accept the mass in kilograms as user input from the command line. Many of the exercises will be similar.

Example 2.16

```
class mc2
{
public static void main (String args[])
{
```

```
double mass;
double c = 2.998E8;   // meters/second
double E;
mass = Double.valueOf(args[0]).doubleValue();
E = mass * c * c;
System.out.println(E + "Joules");
}
}
```

Here's the output:

```
% javac mc2.java
% java mc2 0.0456
4.09853e+15 Joules
%
```

2.26 Ternary if-else Operator

This operator is unusual because it has three operands. It is truly an operator because it produces a value, unlike the ordinary if-else statement that you'll see in the next section of this chapter. The expression is of the form

```
boolean-exp ? value0 : value1
```

If boolean-exp evaluates to true, value0 is evaluated and its result becomes the value produced by the operator. If boolean-exp is false, value1 is evaluated and its result becomes the value produced by the operator.

Of course, you could use an ordinary if-else statement (described later), but the ternary operator is much terser. Although C prides itself on being a terse language, and the ternary operator might have been introduced partly for efficiency, you should be somewhat wary of using it on an everyday basis - it's easy to produce unreadable code.

The conditional operator can be used for its side effects or for the value it produces, but in general you want the value since that's what makes the operator distinct from the if-else. Here's an example:

```
static int ternary(int i)
{
return i < 10 ? i * 100 : i * 10;
}
```

You can see that this code is more compact than what you'd need to write without the ternary operator:

```
static int alternative(int i)
{
if (i < 10)
return i * 100;
return i * 10;
}
```

The second form is easier to understand, and doesn't require a lot more typing. So be sure to ponder your reasons when choosing the ternary operator.

2.27 Arrays

Most of the necessary introduction to arrays is in the last section of Chapter 4, which shows how you define and initialize an array. Holding objects is the focus of this chapter, and an array is just one way to hold objects. But there are a number of other ways to hold objects, so what makes an array special?

There are two issues that distinguish arrays from other types of collections: efficiency and type. The array is the most efficient way that Java provides to store and access a sequence of objects (actually, object handles). The array is a simple linear sequence, which makes element access fast, but you pay for this speed: when you create an array object, its size is fixed and cannot be changed for the lifetime of that array object. You might suggest creating an array of a particular size and then, if you run out of space, creating a new one and moving all the handles from the old one to the new one. This is the behavior of the Vector class, which will be studied later in the chapter. However, because of the overhead of this size flexibility, a Vector is measurably less efficient than an array.

The vector class in C++ does know the type of objects it holds, but it has a different drawback when compared with arrays in Java: the C++ vector's operator[] doesn't do bounds checking, so you can run past the end. (It's possible, however, to ask how big the vector is, and the at( ) method does perform bounds checking.) In Java, you get bounds checking regardless of whether you're using an array or a collection - you'll get a RuntimeException if you exceed the bounds. As you'll learn in Chapter 9, this type of exception indicates a programmer error and thus you don't need to check for it in your code. As an aside, the reason the C++ vector doesn't check bounds with every access is speed - in Java you have the constant performance overhead of bounds checking all the time for both arrays and collections.

The other generic collection classes that will be studied in this chapter, Vector, Stack, and Hashtable, all deal with objects as if they had no specific type. That is, they treat them as type Object, the root class of all classes in Java. This works fine from one standpoint: you need to build only one collection, and any Java object will go into that collection. (Except for primitives - these can be placed in collections as constants using the Java primitive wrapper classes, or as changeable values by wrapping in your own class.) This is the second place where an array is superior to the generic collections: when you create an array, you create it to hold a specific type. This means that you get compile-time type checking to prevent you from putting the wrong type in, or mistaking the type that you're extracting. Of course, Java will prevent you from sending an inappropriate message to an object, either at compile-time or at run-time. So it's not as if it's riskier one way or the other, it's just nicer if the compiler points it out to you, faster at run-time, and there's less likelihood that the end user will get surprised by an exception.

For efficiency and type checking it's always worth trying to use an array if you can. However, when you're trying to solve a more general problem arrays can be too restrictive. After looking at arrays, the rest of this chapter will be devoted to the collection classes provided by Java.

2.27.1 Arrays are first-class objects

Regardless of what type of array you're working with, the array identifier is actually a handle to a true object that's created on the heap. The heap object can be created either implicitly, as part of the array initialization syntax, or explicitly with a new expression. Part of the heap object (in fact, the only field or method you can access) is the read-only length member that tells you how many elements can be stored in that array object. The '[]' syntax is the only other access that you have to the array object.

The following example shows the various ways that an array can be initialized, and how the array handles can be assigned to different array objects. It also shows that arrays of objects and arrays of primitives are almost identical in their use. The only difference is that arrays of objects hold handles while arrays of primitives hold the primitive values directly. (See page 97 if you have trouble executing this program.)

Example 2.17

```
//: ArraySize.java
// Initialization & re-assignment of arrays
package c08;

class Weeble {} // A small mythical creature

public class ArraySize
{
public static void main(String[] args)
{
// Arrays of objects:
Weeble[] a; // Null handle
Weeble[] b = new Weeble[5]; // Null handles
Weeble[] c = new Weeble[4];
for(int i = 0; i < c.length; i++)
c[i] = new Weeble();
Weeble[] d =
{
new Weeble(), new Weeble(), new Weeble()
};
// Compile error: variable a not initialized:
//!System.out.println("a.length=" + a.length);
System.out.println("b.length =" + b.length);
// The handles inside the array are
// automatically initialized to null:
for(int i = 0; i < b.length; i++)
System.out.println("b[" + i + "]=" + b[i]);
System.out.println("c.length =" + c.length);
System.out.println("d.length =" + d.length);
a = d;
System.out.println("a.length =" + a.length);
// Java 1.1 initialization syntax:
a = new Weeble[]
{
new Weeble(), new Weeble()
};
System.out.println("a.length =" + a.length);

// Arrays of primitives:
int[] e; // Null handle
int[] f = new int[5];
int[] g = new int[4];
for(int i = 0; i < g.length; i++)
g[i] = i*i;
int[] h = { 11, 47, 93 };
// Compile error: variable e not initialized:
//!System.out.println("e.length=" + e.length);
```

```
System.out.println("f.length =" + f.length);
// The primitives inside the array are
// automatically initialized to zero:
for(int i = 0; i < f.length; i++)
System.out.println("f[" + i + "]=" + f[i]);
System.out.println("g.length =" + g.length);
System.out.println("h.length =" + h.length);
e = h;
System.out.println("e.length =" + e.length);
// Java 1.1 initialization syntax:
e = new int[] { 1, 2 };
System.out.println("e.length =" + e.length);
}
} ///:~
```

Here's the output from the program:

```
b.length = 5
b[0]=null
b[1]=null
b[2]=null
b[3]=null
b[4]=null
c.length = 4
d.length = 3
a.length = 3
a.length = 2
f.length = 5
f[0]=0
f[1]=0
f[2]=0
f[3]=0
f[4]=0
g.length = 4
h.length = 3
e.length = 3
e.length = 2
```

The array a is initially just a null handle, and the compiler prevents you from doing anything with this handle until you've properly initialized it. The array b is initialized to point to an array of Weeble handles, but no actual Weeble objects are ever placed in that array. However, you can still ask what the size of the array is, since b is pointing to a legitimate object. This brings up a slight drawback: you can't find out how many elements are actually in the array, since length tells you only how many elements can be placed in the array; that is, the size of the array object, not the number of elements it actually holds. However, when an array object is created its handles are automatically initialized to null so you can see whether a particular array slot has an object in it by checking to see whether it's null. Similarly, an array of primitives is automatically initialized to zero for numeric types, null for char, and false for boolean.

Array c shows the creation of the array object followed by the assignment of Weeble objects to all the slots in the array. Array d shows the "aggregate initialization" syntax that causes the array object to be created (implicitly with new on the heap, just like for array c) and initialized with Weeble objects, all in one statement.

The expression

```
a = d;
```

shows how you can take a handle that's attached to one array object and assign it to another array object, just as you can do with any other type of object handle. Now both a and d are pointing to the same array object on the heap.

Java 1.1 adds a new array initialization syntax, which could be thought of as a "dynamic aggregate initialization." The Java 1.0 aggregate initialization used by d must be used at the point of d's definition, but with the Java 1.1 syntax you can create and initialize an array object anywhere. For example, suppose hide( ) is a method that takes an array of Weeble objects. You could call it by saying:

```
hide(d);
```

but in Java 1.1 you can also dynamically create the array you want to pass as the argument:

hide(new Weeble[] { new Weeble(), new Weeble() });

This new syntax provides a more convenient way to write code in some situations.

The second part of the above example shows that primitive arrays work just like object arrays except that primitive arrays hold the primitive values directly.

2.27.2 Declaring Arrays

Like all other variables in Java, an array must have a specific type like byte, int, String or double. Only variables of the appropriate type can be stored in an array. One array cannot store both ints and Strings, for instance.

Like all other variables in Java an array must be declared. When you declare an array variable you suffix the type with [] to indicate that this variable is an array. Here are some examples:

```
int[] k;
float[] yt;
String[] names;
```

This says that k is an array of ints, yt is an array of floats and names is an array of Strings. In other words you declare an array like you declare any other variable except that you append brackets to the end of the type.

You also have the option to append the brackets to the variable instead of the type.

```
int k[];
float yt[];
String names[];
```

The choice is primarily one of personal preference. You can even use both at the same time like this

```
int[] k[];
float[] yt[];
String[] names[];
```

2.27.3 Creating Arrays

Declaring arrays merely says what kind of values the array will hold. It does not create them. Java arrays are objects, and like any other object you use the new keyword to create them. When you create an array, you must tell the compiler how many components will be stored in it. Here's how you'd create the variables declared on the previous page:

```
k = new int[3];
yt = new float[7];
names = new String[50];
```

The numbers in the brackets specify the length of the array; that is, how many slots it has to hold values. With the lengths above k can hold three ints, yt can hold seven floats and names can hold fifty Strings. This step is sometimes called allocating the array since it sets aside the memory the array requires.

2.27.4 Initializing Arrays

Individual components of an array are referenced by the array name and by an integer which represents their position in the array. The numbers you use to identify them are called subscripts or indexes into the array.

Subscripts are consecutive integers beginning with 0. Thus the array k above has components k[0], k[1], and k[2]. Since you start counting at zero there is no k[3], and trying to access it will throw an ArrayIndexOutOfBoundsException. You can use array components wherever you'd use a similarly typed variable that wasn't part of an array. For example this is how you'd store values in the arrays above:

```
k[0] = 2;
k[1] = 5;
k[2] = -2;
yt[17] = 7.5f;
names[4] = "Fred";
```

This step is called initializing the array or, more precisely, initializing the components of the array. Sometimes the phrase "initializing the array" is used to mean when you initialize all the components of the array.

For even medium sized arrays, it's unwieldy to specify each component individually. It is often helpful to use for loops to initialize the array. Here is a loop which fills an array with the squares of the numbers from 0 to 100.

```
float[] squares;
squares = new float[101];
for (int i=0; i <= 100; i++)
{
squares[i] = i*i;
}
```

Two things you should note about this code fragment:

Watch the fenceposts! Since array subscripts begin at zero you need 101 components if you want to include the square of 100.

Although i is an int, it is promoted to a float when it is stored in squares, since squares is declared to be an array of floats.

- **System.arraycopy()**

Although copying an array isn't particularly difficult, it is an operation which benefits from a native implementation. Therefore java.lang.System includes a static System.arraycopy() method you can use to copy one array to another.

public static void arraycopy(Array src, int src_position, Array dst, int dst_position, int n)

System.arraycopy() copies n elements from from the array src, beginning with the element at src_position, to the array dst starting at dst_position. The destination array must already exist when arraycopy is called. The method does not create it. The src and dst arrays must be of the same type.

For example,

```
int[] unicode = new int[65536];
for (int i = 0; i < unicode.length; i++)
{
unicode[i] = i;
}
int[] latin1 = new int[256];
System.arraycopy(unicode, 0, latin1, 0, 256);
```

2.27.5 Array Initialization

Initializing arrays in C is error-prone and tedious. C++ uses aggregate initialization to make it much safer. [22] Java has no "aggregates" like C++, since everything is an object in Java. It does have arrays, and these are supported with array initialization.

An array is simply a sequence of either objects or primitives, all the same type and packaged together under one identifier name. Arrays are defined and used with the square-brackets indexing operator [ ]. To define an array you simply follow your type name with empty square brackets:

```
int[] a1;
```

You can also put the square brackets after the identifier to produce exactly the same meaning:

```
int a1[];
```

This conforms to expectations from C and C++ programmers. The former style, however, is probably a more sensible syntax, since it says that the type is "an int array." That style will be used in this book.

The compiler doesn't allow you to tell it how big the array is. This brings us back to that issue of "handles." All that you have at this point is a handle to an array, and there's been no space allocated for the array. To create storage for the array you must write an initialization expression. For arrays, initialization can appear anywhere in your code, but you can also use a special kind of initialization expression that must occur at the point where the array is created. This special initialization is a set of values surrounded by curly braces. The storage allocation (the equivalent of using new) is taken care of by the compiler in this case. For example:

```
int[] a1 = { 1, 2, 3, 4, 5 };
```

So why would you ever define an array handle without an array?

```
int[] a2;
```

Well, it's possible to assign one array to another in Java, so you can say:

```
a2 = a1;
```

What you're really doing is copying a handle, as demonstrated here:

Example 2.18

```
//: Arrays.java
// Arrays of primitives.

public class Arrays
{
public static void main(String[] args)
```

```
{
int[] a1 = { 1, 2, 3, 4, 5 };
int[] a2;
a2 = a1;
for(int i = 0; i < a2.length; i++)
a2[i]++;
for(int i = 0; i < a1.length; i++)
prt("a1[" + i + "] = " + a1[i]);
}
static void prt(String s)
{
System.out.println(s);
}
} ///:~
```

You can see that a1 is given an initialization value while a2 is not; a2 is assigned later - in this case, to another array.

There's something new here: all arrays have an intrinsic member (whether they're arrays of objects or arrays of primitives) that you can query - but not change - to tell you how many elements there are in the array. This member is length. Since arrays in Java, like C and C++, start counting from element zero, the largest element you can index is length - 1 . If you go out of bounds, C and C++ quietly accept this and allow you to stomp all over your memory, which is the source of many infamous bugs. However, Java protects you against such problems by causing a run-time error (an exception, the subject of Chapter 9) if you step out of bounds. Of course, checking every array access costs time and code and there's no way to turn it off, which means that array accesses might be a source of inefficiency in your program if they occur at a critical juncture. For Internet security and programmer productivity, the Java designers thought that this was a worthwhile tradeoff.

What if you don't know how many elements you're going to need in your array while you're writing the program? You simply use new to create the elements in the array. Here, new works even though it's creating an array of primitives (new won't create a non-array primitive):

Example 2.19

```
//: ArrayNew.java
// Creating arrays with new.
import java.util.*;

public class ArrayNew
{
static Random rand = new Random();
static int pRand(int mod)
{
return Math.abs(rand.nextInt()) % mod;
}
public static void main(String[] args)
{
int[] a;
a = new int[pRand(20)];
prt("length of a =" + a.length);
for(int i = 0; i < a.length; i++)
```

```
prt("a[" + i + "] = " + a[i]);
}
static void prt(String s)
{
System.out.println(s);
}
} ///:~
```

Since the size of the array is chosen at random (using the pRand( ) method defined earlier), it's clear that array creation is actually happening at run-time. In addition, you'll see from the output of this program that array elements of primitive types are automatically initialized to "empty" values. (For numerics, this is zero, for char, it's null, and for boolean, it's false.)

Of course, the array could also have been defined and initialized in the same statement:

```
int[] a = new int[pRand(20)];
```

If you're dealing with an array of non-primitive objects, you must always use new. Here, the handle issue comes up again because what you create is an array of handles. Consider the wrapper type Integer, which is a class and not a primitive:

Example 2.20

```
//: ArrayClassObj.java
// Creating an array of non-primitive objects.
import java.util.*;

public class ArrayClassObj
{
static Random rand = new Random();
static int pRand(int mod)
{
return Math.abs(rand.nextInt()) % mod;
}
public static void main(String[] args)
{
Integer[] a = new Integer[pRand(20)];
prt("length of a =" + a.length);
for(int i = 0; i < a.length; i++)
{
a[i] = new Integer(pRand(500));
prt("a[" + i + "] =" + a[i]);
}
}
static void prt(String s)
{
System.out.println(s);
}
} ///:~
```

Here, even after new is called to create the array:

```
Integer[] a = new Integer[pRand(20)];
```

it's only an array of handles, and not until the handle itself is initialized by creating a new Integer object is the initialization complete:

```
a[i] = new Integer(pRand(500));
```

If you forget to create the object, however, you'll get an exception at run-time when you try to read the empty array location.

Take a look at the formation of the String object inside the print statements. You can see that the handle to the Integer object is automatically converted to produce a String representing the value inside the object.

It's also possible to initialize arrays of objects using the curly-brace-enclosed list. There are two forms, the first of which is the only one allowed in Java 1.0. The second (equivalent) form is allowed starting with Java 1.1:

Example 2.21

```
//: ArrayInit.java
// Array initialization

public class ArrayInit
{
public static void main(String[] args)
{
Integer[] a = {
new Integer(1),
new Integer(2),
new Integer(3),
};

// Java 1.1 only:
Integer[] b = new Integer[] {
new Integer(1),
new Integer(2),
new Integer(3),
};
}
} ///:~
```

This is useful at times, but it's more limited since the size of the array is determined at compile time. The final comma in the list of initializers is optional. (This feature makes for easier maintenance of long lists.)

The second form of array initialization, added in Java 1.1, provides a convenient syntax to create and call methods that can produce the same effect as C's variable argument lists (known as "varargs" in C). These included, if you choose, unknown quantity of arguments as well as unknown type. Since all classes are ultimately inherited from the common root class Object, you can create a method that takes an array of Object and call it like this:

Example 2.22

```
//: VarArgs.java
// Using the Java 1.1 array syntax to create
// variable argument lists
class A { int i; }
```

```
public class VarArgs
{
static void f(Object[] x)
{
for(int i = 0; i < x.length; i++)
System.out.println(x[i]);
}
public static void main(String[] args)
{
f(new Object[] {
new Integer(47), new VarArgs(),
new Float(2.14), new Double(11.11) });
f(new Object[] {"one", "two", "three" });
f(new Object[] {new A(), new A(), new A()});
}
} ///:~
```

At this point, there's not much you can do with these unknown objects, and this program uses the automatic String conversion to do something useful with each Object. In Chapter 11 (run-time type identification or RTTI) you'll learn how to discover the exact type of such objects so that you can do something more interesting with them.

2.28 Multi-Dimensional Arrays

So far all these arrays have been one-dimensional. That is, a single number could locate any value in the array. However sometimes data is naturally represented by more than one number. For instance a position on the earth requires a latitude and a longitude.

The most common kind of multidimensional array is the two-dimensional array. If you think of a one-dimensional array as a column of values, you can think of a two-dimensional array as a table of values like this

c0	c1	c2	c3	
r0	0	1	2	3
r1	1	2	3	4
r2	2	3	4	5
r3	3	4	5	6
r4	4	5	6	7

Here we have an array with five rows and four columns. It has twenty total elements. However we say it has dimension five by four, not dimension twenty. This array is not the same as a four by five array like this one:

c0	c1	c2	c3	c4
r0	0	1	2	3 4
r1	1	2	3	4 5
r2	2	3	4	5 6
r3	3	4	5	6 7

We need to use two numbers to identify a position in a two-dimensional array. These are the element's row and column positions. For instance if the above array is called J then J[0][0] is 0, J[0][1] is 1, J[0][2] is 2, J[0][3] is 3, J[1][0] is 1, and so on.

Here's how the elements in a four by five array called M are referred to:

M[0][0]	M[0][1]	M[0][2]	M[0][3]	M[0][4]
M[1][0]	M[1][1]	M[1][2]	M[1][3]	M[1][4]
M[2][0]	M[2][1]	M[2][2]	M[2][3]	M[2][4]
M[3][0]	M[3][1]	M[3][2]	M[3][3]	M[3][4]

Arrays have lengths and you can access that length by referencing the variable arrayname.length You test the length of the args array as follows.

Example 2.23

```
// This is the Hello program in Java
class Hello
{
public static void main (String args[])
{
if (args.length > 0)
{
System.out.println("Hello" + args[0]);
}
}
}
```

System.out.println(args[0]) was wrapped in a conditional test, if (args.length > 0) { }. The code inside the braces, System.out.println(args[0]), now gets executed if and only if the length of the args array is greater than zero.

The arguments to a conditional statement like if must be a boolean value, that is something that evaluates to true or false. Integers are not permissible.

In Java numerical greater than and lesser than tests are done with the > and < operators respectively. You can test whether a number is less than or equal to or greater than or equal to another number with the <= and >= operators.

Exercise: Give aBoolean a different value.

Answers: Here's osur solution to all three exercises, called MinVariables, with the differences shown in red:

Example 2.24

```
public class MinVariables
{
public static void main(String args[])
{
// integers
byte smallestByte = Byte.MIN_VALUE;
short smallestShort = Short.MIN_VALUE;
int smallestInteger = Integer.MIN_VALUE;
long smallestLong = Long.MIN_VALUE;
// real numbers
float smallestFloat = Float.MIN_VALUE;
double smallestDouble = Double.MIN_VALUE;
```

```
// other primitive types
char aChar = 'S';
boolean aBoolean = false;
// display them all
System.out.println("The smallest byte value is" + smallestByte);
System.out.println("The smallest short value is" + smallestShort);
System.out.println("The smallest integer value is" + smallestInteger);
System.out.println("The smallest long value is" + smallestLong);
System.out.println("The smallest float value is" + smallestFloat);
System.out.println("The smallest double value is" + smallestDouble);
if (Character.isLowerCase(aChar)) {
System.out.println("The character" + aChar +" is lower case.");
} else {
System.out.println("The character" + aChar + "is upper case.");
}
System.out.println("The value of aBoolean is" + aBoolean);
}
}
```

Arrays are also objects. Multidimensional arrays are created via arrays of arrays.

Example 2.25 : Fibonacci Numbers

```
class Fibonacci
{
public static void main (String args[])
{
int low = 1;
int high = 0;
System.out.println(low);
while (high < 50) {
System.out.println(high);
int temp = high;
high = high + low;
low = temp;
}
}
}
```

Java allows you to easily create multidimensional arrays:

Example 2.26

```
//: MultiDimArray.java
// Creating multidimensional arrays.
import java.util.*;

public class MultiDimArray
{
static Random rand = new Random();
static int pRand(int mod)
{
return Math.abs(rand.nextInt()) % mod;
```

```
}
public static void main(String[] args)
{
int[][] a1 = {
{ 1, 2, 3, },
{ 4, 5, 6, },
};
for(int i = 0; i < a1.length; i++)
for(int j = 0; j < a1[i].length; j++)
prt("a1[" + i + "][" + j +
"] = " + a1[i][j]);
// 3-D array with fixed length:
int[][][] a2 = new int[2][2][4];
for(int i = 0; i < a2.length; i++)
for(int j = 0; j < a2[i].length; j++)
for(int k = 0; k < a2[i][j].length;
k++)
prt("a2[" + i + "][" +
j + "][" + k +
"] = " + a2[i][j][k]);
// 3-D array with varied-length vectors:
int[][][] a3 = new int[pRand(7)][][];
for(int i = 0; i < a2.length; i++) {
a3[i] = new int[pRand(5)][];
for(int j = 0; j < a3[i].length; j++)
a3[i][j] = new int[pRand(5)];
}
for(int i = 0; i < a2.length; i++)
for(int j = 0; j < a3[i].length; j++)
for(int k = 0; k < a3[i][j].length;
k++)
prt("a3[" + i + "][" +
j + "][" + k +
"] = " + a3[i][j][k]);
// Array of non-primitive objects:
Integer[][] a4 = {
{ new Integer(1), new Integer(2)},
{ new Integer(3), new Integer(4)},
{ new Integer(5), new Integer(6)},
};
for(int i = 0; i < a4.length; i++)
for(int j = 0; j < a4[i].length; j++)
prt("a4[" + i + "][" + j +
"] = " + a4[i][j]);
Integer[][] a5;
a5 = new Integer[3][];
for(int i = 0; i < a5.length; i++)
{
```

```
a5[i] = new Integer[3];
for(int j = 0; j < a5[i].length; j++)
a5[i][j] = new Integer(i*j);
}
for(int i = 0; i < a5.length; i++)
for(int j = 0; j < a5[i].length; j++)
prt("a5[" + i + "][" + j +
"] =" + a5[i][j]);
}
static void prt(String s)
{
System.out.println(s);
}
} ///:~
```

The code used for printing uses length so that it doesn't depend on fixed array sizes.

The first example shows a multidimensional array of primitives. You delimit each vector in the array with curly braces:

```
int[][] a1 = {
{ 1, 2, 3, },
{ 4, 5, 6, },
};
```

Each set of square brackets moves you into the next level of the array.

The second example shows a three-dimensional array allocated with new. Here, the whole array is allocated at once:

```
int[][][] a2 = new int[2][2][4];
```

But the third example shows that each vector in the arrays that make up the matrix can be of any length:

```
int[][][] a3 = new int[pRand(7)][][];
for(int i = 0; i < a2.length; i++) {
a3[i] = new int[pRand(5)][];
for(int j = 0; j < a3[i].length; j++)
a3[i][j] = new int[pRand(5)];
}
```

The first new creates an array with a random-length first element and the rest undetermined. The second new inside the for loop fills out the elements but leaves the third index undetermined until you hit the third new.

You will see from the output that array values are automatically initialized to zero if you don't give them an explicit initialization value.

You can deal with arrays of non-primitive objects in a similar fashion, which is shown in the fourth example, demonstrating the ability to collect many new expressions with curly braces:

```
Integer[][] a4 =
{
{ new Integer(1), new Integer(2)},
{ new Integer(3), new Integer(4)},
{ new Integer(5), new Integer(6)},
```

```
};
```

The fifth example shows how an array of non-primitive objects can be built up piece by piece:

```
Integer[][] a5;
a5 = new Integer[3][];
for(int i = 0; i < a5.length; i++) {
a5[i] = new Integer[3];
for(int j = 0; j < a5[i].length; j++)
a5[i][j] = new Integer(i*j);
}
```

The i*j is just to put an interesting value into the Integer.

2.29 Declaring, Allocating and Initializing Two Dimensional Arrays

Two dimensional arrays are declared, allocated and initialized much like one dimensional arrays. However you have to specify two dimensions rather than one, and you typically use two nested for loops to fill the array.

This example fills a Two-Dimensional Array with the sum of the row and column indexes

Example 2.27

```
class FillArray
{
public static void main (String args[])
{
int[][] M;
M = new int[4][5];
for (int row=0; row < 4; row++)
{
for (int col=0; col < 5; col++)
{
M[row][col] = row+col;
}
}
}
}
```

Of course the algorithm you use to fill the array depends completely on the use to which the array is to be put. Program 9.3 calculates the identity matrix for a given dimension. The identity matrix of dimension N is a square matrix which contains ones along the diagonal and zeros in all other positions.

Example 2.28

```
class IDMatrix ]
{
public static void main (String args[])
{
double[][] ID;
ID = new double[4][4];
for (int row=0; row < 4; row++)
{
```

```
for (int col=0; col < 4; col++)
{
if (row != col)
{
ID[row][col]=0.0;
}
else
{
ID[row][col] = 1.0;
}
}
}
}
}
```

In two-dimensional arrays ArrayIndexOutOfBoundsExceptions occur whenever you exceed the maximum column index or row index.

You can also declare, allocate, and initialize a a two-dimensional array at the same time by providing a list of the initial values inside nested brackets. For instance the three by three identity matrix could be set up like this:

```
double[][] ID3 = {
{1.0, 0.0 , 0.0},
{0.0, 1.0, 0.0},
{0.0, 0.0, 1.0}
};
```

The spacing and the line breaks used above are purely for the programmer. The compiler doesn't care. The following works equally well:

```
double[][] ID3 = {{1.0, 0.0, 0.0},{0.0, 1.0, 0.0},{0.0, 0.0, 1.0}};
```

2.30 Even Higher Dimensions

You don't have to stop with two dimensional arrays. Java permits arrays of three, four or more dimensions. However chances are pretty good that if you need more than three dimensions in an array, you're probably using the wrong data structure. Even three dimensional arrays are exceptionally rare outside of scientific and engineering applications.

The syntax for three dimensional arrays is a direct extension of that for two-dimensional arrays. The program below declares, allocates and initializes a three-dimensional array. The array is filled with the sum of its indexes.

Example 2.29

```
class Fill3DArray
{
public static void main (String args[])
{
int[][][] M;
M = new int[4][5][3];
for (int row=0; row < 4; row++) {
for (int col=0; col < 5; col++) {
```

```
for (int ver=0; ver < 3; ver++) {
M[row][col][ver] = row+col+ver;
}
}
}
}
}
```

You need the additional nested for loop to handle the extra dimension. The syntax for still higher dimensions is similar. Just add another pair of brackets and another dimension.

Unbalanced Arrays

Like C Java does not have true multidimensional arrays. Java fakes multidimensional arrays using arrays of arrays. This means that it is possible to have unbalanced arrays. An unbalanced array is a multidimensional array where the dimension isn't the same for all rows. In most applications this is a horrible idea and should be avoided.

2.31 Collections of Primitives

Collection classes can hold only handles to objects. An array, however, can be created to hold primitives directly, as well as handles to objects. It is possible to use the "wrapper" classes such as Integer, Double, etc. to place primitive values inside a collection, but as you'll see later in this chapter in the WordCount.java example, the wrapper classes for primitives are only somewhat useful anyway. Whether you put primitives in arrays or wrap them in a class that's placed in a collection is a question of efficiency. It's much more efficient to create and access an array of primitives than a collection of wrapped primitives.

Of course, if you're using a primitive type and you need the flexibility of a collection that automatically expands when more space is needed, the array won't work and you're forced to use a collection of wrapped primitives. You might think that there should be a specialized type of Vector for each of the primitive data types, but Java doesn't provide this for you. Some sort of templatizing mechanism might someday provide a better way for Java to handle this problem.

2.32 Returning an Array

Suppose you're writing a method and you don't just want to return one thing, but a whole bunch of things. Languages like C and C++ make this difficult because you can't just return an array, only a pointer to an array. This introduces problems because it becomes messy to control the lifetime of the array, which easily leads to memory leaks.

Java takes a similar approach, but you just "return an array." Actually, of course, you're returning a handle to an array, but with Java you never worry about responsibility for that array - it will be around as long as you need it, and the garbage collector will clean it up when you're done.

As an example, consider returning an array of String:

Example 2.30

```
//: IceCream.java
// Returning arrays from methods
public class IceCream
{
static String[] flav =
{
```

```
"Chocolate", "Strawberry",
"Vanilla Fudge Swirl", "Mint Chip",
"Mocha Almond Fudge", "Rum Raisin",
"Praline Cream", "Mud Pie"
};
static String[] flavorSet(int n)
{
// Force it to be positive & within bounds:
n = Math.abs(n) % (flav.length + 1);
String[] results = new String[n];
int[] picks = new int[n];
for(int i = 0; i < picks.length; i++)
picks[i] = -1;
for(int i = 0; i < picks.length; i++)
{
retry:
while(true)
{
int t =
(int)(Math.random() * flav.length);
for(int j = 0; j < i; j++)
if(picks[j] == t) continue retry;
picks[i] = t;
results[i] = flav[t];
break;
}
}
return results;
}
public static void main(String[] args) {
for(int i = 0; i < 20; i++) {
System.out.println(
"flavorSet(" + i + ") = ");
String[] fl = flavorSet(flav.length);
for(int j = 0; j < fl.length; j++)
System.out.println("\t" + fl[j]);
}
}
} ///:~
```

The method flavorSet( ) creates an array of String called results. The size of this array is n, determined by the argument you pass into the method. Then it proceeds to choose flavors randomly from the array flav and place them into results, which it finally returns. Returning an array is just like returning any other object - it's a handle. It's not important that the array was created within flavorSet( ), or that the array was created anyplace else, for that matter. The garbage collector takes care of cleaning up the array when you're done with it, and the array will persist for as long as you need it.

As an aside, notice that when flavorSet( ) chooses flavors randomly, it ensures that a random choice hasn't been picked before. This is performed in a seemingly infinite while loop that keeps making random choices until it finds one that's not already in the picks array. (Of course, a String comparison could also have been performed to see if the random choice was already in the results array, but String comparisons are inefficient.) If it's successful it adds the entry and breaks out to go find the next one (i gets incremented). But if t is a number that's already in picks, then a labeled continue is used to jump back two levels, which forces a new t to be selected. It's particularly convincing to watch this happen with a debugger.

main( ) prints out 20 full sets of flavors, so you can see that flavorSet( ) chooses the flavors in a random order each time. It's easiest to see this if you redirect the output into a file. And while you're looking at the file, remember, you're not really hungry. (You just want the ice cream, you don't need it.)

2.33 Multiple Initializers and Incrementers

Sometimes it's necessary to initialize several variables before beginning a for loop. Similarly you may want to increment more than one variable. Java lets you do this by placing a comma between the different initializers and incrementers like this:

```
for (int i = 1,  j = 100;  i < 100;  i = i+1, j = j-1)
{
System.out.println(i + j);
}
```

You can't, however, include multiple test conditions, at least not with commas. The following line is illegal and will generate a compiler error.

```
for (int i = 1,  j = 100;  i <= 100, j > 0;  i = i-1, j = j-1) {
```

To include multiple tests you need to use the boolean logic operators && and II which will be discussed later.

QUESTIONS AND EXERCISES

A1. Variables

1. *Which of the following are valid variable names?*

   int anInt i i1 1 thing1

   1thing ONE-HUNDRED ONE_HUNDRED something2do

2. *Answer the following questions about the BasicsDemo program.*

   (1) *What is the name of each variable declared in the program? Remember that method parameters are also variables.*
   (2) *What is the data type of each variable?*
   (3) *What is the scope of each variable?*

3. *Modify the MaxVariablesDemo program so that aBoolean has a different value.*

4. *Rewrite the MaxVariablesDemo program to display the minimum value of each integer data type. You can guess what the names of these variables are or you can look them up in the API documentation.*

   Can you guess the name of a method in the Character class that you can use instead of isUpperCase to determine the capitalization of a character? Modify the MaxVariablesDemo program to use that method instead of isUpperCase.

5. *Here's the Sort program*

   Example 2.31

```
public class Sort
{
public static void main(String[] args)
{
int[] arrayOfInts = { 32, 87, 3, 589, 12, 1076,
2000, 8, 622, 127 };
```

```
for (int i = arrayOfInts.length; —i >= 0; )
{
for (int j = 0; j < i; j++) {
if (arrayOfInts[j] > arrayOfInts[j+1])
{
int temp = arrayOfInts[j];
arrayOfInts[j] = arrayOfInts[j+1];
arrayOfInts[j+1] = temp;
}
}
}
for (int i = 0; i < arrayOfInts.length; i++)
{
System.out.print(arrayOfInts[i] + " ");
}
System.out.println();
}
}
```

(a) *Identify all of the variables in the program.*

(b) *What is the name of each variable?*

(c) *What is the data type for each variable?*

(d) *What is the scope of each variable?*

ANSWER

(a) Here's the sort program again with the variable declarations shown in underline:

Example 2.32

```
public class Sort
{
public static void main(String[] args)
{
for21.gif
int[] arrayOfInts = { 32, 87, 3, 589, 12, 1076,
2000, 8, 622, 127 };
for (int i = arrayOfInts.length; —i >= 0; ) {
for (int j = 0; j < i; j++) {
if (arrayOfInts[j] > arrayOfInts[j+1]) {
int temp = arrayOfInts[j];
arrayOfInts[j] = arrayOfInts[j+1];
arrayOfInts[j+1] = temp;
}
}
}
for (int i = 0; i < arrayOfInts.length; i++) {
System.out.print(arrayOfInts[i] + " ");
}
System.out.println();
}
}
```

(b) args, arrayOfInts, i, j, temp, and i a second time. This program can use i twice because the two variables have different scope.

(c) args is an array of String objects. arrayOfInts is an array of integers. All of the other variables are integers.

(d) The following diagram shows the scope of each variable declared within the Sort program.

6. Recall the MaxVariables program.

Example 2.32

```
public class MaxVariables
{
public static void main(String args[])
{
// integers
byte largestByte = Byte.MAX_VALUE;
short largestShort = Short.MAX_VALUE;
int largestInteger = Integer.MAX_VALUE;
long largestLong = Long.MAX_VALUE;
// real numbers
float largestFloat = Float.MAX_VALUE;
double largestDouble = Double.MAX_VALUE;
// other primitive types
char aChar = 'S';
boolean aBoolean = true;
// display them all
System.out.println("The largest byte value is " + largestByte);
System.out.println("The largest short value is" + largestShort);
System.out.println("The largest integer value is " + largestInteger);
System.out.println("The largest long value is "+ largestLong);
System.out.println("The largest float value is "+ largestFloat);
System.out.println("The largest double value is "+ largestDouble);
if (Character.isUpperCase(aChar)) {
System.out.println("The character " + aChar + "is upper case.");
} else {
System.out.println("The character " + aChar + " is lower case.");
}
System.out.println("The value of aBoolean is "+ aBoolean);
}
}
```

Rewrite it to display the minimum value of each integer data type. You can either guess at the names of the class variables within each type wrapper class that provides the minimum, you can look them up in the javadocs, or you can calculate the values based on what you know about the size of the primitive types. Can you guess the name of a different method in the Character class that determines whether or not a char is a upper case? Use that method in the program.

Modify the program so that aBoolean has a different value.

Q.7 Now, use what you learned from the javadocs to make the following modifications to the ClickMe applet. To compile this program, you also need the Spot.java file.

Note: This is an exercise in reading code, making guesses, and looking up classes and methods in the javadocs. We haven't yet given you any detailed information about how to write Java code and what it all means. But you might be surprised at how much you can intuit from the code. The main pont of this exercise is to get you to use the javadocs and to read code. Do not worry if you cannot get your solution to work. Do not worry if your solutions do not match ours. Do compare your solutions to ours so that you can get more experience reading code and perhaps learn more about the API in the Java platform.

Modify the applet to draw a green square instead of a red spot.

Modify the applet to display your name in purple instead of a red spot.

8. Extra Credit Exercises

1. *Use the javadocs to find information to help you make these modifications to the ClickMe applet. To compile this program, you also need the Spot.java file. Modify the applet to erase the red spot instead of redrawing the whole applet. Modify the applet to drag the red spot when the mouse is held down.*

Hint: For this exercise, start with the result from the previous exercise (erasing the spot rather than redrawing the applet).

Example 2.33

```
public class Spot
{
public int size;
public int x, y;
public Spot(int size)
{
this.size = size;
this.x = -1;
this.y = -1;
}
}
import java.applet.Applet;
import java.awt.*;
import java.awt.event.*;
public class ClickMe extends Applet implements MouseListener {
private Spot spot = null;
private static final int RADIUS = 7;
public void init() {
addMouseListener(this);
}
public void paint(Graphics g) {
// draw a black border and a white background
g.setColor(Color.white);
g.fillRect(0, 0, getSize().width - 1, getSize().height - 1);
g.setColor(Color.black);
g.drawRect(0, 0, getSize().width - 1, getSize().height - 1);
// draw the spot
g.setColor(Color.red);
if (spot != null) {
g.fillOval(spot.x - RADIUS, spot.y - RADIUS, RADIUS * 2, RADIUS * 2);
}
}
public void mousePressed(MouseEvent event) {
if (spot == null) {
spot = new Spot(RADIUS);
}
spot.x = event.getX();
spot.y = event.getY();
repaint();
}
public void mouseClicked(MouseEvent event) {}
public void mouseReleased(MouseEvent event) {}
```

```
public void mouseEntered(MouseEvent event) {}
public void mouseExited(MouseEvent event) {}
}
```

(a) *Rewrite the MaxVariables program to display the minimum value of each integer data type.*

(b) *Use a different method to discover if aChar is an upper case letter.*

What is the index of Brighton in the following array?

```
String[] skiResorts = {
"Whistler Blackcomb", "Squaw Valley", "Brighton",
"Snowmass", "Sun Valley", "Taos"
};
```

A 2. Operators

1. *Consider the following code snippet:*

```
arrayOfInts[j] > arrayOfInts[j+1]
```

What operators does the code contain?

2. *Consider the following code snippet:*

```
int i = 10;
int n = i++%5;
```

(a) *What are the values of i and n after the code is executed?*

(b) *What are the final values of i and n if instead of using the postfix increment operator (i++), you use the prefix version (++i))?*

(c) *What is the value of i after the following code snippet executes?*

```
int i = 8;
i >>=2;
```

(d) *What is the value of i after the following code snippet executes?*

```
int i = 17;
i >>=1;
```

(3) *Write a program that tests whether a floating point number is zero. (Hint: You shouldn't generally use the equality operator == with floating point numbers, since floating point numbers by nature are hard to match exactly. Instead, test whether the number is close to zero.)*

(4) *Write a program that calculates the number of US dollars equivalent to a given number of French francs. Assume an exchange rate of 6.85062 francs per dollar. If you want to control the format of the numbers your program displays, you can use the DecimalFormat class, which is discussed in Customizing Formats*

EXPRESSIONS AND ASSIGNMENT

1. *Sales tax in New York City is 8.25%. Write a program that accepts a price on the command line and prints out the appropriate tax and total purchase price.*

   Modify the sales tax program to accept an arbitrary number of prices, total them, calculate the sales tax and print the total amount.

2. *Write a program that reads two numbers from the command line, the number of hours worked by an employee and their base pay rate. Then output the total pay due.*

3. *Modify the previous program to meet the U.S. Dept. of Labor's requirement for time and a half pay for hours over forty worked in a given week.*

   Add warning messages to the payroll program if the pay rate is less than the minimum wage ($5.15 an hour as of 1998) or if the employee worked more than the number of hours in a week.

4. *Write a program that reads an integer n from the command line and calculates n! (n factorial).*

There are exactly 2.54 centimeters to an inch. Write a program that takes a number of inches from the command line and converts it to centimeters.

5. Write the inverse program that reads a number of centimeters from the command line and converts it to inches.

6. There are 454 grams in a pound and 1000 grams in a kilogram. Write programs that convert pounds to kilograms and kilograms to pounds. Read the number to be converted from the command line. Can you make this one program instead of two?

7. The equivalent resistance of resistors connected in series is calculated by adding the resistances of the individual resistors. 8. Write a program that accepts a series of resistances from the command line and outputs the equivalent resistance.

   The formula for resistors connected in parallel is a little more complex. Given two resistors with resistances R1 and R2 connected in parallel the equivalent resistance is given by the inverse of the sum of the inverses, i.e.

   1
   Requiv = —— 1 1 — + — R1 R2

   If there are more than two resistors you continue to invert the sum of their inverses; e.g. for four resistors you have:

   1
   Requiv = ———— 1 1 1 1 — + — + — + — R1 R2 R3 R4

8. Write a program that calculates the resistance of a a group of resistors arranged in parallel. The resistances will all be passed as command line arguments.

9. Write a program that prints values from one to 100.

10. Modify Exercise 1 so that the program exits by using the break keyword at value 47. Try using return instead.

11. Create a switch statement that prints a message for each case, and put the switch inside a for loop that tries each case. Put a break after each case and test it, then remove the breaks and see what happens.

Arrays

1. Write an expression that refers to the string Brighton within the array.
2. What is the value of the expression skiResorts.length?
3. What is the index of the last item in the array?
4. What is the value of the expression skiResorts[4]?

EXERCISES

5. The following program, WhatHappens, contains a bug. Find it and fix it.

```
//
// This program compiles but won't run successfully.
//
public class WhatHappens
{
public static void main(String[] args)
{
StringBuffer[] stringBuffers = new StringBuffer[10];
for (int i = 0; i < stringBuffers.length; i ++)
{
stringBuffers[i].append("StringBuffer at index" + i);
}
}
}
```

3

Control Statements

3.1 Control Flow Statements

When you write a program, you type statements into a file. Without control flow statements, the interpreter executes these statements in the order they appear in the file from left to right, top to bottom. You can use control flow statements in your programs to conditionally execute statements, to repeatedly execute a block of statements, and to otherwise change the normal, sequential flow of control. For example, in the following code snippet, the if statement conditionally executes the System.out.println statement within the braces, based on the return value of Character.isUpperCase(aChar):

```
char c;
if (Character.isUpperCase(aChar))
{
System.out.println("The character" + aChar + "is upper case.");
}
```

The Java programming language provides several control flow statements, which are listed in the following table.

Statement	Type Keyword
* looping	while, do-while , for
* decision making	if-else, switch-case
* exception handling	try-catch-finally, throw
* branching break,	continue, label:, return

In the sections that follow, you will see the following notation to describe the general form of a control flow statement:

```
control flow statement details
{
    statement(s)
}
```

Technically, the braces, { and }, are not required if the block contains only one statement. However, we recommend that you always use { and }, because the code is easier to read and it helps to prevent errors when modifying code.

- The while and do-while Statements
- The for Statement
- The if/else Statements
- The switch Statement
- Exception Handling Statements
- Branching Statements

Note : Although goto is a reserved word, currently the Java programming language does not support the goto statement.

3.2 The while Statement

You use a while statement to continually execute a block of statements while a condition remains true. The general syntax of the while statement is:

```
while (expression)
{
    statement
}
```

First, the while statement evaluates expression, which must return a boolean value. If the expression returns true, then the while statement executes the statement(s) associated with it. The while statement continues testing the expression and executing statements until the expression returns false. The example program shown below, called WhileDemo, uses a while statement to iterate over a string, copying the characters from the string into a string buffer until it encounters the letter 'g'.

Example 3.1

```
public class WhileDemo
{
public static void main(String[] args)
{
String copyFromMe = "Copy this string until you encounter the letter
'g'.";
StringBuffer copyToMe = new StringBuffer();
int i = 0;
char c = copyFromMe.charAt(i);
while (c != 'g') {
copyToMe.append(c);
c = copyFromMe.charAt(++i);
}
System.out.println(copyToMe);
}
}
```

3.3 The do-while Statement

Java provides another statement that is similar to the while statement—the do-while statement. The general syntax of the do-while is:

```
do
{
statement
} while (expression);
```

Instead of evaluating the expression at the top of the loop, do-while evaluates the expression at the bottom. Thus the statements associated with a do-while are executed at least once. Here's the previous program re-written to use do-while and renamed to DoWhileDemo:

Example 3.2

```
public class DoWhileDemo
```

```
{
public static void main(String[] args) {
String copyFromMe = "Copy this string until you encounter the letter
'g'.";
StringBuffer copyToMe = new StringBuffer();
int i = 0;
char c = copyFromMe.charAt(i);
do {
copyToMe.append(c);
c = copyFromMe.charAt(++i);
} while (c != 'g');
System.out.println(copyToMe);
}
}
```

Example 3.3

```
// This is the Hello program in Java
class Hello
{
public static void main (String args[])
{
int i;
System.out.print("Hello");    // Say Hello
i = 0;            // Initialize loop counter
while (i < args.length) { // Test and Loop
System.out.print(args[i]);
System.out.print(" ");
i = i + 1;       // Increment Loop Counter
}
System.out.println();  // Finish the line
}
}
```

The Java programming language provides another statement that is similar to the while statement—the do-while statement. The general syntax of the do-while is:

```
do {
statement(s)
} while (expression);
```

Instead of evaluating the expression at the top of the loop, do-while evaluates the expression at the bottom. Thus the statements associated with a do-while are executed at least once.

Here's the previous program rewritten to use do-while and renamed to DoWhileDemo:

Example 3.4

```
public class DoWhileDemo
{
public static void main(String[] args)
{
String copyFromMe = "Copy this string until you" +
```

```
"encounter the letter 'g'.";
StringBuffer copyToMe = new StringBuffer();
int i = 0;
char c = copyFromMe.charAt(i);
do {
copyToMe.append(c);
c = copyFromMe.charAt(++i);
} while (c != 'g');
System.out.println(copyToMe);
}
}
```

The value printed by the last line is: Copy this strin.

3.4 The for Statement

The for statement provides a compact way to iterate over a range of values. The general form of the for statement can be expressed like this:

```
for (initialization; termination; increment)
{
    statement
}
```

The initialization is an expression that initializes the loop-it's executed once at the beginning of the loop. The termination expression determines when to terminate the loop. This expression is evaluated at the top of each iteration of the loop. When the expression evaluates to false, the loop terminates. Finally, increment is an expression that gets invoked after each iteration through the loop. All these components are optional. In fact, to write an infinite loop, you omit all three expressions:

```
for ( ; ; )
{    // infinite loop
...
}
```

Often for loops are used to iterate over the elements in an array, or the characters in a string. The following sample, ForDemo, uses a for statement to iterate over the elements of an array and print them:

```
public class ForDemo
{
public static void main(String[] args)
{
int[] arrayOfInts = { 32, 87, 3, 589, 12, 1076,
2000, 8, 622, 127 };

for (int i = 0; i < arrayOfInts.length; i++)
{
System.out.print(arrayOfInts[i] + " ");
}
System.out.println();
}
}
```

The output of the program is: 32 87 3 589 12 1076 2000 8 622 127.

Note that you can declare a local variable within the initialization expression of a for loop. The scope of this variable extends from its declaration to the end of the block governed by the for statement so it can be used in the termination and increment expressions as well. If the variable that controls a for loop is not needed outside of the loop, it's best to declare the variable in the initialization expression. The names i, j, and k are often used to control for loops; declaring them within the for loop initialization expression limits their life-span and reduces errors.

The for statement provides a compact way to iterate over a range of values. The general form of the for statement can be expressed like this:

```
for (initialization; termination; increment)
{
    statement
}
```

initialization is a statement that initializes the loop—its executed once at the beginning of the loop. termination is an expression that determines when to terminate the loop. This expression is evaluated at the top of each iteration of the loop. When the expression evaluates to false, the loop terminates. Finally, increment is an expression that gets invoked for each iteration through the loop. Any (or all) of these components can be empty statements. Often for loops are used to iterate over the elements in an array, or the characters in a string. The sample shown below, ForDemo, uses a for statement to iterate over the elements of an array and print them:

```
public class ForDemo
{
public static void main(String[] args)
{
int[] arrayOfInts = { 32, 87, 3, 589, 12, 1076,
2000, 8, 622, 127 };
for (int i = 0; i < arrayOfInts.length; i++)
{
System.out.print(arrayOfInts[i] + " ");
}
System.out.println();
}
}
```

Example for loop

```
// This is the Hello program in Java
class Hello
{
public static void main (String args[])
{
System.out.print("Hello");    // Say Hello
for (int i = 0; i < args.length; i = i + 1) { // Test and Loop
System.out.print(args[i]);
System.out.print(" ");
}
System.out.println();  // Finish the line
}
}
```

3.5 The if/else Statements

Java's if-else statement provides your programs with the ability to selectively execute other statements based on some criteria. For example, suppose that your program printed debugging information based on the value of some boolean variable named DEBUG. If DEBUG were set to true, then your program would print debugging information such as the value of some variable like x. Otherwise, your program would proceed normally. A segment of code to implement this might look like this:

```
if (DEBUG)
{
System.out.println("DEBUG: x = " + x);
}
```

This is the simplest version of the if statement: the statement governed by the if is executed if some condition is true. Generally, the simple form of if can be written like this:

```
if (expression)
{
    statement
}
```

So, what if you wanted to perform a different set of statements if the expression is false? Well, you can use the else statement for that. Consider another example. Suppose that your program needs to perform different actions depending on whether the user clicks on the OK button or the Cancel button in an alert window. Your program could do this using an if statement:

```
. . .
// response is either OK or CANCEL depending
// on the button that the user pressed
. . .
if (response == OK)
{
. . .
// code to perform OK action
. . .
} else {
. . .
// code to perform Cancel action
. . .
}
```

This particular use of the else statement is the catch-all form. The else block is executed if the if part is false. There is another form of the else statement, else if which executes a statement based on another expression. For example, suppose that you wrote a program that assigned grades based on the value of a test score, an A for a score of 90% or above, a B for a score of 80% or above and so on. You could use an if statement with a series of companion else if statements, and an else to write this code:

```
int testscore;
char grade;
if (testscore >= 90)
{
```

```
grade = 'A';
} else if (testscore >= 80) {
grade = 'B';
} else if (testscore >= 70) {
grade = 'C';
} else if (testscore >= 60) {
grade = 'D';
} else {
grade = 'F';
}
```

An if statement can have any number of companion else if statements, but only one else. You may have noticed that some values of testscore could satisfy more than one of the expressions in the compound if statement. For instance, a score of 76 would evaluate to true for two of the expressions in the if statement: testscore >= 70 and testscore >= 60. However, as the runtime system processes a compound if statement such as this one, once a condition is satisfied (76 >= 70), the appropriate statements are executed (grade = 'C';), and control passes out of the if statement without evaluating the remaining conditions.

The if statement enables your program to selectively execute other statements, based on some criteria. For example, suppose that your program prints debugging information, based on the value of a boolean variable named DEBUG. If DEBUG is true, your program prints debugging information, such as the value of a variable, such as x. Otherwise, your program proceeds normally. A segment of code to implement this might look like this:

```
if (DEBUG)
{
System.out.println("DEBUG: x = " + x);
}
```

This is the simplest version of the if statement: The block governed by the if is executed if a condition is true. Generally, the simple form of if can be written like this:

```
if (expression)
{
statement(s)
}
```

What if you want to perform a different set of statements if the expression is false? You use the else statement for that. Consider another example. Suppose that your program needs to perform different actions depending on whether the user clicks the OK button or another button in an alert window. Your program could do this by using an if statement along with an else statement:

```
. . .
// response is either OK or CANCEL depending
// on the button that the user pressed
. . .
if (response == OK)
{
// code to perform OK action
} else {
// code to perform Cancel action
}
```

The else block is executed if the if part is false. Another form of the else statement, else if, executes a statement based on another expression. An if statement can have any number of companion else if statements but only one else. Following is a program, IfElseDemo, that assigns a grade based on the value of a test score: an A for a score of 90% or above, a B for a score of 80% or above, and so on:

```
public class IfElseDemo
{
public static void main(String[] args)
{
int testscore = 76;
char grade;

if (testscore >= 90)
{
grade = 'A';
} else if (testscore >= 80)
{
grade = 'B';
} else if (testscore >= 70)
{
grade = 'C';
} else if (testscore >= 60)
{
grade = 'D';
} else {
grade = 'F';
}
System.out.println("Grade =" + grade);
}
}
```

The output from this program is:

Grade = C

You may have noticed that the value of testscore can satisfy more than one of the expressions in the compound if statement: 76 >= 70 and 76 >= 60. However, as the runtime system processes a compound if statement such as this one, once a condition is satisfied, the appropriate statements are executed (grade = 'C';), and control passes out of the if statement without evaluating the remaining conditions.

The Java programming language supports an operator, ?:, that is a compact version of an if statement. Recall this statement from the MaxVariablesDemo program:

```
if (Character.isUpperCase(aChar))
{
System.out.println("The character" + aChar + "is upper case.");
} else
{
System.out.println("The character" + aChar + "is lower case.");
}
```

Here's how you could rewrite that statement using the ?: operator:

```
System.out.println("The character" + aChar + " is " +
(Character.isUpperCase(aChar) ? "upper" : "lower") +
"case.");
```

3.5.1 Else If

if statements are not limited to two cases. You can combine an else and an if to make an else if and test a whole range of mutually exclusive possibilities. For instance, here's a version of the Hello program that handles up to four names on the command line:

```
// This is the Hello program in Java
class Hello {
public static void main (String args[])
{

if (args.length == 0)
{
System.out.println("Hello whoever you are");
}
else if (args.length == 1)
{
System.out.println("Hello" + args[0]);
}
else if (args.length == 2)
{
System.out.println("Hello" + args[0] + " " + args[1]);
}
else if (args.length == 3)
{
System.out.println("Hello" + args[0] + " " + args[1] + " " + args[2]);
}
else if (args.length == 4)
{
System.out.println("Hello" + args[0] +
" " + args[1] + " " args[2] + " " + args[3]);
}
else
{
System.out.println("Hello" + args[0] + " " + args[1] + " " args[2]
+ " " + args[3] + "and all the rest!");
}
}
}
```

You can see that this gets mighty complicated mighty quickly. No experienced Java programmer would write code like this. There is a better solution and you'll explore it in the next section.

3.6 The Switch Statement

Use the switch statement to conditionally perform statements based on an integer expression. Following is a sample program, SwitchDemo, that declares an integer named month whose value supposedly represents the month in a date. The program displays the name of the month, based on the value of month, using the switch statement:

```
public class SwitchDemo
{
public static void main(String[] args)
{
int month = 8;
switch (month)
{
    case 1:  System.out.println("January"); break;
    case 2:  System.out.println("February"); break;
    case 3:  System.out.println("March"); break;
    case 4:  System.out.println("April"); break;
    case 5:  System.out.println("May"); break;
    case 6:  System.out.println("June"); break;
    case 7:  System.out.println("July"); break;
    case 8:  System.out.println("August"); break;
    case 9:  System.out.println("September"); break;
    case 10: System.out.println("October"); break;
    case 11: System.out.println("November"); break;
    case 12: System.out.println("December"); break;
}
}
}
```

The switch statement evaluates its expression, in this case the value of month, and executes the appropriate case statement. Thus, the output of the program is: August. Of course, you could implement this by using an if statement:

```
int month = 8;
if (month == 1)
{
System.out.println("January");
} else if (month == 2) {
System.out.println("February");
}
```

Deciding whether to use an if statement or a switch statement is a judgment call. You can decide which to use, based on readability and other factors. An if statement can be used to make decisions based on ranges of values or conditions, whereas a switch statement can make decisions based only on a single integer value. Also, the value provided to each case statement must be unique.

Another point of interest in the switch statement is the break statement after each case. Each break statement terminates the enclosing switch statement, and the flow of control continues with the first statement following the switch block. The break statements are necessary because without them, the case statements fall through. That is, without an explicit break, control will flow sequentially through subsequent case statements. Following is an example, SwitchDemo2, which illustrates why it might be useful to have case statements fall through:

```
public class SwitchDemo2
{
public static void main(String[] args)
{
int month = 2;
int year = 2000;
int numDays = 0;
switch (month)
{
case 1:
case 3:
case 5:
case 7:
case 8:
case 10:
case 12:
numDays = 31;
break;
case 4:
case 6:
case 9:
case 11:
numDays = 30;
break;
case 2:
if ( ((year % 4 == 0) && !(year % 100 == 0))
|| (year % 400 == 0) )
numDays = 29;
else
numDays = 28;
break;
}
System.out.println("Number of Days =" + numDays);
}
}
```

The output from this program is:

```
Number of Days = 29
```

Technically, the final break is not required because flow would fall out of the switch statement anyway. However, we recommend using a break for the last case statement just in case you need to add more case statements at a later date. This makes modifying the code easier and less error-prone.

You will see break used to terminate loops in Branching Statements.

Finally, you can use the default statement at the end of the switch to handle all values that aren't explicitly handled by one of the case statements.

```
int month = 8;
switch (month)
{
```

```
    case 1:  System.out.println("January"); break;
    case 2:  System.out.println("February"); break;
    case 3:  System.out.println("March"); break;
    case 4:  System.out.println("April"); break;
    case 5:  System.out.println("May"); break;
    case 6:  System.out.println("June"); break;
    case 7:  System.out.println("July"); break;
    case 8:  System.out.println("August"); break;
    case 9:  System.out.println("September"); break;
    case 10: System.out.println("October"); break;
    case 11: System.out.println("November"); break;
    case 12: System.out.println("December"); break;
    default: System.out.println("Hey, that's not a valid month!");break;
}
```

3.7 Branching Statements

The Java programming language supports three branching statements:

- The break statement
- The continue statement
- The return statement

The break statement and the continue statement, which are covered next, can be used with or without a label. A label is an identifier placed before a statement. The label is followed by a colon (:):

statementName: someJavaStatement;

You'll see an example of a label within the context of a program in the next section.

3.7.1 The Break Statement

The break statement has two forms: unlabeled and labeled. You saw the unlabeled form of the break statement used with switch earlier. As noted there, an unlabeled break terminates the enclosing switch statement, and flow of control transfers to the statement immediately following the switch. You can also use the unlabeled form of the break statement to terminate a for, while, or do-while loop. The following sample program, BreakDemo, contains a for loop that searches for a particular value within an array:

```
public class BreakDemo
{
public static void main(String[] args)
{
int[] arrayOfInts = { 32, 87, 3, 589, 12, 1076,
2000, 8, 622, 127 };
int searchfor = 12;

int i = 0;
boolean foundIt = false;

for ( ; i < arrayOfInts.length; i++)
{
if (arrayOfInts[i] == searchfor)
```

```
{

foundIt = true;
break;
}
}
if (foundIt)
{
System.out.println("Found" + searchfor + "at index" + i);
} else {
System.out.println(searchfor + "not in the array");
}
}
}
```

The break statement terminates the for loop when the value is found. The flow of control transfers to the statement following the enclosing for, which is the print statement at the end of the program.

The output of this program is:

Found 12 at index 4

The unlabeled form of the break statement is used to terminate the innermost switch, for, while, or do-while; the labeled form terminates an outer statement, which is identified by the label specified in the break statement. The following program, BreakWithLabelDemo, is similar to the previous one, but it searches for a value in a two-dimensional array. Two nested for loops traverse the array. When the value is found, a labeled break terminates the statement labeled search, which is the outer for loop:

```
public class BreakWithLabelDemo {
public static void main(String[] args) {

int[][] arrayOfInts = { { 32, 87, 3, 589 },
{ 12, 1076, 2000, 8 },
{ 622, 127, 77, 955 }
};
int searchfor = 12;

int i = 0;
int j = 0;
boolean foundIt = false;

search:
for ( ; i < arrayOfInts.length; i++) {
for (j = 0; j < arrayOfInts[i].length; j++) {
if (arrayOfInts[i][j] == searchfor) {
foundIt = true;
break search;
}
}
}
```

```
if (foundIt) {
System.out.println("Found" + searchfor + "at" + i + ", " + j);
} else {
System.out.println(searchfor + "not in the array");
}
}
}
```

The output of this program is:

```
Found 12 at 1, 0
```

This syntax can be a little confusing. The break statement terminates the labeled statement; it does not transfer the flow of control to the label. The flow of control transfers to the statement immediately following the labeled (terminated) statement.

3.7.2 The Continue Statement

You use the continue statement to skip the current iteration of a for, while , or do-while loop. The unlabeled form skips to the end of the innermost loop's body and evaluates the boolean expression that controls the loop, basically skipping the remainder of this iteration of the loop. The following program, ContinueDemo, steps through a string buffer checking each letter. If the current character is not a p, the continue statement skips the rest of the loop and proceeds to the next character. If it is a p, the program increments a counter, and converts the p to an uppercase letter.

```
public class ContinueDemo
{
public static void main(String[] args)
{

StringBuffer searchMe = new StringBuffer(
"peter piper picked a peck of pickled peppers");
int max = searchMe.length();
int numPs = 0;

for (int i = 0; i < max; i++)
{
//interested only in p's
if (searchMe.charAt(i) != 'p')
continue;

//process p's
numPs++;
searchMe.setCharAt(i, 'P');
}
System.out.println("Found" + numPs + "p's in the string.");
System.out.println(searchMe);
}
}
```

Here is the output of this program:

```
Found 9 p's in the string.
```

```
Peter PiPer Picked a Peck of Pickled PePPers
```

The labeled form of the continue statement skips the current iteration of an outer loop marked with the given label. The following example program, ContinueWithLabelDemo, uses nested loops to search for a substring within another string. Two nested loops are required: one to iterate over the substring and one to iterate over the string being searched. This program uses the labeled form of continue to skip an iteration in the outer loop:

```
public class ContinueWithLabelDemo {
public static void main(String[] args) {

String searchMe = "Look for a substring in me";
String substring = "sub";
boolean foundIt = false;

int max = searchMe.length() - substring.length();

test:
for (int i = 0; i <= max; i++) {
int n = substring.length();
int j = i;
int k = 0;
while (n— != 0) {
if (searchMe.charAt(j++) != substring.charAt(k++)) {
continue test;
}
}
foundIt = true;
break test;
}
System.out.println(foundIt ? "Found it" : "Didn't find it");
}
}
```

Here is the output from this program:

```
Found it
```

3.7.3 The Return Statement

The last of Java's branching statements is the return statement. You use return to exit from the current method. The flow of control returns to the statement that follows the original method call. The return statement has two forms: one that returns a value and one that doesn't. To return a value, simply put the value (or an expression that calculates the value) after the return keyword:

```
return ++count;
```

The data type of the value returned by return must match the type of the method's declared return value. When a method is declared void, use the form of return that doesn't return a value:

return;

3.8 Summary of Control Flow Statements

For controlling the flow of a program, the Java programming language has three loop constructs, a flexible if-else statement, a switch statement, exception-handling statements, and branching statements.

3.8.1 Loops

Use the while statement to loop over a block of statements while a boolean expression remains true. The expression is evaluated at the top of the loop.

```
while (boolean expression)
{
    statement(s)
}
```

Use the do-while statement to loop over a block of statements while a boolean expression remains true. The expression is evaluated at the bottom of the loop, so the statements within the do-while block execute at least once:

```
do
{
    statementm (s)
} while (expression);
```

The for statement loops over a block of statements and includes an initialization expression, a termination condition expression, and an increment expression.

```
for (initialization ; termination ; increment)
{
    statement(s)
}
```

3.8.2 Decision-Making Statements

The Java programming language has two decision-making statements: if-else and switch. The more general-purpose statement is if; use switch to make multiple-choice decisions based on a single integer value. The following is the most basic if statement whose single statement block is executed if the boolean expression is true:

```
if (boolean expression)
{
    statement(s)
}
```

Here's an if statement with a companion else statement. The if statement executes the first block if the boolean expression is true; otherwise, it executes the second block:

```
if (boolean expression)
{
    statement(s)
} else {
statement(s)
}
```

You can use else if to construct compound if statements:

```
if (boolean expression)
{
    statement(s)
} else if (boolean expression)
{
statement(s)
} else if (boolean expression)
{
statement(s)
} else {
statement(s)
}
```

The switch statement evaluates an integer expression and executes the appropriate case statement.

```
switch (integer expression)
{
    case integer expression:
    statement(s)
    break;
    ...
    default:
    statement(s)
    break;
}
```

3.8.3 Exception-Handling Statements

Use the try, catch, and finally statements to handle exceptions.

```
try
{
statement(s)
} catch (exceptiontype name)
{
statement(s)
} catch (exceptiontype name)
{
statement(s)
} finally {
statement(s)
}
```

3.8.4 Branching Statements

Some branching statements change the flow of control in a program to a labeled statement. You label a statement by placing a legal identifier (the label) followed by a colon (:) before the statement:

statementName: someJavaStatement;

Use the unlabeled form of the break statement to terminate the innermost switch, for, while, or do-while statement.

break;

Use the labeled form of the break statement to terminate an outer switch, for, while, or do-while statement with the given label:

break label;

A continue statement terminates the current iteration of the innermost loop and evaluates the boolean expression that controls the loop.

continue;

The labeled form of the continue statement terminates the current iteration of the loop with the given label:

continue label;

Use return to terminate the current method.

return;

You can return a value to the method's caller, by using the form of return that takes a value.

return value;

3.9 Common Programming Mistakes

The following is a list of common programming mistakes by novice Java programmers. Make sure one of these isn't what's holding you back.

Did you forget to use break after each case statement in a switch statement?

Did you use the assignment operator = when you really wanted to use the comparison operator ==?

Are the termination conditions on your loops correct? Make sure you're not terminating loops one iteration too early or too late. That is, make sure you are using < or <= and > or >= as appropriate for your situation.

Remember that array indices begin at 0, so iterating over an array looks like this:

```
for (int i = 0; i < array.length; i++)
. . .
```

Are you comparing floating-point numbers using ==? Remember that floats are approximations of the real thing. The greater than and less than (> and <) operators are more appropriate when conditional logic is performed on floating-point numbers.

Make sure that blocks of statements are enclosed in curly brackets { }. The following code looks right because of indentation, but it doesn't do what the indents imply because the brackets are missing:

```
for (int i = 0; i < arrayOfInts.length; i++)
arrayOfInts[i] = i;
System.out.println("[i] = " + arrayOfInts[i]);
```

Are you using the correct conditional operator? Make sure you understand && and || and are using them appropriately.

Do you use the negation operator ! a lot? Try to express conditions without it. Doing so is less confusing and error-prone.

Are you using a do-while? If so, do you know that the loop executes one more time than a similar while loop?

Are you trying to change the value of an argument from a method? Arguments in Java are passed by value and can't be changed in a method.

Did you inadvertently add an extra semicolon (;), thereby terminating a statement prematurely? Notice the extra semicolon at the end of this for statement:

```
for (int i = 0; i < arrayOfInts.length; i++) ;
arrayOfInts[i] = i
```

QUESTIONS

1. *Look at the SortDemo program. What control flow statements does it contain?*

   What's wrong with the following code snippet:

```
if (i = 1)
{
/* do something */
}
```

2. *Look at the WhileDemo program and the DoWhileDemo program. What would the output be from each program if you changed the value of each program's copyFromMe string to golly gee. this is fun. Explain why you think each program will have the predicted output.*

3. *Consider the following code snippet.*

```
if (aNumber >= 0)
if (aNumber == 0) System.out.println("first string");
else System.out.println("second string");
System.out.println("third string");
```

4. *What output do you think the code will produce if aNumber is 3?*

5. *Write a test program containing the code snippet; make aNumber 3. What is the output of the program? Is it what you predicted? Explain why the output is what it is. In other words, what is the control flow for the code snippet?*

6. *Using only spaces and line breaks, reformat the code snippet to make the control flow easier to understand.*

   Use braces { and } to further clarify the code and reduce the possibility of errors by future maintainers of the code.

QUESTIONS AND EXERCISES: CONTROL FLOW

Two questions about WhileDemo and DoWhileDemo.

Q.1 *What would the output be from WhileDemo and DoWhileDemo if you change the value of the string copyFromMe to "golly gee. this is fun"?*

Ans. WhileDemo displays nothing. DoWhileDemo displays golly.

Q.2 *Would the output be different? Defend your answer.*

Ans. The output is different. The expression c != 'g' is evaluated at the top of the loop in WhileDemo. Because the first character of the string is a 'g' the statements within the loop are never executed. In DoWhileDemo the expression is evaluated at the bottom of the loop after the first 'g' is appended to the string buffer. Thus the expression tests the second character in the string, which is an 'o'. The loop continues until the second 'g' in the string.

Q.3 *Identify the control flow statements in the Sort program.*

Ans.

```
public class Sort
{
public static void main(String[] args)
```

```
{
int[] arrayOfInts = { 32, 87, 3, 589, 12, 1076,
2000, 8, 622, 127 };
for (int i = arrayOfInts.length; —i >= 0; )
{
for (int j = 0; j < i; j++) {
if (arrayOfInts[j] > arrayOfInts[j+1])
{
int temp = arrayOfInts[j];
arrayOfInts[j] = arrayOfInts[j+1];
arrayOfInts[j+1] = temp;
}
}
}
for (int i = 0; i < arrayOfInts.length; i++)
{
System.out.print(arrayOfInts[i] + " ");
}
System.out.println();
}
}
```

4. *Look at the SortDemo program. What control flow statements does it contain?*
5. *What's wrong with the following code snippet:*

```
if (i = 1)
{
/* do something */
}
```

6. *Look at the WhileDemo program and the DoWhileDemo program. What would the output be from each program if you changed the value of each program's copyFromMe string to golly gee. this is fun. Explain why you think each program will have the predicted output.*
7. *Consider the following code snippet.*

```
if (aNumber >= 0)
if (aNumber == 0) System.out.println("first string");
else System.out.println("second string");
System.out.println("third string");
```

What output do you think the code will produce if aNumber is 3?

8. *Write a test program containing the code snippet; make aNumber 3. 9. What is the output of the program? Is it what you predicted? 10. Explain why the output is what it is. In other words, what is the control flow for the code snippet?*

Using only spaces and line breaks, reformat the code snippet to make the control flow easier to understand.

Use braces { and } to further clarify the code and reduce the possibility of errors by future maintainers of the code.

4

Object-Oriented Programming Concepts

4.1 What Is an Object?

An object is a computer representation of a physical object. Consider the standard English definition of the word object - all nouns can be treated as objects. By this definition, a person is an object, a table is an object, a chair is an object, a room is an object, etc.

"An object is a self-contained entity with well-defined charateristics and behaviour". An object may correspond to a real-world entity. Objects may be concrete or conceptual.

All objects have attributes. A person has arms, legs, a head and a body. A table has a tabletop and legs. A chair could be made of leather. Every object also has uses. A person can walk or run or talk. A table can be used to hold other objects. A chair is used to sit on.

Object-oriented programming is considered superior to standard approaches because we model the real world as closely as possible.

For example, whenever you look around yourself you see a large number of objects. We organize all of the objects around us in our minds by arranging them in hierarchical categories, or "classes". For example, you have in your hands a book. A book is a general class of object. You might say, "This object I am holding is classified as a book."

A hierarchy of object classes surrounds the class "book", and it extends in two directions. Books are a member of the more general class "publications". Specific types of books also exists: computer books, fiction books, biographical books, and so on. The hierarchy extends both toward the general and the more specific. At this point you are holding a single, particular book. In OOP lingo, you are holding an "instance" of the class "book".

Books have certain attributes that are shared by all books: They have a cover, several chapters, no advertising, and so on. They also have attributes shared by publications in general: a title, a date of publication, a publisher, etc. They have attributes that are shared by all physical objects: a location, size, shape, and weight. This idea of shared attributes is very important in Java and C++. C++ models the concept of shared attributes using inheritance.

There are certain things you do with and to different objects, and those actions change from object to object. For example, you can read a book, and you can flip its pages. You can look at the title, find a specific chapter, look something up in the index, count the number of pages, and so on. These actions are largely unique to publications: you never find yourself flipping the pages of a hammer, for example. However, there are actions that are generic to all physical objects, such as picking them up. C++ takes this fact about the world into account as well, again using inheritance.

As the name object-oriented implies, objects are key to understanding object-oriented technology. You can look around you now and see many examples of real-world objects: your dog, your desk, your television set, your bicycle.

These real-world objects share two characteristics:

- They all have state and
- They all have behavior.

For example, dogs have state (name, color, breed, hungry) and dogs have behavior (barking, fetching, and slobbering on your newly cleaned slacks). Bicycles have state (current gear, current pedal cadence, two wheels, number of gears) and behavior (braking, accelerating, slowing down, changing gears).

Software objects are modeled after real-world objects in that they, too, have state and behavior. A software object maintains its state in variables and implements its behavior with methods.

Definition: An object is a software bundle of variables and related methods.

You can represent real-world objects using software objects. You might want to represent real-world dogs as software objects in an animation program or a real-world bicycle as a software object in the program that controls an electronic exercise bike. However, you can also use software objects to model abstract concepts. For example, an event is a common object used in GUI window systems to represent the action of a user pressing a mouse button or a key on the keyboard.

What kinds of things become objects in object-oriented programs? The answer to this is limited only by your imagination, but here are some typical categories to start you thinking:

Physical objects

- Automobiles in a traffic-flow simulation
- Electrical components in a circuit-design program
- Countries in an economics model
- Aircraft in an air-traffic-control system

Elements of the computer-user environment

- Windows
- Menus
- Graphics object (lines, rectangle, circles)
- The mouse and the keyboard

Programming constructs

- Customized arrays
- Stacks
- Linked lists
- Binary trees

Collections of data

- An inventory
- A personnel file
- A dictionary
- A table of the latitudes and longitudes of world cities

User-defined data types

- Time Angles
- Complex numbers Points on the plane

Components in computer games

- Ghosts in a maze game
- Positions in a board game (chess, checkers)

- Animals in an ecological simulation
- Opponents and friends in adventure games

The match between programming objects and real-world objects is the happy result of combining data and functions. The resulting objects offer a revolution in program design. No such close match between programming constructs and the items being modeled exists in a procedural language.

Shlaer and Mellor in their works on object-oriented analysis method identify five types of objects:

1. Tangible Things Physical objects, eg 'car', 'bar code reader'
4. Roles Of people or organizations, eg 'account holder', 'employer'
3. Incidents Something happening at a particular time, eg 'flight', 'transaction'
4. Interactions A link between objects, eg 'electrical connection', 'contract'
5. Specifications A definition of a set of other objects, eg a description of a particular type of stock item

A more general distinction in terms of object-oriented programming is made by Stroustrup [1991, p.402] when he identifies two kinds of object:

1. Those that directly represent the ideas used to describe the application.

4. Those that are 'artifacts of the implementation'-objects used as programming tools to implement the code.

A Java/C++ program typically consists of a number of objects, which communicate with each other by calling one another's member functions. The organization of a Java/C++ program is shown in Figure 4.1

The Object-oriented Paradigm

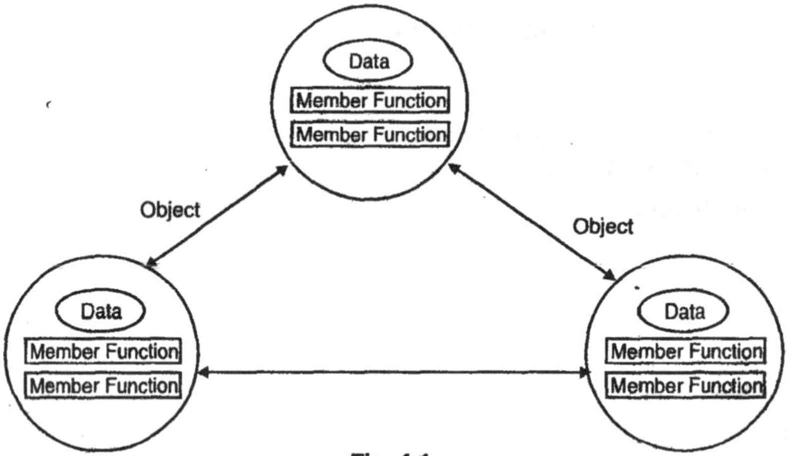

Fig. 4.1

The following illustration is a common visual representation of a software object:

- Everything that the software object knows (state) and can do (behavior) is expressed by the variables and methods within that object. A software object that modelled your real-world bicycle would have variables that indicated the bicycle's current state: its speed is 10 mph, its pedal cadence is 90 rpm, and its current gear is the 5th gear. These variables and methods are formally known as instance variables and instance methods to distinguish them from class variables and class methods (described later in What Is a Class?). The following figure illustrates a bicycle modeled as a software object.

- The software bicycle would also have methods to brake, change the pedal cadence, and change gears. (The bike would not have a method for changing the speed of the bicycle, as the bike's speed is really just a side-effect of what gear it's in, how fast the rider is pedaling, whether the brakes are on, and how steep the hill is.)
- Anything that an object does not know or cannot do is excluded from the object. For example, your bicycle (probably) doesn't have a name, and it can't run, bark, or fetch. Thus there are no variables or methods for those states and behaviors in the bicycle class.

As you can see from the diagrams, the object's variables make up the center or nucleus of the object. Methods surround and hide the object's nucleus from other objects in the program. Packaging an object's variables within the protective custody of its methods is called encapsulation. Typically, encapsulation is used to hide unimportant implementation details from other objects. When you want to change gears on your bicycle, you don't need to know how the gear mechanism works, you just need to know which lever to move. Similarly in software programs, you don't need to know how a class is implemented, you just need to know which methods to invoke. Thus, the implementation details can change at any time without affecting other parts of the program.

This conceptual picture of an object—a nucleus of variables packaged within a protective membrane of methods—is an ideal representation of an object and is the ideal that designers of object-oriented systems strive for. However, it's not the whole story. Often, for implementation or efficiency reasons, an object may wish to expose some of its variables or hide some of its methods.

In many languages, including Java, an object can choose to expose its variables to other objects allowing those other objects to inspect and even modify the variables. Also, an object can choose to hide methods from other objects forbidding those objects from invoking the methods. An object has complete control over whether other objects can access its variables and methods and in fact, can specify which other objects have access. Variable and method access in Java is covered in Controlling Access to Members of a Class.

4.2 Three OOP'S Principle

Object Oriented Programming heavily uses three principles

- Abstraction and Encapsulation
- Inheritence
- Polymorphism

To manage the complexity and enhance the maintenance and reusability of the business logic, developers often use object-oriented (OO) analysis, design, and programming. The focus of these techniques is to build around the objects in the system, rather than the business process flow. To identify objects, the analyst looks at the tangible elements in the system, such as a customer, a dwelling, or a piece of equipment.

For each of these objects the analyst asks what the object should know or what its attributes are. We would expect customers to know their names and dwellings to know their addresses. Next the analyst determines what each object should know how to do or its behavior. The programmer will trigger this behavior by sending a message to the object. A piece of equipment might accept messages to turn a feature on or off, for example. If a designer were modeling a dog using object-oriented programming, then, it might have attributes of a name, hair color, and weight. Its behavior could be how it responds to the messages "speak," "sit," and "roll over."

The analyst must also identify intangible things in the system that might qualify as an object, such as a person's membership in a club. A membership would have attributes such as the beginning date. It might also have behavior that would cause the membership to cease.

The goal of this kind of analysis is to provide a better set of abstractions for building the software solution. The objects form a simplified model of the business problem domain. With an OO design developers can ask, "What object should know that?" or "What object should do that?" This strong sense of belonging created by careful design of the objects leads to systems that are easier to understand, maintain, and extend.

4.3 Abstraction and Encapsulation

Abstraction is the representation of all the essential features of an object, which means its possible states and behaviors. these are 'encapsulated' into an 'abstract data type' which defines how all objects in a class (type) of objects are to be represented and how behave.

Encapsulation is the practice of including in an object everything it needs, (both data and processes) hidden from other objects in the system. The internal state of an object is not directly accessible from outside, and cannot be altered by external changes to the application. similarly, changes to the internal implementation details. Can be made without affecting the external interface.

The most important aspect of an object-oriented software system is that it links together data in the operations that are performed on that data. The reason why this is seen as an advantage in programming is that it reflects objects in the real world and, after all, it is people in the real world that programs are intended to serve.

Any 'real world' object we choose to investigate can be described in terms of what it is called (its identity), what it is (its state) and what it does (its behavior). If we pick up a coffee cup, we might say that it has a name ('coffee cup'), a state (it may be white, hot, full etc.) and has certain fixed behavior (it can be manufactured, filled, drunk from, carried, washed and broken, for example). These elements are all 'encapsulated' into one object-we cannot divorce any one from the others. For example, the state of being full is irrevocably linked to the behavior of being filled-we cannot separate the two. If the cup has not been filled then it cannot be full. It is this kind of link between data ('what it is') and operations ('what it does') that things in the real world have that we are seeking to reflect with object-oriented software.

A further goal of OO programming is to encapsulate the details. For each object, the interface must be carefully designed to hide the details of implementation from the user of the object. When the equipment object gets the message to turn a feature on, the sender of the message does not need to know how that feature is enabled. Encapsulation like this promotes understanding of the system by minimizing the details that a user must know at any one time. If a new way to enable a feature on the equipment emerges, only the equipment object must change. Thus, encapsulation simplifies maintenance of the application.

Two other common attributes of OO programming are inheritance and polymorphism.

4.4 Inheritence

OO programming environments provide an object with the ability to inherit from other objects. For instance, in a business system we might define a person as having attributes such as name, address, and home phone number. We could then create a customer, field technician, or sales representative by inheriting characteristics from the person object. All of these would pick up the name, address, and phone number attributes. Other attributes could then be added to the inheriting objects, such as a sales route for the salesman. Later, if we decided to add a birth date to the person object, all the other objects inheriting from the person will also automatically add the birth date attribute.

4.5 Polymorphism

Polymorphism means 'having many forms', and there are many forms of polymorphism. The general description of polymorphism is that is allows different objects to respond to the same message in different ways, the response specific to the type of object.

Due to Polymorphism objects can respond differently to the same message. To illustrate polymorphism ,let us say that we were modeling a dog, a cat, and a duck. We might send each of them the message to "speak." Each one would carry out the command, but in its own way (i.e., "woof," "meow," and "quack"). So, too, in the business system, we can send a message to all of the objects asking them to store their attributes. Each of them will behave differently in that they have different attributes to store. Yet they all receive and act upon the same message. This is a powerful concept that lets developers build systems that have consistent interfaces yet behave appropriately.

This is achieved by various types of 'overloading'-allowing a symbol (an operator like '+', or a function name like 'show') to have more than one meaning depending on the context in which it is used. Polymorphism is particularly important when object-oriented programs are dynamically creating and destroying objects in a classification hierarchy at run time, so that it is not possible when compiling to predict the number or classes of objects which will receive messages when the program is running. we therefore have to defer decisions about the meaning of a particular symbol until run-time, a practice known as 'dynamic binding'. 'Run-time' polymorphism of this kind is one of the most useful aspects of object-oriented programming.

These three main ideas (encapsulation, inheritance and polymorphism) tend to build on each other, so that once we have encapsulation, then we can build classification hierarchies of inheritance, and from these we can really begin to use the power of polymorphism.

4.6 Information Hiding

We have defined the term 'encapsulation' as meaning that we represent in software some kind of unit which, like real world objects, has both state and behavior. this integration of state and behavior allows us to implement 'information hiding' (a term first coined by David Parnas in 1972). Which means that encapsulation hides private elements of an object behind a public interface. This separation between the public and private parts of an encapsulated object has two aspects-protection of the object's state from unforeseen external influences, and hiding of the implementation details used to define an object's behavior.

Firstly, then, 'information hiding' means that an object's state cannot be altered expect by its fixed methods of behavior. this is crucial, because we are trying to protect the state data inside an object from being changed by unpredictable external influences. If we take the coffee cup example (figure 4.1), we can say that it has a state of 'fullness' (how much coffee is in the cup). Unless we resort to conjuring tricks, this state can only be affected by specific operations: being filled (from kettle, jug etc.) or getting emptied, (drunk or spilled). No other external effect can change the state of 'fullness'. the protection of state data is something which object-orientation provides us with in software. In effect, when programming we need the security of knowing that data in our program won't suddenly changed state because of some apparently unconnected external event, with the same conviction that we know our coffee cup won't suddenly turn from white to black because the sun has gone behind a cloud.

4.7 The Benefits of Encapsulation

Encapsulating related variables and methods into a neat software bundle is a simple yet powerful idea that provides two primary benefits to software developers:

Modularity—The source code for an object can be written and maintained independently of the source code for other objects. Also, an object can be easily passed around in the system. You can give your bicycle to someone else and it will still work.

Information hiding—An object has a public interface that other objects can use to communicate with it. But the object can maintain private information and methods that can be changed at any time without affecting the other objects that depend on it. You don't need to understand the gear mechanism on your bike in order to use it.

4.8 Multiple Objects

In general there will be more than one object in any given class. Reference variables are used to distinguish between different objects of the same class.

For example, the following program creates two two-d point objects and prints their fields:

```
class TwoPointPrinter
{
public static void main(String[] args)
{
TwoDPoint origin; // only declares, does not allocate
TwoDPoint one; // only declares, does not allocate
// The constructor allocates and usually initializes the object
origin = new TwoDPoint();
one = new TwoDPoint();
// set the fields
origin.x = 0.0;
origin.y = 0.0;
one.x = 1.0;
one.y = 0.0;
// print the two-d points
System.out.println("The origin is at " + origin.x + ", " + origin.y);
System.out.println("One is at " + one.x + ", " + one.y);
}  // end main
} // end TwoPointPrinter
```

one and origin are two different reference variables pointing to two different point objects. It's not enough to identify a variable as a member of a class like x or y in the example above. You have to specify which object in the class you're referring to.

It is possible for two different reference variables to point to the same object.

When an object is no longer pointed to by any reference variable (including references stored deep inside the runtime or class library) it will be marked for garbage collection.

For example, the following program declares two TwoDPoint reference variables, creates one two-d point object, and assigns that object to both variables. The two variables are equal.

class EqualPointPrinter {

```
public static void main(String[] args)
{
TwoDPoint origin1; // only declares, does not allocate
TwoDPoint origin2; // only declares, does not allocate
// The constructor allocates and usually initializes the object
```

```
origin1 = new TwoDPoint();
origin2 = origin1;
// set the fields
origin1.x = 0.0;
origin1.y = 0.0;
// print
System.out.println("origin1 is at " + origin1.x + ", " + origin1.y);
System.out.println("origin2 is at " + origin4.x + ", " + origin4.y);
}  // end main
} // end EqualPointPrinter
```

origin1 and origin2 are two different reference variables referring to the same point object.

4.9 The Life Cycle of an Object

A typical Java program creates many objects, which interact with one another by sending each other messages. Through these object interactions, a Java program can implement a GUI, run an animation, or send and receive information over a network. Once an object has completed the work for which it was created, it is garbage-collected and its resources are recycled for use by other objects.

Here's a small program, called CreateObjectDemo, that creates three objects: one Point object and two Rectangle objects. You will need all three source files to compile this program.

```
public class CreateObjectDemo
{
public static void main(String[] args)
{
// create a point object and two rectangle objects
Point origin_one = new Point(23, 94);
Rectangle rect_one = new Rectangle(origin_one, 100, 200);
Rectangle rect_two = new Rectangle(50, 100);
// display rect_one's width, height, and area
System.out.println("Width of rect_one:" + rect_one.width);
System.out.println("Height of rect_one:" + rect_one.height);
System.out.println("Area of rect_one:" + rect_one.area());
// set rect_two's position
rect_two.origin = origin_one;
// display rect_two's position
System.out.println("X Position of rect_two: " + rect_two.origin.x);
System.out.println("Y Position of rect_two: " + rect_two.origin.y);
// move rect_two and display its new position
rect_two.move(40, 72);
System.out.println("X Position of rect_two: " + rect_two.origin.x);
System.out.println("Y Position of rect_two: " + rect_two.origin.y);
}
}
```

After creating the objects, the program manipulates the objects and displays some information about them. Here's the output from the program:

```
Width of rect_one: 100
Height of rect_one: 200
Area of rect_one: 20000
X Position of rect_two: 23
Y Position of rect_two: 94
X Position of rect_two: 40
Y Position of rect_two: 72
```

This section uses this example to describe the life cycle of an object within a program. From this, you can learn how to write code that creates and uses an object and how the system cleans it up.

4.10 Creating Objects

As you know, a class provides the blueprint for objects; you create an object from a class. Each of the following statements taken from the CreateObjectDemo program creates an object:

```
Point origin_one = new Point(23, 94);
Rectangle rect_one = new Rectangle(origin_one, 100, 200);
Rectangle rect_two = new Rectangle(50, 100);
```

The first line creates an object from the Point class and the second and third lines each create an object from the Rectangle class.

Each statement has three parts:

- **Declaration:** The code set in red in the previous listing are all variable declarations that associate a name with a type. When you create an object, you do not have to declare a variable to refer to it. However, a variable declaration often appears on the same line as the code to create an object.
- **Instantiation:** new is a Java operator that creates the new object (allocates space for it).
- **Initialization:** The new operator is followed by a call to a constructor. For example, Point(23, 94) is a call to Point's only constructor. The constructor initializes the new object.

4.10.1 Declaring a Variable to Refer to an Object

From the Variables section in the previous lesson, you learned that to declare a variable, you write:

```
type name
```

This notifies the compiler that you will use name to refer to data whose type is type.

In addition to the primitive types, such as int and boolean, provided directly by the Java platform, classes and interfaces are also types. So to declare a variable to refer to an object, you can use the name of a class or an interface, as the variable's type. The sample program uses both the Point and the Rectangle class names as types to declare variables.

```
Point origin_one = new Point(23, 94);
Rectangle rect_one = new Rectangle(origin_one, 100, 200);
Rectangle rect_two = new Rectangle(50, 100);
```

Declarations do not create new objects. The code Point origin_one does not create a new Point object; it just declares a variable, named origin_one, that will be used to refer to a Point object. The reference is empty until assigned, as illustrated in the next figure. An empty reference is known as a null reference.

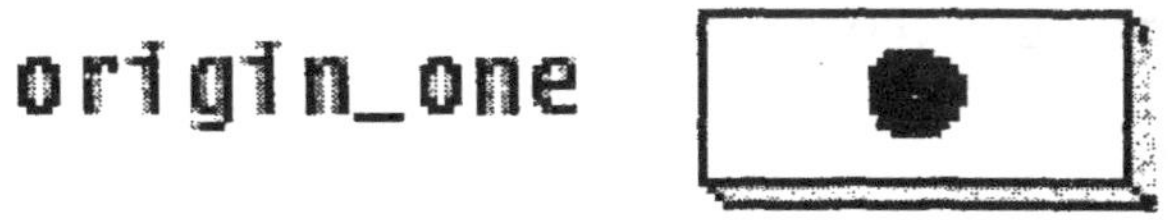

Fig. 4.2

To create an object you must instantiate it with the new operator.

4.10.2 Instantiating an Object

The new operator instantiates a class by allocating memory for a new object. The newoperator requires a single, postfix argument: a call to a constructor. The name of the constructor provides the name of the class to instantiate. The constructor initializes the new object.

The new operator returns a reference to the object it created. Often, this reference is assigned to a variable of the appropriate type. If the reference is not assigned to a variable, the object is unreachable after the statement in which the new operator appears finishes executing.

4.10.3 Initializing an Object

Here's the code for the Point class:

```
public class Point
{
public int x = 0;
public int y = 0;
//A constructor!
public Point(int x, int y)
{
this.x = x;
this.y = y;
}
}
```

This class contains a single constructor. You can recognize a constructor because it has the same name as the class and has no return type. The constructor in the Point class takes two integer arguments, as declared by the code (int x, int y). The following statement provides 23 and 94 as values for those arguments:

Point origin_one = new Point(23, 94);

The effect of the previous line of code can be illustrated in the next figure:

Here's the code for the Rectangle class, which contains four constructors:

```
public class Rectangle
{
public int width = 0;
public int height = 0;
public Point origin;
//Four constructors
public Rectangle()
{
origin = new Point(0, 0);
```

```
}
public Rectangle(Point p)
{
origin = p;
}
public Rectangle(int w, int h)
{
this(new Point(0, 0), w, h);
}
public Rectangle(Point p, int w, int h)
{
origin = p;
width = w;
height = h;
}
//A method for moving the rectangle
public void move(int x, int y)
{
origin.x = x;
origin.y = y;
}
//A method for computing the area of the rectangle
public int area()
{
return width * height;
}
}
```

Each constructor lets you provide initial values for different aspects of the rectangle: the origin; the width, and the height; all three; or none. If a class has multiple constructors, they all have the same name but a different number of arguments or different typed arguments. The Java platform differentiates the constructors, based on the number and the type of the arguments. When the Java platform encounters the following code, it knows to call the constructor in the Rectangle class that requires a Point argument followed by two integer arguments:

```
Rectangle rect_one = new Rectangle(origin_one, 100, 200);
```

This call initializes the rectangle's origin variable to the Point object referred to by origin_one. The code also sets width to 100 and height to 200. Now there are two references to the same Point object; an object can have multiple references to it, as shown in the next figure:

Fig. 4.3

Multiple references can refer to the same object. The following line of code calls the constructor that requires two integer arguments, which provide the initial values for width and height. If you inspect the code within the constructor, you will see that it creates a new Point object whose x and y values are initialized to 0:

```
Rectangle rect_two = new Rectangle(50, 100);
```

The Rectangle constructor used in the following statement doesn't take any arguments, so it's called a no-argument constructor:

```
Rectangle rect = new Rectangle();
```

If a class does not explicitly declare any constructors, the Java platform automatically provides a no-argument constructor, called the default constructor, that does nothing. Thus, all classes have at least one constructor.

This section talked about how to use a constructor. Providing Constructors for Your Classes explains how to write constructors for your classes.

4.10.4 Creating another object.

The following program is given just for perusal purpose only as at this stage it will not be possible for the reader to understand this program. Create objects with the new keyword followed by a constructor. For example, the following program creates a TwoDPoint object and prints its fields:

```
class OriginPrinter
{
public static void main(String[] args)
{
TwoDPoint origin; // only declares, does not allocate
// The constructor allocates and usually initializes the object
origin = new TwoDPoint();
// set the fields
origin.x = 0.0;
origin.y = 0.0;
// print the two-d point
System.out.println("The origin is at" + origin.x +", " + origin.y);
}  // end main
} // end OriginPrinter
```

The . is the member access separator.

A constructor invocation with new is required to allocate an object. There is no C++ like static allocation.

To compile this class, put it in a file called OriginPrinter.java in the same directory as TwoDPoint.java and type:

% javac OriginPrinter.java

What does this produce?

Is this a complete program now? Can you run it?

4.11 Using Objects

Once you've created an object, you probably want to use it for something. You may need information from it, want to change its state, or have it perform some action.

Objects give you two ways to do these things:

- Manipulate or inspect its variables.
- Call its methods.
- Referencing an Object's Variables

The following is the general form of a qualified name, which is also known as a long name:

```
objectReference.variableName
```

You may use a simple name for an instance variable when the instance variable is in scope- that is, within code for the object's class. Code that is outside the object's class must use a qualified name. For example, the code in the CreateObjectDemo class is outside the code for the Rectangle class. So to refer to the origin, width, and height variables within the Rectangle object named rect_one, the CreateObjectDemo class must use the names rect_one.origin, rect_one.width, and rect_one.height, respectively. The program uses two of these names to display the width and the height of rect_one:

```
System.out.println("Width of rect_one:" + rect_one.width);
System.out.println("Height of rect_one:" + rect_one.height);
```

Attempting to use the simple names width and height from the code in the CreateObjectDemo class doesn't make sense-those variables exist only within an object-and results in a compiler error.

Later, the program uses similar code to display information about rect_two. Objects of the same type have their own copy of the same instance variables. Thus, each Rectangle object has variables named origin, width, and height. When you access an instance variable through an object reference, you reference that particular object's variable. The two objects rect_one and rect_two in the CreateObjectDemo program have different origin, width, and height variables.

The first part of the variable's qualified name, objectReference, must be a reference to an object. You can use the name of a reference variable here, as in the previous examples, or you can use any expression that returns an object reference. Recall that the new operator returns a reference to an object. So you could use the value returned from new to access a new object's variables:

int height = new Rectangle().height;

This statement creates a new Rectangle object and immediately gets its height. In essence, the statement calculates the default height of a Rectangle. Note that after this statement has been executed, the program no longer has a reference to the created Rectangle, because the program never stored the reference in a variable. The object is unreferenced, and its resources can be recycled by the Java platform.

4.12 A Word About Variable Access

The direct manipulation of an object's variables by other objects and classes is discouraged because it's possible to set the variables to values that don't make sense. For example, consider the Rectangle class from the previous section. Using that class, you can create a rectangle whose width and height are negative, which, for some applications, doesn't make sense.

Ideally, instead of allowing direct manipulation of variables, a class would provide methods through which other objects can inspect or change variables. These methods ensure that the values of the variables make sense for objects of that type. Thus, the Rectangle class would provide methods called setWidth, setHeight, getWidth, and getHeight for setting and getting the width and the height. The methods for setting the variables would report an error if the caller tried to set the width or the height to a negative number. The other advantage of using methods instead of direct variable access is that the class can change the type and the names of the variables it uses for storing the width and the height without affecting its clients.

However, in practical situations, it sometimes makes sense to allow direct access to an object's variables. For example, both the Point class and the Rectangle class allow free access to their member variables by declaring them public. This keeps these classes small and simple. Also, it keeps them generally useful. Some applications might allow rectangles with negative widths and heights.

The Java programming language provides an access control mechanism whereby classes can determine what other classes can have direct access to its variables. A class should protect variables against direct manipulation by other objects if those manipulations could result in values that don't make sense for objects of that type. Changes to these variables should be controlled by method calls. If a class grants access to its variables, you can assume that you can inspect and change those variables without adverse effects. To learn more about the access control mechanism, refer to Controlling Access to Members of a Class. Also, by making the variables accessible, they become part of the class's API, which means that the writer of the class should not change their names or their types.

4.13 Calling an Object's Methods

You also use qualified names to call an object's method. To form the qualified name of a method, you append the method name to an object reference, with an intervening period (.). Also, you provide, within enclosing parentheses, any arguments to the method. If the method does not require any arguments, use empty parentheses.

```
objectReference.methodName(argumentList);
```

or

```
objectReference.methodName();
```

The Rectangle class has two methods: area to compute the rectangle's area and move to change the rectangle's origin. Here's the CreateObjectDemo code that calls these two methods:

```
System.out.println("Area of rect_one:" + rect_one.area());
...
rect_two.move(40, 72);
```

The first statement calls rect_one's area method and displays the results. The second line moves rect_two because the move method assigns new values to the object's origin.x and origin.y.

As with instance variables, objectReference must be a reference to an object. You can use a variable name, but you also can use any expression that returns an object reference. The new operator returns an object reference, so you can use the value returned from new to call a new object's methods:

```
new Rectangle(100, 50).area()
```

The expression new Rectangle(100, 50) returns an object reference that refers to a Rectangle object. As shown, you can use the dot notation to call the new Rectangle's area method to compute the area of the new rectangle.

Some methods, such as area, return a value. For methods that return a value, you can use the method call in expressions. You can assign the return value to a variable, use it to make decisions, or control a loop. This code assigns the value returned by areato a variable:

```
int areaOfRectangle = new Rectangle(100, 50).area();
```

Remember, invoking a method on a particular object is the same as sending a message to that object. In this case, the object that areais invoked on is the rectangle returned by the constructor.

4.13.1 A Word about Method Access

The methods in our Point and Rectangle classes are all declared public, so they are accessible to any other class. Sometimes, a class needs to restrict access to its methods. For example, a class might have a method that only subclasses are allowed to call. A class can use the same mechanism to control access to its methods as it uses to control access to its variables. To learn more about the access control mechanism, refer to Controlling Access to Members of a Class.

4.14 Cleaning Up Unused Objects

Some object-oriented languages require that you keep track of all the objects you create and that you explicitly destroy them when they are no longer needed. Managing memory explicitly is tedious and error prone. The Java platform allows you to create as many objects as you want (limited, of course, by what your system can handle), and you don't have to worry about destroying them. The Java runtime environment deletes objects when it determines that they are no longer being used. This process is called garbage collection.

An object is eligible for garbage collection when there are no more references to that object. References that are held in a variable are usually dropped when the variable goes out of scope. Or, you can explicitly drop an object reference by setting the variable to the special value null. Remember that a program can have multiple references to the same object; all references to an object must be dropped before the object is eligible for garbage collection.

4.15 The Garbage Collector

The Java runtime environment has a garbage collector that periodically frees the memory used by objects that are no longer referenced. The garbage collector does its job automatically, although, in some situations, you may want to run the garbage collection explicitly by calling the gc method in the System class. For instance, you might want to run the garbage collector after a section of code that creates a large amount of garbage or before a section of code that needs a lot of memory.

4.16 Finalization

Before an object gets garbage-collected, the garbage collector gives the object an opportunity to clean up after itself through a call to the object's finalize method. This process is known as finalization.

Most programmers don't have to worry about implementing the finalize method. In rare cases, however, a programmer might have to implement a finalize method to release resources, such as native peers, that aren't under the control of the garbage collector.

The finalize method is a member of the Object class, which is the top of the Java platform's class hierarchy and a superclass of all classes. A class can override the finalize method to perform any finalization necessary for objects of that type. If you override finalize, your implementation of the method should call super.finalize as the last thing it does. Overriding Methods talks more about how to override methods.

QUESTIONS AND EXERCISES

1. *What's wrong with the following program?*

```
//
// This program won't compile because something is wrong.
//
```

```
public class SomethingIsWrong
{
public static void main(String[] args)
{
Rectangle myRect;
myRect.width = 40;
myRect.height = 50;
System.out.println("myRect's area is" + myRect.area());
}
}
```

2. *The following code creates one Point object and one Rectangle object. How many references to those objects exist after the code executes? Is either object eligible for garbage collection?*

```
...
Point point = new Point(2,4);
Rectangle rectangle = new Rectangle(point, 20, 20);
point = null;
...
```

3. *How does a program destroy an object that it creates?*

EXERCISES

1. *Fix the program called SomethingIsWrong shown in Question 1.*

Given the following class, called NumberHolder, write some code that creates an instance of the class, initializes its two member variables, and then displays the value of each member variable.

```
public class NumberHolder
{
public int anInt;
public float aFloat;
}
```

PART II OBJECTIVE TYPE QUESTIONS

A1 Select the most appropriate alternative from following

1. In OOP, a function contained within a class is called

(a) a member function
(b) an operator
(c) a class function
(d) a method

2. *Which of the following are good reasons to use an object-oriented language?*

(a) you can define your own data types.
(b) Program statements are simpler than in procedural language.
(c) An OO program can be taught to correct its own errors.
(d) It's easier to conceptualize an OO program.

3. *When a language has the capability to produce new data types, it is said to be*

(a) reprehensible
(b) encapsulated
(c) overloaded
(d) extensible

4. *Which of the following are good reasons to use an object-oriented language?*

(a) *you can define your own data types.*
(b) *Program statements are simpler than in procedural language.*
(c) *An OO program can be taught to correct its own errors.*
(d) *It's easier to conceptualize an OO program.*

B1 Fill in the blanks

1. *Pascal, BASIC, and C are .... languages, while vb or C++ is an a .... language.*
2. *The two major components of an object are ...... and functions that ....*
3. *Protecting data from access by unauthorized function is called ....*
4. *...... model entities in the real world more closely than do functions.*
5. *The ability of a function or operator to act in different ways on different data types is called ....*

ANSWER TO QUESTIONS

A1 1. a 2.a,d 3.d 4. a , d

B1 1. procedural, object-oriented

2. data, act on that data
3. encapsulation
4. objects
5. polymorphism

5

Introduction to Classes

5.1 What is Object Oriented Programming?

In classic, procedural programming you try to make the real world problem you're attempting to solve fit a few, pre-determined data types: integers, floats, Strings, and arrays perhaps. In object oriented programming you create a model for a real world system.

5.2 Classes

Classes are programmer-defined types that model the parts of the system. A class is a programmer defined type that serves as a blueprint for instances of the class. You can still have ints, floats, Strings, and arrays; but you can also have cars, motorcycles, people, buildings, clouds, dogs, angles, students, courses, bank accounts, and any other type that's important to your problem.

Classes specify the data and behavior possessed both by themselves and by the objects built from them. A class has two parts:

- Fields
- Methods.

Fields describe what the class is. Methods describe what the class does. Using the blueprint provided by a class, you can create any number of objects, each of which is called an instance of the class. Different objects of the same class have the same fields and methods, but the values of the fields will in general differ. For example, all humans have eye color but the color of each human's eyes can be different from others.

On the other hand, objects have the same methods as all other objects in the class except in so far as the methods depend on the value of the fields and arguments to the method.

This dichotomy is reflected in the runtime form of objects. Every object has a separate block of memory to store its fields, but the bytes in the actual methods are shared between all objects in a class.

Another common analogy is that a class is to an object as a cookie cutter is to a cookie. One cookie cutter can make many cookies. There may be only one class, but there can be many objects in that class. Each object is an instance of one class.

5.2.1 The Class Body

The class body follows the class declaration and is embedded within curly braces { and }. The class body contains declarations for all instance variables and class variables (known collectively as member variables) for the class. In addition, the class body contains declarations and implementations for all instance methods and class methods (known collectively as methods) for the class.

The class body contains all of the code that provides for the life cycle of the objects created from it:

constructors for initializing new objects, declarations for the variables that provide the state of the class and its objects, methods to implement the behavior of the class and its objects, and in rare cases, a finalize method to provide for cleaning up an object after it has done its job. Variables and methods collectively are called members.

Note: Constructors are not methods. Nor are they members. The Stack class defines one member variable in its body to contain its elements—the items Vector. It also defines one constructor—a no-argument constructor—and three methods: push, pop, and isEmpty.

5.3 Creating Classes

Now that we've covered how to create and use objects, and how objects are cleaned up, it's time to show you how to write the classes from which objects are created. This section shows you the main components of a class through a small example that implements a last-in-first-out (LIFO) stack. The following diagram lists the class and identifies the structure of the code.

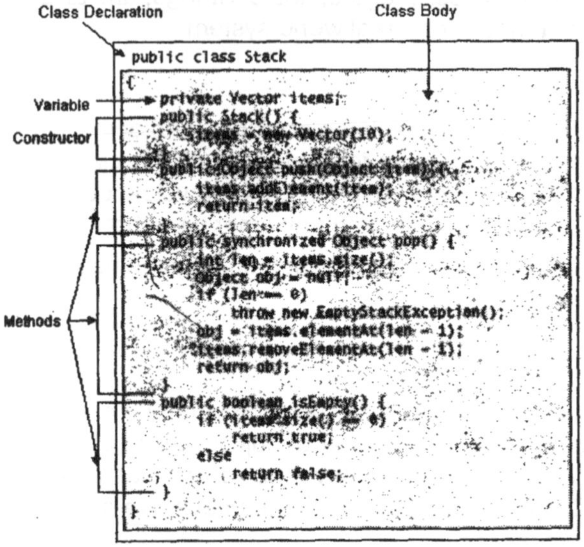

This implementation of a stack uses another object, a Vector, to store its elements. Vector is a growable array of objects and does a nice job of allocating space for new objects as space is required. The Stack class makes use of this code by using a Vector to store its elements. However, it imposes LIFO restrictions on the Vector— that is, you can only add elements to and remove elements from the top of the stack.

5.3.1 The Class Declaration

The previous diagram shows that two primary components make up the implementation of a class: the class declaration and the class body. The class declaration declares the name of the class along with other attributes. The class declaration for the Stack class is fairly simple and indicates that the class is public and that its name is Stack. Often, a minimal class declaration such as this one is all you'll need. However, the class declaration can say more about the class, such as the name of the superclass and if it can be subclassed.

Now that we've covered how to create and use objects, and how objects are cleaned up, it's time to show you how to write the classes from which objects are created. This section shows you the main components of a class through a small example that implements a last-in-first-out (LIFO) stack. The following diagram lists the class and identifies the structure of the code.

5.4 The Class Body

The class body follows the class declaration and is embedded within curly braces { and }. The class body contains declarations for all instance variables and class variables (known collectively as member variables) for the class. In addition, the class body contains declarations and implementations for all instance methods and class methods (known collectively as methods) for the class.

The class body contains all of the code that provides for the life cycle of the objects created from it: constructors for initializing new objects, declarations for the variables that provide the state of the class and its objects, methods to implement the behavior of the class and its objects, and in rare cases, a finalize method to provide for cleaning up an object after it has done its job. Variables and methods collectively are called members.

Note: Constructors are not methods. Nor are they members. The Stack class defines one member variable in its body to contain its elements—the items Vector. It also defines one constructor—a no-argument constructor—and three methods: push, pop, and isEmpty.

The class body follows the class declaration and is embedded within curly braces { and }. The class body contains declarations for all instance variables and class variables (known collectively as member variables) for the class. In addition, the class body contains declarations and implementations for all instance methods and class methods (known collectively as methods) for the class.

5.5 Providing Constructors for Your Classes

A class may contain one or more constructors that provide for the initialization of an object created from the class. This section shows you how to write a constructor.

Declaring Member Variables

A class's state is represented by its member variables. You declare a class's member variables in the body of the class. Typically, you declare a class's variables before you declare its methods, although this is not required.

```
classDeclaration
{
member variable declarations
method declarations
}
```

Note: To declare variables that are members of a class, the declarations must be within the class body, but not within the body of a method. Variables declared within the body of a method are local to that method.

Implementing Methods

As you know, objects have behavior that is implemented by its methods. Other objects can ask an object to do something by invoking its methods. This section tells you everything you need to know about writing methods for your Java classes. For more information about how to call methods see Using Objects.

In Java, you define a class's methods in the body of the class for which the method implements some behavior. Typically, you declare a class's methods after its variables in the class body although this is not required.

5.6 Controlling Access to Members of a Class

Member variables and methods are known collectively as members. When you declare a member of a Java class, you can allow or disallow other objects of other types access to that member through the use of access specifiers.

Understanding Instance and Class Members

A Java class can contain two different types of members: instance members and class members. This page shows you how to declare both types of members and how to use them.

How Do These Concepts Translate into Code? in the Object-Oriented Programming Concepts lesson, showed you a subclass of Applet and talked briefly about the responsibilities and benefits of subclasses. Managing Inheritance goes into further detail on this subject.

- **Implements Interfaces**

To declare that your class implements one or more interfaces, use the keyword implements followed by a comma-separated list of the names of the interfaces implemented by the class. How Do These Concepts Translate into Code? explained how the ClickMe applet implements an interface. Details about writing your own interfaces and how to use them can be found in Creating Interfaces.

5.7 The Class Body

The class body contains all of the code that provides for the life cycle of the objects created from it: constructors for initializing new objects, declarations for the variables that provide the state of the class and its objects, methods to implement the behavior of the class and its objects, and in rare cases, a finalize method to provide for cleaning up an object after it has done its job.

Variables and methods collectively are called members.

Note: Constructors are not methods. Nor are they members.

The Stack class defines one member variable in its body to contain its elements—the items Vector. It also defines one constructor—a no-argument constructor—and three methods: push, pop, and isEmpty.

5.8 Providing Constructors for Your Classes

All Java classes have constructors that are used to initialize a new object of that type. A constructor has the same name as the class. For example, the name of the Stack class's constructor is Stack, the name of the Rectangle class's constructor is Rectangle, and the name of the Thread class's constructor is Thread. Stack defines a single constructor:

```
public Stack(){
items = new Vector(10);
}
```

Java supports name overloading for constructors so that a class can have any number of constructors, all of which have the same name. Following is another constructor that could be defined by Stack. This particular constructor sets the initial size of the stack according to its parameter:

```
public Stack(int initialSize){
    items = new Vector(initialSize);
}
```

Both constructors share the same name, Stack, but they have different parameter lists. The compiler differentiates these constructors based on the number of parameters in the list and their types.

Typically, a constructor uses its arguments to initialize the new object's state. When creating an object, choose the constructor whose arguments best reflect how you want to initialize the new object.

Based on the number and type of the arguments that you pass into the constructor, the compiler can determine which constructor to use. The compiler knows that when you write the following code, it should use the constructor that requires a single integer argument:

```
new Stack(10);
```

Similarly, when you write the following code, the compiler chooses the no-argument constructor or the default constructor:

```
new Stack();
```

When writing your own class, you don't have to provide constructors for it. The default constructor is automatically provided by the runtime system for any class that contains no constructors. The default provided by the runtime system doesn't do anything. So, if you want to perform some initialization, you will have to write some constructors for your class.

The constructor for the following subclass of Thread performs animation, sets up some default values, such as the frame speed and the number of images, and then loads the images:

```
class AnimationThread extends Thread {
    int framesPerSecond;
    int numImages;
    Image[] images;
AnimationThread(int fps, int num){
    super("AnimationThread");
    this.framesPerSecond = fps;
    this.numImages = num;
    this.images = new Image[numImages];
    for (int i = 0; i <= numImages; i++)
{
    . . .
    // Load all the images.
    . . .
    }
   .}
. . .
}
```

Note how the body of a constructor is like the body of a method; that is, it contains local variable declarations, loops, and other statements. However, one line in the AnimationThread constructor that you wouldn't see in a method is the second line:

```
super("AnimationThread");
```

This line invokes a constructor provided by the superclass of AnimationThread, namely, Thread. This particular Thread constructor takes a String that sets the name of Thread. Often a constructor wants to take advantage of initialization code written in a class's superclass. Indeed, some classes must call their superclass constructor in order for the object to work properly. If present, the superclass constructor must be the first statement in the subclass's constructor: An object should perform the higher-level initialization first.

You can specify what other objects can create instances of your class by using an access specifier in the constructors' declaration:

- **Private**

No other class can instantiate your class. Your class may contain public class methods (sometimes called factory methods), and those methods can construct an object and return it, but no other classes can.

- **Protected**

Only subclasses of the class and classes in the same package can create instances of it.

- **Public**

Any class can create an instance of your class.

no specifier gives package access

Only classes within the same package as your class can construct an instance of it.

Constructors provide a way to initialize a new object. Initializing Instance and Class Members describes other ways you can provide for the initialization of your class and a new object created from the class. That section also discusses when and why you would use each technique.

5.9 Declaring Member Variables

Stack uses the following line of code to define its single member variable:

```
private Vector items;
```

This declares a member variable and not some other type of variable (like a local variable) because the declaration appears within the class body but outside of any methods or constructors. The member variable declared is named items, and its data type is Vector. Also, the private keyword identifies items as a private member. This means that only code within the Stack class can access it.

accessLevel	Indicates the access level for this member.
`static`	Declares a class member.
`final`	Indicates that it is constant.
`transient`	This variable is transient.
`volatile`	This variable is volatile.
type name	The type and name of the variable.

This is a relatively simple member variable declaration, but declarations can be more complex. You can specify not only type, name, and access level, but also other attributes, including whether the variable is a class or instance variable and whether it's a constant. Each component of a member variable declaration is further defined below:

accessLevel

Lets you control which other classes have access to a member variable by using one of four access levels: public, protected, package, and private. You control access to methods in the same way. Controlling Access to Members of a Class covers access levels in detail.

static

Declares this is a class variable rather than an instance variable. You also use static to declare class methods. Understanding Instance and Class Members later in this lesson talks about declaring instance and class variables.

final

Indicates that the value of this member cannot change. The following variable declaration defines a constant named AVOGADRO, whose value is Avogadro's number (6.022 * 1023) and cannot be changed:

```
final double AVOGADRO = 6.022e23;
```

It's a compile-time error if your program ever tries to change a final variable. By convention, the name of constant values are spelled in uppercase letters.

transient

The transient marker is not fully specified by The Java Language Specification but is used in object serialization which is covered in Object Serialization to mark member variables that should not be serialized.

volatile

The volatile keyword is used to prevent the compiler from performing certain optimizations on a member. This is an advanced Java feature, used by only a few Java programmers, and is outside the scope of this tutorial.

type

Like other variables, a member variable must have a type. You can use primitive type names such as int, float, or boolean. Or you can use reference types, such as array, object, or interface names.

name

A member variable's name can be any legal Java identifier and, by convention, begins with a lowercase letter. You cannot declare more than one member variable with the same name in the same class, but a subclass can hide a member variable of the same name in its superclass. Additionally, a member variable and a method can have the same name. For example, the following code is legal:

```
public class Stack {
    private Vector items;
    // a method with same name as a member variable
    public Vector items(){
    . . .
    }
}
```

5.10 Implementing Methods

This figure shows the code for Stack's push method. This method pushes an object, the one passed in as an argument, onto the top of the stack, and returns it.

Like a class, a method has two major parts: method declaration and method body. The method declaration defines all of the method's attributes, such as access level, return type, name, and arguments, as illustrated here:

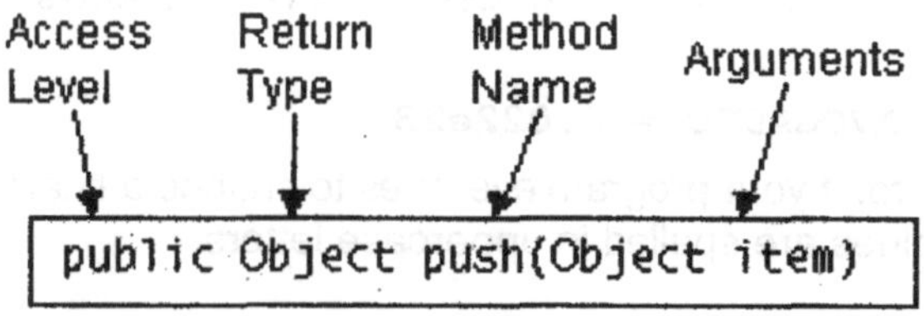

The method body is where all the action takes place. It contains the Java instructions that implement the method.

5.10.1 The Method Declaration

At minimum, a method declaration has a name and a return type indicating the data type of the value returned by the method:

```
returnType methodName(){
. . .
}
```

This method declaration is very basic. Methods have many other attributes such as arguments, access control, and so on. This section will cover these topics as well as expand upon the features illustrated in the method declaration above.

5.10.2 Passing Information into a Method

Perhaps the most commonly used optional component of a method declaration are method parameters. Similar to functions in other programming languages, Java methods accept input from the caller through its parameters. Parameters provide information to the method from outside the scope of the method.

5.10.3 Details of a Method Declaration

A method's declaration provides a lot of information about the method to the compiler, to the runtime system, and to other classes and objects. Included is not only the name of the method, but also such information as the return type of the method, the number and type of the arguments required by the method, and which other classes and objects can call the method.

While this may sound like writing a novel rather than simply declaring a method, most method attributes can be declared implicitly. The only required elements of a method declaration are the method's name, its return type, and a pair of parentheses ( ). This figure shows the elements of a method declaration.

accessLevel	Access level for this method.
static	This is a class method.
abstract	This method is not implemented.
final	Method cannot be overridden.
native	Method implemented in another language.
synchronized	Method requires a monitor to run.
returnType methodName	The return type and method name.
(*paramList*)	The list of arguments.
throws *exceptions*	The exceptions thrown by this method.

Each element of a method declaration is further defined below:

accessLevel

As with member variables, you control which other classes have access to a method using one of four access levels: public, protected, package, and private.

static

As with member variables, static declares this method as a class method rather than an instance method.

abstract

An abstract method has no implementation and must be a member of an abstract class.

5.10.4 Final

A final method cannot be overridden by subclasses.

native

If you have a significant library of functions written in another language such as C, you may wish to preserve that investment and use those functions from Java. Methods implemented in a language other than Java are called native methods and are declared as such using the native keyword.

synchronized

Concurrently running threads often invoke methods that operate on the same data. These methods may be declared synchronized to ensure that the threads access information in a thread-safe manner.

return type

Java requires that a method declare the data type of the value that it returns. If your method does not return a value, use the keyword void for the return type. Returning a Value from a Method talks about the issues related to returning values from a method.

Method Name

A method name can be any legal Java identifier. You need to consider several issues in regards to Java method names. These are covered in Method Names.

(Paramlist)

You pass information into a method through its arguments. See the next section, Passing Information into a Method.

[Throws exceptions]

If your method throws any checked exceptions, your method declaration must indicate the type of those exceptions. See Handling Errors with Exceptionsfor information. In particular, refer to Specifying the Exceptions Thrown by a Method.

5.10.5 Returning a Value from a Method

You declare a method's return type in its method declaration. Within the body of the method, you use the return operator to return the value. Any method that is not declared void must contain a return statement. The Stack class declares the isEmpty method, which returns a boolean:

```
public boolean isEmpty() {
    if (items.size() == 0)
    return true;
    else
    return false;
}
```

The data type of the return value must match the method's return type; you can't return an Object type from a method declared to return an integer. The isEmpty method returns either the boolean value true or false, depending on the outcome of a test. A compiler error results if you try to write a method in which the return value doesn't match the return type.

The isEmpty method returns a primitive type. Methods also can return a reference type. For example, Stack declares the pop method that returns the Object reference type:

```
public synchronized Object pop() {
int len = items.size();
Object obj = null;
if (len == 0)
    throw new EmptyStackException();
obj = items.elementAt(len - 1);
items.removeElementAt(len - 1);
return obj;
}
```

When a method returns an object such as pop does, the class of the returned object must be either a subclass of or the exact class of the return type. This can be a source of confusion, so let's look at this more closely. Suppose you have a class hierarchy where ImaginaryNumber is a subclass of java.lang.Number, which is, in turn, a subclass of Object, as illustrated here:

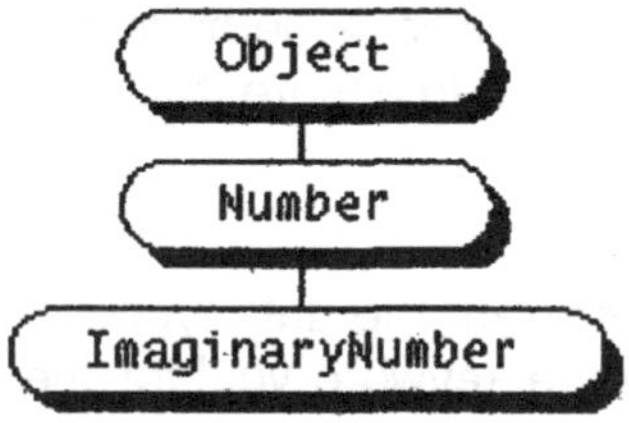

Now suppose you have a method declared to return a Number:

```
public Number returnANumber() {
. . .
}
```

The returnANumber method can return an ImaginaryNumber but not an Object. ImaginaryNumber "is a" Number because it's a subclass of Number. However, an Object is not necessarily a Number—it could be a String or some other type. You also can use interface names as return types. In this case, the object returned must implement the specified interface.

5.10.6 A Method's Name

Java supports method name overloading so that multiple methods can share the same name. For example, suppose you are writing a class that can render various types of data (strings, integers, and so on) to its drawing area. You need to write a method that knows how to render each data type. In other languages, you have to think of a new name for each method, for example, drawString, drawInteger, drawFloat, and so on. In Java, you can use the same name for all of the drawing methods but pass a different type of parameter to each method. So, in your data rendering class, you can declare three methods named draw, each of which takes a different type of parameter:

```
class DataRenderer {
    void draw(String s) {
    . . .
    }
    void draw(int i)
```

```
        {
        . . .
        }
        void draw(float f)
        {
        . . .
        }
    }
```

Overloaded methods are differentiated by the number and type of the arguments passed into the method. In the code sample, draw(String s) and draw(int i) are distinct and unique methods because they require different argument types. You cannot declare more than one method with the same name and the same number and type of arguments because the compiler cannot differentiate them. So, draw(String s) and draw(String t) are identical and result in a compiler error.

A class may override a method in its superclass. The overriding method must have the same name, return type, and parameter list as the method it overrides. Overriding Methods shows you how to override methods.

5.10.7 Passing Information

The method body is where all of the action of a method takes place; the method body contains all of the legal Java instructions that implement the method.

When you write your method, you declare the number and type of the arguments required by that method. You declare the type and name for each argument in the method signature. For example, the following is a method that computes the monthly payments for a home loan based on the amount of the loan, the interest rate, the length of the loan (the number of periods), and the future value of the loan (presumably the future value of the loan is zero because at the end of the loan, you've paid it off):

```
double computePayment(double loanAmt,    double rate,
                                         double futureValue,
                                         int numPeriods){
double I, partial1, denominator, answer;
I = rate / 100.0;
partial1 = Math.pow((1 + I), (0.0 - numPeriods));
denominator = (1 - partial1) / I;
answer = ((-1 * loanAmt) / denominator)
    - ((futureValue * partial1) / denominator);
return answer;
}
```

This method takes four arguments: the loan amount, the interest rate, the future value and the number of periods. The first three are double-precision floating point numbers, and the fourth is an integer.

As with this method, the set of arguments to any method is a comma-separated list of variable declarations where each variable declaration is a type/name pair:

```
type name
```

As you can see from the body of the computePayment method, you simply use the argument name to refer to the argument's value.

- **Argument Types**

In Java, you can pass an argument of any valid Java data type into a method. This includes primitive data types such as doubles, floats and integers as you saw in the computePayment method, and reference data types such as objects and arrays. Here's an example of a factory method that accepts an array as an argument. In this example, the method creates a new Polygon object and initializes it from a list of Points (Point is a class that represents an x, y coordinate):

```
static Polygon polygonFrom(Point[] listOfPoints){
. . .
}
```

Unlike some other languages, you cannot pass methods into Java methods. But you can pass an object into a method and then invoke the object's methods.

Argument Names

When you declare an argument to a Java method, you provide a name for that argument. This name is used within the method body to refer to the item.

A method argument can have the same name as one of the class's member variables. If this is the case, then the argument is said to hide the member variable. Arguments that hide member variables are often used in constructors to initialize a class. For example, take the following Circle class and its constructor:

```
class Circle {
    int x, y, radius;
    public Circle(int x, int y, int radius){
    . . .
}
}
```

The Circle class has three member variables: x, y and radius. In addition, the constructor for the Circle class accepts three arguments each of which shares its name with the member variable for which the argument provides an initial value.

The argument names hide the member variables. So using x, y or radius within the body of the constructor refers to the argument, not to the member variable. To access the member variable, you must reference it through this—the current object:

```
class Circle {
    int x, y, radius;
    public Circle (int x, int y, int radius){
    this.x = x;
    this.y = y;
    this.radius = radius;
    }
}
```

Names of method arguments cannot be the same as another argument name for the same method, the name of any variable local to the method, or the name of any parameter to a catch clause within the same method.

5.11 Pass by Value

In Java methods, arguments are passed by value. When invoked, the method receives the value of the variable passed in. When the argument is of primitive type, pass-by-value means that the method cannot change its value. When the argument is of reference type, pass-by-value means that the method cannot change the object reference, but can invoke the object's methods and modify the accessible variables within the object.

This is often the source of confusion—a programmer writes a method that attempts to modify the value of one its arguments and the method doesn't work as expected. Let's look at such method and then investigate how to change it so that it does what the programmer originally intended.

Consider this series of Java statements which attempts to retrieve the current color of a Pen object in a graphics application:

```
int r = -1, g = -1, b = -1;
pen.getRGBColor(r, g, b);
System.out.println      ("red =" + r +
                         ", green =" + g +
                         ", blue =" + b);
```

At the time when the getRGBColor method is called, the variables r, g, and b all have the value -1. The caller is expecting the getRGBColor method to pass back the red, green and blue values of the current color in the r, g, and b variables.

However, the Java runtime passes the variables' values (-1) into the getRGBColor method; not a reference to the r, g, and b variables. So you could visualize the call to getRGBColor like this: getRGBColor(-1, -1, -1).

When control passes into the getRGBColor method, the arguments come into scope (get allocated) and are initialized to the value passed into the method:

```
class Pen {
    int redValue, greenValue, blueValue;
    void getRGBColor(int red, int green, int blue) {
    // red, green, and blue have been created
    // and their values are -1
    . . .
    }
}
```

So getRGBColor gets access to the values of r, g, and b in the caller through its arguments red, green, and blue, respectively. The method gets its own copy of the values to use within the scope of the method. Any changes made to those local copies are not reflected in the original variables from the caller.

Now, let's look at the implementation of getRGBColor within the Pen class that the method signature above implies:

```
class Pen {
    int redValue, greenValue, blueValue;
    . . .
    // this method does not work as intended
void getRGBColor(int red, int green, int blue) {
        red = redValue;
        green = greenValue;
        blue = blueValue;
    }
}
```

This method will not work as intended. When control gets to the println statement in the following code, which was shown previously, getRGBColor's arguments, red, green, and blue, no longer exist. Therefore the assignments made to them within the method had no effect; r, g, and b are all still equal to -1.

```
int r = -1, g = -1, b = -1;
pen.getRGBColor(r, g, b);
System.out.println      ("red =" + r +
                         ", green =" + g +
                         ", blue =" + b);
```

Passing variables by value affords the programmer some safety: Methods cannot unintentionally modify a variable that is outside of its scope. However, you often want a method to be able to modify one or more of its arguments. The getRGBColor method is a case in point. The caller wants the method to return three values through its arguments. However, the method cannot modify its arguments, and, furthermore, a method can only return one value through its return value. So, how can a method return more than one value, or have an effect (modify some value) outside of its scope?

For a method to modify an argument, it must be of a reference type such as an object or array. Objects and arrays are also passed by value, but the value of an object is a reference. So the effect is that arguments of reference types are passed in by reference. Hence the name. A reference to an object is the address of the object in memory. Now, the argument in the method is referring to the same memory location as the caller.

Let's rewrite the getRGBColor method so that it actually does what you want. First, you must introduce a new type of object, RGBColor, that can hold the red, green and blue values of a color in RGB space:

```
class RGBColor {
    public int red, green, blue;
}
```

Now, we can rewrite getRGBColor so that it accepts an RGBColor object as an argument. The getRGBColor method returns the current color of the pen by setting the red, green and blue member variables of its RGBColor argument:

```
class Pen {
int redValue, greenValue, blueValue;
void getRGBColor(RGBColor aColor)
{
        aColor.red = redValue;
        aColor.green = greenValue;
        aColor.blue = blueValue;
    }
}
```

And finally, let's rewrite the calling sequence:

```
RGBColor penColor = new RGBColor();
pen.getRGBColor(penColor);
System.out.println      ("red =" + penColor.red +
                         ", green =" + penColor.green +
                         ", blue =" + penColor.blue);
```

The modifications made to the RGBColor object within the getRGBColor method affect the object created in the calling sequence because the names penColor (in the calling sequence) and aColor (in the getRGBColor method) refer to the same object.

5.12 The Method Body

In the code sample that follows, the method bodies for the isEmpty and pop methods are shown in bold:

```
class Stack {
    static final int STACK_EMPTY = -1;
    Object[] stackelements;
    int topelement = STACK_EMPTY;
    . . .
    boolean isEmpty() {
    if (topelement == STACK_EMPTY)
    return true;
else
    return false;
}
Object pop() {
if (topelement == STACK_EMPTY)
    return null;
else {
        return stackelements[topelement--];
    }
  }
}
```

Besides regular Java language elements, you can use this in the method body to refer to members in the current object. The current object is the object whose method is being called. You can also use super to refer to members in the superclass that the current object has hidden or overridden. Also, a method body may contain declarations for variables that are local to that method.

5.12.1 This

Typically, within an object's method body you can just refer directly to the object's member variables. However, sometimes you need to disambiguate the member variable name if one of the arguments to the method has the same name.

For example, the following constructor for the HSBColor class initializes some of an object's member variables according to the arguments passed into the constructor. Each argument to the constructor has the same name as the object's member variable whose initial value the argument contains.

```
class HSBColor {
    int hue, saturation, brightness;
    HSBColor (int hue, int saturation, int brightness) {
       this.hue = hue;
       this.saturation = saturation;
       this.brightness = brightness;
}
```

You must use the this keyword in this constructor because you have to disambiguate the argument hue from the member variable hue (and so on with the other arguments). Writing hue = hue; makes no sense. Argument names take precedence and hide member variables with the same name. So to refer to the member variable you must do so through the current object—using the this keyword to refer to the current object—explicitly.

Some programmers prefer to always use the this keywrod when referring to a member variable of the object whose method the reference appears. Doing so makes the intent of the code explicit and reduces errors based on name sharing.

You can also use the this keyword to call one of the current object's methods. Again this is only necessary if there is some ambiguity in the method name and is often used to make the intent of the code clearer.

5.12.2 Super

If your method hides one of its superclass's member variables, your method can refer to the hidden variable through the use of the super keyword. Similarly, if your method overrides one of its superclass's methods, your method can invoke the overridden method through the use of the super keyword.

Consider this class:

```
class ASillyClass {
    boolean aVariable;
    void aMethod() {
aVariable = true;
    }
}
```

and its subclass which hides aVariable and overrides aMethod:

```
class ASillierClass extends ASillyClass {
    boolean aVariable;
    void aMethod() {
        aVariable = false;
        super.aMethod();
        System.out.println(aVariable);
        System.out.println(super.aVariable);
    }
}
```

First aMethod sets aVariable (the one declared in ASillierClass that hides the one declared in ASillyClass) to false. Next aMethod invoked its overridden method with this statement:

```
super.aMethod();
```

This sets the hidden version of the aVariable (the one declared in ASillyClass) to true. Then aMethod displays both versions of aVariable which have different values:

```
false
true
```

5.13 Local Variables

Within the body of the method you can declare more variables for use within that method. These variables are local variables and live only while control remains within the method. This method declares a local variable i that it uses to iterate over the elements of its array argument.

```
Object findObjectInArray(Object o, Object[] arrayOfObjects)
{
int i;        // local variable
for (i = 0; i < arrayOfObjects.length; i++)
```

```
if (arrayOfObjects[i] == o)
return o;
}
return null;
}
```

After this method returns, i no longer exists.

5.14 Controlling Access to Members of a Class

One of the benefits of classes is that classes can protect their member variables and methods from access by other objects. Why is this important? Well, consider this. You're writing a class that represents a query on a database that contains all kinds of secret information, say employee records or income statements for your startup company.

Certain information and queries contained in the class, the ones supported by the publicly accessible methods and variables in your query object, are OK for the consumption of any other object in the system. Other queries contained in the class are there simply for the personal use of the class. They support the operation of the class but should not be used by objects of another type—you've got secret information to protect. You'd like to be able to protect these personal variables and methods at the language level and disallow access by objects of another type.

In Java, you can use access specifiers to protect both a class's variables and its methods when you declare them. The Java language supports four distinct access levels for member variables and methods: private, protected, public, and, if left unspecified, package.

Note: The 1.0 release of the Java language supported five access levels: the four listed above plus private protected. The private protected access level is not supported in versions of Java higher than 1.0; you should no longer be using it in your Java programs.

The following chart shows the access level permitted by each specifier.

Specifier	class	subclass	package	world
private	X			
protected	X	X	* X	
public	X	X	X	X
package	X	X		

The first column indicates whether the class itself has access to the member defined by the access specifier. As you can see, a class always has access to its own members. The second column indicates whether subclasses of the class (regardless of which package they are in) have access to the member. The third column indicates whether classes in the same package as the class (regardless of their parentage) have access to the member. The fourth column indicates whether all classes have access to the member.

Note that the protected/subclass intersection has an "*" . This particular access case has a special caveat discussed in detail later.

Let's look at each access level in more detail.

5.15 Private

The most restrictive access level is private. A private member is accessible only to the class in which it is defined. Use this access to declare members that should only be used by the class. This includes variables that contain information that if accessed by an outsider could put the object in an inconsistent state, or methods that, if invoked by an outsider, could jeopardize the state of the object or the program in which it's running. Private members are like secrets you never tell anybody.

To declare a private member, use the private keyword in its declaration. The following class contains one private member variable and one private method:

```
class Alpha {
    private int iamprivate;
    private void privateMethod() {
        System.out.println("privateMethod");
    }
}
```

Objects of type Alpha can inspect or modify the iamprivate variable and can invoke privateMethod, but objects of other types cannot. For example, the Beta class defined here:

```
class Beta {
    void accessMethod() {
        Alpha a = new Alpha();
        a.iamprivate = 10;          // illegal
        a.privateMethod();          // illegal
    }
}
```

cannot access the iamprivate variable or invoke privateMethod on an object of type Alpha because Beta is not of type Alpha.

When one of your classes is attempting to access a member varible to which it does not have access, the compiler prints an error message similar to the following and refuses to compile your program:

```
Beta.java:9: Variable iamprivate in class Alpha not
accessible from class Beta.
        a.iamprivate = 10;      // illegal
        ^
1 error
```

Also, if your program is attempting to access a method to which it does not have access, you will see a compiler error like this:

```
Beta.java:12: No method matching privateMethod()
found in class Alpha.
a.privateMethod();          // illegal
1 error
```

New Java programmers might ask if one Alpha object can access the private members of another Alpha object. This is illustrated by the following example. Suppose the Alpha class contained an instance method that compared the current Alpha object (this) to another object based on their iamprivate variables:

```
class Alpha {
    private int iamprivate;
    boolean isEqualTo(Alpha anotherAlpha)
{
        if (this.iamprivate == anotherAlpha.iamprivate)
        return true;
        else
```

```
            return false;
        }
    }
```

This is perfectly legal. Objects of the same type have access to one another's private members. This is because access restrictions apply at the class or type level (all instances of a class) rather than at the object level (this particular instance of a class).

Note: this is a Java language keyword that refers to the current object. For more information about how to use this see The Method Body.

5.16 Protected

The next access level specifier is protected, which allows the class itself, subclasses (with the caveat that we referred to earlier), and all classes in the same package to access the members. Use the protected access level when it's appropriate for a class's subclasses to have access to the member, but not unrelated classes. Protected members are like family secrets—you don't mind if the whole family knows, and even a few trusted friends but you wouldn't want any outsiders to know.

To declare a protected member, use the keyword protected. First, let's look at how the protected specifier affects access for classes in the same package. Consider this version of the Alpha class which is now declared to be within a package named Greek and which has one protected member variable and one protected method declared in it:

```
package Greek;
public class Alpha {
    protected int iamprotected;
    protected void protectedMethod() {
        System.out.println("protectedMethod");
    }
}
```

Now, suppose that the class Gamma was also declared to be a member of the Greek package (and is not a subclass of Alpha). The Gamma class can legally access an Alpha object's iamprotected member variable and can legally invoke its protectedMethod:

```
package Greek;
class Gamma {
    void accessMethod() {
        Alpha a = new Alpha();
        a.iamprotected = 10;     // legal
        a.protectedMethod();     // legal
    }
}
```

That's pretty straightforward. Now, let's investigate how the protected specifier affects access for subclasses of Alpha.

Let's introduce a new class, Delta, that derives from Alpha but lives in a different package—Latin. The Delta class can access both iamprotected and protectedMethod, but only on objects of type Delta or its subclasses. The Delta class cannot access iamprotected or protectedMethod on objects of type Alpha. accessMethod in the following code sample attempts to access the iamprotected member variable on an object of type Alpha, which is illegal, and on an object of type Delta, which is legal. Similarly, accessMethod attempts to invoke an Alpha object's protectedMethod which is also illegal:

```
package Latin;
import Greek.*;
class Delta extends Alpha {
    void accessMethod(Alpha a, Delta d) {
        a.iamprotected = 10;    // illegal
        d.iamprotected = 10;    // legal
        a.protectedMethod();    // illegal
        d.protectedMethod();    // legal
    }
}
```

If a class is both a subclass of and in the same package as the class with the protected member, then the class has access to the protected member.

5.17 Public

The easiest access specifier is public. Any class, in any package, has access to a class's public members. Declare public members only if such access cannot produce undesirable results if an outsider uses them. There are no personal or family secrets here; this is for stuff you don't mind anybody else knowing.

To declare a public member, use the keyword public. For example,

```
package Greek;
public class Alpha {
    public int iampublic;
    public void publicMethod() {
        System.out.println("publicMethod");
    }
}
```

Let's rewrite our Beta class one more time and put it in a different package than Alpha and make sure that it is completely unrelated to (not a subclass of) Alpha:

```
package Roman;
import Greek.*;
class Beta {
    void accessMethod() {
        Alpha a = new Alpha();
        a.iampublic = 10;       // legal
        a.publicMethod();       // legal
    }
}
```

As you can see from the above code snippet, Beta can legally inspect and modify the iampublic variable in the Alpha class and can legally invoke publicMethod.

Package

The package access level is what you get if you don't explicitly set a member's access to one of the other levels. This access level allows classes in the same package as your class to access the members. This level of access assumes that classes in the same package are trusted friends. This level of trust is like that which you extend to your closest friends but wouldn't trust even to your family.

For example, this version of the Alpha class declares a single package-access member variable and a single package-access method. Alpha lives in the Greek package:

```
package Greek;
class Alpha {
    int iampackage;
    void packageMethod() {
        System.out.println("packageMethod");
    }
}
```

The Alpha class has access both to iampackage and packageMethod. In addition, all the classes declared within the same package as Alpha also have access to iampackage and packageMethod. Suppose that both Alpha and Beta were declared as part of the Greek package:

```
package Greek;
class Beta {
    void accessMethod() {
        Alpha a = new Alpha();
        a.iampackage = 10;      // legal
        a.packageMethod();      // legal
    }
}
```

Beta can legally access iampackage and packageMethod as shown.

5.18 Understanding Instance and Class Members

When you declare a member variable such as aFloat in MyClass:

```
class MyClass {
    float aFloat;
}
```

you declare an instance variable. Every time you create an instance of a class, the runtime system creates one copy of each the class's instance variables for the instance.

Instance variables are in contrast to class variables (which you declare using the static modifier). The runtime system allocates class variables once per class regardless of the number of instances created of that class. The system allocates memory for class variables the first time it encounters the class. All instances share the same copy of the class's class variables. You can access class variables through an instance or through the class itself.

Methods are similar: Your classes can have instance methods and class methods. Instance methods operate on the current object's instance variables but also have access to the class variables. Class methods, on the other hand, cannot access the instance variables declared within the class (unless they create a new object and access them through the object). Also, class methods can be invoked on the class, you don't need an instance to call a class method.

By default, unless otherwise specified, a member declared within a class is an instance member. The class defined below has one instance variable—an integer named x—and two instance methods—x and setX—that let other objects set and query the value of x:

```
class AnIntegerNamedX {
int x;
public int x() {
```

```
            return x;
    }
    public void setX(int newX) {
            x = newX;
        }
    }
```

Every time you instantiate a new object from a class, you get a new copy of each of the class's instance variables. These copies are associated with the new object. So, every time you instantiate a new AnIntegerNamedX object from the class, you get a new copy of x that is associated with the new AnIntegerNamedX object.

All instances of a class share the same implementation of an instance method; all instances of AnIntegerNamedX share the same implementation of x and setX. Note that both methods, x and setX, refer to the object's instance variable x by name. "But", you ask, "if all instances of AnIntegerNamedX share the same implementation of x and setX isn't this ambiguous?" The answer is "no." Within an instance method, the name of an instance variable refers to the current object's instance variable, assuming that the instance variable isn't hidden by a method parameter. So, within x and setX, x is equivalent to this.x.

Objects outside of AnIntegerNamedX that wish to access x must do so through a particular instance of AnIntegerNamedX. Suppose that this code snippet was in another object's method. It creates two different objects of type AnIntegerNamedX, sets their x values to different values, then displays them:

```
AnIntegerNamedX myX = new AnIntegerNamedX();
AnIntegerNamedX anotherX = new AnIntegerNamedX();
myX.setX(1);
anotherX.x = 2;
System.out.println("myX.x =" + myX.x());
System.out.println("anotherX.x =" + anotherX.x());
```

Notice that the code used setX to set the x value for myX but just assigned a value to anotherX.x directly. Either way, the code is manipulating two different copies of x: the one contained in the myX object and the one contained in the anotherX object. The output produced by this code snippet is:

```
myX.x = 1
anotherX.x = 2
```

showing that each instance of the class AnIntegerNamedX has its own copy of the instance variable x and each x has a different value.

You can, when declaring a member variable, specify that the variable is a class variable rather than an instance variable. Similarly, you can specify that a method is a class method rather than an instance method. The system creates a single copy of a class variable the first time it encounters the class in which the variable is defined. All instances of that class share the same copy of the class variable. Class methods can only operate on class variables—they cannot access the instance variables defined in the class.

To specify that a member variable is a class variable, use the static keyword. For example, let's change the AnIntegerNamedX class such that its x variable is now a class variable:

```
class AnIntegerNamedX {
        static int x;
```

```
        public int x() {
        return x;
}
public void setX(int newX) {
        x = newX;
    }
}
```

Now the exact same code snippet from before that creates two instances of AnIntegerNamedX, sets their x values, and then displays them produces this, different, output.

```
myX.x = 2
anotherX.x = 2
```

The output is different because x is now a class variable so there is only one copy of the variable and it is shared by all instances of AnIntegerNamedX, including myX and anotherX. When you invoke setX on either instance, you change the value of x for all instances of AnIntegerNamedX.

You use class variables for items that you need only one copy of and which must be accessible by all objects inheriting from the class in which the variable is declared. For example, class variables are often used with final to define constants; this is more memory efficient than final instance variables because constants can't change, so you really only need one copy).

Similarly, when declaring a method, you can specify that method to be a class method rather than an instance method. Class methods can only operate on class variables and cannot access the instance variables defined in the class.

To specify that a method is a class method, use the static keyword in the method declaration. Let's change the AnIntegerNamedX class such that its member variable x is once again an instance variable, and its two methods are now class methods:

```
class AnIntegerNamedX {
        int x;
        static public int x() {
        return x;
}
static public void setX(int newX)
{
        x = newX;
    }
}
```

When you try to compile this version of AnIntegerNamedX, the compiler displays an error like this one:

```
AnIntegerNamedX.java:4: Can't make a static reference to
nonstatic variable x in class AnIntegerNamedX.
return x;
^
```

This is because class methods cannot access instance variables unless the method created an instance of AnIntegerNamedX first and accessed the variable through it.

Let's fix AnIntegerNamedX by making its x variable a class variable:

```
class AnIntegerNamedX {
```

```
            static int x;
            static public int x() {
            return x;
    }
    static public void setX(int newX) {
            x = newX;
        }
    }
```

Now the class will compile and the same code snippet from before that creates two instances of AnIntegerNamedX, sets their x values, and then prints the x values produces this output:

```
myX.x = 2
anotherX.x = 2
```

Again, changing x through myX also changes it for other instances of AnIntegerNamedX.

Another difference between instance members and class members is that class members are accessible from the class itself. You don't need to instantiate a class to access its class members. Let's rewrite the code snippet from before to access x and setX directly from the AnIntegerNamedX class:

AnIntegerNamedX.setX(1);

```
System.out.println("AnIntegerNamedX.x =" + AnIntegerNamedX.x());
```

Notice that you no longer have to create myX and anotherX. You can set x and retrieve x directly from the AnIntegerNamedX class. You cannot do this with instance members, you can only invoke instance methods from an object and can only access instance variables from an object. You can access class variables and methods either from an instance of the class or from the class itself.

Initializing Instance and Class Members

You can use static initializers and instance initializers to provide initial values for class and instance members when you declare them in a class:

```
class BedAndBreakfast {
        static final int MAX_CAPACITY = 10;
        boolean full = false;
}
```

This works well for members of primitive data type. Sometimes, it even works when creating arrays and objects. But this form of initialization has limitations, as follows:

1. Initializers can perform only initializations that can be expressed in an assignment statement.
2. Initializers cannot call any method that can throw a checked exception.
3. If the initializer calls a method that throws a runtime exception, then it cannot do error recovery.

If you have some initialization to perform that cannot be done in an initializer because of one of these limitations, you have to put the initialization code elsewhere. To initialize class members, put the initialization code in a static initialization block. To initialize instance members, put the initialization code in a constructor.

5.19 Using Static Initialization Blocks

Here's an example of a static initialization block:

```
import java.util.ResourceBundle;
class Errors {
    static ResourceBundle errorStrings;
    static {
        try {
            errorStrings = ResourceBundle.
                              getBundle("ErrorStrings");
        } catch (java.util.MissingResourceException e) {
            // error recovery code here
        }
    }
}
```

The errorStrings resource bundle must be initialized in a static initialization block. This is because rror recovery must be performed if the bundle cannot be found. Also, errorStrings is a class member and it doesn't make sense for it to be initialized in a constructor. As the previous example shows, a static initialization block begins with the static keyword and is a normal block of Java code enclosed in curly braces {}.

A class can have any number of static initialization blocks that appear anywhere in the class body. The runtime system guarantees that static initialization blocks and static initializers are called in the order (left-to-right, top-to-bottom) that they appear in the source code.

5.20 Initializing Instance Members

If you want to initialize an instance variable and cannot do it in the variable declaration for the reasons cited previously, then put the initialization in the constructor(s) for the class. Suppose the errorStrings bundle in the previous example is an instance variable rather than a class variable. Then you'd use the following code to initialize it:

```
import java.util.ResourceBundle;
class Errors {
    ResourceBundle errorStrings;
    Errors() {
        try {
        errorStrings = ResourceBundle.
        getBundle("ErrorStrings");
        } catch (java.util.MissingResourceException e) {
// error recovery code here
        }
    }
}
```

The code that initializes errorStrings is now in a constructor for the class.

Sometimes a class contains many constructors and each constructor allows the caller to provide initial values for different instance variables of the new object. For example, java.awt.Rectangle has these three constructors:

```
Rectangle();
Rectangle(int width, int height);
Rectangle(int x, int y, int width, int height);
```

The no-argument constructor doesn't let the caller provide initial values for anything, and the other two constructors let the caller set initial values either for the size or for the origin and size. Yet, all of the instance variables, the origin and the size, for Rectangle must be initialized. In this case, classes often have one constructor that does all of the work. The other constructors call this constructor and provide it either with the values from their parameters or with default values. For example, here are the possible implementations of the three Rectangle constructors shown previously (assume x, y, width, and height are the names of the instance variables to be initialized):

```
Rectangle() {
    this(0,0,0,0);
}
Rectangle(int width, int height)
{
    this(0,0,width,height);
}
Rectangle(int x, int y, int width, int height) {
    this.x = x;
    this.y = y;
    this.width = width;
    this.height = height;
}
```

The Java language supports instance initialization blocks, which you could use instead. However, these are intended to be used with anonymous classes, which cannot declare constructors.

The approach described here that uses constructors is better for these reasons:

- All of the initialization code is in one place, thus making the code easier to maintain and read.
- Defaults are handled explicitly.
- Constructors are widely understood by the Java community, including relatively new Java programmers, while instance initializers are not and may cause confusion to others reading your code.

Example 5.1 : The Car Class

Suppose you need to write a traffic simulation program that watches cars going past an intersection. Each car has a speed, a maximum speed, and a license plate that uniquely identifies it. In traditional programming languages you'd have two floating point and one string variable for each car. With a class you combine these into one thing like this.

```
class Car
{
String licensePlate;
double speed;
double maxSpeed;
}
```

These variables (licensePlate, speed and maxSpeed) are called the member variables, instance variables, or fields of the class.

Fields tell you what a class is and what its properties are.

An object is a specific instance of a class with particular values (possibly mutable) for the fields. While a class is a general blueprint for objects, an instance is a particular object.

5.21 Constructing Objects with New

```
class Car
{
String licensePlate;
double speed;
double maxSpeed;
}
```

To instantiate an object in Java, use the keyword new followed by a call to the class's constructor. Here's how you'd create a new Car variable called c:

```
Car c;
c = new Car();
```

The first word, Car, declares the type of the variable c. Classes are types and variables of a class type need to be declared just like variables that are ints or doubles.

The equals sign is the assignment operator and new is the construction operator.

Finally notice the Car() method. The parentheses tell you this is a method and not a data type like the Car on the left hand side of the assignment. This is a constructor, a method that creates a new instance of a class. You'll learn more about constructors shortly. However if you do nothing, then the compiler inserts a default constructor that takes no arguments.

This is often condensed into one line like this:

Car c = new Car();

5.22 Class access

In Java, the access specifiers can also be used to determine which classes within a library will be available to the users of that library. If you want a class to be available to a client programmer, you place the public keyword somewhere before the opening brace of the class body. This controls whether the client programmer can even create an object of the class.

To control the access of a class, the specifier must appear before the keyword class. Thus you can say:

```
public class Widget
{
```

That is, if the name of your library is mylib any client programmer can access Widget by saying

```
import mylib.Widget;
or
import mylib.*;
```

However, there's an extra pair of constraints:

There can be only one public class per compilation unit (file). The idea is that each compilation unit has a single public interface represented by that public class. It can have as many supporting "friendly" classes as you want. If you have more than one public class inside a compilation unit, the compiler will give you an error message.

The name of the public class must exactly match the name of the file containing the compilation unit, including capitalization. So for Widget, the name of the file must be Widget.java, not widget.java or WIDGET.java. Again, you'll get a compile-time error if they don't agree.

It is possible, though not typical, to have a compilation unit with no public class at all. In this case, you can name the file whatever you like.

What if you've got a class inside mylib that you're just using to accomplish the tasks performed by Widget or some other public class in mylib? You don't want to go to the bother of creating documentation for the client programmer, and you think that sometime later you might want to completely change things and rip out your class altogether, substituting a different one. To give you this flexibility, you need to ensure that no client programmers become dependent on your particular implementation details hidden inside mylib. To accomplish this, you just leave the public keyword off the class, in which case it becomes friendly. (That class can be used only within that package.)

Note that a class cannot be private (that would make it accessible to no one but the class), or protected.[26] So you have only two choices for class access: "friendly" or public. If you don't want anyone else to have access to that class, you can make all the constructors private, thereby preventing anyone but you, inside a static member of the class, from creating an object of that class. [27] Here's an example:

```
//: Lunch.java
// Demonstrates class access specifiers.
// Make a class effectively private
// with private constructors:

class Soup
{
private Soup() {}
// (1) Allow creation via static method:
public static Soup makeSoup()
{
return new Soup();
}
// (2) Create a static object and
// return a reference upon request.
// (The "Singleton" pattern):
private static Soup ps1 = new Soup();
public static Soup access()
{
return ps1;
}
public void f() {}
}

class Sandwich { // Uses Lunch
void f() { new Lunch();
}
}

// Only one public class allowed per file:
public class Lunch
```

```
{
void test()
{
// Can't do this! Private constructor:
//! Soup priv1 = new Soup();
Soup priv2 = Soup.makeSoup();
Sandwich f1 = new Sandwich();
Soup.access().f();
}
} ///:~
```

Up to now, most of the methods have been returning either void or a primitive type so the definition:

```
public static Soup access()
{
return ps1;
}
```

might look a little confusing at first. The word before the method name (access) tells what the method returns. So far this has most often been void, which means it returns nothing. But you can also return a handle to an object, which is what happens here. This method returns a handle to an object of class Soup.

The class Soup shows how to prevent direct creation of a class by making all the constructors private. Remember that if you don't explicitly create at least one constructor, the default constructor (a constructor with no arguments) will be created for you. By writing the default constructor, it won't be created automatically. By making it private, no one can create an object of that class. But now how does anyone use this class? The above example shows two options. First, a static method is created that creates a new Soup and returns a handle to it. This could be useful if you want to do some extra operations on the Soup before returning it, or if you want to keep count of how many Soup objects to create (perhaps to restrict their population).

The second option uses what's called a design pattern , which will be discussed later in this book. This particular pattern is called a "singleton" because it allows only a single object to ever be created. The object of class Soup is created as a static private member of Soup, so there's one and only one, and you can't get at it except through the public method access( ).

As previously mentioned, if you don't put an access specifier for class access it defaults to "friendly." This means that an object of that class can be created by any other class in the package, but not outside the package. (Remember, all the files within the same directory that don't have explicit package declarations are implicitly part of the default package for that directory.) However, if a static member of that class is public, the client programmer can still access that static member even though they cannot create an object of that class.

5.22.1 The Member Access Separator

```
class Car
{
String licensePlate;
double speed;
double maxSpeed;
}
```

Once you've consturcted a car, you want to do something with it. To access the fields of the car you use the . separator. The Car class has three fields

- licensePlate
- speed
- maxSpeed

Therefore if c is a Car object, c has three fields as well:

- c.licensePlate
- c.speed
- c.maxSpeed

You use these just like you'd use any other variables of the asem type. For instance:

```
Car c = new Car();
c.licensePlate = "New York A45 636";
c.speed = 70.0;
c.maxSpeed = 123.45;
System.out.println(c.licensePlate +" is moving at" + c.speed +
"kilometers per hour.");
```

The . separator selects a specific member of a Car object by name.

5.23 Using a Car object in a different class

```
class Car
{
String licensePlate;
double speed;
double maxSpeed;
}
```

The next program creates a new website, sets its fields, and prints the result:

```
class CarTest
{
public static void main(String args[])
{
Car c = new Car();
c.licensePlate = "New York A45 636";
c.speed = 70.0;
c.maxSpeed = 123.45;
System.out.println(c.licensePlate + " is moving at " + c.speed +
"kilometers per hour.");
}
}
```

This program requires not just the CarTest class but also the Car class. To make them work together put the Car class in a file called Car.java. Put the CarTest class in a file called CarTest.java. Put both these files in the same directory. Then compile both files in the usual way. Finally run CarTest. For example,

```
% javac Car.java
% javac CarTest.java
% java CarTest
```

New York A45 636 is moving at 70.0 kilometers per hour.

Note that Car does not have a main() method so you cannot run it. It can exist only when called by other programs that do have main() methods.

Many of the applications you write from now on will use multiple classes. It is customary in Java to put every class in its own file. Next week, you'll learn how to use packages to organize your commonly used classes in different directories. For now keep all your .java source code and .class byte code files in one directory.

5.24 Member Variables vs. Local Variables

```
class Car
{
String licensePlate; // member variable
double speed;        // member variable
double maxSpeed;     // member variable
}
```

Until now all the programs you've seen quite simple in structure. Each had exactly one class. This class had a single method, main(), which contained all the program logic and variables. The variables in those classes were all local to the main() method. They could not be accessed by anything outside the main() method. These are called local variables.

This sort of program is the amoeba of Java. Everything the program needs to live is contained inside a single cell. It's quite an efficient arrangement for small organisms, but it breaks down when you want to design something bigger or more complex.

The licensePlate, speed and maxSpeed variables of the Car class, however, belong to a Car object, not to any individual method. They are defined outside of any methods but inside the class and are used in different methods. They are called member variables or fields.

Member variable, instance variable, and field are different words that mean the same thing. Field is the preferred term in Java. Member variable is the preferred term in C++.

A member is not the same as a member variable or field. Members include both fields and methods.

5.25 Constructors

A constructor creates a new instance of the class. It initializes all the variables and does any work necessary to prepare the class to be used. In the line

```
Car c = new Car();
```

Car() is the constructor. A constructor has the same name as the class.

If no constructor exists Java provides a generic one that takes no arguments (a noargs constructor), but it's better to write your own. You make a constructor by writing a method that has the same name as the class. Thus the website constructor is called Website().

Constructors do not have return types. They do return an instance of their own class, but this is implicit, not explicit.

The following method is a constructor that initializes license plate to an empty string, speed to zero, and maximum speed to 100.0.

```
Car() {
this.licensePlate = "";
this.speed  = 0.0;
this.maxSpeed = 100.0;
```

```
}
```

Better yet, you can create a constructor that accepts three arguments and use those to initialize the fields as below.

```
Car(String licensePlate, double speed, double maxSpeed)
{
this.licensePlate = licensePlate;
this.speed  = speed;
this.maxSpeed = maxSpeed;
}
```

Or perhaps you always want the initial speed to be zero, but require the maximum speed and license plate to be specified:

```
Car(String licensePlate, double maxSpeed)
{
this.licensePlate = licensePlate;
this.speed  = 0.0;
this.maxSpeed = maxSpeed;
}
```

Here's the complete class:

```
class Car
{
String licensePlate; // e.g. "New York A456 324"
double speed;        // kilometers per hour
double maxSpeed;     // kilometers per hour
Car(String licensePlate, double maxSpeed)
{
this.licensePlate = licensePlate;
this.speed  = 0.0;
this.maxSpeed = maxSpeed;
}
// getter (accessor) methods
String getLicensePlate()
{
return this.licensePlate;
}
double getMaxSpeed()
{
return this.speed;
}
double getSpeed()
{
return this.maxSpeed;
}
// setter method for the license plate property
void setLicensePlate(String licensePlate)
{
this.licensePlate = licensePlate;
```

```
}
// accelerate to maximum speed
// put the pedal to the metal
void floorIt() {
this.speed = this.maxSpeed;
}
void accelerate(double deltaV)
{
this.speed = this.speed + deltaV;
if (this.speed > this.maxSpeed)
{
this.speed = this.maxSpeed;
}
if (this.speed <  0.0)
{
this.speed = 0.0;
}
}
}
```

5.26 Constraints

One of the reasons to use constructors and setter methods rather than directly accessing fields is to enforce constraints. For instance, in the Car class it's important to make sure that the speed is always less than or equal to the maximum speed and that both speed and maximum speed are greater than or equal to zero.

You've already seen one example of this in the accelerate() method which will not accelerate a car past its maximum speed.

```
void accelerate(double deltaV)
{
this.speed = this.speed + deltaV;
if (this.speed > this.maxSpeed)
{
this.speed = this.maxSpeed;
}
if (this.speed < 0.0)
{
this.speed = 0.0;
}
}
```

We can also insert constraints like that in the constructor. For example, this Car constructor makes sure that the maximum speed is greater than or equal to zero:

```
Car(String licensePlate, double maxSpeed) {
this.licensePlate = licensePlate;
this.speed  = 0.0;
if (maxSpeed >= 0.0)
{
this.maxSpeed = maxSpeed;
```

```
}
else
{
maxSpeed = 0.0;
}
}
```

5.27 Providing Constructors for Your Classes

A class may contain one or more constructors that provide for the initialization of an object created from the class. This method shows you how to write a constructor.

5.27.1 Declaring Member Variables

A class's state is represented by its member variables. You declare a class's member variables in the body of the class. Typically, you declare a class's variables before you declare its methods, although this is not required.

```
classDeclaration
{
member variable declarations
method declarations
}
```

Note: To declare variables that are members of a class, the declarations must be within the class body, but not within the body of a method. Variables declared within the body of a method are local to that method.

5.27.2 Implementing Methods

As you know, objects have behavior that is implemented by its methods. Other objects can ask an object to do something by invoking its methods. This section tells you everything you need to know about writing methods for your Java classes. For more information about how to call methods see Using Objects. In Java, you define a class's methods in the body of the class for which the method implements some behavior. Typically, you declare a class's methods after its variables in the class body although this is not required.

5.27.3 Cleaning Up Unused Objects

Many other object-oriented languages require that you keep track of all of the objects you create and that you explicitly destroy them when they are no longer needed. This technique of managing memory is tedious and often error-prone. Java allows you to create as many objects as you want (limited, of course, by what your system can handle), and you never have to worry about destroying them. The Java runtime environment deletes objects when it determines that they are no longer being used. This process is called garbage collection. The next section discusses this in more detail. An object is eligible for garbage collection when there are no more references to that object. References that are held in a variable are naturally dropped when the variable goes out of scope. Or you can explicitly drop an object reference by setting the variable to null.

5.27.4 The Garbage Collector

The Java platform has a garbage collector that periodically frees the memory used by objects that are no longer needed. The Java garbage collector is a mark-sweep garbage collector. A mark-sweep garbage collector scans dynamic memory areas for objects and marks those that are referenced.

After all possible paths to objects are investigated, unmarked objects (unreferenced objects) are known to be garbage and are collected. (A more complete description of Java's garbage collection algorithm might be "a compacting, mark-sweep collector with some conservative scanning.") The garbage collector runs in a low-priority thread and runs either synchronously or asynchronously depending on the situation and the system on which Java is running. It runs synchronously when the system runs out of memory or in response to a request from a Java program.

The Java garbage collector runs asynchronously when the system is idle, but it does so only on systems, such as Windows 95/NT, that allow the Java runtime environment to note when a thread has begun and to interrupt another thread. As soon as another thread becomes active, the garbage collector is asked to get to a consistent state and terminate.

5.27.5 Finalization

Before an object gets garbage-collected, the garbage collector gives the object an opportunity to clean up after itself through a call to the object's finalize method. This process is known as finalization. Most programmers don't have to worry about implementing finalize. In rare cases, however, a programmer might have to implement a finalize method to release resources, such as native peers, that aren't under the control of the garbage collector.

The finalize method is a member of the Object class, which is the top of Java's class hierarchy and the parent of everything. A class can override the finalize method to perform any finalization necessary for objects of that type. If you override finalize, then your implementation of the method should call super.finalize as the last thing it does. Overriding Methods talks more about how to override methods.

5.28 Using Objects

Once you've created an object, you probably want to use it for something. You may need information from it, want to change its state, or have it perform some action.

Objects give you two ways to do these things:

- Manipulate or inspect its variables.
- Call its methods.

Ideal object-oriented programming discourages the direct manipulation of an object's variables; you could potentially put the object into an inconsistent state. Instead, an ideal object provides methods through which you can inspect or change its state. These methods ensure that the object never gets into an inconsistent state. However, in practical situations, it sometimes makes sense to use an object's variables directly. Both the Point class and the Rectangle class allow free access to their member variables. You cannot put a Point object in an inconsistent state by setting x or y directly, and you cannot put a Rectangle object in an inconsistent state by setting width, height, or origin.

Java provides an access control mechanism whereby classes can restrict or allow access to its variables and methods. A class should protect variables against direct manipulation by other objects if those manipulations could endanger the object's state. State changes should then be affected and therefore controlled by method calls. If an object grants access to its variables, you can assume that you can inspect and change them without adverse effects. To learn more about Java's access control mechanism, refer to Controlling Access to Members of a Class.

So, back to the Rectangle object. Suppose a Rectangle object represents a rectangular object in a drawing program and the user just dragged it to a new location. You need to update the Rectangle object's point of origin. The Rectangle class provides two equivalent ways of doing this:

- Manipulate the object's origin variable directly.

- Call the move method.
- Rectangle's origin member is accessible to other classes (it's declared public), so you can assume that manipulating a Rectangle's origin member directly is safe.
- Referencing an Object's Variables This section focuses on how to move the Rectangle by modifying its origin variable directly. The next section shows you how to move the rectangle by calling the move method. Assume you created a rectangle named rect as described in the previous section. To move rect to a new location, you would write:

```
rect.origin = new Point(15, 37);
```

This statement moves the rectangle by setting its point of origin to a new position. rect.origin is the name of rect's origin variable. You can use these kinds of object variable names in the same manner as you use other variables names. Thus, as in the previous example code, you can use the = operator to assign a value to rect.origin. The Rectangle class has two other variables— width and height— that are accessible to objects outside of the class. You can use the same notation to access them and calculate the rectangle's area using this statement (or you could just call the area method):

```
area = rect.height * rect.width;
```

In general, to refer to an object's variables, append the name of the variable to an object reference with an intervening period (.):

```
objectReference.variable
```

The first part of the variable's name, objectReference, must be a reference to an object. You can use an object name here just as was done in the previous examples with rect. You also can use any expression that returns an object reference. Recall that the new operator returns a reference to an object. So you could use the value returned from new to access a new object's variables:

```
height = new Rectangle().height;
```

This statement creates a new Rectangle object and immediately gets its height. Effectively, the statement calculates the default height of a Rectangle. Note that after this statement has been executed, the program no longer has a reference to the Rectangle that was created because the program never stored the reference in a variable. Thus the object becomes eligible for garbage collection. Here's a final word about accessing an object's variables to clear up a point of some confusion that beginning Java programmers often have. All objects of the same type have the same variables. All Rectangle objects have origin, width, and height variables that they got from the Rectangle class. When you access a variable through an object reference, you reference that particular object's variables. Suppose that bob is also a rectangle in your drawing program and it has a different height and width than rect. The following instruction calculates the area of the rectangle named bob, which differs from the previous instruction that calculated the area of rect:

```
area = bob.height * bob.width;
```

5.29 Calling an Object's Methods

To move rect to a new location using its move method, you write this:

```
rect.move(15, 37);
```

This Java statement calls rect's move method with two integer parameters, 15 and 37. It moves the rect object because the rect method assigns new values to origin.x and origin.y and is equivalent to the assignment statement used previously:

```
rect.origin = new Point(15, 37);
```

The notation used to call an object's method is similar to that used when referring to its variables: You append the method name to an object reference with an intervening period (.). Also, you provide any arguments to the method within enclosing parentheses. If the method does not require any arguments, use empty parentheses.

```
objectReference.methodName(argumentList);

or

objectReference.methodName();
```

As stated previously in this lesson, objectReference must be a reference to an object. You can use a variable name here, but you also can use any expression that returns an object reference. The new operator returns an object reference, so you can use the value returned from new to call a new object's methods:

```
new Rectangle(100, 50).area()
```

The expression new Rectangle(100, 50) returns an object reference that refers to a Rectangle object. As shown, you can use the dot notation to call the new Rectangle's area method to compute the area of the new rectangle. Some methods, like area, return a value. For methods that return a value, you can use the method call in expressions. You can assign the return value to a variable, use it to make decisions, or control a loop. This code assigns the value returned by area to a variable:

```
int areaOfRectangle = new Rectangle(100, 50).area();
```

Remember, invoking a method on a particular object is the same as sending a message to that object. In this case, the object is the rectangle returned by the constructor.

5.30 Creating Objects

In Java, you create an object by creating an instance of a class or, in other words, instantiating a class. Often, you will see a Java object created with a statement like the following, which creates a new Rectangle object from the Rectangle class given in the previous section:

```
Rectangle rect = new Rectangle();
```

This single statement performs three actions:

Declaration: Rectangle rect is a variable declaration that declares to the compiler that the name rect will be used to refer to a Rectangle object. Notice that a class name is used as the variable's type.

Instantiation: new is a Java operator that creates the new object (allocates space for it).

Initialization: Rectangle() is a call to Rectangle's constructor, which initializes the object.

5.31 Declaring an Object

The declaration of an object is not a necessary part of object creation, although it often appears on the same line. Like other variable declarations, object declarations can also appear alone, like this:

Rectangle rect;

Variables in the previous lesson discussed variable declarations in detail. To declare an object, you just follow the same rules and declare a variable to refer to that object by declaring its type and name:

type name

In Java, classes and interfaces can be used as data types. So type can be the name of a class such as the Rectangle class or the name of an interface. Classes and interfaces are both reference types (the variable's actual value is a reference to the value or set of values represented by the variable). In this tutorial, a reference may also be called an object reference or an array reference, depending on the data to which the reference refers. Declarations notify the compiler that you will use name to refer to a variable whose type is type. Declarations do not create new objects. Rectangle rect does not create a new Rectangle object, just a variable named rect to hold a Rectangle object. To create a Rectangle object, or any other object, use the new operator.

5.32 Instantiating an Object

The new operator instantiates a class by allocating memory for a new object of that type. new requires a single, postfix argument: a call to a constructor. Each Java class provides a set of constructors used to initialize new objects of that type. The new operator creates the object, and the constructor initializes it. Here's an example of using the new operator to create a Rectangle object:

```
new Rectangle(100, 200);
```

Here, Rectangle(100, 200) is the argument to new. The new operator returns a reference to the newly created object. This reference can be assigned to a variable of the appropriate type, as shown here.

```
Rectangle rect = new Rectangle(100, 200);
```

After this statement, rect refers to a Rectangle object whose origin is at (0, 0), width is 100, and height is 200.

5.33 Initializing an Object

As shown in the code for the Rectangle class, classes can provide one or more constructors to initialize a new object of that type. You can recognize a class's constructors because they have the same name as the class and have no return type. Here are the declarations for Rectangle's constructors:

- public Rectangle(Point p)
- public Rectangle(int w, int h)
- public Rectangle(Point p, int w, int h)
- public Rectangle()

Each of these constructors lets you provide initial values for different aspects of the rectangle: the origin, the width and height, all three, or none. If a class has multiple constructors, they all have the same name but a different number of arguments or different typed arguments. The compiler differentiates the constructors, and knows which one to call, depending on the arguments. So when the compiler encounters the following code, it knows to call the constructor that requires two integer arguments (which initializes the width and height of the new rectangle to the values provided by the arguments):

```
Rectangle rect = new Rectangle(100, 200);
```

And when the compiler encounters the next line of code, it knows to call the constructor that requires a Point (which provides the initial values for the origin of the new Rectangle):

```
Rectangle rect = new Rectangle(new Point(44,78));
```

The Rectangle constructor used below doesn't take any arguments:

```
Rectangle rect = new Rectangle();
```

A constructor that takes no arguments, such as the one shown, is called a no-argument constructor. If a class (like the SimplePoint and SimpleRectangle classes shown at the very beginning of this lesson) does not explicitly define any constructors at all, Java automatically provides a no-argument constructor, called the default constructor, that does nothing. Thus all classes have at least one constructor. This section talked about how to use a constructor. Providing Constructors for Your Classes later in this lesson explains how to write constructors for your classes.

5.34 The Life Cycle of an Object

Typically, a Java program creates many objects from a variety of classes. These objects interact with one another by sending each other messages. Through these object interactions, a Java program can implement a GUI, run an animation, or send and receive information over a network. Once an object has completed the work for which it was created, it is garbage-collected and its resources are recycled for use by other objects. Follow the links below to learn about the typical phases of the life of an object:

dfdHere, you will learn how to create a Rectangle object from the Rectangle class and use it. This section also discusses briefly how the system cleans up the object when it's no longer needed.

5.35 "Friendly"

What if you give no access specifier at all, as in all the examples before this chapter? The default access has no keyword, but it is commonly referred to as "friendly." It means that all the other classes in the current package have access to the friendly member, but to all the classes outside of this package the member appears to be private. Since a compilation unit - a file - can belong only to a single package, all the classes within a single compilation unit are automatically friendly with each other. Thus, friendly elements are also said to have package access .

Friendly access allows you to group related classes together in a package so that they can easily interact with each other. When you put classes together in a package (thus granting mutual access to their friendly members; e.g. making them "friends") you "own" the code in that package. It makes sense that only code that you own should have friendly access to other code that you own. You could say that friendly access gives a meaning or a reason for grouping classes together in a package. In many languages the way you organize your definitions in files can be willy-nilly, but in Java you're compelled to organize them in a sensible fashion. In addition, you'll probably want to exclude classes that shouldn't have access to the classes being defined in the current package.

An important question in any relationship is "Who can access my private implementation?" The class controls which code has access to its members. There's no magic way to "break in;" someone in another package can't declare a new class and say, "Hi, I'm a friend of Bob's!" and expect to see the protected, friendly, and private members of Bob. The only way to grant access to a member is to:

- Make the member public. Then everybody, everywhere, can access it.
- Make the member friendly by leaving off any access specifier, and put the other classes in the same package. Then the other classes can access the member.

As you'll see in a later chapter where inheritance is introduced, an inherited class can access a protected member as well as a public member (but not private members). It can access friendly members only if the two classes are in the same package. But don't worry about that now.

Provide "accessor/mutator" methods (also known as "get/set" methods) that read and change the value. This is the most civilized approach in terms of OOP, and it is fundamental to Java Beans, as you'll see in Chapter 13.

`public: interface access`

When you use the public keyword, it means that the member declaration that immediately follows public is available to everyone, in particular to the client programmer who uses the library. Suppose you define a package dessert containing the following compilation unit: (See page 97 if you have trouble executing this program.)

```
//: Cookie.java
// Creates a library
package c05.dessert;
public class Cookie
{
public Cookie()
{
System.out.println("Cookie constructor");
}
void foo() { System.out.println("foo"); }
} ///:~
```

Remember, Cookie.java must reside in a subdirectory called dessert, in a directory under C05 (indicating Chapter 5 of this book) that must be under one of the CLASSPATH directories. Don't make the mistake of thinking that Java will always look at the current directory as one of the starting points for searching. If you don't have a '.' as one of the paths in your CLASSPATH, Java won't look there.

Now if you create a program that uses Cookie:

```
//: Dinner.java
// Uses the library
import c05.dessert.*;
public class Dinner
{
public Dinner()
{
System.out.println("Dinner constructor");
}
public static void main(String[] args)
{
Cookie x = new Cookie();
//! x.foo(); // Can't access
}
} ///:~
```

You can create a Cookie object, since its constructor is public and the class is public. (We'll look more at the concept of a public class later.) However, the foo( ) member is inaccessible inside Dinner.java since foo( ) is friendly only within package dessert.

5.36 The default package

You might be surprised to discover that the following code compiles, even though it would appear that it breaks the rules:

```
//: Cake.java
// Accesses a class in a separate
// compilation unit.
class Cake
{
public static void main(String[] args)
{
```

```
Pie x = new Pie();
x.f();
}
} ///:~
```

In a second file, in the same directory:

```
//: Pie.java
// The other class
class Pie {
void f() { System.out.println("Pie.f()"); }
} ///:~
```

You might initially view these as completely foreign files, and yet Cake is able to create a Pie object and call its f( ) method! You'd typically think that Pie and f( ) are friendly and therefore not available to Cake. They are friendly - that part is correct. The reason that they are available in Cake.java is because they are in the same directory and have no explicit package name. Java treats files like this as implicitly part of the "default package" for that directory, and therefore friendly to all the other files in that directory.

5.37 Private: you can't touch that!

The private keyword that means no one can access that member except that particular class, inside methods of that class. Other classes in the same package cannot access private members, so it's as if you're even insulating the class against yourself. On the other hand, it's not unlikely that a package might be created by several people collaborating together, so private allows you to freely change that member without concern that it will affect another class in the same package. The default "friendly" package access is often an adequate amount of hiding; remember, a "friendly" member is inaccessible to the user of the package. This is nice, since the default access is the one that you normally use. Thus, you'll typically think about access for the members that you explicitly want to make public for the client programmer, and as a result, you might not initially think you'll use the private keyword often since it's tolerable to get away without it. (This is a distinct contrast with C++.) However, it turns out that the consistent use of private is very important, especially where multithreading is concerned.

Here's an example of the use of private:

```
//: IceCream.java
// Demonstrates "private" keyword
class Sundae
{
private Sundae() {}
static Sundae makeASundae()
{
return new Sundae();
}
}
public class IceCream
{
public static void main(String[] args)
{
//! Sundae x = new Sundae();
Sundae x = Sundae.makeASundae();
```

```
}
} ///:~
```

This shows an example in which private comes in handy: you might want to control how an object is created and prevent someone from directly accessing a particular constructor (or all of them). In the example above, you cannot create a Sundae object via its constructor; instead you must call the makeASundae( ) method to do it for you.

Any method that you're certain is only a "helper" method for that class can be made private to ensure that you don't accidentally use it elsewhere in the package and thus prohibit you from changing or removing the method. Making a method private guarantees that you retain this option. (However, just because the handle is private doesn't mean that some other object can't have a public handle to the same object. See Chapter 12 for issues about aliasing.)

5.38 Protected: "sort of friendly"

The protected access specifier requires a jump ahead to understand. First, you should be aware that you don't need to understand this section to continue through the book up through the inheritance chapter. But for completeness, here is a brief description and example using protected.

The protected keyword deals with a concept called inheritance, which takes an existing class and adds new members to that class without touching the existing class, which we refer to as the base class. You can also change the behavior of existing members of the class. To inherit from an existing class, you say that your new class extends an existing class, like this:

```
class Foo extends Bar {
```

The rest of the class definition looks the same.

If you create a new package and you inherit from a class in another package, the only members you have access to are the public members of the original package. (Of course, if you perform the inheritance in the same package, you have the normal package access to all the "friendly" members.) Sometimes the creator of the base class would like to take a particular member and grant access to derived classes but not the world in general. That's what protected does. If you refer back to the file Cookie.java on page 203, the following class cannot access the "friendly" member:

```
//: ChocolateChip.java
// Can't access friendly member
// in another class
import c05.dessert.*;
public class ChocolateChip extends Cookie
{
public ChocolateChip()
{
System.out.println(
"ChocolateChip constructor");
}
public static void main(String[] args)
{
ChocolateChip x = new ChocolateChip();
//! x.foo(); // Can't access foo
}
```

```
} ///:~
```

One of the interesting things about inheritance is that if a method foo( ) exists in class Cookie, then it also exists in any class inherited from Cookie. But since foo( ) is "friendly" in a foreign package, it's unavailable to us in this one. Of course, you could make it public, but then everyone would have access and maybe that's not what you want. If we change the class Cookie as follows:

```
public class Cookie
{
public Cookie()
{
System.out.println("Cookie constructor");
}
protected void foo()
{
System.out.println("foo");
}
}
```

then foo( ) still has "friendly" access within package dessert, but it is also accessible to anyone inheriting from Cookie. However, it is not public.

There's another effect in this case: Since the default constructor is the only one defined, and it's private, it will prevent inheritance of this class.

5.39 Methods

Data types aren't much use unless you can do things with them. For this purpose classes have methods. Fields say what a class is. Methods say what a class does. The fields and methods of a class are collectively referred to as the members of the class.

The classes you've encountered up till now have mostly had a single method, main(). However, in general classes can have many different methods that do many different things. For instance the Car class might have a method to make the car go as fast as it can. For example,

```
class Car
{
String licensePlate; // e.g. "New York A456 324"
double speed;        // kilometers per hour
double maxSpeed;     // kilometers per hour
// accelerate to maximum speed
// put the pedal to the metal
void floorIt()
{
this.speed = this.maxSpeed;
}
}
```

The fields are the same as before, but now there's also a method called floorIt(). It begins with the Java keyword void which is the return type of the method. Every method must have a return type which will either be void or some data type like int, byte, float, or String. The return type says what kind of the value will be sent back to the calling method when all calculations inside the method are finished. If the return type is int, for example, you can use the method anywhere you use an int constant. If the return type is void then no value will be returned.

floorIt is the name of this method. The name is followed by two empty parentheses. Any arguments passed to the method would be passed between the parentheses, but this method has no arguments. Finally an opening brace ({) begins the body of the method.

There is one statement inside the method

```
this.speed = this.maxSpeed;
```

Notice that within the Car class the field names are prefixed with the keyword this to indicate that I'm referring to fields in the current object.

Finally the floorIt() method is closed with a } and the class is closed with another }.

Question: what are some other methods this class might need? Or, another way of putting it, what might you want to do with a Car object?

5.40 Invoking Methods

```
class Car {
String licensePlate; // e.g. "New York A456 324"
double speed;        // kilometers per hour
double maxSpeed;     // kilometers per hour
// accelerate to maximum speed
// put the pedal to the metal
void floorIt()
{
this.speed = this.maxSpeed;
}
}
```

Outside the Car class, you call the floorIt() method just like you reference fields, using the name of the object you want to accelerate to maximum and the . separator as demonstrated below

```
class CarTest2
{
public static void main(String args[])
{
Car c = new Car();
c.licensePlate = "New York A45 636";
c.speed = 0.0;
c.maxSpeed = 123.45;
System.out.println(this.licensePlate + " is moving at " + this.speed
+ " kilometers per hour.");
c.floorIt();
System.out.println(this.licensePlate + " is moving at " + this.speed
+ " kilometers per hour.");
}
}
```

The output is:

New York A45 636 is moving at 0.0 kilometers per hour.

New York A45 636 is moving at 123.45 kilometers per hour.

The floorIt() method is completely enclosed within the Car class. Every method in a Java program must belong to a class. Unlike C++ programs, Java programs cannot have a method hanging around in global space that does everything you forgot to do inside your classes.

5.41 Implied this

```
class Car
{
String licensePlate; // e.g. "New York A456 324"
double speed;         // kilometers per hour
double maxSpeed;      // kilometers per hour
void floorIt() {
this.speed = this.maxSpeed;
}
}
```

Within the Car class, you don't absolutely need to prefix the field names with this. like this.licensePlate or this.speed. Just licensePlate and speed are sufficient. The this. may be implied. That's because the floorIt() method must be called by a specific instance of the Car class, and this instance knows what its data is. Or, another way of looking at it, the every object has its own floorIt() method.

For clarity, I will use an explicit this today, and I recommend you do so too, at least initially. As you become more comfortable with Java, classes, references, and OOP, you will be able to leave out the this without fear of confusion. Most real-world code does not use an explicit this.

5.42 Passifgng Arguments to Methods

It's generally considered bad form to access fields directly. Instead it is considered good object oriented practice to access the fields only through methods. This allows you to change the implementation of a class without changing its interface. This also allows you to enforce constraints on the values of the fields.

To do this you need to be able to send information into the Car class. This is done by passing arguments. For example, to allow other objects to change the value of the speed field in a Car object, the Car class could provide an accelerate() method. This method does not allow the car to exceed its maximum speed, or to go slower than 0 kph.

```
void accelerate(double deltaV)
{
0this.speed = this.speed + deltaV;
if (this.speed > this.maxSpeed)
{
this.speed = this.maxSpeed;
}
if (this.speed <  0.0)
{
this.speed = 0.0;
}
}
```

The first line of the method is called its signature. The signature

void accelerate(double deltaV)

indicates that accelerate() returns no value and takes a single argument, a double which will be referred to as deltaV inside the method.

deltaV is a purely formal argument.

Java passes method arguments by value, not by reference.

5.42.1 Passing Arguments to Methods, An Example

```
class Car
{
String licensePlate; // e.g. "New York A456 324"
double speed;        // kilometers per hour
double maxSpeed;     // kilometers per hour
// accelerate to maximum speed
// put the pedal to the metal
void floorIt()
{
this.speed = this.maxSpeed;
}
void accelerate(double deltaV)
{
this.speed = this.speed + deltaV;
if (this.speed > this.maxSpeed)
{
this.speed = this.maxSpeed;
}
if (this.speed <  0.0)
{
this.speed = 0.0;
}
}
}

class CarTest3 {
public static void main(String args[])
{
Car c = new Car();
c.licensePlate = "New York A45 636";
c.speed = 0.0;
c.maxSpeed = 123.45;
System.out.println(c.licensePlate + " is moving at " + c.speed +
"kilometers per hour.");
for (int i = 0; i < 15; i++) {
c.accelerate(10.0);
System.out.println(c.licensePlate + " is moving at " + c.speed +
" kilometers per hour.");
}
}
}
```

Here's the output:

utopia% java CarTest3

New York A45 636 is moving at 0.0 kilometers per hour.

New York A45 636 is moving at 10.0 kilometers per hour.

New York A45 636 is moving at 20.0 kilometers per hour.

New York A45 636 is moving at 30.0 kilometers per hour.

New York A45 636 is moving at 40.0 kilometers per hour.

New York A45 636 is moving at 50.0 kilometers per hour.

New York A45 636 is moving at 60.0 kilometers per hour.

New York A45 636 is moving at 70.0 kilometers per hour.

New York A45 636 is moving at 80.0 kilometers per hour.

New York A45 636 is moving at 90.0 kilometers per hour.

New York A45 636 is moving at 100.0 kilometers per hour.

New York A45 636 is moving at 110.0 kilometers per hour.

New York A45 636 is moving at 120.0 kilometers per hour.

New York A45 636 is moving at 123.45 kilometers per hour.

New York A45 636 is moving at 123.45 kilometers per hour.

New York A45 636 is moving at 123.45 kilometers per hour.

5.42.2 Setter Methods

Setter methods, also known as mutator methods, merely set the value of a field to a value specified by the argument to the method. These methods almost always return void.

One common idiom in setter methods is to use this.name to refer to the field and give the argument the same name as the field. For example,

```
class Car
{
String licensePlate; // e.g. "New York A456 324"
double speed;        // kilometers per hour
double maxSpeed;     // kilometers per hour
// setter method for the license plate property
void setLicensePlate(String licensePlate)
{
this.licensePlate = licensePlate;
}
// accelerate to maximum speed
// put the pedal to the metal
void floorIt() {
this.speed = this.maxSpeed;
}
void accelerate(double deltaV)
{
this.speed = this.speed + deltaV;
if (this.speed > this.maxSpeed)
{
this.speed = this.maxSpeed;
```

```
}
if (this.speed <  0.0) {
this.speed = 0.0;
}
}
}
```

5.42.3 Returning Values From Methods

It's often useful to have a method return a value to the class that called it. This is accomplished by the return keyword at the end of a method and by declaring the data type that is returned by the method at the beginning of the method.

For example, the following getLicensePlate() method returns the current value of the licensePlate field in the Car class.

```
String getLicensePlate()
{
return this.licensePlate;
}
```

A method like this that merely returns the value of an object's field or property is called a getter or accessor method.

The signature String getLicensePlate() indicates that getLicensePlate() returns a value of type String and takes no arguments. Inside the method the line

return this.licensePlate;

returns the String contained in the licensePlate field to whoever called this method. It is important that the type of value returned by the return statement match the type declared in the method signature. If it does not, the compiler will complain.

5.42.4 Returning Multiple Values From Methods

It is not possible to return more than one value from a method. You cannot, for example, return the licensePlate, speed and maxSpeed fields from a single single method. You could combine them into an object of some kind and return the object. However this would be poor object oriented design.

The right way to solve this problem is to define three separate methods, getSpeed(), getMaxSpeed(), and getLicensePlate(), each of which returns its respective value. For example,

```
class Car {
String licensePlate; // e.g. "New York A456 324"
double speed;         // kilometers per hour
double maxSpeed;      // kilometers per hour
// getter (accessor) methods
String getLicensePlate() {
return this.licensePlate;
}
double getMaxSpeed() {
return this.maxSpeed;
}
double getSpeed()
{
return this.speed;
```

```
}
// accelerate to maximum speed
// put the pedal to the metal
void floorIt()
{
this.speed = this.maxSpeed;
}
void accelerate(double deltaV)
{
this.speed = this.speed + deltaV;
if (this.speed > this.maxSpeed)
{
this.speed = this.maxSpeed;
}
if (this.speed <  0.0)
{
this.speed = 0.0;
}
}
}
```

5.43 Access Protection

Global variables are a classic cause of bugs in most programming languages. Some unknown function can change the value of a variable when the programmer isn't expecting it to change. This plays all sorts of havoc.

Most OOP languages including Java allow you to protect variables from external modification. This allows you to guarantee that your class remains consistent with what you think it is as long as the methods of the class themselves are bug-free. For example, int the Car class we'd like to make sure that no block of code in some other class is allowed to make the speed greater than the maximum speed. We want a way to make the following illegal:

```
Car c = new Car("New York A234 567", 100.0);
c.speed = 150.0;
```

This code violates the constraints we've placed on the class. We want to allow the compiler to enforce these constraints.

A class presents a picture of itself to the world. (This picture is sometimes called an interface, but the word interface has a more specific meaning in Java.) This picture says that the class has certain methods and certain fields. Everything else about the class including the detailed workings of the class's methods is hidden. As long as the picture the class shows to the world doesn't change, the programmer can change how the class implements that picture. Among other advantages this allows the programmer to change and improve the algorithms a class uses without worrying that some piece of code depends in unforeseen ways on the details of the algorithm used. This is called encapsulation.

Another way to think about encapsulation is that a class signs a contract with all the other classes in the program. This contract says that a class has methods with unambiguous names which take particular types of arguments and return a particular type of value. The contract may also say that a class has fields with given names and of a given type. However the contract does not specify how the methods are implemented. Furthermore, it does not say that there aren't other private fields and methods which the class may use. A contract guarantees the presence of certain methods and fields. It does not exclude all other methods and fields. This contract is implemented through access protection. Every class, field and method in a Java program is defined as either public, private, protected or unspecified.

You're closer to your immediate family (your parents and your children) than you are to your cousins. You're closer to your cousins than to the general public at large, but there are some things you don't tell anybody. Furthermore, your family is not my family.

5.43.1 Examples of Access Protection

This is how the Car class would probably be written in practice. Notice that all the fields are now declared private, and they are accessed only through public methods. This is the normal pattern for all but the simplest classes.

```
public class Car
{
private String licensePlate; // e.g. "New York A456 324"
private double speed;        // kilometers per hour
private double maxSpeed;     // kilometers per hour
public Car(String licensePlate, double maxSpeed)
{
this.licensePlate = licensePlate;
this.speed  = 0.0;
if (maxSpeed >= 0.0) {
this.maxSpeed = maxSpeed;
}
else {
maxSpeed = 0.0;
}
}
// getter (accessor) methods
public String getLicensePlate()
{
return this.licensePlate;
}
public double getMaxSpeed()
{
return this.speed;
}
public double getSpeed()
{
return this.maxSpeed;
}
// setter method for the license plate property
public void setLicensePlate(String licensePlate)
{
this.licensePlate = licensePlate;
}
```

```
// accelerate to maximum speed
// put the pedal to the metal
public void floorIt() {
this.speed = this.maxSpeed;
}
public void accelerate(double deltaV)
{
this.speed = this.speed + deltaV;
if (this.speed > this.maxSpeed)
{
this.speed = this.maxSpeed;
}
if (this.speed <  0.0)
{
this.speed = 0.0;
}
}
}
```

Example of attempting to access private field from outside the class.

In many cases there will also be private, protected and default access methods as well. Collectively these are called non-public methods.

In many cases, the fields may be protected or default access. However public fields are rare. This allows programmers to change the implementation of a class while still maintaining the same contract with the outside world.

5.43.2 The Four Levels of Access Protection

Any two different Java objects have one of four relations to each other. The four relations are:

- The objects are in the same class.
- One object is a subclass of the other object's class.
- The objects are in the same package.

None of the above. (Both objects are members of the general public.)

These relationships are not mutually exclusive. One object can be a subclass of another object in the same package, for example.

You can define which of your class's members, that is its fields and its methods, are accessible to other objects in each of these four groups, relative to the current class.

If you want any object at all to be able to call a method or change a field, declare it public.

If you want only objects in the same class to be able to get or set the value of a field or invoke a method, declare it private.

If you want access restricted to subclasses and members of the same package, declare it protected.

Finally, to restrict access only to objects in the same package, use no access declaration at all. This is called "package" or "default" access, but it has no keyword. The default keyword means something else entirely.

By default, all classes you write are in the same package. However, they are in different packages from the Java classes like System or Applet.

The public fields and methods of an object can be accessed from anywhere the object itself can be seen. Anyone can touch an object's public members. They should be kept to a minimum. Public fields should relate very closely to the core functionality of the class. They should not show intimate details of the inner workings of the class. Except in very simple instances fields should probably not be public.

The private fields and methods of an object can only be accessed by the object itself and by other objects of the same class (siblings). An object may touch its sibling's private parts. A sibling is an object in the same class but which is not the same object.

5.43.3 The Three Benefits of Access Protection

Access protection has three main benefits:

- It allows you to enforce constraints on an object's state.
- It provides a simpler client interface. Client programmers don't need to know everything that's in the class, only the public parts.
- It separates interface from implementation, allowing them to vary independently. For instance consider making the licensePlate field of Car an instance of a new LicensePlate class instead of a String.

What should be public? What should be private?

As a rule of thumb:

- Classes are public.
- Fields are private.
- Constructors are public.
- Getter and setter methods are public.

Other methods must be decided on a case-by-case basis.

All of these rules may be freely violated if you have a reason for doing so. These are simply the defaults that handle 90% of the cases.

5.44 Controlling Access to Members of a Class

One of the benefits of classes is that classes can protect their member variables and methods from access by other objects. Why is this important? Well, consider this. You're writing a class that represents a query on a database that contains all kinds of secret information, say employee records or income statements for your startup company. Certain information and queries contained in the class, the ones supported by the publicly accessible methods and variables in your query object, are OK for the consumption of any other object in the system. Other queries contained in the class are there simply for the personal use of the class. They support the operation of the class but should not be used by objects of another type—you've got secret information to protect. You'd like to be able to protect these personal variables and methods at the language level and disallow access by objects of another type.

In Java, you can use access specifiers to protect both a class's variables and its methods when you declare them. The Java language supports four distinct access levels for member variables and methods: private, protected, public, and, if left unspecified, package.

Note: The 1.0 release of the Java language supported five access levels: the four listed above plus private protected. The private protected access level is not supported in versions of Java higher than 1.0; you should no longer be using it in your Java programs. The following chart shows the access level permitted by each specifier.

Specifier class subclass package world

```
private X
protected X X* X
public X X X X
package X   X
```

The first column indicates whether the class itself has access to the member defined by the access specifier. As you can see, a class always has access to its own members. The second column indicates whether subclasses of the class (regardless of which package they are in) have access to the member. The third column indicates whether classes in the same package as the class (regardless of their parentage) have access to the member. The fourth column indicates whether all classes have access to the member.

Note that the protected/subclass intersection has an '*' . This particular access case has a special caveat discussed in detail later.

Let's look at each access level in more detail.

5.44.1 Private

The most restrictive access level is private. A private member is accessible only to the class in which it is defined. Use this access to declare members that should only be used by the class. This includes variables that contain information that if accessed by an outsider could put the object in an inconsistent state, or methods that, if invoked by an outsider, could jeopardize the state of the object or the program in which it's running. Private members are like secrets you never tell anybody. To declare a private member, use the private keyword in its declaration. The following class contains one private member variable and one private method:

```
class Alpha
{
private int iamprivate;
private void privateMethod()
{
System.out.println("privateMethod");
}
}
```

Objects of type Alpha can inspect or modify the iamprivate variable and can invoke privateMethod, but objects of other types cannot. For example, the Beta class defined here:

```
class Beta
{
void accessMethod()
{
Alpha a = new Alpha();
a.iamprivate = 10;        // illegal
a.privateMethod();        // illegal
}
}
```

cannot access the iamprivate variable or invoke privateMethod on an object of type Alpha because Beta is not of type Alpha.

When one of your classes is attempting to access a member varible to which it does not have access, the compiler prints an error message similar to the following and refuses to compile your program:

```
Beta.java:9: Variable iamprivate in class Alpha not
accessible from class Beta.
a.iamprivate = 10;      // illegal
^
1 error
```

Also, if your program is attempting to access a method to which it does not have access, you will see a compiler error like this:

```
Beta.java:12: No method matching privateMethod()
found in class Alpha.
a.privateMethod();          // illegal
1 error
```

New Java programmers might ask if one Alpha object can access the private members of another Alpha object. This is illustrated by the following example. Suppose the Alpha class contained an instance method that compared the current Alpha object (this) to another object based on their iamprivate variables:

```
class Alpha
{
private int iamprivate;
boolean isEqualTo(Alpha anotherAlpha)
{
if (this.iamprivate == anotherAlpha.iamprivate)
return true;
else
return false;
}
}
```

This is perfectly legal. Objects of the same type have access to one another's private members. This is because access restrictions apply at the class or type level (all instances of a class) rather than at the object level (this particular instance of a class).

Note: this is a Java language keyword that refers to the current object. For more information about how to use this see The Method Body.

5.44.2 Protected

The next access level specifier is protected, which allows the class itself, subclasses (with the caveat that we referred to earlier), and all classes in the same package to access the members. Use the protected access level when it's appropriate for a class's subclasses to have access to the member, but not unrelated classes. Protected members are like family secrets—you don't mind if the whole family knows, and even a few trusted friends but you wouldn't want any outsiders to know. To declare a protected member, use the keyword protected. First, let's look at how the protected specifier affects access for classes in the same package. Consider this version of the Alpha class which is now declared to be within a package named Greek and which has one protected member variable and one protected method declared in it:

```
package Greek;
class Alpha {
```

```
protected int iamprotected;
protected void protectedMethod()
{
System.out.println("protectedMethod");
}
}
```

Now, suppose that the class Gamma was also declared to be a member of the Greek package (and is not a subclass of Alpha). The Gamma class can legally access an Alpha object's iamprotected member variable and can legally invoke its protectedMethod:

```
package Greek;
class Gamma
{
void accessMethod()
{
Alpha a = new Alpha();
a.iamprotected = 10;     // legal
a.protectedMethod();     // legal
}
}
```

That's pretty straightforward. Now, let's investigate how the protected specifier affects access for subclasses of Alpha. Let's introduce a new class, Delta, that derives from Alpha but lives in a different package—Latin. The Delta class can access both iamprotected and protectedMethod, but only on objects of type Delta or its subclasses. The Delta class cannot access iamprotected or protectedMethod on objects of type Alpha. accessMethod in the following code sample attempts to access the iamprotected member variable on an object of type Alpha, which is illegal, and on an object of type Delta, which is legal. Similarly, accessMethod attempts to invoke an Alpha object's protectedMethod which is also illegal:

```
import Greek.*;
package Latin;
class Delta extends Alpha
{
void accessMethod(Alpha a, Delta d)
{
a.iamprotected = 10;     // illegal
d.iamprotected = 10;     // legal
a.protectedMethod();     // illegal
d.protectedMethod();     // legal
}
}
```

If a class is both a subclass of and in the same package as the class with the protected member, then the class has access to the protected member.

5.44.3 Public

The easiest access specifier is public. Any class, in any package, has access to a class's public members. Declare public members only if such access cannot produce undesirable results if an outsider uses them. There are no personal or family secrets here; this is for stuff you don't mind anybody else knowing.

To declare a public member, use the keyword public. For example,

```
package Greek;
public class Alpha
{
public int iampublic;
public void publicMethod()
{
System.out.println("publicMethod");
}
}
```

Let's rewrite our Beta class one more time and put it in a different package than Alpha and make sure that it is completely unrelated to (not a subclass of) Alpha:

```
import Greek.*;
package Roman;
class Beta
{
void accessMethod()
{
Alpha a = new Alpha();
a.iampublic = 10;          // legal
a.publicMethod();          // legal
}
}
```

As you can see from the above code snippet, Beta can legally inspect and modify the iampublic variable in the Alpha class and can legally invoke publicMethod.

5.44.4 Package

The package access level is what you get if you don't explicitly set a member's access to one of the other levels. This access level allows classes in the same package as your class to access the members. This level of access assumes that classes in the same package are trusted friends. This level of trust is like that which you extend to your closest friends but wouldn't trust even to your family. For example, this version of the Alpha class declares a single package-access member variable and a single package-access method. Alpha lives in the Greek package:

```
package Greek;
class Alpha
{
int iampackage;
void packageMethod()
{
System.out.println("packageMethod");
}
}
```

The Alpha class has access both to iampackage and packageMethod. In addition, all the classes declared within the same package as Alpha also have access to iampackage and packageMethod. Suppose that both Alpha and Beta were declared as part of the Greek package:

```
package Greek;
class Beta
{
void accessMethod()
{
Alpha a = new Alpha();
a.iampackage = 10;      // legal
a.packageMethod();      // legal
}
}
```

Beta can legally access iampackage and packageMethod as shown.

5.45 toString() Methods

Print methods are common in some languages, but most Java programs operate differently. You can use System.out.println() to print any object. However for good results your class should have a toString() method that formats the object's data in a sensible way and returns a string. Otherwise all that's printed is the name of the class which is normally not what you want. For example, a good toString() method for the Car class might be .

```
public String toString()
{
return  (this.licensePlate + " is moving at " + this.speed
+ "kph and has a maximum speed of" + this.maxSpeed +"kph.");
}
```

5.45.1 Using toString() Methods

Below is a version of CarTest that uses toString() and System.out.println() instead of printing the fields directly and thus works with the new Car class that makes its fields private.

```
class CarTest5
{
public static void main(String args[])
{
Car c = new Car("New York A45 636", 123.45);
System.out.println(c);
for (int i = 0; i < 15; i++)
{
c.accelerate(10.0);
System.out.println(c);
}
}
```

5.45.2 Class or static Members

A method or a field in a Java program can be declared static. This means the member belongs to the class rather than to an individual object.

If a variable is static, then when any object in the class changes the value of the variable, that value changes for all objects in the class.

One possible use of static methods and members is to add version information to a class. A static

String field called version can be used to store the version information and a static method called getVersion() can return it. Since the version is a property of the class rather than of an object it is properly static.

Below is a Car class with such a version field and getVersion() method.

```
public class Car
{
private String licensePlate; // e.g. "New York A456 324"
private double speed;        // kilometers per hour
private double maxSpeed;     // kilometers per hour
static String version = "1.0";
public Car(String licensePlate, double maxSpeed)
{
this.licensePlate = licensePlate;
this.speed  = 0.0;
if (maxSpeed >= 0.0)
{
this.maxSpeed = maxSpeed;
}
else {
maxSpeed = 0.0;
}
}
// getter (accessor) methods
public String getLicensePlate()
{
return this.licensePlate;
}
public double getMaxSpeed()
{
return this.speed;
}
public double getSpeed()
{
return this.maxSpeed;
}
public static String getVersion()
{
return version;
}
// setter method for the license plate property
public void setLicensePlate(String licensePlate)
{
this.licensePlate = licensePlate;
}
// accelerate to maximum speed
// put the pedal to the metal
public void floorIt()
```

```
{
this.speed = this.maxSpeed;
}
public void accelerate(double deltaV)
{
this.speed = this.speed + deltaV;
if (this.speed > this.maxSpeed)
{
this.speed = this.maxSpeed;
}
if (this.speed <  0.0)
{
this.speed = 0.0;
}
}
}
```

5.45.3 Rules for toString() Methods

- toString() methods should return a single line of text that does not contain any carriage returns or linefeeds.
- toString() methods are primarily for debugging.
- toString() should not do a lot of fancy processing. toString() methods should be quick.

The string returned by toString() should contain the name of the class, and names and values of the fields that represent the state of the object, unless there are an excessive number of such fields, in which case only the most important should be returned.

```
A better Website toString() method would be:
public String toString()
{
return "[Website: name=" + this.name
+ "URL=" + this.url + "]");
}
```

description is not included because it might be excessively long.

These rules are conventions, not requirements of the language.

5.46 Further Examples

5.46.1 Money

What is money?

What is the essential information a program needs to know about money? How can these be represented as fields in a Money class?

Is this the only way to represent Money?

What should the constructor for Money look like?

What should the toString() method for Money look like?

Do you need any getter or setter methods? (Can money change its state or should it be immutable?)

What do you want to do with money? What methods should you write?

Angles

5.47 Importing Classes

Fully qualifed names like java.net.URL are not the most convenient thing to have to type. You can use the shorter class names like URL without the java.net part if you first import the class by adding an import statement at the top of the file. For example,

```
import java.net.URL;
import java.net.MalformedURLException;
public class URLSplitter
{
public static void main(String[] args)
{
for (int i = 0; i < args.length; i++)
{
try
{
URL u = new URL(args[i]);
System.out.println("Protocol: " + u.getProtocol());
System.out.println("Host: " + u.getHost());
System.out.println("Port: " + u.getPort());
System.out.println("File: " + u.getFile());
System.out.println("Ref: " + u.getRef());
}
catch (MalformedURLException e) {
System.err.println(args[i] + "is not a valid URL");
}
}
}
}
```

5.48 Inner Classes

In Java 1.1 and later, you can define an inner class. This is a class whose body is defined inside another class, referred to as the top-level class. For example

```
public class Queue
{
Element back = null;
public void add(Object o)
{
Element e = new Element();
e.data = o;
e.next = back;
back = e;
}
public Object remove()
{
if (back == null) return null;
Element e = back;
while (e.next != null) e = e.next;
```

```
Object o = e.data;
Element f = back;
while (f.next != e) f = f.next;
f.next = null;
return o;
}
public boolean isEmpty()
{
return back == null;
}
// Here's the inner class
class Element
{
Object data = null;
Element next = null;
}
}
```

Inner classes may also contain methods. They may not contain static members. Inner classes in a class scope can be public, private, protected, final, abstract.

Inner classes can also be used inside methods, loops, and other blocks of code surrounded by braces ({}). Such a class is not a member, and therefore cannot be declared public, private, protected, or static.

The inner class has access to all the methods and fields of the top-level class, even the private ones.

The inner class's short name may not be used outside its scope. If you absolutely must use it, you can use the fully qualified name instead. (For example, Queue$Element) However, if you need to do this you should almost certainly have made it a top-level class instead or at least an inner class within a broader scope.

Inner classes are most useful for the adapter classes required by 1.1 AWT and Java Beans event handling protocols. They allow you to implement callbacks. In most other languages this would bo done with function pointers.

5.49 The static keyword

Ordinarily, when you create a class you are describing how objects of that class look and how they will behave. You don't actually get anything until you create an object of that class with new, and at that point data storage is created and methods become available.

But there are two situations in which this approach is not sufficient. One is if you want to have only one piece of storage for a particular piece of data, regardless of how many objects are created, or even if no objects are created. The other is if you need a method that isn't associated with any particular object of this class. That is, you need a method that you can call even if no objects are created. You can achieve both of these effects with the static keyword. When you say something is static, it means that data or method is not tied to any particular object instance of that class. So even if you've never created an object of that class you can call a static method or access a piece of static data. With ordinary, non- static data and methods you must create an object and use that object to access the data or method, since non- static data and methods must know the particular object they are working with. Of course, since static methods don't need any objects to be created before they are used, they cannot directly access non- static members or methods by simply calling those other members without referring to a named object (since non- static members and methods must be tied to a particular object).

Some object-oriented languages use the terms class data and class methods, meaning that the data and methods exist only for the class as a whole, and not for any particular objects of the class. Sometimes the Java literature uses these terms too.

To make a data member or method static, you simply place the keyword before the definition. For example, this produces a static data member and initializes it:

```
class StaticTest
{
static int i = 47;
}
```

Now even if you make two StaticTest objects, there will still be only one piece of storage for StaticTest.i. Both objects will share the same i. Consider:

StaticTest st1 = new StaticTest();

StaticTest st2 = new StaticTest();

At this point, both st1.i and st2.i have the same value of 47 since they refer to the same piece of memory.

There are two ways to refer to a static variable. As indicated above, you can name it via an object, by saying, for example, st2.i. You can also refer to it directly through its class name, something you cannot do with a non-static member. (This is the preferred way to refer to a static variable since it emphasizes that variable's static nature.)

StaticTest.i++;

The ++ operator increments the variable. At this point, both st1.i and st2.i will have the value 48.

Similar logic applies to static methods. You can refer to a static method either through an object as you can with any method, or with the special additional syntax classname.method( ). You define a static method in a similar way:

```
class StaticFun
{
static void incr() { StaticTest.i++; }
}
```

You can see that the StaticFun method incr( ) increments the static data i. You can call incr( ) in the typical way, through an object:

```
StaticFun sf = new StaticFun();
sf.incr();
```

Or, because incr( ) is a static method, you can call it directly through its class:

```
StaticFun.incr();
```

While static, when applied to a data member, definitely changes the way the data is created (one for each class vs. the non- static one for each object), when applied to a method it's not so dramatic. An important use of static for methods is to allow you to call that method without creating an object. This is essential, as we will see, in defining the main( ) method that is the entry point for running an application.

Like any method, a static method can create or use named objects of its type, so a static method is often used as a "shepherd" for a flock of instances of its own type.

5.50 Initialization and cleanup

As the computer revolution progresses, "unsafe" programming has become one of the major culprits that makes programming expensive.

Two of these safety issues are

- initialization and
- cleanup.

Many C bugs occur when the programmer forgets to initialize a variable. This is especially true with libraries when users don't know how to initialize a library component, or even that they must. Cleanup is a special problem because it's easy to forget about an element when you're done with it, since it no longer concerns you. Thus, the resources used by that element are retained and you can easily end up running out of resources (most notably memory).

C++ introduced the concept of a constructor, a special method automatically called when an object is created. Java also adopted the constructor, and in addition has a garbage collector that automatically releases memory resources when they're no longer being used. This chapter examines the issues of initialization and cleanup and their support in Java.

5.50.1 Guaranteed initialization with the constructor

You can imagine creating a method called initialize( ) for every class you write. The name is a hint that it should be called before using the object. Unfortunately, this means the user must remember to call the method. In Java, the class designer can guarantee initialization of every object by providing a special method called a constructor. If a class has a constructor, Java automatically calls that constructor when an object is created, before users can even get their hands on it. So initialization is guaranteed.

The next challenge is what to name this method. There are two issues. The first is that any name you use could clash with a name you might like to use as a member in the class. The second is that because the compiler is responsible for calling the constructor, it must always know which method to call. The C++ solution seems the easiest and most logical, so it's also used in Java: The name of the constructor is the same as the name of the class. It makes sense that such a method will be called automatically on initialization.

Here's a simple class with a constructor: (See page 97 if you have trouble executing this program.)

```
//: SimpleConstructor.java
// Demonstration of a simple constructor
package c04;
class Rock {
Rock() { // This is the constructor
System.out.println("Creating Rock");
}
}
public class SimpleConstructor {
public static void main(String[] args) {
for(int i = 0; i < 10; i++)
new Rock();
}
} ///:~
```

Now, when an object is created:

new Rock();

storage is allocated and the constructor is called. It is guaranteed that the object will be properly initialized before you can get your hands on it.

Note that the coding style of making the first letter of all methods lower case does not apply to constructors, since the name of the constructor must match the name of the class exactly.

Like any method, the constructor can have arguments to allow you to specify how an object is created. The above example can easily be changed so the constructor takes an argument:

```
class Rock {
Rock(int i) {
System.out.println(
"Creating Rock number " + i);
}
}
public class SimpleConstructor {
public static void main(String[] args) {
for(int i = 0; i < 10; i++)
new Rock(i);
}
}
```

Constructor arguments provide you with a way to provide parameters for the initialization of an object. For example, if the class Tree has a constructor that takes a single integer argument denoting the height of the tree, you would create a Tree object like this:

```
Tree t = new Tree(12); // 12-foot tree
```

If Tree(int) is your only constructor, then the compiler won't let you create a Tree object any other way.

Constructors eliminate a large class of problems and make the code easier to read. In the preceding code fragment, for example, you don't see an explicit call to some initialize( ) method that is conceptually separate from definition. In Java, definition and initialization are unified concepts - you can't have one without the other.

The constructor is an unusual type of method because it has no return value. This is distinctly different from a void return value, in which the method returns nothing but you still have the option to make it return something else. Constructors return nothing and you don't have an option. If there were a return value, and if you could select your own, the compiler would somehow need to know what to do with that return value.

5.51 Overloading Method

One of the important features in any programming language is the use of names. When you create an object, you give a name to a region of storage. A method is a name for an action. By using names to describe your system, you create a program that is easier for people to understand and change. It's a lot like writing prose - the goal is to communicate with your readers.

You refer to all objects and methods by using names. Well-chosen names make it easier for you and others to understand your code.

A problem arises when mapping the concept of nuance in human language onto a programming language. Often, the same word expresses a number of different meanings - it's overloaded. This is useful, especially when it comes to trivial differences. You say "wash the shirt," "wash the car," and "wash the dog." It would be silly to be forced to say, "shirtWash the shirt," "carWash the car," and "dogWash the dog" just so the listener doesn't need to make any distinction about the action performed. Most human languages are redundant, so even if you miss a few words, you can still determine the meaning. We don't need unique identifiers - we can deduce meaning from context.

Most programming languages (C in particular) require you to have a unique identifier for each function. So you could not have one function called print( ) for printing integers and another called print( ) for printing floats - each function requires a unique name.

In Java, another factor forces the overloading of method names: the constructor. Because the constructor's name is predetermined by the name of the class, there can be only one constructor name. But what if you want to create an object in more than one way? For example, suppose you build a class that can initialize itself in a standard way and by reading information from a file. You need two constructors, one that takes no arguments (the default constructor), and one that takes a String as an argument, which is the name of the file from which to initialize the object. Both are constructors, so they must have the same name - the name of the class. Thus method overloading is essential to allow the same method name to be used with different argument types. And although method overloading is a must for constructors, it's a general convenience and can be used with any method.

Here's an example that shows both overloaded constructors and overloaded ordinary methods:

```
//: Overloading.java
// Demonstration of both constructor
// and ordinary method overloading.
import java.util.*;
class Tree {
int height;
Tree() {
prt("Planting a seedling");
height = 0;
}
Tree(int i) {
prt("Creating new Tree that is"
+ i + "feet tall");
height = i;
}
void info() {
prt("Tree is "+ height
+ "feet tall");
}
void info(String s)
{
prt(s + ": Tree is "
+ height + "feet tall");
}
static void prt(String s)
{
System.out.println(s);
}
}
```

```
public class Overloading
{
public static void main(String[] args)
{
for(int i = 0; i < 5; i++)
{
Tree t = new Tree(i);
t.info();
t.info("overloaded method");
}
// Overloaded constructor:
new Tree();
}
} ///:~
```

A Tree object can be created either as a seedling, with no argument, or as a plant grown in a nursery, with an existing height. To support this, there are two constructors, one that takes no arguments (we call constructors that take no arguments default constructors [17]) and one that takes the existing height.

You might also want to call the info( ) method in more than one way. For example, with a String argument if you have an extra message you want printed, and without if you have nothing more to say. It would seem strange to give two separate names to what is obviously the same concept. Fortunately, method overloading allows you to use the same name for both.

5.51.1 Distinguishing overloaded methods

If the methods have the same name, how can Java know which method you mean? There's a simple rule: Each overloaded method must take a unique list of argument types.

If you think about this for a second, it makes sense: how else could a programmer tell the difference between two methods that have the same name, other than by the types of their arguments?

Even differences in the ordering of arguments is sufficient to distinguish two methods: (Although you don't normally want to take this approach, as it produces difficult-to-maintain code.)

```
//: OverloadingOrder.java
// Overloading based on the order of
// the arguments.

public class OverloadingOrder
{
static void print(String s, int i)
{
System.out.println(
"String: " + s +
", int: " + i);
}
static void print(int i, String s)
{
System.out.println(
"int: " + i +
", String: " + s);
}
```

```
public static void main(String[] args)
{
print("String first", 11);
print(99, "Int first");
}
} ///:~
```

The two print( ) methods have identical arguments, but the order is different, and that's what makes them distinct.

Overloading with primitives

Primitives can be automatically promoted from a smaller type to a larger one and this can be slightly confusing in combination with overloading. The following example demonstrates what happens when a primitive is handed to an overloaded method:

```
//: PrimitiveOverloading.java
// Promotion of primitives and overloading
public class PrimitiveOverloading
{
// boolean can't be automatically converted
static void prt(String s)
{
System.out.println(s); }
void f1(char x) { prt("f1(char)"); }
void f1(byte x) { prt("f1(byte)"); }
void f1(short x) { prt("f1(short)"); }
void f1(int x) { prt("f1(int)"); }
void f1(long x) { prt("f1(long)"); }
void f1(float x) { prt("f1(float)"); }
void f1(double x) { prt("f1(double)"); }
void f2(byte x) { prt("f2(byte)"); }
void f2(short x) { prt("f2(short)"); }
void f2(int x) { prt("f2(int)"); }
void f2(long x) { prt("f2(long)"); }
void f2(float x) { prt("f2(float)"); }
void f2(double x) { prt("f2(double)"); }
void f3(short x) { prt("f3(short)"); }
void f3(int x) { prt("f3(int)"); }
void f3(long x) { prt("f3(long)"); }
void f3(float x) { prt("f3(float)"); }
void f3(double x) { prt("f3(double)"); }
void f4(int x) { prt("f4(int)"); }
void f4(long x) { prt("f4(long)"); }
void f4(float x) { prt("f4(float)"); }
void f4(double x) { prt("f4(double)"); }
void f5(long x) { prt("f5(long)"); }
void f5(float x) { prt("f5(float)"); }
void f5(double x) { prt("f5(double)"); }
void f6(float x) { prt("f6(float)"); }
void f6(double x) { prt("f6(double)"); }
```

```
void f7(double x) { prt("f7(double)"); }
void testConstVal() {
prt("Testing with 5");
f1(5);f2(5);f3(5);f4(5);f5(5);f6(5);f7(5);
}
void testChar()
{
char x = 'x';
prt("char argument:");
f1(x);f2(x);f3(x);f4(x);f5(x);f6(x);f7(x);
}
void testByte()
{
byte x = 0;
prt("byte argument:");
f1(x);f2(x);f3(x);f4(x);f5(x);f6(x);f7(x);
}
void testShort()
{
short x = 0;
prt("short argument:");
f1(x);f2(x);f3(x);f4(x);f5(x);f6(x);f7(x);
}
void testInt()
{
int x = 0;
prt("int argument:");
f1(x);f2(x);f3(x);f4(x);f5(x);f6(x);f7(x);
}
void testLong()
{
long x = 0;
prt("long argument:");
f1(x);f2(x);f3(x);f4(x);f5(x);f6(x);f7(x);
}
void testFloat()
{
float x = 0;
prt("float argument:");
f1(x);f2(x);f3(x);f4(x);f5(x);f6(x);f7(x);
}
void testDouble() {
double x = 0;
prt("double argument:");
f1(x);f2(x);f3(x);f4(x);f5(x);f6(x);f7(x);
}
public static void main(String[] args)
{
```

```
PrimitiveOverloading p =
new PrimitiveOverloading();
p.testConstVal();
p.testChar();
p.testByte();
p.testShort();
p.testInt();
p.testLong();
p.testFloat();
p.testDouble();
}
} ///:~
```

If you view the output of this program, you'll see that the constant value 5 is treated as an int, so if an overloaded method is available that takes an int it is used. In all other cases, if you have a data type that is smaller than the argument in the method, that data type is promoted. char produces a slightly different effect, since if it doesn't find an exact char match, it is promoted to int.

What happens if your argument is bigger than the argument expected by the overloaded method? A modification of the above program gives the answer:

```
//: Demotion.java
// Demotion of primitives and overloading
public class Demotion
{
static void prt(String s)
{
System.out.println(s);
}
void f1(char x) { prt("f1(char)"); }
void f1(byte x) { prt("f1(byte)"); }
void f1(short x) { prt("f1(short)"); }
void f1(int x) { prt("f1(int)"); }
void f1(long x) { prt("f1(long)"); }
void f1(float x) { prt("f1(float)"); }
void f1(double x) { prt("f1(double)"); }
void f2(char x) { prt("f2(char)"); }
void f2(byte x) { prt("f2(byte)"); }
void f2(short x) { prt("f2(short)"); }
void f2(int x) { prt("f2(int)"); }
void f2(long x) { prt("f2(long)"); }
void f2(float x) { prt("f2(float)"); }
void f3(char x) { prt("f3(char)"); }
void f3(byte x) { prt("f3(byte)"); }
void f3(short x) { prt("f3(short)"); }
void f3(int x) { prt("f3(int)"); }
void f3(long x) { prt("f3(long)"); }
void f4(char x) { prt("f4(char)"); }
void f4(byte x) { prt("f4(byte)"); }
```

```
void f4(short x) { prt("f4(short)"); }
void f4(int x) { prt("f4(int)"); }
void f5(char x) { prt("f5(char)"); }
void f5(byte x) { prt("f5(byte)"); }
void f5(short x) { prt("f5(short)"); }
void f6(char x) { prt("f6(char)"); }
void f6(byte x) { prt("f6(byte)"); }
void f7(char x) { prt("f7(char)"); }
void testDouble() {
double x = 0;
prt("double argument:");
f1(x);f2((float)x);f3((long)x);f4((int)x);
f5((short)x);f6((byte)x);f7((char)x);
}
public static void main(String[] args) {
Demotion p = new Demotion();
p.testDouble();
}
} ///:~
```

Here, the methods take narrower primitive values. If your argument is wider then you must cast to the necessary type using the type name in parentheses. If you don't do this, the compiler will issue an error message.

You should be aware that this is a narrowing conversion, which means you might lose information during the cast. This is why the compiler forces you to do it - to flag the narrowing conversion.

5.51.2 Overloading on Return Values

It is common to wonder "Why only class names and method argument lists? Why not distinguish between methods based on their return values?" For example, these two methods, which have the same name and arguments, are easily distinguished from each other:

```
void f() {}
int f() {}
```

This works fine when the compiler can unequivocally determine the meaning from the context, as in int x = f( ) . However, you can call a method and ignore the return value; this is often referred to as calling a method for its side effect since you don't care about the return value but instead want the other effects of the method call. So if you call the method this way:

f();

how can Java determine which f( ) should be called? And how could someone reading the code see it? Because of this sort of problem, you cannot use return value types to distinguish overloaded methods.

5.52 Overriding vs. overloading

Let's take a different look at the first example in this chapter. In the following program, the interface of the method play( ) is changed in the process of overriding it, which means that you haven't overridden the method, but instead overloaded it. The compiler allows you to overload methods so it gives no complaint. But the behavior is probably not what you want. Here's the example:

```
//: WindError.java
// Accidentally changing the interface

class NoteX {
public static final int
MIDDLE_C = 0, C_SHARP = 1, C_FLAT = 2;
}
class InstrumentX
{
public void play(int NoteX) {
System.out.println("InstrumentX.play()");
}
}
class WindX extends InstrumentX
{
// OOPS! Changes the method interface:
public void play(NoteX n)
{
System.out.println("WindX.play(NoteX n)");
}
}
public class WindError
{
public static void tune(InstrumentX i)
{
// ...
i.play(NoteX.MIDDLE_C);
}
public static void main(String[] args)
{
WindX flute = new WindX();
tune(flute); // Not the desired behavior!
}
} ///:~
```

There's another confusing aspect thrown in here. In InstrumentX, the play( ) method takes an int that has the identifier NoteX. That is, even though NoteX is a class name, it can also be used as an identifier without complaint. But in WindX, play( ) takes a NoteX handle that has an identifier n. (Although you could even say play(NoteX NoteX) without an error.) Thus it appears that the programmer intended to override play( ) but mistyped the method a bit. The compiler, however, assumed that an overload and not an override was intended. Note that if you follow the standard Java naming convention, the argument identifier would be noteX, which would distinguish it from the class name.

In tune, the InstrumentX i is sent the play( ) message, with one of NoteX's members (MIDDLE_C) as an argument. Since NoteX contains int definitions, this means that the int version of the now-overloaded play( ) method is called, and since that has not been overridden the base-class version is used.

The output is:

InstrumentX.play()

This certainly doesn't appear to be a polymorphic method call. Once you understand what's happening, you can fix the problem fairly easily, but imagine how difficult it might be to find the bug if it's buried in a program of significant size.

5.52.1 Passing and Returning Objects

By this time you should be reasonably comfortable with the idea that when you're "passing" an object, you're actually passing a handle.

In many programming languages, if not all of them, you can use that language's "regular" way to pass objects around and most of the time everything works fine. But it always seems that there comes a point at which you must do something irregular and suddenly things get a bit more complicated (or in the case of C++, quite complicated). Java is no exception, and it's important that you understand exactly what's happening with them as you pass them around and assign to them. This chapter will provide that insight.

Another way to pose the question of this chapter, if you're coming from a programming language so equipped, is "Does Java have pointers?" Some have claimed that pointers are hard and dangerous and therefore bad, and since Java is all goodness and light and will lift your earthly programming burdens, it cannot possibly contain such things. However, it's more accurate to say that Java has pointers; indeed, every object identifier in Java (except for primitives) is one of these pointers, but their use is restricted and guarded not only by the compiler but by the run-time system. Or to put in another way, Java has pointers, but no pointer arithmetic. These are what I've been calling "handles," and you can think of them as "safety pointers," not unlike the safety scissors of elementary school-they aren't sharp so you cannot hurt yourself without great effort, but they can sometimes be slow and tedious.

5.52.2 Passing Handles Around

When you pass a handle into a method, you're still pointing to the same object. A simple experiment demonstrates this: (See page 97 if you have trouble executing this program.)

```
//: PassHandles.java
// Passing handles around
package c12;
public class PassHandles
{
static void f(PassHandles h) {
System.out.println("h inside f(): " + h);
}
public static void main(String[] args) {
PassHandles p = new PassHandles();
System.out.println("p inside main(): "+ p);
f(p);
}
} ///:~
```

The method toString( ) is automatically invoked in the print statements, and PassHandles inherits directly from Object with no redefinition of toString( ). Thus, Object's version of toString( ) is used, which prints out the class of the object followed by the address where that object is located (not the handle, but the actual object storage). The output looks like this:

p inside main(): PassHandles@1653748

h inside f(): PassHandles@1653748

You can see that both p and h refer to the same object. This is far more efficient than duplicating a new PassHandles object just so that you can send an argument to a method. But it brings up an important issue.

5.52.3 Aliasing

Aliasing means that more than one handle is tied to the same object, as in the above example. The problem with aliasing occurs when someone writes to that object. If the owners of the other handles aren't expecting that object to change, they'll be surprised. This can be demonstrated with a simple example:

```
//: Alias1.java
// Aliasing two handles to one object
public class Alias1
{
int i;
Alias1(int ii) { i = ii; }
public static void main(String[] args)
{
Alias1 x = new Alias1(7);
Alias1 y = x; // Assign the handle
System.out.println("x: " + x.i);
System.out.println("y: " + y.i);
System.out.println("Incrementing x");
x.i++;
System.out.println("x: " + x.i);
System.out.println("y: " + y.i);
}
} ///:~
```

In the line:

Alias1 y = x; // Assign the handle

a new Alias1 handle is created, but instead of being assigned to a fresh object created with new, it's assigned to an existing handle. So the contents of handle x, which is the address of the object x is pointing to, is assigned to y, and thus both x and y are attached to the same object. So when x's i is incremented in the statement:

```
x.i++;
y's i will be affected as well. This can be seen in the output:
x: 7
y: 7
Incrementing x
x: 8
y: 8
```

One good solution in this case is to simply not do it: don't consciously alias more than one handle to an object at the same scope. Your code will be much easier to understand and debug. However, when you're passing a handle in as an argument - which is the way Java is supposed to work - you automatically alias because the local handle that's created can modify the "outside object" (the object that was created outside the scope of the method). Here's an example:

```
//: Alias2.java
// Method calls implicitly alias their
// arguments.

public class Alias2
{
int i;
Alias2(int ii) { i = ii; }
static void f(Alias2 handle)
{
handle.i++;
}
public static void main(String[] args)
{
Alias2 x = new Alias2(7);
System.out.println("x: " + x.i);
System.out.println("Calling f(x)");
f(x);
System.out.println("x: " + x.i);
}
} ///:~
```

The output is:

x: 7

Calling f(x)

x: 8

The method is changing its argument, the outside object. When this kind of situation arises, you must decide whether it makes sense, whether the user expects it, and whether it's going to cause problems.

In general, you call a method in order to produce a return value and/or a change of state in the object that the method is called for . (A method is how you "send a message" to that object.) It's much less common to call a method in order to manipulate its arguments; this is referred to as "calling a method for its side effects ." Thus, when you create a method that modifies its arguments the user must be clearly instructed and warned about the use of that method and its potential surprises. Because of the confusion and pitfalls, it's much better to avoid changing the argument.

If you need to modify an argument during a method call and you don't intend to modify the outside argument, then you should protect that argument by making a copy inside your method. That's the subject of much of this chapter.

5.53 Default Constructors

As mentioned previously, a default constructor is one without arguments, used to create a "vanilla object." If you create a class that has no constructors, the compiler will automatically create a default constructor for you. For example:

```
//: DefaultConstructor.java
class Bird
{
```

```
int i;
}
public class DefaultConstructor
{
public static void main(String[] args)
{
Bird nc = new Bird(); // default!
}
} ///:~
```

The line

new Bird();

creates a new object and calls the default constructor, even though one was not explicitly defined. Without it we would have no method to call to build our object. However, if you define any constructors (with or without arguments), the compiler will not synthesize one for you:

```
class Bush {
Bush(int i) {}
Bush(double d) {}
}
```

Now if you say:
new Bush();

the compiler will complain that it cannot find a constructor that matches. It's as if when you don't put in any constructors, the compiler says "You are bound to need some constructor, so let me make one for you." But if you write a constructor, the compiler says "You've written a constructor so you know what you're doing; if you didn't put in a default it's because you meant to leave it out."

5.54 The this Keyword

If you have two objects of the same type called a and b, you might wonder how it is that you can call a method f( ) for both those objects:

class Banana { void f(int i) { /* ... */ } }
Banana a = new Banana(), b = new Banana();
a.f(1);
b.f(2);

If there's only one method called f( ), how can that method know whether it's being called for the object a or b?

To allow you to write the code in a convenient object-oriented syntax in which you "send a message to an object," the compiler does some undercover work for you. There's a secret first argument passed to the method f( ), and that argument is the handle to the object that's being manipulated. So the two method calls above become something like:

Banana.f(a,1);
Banana.f(b,2);

This is internal and you can't write these expressions and get the compiler to accept them, but it gives you an idea of what's happening.

Suppose you're inside a method and you'd like to get the handle to the current object. Since that handle is passed secretly by the compiler, there's no identifier for it. However, for this purpose there's a keyword: this. The this keyword - which can be used only inside a method - produces the handle to the object the method has been called for. You can treat this handle just like any other object handle. Keep in mind that if you're calling a method of your class from within another method of your class, you don't need to use this; you simply call the method. The current this handle is automatically used for the other method. Thus you can say:

```
class Apricot {
void pick() { /* ... */ }
void pit() { pick(); /* ... */ }
}
```

Inside pit( ), you could say this.pick( ) but there's no need to. The compiler does it for you automatically. The this keyword is used only for those special cases in which you need to explicitly use the handle to the current object. For example, it's often used in return statements when you want to return the handle to the current object:

```
//: Leaf.java
// Simple use of the "this" keyword
public class Leaf {
private int i = 0;
Leaf increment() {
i++;
return this;
}
void print() {
System.out.println("i = " + i);
}
public static void main(String[] args)
{
Leaf x = new Leaf();
x.increment().increment().increment().print();
}
} ///:~
```

Because increment( ) returns the handle to the current object via the this keyword, multiple operations can easily be performed on the same object.

5.55 Calling Constructors from Constructors

When you write several constructors for a class, there are times when you'd like to call one constructor from another to avoid duplicating code. You can do this using the this keyword.

Normally, when you say this, it is in the sense of "this object" or "the current object," and by itself it produces the handle to the current object. In a constructor, the this keyword takes on a different meaning when you give it an argument list: it makes an explicit call to the constructor that matches that argument list. Thus you have a straightforward way to call other constructors:

```
//: Flower.java
// Calling constructors with "this"
public class Flower
{
private int petalCount = 0;
private String s = new String("null");
```

```
Flower(int petals)
{
petalCount = petals;
System.out.println(
"Constructor w/ int arg only, petalCount= "
+ petalCount);
}
Flower(String ss)
{
System.out.println(
"Constructor w/ String arg only, s=" + ss);
s = ss;
}
Flower(String s, int petals)
{
this(petals);
//!     this(s); // Can't call two!
this.s = s; // Another use of "this"
System.out.println("String & int args");
}
Flower()
{
this("hi", 47);
System.out.println(
"default constructor (no args)");
}
void print()
{
//!     this(11); // Not inside non-constructor!
System.out.println(
"petalCount = " + petalCount + " s = "+ s);
}
public static void main(String[] args)
{
Flower x = new Flower();
x.print();
}
} ///:~
```

The constructor Flower(String s, int petals) shows that, while you can call one constructor using this, you cannot call two. In addition, the constructor call must be the first thing you do or you'll get a compiler error message.

This example also shows another way you'll see this used. Since the name of the argument s and the name of the member data s are the same, there's an ambiguity. You can resolve it by saying this.s to refer to the member data. You'll often see this form used in Java code, and it's used in numerous places in this book.

In print( ) you can see that the compiler won't let you call a constructor from inside any method other than a constructor.

5.56 The Meaning of Static

With the this keyword in mind, you can more fully understand what it means to make a method static. It means that there is no this for that particular method. You cannot call non- static methods from inside static methods [18] (although the reverse is possible), and you can call a static method for the class itself, without any object. In fact, that's primarily what a static method is for. It's as if you're creating the equivalent of a global function (from C). Except global functions are not permitted in Java, and putting the static method inside a class allows it access to other static methods and to static fields.

Some people argue that static methods are not object-oriented since they do have the semantics of a global function; with a static method you don't send a message to an object, since there's no this. This is probably a fair argument, and if you find yourself using a lot of static methods you should probably rethink your strategy. However, statics are pragmatic and there are times when you genuinely need them, so whether or not they are "proper OOP" should be left to the theoreticians. Indeed, even Smalltalk has the equivalent in its "class methods."

In some of the Java literature from Sun they instead refer to these with the clumsy but descriptive name "no-arg constructors." The term "default constructor" has been in use for many years and so I will use that.

The one case in which this is possible occurs if you pass a handle to an object into the static method. Then, via the handle (which is now effectively this), you can call non- static methods and access non-static fields. But typically if you want to do something like this you'll just make an ordinary, non- static method.

5.57 Cleanup: Finalization and Garbage Collection

Programmers know about the importance of initialization, but often forget the importance of cleanup. After all, who needs to clean up an int? But with libraries, simply "letting go" of an object once you're done with it is not always safe. Of course, Java has the garbage collector to reclaim the memory of objects that are no longer used. Now consider a very special and unusual case. Suppose your object allocates "special" memory without using new. The garbage collector knows only how to release memory allocated with new, so it won't know how to release the object's "special" memory. To handle this case, Java provides a method called finalize( ) that you can define for your class. Here's how it's supposed to work. When the garbage collector is ready to release the storage used for your object, it will first call finalize( ), and only on the next garbage-collection pass will it reclaim the object's memory. So if you choose to use finalize( ), it gives you the ability to perform some important cleanup at the time of garbage collection .

This is a potential programming pitfall because some programmers, especially C++ programmers, might initially mistake finalize( ) for the destructor in C++, which is a function that is always called when an object is destroyed. But it is important to distinguish between C++ and Java here, because in C++ objects always get destroyed (in a bug-free program), whereas in Java objects do not always get garbage-collected. Or, put another way:

5.57.1 Garbage collection is not destruction.

If you remember this, you will stay out of trouble. What it means is that if there is some activity that must be performed before you no longer need an object, you must perform that activity yourself. Java has no destructor or similar concept, so you must create an ordinary method to perform this cleanup. For example, suppose in the process of creating your object it draws itself on the screen. If you don't explicitly erase its image from the screen, it might never get cleaned up. If you put some kind of erasing functionality inside finalize( ), then if an object is garbage-collected, the image will first be removed from the screen, but if it isn't, the image will remain. So a second point to remember is:

5.57.2 Your Objects Might not Get Garbage Collected

You might find that the storage for an object never gets released because your program never nears the point of running out of storage. If your program completes and the garbage collector never gets around to releasing the storage for any of your objects, that storage will be returned to the operating system en masse as the program exits. This is a good thing, because garbage collection has some overhead, and if you never do it you never incur that expense.

5.57.3 Finalize() Method

You might believe at this point that you should not use finalize( ) as a general-purpose cleanup method. What good is it?

A third point to remember is:

5.57.4 Garbage Collection is only about Memory

That is, the sole reason for the existence of the garbage collector is to recover memory that your program is no longer using. So any activity that is associated with garbage collection, most notably your finalize( ) method, must also be only about memory and its deallocation.

Does this mean that if your object contains other objects finalize( ) should explicitly release those objects? Well, no - the garbage collector takes care of the release of all object memory regardless of how the object is created. It turns out that the need for finalize( ) is limited to special cases, in which your object can allocate some storage in some way other than creating an object. But, you might observe, everything in Java is an object so how can this be?

It would seem that finalize( ) is in place because of the possibility that you'll do something C-like by allocating memory using a mechanism other than the normal one in Java. This can happen primarily through native methods , which are a way to call non-Java code from Java. (Native methods are discussed in Appendix A.) C and C++ are the only languages currently supported by native methods, but since they can call subprograms in other languages, you can effectively call anything. Inside the non-Java code, C's malloc( ) family of functions might be called to allocate storage, and unless you call free( ) that storage will not be released, causing a memory leak. Of course, free( ) is a C and C++ function, so you'd need call it in a native method inside your finalize( ).

After reading this, you probably get the idea that you won't use finalize( ) much. You're correct; it is not the appropriate place for normal cleanup to occur. So where should normal cleanup be performed?

5.57.5 Cleanup : An Necessary Requirement

To clean up an object, the user of that object must call a cleanup method at the point the cleanup is desired. This sounds pretty straightforward, but it collides a bit with the C++ concept of the destructor. In C++, all objects are destroyed. Or rather, all objects should be destroyed. If the C++ object is created as a local, i.e. on the stack (not possible in Java), then the destruction happens at the closing curly brace of the scope in which the object was created. If the object was created using new (like in Java) the destructor is called when the programmer calls the C++ operator delete (which doesn't exist in Java). If the programmer forgets, the destructor is never called and you have a memory leak, plus the other parts of the object never get cleaned up.

In contrast, Java doesn't allow you to create local objects - you must always use new. But in Java, there's no "delete" to call for releasing the object since the garbage collector releases the storage for you. So from a simplistic standpoint you could say that because of garbage collection, Java has no destructor. You'll see as this book progresses, however, that the presence of a garbage collector does not remove the need or utility of destructors. (And you should never call finalize( ) directly, so that's not an appropriate avenue for a solution.) If you want some kind of cleanup performed other than storage release you must still call a method in Java, which is the equivalent of a C++ destructor without the convenience.

One of the things finalize( ) can be useful for is observing the process of garbage collection. The following example shows you what's going on and summarizes the previous descriptions of garbage collection:

```
//: Garbage.java
// Demonstration of the garbage
// collector and finalization
class Chair
{
static boolean gcrun = false;
static boolean f = false;
static int created = 0;
static int finalized = 0;
int i;
Chair()
{
i = ++created;
if(created == 47)
System.out.println("Created 47");
}
protected void finalize()
{
if(!gcrun)
{
gcrun = true;
System.out.println(
"Beginning to finalize after " +
created + "Chairs have been created");
}
if(i == 47) {
System.out.println(
"Finalizing Chair #47," +
"Setting flag to stop Chair creation");
f = true;
}
finalized++;
if(finalized >= created)
System.out.println(
"All "+ finalized + "finalized");
}
}
public class Garbage
{
```

```
public static void main(String[] args)
{
if(args.length == 0) {
System.err.println("Usage: \n" +
"java Garbage before\n  or:\n" +
"java Garbage after");
return;
}
while(!Chair.f)
{
new Chair();
new String("To take up space");
}
System.out.println(
"After all Chairs have been created:\n" +
"total created = " + Chair.created +
", total finalized = " + Chair.finalized);
if(args[0].equals("before")) {
System.out.println("gc():");
System.gc();
System.out.println("runFinalization():");
System.runFinalization();
}
System.out.println("bye!");
if(args[0].equals("after"))
System.runFinalizersOnExit(true);
}
} ///:~
```

The above program creates many Chair objects, and at some point after the garbage collector begins running, the program stops creating Chairs. Since the garbage collector can run at any time, you don't know exactly when it will start up, so there's a flag called gcrun to indicate whether the garbage collector has started running yet. A second flag f is a way for Chair to tell the main( ) loop that it should stop making objects. Both of these flags are set within finalize( ), which is called during garbage collection.

Two other static variables, created and finalized, keep track of the number of objs created versus the number that get finalized by the garbage collector. Finally, each Chair has its own (non- static) int i so it can keep track of what number it is. When Chair number 47 is finalized, the flag is set to true to bring the process of Chair creation to a stop.

All this happens in main( ), in the loop

```
while(!Chair.f) {
new Chair();
new String("To take up space");
}
```

You might wonder how this loop could ever finish, since there's nothing inside that changes the value of Chair.f. However, the finalize( ) process will, eventually, when it finalizes number 47.

The creation of a String object during each iteration is simply extra garbage being created to encourage the garbage collector to kick in, which it will do when it starts to get nervous about the amount of memory available.

When you run the program, you provide a command-line argument of "before" or "after." The "before" argument will call the System.gc( ) method (to force execution of the garbage collector) along with the System.runFinalization( ) method to run the finalizers. These methods were available in Java 1.0, but the runFinalizersOnExit( ) method that is invoked by using the "after" argument is available only in Java 1.1[19] and beyond. (Note you can call this method any time during program execution, and the execution of the finalizers is independent of whether the garbage collector runs).

The preceding program shows that, in Java 1.1, the promise that finalizers will always be run holds true, but only if you explicitly force it to happen yourself. If you use an argument that isn't "before" or "after" (such as "none"), then neither finalization process will occur, and you'll get an output like this:

Created 47

```
Beginning to finalize after 8694 Chairs have been created
Finalizing Chair #47, Setting flag to stop Chair creation
After all Chairs have been created:
total created = 9834, total finalized = 108
bye!
```

Thus, not all finalizers get called by the time the program completes. [20] To force finalization to happen, you can call System.gc( ) followed by System.runFinalization( ). This will destroy all the objects that are no longer in use up to that point. The odd thing about this is that you call gc( ) before you call runFinalization( ), which seems to contradict the Sun documentation, which claims that finalizers are run first, and then the storage is released. However, if you call runFinalization( ) first, and then gc( ), the finalizers will not be executed.

One reason that Java 1.1 might default to skipping finalization for all objects is because it seems to be expensive. When you use either of the approaches that force garbage collection you might notice longer delays than you would without the extra finalization.

Unfortunately, the implementations of the garbage collector in Java 1.0 would never call finalize( ) correctly. As a result, finalize( ) methods that were essential (such as those to close a file) often didn't get called. The documentation claimed that all finalizers would be called at the exit of a program, even if the garbage collector hadn't been run on those objects by the time the program terminated. This wasn't true, so as a result you couldn't reliably expect finalize( ) to be called for all objects. Effectively, finalize( ) was useless in Java 1.0.

By the time you read this, some Java Virtual Machines may show different behavior.

5.58 Member Initialization

Java goes out of its way to guarantee that any variable is properly initialized before it is used. In the case of variables that are defined locally to a method, this guarantee comes in the form of a compile-time error. So if you say:

```
void f() {
int i;
i++;
}
```

You'll get an error message that says that i might not have been initialized. Of course, the compiler could have given i a default value, but it's more likely that this is a programmer error and a default value would have covered that up. Forcing the programmer to provide an initialization value is more likely to catch a bug.

If a primitive is a data member of a class, however, things are a bit different. Since any method can initialize or use that data, it might not be practical to force the user to initialize it to its appropriate value before the data is used. However, it's unsafe to leave it with a garbage value, so each primitive data member of a class is guaranteed to get an initial value. Those values can be seen here:

```
//: InitialValues.java
// Shows default initial values
class Measurement {
boolean t;
char c;
byte b;
short s;
int i;
long l;
float f;
double d;
void print()
{
System.out.println(
"Data type      Inital value\n" +
"boolean        " + t + "\n" +
"char           " + c + "\n" +
"byte           " + b + "\n" +
"short          " + s + "\n" +
"int            " + i + "\n" +
"long           " + l + "\n" +
"float          " + f + "\n" +
"double         " + d);
}
}
public class InitialValues
{
public static void main(String[] args)
{
Measurement d = new Measurement();
d.print();
/* In this case you could also say:
new Measurement().print();
*/
}
} ///:~
```

The output of this program is:

Data type	**Inital value**
boolean	false
char	
byte	0
short	0

int	0
long	0
float	0.0
double	0.0

The char value is a null, which doesn't print.

You'll see later that when you define an object handle inside a class without initializing it to a new object, that handle is given a value of null.

You can see that even though the values are not specified, they automatically get initialized. So at least there's no threat of working with uninitialized variables.

5.58.1 Specifying Initialization

What happens if you want to give a variable an initial value? One direct way to do this is simply to assign the value at the point you define the variable in the class. (Notice you cannot do this in C++, although C++ novices always try.) Here the field definitions in class Measurement are changed to provide initial values:

```
class Measurement
{
boolean b = true;
char c = 'x';
byte B = 47;
short s = 0xff;
int i = 999;
long l = 1;
float f = 3.14f;
double d = 3.14159;    //. . .
```

You can also initialize non-primitive objects in this same way. If Depth is a class, you can insert a variable and initialize it like so:

```
class Measurement {
Depth o = new Depth();
boolean b = true;    // . . .
```

If you haven't given o an initial value and you go ahead and try to use it anyway, you'll get a run-time error called an exception (covered in Chapter 9).

You can even call a method to provide an initialization value:

```
class CInit {
int i = f();
//...
}
```

This method can have arguments, of course, but those arguments cannot be other class members that haven't been initialized yet. Thus, you can do this:

```
class CInit {
int i = f();
int j = g(i);
//...
}
```

But you cannot do this:

```
class CInit {
int j = g(i);
int i = f();
//...
}
```

This is one place in which the compiler, appropriately, does complain about forward referencing, since this has to do with the order of initialization and not the way the program is compiled.

This approach to initialization is simple and straightforward. It has the limitation that every object of type Measurement will get these same initialization values. Sometimes this is exactly what you need, but at other times you need more flexibility.

5.58.2 Constructor Initialization

The constructor can be used to perform initialization, and this gives you greater flexibility in your programming since you can call methods and perform actions at run time to determine the initial values. There's one thing to keep in mind, however: you aren't precluding the automatic initialization, which happens before the constructor is entered. So, for example, if you say:

```
class Counter
{
int i;
Counter() { i = 7; }
// . . .
```

then i will first be initialized to zero, then to 7. This is true with all the primitive types and with object handles, including those that are given explicit initialization at the point of definition. For this reason, the compiler doesn't try to force you to initialize elements in the constructor at any particular place, or before they are used - initialization is already guaranteed.

5.58.3 Order of Initialization

Within a class, the order of initialization is determined by the order that the variables are defined within the class. Even if the variable definitions are scattered throughout in between method definitions, the variables are initialized before any methods can be called - even the constructor. For example:

```
//: OrderOfInitialization.java
// Demonstrates initialization order.
// When the constructor is called, to create a
// Tag object, you'll see a message:
class Tag {
Tag(int marker) {
System.out.println("Tag(" + marker + ")");
}
}
class Card
{
Tag t1 = new Tag(1); // Before constructor
Card() {
// Indicate we're in the constructor:
```

```
System.out.println("Card()");
t3 = new Tag(33); // Re-initialize t3
}
Tag t2 = new Tag(2); // After constructor
void f() {
System.out.println("f()");
}
Tag t3 = new Tag(3); // At end
}
public class OrderOfInitialization
{
public static void main(String[] args)
{
Card t = new Card();
t.f(); // Shows that construction is done
}
} ///:~
```

In Card, the definitions of the Tag objects are intentionally scattered about to prove that they'll all get initialized before the constructor is entered or anything else can happen. In addition, t3 is re-initialized inside the constructor. The output is:

```
Tag(1)
Tag(2)
Tag(3)
Card()
Tag(33)
f()
```

Thus, the t3 handle gets initialized twice, once before and once during the constructor call. (The first object is dropped, so it can be garbage-collected later.) This might not seem efficient at first, but it guarantees proper initialization - what would happen if an overloaded constructor were defined that did not initialize t3 and there wasn't a "default" initialization for t3 in its definition?

5.58.4 Static Data Initialization

When the data is static the same thing happens; if it's a primitive and you don't initialize it, it gets the standard primitive initial values. If it's a handle to an object, it's null unless you create a new object and attach your handle to it.

If you want to place initialization at the point of definition, it looks the same as for non-statics. But since there's only a single piece of storage for a static, regardless of how many objects are created the question of when that storage gets initialized arises. An example makes this question clear:

```
//: StaticInitialization.java
// Specifying initial values in a
// class definition.
class Bowl {
Bowl(int marker) {
System.out.println("Bowl(" + marker + ")");
}
void f(int marker)
{
```

```
System.out.println("f(" + marker + ")");
}
}
class Table
{
static Bowl b1 = new Bowl(1);
Table() {
System.out.println("Table()");
b2.f(1);
}
void f2(int marker) {
System.out.println("f2(" + marker + ")");
}
static Bowl b2 = new Bowl(2);
}
class Cupboard
{
Bowl b3 = new Bowl(3);
static Bowl b4 = new Bowl(4);
Cupboard()
{
System.out.println("Cupboard()");
b4.f(2);
}
void f3(int marker)
{
System.out.println("f3(" + marker + ")");
}
static Bowl b5 = new Bowl(5);
}

public class StaticInitialization {
public static void main(String[] args) {
System.out.println(
"Creating new Cupboard() in main");
new Cupboard();
System.out.println(
"Creating new Cupboard() in main");
new Cupboard();
t2.f2(1);
t3.f3(1);
}
static Table t2 = new Table();
static Cupboard t3 = new Cupboard();
} ///:~
```

Bowl allows you to view the creation of a class, and Table and Cupboard create static members of Bowl scattered through their class definitions. Note that Cupboard creates a non- static Bowl b3 prior to the static definitions. The output shows what happens:

```
Bowl(1)
Bowl(2)
Table()
f(1)
Bowl(4)
Bowl(5)
Bowl(3)
Cupboard()
f(2)
Creating new Cupboard() in main
Bowl(3)
Cupboard()
f(2)
Creating new Cupboard() in main
Bowl(3)
Cupboard()
f(2)
f2(1)
f3(1)
```

The static initialization occurs only if it's necessary. If you don't create a Table object and you never refer to Table.b1 or Table.b2, the static Bowl b1 and b2 will never be created. However, they are created only when the first Table object is created (or the first static access occurs). After that, the static object is not re-initialized.

The order of initialization is statics first, if they haven't already been initialized by a previous object creation, and then the non- static objects. You can see the evidence of this in the output.

It's helpful to summarize the process of creating an object. Consider a class called Dog:

The first time an object of type Dog is created, or the first time a static method or static field of class Dog is accessed, the Java interpreter must locate Dog.class, which it does by searching through the classpath.

As Dog.class is loaded (which creates a Class object, which you'll learn about later), all of its static initializers are run. Thus, static initialization takes place only once, as the Class object is loaded for the first time.

When you create a new Dog( ) , the construction process for a Dog object first allocates enough storage for a Dog object on the heap.

This storage is wiped to zero, automatically setting all the primitives in Dog to their default values (zero for numbers and the equivalent for boolean and char).

Any initializations that occur at the point of field definition are executed.

Constructors are executed. As you shall see in Chapter 6, this might actually involve a fair amount of activity, especially when inheritance is involved.

Explicit static initialization

Java allows you to group other static initializations inside a special "static construction clause" (sometimes called a static block) in a class. It looks like this:

```
class Spoon {
static int i;
```

```
static {
i = 47;
}
// . . .
```

So it looks like a method, but it's just the static keyword followed by a method body. This code, like the other static initialization, is executed only once, the first time you make an object of that class or you access a static member of that class (even if you never make an object of that class). For example:

```
//: ExplicitStatic.java
// Explicit static initialization
// with the "static" clause.
class Cup {
Cup(int marker) {
System.out.println("Cup(" + marker + ")");
}
void f(int marker) {
System.out.println("f(" + marker + ")");
}
}
class Cups {
static Cup c1;
static Cup c2;
static {
c1 = new Cup(1);
c2 = new Cup(2);
}
Cups() {
System.out.println("Cups()");
}
}

public class ExplicitStatic {
public static void main(String[] args) {
System.out.println("Inside main()");
Cups.c1.f(99);  // (1)
}
static Cups x = new Cups();  // (2)
static Cups y = new Cups();  // (2)   } ///:~
```

The static initializers for Cups will be run when either the access of the static object c1 occurs on the line marked (1), or if line (1) is commented out and the lines marked (2) are uncommented. If both (1) and (2) are commented out, the static initialization for Cups never occurs.

5.58.5 Non-static Instance Initialization

Java 1.1 provides a similar syntax for initializing non-static variables for each object. Here's an example:

```
//: Mugs.java
// Java 1.1 "Instance Initialization"
class Mug {
```

```
Mug(int marker) {
System.out.println("Mug(" + marker + ")");
}
void f(int marker) {
System.out.println("f(" + marker + ")");
}
}
public class Mugs {
Mug c1;
Mug c2;
{
c1 = new Mug(1);
c2 = new Mug(2);
System.out.println("c1 & c2 initialized");
}
Mugs() {
System.out.println("Mugs()");
}
public static void main(String[] args) {
System.out.println("Inside main()");
Mugs x = new Mugs();
}
} ///:~
```

You can see that the instance initialization clause:

```
{
c1 = new Mug(1);
c2 = new Mug(2);
System.out.println("c1 & c2 initialized");
}
```

looks exactly like the static initialization clause except for the missing static keyword. This syntax is necessary to support the initialization of anonymous inner classes.

In contrast, C++ has the constructor initializer list that causes initialization to occur before entering the constructor body, and is enforced for objects. See Thinking in C++ .

5.58.6 Array Initialization

Initializing arrays in C is error-prone and tedious. C++ uses aggregate initialization to make it much safer. [22] Java has no "aggregates" like C++, since everything is an object in Java. It does have arrays, and these are supported with array initialization.

An array is simply a sequence of either objects or primitives, all the same type and packaged together under one identifier name. Arrays are defined and used with the square-brackets indexing operator [ ]. To define an array you simply follow your type name with empty square brackets:

int[] a1;

You can also put the square brackets after the identifier to produce exactly the same meaning:

int a1[];

This conforms to expectations from C and C++ programmers. The former style, however, is probably a more sensible syntax, since it says that the type is "an int array." That style will be used in this book.

The compiler doesn't allow you to tell it how big the array is. This brings us back to that issue of "handles." All that you have at this point is a handle to an array, and there's been no space allocated for the array. To create storage for the array you must write an initialization expression. For arrays, initialization can appear anywhere in your code, but you can also use a special kind of initialization expression that must occur at the point where the array is created. This special initialization is a set of values surrounded by curly braces. The storage allocation (the equivalent of using new) is taken care of by the compiler in this case. For example:

int[] a1 = { 1, 2, 3, 4, 5 };

So why would you ever define an array handle without an array?

int[] a2;

Well, it's possible to assign one array to another in Java, so you can say:

a2 = a1;

What you're really doing is copying a handle, as demonstrated here:

```
//: Arrays.java
// Arrays of primitives.
public class Arrays {
public static void main(String[] args) {
int[] a1 = { 1, 2, 3, 4, 5 };
int[] a2;
a2 = a1;
for(int i = 0; i < a2.length; i++)
a2[i]++;
for(int i = 0; i < a1.length; i++)
prt("a1[" + i + "] = " + a1[i]);
}
static void prt(String s) {
System.out.println(s);
}
} ///:~
```

You can see that a1 is given an initialization value while a2 is not; a2 is assigned later - in this case, to another array.

There's something new here: all arrays have an intrinsic member (whether they're arrays of objects or arrays of primitives) that you can query - but not change - to tell you how many elements there are in the array. This member is length. Since arrays in Java, like C and C++, start counting from element zero, the largest element you can index is length - 1 . If you go out of bounds, C and C++ quietly accept this and allow you to stomp all over your memory, which is the source of many infamous bugs. However, Java protects you against such problems by causing a run-time error (an exception, the subject of Chapter 9) if you step out of bounds. Of course, checking every array access costs time and code and there's no way to turn it off, which means that array accesses might be a source of inefficiency in your program if they occur at a critical juncture. For Internet security and programmer productivity, the Java designers thought that this was a worthwhile tradeoff.

What if you don't know how many elements you're going to need in your array while you're writing the program? You simply use new to create the elements in the array. Here, new works even though it's creating an array of primitives (new won't create a non-array primitive):

```
//: ArrayNew.java
// Creating arrays with new.
import java.util.*;
public class ArrayNew {
static Random rand = new Random();
static int pRand(int mod) {
return Math.abs(rand.nextInt()) % mod;
}
public static void main(String[] args) {
int[] a;
a = new int[pRand(20)];
prt("length of a = " + a.length);
for(int i = 0; i < a.length; i++)
prt("a[" + i + "] = " + a[i]);
}
static void prt(String s) {
System.out.println(s);
}
} ///:~
```

Since the size of the array is chosen at random (using the pRand( ) method defined earlier), it's clear that array creation is actually happening at run-time. In addition, you'll see from the output of this program that array elements of primitive types are automatically initialized to "empty" values. (For numerics, this is zero, for char, it's null, and for boolean, it's false.)

Of course, the array could also have been defined and initialized in the same statement:

int[] a = new int[pRand(20)];

If you're dealing with an array of non-primitive objects, you must always use new. Here, the handle issue comes up again because what you create is an array of handles. Consider the wrapper type Integer, which is a class and not a primitive:

```
//: ArrayClassObj.java
// Creating an array of non-primitive objects.
import java.util.*;
public class ArrayClassObj {
static Random rand = new Random();
static int pRand(int mod) {
return Math.abs(rand.nextInt()) % mod;
}
public static void main(String[] args) {
Integer[] a = new Integer[pRand(20)];
prt("length of a = " + a.length);
for(int i = 0; i < a.length; i++) {
a[i] = new Integer(pRand(500));
prt("a[" + i + "] = " + a[i]);
}
}
static void prt(String s) {
System.out.println(s);
}
```

```
} ///:~
```

Here, even after new is called to create the array:

Integer[] a = new Integer[pRand(20)];

it's only an array of handles, and not until the handle itself is initialized by creating a new Integer object is the initialization complete:

a[i] = new Integer(pRand(500));

If you forget to create the object, however, you'll get an exception at run-time when you try to read the empty array location.

Take a look at the formation of the String object inside the print statements. You can see that the handle to the Integer object is automatically converted to produce a String representing the value inside the object.

It's also possible to initialize arrays of objects using the curly-brace-enclosed list. There are two forms, the first of which is the only one allowed in Java 1.0. The second (equivalent) form is allowed starting with Java 1.1:

```
//: ArrayInit.java
// Array initialization
public class ArrayInit {
public static void main(String[] args) {
Integer[] a = {
new Integer(1),
new Integer(2),
new Integer(3),
};
// Java 1.1 only:
Integer[] b = new Integer[] {
new Integer(1),
new Integer(2),
new Integer(3),
};
}
} ///:~
```

This is useful at times, but it's more limited since the size of the array is determined at compile time. The final comma in the list of initializers is optional. (This feature makes for easier maintenance of long lists.)

The second form of array initialization, added in Java 1.1, provides a convenient syntax to create and call methods that can produce the same effect as C's variable argument lists (known as "varargs" in C). These included, if you choose, unknown quantity of arguments as well as unknown type. Since all classes are ultimately inherited from the common root class Object, you can create a method that takes an array of Object and call it like this:

```
//: VarArgs.java
// Using the Java 1.1 array syntax to create
// variable argument lists
class A { int i; }
public class VarArgs {
static void f(Object[] x) {
```

```
for(int i = 0; i < x.length; i++)
System.out.println(x[i]);
}
public static void main(String[] args)
{
f(new Object[] {
new Integer(47), new VarArgs(),
new Float(3.14), new Double(11.11) });
f(new Object[] {"one", "two", "three" });
f(new Object[] {new A(), new A(), new A()});
}
} ///:~
```

At this point, there's not much you can do with these unknown objects, and this program uses the automatic String conversion to do something useful with each Object. In Chapter 11 (run-time type identification or RTTI) you'll learn how to discover the exact type of such objects so that you can do something more interesting with them.

5.59 Multidimensional Arrays

Java allows you to easily create multidimensional arrays:

```
//: MultiDimArray.java
// Creating multidimensional arrays.
import java.util.*;
public class MultiDimArray {
static Random rand = new Random();
static int pRand(int mod) {
return Math.abs(rand.nextInt()) % mod;
}
public static void main(String[] args) {
int[][] a1 = {
{ 1, 2, 3, },
{ 4, 5, 6, },
};
for(int i = 0; i < a1.length; i++)
for(int j = 0; j < a1[i].length; j++)
prt("a1[" + i + "][" + j +
"] = " + a1[i][j]);
// 3-D array with fixed length:
int[][][] a2 = new int[2][2][4];
for(int i = 0; i < a2.length; i++)
for(int j = 0; j < a2[i].length; j++)
for(int k = 0; k < a2[i][j].length;
k++)
prt("a2[" + i + "][" +
j + "][" + k +
"] = " + a2[i][j][k]);
// 3-D array with varied-length vectors:
int[][][] a3 = new int[pRand(7)][][];
```

```
for(int i = 0; i < a3.length; i++) {
a3[i] = new int[pRand(5)][];
for(int j = 0; j < a3[i].length; j++)
a3[i][j] = new int[pRand(5)];
}
for(int i = 0; i < a3.length; i++)
for(int j = 0; j < a3[i].length; j++)
for(int k = 0; k < a3[i][j].length;
k++)
prt("a3[" + i + "][" +
j + "][" + k +
"] = "+ a3[i][j][k]);
// Array of non-primitive objects:
Integer[][] a4 = {
{ new Integer(1), new Integer(2)},
{ new Integer(3), new Integer(4)},
{ new Integer(5), new Integer(6)},
};
for(int i = 0; i < a4.length; i++)
for(int j = 0; j < a4[i].length; j++)
prt("a4[" + i + "][" + j +
"] =" + a4[i][j]);
Integer[][] a5;
a5 = new Integer[3][];
for(int i = 0; i < a5.length; i++) {
a5[i] = new Integer[3];
for(int j = 0; j < a5[i].length; j++)
a5[i][j] = new Integer(i*j);
}
for(int i = 0; i < a5.length; i++)
for(int j = 0; j < a5[i].length; j++)
prt("a5[" + i + "][" + j +
"] = " + a5[i][j]);
}
static void prt(String s) {
System.out.println(s);
}
} ///:~
```

The code used for printing uses length so that it doesn't depend on fixed array sizes.

The first example shows a multidimensional array of primitives. You delimit each vector in the array with curly braces:

```
int[][] a1 = {
{ 1, 2, 3, },
{ 4, 5, 6, },
};
```

Each set of square brackets moves you into the next level of the array.

The second example shows a three-dimensional array allocated with new. Here, the whole array is allocated at once:

```
int[][][] a2 = new int[2][2][4];
```

But the third example shows that each vector in the arrays that make up the matrix can be of any length:

```
int[][][] a3 = new int[pRand(7)][][];
for(int i = 0; i < a3.length; i++) {
a3[i] = new int[pRand(5)][];
for(int j = 0; j < a3[i].length; j++)
a3[i][j] = new int[pRand(5)];
}
```

The first new creates an array with a random-length first element and the rest undetermined. The second new inside the for loop fills out the elements but leaves the third index undetermined until you hit the third new.

You will see from the output that array values are automatically initialized to zero if you don't give them an explicit initialization value.

You can deal with arrays of non-primitive objects in a similar fashion, which is shown in the fourth example, demonstrating the ability to collect many new expressions with curly braces:

```
Integer[][] a4 = {
{ new Integer(1), new Integer(2)},
{ new Integer(3), new Integer(4)},
{ new Integer(5), new Integer(6)},
};
```

The fifth example shows how an array of non-primitive objects can be built up piece by piece:

```
Integer[][] a5;
a5 = new Integer[3][];
for(int i = 0; i < a5.length; i++) {
a5[i] = new Integer[3];
for(int j = 0; j < a5[i].length; j++)
a5[i][j] = new Integer(i*j);
}
```

The i*j is just to put an interesting value into the Integer.

5.60 Reusing Classes

One of the most compelling features about Java is code reuse. But to be revolutionary, you've got to be able to do a lot more than copy code and change it.

That's the approach used in procedural languages like C, and it hasn't worked very well. Like everything in Java, the solution revolves around the class. You reuse code by creating new classes, but instead of creating them from scratch, you use existing classes that someone has already built and debugged.

The trick is to use the classes without soiling the existing code. In this chapter you'll see two ways to accomplish this. The first is quite straightforward: You simply create objects of your existing class inside the new class. This is called composition because the new class is composed of objects of existing classes. You're simply reusing the functionality of the code, not its form.

The second approach is more subtle. It creates a new class as a type of an existing class. You literally take the form of the existing class and add code to it without modifying the existing class. This magical act is called inheritance, and the compiler does most of the work. Inheritance is one of the cornerstones of object-oriented programming and has additional implications that will be explored in the next chapter.

It turns out that much of the syntax and behavior are similar for both composition and inheritance (which makes sense because they are both ways of making new types from existing types). In this chapter, you'll learn about these code reuse mechanisms.

5.61 The final keyword

The final keyword has slightly different meanings depending on the context, but in general it says "This cannot be changed." You might want to prevent changes for two reasons: design or efficiency. Because these two reasons are quite different, it's possible to misuse the final keyword.

The following sections discuss the three places where final can be used: for data, methods and for a class.

5.61.1 Final Data

Many programming languages have a way to tell the compiler that a piece of data is "constant." A constant is useful for two reasons:

- It can be a compile-time constant that won't ever change.
- It can be a value initialized at run-time that you don't want changed.

In the case of a compile-time constant the compiler is allowed to "fold" the constant value into any calculations in which it's used; that is, the calculation can be performed at compile time, eliminating some run-time overhead. In Java, these sorts of constants must be primitives and are expressed using the final keyword. A value must be given at the time of definition of such a constant.

A field that is both static and final has only one piece of storage that cannot be changed.

When using final with object handles rather than primitives the meaning gets a bit confusing. With a primitive, final makes the value a constant, but with an object handle, final makes the handle a constant. The handle must be initialized to an object at the point of declaration, and the handle can never be changed to point to another object. However, the object can be modified; Java does not provide a way to make any arbitrary object a constant. (You can, however, write your class so that objects have the effect of being constant.) This restriction includes arrays, which are also objects.

Here's an example that demonstrates final fields:

```
//: FinalData.java
// The effect of final on fields
class Value {
int i = 1;
}
public class FinalData {
// Can be compile-time constants
final int i1 = 9;
static final int I2 = 99;
// Typical public constant:
public static final int I3 = 39;
```

```
// Cannot be compile-time constants:
final int i4 = (int)(Math.random()*20);
static final int i5 = (int)(Math.random()*20);
Value v1 = new Value();
final Value v2 = new Value();
static final Value v3 = new Value();
//! final Value v4; // Pre-Java 1.1 Error:
// no initializer
// Arrays:
final int[] a = { 1, 2, 3, 4, 5, 6 };
public void print(String id) {
System.out.println(
id + ": " + "i4 = " + i4 +
", i5 = " + i5);
}
public static void main(String[] args) {
FinalData fd1 = new FinalData();
//! fd1.i1++; // Error: can't change value
fd1.v2.i++; // Object isn't constant!
fd1.v1 = new Value(); // OK — not final
for(int i = 0; i < fd1.a.length; i++)
fd1.a[i]++; // Object isn't constant!
//! fd1.v2 = new Value(); // Error: Can't
//! fd1.v3 = new Value(); // change handle
//! fd1.a = new int[3];
fd1.print("fd1");
System.out.println("Creating new FinalData");
FinalData fd2 = new FinalData();
fd1.print("fd1");
fd2.print("fd2");
}
} ///:~
```

Since i1 and I2 are final primitives with compile-time values, they can both be used as compile-time constants and are not different in any important way. I3 is the more typical way you'll see such constants defined: public so they're usable outside the package, static to emphasize that there's only one, and final to say that it's a constant. Note that final static primitives with constant initial values (that is, compile-time constants) are named with all capitals by convention. Also note that i5 cannot be known at compile time, so it is not capitalized.

Just because something is final doesn't mean that its value is known at compile-time. This is demonstrated by initializing i4 and i5 at run-time using randomly generated numbers. This portion of the example also shows the difference between making a final value static or non- static. This difference shows up only when the values are initialized at run-time, since the compile-time values are treated the same by the compiler. (And presumably optimized out of existence.) The difference is shown in the output from one run:

```
fd1: i4 = 15, i5 = 9
Creating new FinalData
fd1: i4 = 15, i5 = 9
```

```
fd2: i4 = 10, i5 = 9
```

Note that the values of i4 for fd1 and fd2 are unique, but the value for i5 is not changed by creating the second FinalData object. That's because it's static and is initialized once upon loading and not each time a new object is created.

The variables v1 through v4 demonstrate the meaning of a final handle. As you can see in main( ), just because v2 is final doesn't mean that you can't change its value. However, you cannot re-bind v2 to a new object, precisely because it's final. That's what final means for a handle. You can also see the same meaning holds true for an array, which is just another kind of handle. (There is know way that I know of to make the array handles themselves final.) Making handles final seems less useful than making primitives final.

5.61.2 Blank finals

Java 1.1 allows the creation of blank finals , which are fields that are declared as final but are not given an initialization value. In all cases, the blank final must be initialized before it is used, and the compiler ensures this. However, blank finals provide much more flexibility in the use of the final keyword since, for example, a final field inside a class can now be different for each object and yet it retains its immutable quality. Here's an example:

```
//: BlankFinal.java
// "Blank" final data members
class Poppet { }
class BlankFinal {
final int i = 0; // Initialized final
final int j; // Blank final
final Poppet p; // Blank final handle
// Blank finals MUST be initialized
// in the constructor:
BlankFinal() {
j = 1; // Initialize blank final
p = new Poppet();
}
BlankFinal(int x) {
j = x; // Initialize blank final
p = new Poppet();
}
public static void main(String[] args) {
BlankFinal bf = new BlankFinal();
}
} ///:~
```

You're forced to perform assignments to finals either with an expression at the point of definition of the field or in every constructor. This way it's guaranteed that the final field is always initialized before use.

5.61.3 Final arguments

Java 1.1 allows you to make arguments final by declaring them as such in the argument list. This means that inside the method you cannot change what the argument handle points to:

```
//: FinalArguments.java
// Using "final" with method arguments
```

```
class Gizmo {
public void spin() {}
}
public class FinalArguments {
void with(final Gizmo g) {
//! g = new Gizmo(); // Illegal — g is final
g.spin();
}
void without(Gizmo g) {
g = new Gizmo(); // OK — g not final
g.spin();
}
// void f(final int i) { i++; } // Can't change
// You can only read from a final primitive:
int g(final int i) { return i + 1; }
public static void main(String[] args) {
FinalArguments bf = new FinalArguments();
bf.without(null);
bf.with(null);
}
} ///:~
```

Note that you can still assign a null handle to an argument that's final without the compiler catching it, just like you can with a non-final argument.

The methods f( ) and g( ) show what happens when primitive arguments are final: you can only read the argument, but you can't change it.

5.61.4 Final Methods

There are two reasons for final methods. The first is to put a "lock" on the method to prevent any inheriting class from changing its meaning. This is done for design reasons when you want to make sure that a method's behavior is retained during inheritance and cannot be overridden.

The second reason for final methods is efficiency. If you make a method final, you are allowing the compiler to turn any calls to that method into inline calls. When the compiler sees a final method call it can (at its discretion) skip the normal approach of inserting code to perform the method call mechanism (push arguments on the stack, hop over to the method code and execute it, hop back and clean off the stack arguments, and deal with the return value) and instead replace the method call with a copy of the actual code in the method body. This eliminates the overhead of the method call. Of course, if a method is big, then your code begins to bloat and you probably won't see any performance gains from inlining since any improvements will be dwarfed by the amount of time spent inside the method. It is implied that the Java compiler is able to detect these situations and choose wisely whether to inline a final method. However, it's better to not trust that the compiler is able to do this and make a method final only if it's quite small or if you want to explicitly prevent overriding.

Any private methods in a class are implicitly final. Because you can't access a private method, you can't override it (the compiler gives an error message if you try). You can add the final specifier to a private method but it doesn't give that method any extra meaning.

5.61.5 Final Classes

When you say that an entire class is final (by preceding its definition with the final keyword), you state that you don't want to inherit from this class or allow anyone else to do so. In other words, for some reason the design of your class is such that there is never a need to make any changes, or for safety or security reasons you don't want subclassing. Alternatively, you might be dealing with an efficiency issue and you want to make sure that any activity involved with objects of this class is as efficient as possible.

```
//: Jurassic.java
// Making an entire class final
class SmallBrain {}
final class Dinosaur {
int i = 7;
int j = 1;
SmallBrain x = new SmallBrain();
void f() {}
}
//! class Further extends Dinosaur {}
// error: Cannot extend final class 'Dinosaur'
public class Jurassic {
public static void main(String[] args) {
Dinosaur n = new Dinosaur();
n.f();
n.i = 40;
n.j++;
}
} ///:~
```

Note that the data members can be final or not, as you choose. The same rules apply to final for data members regardless of whether the class is defined as final. Defining the class as final simply prevents inheritance - nothing more. However, because it prevents inheritance all methods in a final class are implicitly final, since there's no way to override them. So the compiler has the same efficiency options as it does if you explicitly declare a method final.

You can add the final specifier to a method in a final class, but it doesn't add any meaning.

5.61.6 Final Caution

It can seem to be sensible to make a method final while you're designing a class. You might feel that efficiency is very important when using your class and that no one could possibly want to override your methods anyway. Sometimes this is true.

But be careful with your assumptions. In general, it's difficult to anticipate how a class can be reused, especially a general-purpose class. If you define a method as final you might prevent the possibility of reusing your class through inheritance in some other programmer's project simply because you couldn't imagine it being used that way.

The standard Java library is a good example of this. In particular, the Vector class is commonly used and might be even more useful if, in the name of efficiency, all the methods hadn't been made final. It's easily conceivable that you might want to inherit and override with such a fundamentally useful class, but the designers somehow decided this wasn't appropriate. This is ironic for two reasons. First, Stack is inherited from Vector, which says that a Stack is a Vector, which isn't really true. Second, many of the most important methods of Vector, such as addElement( ) and elementAt( ) are synchronized, which as you will see in Chapter 14 incurs a significant performance overhead that probably wipes out any gains provided by final. This lends credence to the theory that programmers are consistently bad at guessing where optimizations should occur. It's just too bad that such a clumsy design made it into the standard library where we must all cope with it.

It's also interesting to note that Hashtable, another important standard library class, does not have any final methods. As mentioned elsewhere in this book, it's quite obvious that some classes were designed by completely different people than others. (Notice the brevity of the method names in Hashtable compared to those in Vector.) This is precisely the sort of thing that should not be obvious to consumers of a class library. When things are inconsistent it just makes more work for the user. Yet another paean to the value of design and code walkthroughs.

5.62 Forcing Finalization and Garbage Collection

The Java runtime system performs memory management tasks for you. When your program has finished using an object, that is, when there are no more references to an object, the object is finalized and is then garbage collected. These tasks happen asynchronously in the background. However, you can force object finalization and garbage collection using the appropriate method in the System class.

Finalizing Objects

Before an object is garbage collected, the Java runtime system gives the object a chance to clean up after itself. This step is known as finalization and is achieved through a call to the object's finalize method. The object should override the finalize method to perform any final cleanup tasks such as freeing system resources like files and sockets. For information about the finalize method, see Writing a finalize Method.

You can force object finalization to occur by calling System's runFinalization method.

System.runFinalization();

This method calls the finalize methods on all objects that are waiting to be garbage collected.

Running the Garbage Collector

You can ask the garbage collector to run at any time by calling System's gc method:

System.gc();

You might want to run the garbage collector to ensure that it runs at the best time for your program rather than when it's most convenient for the runtime system to run it. For example, your program may wish to run the garbage collector right before it enters a compute or memory intensive section of code or when it knows there will be some idle time.

Note that the garbage collector requires time to complete its task. The amount of time that gc requires to complete varies depending on certain factors: How big your heap is and how fast your processor is, for example. Your program should only run the garbage collector when doing so will have no performance impact on your program.

}

5.63 Command-Line Arguments

A Java application can accept any number of arguments from the command line. Command-line arguments allow the user to affect the operation of an application for one invocation. For example, an application might allow the user to specify verbose mode—that is, specify that the application display a lot of trace information. This is done using the command-line argument -verbose.

Purity Tip: Programs that use command-line arguments are not 100% Pure Java because some systems, like the Mac OS, don't normally have a command line or command-line arguments. Consider using properties instead so that your programs fit more naturally into the environment. If you really must use command-line arguments, have them comply with the POSIX conventions.

The user enters command-line arguments when invoking the application and specifies them after the name of the class to run. For example, suppose you have a Java application, called Sort, that sorts lines in a file. To sort the data in a file named friends.txt, you would run it like this:

java Sort friends.txt

In the Java language, when you invoke an application, the runtime system passes the command-line arguments to the application's main method via an array of Strings. Each String in the array contains one of the command-line arguments. In the previous example, the command-line arguments passed to the Sort application is an array that contains a single String: "friends.txt".

Note to C and C++ Programmers: The command-line arguments passed to a Java application differ in number and in type than those passed to a C or C++ program. When you invoke a Java application, the system passes only one parameter to it:

args: An array of strings that contains the arguments

You can derive the number of command-line arguments with the array's length attribute:

numberOfArgs = args.length;

In Java, you always know the name of the application because it's the name of the class in which the main method is defined. So the Java runtime system does not pass the class name you invoke to the main method. Rather, it passes only the items on the command line that appear after the class name. For example, consider the following statement, which is used to invoke a Java application:

java diff file1 file2

The command-line arguments are in a different font.

Echoing Command-Line Arguments

The following simple application displays each of its command-line arguments on a line by itself:

```
public class Echo {
public static void main (String[] args) {
for (int i = 0; i < args.length; i++)
System.out.println(args[i]);
}
}
```

Here's an example of how to invoke the application using Windows 95/NT. You enter the words that are shown here in a different font:

```
java Echo Drink Hot Java
Drink
Hot
Java
```

Note that the application displays each word—Drink, Hot, and Java—on a line by itself. This is because the space character separates command-line arguments. If you want Drink, Hot, and Java to be interpreted as a single argument, you would join them by enclosing them within double quotation marks. On Windows 95/NT, you run it like this:

```
java Echo "Drink Hot Java"
Drink Hot Java
```

5.63.1 Parsing Numeric Command-Line Arguments

If your program needs to support a numeric command-line argument, it must convert a String argument that represents a number, such as "34", to a number. Here's a code snippet that converts a command-line argument to an int:

```
int firstArg;
if (args.length > 0)
firstArg = Integer.parseInt(args[0]);
```

parseInt throws a NumberFormatException if the format of args[0] isn't valid. All of the Number classes—Integer, Float, Double, and so on—have parseXXX methods that convert a String representing a number to an object of their type.

6 Inheritance

6.1 Managing Inheritance

Recall from the previous lesson that the extends clause declares that your class is a subclass of another. You can specify only one superclass for your class (Java does not support multiple class inheritance), and even though you can omit the extends clause from your class declaration, your class has a superclass. So, every class in Java has one and only one immediate superclass. This statement leads to the question, "Where does it all begin?" As depicted in the following figure, the top-most class, the class from which all other classes are derived, is the Object class defined in java.lang.

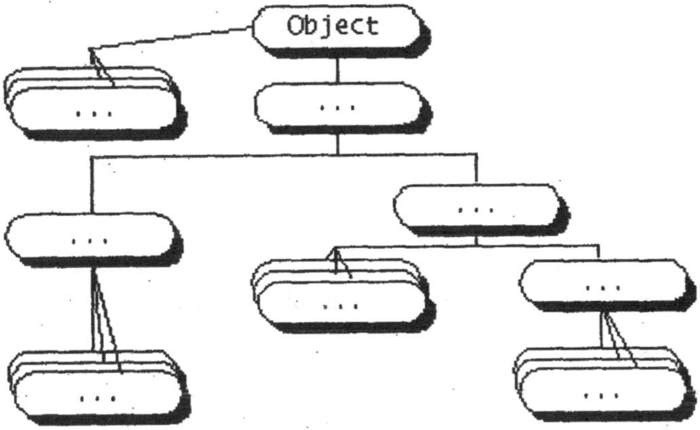

Fig. 6.1

The Object class defines and implements behavior that every class in the Java system needs. It is the most general of all classes. Its immediate subclasses, and other classes near top of the hierarchy, implement general behavior; classes near the bottom of the hierarchy provide for more specialized behavior.

Definition: *A subclass is a class that extends another class. A subclass inherits state and behavior from all of its ancestors. The term "superclass" refers to a class's direct ancestor as well as to all of its ascendant classes.*

The next section, Understanding Inheritance, talks about the various issues involved in extending any class, such as which members it inherits, which members it can override or hide, and which it cannot. The section that follows, Being a Descendent of Object, describes what all classes inherit from the Object class and how these classes implement their inherited functionality.

6.2 Understanding Inheritance

A subclass inherits variables and methods from its superclass and all of its ancestors. The subclass can use these members as is, or it can hide the member variables or override the methods.

6.2.1 What Members Does a Subclass Inherit?

Rule: A subclass inherits all of the members in its superclass that are accessible to that subclass unless the subclass explicitly hides a member variable or overrides a method. Note that constructors are not members and are not inherited by subclasses.

The following list itemizes the members that are inherited by a subclass:

- Subclasses inherit those superclass members declared as public or protected.
- Subclasses inherit those superclass members declared with no access specifier as long as the subclass is in the same package as the superclass.
- Subclasses don't inherit a superclass's member if the subclass declares a member with the same name. In the case of member variables, the member variable in the subclass hides the one in the superclass. In the case of methods, the method in the subclass overrides the one in the superclass.
- Creating a subclass can be as simple as including the extends clause in your class declaration. However, you usually have to make other provisions in your code when subclassing a class, such as overriding methods or providing implementations for abstract methods.

6.2.2 Hiding Member Variables

As mentioned in the previous section, member variables defined in the subclass hide member variables that have the same name in the superclass.

While this feature of the Java language is powerful and convenient, it can be a fruitful source of errors. When naming your member variables, be careful to hide only those member variables that you actually wish to hide.

One interesting feature of Java member variables is that a class can access a hidden member variable through its superclass. Consider the following superclass and subclass pair:

```
class Super {
Number aNumber;
}
class Subbie extends Super {
Float aNumber;
}
```

The aNumber variable in Subbie hides aNumber in Super. But you can access Super's aNumber from Subbie with

```
super.aNumber
```

super is a Java language keyword that allows a method to refer to hidden variables and overridden methods of the superclass.

Overriding Methods

The ability of a subclass to override a method in its superclass allows a class to inherit from a superclass whose behavior is "close enough" and then supplement or modify the behavior of that superclass.

6.3 Inheritance

Code reusability is claimed to be a key advantage of object-oriented languages over non-object-oriented languages. Inheritance is the mechanism by which this is achieved. An object can inherit the variables and methods of another object. It can keep those it wants, and replace those it doesn't want.

For example, let us also expand the Car class so that a car also has a make, a model, a year, a number of passengers it can carry, four wheels, either two or four doors. That class might look like this:

```
public class Car {
private String licensePlate;      // e.g. "New York A456 324"
private double speed;             // kilometers per hour
private double maxSpeed;          // kilometers per hour
private String make;              // e.g. "Ford"
private String model;             // e.g. "Taurus"
private int   year;           // e.g. 1997, 1998, 1999, 2000, 2001,
etc.
private int    numberPassengers;  // e.g. 4
private int    numberWheels = 4;  // all cars have four wheels
private int    numberDoors;       // e.g. 4
// constructors
public Car(String licensePlate, double maxSpeed,
String make, String model, int year, int numberOfPassengers,
int numberOfDoors) {
this(licensePlate, maxSpeed, make, model, year, numberOfPassengers,
numberOfDoors);
}
public Car(String licensePlate, double speed, double maxSpeed,
String make, String model, int year, int numberOfPassengers) {
this(licensePlate, speed, maxSpeed, make, model, year,
numberOfPassengers, 4);
}
public Car(String licensePlate, double speed, double maxSpeed,
String make, String model, int year, int numberOfPassengers,
int numberOfDoors) {

// I could add some more constraints like the
// number of doors being positive but I won't
// so that this example doesn't get too big.
this.licensePlate = licensePlate;
this.make = make;
this.model = model;
this.year = year;
this.numberPassengers = numberOfPassengers;
this.numberDoors = numberOfDoors;
if (maxSpeed >= 0.0) {
this.maxSpeed = maxSpeed;
```

```
}
else {
maxSpeed = 0.0;
}
if (speed < 0.0) {
speed = 0.0;
}
if (speed <= maxSpeed) {
this.speed = speed;
}
else {
this.speed = maxSpeed;
}
}
// getter (accessor) methods
public String getLicensePlate() {
return this.licensePlate;
}
public String getMake() {
return this.make;
}
public String getModel() {
return this.model;
}
public int getYear() {
return this.year;
}
public int getNumberOfPassengers() {
return this.numberPassengers;
}
public int getNumberOfPassengers() {
return this.numberWheels;
}
public int getNumberOfDoors() {
return this.numberDoors;
}

public double getMaxSpeed() {
return this.speed;
}
public double getSpeed() {
return this.maxSpeed;
}
// setter method for the license plate property
public void setLicensePlate(String licensePlate) {
this.licensePlate = licensePlate;
}
// accelerate to maximum speed
```

```
// put the pedal to the metal
public void floorIt() {
this.speed = this.maxSpeed;
}
public void accelerate(double deltaV) {
this.speed = this.speed + deltaV;
if (this.speed > this.maxSpeed) {
this.speed = this.maxSpeed;
}
if (this.speed <  0.0) {
this.speed = 0.0;
}
}
}
```

Obviously this doesn't exhaust everything there is to say about a car. Which properties you choose to include in your class depends on your application.

6.4 Using the Superclass

In this example you begin by defining a more general MotorVehicle class.

```
public class MotorVehicle {
protected String licensePlate;      // e.g. "New York A456 324"
protected double speed;             // kilometers per hour
protected double maxSpeed;          // kilometers per hour
protected String make;            // e.g. "Harley-Davidson", "Ford"
protected String model;             // e.g. "Fatboy", "Taurus"
protected int    year;             // e.g. 1998, 1999, 2000, 2001,
etc.
protected int    numberPassengers;  // e.g. 4

// constructors
```

public MotorVehicle(String licensePlate, double maxSpeed,

```
String make, String model, int year, int numberOfPassengers) {
this(licensePlate, maxSpeed, make, model, year,
numberOfPassengers);
}
```

public MotorVehicle(String licensePlate, double speed, double maxSpeed,

```
String make, String model, int year, int numberOfPassengers) {
this(licensePlate, speed, maxSpeed, make, model, year,
numberOfPassengers);
}
```

public MotorVehicle(String licensePlate, double speed, double maxSpeed,
String make, String model, int year, int numberOfPassengers) {

```
// I could add some more constraints like the
// number of doors being positive but I won't
// so that this example doesn't get too big.
```

```
this.licensePlate = licensePlate;
this.make = make;
this.model = model;
this.year = year;
this.numberPassengers = numberOfPassengers;
if (maxSpeed >= 0.0) {
this.maxSpeed = maxSpeed;
}
else {
maxSpeed = 0.0;
}
if (speed < 0.0) {
speed = 0.0;
}
if (speed <= maxSpeed) {
this.speed = speed;
}
else {
this.speed = maxSpeed;
}

}
// getter (accessor) methods
public String getLicensePlate() {
return this.licensePlate;
}
public String getMake() {
return this.make;
}
public String getModel() {
return this.model;
}
public int getYear() {
return this.year;
}

public int getNumberOfPassengers() {
return this.numberPassengers;
}
public int getNumberOfPassengers() {
return this.numberWheels;
}
public double getMaxSpeed() {
return this.speed;
}
public double getSpeed() {
return this.maxSpeed;
}
```

```
// setter method for the license plate property
protected void setLicensePlate(String licensePlate) {
this.licensePlate = licensePlate;
}
// accelerate to maximum speed
// put the pedal to the metal
public void floorIt() {
this.speed = this.maxSpeed;
}
public void accelerate(double deltaV) {
this.speed = this.speed + deltaV;
if (this.speed > this.maxSpeed) {
this.speed = this.maxSpeed;
}
if (this.speed < 0.0) {
this.speed = 0.0;
}
}
}
```

The MotorVehicle class has all the characteristics shared by motorcycles and cars, but it leaves the number of wheels unspecified, and it doesn't have a numberDoors field since not all motor vehicles have doors. It also makes the fields and the setLicensePlate() method protected instead of private and public.

6.4.1 Inheritance: the Motorcycle Subclass

The MotorVehicle class has all the characteristics shared by motorcycles and cars, but it leaves the number of wheels unspecified, and it doesn't have a numberDoors field since not all motor vehicles have doors.

Next you define two subclasses of MotorVehicle, one for cars and one for motorcycles. To do this you use the keyword extends.

```
public class Motorcycle extends MotorVehicle {
protected int numberWheels = 2;
// constructors
public Motorcycle(String licensePlate, double maxSpeed,
String make, String model, int year, int numberOfPassengers) {
this(licensePlate, 0.0, maxSpeed, make, model, year,
numberOfPassengers);
}
public Motorcycle(String licensePlate, double speed, double maxSpeed,
String make, String model, int year, int numberOfPassengers) {
// invoke superclass constructor
super(licensePlate, speed, maxSpeed, make, model, year,
numberOfPassengers);
}
public int getNumberOfWheels() {
return this.numberWheels;
}
```

```
}
```

6.4.2 Inheritance: The Car subclass

```
public class Car extends MotorVehicle {
protected int numberWheels = 4;
protected int numberDoors;
// constructors
public Car(String licensePlate, double maxSpeed,
String make, String model, int year, int numberOfPassengers,
int numberOfDoors) {
this(licensePlate, maxSpeed, make, model, year, numberOfPassengers,
numberOfDoors);
}
public Car(String licensePlate, double speed, double maxSpeed,
String make, String model, int year, int numberOfPassengers) {
this(licensePlate, speed, maxSpeed, make, model, year,
numberOfPassengers, 4);
}
public Car(String licensePlate, double speed, double maxSpeed,
String make, String model, int year, int numberOfPassengers,
int numberOfDoors) {
super(licensePlate, speed, maxSpeed, make, model,
year, numberOfPassengers);
this.numberDoors = numberOfDoors;
}
public int getNumberOfWheels() {
return this.numberWheels;
}
public int getNumberOfDoors() {
return this.numberDoors;
}
}
```

It may look like these classes aren't as complete as the earlier ones, but that's incorrect. Car and Motorcycle each inherit the members of their superclass, MotorVehicle. Since a MotorVehicle has a make, a model, a year, a speed, a maximum speed, a number of passengers, cars and motorcycles also have makes, models, years, speeds, maximum speeds, and numbers of passengers. They alse have all the public methods the superclass has. They do not have the same constructors, though they can invoke the superclass constructor through the super keyword, much as a constructor in the same class can be invoked with the this keyword.

6.5 Subclasses and Polymorphism

Car and Motorcycle are subclasses of MotorVehicle. If you instantiate a Car or a Motorcycle with new, you can use that object anywhere you can use a MotorVehicle, because cars are motor vehicles. Similarly you can use a Motorcycle anywhere you can use a MotorVehicle. This use of a subclass object in place of a superclass object is the beginning of polymorphism. I'll say more about polymorphism later.

The converse is not true. Although all cars are motor vehicles, not all motor vehicles are cars. Some are motorcycles. Therefore if a method expects a Car object you shouldn't give it a MotorVehicle object instead.

Note that I said you shouldn't give a method that expects a Car a MotorVehicle. I didn't say you couldn't. Objects can be cast into their subclasses. This is useful when using data structures like Vectors that only handle generic objects. It's up to the programmer to keep track of what kind of object is stored in a Vector, and to use it accordingly.

The proper choice of classes and subclasses is a skill learned primarily through experience. There are often different ways to define classes.

6.6 Multilevel Hierarchy Inheritance

The Car-Motorcycle-MotorVehicle example showed single-level inheritance. There's nothing to stop you from going further. You can define subclasses of cars for compacts, station wagons, sports coupes and more. For example, this class defines a compact as a car with two doors:

```
public class Compact extends Car {
// constructors
public Compact(String licensePlate, double maxSpeed,
String make, String model, int year, int numberOfPassengers) {
this(licensePlate, maxSpeed, make, model, year,
numberOfPassengers);
}
public Compact(String licensePlate, double speed, double  maxSpeed,
String make, String model, int year, int numberOfPassengers) {
super(licensePlate, speed, maxSpeed, make, model,
year, numberOfPassengers, 2);
}
}
```

Compact not only inherits from its immediate superclass, Car, but also from Car's superclass, MotorVehicle. Thus the Compact class also has a make, a model, a year and so on. There's no limit to this chain of inheritance, though getting more than four or five classes deep makes code excessively complex.

6.7 Multiple Inheritance

Some object oriented languages, notably C++, allow a class to inherit from more than one unrelated class. This is called multiple inheritance and is different from the multi-level inheritance in this section. Most of the things that can be accomplished via multiple inheritance in C++ can be handled by interfaces in Java.

6.8 Overriding Methods

The ability of a subclass to override a method in its superclass allows a class to inherit from a superclass whose behavior is "close enough" and then override methods as needed. For example, all classes are descendents of the Object class. Object contains the toString method, which returns a String object containing the name of the object's class and its hash code. Most, if not all, classes will want to override this method and print out something meaningful for that class.

Let's resurrect the Stack class example and override the toString method. The output of toString should be a textual representation of the object. For the Stack class, a list of the items in the stack would be appropriate

```
public class Stack
{
    private Vector items;
    // code for Stack's methods and constructor not shown
    // overrides Object's toString method
    public String toString() {
    int n = items.size();
    StringBuffer result = new StringBuffer();
    result.append("[");
    for (int i = 0; i < n; i++) {
        result.append(items.elementAt(i).toString());
        if (i < n-1) result.append(",");
    }
        result.append("]");
        return result.toString();
    }
}
```

The return type, method name, and number and type of the parameters for the overriding method must match those in the overridden method. The overriding method can have a different throws clause as long as it doesn't declare any types not declared by the throws clause in the overridden method. Also, the access specifier for the overriding method can allow more access than the overridden method, but not less. For example, a protected method in the superclass can be made public but not private.

6.8.1 Calling the Overridden Method

Sometimes, you don't want to completely override a method. Rather, you want to add more functionality to it. To do this, simply call the overridden method using the super keyword. For example,

```
super.overriddenMethodName();
```

6.8.2 Methods a Subclass Cannot Override

A subclass cannot override methods that are declared final in the superclass (by definition, final methods cannot be overridden). If you attempt to override a final method, the compiler displays an error message similar to the following and refuses to compile the program:

```
FinalTest.java:7: Final methods can't be overridden.
Method void iamfinal() is final in class ClassWithFinalMethod.
    void iamfinal() {
^
1 error
```

Also, a subclass cannot override methods that are declared static in the superclass. In other words, a subclass cannot override a class method. A subclass can hide a static method in the superclass by declaring a static method in the subclass with the same signature as the static method in the superclass.

6.8.3 Overriding Methods

Suppose that one day you've just finished your Car class. It's been plugged into your traffic simulation which is chugging along merrily simulating traffic. Then your pointy haired boss rolls in the door, and tells you that he needs the Car class to not accelerate past the 70 miles per hour (pointy haired bosses rarely understand the metric system) even if the car's a Ferrari with a maximum speed in excess of 200 miles per hour.

What are you going to do? Your first reaction may be to change the class that you already wrote so that it limits the speed of all the cars. However you're using that class elsewhere and things will break if you change it.

You could create a completely new class in a different file, either by starting from scratch or by copying and pasting. This would work, but it would mean that if you found a bug in the Car class now you'd have to fix it in two files. And if you wanted to add new methods to the Car class, you'd have to add them in two files. Still this is the best you could do if you were writing in C or some other traditional language.

6.8.4 Overriding Methods: The Solution

The object oriented solution to this problem is to define a new class, call it SlowCar, which inherits from Car and imposes the additional constraint that a car may not go faster than 70 mph (112.65 kph).

To do this you'll need to adjust the two places that speed can be changed, the constructor and the accelerate() method. The constructor has a different name because all constructors are named after their classes but the accelerate() method must be overridden. This means the subclass has a method with the same signature as the method in the superclass.

```
public class SlowCar extends Car {
private double speedLimit = 112.65408; // kph == 70 mph
public SlowCar(String licensePlate, double speed, double    maxSpeed,
String make, String model, int year, int numberOfPassengers,    int
numDoors) {
super(licensePlate, (speed < speedLimit) ? speed :      speedLimit,
maxSpeed, make, model, year, numberOfPassengers, numDoors);
}
public void accelerate(double deltaV) {
double speed = this.speed + deltaV;
if (speed > this.maxSpeed) {
speed = this.maxSpeed;
}
if (speed > speedLimit) {
speed = speedLimit;
}
if (speed < 0.0) {
speed = 0.0;
}
this.speed = speed;
}
}
```

The first thing to note about this class is what it doesn't have, getSpeed(), getLicensePlate(), getMaximumSpeed(), setLicensePlate() methods or speed, maxSpeed and numDoors fields. All of these are provided by the superclass Car. Nothing about them has changed so they don't need to be repeated here.

Next look at the accelerate() method. This is different than the accelerate() method in Car. It imposes the additional constraint. Since the speed and maxSpeed fields from Car are protected, they're accessible from this subclass.

The constructor is a little more complicated. First note that if you're going to use a non-default constructor, that is a constructor with arguments, you do need to write a constructor for the subclass, even if it's just going to do the exact same thing as the matching constructor in the superclass. You cannot simply inherit Car's constructor because that constructor is named Car() and this one must be named SlowCar().

The constructor needs to set the value of name, url, and description. However they're not accessible from the subclass. Instead they are set by calling the superclass's constructor using the keyword super. When super is used as a method in the first non-blank line of a constructor, it stands for the constructor of this class's superclass.

The immediate superclass's constructor will be called in the first non-blank line of the subclass's constructor. If you don't call it explicitly, then Java will call it for you with no arguments. It's a compile time error if the immediate superclass doesn't have a constructor with no arguments and you don't call a different constructor in the first line of the subclass's constructor.

The use of the ternary operator in the constructor call is unusual. However, it's necessary to meet the compiler's requirement that the invocation of super be the first line in the subclass constructor. Otherwise this could be written more clearly using only if-else.

6.8.5 Adding Methods

A subclass isn't restricted to changing the behavior of its superclass. It can also add completely new methods and fields that are not shared with the superclass. For instance if a class represents a user of a multi-user database, the user class might start off with no access. Secretaries could be given read-only access. Therefore the secretary class would have additional methods to read data that aren't part of the user class.

Data entry clerks might be allowed to read the database and to create new records but not to modify old records. Therefore the data entry class would inherit from the secretary class and have methods to allow adding new records. A supervisor class would inherit from the data entry class and also have methods that allows modification of existing records. Finally a database manager would inherit from supervisor, but have new methods that allowed database managers to change the structure of the database.

As a practical example, recall that the Car class added a numberDoors field and a getNumberOfDoors() method that the MotorVehicle class didn't have.

6.9 Inheritance Syntax

Inheritance is such an integral part of Java (and OOP languages in general) that it was introduced in Chapter 1 and has been used occasionally in chapters before this one because certain situations required it. In addition, you're always doing inheritance when you create a class, because if you don't say otherwise you inherit from Java's standard root class Object.

The syntax for composition is obvious, but to perform inheritance there's a distinctly different form. When you inherit, you say "This new class is like that old class." You state this in code by giving the name of the class as usual, but before the opening brace of the class body, put the keyword extends followed by the name of the base class . When you do this, you automatically get all the data members and methods in the base class. Here's an example:

```
//: Detergent.java
// Inheritance syntax & properties
```

```
class Cleanser {
private String s = new String("Cleanser");
public void append(String a) { s += a; }
public void dilute() { append(" dilute()"); }
public void apply() { append(" apply()"); }
public void scrub() { append(" scrub()"); }
public void print() { System.out.println(s); }
public static void main(String[] args) {
Cleanser x = new Cleanser();
x.dilute(); x.apply(); x.scrub();
x.print();
}
}
public class Detergent extends Cleanser {
// Change a method:
public void scrub() {
append(" Detergent.scrub()");
super.scrub(); // Call base-class version
}
// Add methods to the interface:
public void foam() { append(" foam()"); }
// Test the new class:
public static void main(String[] args) {
Detergent x = new Detergent();
x.dilute();
x.apply();
x.scrub();
x.foam();
x.print();
System.out.println("Testing base class:");
Cleanser.main(args);
}
} ///:~
```

This demonstrates a number of features. First, in the Cleanser append( ) method, Strings are concatenated to s using the += operator, which is one of the operators (along with '+') that the Java designers "overloaded" to work with Strings.

Second, both Cleanser and Detergent contain a main( ) method. You can create a main( ) for each one of your classes, and it's often recommended to code this way so that your test code is wrapped in with the class. Even if you have a lot of classes in a program only the main( ) for the public class invoked on the command line will be called. (And you can have only one public class per file.) So in this case, when you say java Detergent , Detergent.main( ) will be called. But you can also say java Cleanser to invoke Cleanser.main( ), even though Cleanser is not a public class. This technique of putting a main( ) in each class allows easy unit testing for each class. And you don't need to remove the main( ) when you're finished testing; you can leave it in for later testing.

Here, you can see that Detergent.main( ) calls Cleanser.main( ) explicitly.

It's important that all of the methods in Cleanser are public. Remember that if you leave off any access specifier the member defaults to "friendly," which allows access only to package members.

Thus, within this package, anyone could use those methods if there were no access specifier. Detergent would have no trouble, for example. However, if a class from some other package were to inherit Cleanser it could access only public members. So to plan for inheritance, as a general rule make all fields private and all methods public. (protected members also allow access by derived classes; you'll learn about this later.) Of course, in particular cases you must make adjustments, but this is a useful guideline.

Note that Cleanser has a set of methods in its interface: append( ), dilute( ), apply( ), scrub( ) and print( ). Because Detergent is derived from Cleanser (via the extends keyword) it automatically gets all these methods in its interface, even though you don't see them all explicitly defined in Detergent. You can think of inheritance, then, as reusing the interface. (The implementation comes along for free, but that part isn't the primary point.)

As seen in scrub( ), it's possible to take a method that's been defined in the base class and modify it. In this case, you might want to call the method from the base class inside the new version. But inside scrub( ) you cannot simply call scrub( ), since that would produce a recursive call, which isn't what you want. To solve this problem Java has the keyword super that refers to the "superclass" that the current class has been inherited from. Thus the expression super.scrub( ) calls the base-class version of the method scrub( ).

When inheriting you're not restricted to using the methods of the base class. You can also add new methods to the derived class exactly the way you put any method in a class: just define it. The extends keyword suggests that you are going to add new methods to the base-class interface, and the method foam( ) is an example of this.

In Detergent.main( ) you can see that for a Detergent object you can call all the methods that are available in Cleanser as well as in Detergent (i.e. foam( )).

6.10 Initializing the Base Class

Since there are now two classes involved - the base class and the derived class - instead of just one, it can be a bit confusing to try to imagine the resulting object produced by a derived class. From the outside, it looks like the new class has the same interface as the base class and maybe some additional methods and fields. But inheritance doesn't just copy the interface of the base class. When you create an object of the derived class, it contains within it a subobject of the base class. This subobject is the same as if you had created an object of the base class by itself. It's just that, from the outside, the subobject of the base class is wrapped within the derived-class object.

Of course, it's essential that the base-class subobject be initialized correctly and there's only one way to guarantee that: perform the initialization in the constructor, by calling the base-class constructor, which has all the appropriate knowledge and privileges to perform the base-class initialization. Java automatically inserts calls to the base-class constructor in the derived-class constructor. The following example shows this working with three levels of inheritance:

```
//: Cartoon.java
// Constructor calls during inheritance
class Art {
Art() {
System.out.println("Art constructor");
}
}
class Drawing extends Art {
Drawing() {
```

```
System.out.println("Drawing constructor");
}
}
public class Cartoon extends Drawing {
Cartoon() {
System.out.println("Cartoon constructor");
}
public static void main(String[] args) {
Cartoon x = new Cartoon();
}
} ///:~
```

The output for this program shows the automatic calls:

- Art constructor
- Drawing constructor
- Cartoon constructor

You can see that the construction happens from the base "outward," so the base class is initialized before the derived-class constructors can access it.

Even if you don't create a constructor for Cartoon( ), the compiler will synthesize a default constructor for you that calls the base class constructor.

6.10.1 Constructors with Arguments

The above example has default constructors; that is, they don't have any arguments. It's easy for the compiler to call these because there's no question about what arguments to pass. If your class doesn't have default arguments or if you want to call a base-class constructor that has an argument you must explicitly write the calls to the base-class constructor using the super keyword and the appropriate argument list:

```
//: Chess.java
// Inheritance, constructors and arguments
class Game {
Game(int i) {
System.out.println("Game constructor");
}
}
class BoardGame extends Game {
BoardGame(int i) {
super(i);
System.out.println("BoardGame constructor");
}
}

public class Chess extends BoardGame {
Chess() {
super(11);
System.out.println("Chess constructor");
}
public static void main(String[] args) {
Chess x = new Chess();
```

```
}
} ///:~
```

If you don't call the base-class constructor in BoardGame( ), the compiler will complain that it can't find a constructor of the form Game( ). In addition, the call to the base-class constructor must be the first thing you do in the derived-class constructor. (The compiler will remind you if you get it wrong.)

6.10.2 Catching Base Constructor Exceptions

As just noted, the compiler forces you to place the base-class constructor call first in the body of the derived-class constructor. This means nothing else can appear before it. This also prevents a derived-class constructor from catching any exceptions that come from a base class. This can be inconvenient at times.

6.10.3 Combining Composition and Inheritance

It is very common to use composition and inheritance together. The following example shows the creation of a more complex class, using both inheritance and composition, along with the necessary constructor initialization:

```
//: PlaceSetting.java
// Combining composition & inheritance
class Plate {
Plate(int i) {
System.out.println("Plate constructor");
}
}

class DinnerPlate extends Plate {
DinnerPlate(int i) {
super(i);
System.out.println(
"DinnerPlate constructor");
}
}

class Utensil {
Utensil(int i) {
System.out.println("Utensil constructor");
}
}

class Spoon extends Utensil {
Spoon(int i) {
super(i);
System.out.println("Spoon constructor");
}
}

class Fork extends Utensil {
Fork(int i) {
super(i);
```

```
System.out.println("Fork constructor");
}
}

class Knife extends Utensil {
Knife(int i) {
super(i);
System.out.println("Knife constructor");
}
}

// A cultural way of doing something:
class Custom {
Custom(int i) {
System.out.println("Custom constructor");
}
}

public class PlaceSetting extends Custom {
Spoon sp;
Fork frk;
Knife kn;
DinnerPlate pl;
PlaceSetting(int i) {
super(i + 1);
sp = new Spoon(i + 2);
frk = new Fork(i + 3);
kn = new Knife(i + 4);
pl = new DinnerPlate(i + 5);
System.out.println(
"PlaceSetting constructor");
}
public static void main(String[] args) {
PlaceSetting x = new PlaceSetting(9);
}
} ///:~
```

While the compiler forces you to initialize the base classes, and requires that you do it right at the beginning of the constructor, it doesn't watch over you to make sure that you initialize the member objects, so you must remember to pay attention to that.

6.11 Guaranteeing Proper Cleanup

Java doesn't have the C++ concept of a destructor, a method that is automatically called when an object is destroyed. The reason is probably that in Java the practice is simply to forget about objects rather than to destroy them, allowing the garbage collector to reclaim the memory as necessary.

Often this is fine, but there are times when your class might perform some activities during its lifetime that require cleanup. As mentioned in Chapter 4, you can't know when the garbage collector will be called, or if it will be called. So if you want something cleaned up for a class, you must write a special method to do it explicitly, and make sure that the client programmer knows that they must call this method. On top of this, as described in Chapter 9 (exception handling), you must guard against an exception by putting such cleanup in a finally clause.

Consider an example of a computer-aided design system that draws pictures on the screen:

```
//: CADSystem.java
// Ensuring proper cleanup
import java.util.*;
class Shape {
Shape(int i) {
System.out.println("Shape constructor");
}
void cleanup() {
System.out.println("Shape cleanup");
}
}
class Circle extends Shape {
Circle(int i) {
super(i);
System.out.println("Drawing a Circle");
}
void cleanup() {
System.out.println("Erasing a Circle");
super.cleanup();
}
}
class Triangle extends Shape {
Triangle(int i) {
super(i);
System.out.println("Drawing a Triangle");
}
void cleanup() {
System.out.println("Erasing a Triangle");
super.cleanup();
}
}
class Line extends Shape {
private int start, end;
Line(int start, int end) {
super(start);
this.start = start;
this.end = end;
System.out.println("Drawing a Line: " +
start + ", " + end);
}
void cleanup() {
System.out.println("Erasing a Line: " +
start + ", " + end);
```

```
super.cleanup();
}
}

public class CADSystem extends Shape {
private Circle c;
private Triangle t;
private Line[] lines = new Line[10];
CADSystem(int i) {
super(i + 1);
for(int j = 0; j < 10; j++)
lines[j] = new Line(j, j*j);
c = new Circle(1);
t = new Triangle(1);
System.out.println("Combined constructor");
}
void cleanup() {
System.out.println("CADSystem.cleanup()");
t.cleanup();
c.cleanup();
for(int i = 0; i < lines.length; i++)
lines[i].cleanup();
super.cleanup();
}
public static void main(String[] args) {
CADSystem x = new CADSystem(47);
try {
// Code and exception handling...
} finally {
x.cleanup();
}
}
} ///:~
```

Everything in this system is some kind of Shape (which is itself a kind of Object since it's implicitly inherited from the root class). Each class redefines Shape's cleanup( ) method in addition to calling the base-class version of that method using super. The specific Shape classes Circle, Triangle and Line all have constructors that "draw," although any method called during the lifetime of the object could be responsible for doing something that needs cleanup. Each class has its own cleanup( ) method to restore non-memory things back to the way they were before the object existed.

In main( ), you can see two keywords that are new, and won't officially be introduced until Chapter 9: try and finally. The try keyword indicates that the block that follows (delimited by curly braces) is a guarded region , which means that it is given special treatment. One of these special treatments is that the code in the finally clause following this guarded region is always executed, no matter how the try block exits. (With exception handling, it's possible to leave a try block in a number of non-ordinary ways.) Here, the finally clause is saying "always call cleanup( ) for x, no matter what happens." These keywords will be explained thoroughly in Chapter 9.

Note that in your cleanup method you must also pay attention to the calling order for the base-class and member-object cleanup methods in case one subobject depends on another. In general, you should follow the same form that is imposed by a C++ compiler on its destructors: First perform all of the work specific to your class (which might require that base-class elements still be viable) then call the base-class cleanup method, as demonstrated here.

There can be many cases in which the cleanup issue is not a problem; you just let the garbage collector do the work. But when you must do it explicitly, diligence and attention is required.

6.12 Order of Garbage Collection

There's not much you can rely on when it comes to garbage collection. The garbage collector might never be called. If it is, it can reclaim objects in any order it wants. In addition, implementations of the garbage collector in Java 1.0 often don't call the finalize( ) methods. It's best to not rely on garbage collection for anything but memory reclamation. If you want cleanup to take place, make your own cleanup methods and don't rely on finalize( ). (As mentioned earlier, Java 1.1 can be forced to call all the finalizers.)

6.12.1 Name Hiding

Only C++ programmers might be surprised by name hiding, since it works differently in that language. If a Java base class has a method name that's overloaded several times, redefining that method name in the derived class will not hide any of the base-class versions. Thus overloading works regardless of whether the method was defined at this level or in a base class:

```
//: Hide.java
// Overloading a base-class method name
// in a derived class does not hide the
// base-class versions
class Homer {
char doh(char c) {
System.out.println("doh(char)");
return 'd';
}
float doh(float f) {
System.out.println("doh(float)");
return 1.0f;
}
}
class Milhouse {}
class Bart extends Homer {
void doh(Milhouse m) {}
}
class Hide {
public static void main(String[] args) {
Bart b = new Bart();
b.doh(1); // doh(float) used
b.doh('x');
b.doh(1.0f);
b.doh(new Milhouse());
}
} ///:~
```

As you'll see in the next chapter, it's far more common to override methods of the same name using exactly the same signature and return type as in the base class. It can be confusing otherwise (which is why C++ disallows it, to prevent you from making what is probably a mistake).

6.13 Choosing Composition vs. Inheritance

Both composition and inheritance allow you to place subobjects inside your new class. You might wonder about the difference between the two, and when to choose one over the other.

Composition is generally used when you want the features of an existing class inside your new class, but not its interface. That is, you embed an object so that you can use it to implement features of your new class, but the user of your new class sees the interface you've defined rather than the interface from the embedded object. For this effect, you embed private objects of existing classes inside your new class.

Sometimes it makes sense to allow the class user to directly access the composition of your new class; that is, to make the member objects public. The member objects use implementation hiding themselves, so this is a safe thing to do and when the user knows you're assembling a bunch of parts, it makes the interface easier to understand. A car object is a good example:

```
//: Car.java
// Composition with public objects
class Engine {
public void start() {}
public void rev() {}
public void stop() {}
}
class Wheel {
public void inflate(int psi) {}
}
class Window {
public void rollup() {}
public void rolldown() {}
}
class Door {
public Window window = new Window();
public void open() {}
public void close() {}
}
public class Car {
public Engine engine = new Engine();
public Wheel[] wheel = new Wheel[4];
public Door left = new Door(),
right = new Door(); // 2-door
Car() {
for(int i = 0; i < 4; i++)
wheel[i] = new Wheel();
}
public static void main(String[] args) {
Car car = new Car();
```

```
        car.left.window.rollup();
        car.wheel[0].inflate(72);
        }
        } ///:~
```

Because the composition of a car is part of the analysis of the problem (and not simply part of the underlying design), making the members public assists the client programmer's understanding of how to use the class and requires less code complexity for the creator of the class.

When you inherit, you take an existing class and make a special version of it. In general, this means that you're taking a general-purpose class and specializing it for a particular need. With a little thought, you'll see that it would make no sense to compose a car using a vehicle object - a car doesn't contain a vehicle, it is a vehicle. The is-a relationship is expressed with inheritance, and the has-a relationship is expressed with composition.

6.14 Incremental Development

One of the advantages of inheritance is that it supports incremental development by allowing you to introduce new code without causing bugs in existing code. This also isolates new bugs to the new code. By inheriting from an existing, functional class and adding data members and methods (and redefining existing methods), you leave the existing code - that someone else might still be using - untouched and unbugged. If a bug happens, you know that it's in your new code, which is much shorter and easier to read than if you had modified the body of existing code.

It's rather amazing how cleanly the classes are separated. You don't even need the source code for the methods in order to reuse the code. At most, you just import a package. (This is true for both inheritance and composition.)

It's important to realize that program development is an incremental process, just like human learning. You can do as much analysis as you want, but you still won't know all the answers when you set out on a project. You'll have much more success - and more immediate feedback - if you start out to "grow" your project as an organic, evolutionary creature, rather than constructing it all at once like a glass-box skyscraper.

Although inheritance for experimentation can be a useful technique, at some point after things stabilize you need to take a new look at your class hierarchy with an eye to collapsing it into a sensible structure. Remember that underneath it all, inheritance is meant to express a relationship that says "This new class is a type of that old class." Your program should not be concerned with pushing bits around, but instead with creating and manipulating objects of various types to express a model in the terms that come from the problem space.

6.15 Upcasting

The most important aspect of inheritance is not that it provides methods for the new class. It's the relationship expressed between the new class and the base class. This relationship can be summarized by saying "The new class is a type of the existing class."

This description is not just a fanciful way of explaining inheritance - it's supported directly by the language. As an example, consider a base class called Instrument that represents musical instruments and a derived class called Wind. Because inheritance means that all of the methods in the base class are also available in the derived class, any message you can send to the base class can also be sent to the derived class. If the Instrument class has a play( ) method, so will Wind instruments. This means we can accurately say that a Wind object is also a type of Instrument. The following example shows how the compiler supports this notion:

```
//: Wind.java
// Inheritance & upcasting
import java.util.*;
class Instrument {
public void play() {}
static void tune(Instrument i) {
// ...
i.play();
}
}
// Wind objects are instruments
// because they have the same interface:
class Wind extends Instrument {
public static void main(String[] args) {
Wind flute = new Wind();
Instrument.tune(flute); // Upcasting
}
} ///:~
```

What's interesting in this example is the tune( ) method, which accepts an Instrument handle. However, in Wind.main( ) the tune( ) method is called by giving it a Wind handle. Given that Java is particular about type checking, it seems strange that a method that accepts one type will readily accept another type, until you realize that a Wind object is also an Instrument object, and there's no method that tune( ) could call for an Instrument that isn't also in Wind. Inside tune( ), the code works for Instrument and anything derived from Instrument, and the act of converting a Wind handle into an Instrument handle is called upcasting.

6.15.1 Why "upcasting"?

The reason for the term is historical and is based on the way class inheritance diagrams have traditionally been drawn with the root at the top of the page, growing downward. (Of course, you can draw your diagrams any way you find helpful.) The inheritance diagram for Wind.java is then:

Casting from derived to base moves up on the inheritance diagram, so it's commonly referred to as upcasting. Upcasting is always safe because you're going from a more specific type to a more general type. That is, the derived class is a superset of the base class. It might contain more methods than the base class, but it must contain at least the methods in the base class. The only thing that can occur to the class interface during the upcast is that it can lose methods, not gain them. This is why the compiler allows upcasting without any explicit casts or other special notation.

6.16 Composition vs. Inheritance Revisited

In object-oriented programming, the most likely way that you'll create and use code is by simply packaging data and methods together into a class, and using objects of that class. Occasionally, you'll use existing classes to build new classes with composition. Even less frequently than that you'll use inheritance. So although inheritance gets a lot of emphasis while learning OOP, it doesn't mean that you should use it everywhere you possibly can. On the contrary, you should use it sparingly, only when it's clear that inheritance is useful. One of the clearest ways to determine whether you should use composition or inheritance is to ask whether you'll ever need to upcast from your new class to the base class. If you must upcast, then inheritance is necessary, but if you don't need to upcast, then you should look closely at whether you need inheritance. The next chapter (polymorphism) provides one of the most compelling reasons for upcasting, but if you remember to ask "Do I need to upcast?", you'll have a good tool for deciding between composition and inheritance.

6.17 Designing with Inheritance

Once you learn about polymorphism, it can seem that everything ought to be inherited because polymorphism is such a clever tool. This can burden your designs; in fact if you choose inheritance first when you're using an existing class to make a new class things can become needlessly complicated.

A better approach is to choose composition first, when it's not obvious which one you should use. Composition does not force a design into an inheritance hierarchy. But composition is also more flexible since it's possible to dynamically choose a type (and thus behavior) when using composition, whereas inheritance requires an exact type to be known at compile time. The following example illustrates this:

```
//: Transmogrify.java
// Dynamically changing the behavior of
// an object via composition.
interface Actor {
void act();
}
class HappyActor implements Actor {
public void act() {
System.out.println("HappyActor");
}
}
class SadActor implements Actor {
public void act() {
System.out.println("SadActor");
}
}
class Stage {
Actor a = new HappyActor();
void change() { a = new SadActor(); }
void go() { a.act(); }.
}
public class Transmogrify {
public static void main(String[] args) {
Stage s = new Stage();
s.go(); // Prints "HappyActor"
s.change();
s.go(); // Prints "SadActor"
}
} ///:~
```

A Stage object contains a handle to an Actor, which is initialized to a HappyActor object. This means go( ) produces a particular behavior. But since a handle can be re-bound to a different object at run time, a handle for a SadActor object can be substituted in a and then the behavior produced by go( ) changes. Thus you gain dynamic flexibility at run time. In contrast, you can't decide to inherit differently at run time; that must be completely determined at compile time.

A general guideline is "Use inheritance to express differences in behavior, and member variables to express variations in state." In the above example, both are used: two different classes are inherited to express the difference in the act( ) method, and Stage uses composition to allow its state to be changed. In this case, that change in state happens to produce a change in behavior.

6.18 Pure Inheritance Vs. Extension

When studying inheritance, it would seem that the cleanest way to create an inheritance hierarchy is to take the "pure" approach. That is, only methods that have been established in the base class or interface are to be overridden in the derived class, as seen in this diagram:

This can be termed a pure "is-a" relationship because the interface of a class establishes what it is. Inheritance guarantees that any derived class will have the interface of the base class and nothing less. If you follow the above diagram, derived classes will also have no more than the base class interface.

This can be thought of as pure substitution , because derived class objects can be perfectly substituted for the base class, and you never need to know any extra information about the subclasses when you're using them:

That is, the base class can receive any message you can send to the derived class because the two have exactly the same interface. All you need to do is upcast from the derived class and never look back to see what exact type of object you're dealing with. Everything is handled through polymorphism.

When you see it this way, it seems like a pure "is-a" relationship is the only sensible way to do things, and any other design indicates muddled thinking and is by definition broken. This too is a trap. As soon as you start thinking this way, you'll turn around and discover that extending the interface (which, unfortunately, the keyword extends seems to promote) is the perfect solution to a particular problem. This could be termed an "is-like-a" relationship because the derived class is like the base class - it has the same fundamental interface - but it has other features that require additional methods to implement:

While this is also a useful and sensible approach (depending on the situation) it has a drawback. The extended part of the interface in the derived class is not available from the base class, so once you upcast you can't call the new methods:

If you're not upcasting in this case, it won't bother you, but often you'll get into a situation in which you need to rediscover the exact type of the object so you can access the extended methods of that type. The following sections show how this is done.

6.19 Downcasting and Run-Time Type Identification

Since you lose the specific type information via an upcast (moving up the inheritance hierarchy), it makes sense that to retrieve the type information - that is, to move back down the inheritance hierarchy - you use a downcast. However, you know an upcast is always safe; the base class cannot have a bigger interface than the derived class, therefore every message you send through the base class interface is guaranteed to be accepted. But with a downcast, you don't really know that a shape (for example) is actually a circle. It could instead be a triangle or square or some other type.

To solve this problem there must be some way to guarantee that a downcast is correct, so you won't accidentally cast to the wrong type and then send a message that the object can't accept. This would be quite unsafe.

In some languages (like C++) you must perform a special operation in order to get a type-safe downcast, but in Java every cast is checked! So even though it looks like you're just performing an ordinary parenthesized cast, at run time this cast is checked to ensure that it is in fact the type you think it is. If it isn't, you get a ClassCastException. This act of checking types at run time is called run-time type identification (RTTI). The following example demonstrates the behavior of RTTI:

```
//: RTTI.java
// Downcasting & Run-Time Type
// Identification (RTTI)
import java.util.*;
class Useful {
public void f() {}
public void g() {}
}
class MoreUseful extends Useful {
public void f() {}
public void g() {}
public void u() {}
public void v() {}
public void w() {}
}
public class RTTI {
public static void main(String[] args) {
Useful[] x = {
new Useful(),
new MoreUseful()
};
x[0].f();
x[1].g();
// Compile-time: method not found in Useful:
//! x[1].u();
((MoreUseful)x[1]).u(); // Downcast/RTTI
((MoreUseful)x[0]).u(); // Exception thrown
}
} ///:~
```

As in the diagram, MoreUseful extends the interface of Useful. But since it's inherited, it can also be upcast to a Useful. You can see this happening in the initialization of the array x in main( ). Since both objects in the array are of class Useful, you can send the f( ) and g( ) methods to both, and if you try to call u( ) (which exists only in MoreUseful) you'll get a compile-time error message.

If you want to access the extended interface of a MoreUseful object, you can try to downcast. If it's the correct type, it will be successful. Otherwise, you'll get a ClassCastException. You don't need to write any special code for this exception, since it indicates a programmer error that could happen anywhere in a program.

There's more to RTTI than a simple cast. For example, there's a way to see what type you're dealing with before you try to downcast it. All of Chapter 11 is devoted to the study of different aspects of Java run-time type identification.

6.20 Deciding What SecurityManager Methods to Override

You may have to override several of SecurityManager's checkXXX() methods depending on which operations you want your security manager to impose restrictions on.

The first column in the following table are objects on which you can perform various operations. The second column lists the SecurityManager methods that approve the operations on the objects in the first column.

Operations On	Approved By
socketscheckAccept	(String host, int port)
check Connect	(String host, int port)
checkConnect	(String host, int port, Object executionContext)
checkListen	(int port)
threads checkAccess	(Thread thread)
checkAccess	(ThreadGroup threadgroup)
class loader check	CreateClassLoader()
file system checkDelete	(String filename)
checkLink	(String library)
checkRead	(FileDescriptor filedescriptor)
checkRead	(String filename)
checkRead	(String filename, Object executionContext)
checkWrite	(FileDescriptor filedescriptor)
checkWrite	(String filename)
system commands checkExec	(String command)
interpreter checkExit	(int status)
package checkPackageAccess	(String packageName)
checkPackageDefinition	(String packageName)
properties	checkPropertiesAccess()
checkPropertyAccess	(String key)
checkPropertyAccess	(String key, String def)
networking	checkSetFactory()
windows	checkTopLevelWindow(Object window)

Depending on your security policy, you can override some or all of these methods. For example, suppose you are writing a Web browser or applet viewer and want to disallow applets from using sockets altogether. To do this you override the four methods that affect socket access.

Many of the checkXXX() methods are called in multiple situations. You saw this when writing the PasswordSecurityManager in Writing a Security Manager—the checkAccess(ThreadGroup g) method is invoked when you create a ThreadGroup, set its daemon status, stop it, and so on. When overriding a checkXXX() method make sure that you understand all the situations in which it can be invoked.

The default implementation provided by the SecurityManager class for all checkXXX() methods is:

```
public void checkXXX(. . .) {
throw new SecurityException();
}
```

Most security policies that you want to implement will likely be more selective than disallowing everything! So you may find that you have to override all SecurityManager's checkXXX() methods.

6.21 Writing Final Classes and Methods

You can declare that your class is final, that is, that your class cannot be subclassed. There are (at least) two reasons why you might want to do this:

- To increase system security by preventing system subversion, and
- For reasons of good object-oriented design.

6.21.1 Security:

One mechanism that hackers use to subvert systems is to create a subclass of a class and then substitute their class for the original. The subclass looks and feels like the original class but does vastly different things, possibly causing damage or getting into private information. To prevent this kind of subversion, you can declare your class to be final and thereby prevent any subclasses from being created. The String class in the java.lang package is a final class for just this reason. This class is so vital to the operation of the compiler and the interpreter that the Java system must guarantee that whenever a method or object uses a String it gets exactly a java.lang.String and not some other string. This ensures that all strings have no strange, inconsistent, undesirable, or unpredictable properties. If you try to compile a subclass of a final class, the compiler prints an error message and refuses to compile your program. In addition, the bytecode verifier ensures that the subversion is not taking place at the bytecode level. It does this by checking to make sure that a class is not a subclass of a final class.

6.21.2 Design:

You may also wish to declare a class as final for object-oriented design reasons. You may think that your class is "perfect" or that, conceptually, your class should have no subclasses. To specify that your class is final, use the keyword final before the class keyword in your class declaration.

For example, if you wanted to declare your (perfect) ChessAlgorithm class as final, its declaration should look like this:

```
final class ChessAlgorithm {
. . .
}
```

Any subsequent attempts to subclass ChessAlgorithm will result in a compiler error such as the following:

Chess.java:6: Can't subclass final classes: class ChessAlgorithm

```
class BetterChessAlgorithm extends ChessAlgorithm {
^
1 error
```

6.22 Final Methods

Does creating a final class seem heavy-handed for your needs? Do you really just want to protect some of your class's methods from being overridden? You can use the final keyword in a method declaration to indicate to the compiler that the method cannot be overridden by subclasses. As just shown, the Object class does this; some of its methods are final and some are not. You might wish to make a method final if it has an implementation that should not be changed and it is critical to the consistent state of the object. For example, instead of making your ChessAlgorithm class final, you might want instead to make the nextMove method final:

```
class ChessAlgorithm {
```

```
. . .
final void nextMove(ChessPiece pieceMoved,
BoardLocation newLocation)
{
...
}
. . .
}
```

6.22.1 Being a Descendent of Object

The Object class sits at the top of the class hierarchy tree in the Java platform. Every class in the Java system is a descendent, direct or indirect, of the Object class. This class defines the basic state and behavior that all objects must have, such as the ability to compare oneself to another object, to convert to a string, to wait on a condition variable, to notify other objects that a condition variable has changed, and to return the class of the object. Your classes may want to override the following Object methods. The equals/hashCode are listed together as they must be overridden together.

```
clone
equals/hashCode
finalize
toString
Your class cannot override these Object methods (they are final):
getClass
notify
notifyAll
wait
The clone Method
```

You use the clone method to create an object from an existing object. To create a clone, you write:

```
aCloneableObject.clone();
```

Object's implementation of this method checks to see if the object on which clone was invoked implements the Cloneable interface, and throws a CloneNotSupportedException if it does not. Note that Object itself does not implement Cloneable, so subclasses of Object that don't explicitly implement the interface are not cloneable. If the object on which clone was invoked does implement the Cloneable interface, Object's implementation of the clone method creates an object of the same type as the original object and initializes the new object's member variables to have the same values as the original object's corresponding member variables.

The simplest way to make your class cloneable then, is to add implements Cloneable to your class's declaration. For some classes the default behavior of Object's clone method works just fine. Other classes need to override clone to get correct behavior. Consider the Stack class, which contains a member variable that refers to a Vector. If Stack relies on Object's implementation of clone, then the original stack and its clone will refer to the same vector. Changing one stack will change the other, which is undesirable behavior.

Here then is an appropriate implementation of clone for our Stack class, which clones the vector to ensure that the original stack and its clone do not refer to the same vector (changes are indicated with a change in font):

```
public class Stack implements Cloneable
{
```

```
private Vector items;
// code for Stack's methods and constructor not shown
protected Object clone() {
try {
Stack s = (Stack)super.clone();   // clone the stack
s.items = (Vector)items.clone(); // clone the vector
return s;                        // return the clone
} catch (CloneNotSupportedException e) {
// this shouldn't happen because Stack is Cloneable
throw new InternalError();
}
}
}
```

The implementation for Stack's clone method is relatively simple: It calls super.clone, which Stack inherits from Object and which creates and initializes an instance of the correct type. At this point, the original stack and its clone refer to the same vector. Next the method clones the vector.

Be careful: clone should never use new to create the clone and should not call constructors. Instead, the method should call super.clone, which creates an object of the correct type and allows the hierarchy of superclasses to perform the copying necessary to get a proper clone.

6.22.2 The equals and HashCode Methods

You must override the equals and hashCode methods together.

The equals method compares two objects for equality and returns true if they are equal. The equals method provided in the Object class uses the identity function to determine if objects are equal (if the objects compared are the exact same object the method returns true).

However, for some classes, two distinct objects of that type might be considered equal if they contain the same information. Consider this code that tests two Integers, one and anotherOne, for equality:

```
Integer one = new Integer(1), anotherOne = new Integer(1);
if (one.equals(anotherOne))
System.out.println("objects are equal");
```

This program displays objects are equal even though one and anotherOne reference two distinct objects. They are considered equal because the objects compared contain the same integer value. Your classes should only override the equals method if the identity function is not appropriate for your class. If you override equals, then override hashCode as well.

The value returned by hashCode is an int that maps an object into a bucket in a hash table. An object must always produce the same hash code. However, objects can share hash codes (they aren't necessarily unique). Writing a "correct" hashing function is easy—always return the same hash code for the same object. Writing an "efficient" hashing function, one that provides a sufficient distribution of objects over the buckets, is difficult and is out of the scope of the tutorial. Even so, the hashing function for some classes is relatively obvious. For example, an obvious hash code for an Integer object is its integer value. For an example of a class that overrides the equals and hashCode methods, see the BingoBall class in BINGO!.

6.22.3 The finalize Method

The Object class provides a method, finalize, that cleans up an object before it is garbage collected. This method's role during garbage collection was discussed previously in Cleaning Up Unused Objects. The finalize method is called automatically by the system and most classes you write do not need to override it. So you can generally ignore this method.

The toString Method

Object's toString method returns a String representation of the object. You can use toString along with System.out.println to display a text representation of an object, such as the current thread:

System.out.println(Thread.currentThread().toString());

The String representation for an object depends entirely on the object. The String representation of an Integer object is the integer value displayed as text. The String representation of a Thread object contains various attributes about the thread, such as its name and priority. For example, the previous line of code displays the following output:

Thread[main,5,main]

The toString method is very useful for debugging. It behooves you to override this method in all your classes.

6.22.4 The GetClass Method

The getClass method is a final method that returns a runtime representation of the class of an object. This method returns a Class object. Once you have a Class object you can query it for various information about the class, such as its name, its superclass, and the names of the interfaces that it implements. The following method gets and displays the class name of an object:

```
void PrintClassName(Object obj) {
System.out.println("The Object's class is " +
obj.getClass().getName());
}
```

One handy use of a Class object is to create a new instance of a class without knowing what the class is at compile time. The following sample method creates a new instance of the same class as obj, which can be any class that inherits from Object (which means that it could be any class):

```
Object createNewInstanceOf(Object obj) {
return obj.getClass().newInstance();
}
```

Note: . Take particular note of the section titled Synchronizing Threads.

7 Packages and Interfaces

7.1 What Is an Interface?

A Java interface defines a set of methods but does not implement them. A class that implements the interface agrees to implement all of the methods defined in the interface, thereby agreeing to certain behavior.

Definition: An interface is a named collection of method definitions (without implementations). An interface can also include constant declarations.

Interfaces are best understood through examples, so let's look at a concrete example of an interface and two classes that use it to interact. Then we'll talk more about interfaces in the abstract and clear up some common confusion.

An interface is an idea taken from Objective C. It describes the public methods that a class implements and their calling conventions without saying anything about how those methods are implemented. It is the responsibility of each class that implements an interface to provide code to handle the cases where the methods of the interface are called.

For example suppose you're writing an inventory database. The inventory may include many different items of many different types and classes. However each item in the warehouse needs to be able to tell you its price. Normally you would implement this by having each class extend a common superclass. However that's not always convenient. Instead you can declare an interface called Price with a price() method like this:

```
public interface Price {
public float price();
}
```

Any class which implements the Price interface must contain a method with the signature public float price(). The code of the price() method is included separately in each separate class which implements Price, not in the Price interface itself.

Different classes in your warehouse can each implement the Price interface like this:

```
public class Monopoly extends BoardGame implements Price {
// other methods
public float price() {
return 14.95;
}
}
```

When other code is passed an object, it can test whether the object implements Price with the instanceof operator. For example,

```
if (o instanceof Price) System.out.println("Subtotal is " + o.price());
```

In fact, interfaces can be used to tag objects. The java.rmi.Remote interface declares no methods. Its sole purpose is to indicate that an object is a remote object. In general, sub-interfaces of java.rmi.Remote will declare remote methods, however. For example,

```
public interface Hello extends java.rmi.Remote {
public String sayHello();
}
public class HelloImpl extends UnicastRemoteServer implements Hello
{
public String sayHello() {
return "Hello";
}
}
```

Interfaces are the next level of abstraction. An interface is like a class with nothing but abstract methods and final, static fields. All methods and fields of an interface must be public.

However, unlike a class, an interface can be added to a class that is already a subclass of another class. Furthermore an interface can apply to members of many different classes. For instance you can define an Import interface with the single method calculateTariff().

```
public interface Import {
public double calculateTariff();
}
```

You might want to use this interface on many different classes, cars among them but also for clothes, food, electronics and more. It would be inconvenient to make all these objects derive from a single class. Furthermore, each different type of item is likely to have a different means of calculating the tariff. Therefore you define an Import interface and declare that each class implements Import.

The syntax is simple. Import is declared public so that it can be accessed from any class. It is also possible to declare that an interface is protected so that it can only be implemented by classes in a particular package. However this is very unusual. Almost all interfaces will be public. No interface may be private because the whole purpose of an Interface is to be inherited by other classes.

The interface keyword takes the place of the class keyword. Line 3 looks like a classic method definition. It's public (as it must be). It's abstract, also as it must be. And it returns a double. The method's name is calculateTariff() and it takes no arguments. The difference between this and a method in a class is that there is no method body. That remains to be created in each class that implements the interface.

You can declare many different methods in an interface. These methods may be overloaded.

An interface can also have fields, but if so they must be final and static (in other words constants).

Example 7.1 : AlarmClock and Sleeper

This example is fairly simple, but it shows you how to create and use an interface. It also gives you some insight as to why you need them and how to decide when to use an interface versus when to use a class or an abstract class.

The AlarmClock class is a service provider— it notifies objects after a certain amount of time has elapsed.

To get on AlarmClock's list of "sleepers," an object must do two things:

- Ask the alarm clock to wake it up.

- Implement the wakeUp method.

To satisfy the first requirement, an object calls AlarmClock's letMeSleepFor method, which is implemented like this:

```
public synchronized boolean letMeSleepFor(Sleeper theSleeper,
                                          long time) {
int index = findNextSlot();
if (index == NOROOM) {
   return false;
} else {
      sleepers[index] = theSleeper;
      sleepFor[index] = time;
      new AlarmThread(index).start();
      return true;
   }
}
```

If AlarmClock has space, then it registers the sleeper, starts a new AlarmThread for it, and returns true. After the specified amount of time has elapsed the AlarmClock will call theSleeper's wakeUp method.

This leads to the second requirement. An object that wants to use AlarmClock must implement the wakeUp method (so that AlarmClock can call it to notify the object after the time has elapsed). But how is this enforced? It's enforced through the data type of the object being registered.

The first argument to the letMeSleepFor method is the object that wants to get woken up. The data type of this argument is Sleeper, which is the name of this interface:

```
public interface Sleeper {
    public void wakeUp();
    public long ONE_SECOND = 1000; // in milliseconds
}
```

The Sleeper interface defines the wakeUp method but does not implement it. It also defines two useful constants. Classes that implement this interface "inherit" the constants and must implement wakeUp.

Any object that is a Sleeper (and can therefore be passed into letMeSleepFor) implements this interface. This means it implements all of the methods defined by the interface. Thus a Sleeper object implements the wakeUp method, thereby satisfying AlarmClock's second requirement.

For example, check out the following small class that implements the Sleeper interface. The GUIClock class is an applet that displays the current time and uses an AlarmClock object to wake it up every second so that it can update its display:

```
class GUIClock extends Applet implements Sleeper {
    . . .
    public void wakeUp() {
        repaint();
        clock.letMeSleepFor(this, ONE_SECOND);
    }
}
```

Here's the GUIClock applet running:

Fig.7.1

Note: Because some old browsers don't support 1.1, the above applet is a 1.0 version (here is the 1.0 code; here's the 1.1 code). To run the 1.1 version of the applet, go to example-1dot1/GUIClock.html. For more information about running applets, refer to About Our Examples.

Now that you've seen an interface in action, we'll answer some of the inevitable questions.

Why Can't I Just Use an Abstract Class?

At this point, many programmers wonder how an interface differs from an abstract class. An interface is simply a list of unimplemented, and therefore abstract, methods. Wouldn't the following Sleeper class do the same thing as the Sleeper interface?

```
abstract class Sleeper {
    public abstract void wakeUp();
}
```

No. The two are not equivalent. If Sleeper is an abstract class, then all objects that wish to use AlarmClock must be instances of a class inherited from Sleeper. However, many objects that wish to use AlarmClock already have a superclass. For example, the GUIClock is an Applet; it must be an applet to run inside a browser. But Java doesn't support multiple inheritance. So GUIClock can't be both a Sleeper and an Applet. Hence, you use an interface instead.

This is the practical explanation of the problem. The conceptual explanation is this: AlarmClock should not force a class relationship on its users. It doesn't matter what their class is. It simply matters that they implement a specific method.

7.2 Interfaces Provide for Multiple Inheritance

Often interfaces are touted as an alternative to multiple class inheritance. While interfaces may solve similar problems, interface and multiple class inheritance are quite different animals, in particular:

- A class inherits only constants from an interface.
- A class cannot inherit method implementations from an interface.
- The interface hierarchy is independent of the class hierarchy. * Classes that implement the same interface may or may not be related through the class hierarchy. This is not true for multiple inheritance.

Yet, Java does allow multiple interface inheritance. That is, an interface can have multiple superinterfaces.

So Tell Me, What Can I Use Interfaces For?

You use an interface to define a protocol of behavior that can be implemented by any class anywhere in the class hierarchy. Interfaces are useful for the following:

- Capturing similarities between unrelated classes without artificially forcing a class relationship
- Declaring methods that one or more classes are expected to implement
- Revealing an object's programming interface without revealing its class. (Objects such as these

are called anonymous objects and can be useful when shipping a package of classes to other developers.)

7.3 Defining an Interface

The following figure shows that an interface definition has two components: the interface declaration and the interface body. The interface declaration declares various attributes about the interface such as its name and whether it extends another interface. The interface body contains the constant and method declarations within that interface.

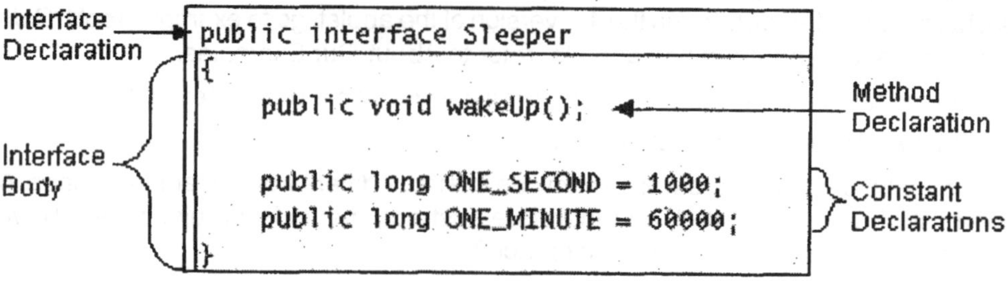

Fig. 7.2

7.4 The Interface Declaration

The declaration for the Sleeper interface uses the two required elements of an interface declaration—the interface keyword and the name of the interface—plus the public access modifier :

```
public interface Sleeper {
    . . .
}
```

An interface declaration can have one other component: the public access specifier and a list of superinterfaces. The full interface declaration looks like this figure:

`public`	Makes this interface public.
`interface InterfaceName`	Class cannot be instantiated.
`Extends SuperInterfaces`	This interface's superinterfaces.

```
{
    InterfaceBody
}
```

Fig. 7.3

The public access specifier indicates that the interface can be used by any class in any package. If you do not specify that your interface is public, then your interface will be accessible only to classes that are defined in the same package as the interface.

An interface can extend other interfaces just as a class can extend or subclass another class. However, while a class can extend only one other class, an interface can extend any number of interfaces. The list of superinterfaces is a comma-separated list of all of the interfaces extended by the new interface. An interface inherits all constants and methods from its superinterfaces, unless the interface hides a constant with another of the same name or redeclares a method with a new method declaration.

7.5 The Interface Body

The interface body contains method declarations for all of the methods included in the interface. Here's the body of the Sleeper interface:

```
public interface Sleeper {
    public void wakeUp();
    public long ONE_SECOND = 1000;
}
```

The method declaration for wakeUp is followed by a semicolon (;) because an interface does not provide implementations for the methods declared within it. All methods declared in an interface are implicitly public and abstract. The use of these modifiers on a method declaration in an interface is discouraged as a matter of style.

An interface can contain constant declarations in addition to method declarations. The Sleeper interface declares two constants that are useful arguments to letMeSleepFor. All constant values defined in an interface are implicitly public, static, and final. The use of these modifiers on a constant declaration in an interface is discouraged as a matter of style.

Any class can use an interface's constants from the name of the interface, like this:

```
Sleeper.ONE_SECOND
```

Classes that implement an interface can treat the constants as though they were inherited. This is why GUIClock can use ONE_SECOND directly when calling letMeSleepFor:

```
public class GUIClock extends Applet implements Sleeper {
    . . .
public void wakeUp() {
        repaint();
        clock.letMeSleepFor(this, ONE_SECOND);
    }
}
```

Member declarations in an interface disallow the use of some declaration modifiers; you may not use transient, volatile, or synchronized in a member declaration in an interface. Also, you may not use the private and protected specifiers when declaring members of an interface.

Note: Previous releases of the Java platform allowed you to use the abstract modifier on interface declarations and on method declarations within interfaces. However this is unnecessary, since interfaces and their methods are implicitly abstract. You should no longer be using abstract in your interface declarations or in your method declarations within interfaces.

7.6 Implementing Interfaces

To actually use this interface you create a class that includes a public double calculateTariff() method and declare that the class implements Import. For instance here's one such class:

```
public class Car extends MotorVehicle implements Import {
int numWheels = 4;
public double calculateTariff() {
return this.price * 0.1;
}
}
```

One of the advantages of interfaces over classes is that a single class may implement more than one interface. For example, this Car class implements three interfaces: Import, Serializable, and Cloneable

```
import java.io.*;
public class Car extends MotorVehicle
implements Import, Serializable, Cloneable {
int numWheels = 4;
public double calculateTariff() {
return this.price * 0.1;
}
}
```

Serializable and Cloneable are marker interfaces from the class library that only add a type to a class, but do not declare any additional methods.

7.7 Implementing the Sleeper Interface

An interface defines a protocol of behavior. A class that implements an interface adheres to the protocol defined by that interface. To declare a class that implements an interface, include an implements clause in the class declaration. Your class can implement more than one interface (the Java platform supports multiple interface inheritance), so the implements keyword is followed by a comma-separated list of the interfaces implemented by the class.

By Convention: The implements clause follows the extends clause, if it exists.

The GUIClock class implements the Sleeper interface, which contains a single method declaration for the wakeUp method. Thuse GUIClock must implement the wakeUp method:

```
public class GUIClock extends Applet implements Sleeper {
    . . .
    public void wakeUp() {
        // update the display
    }
}
```

Remember that when a class implements an interface, it is essentially signing a contract. The class must provide method implementations for all of the methods declared in the interface and its superinterfaces. Or, the class must be declared abstract. The method signature (the name and the number and type of arguments) for the method in the class must match the method signature as it appears in the interface.

7.8 Using an Interface as a Type

When you define a new interface, you are in essence defining a new reference data type. You can use interface names anywhere you can use any other data type name.

For example, the AlarmClock class uses the Sleeper type in two places:

- To declare an array of Sleepers (shown in bold):

```
private Sleeper[] sleepers = new Sleeper[MAX_CAPACITY];
```

- As an argument to letMeSleepFor (shown in bold):

```
private boolean letMeSleepFor(Sleeper theSleeper, int time)
{
. . .
```

```
}
```

7.9 Warning! Interfaces Cannot Grow

Suppose you want to add some functionality to AlarmClock for its 2.0 release. For example, GUIClock needs to update its display every second so that it makes continual requests to be woken up. Really, GUIClock just wants AlarmClock to beep at it every second. It would be preferable to register a single request with AlarmClock, for two reasons:

- It's more efficient because it involves fewer method calls.
  GUIClock wouldn't have to maintain its own AlarmClock because it wouldn't risk losing its bed.
- AlarmClock needs to differentiate such "beeps" from an actual wake up call. So now the Sleeper interface must include a beep method:

```
public interface Sleeper {
    public void wakeUp();
    public void beep();
    public long ONE_SECOND = 1000;
}
```

However, if you make this change to Sleeper, all classes that implement the old Sleeper will break because they don't implement the interface anymore! Programmers relying on this interface will protest loudly.

Try to anticipate all uses for your interface up front and specify it completely from the beginning. Given that this is often impossible, you may need either to create more interfaces later or to break your customer's code.

7.10 Implementing the Cloneable Interface

The java.lang.Object class contains a clone() method that returns a bitwise copy of the current object.

protected native Object clone() throws CloneNotSupportedException

Not all objects are cloneable. It particular only instances of classes that implement the Cloneable interface can be cloned. Trying to clone an object that does not implement the Cloneable interface throws a CloneNotSupportedException.

For example, to make the Car class cloneable, you simply declare that it implements the Cloneable interface. Since this is only a marker interface, you do not need to add any methods to the class.

```
public class Car extends MotorVehicle implements Cloneable {
// ...
}
```

For example

```
Website w1=new Website("Yahoo", "http://www.yahoo.com", "Useful");
Website w2 = w1.clone();
```

Most classes in the class library do not implement Cloneable so their instances are not cloneable.

Most of the time, clones are shallow copies. In other words if the object being cloned contains a reference to another object A, then the clone contains a reference to the same object A, not to a clone of A. If this isn't the behavior you want, you can override clone() yourself.

You may also override clone() if you want to make a subclass uncloneable, when one of its superclasses does implement Cloneable. In this case simply use a clone() method that throws a

CloneNotSupportedException. For example,

```
public Object clone() throws CloneNotSupportedException {
throw new CloneNotSupportedException("Can't clone a SlowCar");
// never get here
return this;
}
```

You may also want to override clone() to make it public instead of protected. In this case, you can simply fall back on the superclass implementation. For example,

```
public Object clone() throws CloneNotSupportedException {
return super.clone();
}
```

7.11 Interface and Implementation

Access control is often referred to as implementation hiding. Wrapping data and methods within classes (combined with implementation hiding this is often called encapsulation) produces a data type with characteristics and behaviors, but access control puts boundaries within that data type for two important reasons. The first is to establish what the client programmers can and can't use. You can build your internal mechanisms into the structure without worrying that the client programmers will think it's part of the interface that they should be using.

This feeds directly into the second reason, which is to separate the interface from the implementation. If the structure is used in a set of programs, but users can't do anything but send messages to the public interface, then you can change anything that's not public (e.g. "friendly," protected, or private) without requiring modifications to their code.

We're now in the world of object-oriented programming, where a class is actually describing "a class of objects," as you would describe a class of fishes or a class of birds. Any object belonging to this class will share these characteristics and behaviors. The class is a description of the way all objects of this type will look and act.

In the original OOP language, Simula-67, the keyword class was used to describe a new data type. The same keyword has been used for most object-oriented languages. This is the focal point of the whole language: the creation of new data types that are more than just boxes containing data and methods.

The class is the fundamental OOP concept in Java. It is one of the keywords that will not be set in bold in this book - it becomes annoying with a word repeated as often as "class."

For clarity, you might prefer a style of creating classes that puts the public members at the beginning, followed by the protected, friendly and private members. The advantage is that the user of the class can then read down from the top and see first what's important to them (the public members, because they can be accessed outside the file) and stop reading when they encounter the non-public members, which are part of the internal implementation. However, with the comment documentation supported by javadoc (described in Chapter 2) the issue of code readability by the client programmer becomes less important.

```
public class X {
public void pub1( ) { /* . . . */ }
public void pub2( ) { /* . . . */ }
public void pub3( ) { /* . . . */ }
private void priv1( ) { /* . . . */ }
```

```
    private void priv2( ) { /* . . . */ }
    private void priv3( ) { /* . . . */ }
    private int i;   // . . . }
```

This will make it only partially easier to read because the interface and implementation are still mixed together. That is, you still see the source code - the implementation - because it's right there in the class. Displaying the interface to the consumer of a class is really the job of the class browser , a tool whose job is to look at all the available classes and show you what you can do with them (i.e. what members are available) in a useful fashion. By the time you read this, good browsers should be an expected part of any good Java development tool.

7.12 Interface Keyword

The interface keyword takes the abstract concept one step further. You could think of it as a "pure" abstract class. It allows the creator to establish the form for a class: method names, argument lists and return types, but no method bodies. An interface can also contain data members of primitive types, but these are implicitly static and final. An interface provides only a form, but no implementation.

An interface says: "This is what all classes that implement this particular interface will look like." Thus, any code that uses a particular interface knows what methods might be called for that interface, and that's all. So the interface is used to establish a "protocol" between classes. (Some object-oriented programming languages have a keyword called protocol to do the same thing.)

To create an interface, use the interface keyword instead of the class keyword. Like a class, you can add the public keyword before the interface keyword (but only if that interface is defined in a file of the same name) or leave it off to give "friendly" status.

To make a class that conforms to a particular interface (or group of interfaces) use the implements keyword. You're saying "The interface is what it looks like and here's how it works." Other than that, it bears a strong resemblance to inheritance. The diagram for the instrument example shows this:

Once you've implemented an interface, that implementation becomes an ordinary class that can be extended in the regular way.

You can choose to explicitly declare the method declarations in an interface as public. But they are public even if you don't say it. So when you implement an interface, the methods from the interface must be defined as public. Otherwise they would default to "friendly" and you'd be restricting the accessibility of a method during inheritance, which is not allowed by the Java compiler.

You can see this in the modified version of the Instrument example. Note that every method in the interface is strictly a declaration, which is the only thing the compiler allows. In addition, none of the methods in Instrument5 are declared as public, but they're automatically public anyway:

```
//: Music5.java
// Interfaces
import java.util.*;

interface Instrument5 {
    // Compile-time constant:
    int i = 5; // static & final
    // Cannot have method definitions:
    void play(); // Automatically public
    String what();
    void adjust();
```

```
}
class Wind5 implements Instrument5 {
    public void play() {
    System.out.println("Wind5.play()");
}
public String what() { return "Wind5"; }
public void adjust() {}
}
class Percussion5 implements Instrument5 {
    public void play() {
    System.out.println("Percussion5.play()");
}
    public String what() { return "Percussion5"; }
    public void adjust() {}
}
class Stringed5 implements Instrument5 {
    public void play() {
    System.out.println("Stringed5.play()");
}
public String what() { return "Stringed5"; }
public void adjust() {}
}
class Brass5 extends Wind5 {
    public void play() {
    System.out.println("Brass5.play()");
}
public void adjust() {
    System.out.println("Brass5.adjust()");
}
}
class Woodwind5 extends Wind5 {
    public void play() {
    System.out.println("Woodwind5.play()");
}
public String what() { return "Woodwind5"; }
}

public class Music5 {
    // Doesn't care about type, so new types
    // added to the system still work right:
    static void tune(Instrument5 i) {
// ...
i.play();
}
static void tuneAll(Instrument5[] e) {
    for(int i = 0; i < e.length; i++)
    tune(e[i]);
}
```

```
public static void main(String[] args) {
Instrument5[] orchestra = new Instrument5[5];
int i = 0;
// Upcasting during addition to the array:
orchestra[i++] = new Wind5();
orchestra[i++] = new Percussion5();
orchestra[i++] = new Stringed5();
orchestra[i++] = new Brass5();
orchestra[i++] = new Woodwind5();
tuneAll(orchestra);
}
} ///:~
```

The rest of the code works the same. It doesn't matter if you are upcasting to a "regular" class called Instrument5, an abstract class called Instrument5, or to an interface called Instrument5. The behavior is the same. In fact, you can see in the tune( ) method that there isn't any evidence about whether Instrument5 is a "regular" class, an abstract class or an interface. This is the intent: Each approach gives the programmer different control over the way objects are created and used.

7.13 "Multiple inheritance" in Java

The interface isn't simply a "more pure" form of abstract class. It has a higher purpose than that. Because an interface has no implementation at all - that is, there is no storage associated with an interface - there's nothing to prevent many interfaces from being combined. This is valuable because there are times when you need to say "An x is an a and a b and a c." In C++, this act of combining multiple class interfaces is called multiple inheritance , and it carries some rather sticky baggage because each class can have an implementation. In Java, you can perform the same act, but only one of the classes can have an implementation, so the problems seen in C++ do not occur with Java when combining multiple interfaces:

In a derived class, you aren't forced to have a base class that is either an abstract or "concrete" (one with no abstract methods). If you do inherit from a non- interface, you can inherit from only one. All the rest of the base elements must be interfaces. You place all the interface names after the implements keyword and separate them with commas. You can have as many interfaces as you want and each one becomes an independent type that you can upcast to. The following example shows a concrete class combined with several interfaces to produce a new class:

```
//: Adventure.java
// Multiple interfaces
import java.util.*;

interface CanFight {
    void fight();
}
interface CanSwim {
    void swim();
}
interface CanFly {
    void fly();
}
class ActionCharacter {
```

```
    public void fight() {}
}
class Hero extends ActionCharacter
    implements CanFight, CanSwim, CanFly {
    public void swim() {}
    public void fly() {}
}
public class Adventure {
    static void t(CanFight x) { x.fight(); }
    static void u(CanSwim x) { x.swim(); }
    static void v(CanFly x) { x.fly(); }
    static void w(ActionCharacter x) { x.fight(); }
    public static void main(String[] args) {
        Hero i = new Hero();
        t(i); // Treat it as a CanFight
        u(i); // Treat it as a CanSwim
        v(i); // Treat it as a CanFly
        w(i); // Treat it as an ActionCharacter
    }
} ///:~
```

You can see that Hero combines the concrete class ActionCharacter with the interfaces CanFight, CanSwim, and CanFly. When you combine a concrete class with interfaces this way, the concrete class must come first, then the interfaces. (The compiler gives an error otherwise.)

Note that the signature for fight( ) is the same in the interface CanFight and the class ActionCharacter, and that fight( ) is not provided with a definition in Hero. The rule for an interface is that you can inherit from it (as you will see shortly), but then you've got another interface. If you want to create an object of the new type, it must be a class with all definitions provided. Even though Hero does not explicitly provide a definition for fight( ), the definition comes along with ActionCharacter so it is automatically provided and it's possible to create objects of Hero.

In class Adventure, you can see that there are four methods that take as arguments the various interfaces and the concrete class. When a Hero object is created, it can be passed to any of these methods, which means it is being upcast to each interface in turn. Because of the way interfaces are designed in Java, this works without a hitch and without any particular effort on the part of the programmer.

Keep in mind that the core reason for interfaces is shown in the above example: to be able to upcast to more than one base type. However, a second reason for using interfaces is the same as using an abstract base class: to prevent the client programmer from making an object of this class and to establish that it is only an interface. This brings up a question: Should you use an interface or an abstract class? An interface gives you the benefits of an abstract class and the benefits of an interface, so if it's possible to create your base class without any method definitions or member variables you should always prefer interfaces to abstract classes. In fact, if you know something is going to be a base class, your first choice should be to make it an interface, and only if you're forced to have method definitions or member variables should you change to an abstract class.

7.14 Extending an Interface with Inheritance

You can easily add new method declarations to an interface using inheritance, and you can also combine several interfaces into a new interface with inheritance. In both cases you get a new interface, as seen in this example:

```
//: HorrorShow.java
// Extending an interface with inheritance
interface Monster {
    void menace();
}
interface DangerousMonster extends Monster {
    void destroy();
}
interface Lethal {
    void kill();
}
class DragonZilla implements DangerousMonster {
    public void menace() {}
    public void destroy() {}
}
interface Vampire
    extends DangerousMonster, Lethal {
    void drinkBlood();
}
class HorrorShow {
    static void u(Monster b) { b.menace(); }
    static void v(DangerousMonster d) {
        d.menace();
        d.destroy();
}
public static void main(String[] args) {
        DragonZilla if2 = new DragonZilla();
        u(if2);
        v(if2);
    }
} ///:~
```

DangerousMonster is a simple extension to Monster that produces a new interface. This is implemented in DragonZilla.

The syntax used in Vampire works only when inheriting interfaces. Normally, you can use extends with only a single class, but since an interface can be made from multiple other interfaces, extends can refer to multiple base interfaces when building a new interface. As you can see, the interface names are simply separated with commas.

7.15 Grouping Constants

Because any fields you put into an interface are automatically static and final, the interface is a convenient tool for creating groups of constant values, much as you would with an enum in C or C++. **For example:**

```
//: Months.java
// Using interfaces to create groups of constants
package c07;
```

```
public interface Months {
    int
        JANUARY = 1, FEBRUARY = 2, MARCH = 3,
        APRIL = 4, MAY = 5, JUNE = 6, JULY = 7,
        AUGUST = 8, SEPTEMBER = 9, OCTOBER = 10,
        NOVEMBER = 11, DECEMBER = 12;
} ///:~
```

Notice the Java style of using all uppercase letters (with underscores to separate multiple words in a single identifier) for static final primitives that have constant initializers - that is, for compile-time constants.

The fields in an interface are automatically public, so it's unnecessary to specify that.

Now you can use the constants from outside the package by importing c07.* or c07.Months just as you would with any other package, and referencing the values with expressions like Months.JANUARY. Of course, what you get is just an int so there isn't the extra type safety that C++'s enum has, but this (commonly-used) technique is certainly an improvement over hard-coding numbers into your programs. (This is often referred to as using "magic numbers" and it produces very difficult-to-maintain code.)

If you do want extra type safety, you can build a class like this: [28]

```
//: Month2.java
// A more robust enumeration system
package c07;
public final class Month2 {
    private String name;
    private Month2(String nm) { name = nm; }
    public String toString() { return name; }
    public final static Month2
        JAN = new Month2("January"),
        FEB = new Month2("February"),
        MAR = new Month2("March"),
        APR = new Month2("April"),
        MAY = new Month2("May"),
        JUN = new Month2("June"),
        JUL = new Month2("July"),
        AUG = new Month2("August"),
        SEP = new Month2("September"),
        OCT = new Month2("October"),
        NOV = new Month2("November"),
        DEC = new Month2("December");
    public final static Month2[] month =  {
    JAN, JAN, FEB, MAR, APR, MAY, JUN,
    JUL, AUG, SEP, OCT, NOV, DEC
};
public static void main(String[] args) {
    Month2 m = Month2.JAN;
    System.out.println(m);
    m = Month2.month[12];
```

```
System.out.println(m);
System.out.println(m == Month2.DEC);
System.out.println(m.equals(Month2.DEC));
}
} ///:~
```

The class is called Month2 since there's already a Month in the standard Java library. It's a final class with a private constructor so no one can inherit from it or make any instances of it. The only instances are the final static ones created in the class itself: JAN, FEB, MAR, etc. These objects are also used in the array month, which lets you choose months by number instead of by name. (Notice the extra JAN in the array to provide an offset by one, so that December is month 12.) In main( ) you can see the type safety: m is a Month2 object so it can be assigned only to a Month2. The previous example Months.java provided only int values, so an int variable intended to represent a month could actually be given any integer value, which wasn't too safe.

This approach also allows you to use == or equals( ) interchangeably, as shown at the end of main( ).

7.16 Initializing Fields in Interfaces

Fields defined in interfaces are automatically static and final. These cannot be "blank finals," but they can be initialized with non-constant expressions. For example:

```
//: RandVals.java
// Initializing interface fields with
// non-constant initializers
import java.util.*;

public interface RandVals {
    int rint = (int)(Math.random() * 10);
    long rlong = (long)(Math.random() * 10);
    float rfloat = (float)(Math.random() * 10);
    double rdouble = Math.random() * 10;
} ///:~
```

Since the fields are static, they are initialized when the class is first loaded, upon first access of any of the fields. Here's a simple test:

```
//: TestRandVals.java
public class TestRandVals {
    public static void main(String[] args) {
        System.out.println(RandVals.rint);
        System.out.println(RandVals.rlong);
        System.out.println(RandVals.rfloat);
        System.out.println(RandVals.rdouble);
}
} ///:~
```

The fields, of course, are not part of the interface but instead are stored in the static storage area for that interface.

7.17 Creating and Using Packages

To make classes easier to find and use, to avoid naming conflicts, and to control access, programmers bundle groups of related classes into packages.

Definition: A package is a collection of related classes and interfaces that provides access protection and namespace management.

The classes and interfaces that are part of the JDK are members of various packages that bundle classes by function: applet classes are in java.applet, I/O classes are in java.io, and the GUI widget classes are in java.awt. You can put your classes and interfaces in packages, too.

Let's look at a set of classes and examine why you might want to put them in a package. Suppose you write a group of classes that represent a collection of graphics objects such as circles, rectangles, lines, and points. You also write an interface Draggable that classes implement if they can be dragged with the mouse by the user.

```
in the Graphics.java file
abstract class Graphic {
. . .
}
in the Circle.java file
public class Circle extends Graphic implements Draggable {
. . .
}
in the Rectangle.java file
public class Rectangle extends Graphic implements Draggable {
. . .
}
in the Draggable.java file
public interface Draggable {
. . .
}
```

You should bundle these classes and the interface together in a package, for several reasons:

- You and other programmers can easily determine that these classes and interfaces are related.
- You and other programmers know where to find classes and interfaces that provide graphics-related functions.
- The names of your classes won't conflict with class names in other packages because the package creates a new namespace.
- You can allow classes within the package to have unrestricted access to each other, yet still restrict access for classes outside the package.

7.18 Creating a Package

You can easily create your own packages and put any number of class and interface definitions in them.

To create a package, you simply put a class or interface in it. To do this, you put a package statement at the top of the source file in which the class or interface is defined. For example, the following code appears in the source file Circle.java and puts the Circle class in the graphics package:

```
package graphics;
public class Circle extends Graphic implements Draggable {
. . .
}
```

The Circle class is a public member of the graphics package.

You must include a package statement at the top of every source file that defines a class or interface that is to be a member of the graphics package. So you would also include the statement in Rectangle.java and so on:

```
package graphics;
public class Rectangle extends Graphic implements Draggable {
. . .
}
```

The scope of the package statement is the entire source file, so all classes and interfaces defined in Circle.java and Rectangle.java are also members of the graphics package. If you put multiple classes in a single source file, only one may be declared public and it must share the name of the source file's basename. Only public package members are accessible from outside the package.

Note: Some compilers might allow more than one public file per .java file. However, we recommend that you use the one-public-class-per-file convention, since it makes public classes easier to find and works for all compilers.

If you do not use a package statement, your class or interface ends up in the default package, which is a package that has no name. Generally speaking, the default package is only for small or temporary applications or when you are just beginning development. Otherwise, classes and interfaces belong in named packages.

7.19 Naming a Package

With programmers all over the world writing Java classes and interfaces, it is conceivable and even likely that two programmers will use the same name for two different classes. In fact, the previous example does just that: It defines a Rectangle class when there is already a Rectangle class in the java.awt package. Yet, the compiler allows both classes to have the same name. Why? Because they are in different packages and the actual name of each class includes the package name. That is, the name of the Rectangle class in the graphics package is really graphics.Rectangle, and the name of the Rectangle class in the java.awt package is really java.awt.Rectangle.

This works just fine unless two independent programmers use the same name for their packages. What prevents this? Convention.

By Convention: Companies use their reversed Internet domain name in their package names, like this: com.company.package. Name collisions that occur within a single company need to be handled by convention within that company, perhaps by including the region or project name after the company name, for example, com.company.region.package.

7.19.1 Problems with Naming Packages

As you saw earlier name space conflicts arise if two pieces of code declare the same name. Java keeps track of what belongs to each package internally. Thus if Sun decides to put a Website class in java.lang in Java 2.0, it won't conflict with a Website class defined in an http package. Since they're in different packages Java can tell them apart. Just as you tell John Smith apart from John Jones by their last names, so too does Java tell two Website classes apart by their package names.

However this scheme breaks down if two different classes share the same package name as well as class name. In a world in which many different packages can be downloaded from many different sites, all landing in the user's CLASSPATH, it's not unthinkable that two different people might write packages called http with a class called Website.

To ensure that package names don't conflict with each other, Sun asks that you prefix all your packages with a reversed domain name. Thus if your domain name is poly.edu, your package names should begin with edu.poly. Within that domain you are responsible for making sure that no one else writes a package that conflicts with yours.

If you don't have a personal domain name, only an account with an Internet service provider, then add your username to this as well. For instance under this scheme the package prefix for foo@utopia.poly.edu would be edu.poly.utopia.foo.

This is primarily of interest to applet writers, not applet users. If you're surfing the net and you load one applet from MIT that has a http.Website class and another from Polytechnic that has a different http.Website class, Java can still tell them apart because before it runs any package it downloads off the net it prefixes everything with the site from which it got it. In other words it sees edu.poly.www.http.Website and edu.mit.www.http.Website. It's only when you download a package manually and install it in one directory in your CLASSPATH and install another package elsewhere in your CLASSPATH that real name conflicts can arise if packages aren't carefully prefixed with a domain or email address.

7.20 Using Package Members

Only public package members are accessible outside the package in which they are defined. To use a public package member from outside its package, you must either

- refer to the member by its long (disambiguated) name,
- import the package member, or
- import the member's entire package.

Each is appropriate for different situations, as explained in the following sections.

7.20.1 Referring to a Package Member by Name

So far, the examples in this book have referred to classes and interfaces by the name specified in their declaration (such as Rectangle, AlarmClock, and Sleeper). Such names are called short names. You can use a package member's short name if the code you are writing is in the same package as that member or if the member's package has been imported.

However, if you are trying to use a member from a different package and that package has not been imported, then you must use the member's long name, which includes the package name. This is the long name for the Rectangle class declared in the graphics package in the previous example:

```
graphics.Rectangle
```

You could use this long name to create an instance of graphics.Rectangle:

```
graphics.Rectangle myRect = new graphics.Rectangle();
```

You'll find that using long names is okay for one-shot uses. But you'd likely get annoyed if you had to write graphics.Rectangle again and again. Also, your code would get very messy and difficult to read. In such cases, you can just import the member instead.

7.21 Importing a Package Member

To import a specific member into the current file, put an import statement at the beginning of your file before any class or interface definitions (but after the package statement, if there is one). Here's how you would import the Circle class from the graphics package created in the previous section:

```
import graphics.Circle;
```

Now you can refer to the Circle class by its short name:

```
Circle myCircle = new Circle();
```

This approach works just fine if you use just a few members from the graphics package. But if you use many classes and interfaces from a package, you really just want to import the whole package and forget about it.

7.22 Importing an Entire Package

To import all of the classes and interfaces contained in a particular package, use the import statement with the asterisk * wildcard character:

```
import graphics.*;
```

Now you can refer to any class or interface in the graphics package by its short name:

```
Circle myCircle = new Circle();
Rectangle myRectangle = new Rectangle();
```

The asterisk in the import statement can be used only to specify all of the classes within a package, as shown here. It cannot be used to match a subset of the classes in a package. For example, the following does not match all of the classes in the graphics package that begin with "A":

```
import graphics.A*; // does not work
```

Instead, it generates a compiler error. With the import statement, you can import only a single package member or an entire package.

For your convenience, the Java runtime system automatically imports three packages for you:

- The default package (the package with no name)
- The ava.lang package
- The current package

7.23 Disambiguating a Name

If by some chance a member in one package shares the same name with a member in another package and both packages are imported, you must refer to the member by its long name. For example, the previous example defined a class named Rectangle in the graphics package. The java.awt package also contains a Rectangle class. If both graphics and java.awt have been imported, then the following is ambiguous:

```
Rectangle rect;
```

In such a situation, you have to be more specific and indicate exactly which Rectangle class you want by using the member's long name:

```
graphics.Rectangle rect;
```

7.24 Managing Source and Class Files

The JDK relies on hierarchical file systems to manage source and class files for Java programs, although The Java Language Specification does not require this. The strategy is as follows.

You put the source code for a class or interface in a text file whose name is the short name of the class or interface and whose extension is .java (the JDK requires this extension for public classes and it's a good idea for other classes). Then, you put the source file in a directory whose name reflects the name of the package to which the class or interface belongs. For example, the source code for the Rectangle class would be in a file named Rectangle.java and the file would be in a directory named graphics. The graphics directory may be anywhere on the file system. The following diagram shows how this works.

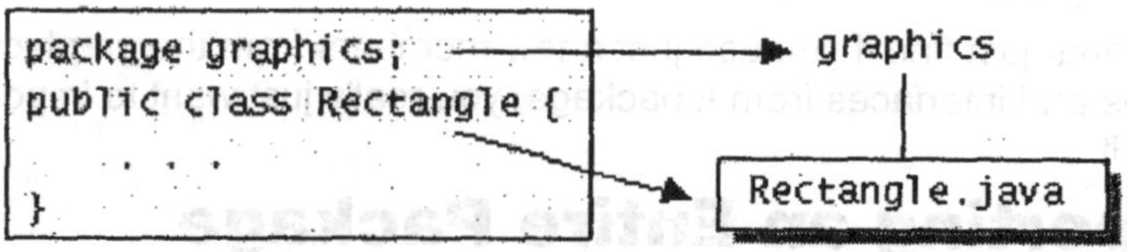

Fig. 7.4

The long name of the package member and the pathname to the file are parallel (assuming the UNIX filename separator slash /):

```
graphics.Rectangle          class name
graphics/Rectangle.java     pathname to file
```

Furthermore, by convention, each company uses its reversed Internet domain name in its package names. (However, some companies now choose to drop "com" from their package names.) The fictional company called Taranis Interactive whose Internet domain name is taranis.com would precede all of its package names with com.taranis. Each component of the package name corresponds to a subdirectory. So, if Taranis had a graphics package that contained a Rectangle.java source file, it would be contained in a series of subdirectories, as shown here:

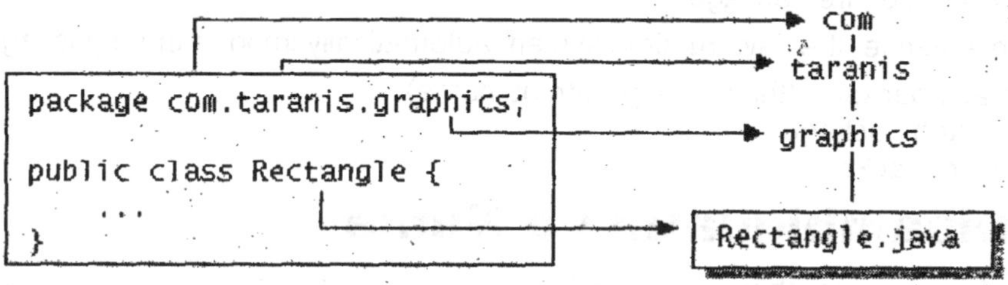

Fig. 7.5

When you compile a source file, the compiler creates a different output file for each class and interface defined in it. The basename of the output file is the name of the class or interface, and its extension is .class:

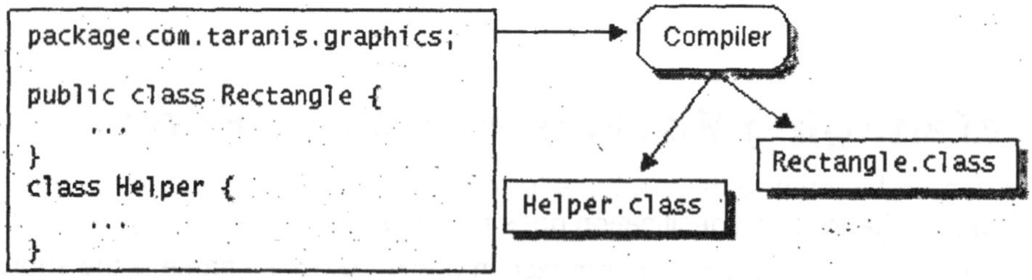

Fig. 7.6

Like a .java file, a .class file should also be in a series of directories that reflect the package name. However, it does not have to be in the same directory as its source. You could arrange your source and class directories separately, like this:

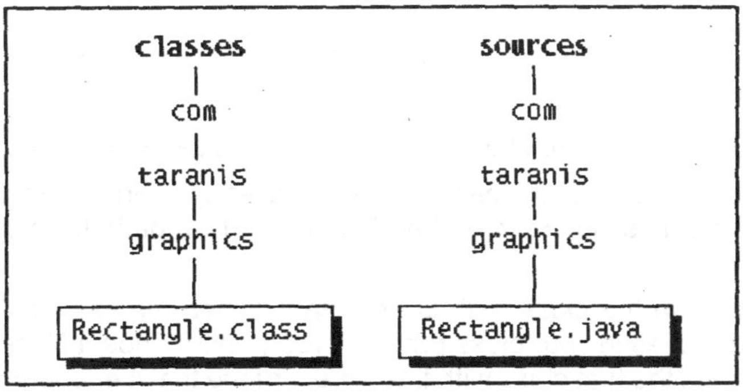

Fig. 7.7

By doing this, you can give the classes directory to other programmers without revealing your sources.

Why all the bother about directories and filenames? You need to manage your source and class files in this manner so that the compiler and the interpreter can find all of the classes and interfaces used by your program. When the compiler encounters a new class as it's compiling your program, it must be able to find the class so as to resolve names, do type checking, and so on. Similarly, when the interpreter encounters a new class as it's running your program, it must be able to find the class to invoke its methods, and so on. Both the compiler and the interpreter search for classes in each directory or zip file listed in your class path..

Definition: A class path is a list of directories or zip files to search for class files.

Each directory listed in the class path is a top-level directory in which package directories appear. From the top-level directory, the compiler and the interpreter can construct the rest of the path based on the package and class name for the class. For example, the class path entry for the directory structure shown in the previous diagram page would include classes, but not com or any of the directories below com. Both the compiler and the interpreter construct the path name to a .class file with its full package name.

By default, the compiler and the interpreter search the current directory and the zip file containing the JDK class files. In other words, the current directory and the JDK class files are automatically in your class path. Most, if not all, classes can be found in these two locations. So it's likely that you don't have to worry about your class path. In some cases, however, you may have to set your class path.

7.25 Setting the Class Path

If you must, you can change your class path. This can be done in either of two ways:

- Set the CLASSPATH environment variable (not recommended).
- Use the -classpath runtime option when you invoke the compiler or the interpreter.

We don't recommend setting the CLASSPATH environment variable because it can be long-lived (particularly if you set it in a login or startup script). It's also easy to forget about, and then one day, your programs won't work because the compiler or interpreter loads a crusty old class file instead of the one you want. An old, out-of-date CLASSPATH variable is a fruitful source of confusing problems.

The second option, setting the class path with the runtime option, is preferable because it sets the class path only for the current invocation of the compiler or the interpreter. Here's how to use the runtime option -classpath to set your class path.

Platform-specific Details: Using the -classpath Runtime Option:

UNIX:

```
javac -classpath .:~/classes:/JDK/lib/classes.zip
```

DOS shell (Windows 95/NT):

```
javac -classpath .;C:\classes;C:\JDK\lib\classes.zip
```

When you specify a class path in this manner, you completely override the current class path. Thus you must include the classes.zip file from the JDK in the class path. It's a good idea to include the current directory as well.

The order of the entries in the class path is important. When the Java interpreter is looking for a class, it searches the entries in your class path, in order, until it finds a class with the correct name. The Java interpreter runs the first class with the correct name that it encounters and does not search the remaining entries.

Note: If you load an applet into a Java application such as HotJava or the Applet Viewer and the loaded class is in the class path, the applet doesn't have the restrictions that applets loaded over the network do, so it can never be reloaded. We recommend never starting an application such as HotJava in the same directory as an Applet class because the current directory "." is usually part of the class path.

7.26 Inner Classes

To help you get a handle on inner classes and what they are good for, let's revisit the Stack class. Suppose you want to add a feature to this class that lets another class enumerate over the elements in the stack using the interface defined in java.util.Enumeration. This interface contains two method declarations:

```
public boolean hasMoreElements();
public Object nextElement();
```

The Enumeration interface defines the interface for a single loop over the elements:

```
while (hasMoreElements())
    nextElement()
```

If Stack implemented the Enumeration interface itself, you could not restart the loop and you could not enumerate the contents more than once. Also, you couldn't allow two enumerations to happen simultaneously. So Stack shouldn't implement Enumeration. Rather, a helper class should do the work for Stack. The helper class must have access to the Stack's elements. It also must be able to access them directly because the Stack's public interface supports only LIFO access. This is where inner classes come in.

Here's an implementation of Stack that defines a helper class (called an adapter class) for enumerating over its elements:

```
public class Stack {
    private Vector items;
    ...//code for Stack's methods and constructors not shown...
public Enumeration enumerator() {
    return new StackEnum();
}
class StackEnum implements Enumeration {
    int currentItem = items.size() - 1;
    public boolean hasMoreElements() {
```

```
            return (currentItem >= 0);
        }
        public Object nextElement() {
        if (!hasMoreElements())
            throw new NoSuchElementException();
        else
            return items.elementAt(currentItem—);
          }
      }
  }
```

Note that the StackEnum class refers directly to Stack's items instance variable. Inner classes are used primarily to implement adapter classes like the one shown in this example. If you plan on handling events from the AWT, then you'll want to know about using adapter classes because the event-handling mechanism in the AWT makes extensive use of them.

7.27 Anonymous Classes

As shown in Using an Inner Class to Implement an Adapter, you can declare a class without a name. Here's yet another version of the now-tired Stack class, in this case using an anonymous class for its enumerator:

```
  public class Stack {
      private Vector items;
      ...//code for Stack's methods and constructors not shown...
  public Enumeration enumerator() {
      return new Enumeration() {
      int currentItem = items.size() - 1;
      public boolean hasMoreElements() {
      return (currentItem >= 0);
  }
      public Object nextElement() {
      if (!hasMoreElements())
      throw new NoSuchElementException();
  else
          return items.elementAt(currentItem—);
        }
      }
    }
  }
```

Anonymous classes can make code difficult to read. You should limit their use to those classes that are very small (no more than a method or two) and whose use is well-understood (like the AWT event-handling adapter classes).

7.28 Implementing Nested Classes

As you learned in Using an Inner Class to Implement an Adapter Java lets you define a class as a member of another class. Such a class is called a nested class and is illustrated here:

```
  class EnclosingClass{
        . . .
```

```
        class ANestedClass {
        . . .
    }
}
```

Definition: A nested class is a class that is a member of another class.

You use nested classes to reflect and enforce the relationship between two classes. You should define a class within another class when the nested class makes sense only in the context of its enclosing class or when it relies on the enclosing class for its function. For example, a text cursor makes sense only in the context of a particular text component.

As a member of its enclosing class, a nested class has a special privilege: It has unlimited access to its enclosing class's members, even if they are declared private. However, this special privilege isn't really special at all. It is fully consistent with the meaning of private and the other access specifiers. The access specifiers restrict access to members for classes outside of the enclosing class. The nested class is inside of its enclosing class so that it has access to its enclosing class's members.

Like other members, a nested class can be declared static (or not). A static nested class is called just that: a static nested class. A nonstatic nested class is called an inner class. These are illustrated in the following code:

```
class EnclosingClass{
        . . .
        static class AStaticNestedClass {
        . . .
    }
class InnerClass {
. . .
}
}
```

As with static methods and variables (normally called class methods and variables), a static nested class is associated with its enclosing class. And like class methods, a static nested class cannot refer directly to instance variables or methods defined in its enclosing class-it can use them only through an object reference.

As with instance methods and variables, an inner class is associated with an instance of its enclosing class and has direct access to that object's instance variables and methods. Also, because an inner class is associated with an instance, it cannot define any static members itself.

To help differentiate the terms nested class and inner class further, we suggest you think about them in the following way. The term "nested class" reflects the syntactic relationship between two classes; that is, syntactically, the code for one class appears within the code of another. In contrast, the term "inner class" reflects the relationship between instances of the two classes. Consider the following classes:

```
class EnclosingClass {
        . . .
        class InnerClass {
        . . .
    }
}
```

The interesting feature about the relationship between these two classes is not that InnerClass is syntactically defined within EnclosingClass. Rather, it's that an instance of InnerClass can exist only within an instance of EnclosingClass and that it has direct access to instance variables and methods of its enclosing instance. The following diagram illustrates this idea.

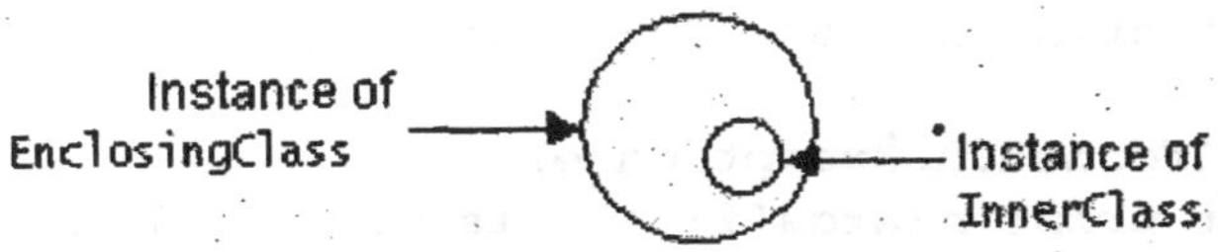

Fig. 7.8

You may encounter nested classes of both kinds in the Java API and be required to use them. However, most nested classes that you write will be inner classes.

Definition: An inner class is a nested class whose instance exists within an instance of its enclosing class and has direct access to the instance members of its enclosing instance.

7.28.1 Other Facts about Nested Classes

Like other classes, nested classes can be declared abstract or final. The meaning of these two modifiers for nested classes is the same as for other classes. Also, the access specifiers—private, public, protected, and package— may be used to restrict access to nested classes just as they do to other class members. Any nested class, not just anonymous ones, can be declared in any block of code. A nested class declared within a method or other smaller block of code has access to any final, local variables in scope.

7.29 Wrapping Your Own Packages

Java does not limit you to using only the system supplied packages. You can write your own as well. You write packages just like you write any other Java program. Make sure you follow these rules:

- There must be no more than one public class per file.
- All files in the package must be named classname.java where classname is the name of the single public class in the file.
- At the very top of each file in the package, before any import statements, put the statement

```
package myPackage;
```

- To use the package in other programs, compile the .java files as usual and then move the resulting .class files into the appropriate subdirectory of one of the directories referenced in your CLASSPATH environment variable. For instance if /home/elharo/classes is in your CLASSPATH and your package is called package1, then you would make a directory called package1 in /home/elharo/classes and then put all the .class files in the package in /home/elharo/classes/package1.

For example,

```
package com.macfaq.net;
import java.net.*;
public class URLSplitter {
public static void main(String[] args) {
for (int i = 0; i < args.length; i++) {
try {
URL u = new URL(args[i]);
System.out.println("Protocol: " + u.getProtocol());
```

```
System.out.println("Host: " + u.getHost());
System.out.println("Port: " + u.getPort());
System.out.println("File: " + u.getFile());
System.out.println("Ref: " + u.getRef());
}
catch (MalformedURLException e) {
System.err.println(args[i] + " is not a valid URL");
}
}
}
}
% javac -d /home/elharo/classes SplitURL.java
```

The -d flag to the compiler tells it to create the necessary directories such as elharo/net in the specified directory. In this example, URLSplitter.class is placed in /home/elharo/classes/com/macfaq/net. You can use the usual shell syntax such as . for the current directory or ~ for your home directory.

7.30 Interchangeable Objects with Polymorphism

Inheritance usually ends up creating a family of classes, all based on the same uniform interface. We express this with an inverted tree diagram:

One of the most important things you do with such a family of classes is to treat an object of a derived class as an object of the base class. This is important because it means you can write a single piece of code that ignores the specific details of type and talks just to the base class. That code is then decoupled from type-specific information, and thus is simpler to write and easier to understand. And, if a new type - a Triangle, for example - is added through inheritance, the code you write will work just as well for the new type of Shape as it did on the existing types. Thus the program is extensible.

Consider the above example. If you write a function in Java:

```
void doStuff(Shape s) {
s.erase();
// ...
s.draw();
}
```

This function speaks to any Shape, so it is independent of the specific type of object it's drawing and erasing. If in some other program we use the doStuff( ) function:

```
Circle c = new Circle();
Triangle t = new Triangle();
Line l = new Line();
doStuff(c);
doStuff(t);
doStuff(l);
```

The calls to doStuff( ) automatically work right, regardless of the exact type of the object.

This is actually a pretty amazing trick. Consider the line:

```
doStuff(c);
```

What's happening here is that a Circle handle is being passed into a function that's expecting a Shape handle. Since a Circle is a Shape it can be treated as one by doStuff( ). That is, any message that doStuff( ) can send to a Shape, a Circle can accept. So it is a completely safe and logical thing to do.

We call this process of treating a derived type as though it were its base type upcasting. The name cast is used in the sense of casting into a mold and the up comes from the way the inheritance diagram is typically arranged, with the base type at the top and the derived classes fanning out downward. Thus, casting to a base type is moving up the inheritance diagram: upcasting.

An object-oriented program contains some upcasting somewhere, because that's how you decouple yourself from knowing about the exact type you're working with. Look at the code in doStuff( ):

```
s.erase();
// ...
s.draw();
```

Notice that it doesn't say "If you're a Circle, do this, if you're a Square, do that, etc." If you write that kind of code, which checks for all the possible types a Shape can actually be, it's messy and you need to change it every time you add a new kind of Shape. Here, you just say "You're a shape, I know you can erase( ) yourself, do it and take care of the details correctly."

7.31 Dynamic Binding

What's amazing about the code in doStuff( ) is that somehow the right thing happens. Calling draw( ) for Circle causes different code to be executed than when calling draw( ) for a Square or a Line, but when the draw( ) message is sent to an anonymous Shape, the correct behavior occurs based on the actual type that the Shape handle happens to be connected to. This is amazing because when the Java compiler is compiling the code for doStuff( ), it cannot know exactly what types it is dealing with. So ordinarily, you'd expect it to end up calling the version of erase( ) for Shape, and draw( ) for Shape and not for the specific Circle, Square, or Line. And yet the right thing happens. Here's how it works.

When you send a message to an object even though you don't know what specific type it is, and the right thing happens, that's called polymorphism. The process used by object-oriented programming languages to implement polymorphism is called dynamic binding . The compiler and run-time system handle the details; all you need to know is that it happens and more importantly how to design with it.

Some languages require you to use a special keyword to enable dynamic binding. In C++ this keyword is virtual. In Java, you never need to remember to add a keyword because functions are automatically dynamically bound. So you can always expect that when you send a message to an object, the object will do the right thing, even when upcasting is involved.

7.32 Abstract Base Classes and Interfaces

Often in a design, you want the base class to present only an interface for its derived classes. That is, you don't want anyone to actually create an object of the base class, only to upcast to it so that its interface can be used. This is accomplished by making that class abstract using the abstract keyword. If anyone tries to make an object of an abstract class, the compiler prevents them. This is a tool to enforce a particular design.

You can also use the abstract keyword to describe a method that hasn't been implemented yet - as a stub indicating "here is an interface function for all types inherited from this class, but at this point I don't have any implementation for it." An abstract method may be created only inside an abstract class. When the class is inherited, that method must be implemented, or the inherited class becomes abstract as well. Creating an abstract method allows you to put a method in an interface without being forced to provide a possibly meaningless body of code for that method.

The interface keyword takes the concept of an abstract class one step further by preventing any function definitions at all. The interface is a very useful and commonly-used tool, as it provides the perfect separation of interface and implementation. In addition, you can combine many interfaces together, if you wish. (You cannot inherit from more than one regular class or abstract class .)

package: the library unit

A package is what you get when you use the import keyword to bring in an entire library, such as

```
import java.util.*;
```

This brings in the entire utility library that's part of the standard Java distribution. Since Vector is in java.util, you can now either specify the full name java.util.Vector (which you can do without the import statement), or you can simply say Vector (because of the import).

If you want to bring in a single class, you can name that class in the import statement

```
import java.util.Vector;
```

Now you can use Vector with no qualification. However, none of the other classes in java.util are available.

The reason for all this importing is to provide a mechanism to manage "name spaces." The names of all your class members are insulated from each other. A method f( ) inside a class A will not clash with an f( ) that has the same signature (argument list) in class B. But what about the class names? Suppose you create a stack class that is installed on a machine that already has a stack class that's written by someone else? With Java on the Internet, this can happen without the user knowing it since classes can get downloaded automatically in the process of running a Java program.

This potential clashing of names is why it's important to have complete control over the name spaces in Java, and to be able to create a completely unique name regardless of the constraints of the Internet.

So far, most of the examples in this book have existed in a single file and have been designed for local use, and haven't bothered with package names. (In this case the class name is placed in the "default package.") This is certainly an option, and for simplicity's sake this approach will be used whenever possible throughout the rest of the book. If you're planning to create a program that is "Internet friendly," however, you must think about preventing class name clashes.

When you create a source-code file for Java, it's commonly called a compilation unit (sometimes a translation unit). Each compilation unit must have a name ending in .java, and inside the compilation unit there can be a public class that must have the same name as the file (including capitalization, but excluding the .java filename extension). If you don't do this, the compiler will complain. There can be only one public class in each compilation unit (again, the compiler will complain). The rest of the classes in that compilation unit, if there are any, are hidden from the world outside that package because they're not public, and they comprise "support" classes for the main public class.

When you compile a .java file you get an output file with exactly the same name but an extension of .class for each class in the .java file. Thus you can end up with quite a few .class files from a small number of .java files. If you've programmed with a compiled language, you might be used to the compiler spitting out an intermediate form (usually an "obj" file) that is then packaged together with others of its kind using a linker (to create an executable file) or a librarian (to create a library). That's not how Java works. A working program is a bunch of .class files, which can be packaged and compressed into a JAR file (using the jar utility in Java 1.1). The Java interpreter is responsible for finding, loading and interpreting these files.

A library is also a bunch of these class files. Each file has one class that is public (you're not forced to have a public class, but it's typical), so there's one component for each file. If you want to say that all these components (that are in their own separate .java and .class files) belong together, that's where the package keyword comes in.

When you say:

```
package mypackage;
```

at the beginning of a file, where the package statement must appear as the first non-comment in the file, you're stating that this compilation unit is part of a library named mypackage. Or, put another way, you're saying that the public class name within this compilation unit is under the umbrella of the name mypackage, and if anyone wants to use the name they must either fully specify the name or use the import keyword in combination with mypackage (using the choices given previously). Note that the convention for Java packages is to use all lowercase letters, even for intermediate words.

For example, suppose the name of the file is MyClass.java. This means there can be one and only one public class in that file, and the name of that class must be MyClass (including the capitalization):

```
package mypackage;
public class MyClass {    // . . .
```

Now, if someone wants to use MyClass or, for that matter, any of the other public classes in mypackage, they must use the import keyword to make the name or names in mypackage available. The alternative is to give the fully-qualified name:

```
mypackage.MyClass m = new mypackage.MyClass();
```

The import keyword can make this much cleaner:

```
import mypackage.*;
// . . .
MyClass m = new MyClass();
```

It's worth keeping in mind that what the package and import keywords allow you to do, as a library designer, is to divide up the single global name space so you won't have clashing names, no matter how many people get on the Internet and start writing classes in Java.

7.33 Creating Unique Package Names

You might observe that, since a package never really gets "packaged" into a single file, a package could be made up of many .class files, and things could get a bit cluttered. To prevent this, a logical thing to do is to place all the .class files for a particular package into a single directory; that is, use the hierarchical file structure of the operating system to your advantage. This is how Java handles the problem of clutter.

It also solves two other problems: creating unique package names and finding those classes that might be buried in a directory structure someplace. This is accomplished, as was introduced in Chapter 2, by encoding the path of the location of the .class file into the name of the package. The compiler enforces this, but by convention, the first part of the package name is the Internet domain name of the creator of the class, reversed. Since Internet domain names are guaranteed to be unique (by InterNIC, [24] who controls their assignment) if you follow this convention it's guaranteed that your package name will be unique and thus you'll never have a name clash. (That is, until you lose the domain name to someone else who starts writing Java code with the same path names as you did.) Of course, if you don't have your own domain name then you must fabricate an unlikely combination (such as your first and last name) to create unique package names. If you've decided to start publishing Java code it's worth the relatively small effort to get a domain name.

The second part of this trick is resolving the package name into a directory on your machine, so when the Java program runs and it needs to load the .class file (which it does dynamically, at the point in the program where it needs to create an object of that particular class, or the first time you access a static member of the class), it can locate the directory where the .class file resides.

The Java interpreter proceeds as follows. First, it finds the environment variable CLASSPATH (set via the operating system when Java, or a tool like a Java-enabled browser, is installed on a machine). CLASSPATH contains one or more directories that are used as roots for a search for .class files. Starting at that root, the interpreter will take the package name and replace each dot with a slash to generate a path name from the CLASSPATH root (so package foo.bar.baz becomes foo\bar\baz or foo/bar/baz depending on your operating system). This is then concatenated to the various entries in the CLASSPATH. That's where it looks for the .class file with the name corresponding to the class you're trying to create. (It also searches some standard directories relative to where the Java interpreter resides).

To understand this, consider my domain name, which is bruceeckel.com. By reversing this, com.bruceeckel establishes my unique global name for my classes. (The com, edu, org, etc. extension was formerly capitalized in Java packages, but this was changed in Java 1.2 so the entire package name is lowercase.) I can further subdivide this by deciding that I want to create a library named util, so I'll end up with a package name:

```
package com.bruceeckel.util;
```

Now this package name can be used as an umbrella name space for the following two files:

```
//: Vector.java
// Creating a package
package com.bruceeckel.util;
public class Vector {
public Vector() {
System.out.println(
"com.bruceeckel.util.Vector");
}
} ///:~
```

When you create your own packages, you'll discover that the package statement must be the first non-comment code in the file. The second file looks much the same:

```
//: List.java
// Creating a package
package com.bruceeckel.util;
public class List {
    public List() {
    System.out.println(
        "com.bruceeckel.util.List");
    }
} ///:~
```

Both of these files are placed in the subdirectory on my system:

```
C:\DOC\JavaT\com\bruceeckel\util
```

If you walk back through this, you can see the package name com.bruceeckel.util, but what about the first portion of the path? That's taken care of in the CLASSPATH environment variable, which is, on my machine:

```
CLASSPATH=.;D:\JAVA\LIB;C:\DOC\JavaT
```

You can see that the CLASSPATH can contain a number of alternative search paths. There's a variation when using JAR files, however. You must put the name of the JAR file in the classpath, not just the path where it's located. So for a JAR named grape.jar your classpath would include:

```
CLASSPATH=.;D:\JAVA\LIB;C:\flavors\grape.jar
```

Once the classpath is set up properly, the following file can be placed in any directory: (See page 97 if you have trouble executing this program.):

```
//: LibTest.java
// Uses the library
package c05;
import com.bruceeckel.util.*;
public class LibTest {
    public static void main(String[] args) {
        Vector v = new Vector();
        List l = new List();
    }
} ///:~
```

When the compiler encounters the import statement, it begins searching at the directories specified by CLASSPATH, looking for subdirectory com\bruceeckel\util, then seeking the compiled files of the appropriate names (Vector.class for Vector and List.class for List). Note that both the classes and the desired methods in Vector and List must be public.

7.34 Automatic Compilation

The first time you create an object of an imported class (or you access a static member of a class), the compiler will hunt for the .class file of the same name (so if you're creating an object of class X, it looks for X.class) in the appropriate directory. If it finds only X.class , that's what it must use. However, if it also finds an X.java in the same directory, the compiler will compare the date stamp on the two files, and if X.java is more recent than X.class, it will automatically recompile X.java to generate an up-to-date X.class.

If a class is not in a .java file of the same name as that class, this behavior will not occur for that class.

7.35 Collisions

What happens if two libraries are imported via * and they include the same names? For example, suppose a program does this:

```
import com.bruceeckel.util.*;
import java.util.*;
```

Since java.util.* also contains a Vector class, this causes a potential collision. However, as long as the collision doesn't actually occur, everything is OK - this is good because otherwise you might end up doing a lot of typing to prevent collisions that would never happen.

The collision does occur if you now try to make a Vector:

```
Vector v = new Vector();
```

Which Vector class does this refer to? The compiler can't know, and the reader can't know either. So the compiler complains and forces you to be explicit. If I want the standard Java Vector, for example, I must say:

```
java.util.Vector v = new java.util.Vector();
```

Since this (along with the CLASSPATH) completely specifies the location of that Vector, there's no need for the import java.util.* statement unless I'm using something else from java.util.

7.35.1 A Custom tool Library

With this knowledge, you can now create your own libraries of tools to reduce or eliminate duplicate code. Consider, for example, creating an alias for System.out.println( ) to reduce typing. This can be part of a package called tools:

```
//: P.java
// The P.rint & P.rintln shorthand
package com.bruceeckel.tools;

public class P {
    public static void rint(Object obj) {
        System.out.print(obj);
}
public static void rint(String s) {
    System.out.print(s);
}
public static void rint(char[] s) {
    System.out.print(s);
}
public static void rint(char c) {
    System.out.print(c);
}
public static void rint(int i) {
    System.out.print(i);
}
public static void rint(long l) {
    System.out.print(l);
}
public static void rint(float f) {
    System.out.print(f);
}
public static void rint(double d) {
    System.out.print(d);
}
public static void rint(boolean b) {
    System.out.print(b);
}
public static void rintln() {
    System.out.println();
}
public static void rintln(Object obj) {
    System.out.println(obj);
}
public static void rintln(String s) {
    System.out.println(s);
}
public static void rintln(char[] s) {
```

```
        System.out.println(s);
    }
    public static void rintln(char c) {
        System.out.println(c);
    }
    public static void rintln(int i) {
        System.out.println(i);
    }
    public static void rintln(long l) {
        System.out.println(l);
    }
    public static void rintln(float f) {
        System.out.println(f);
    }
    public static void rintln(double d) {
        System.out.println(d);
    }
    public static void rintln(boolean b) {
        System.out.println(b);
    }
    } ///:~
```

All the different data types can now be printed out either with a newline (P.rintln( )) or without a newline (P.rint( )).

You can guess that the location of this file must be in a directory that starts at one of the CLASSPATH locations, then continues com/bruceeckel/tools. After compiling, the P.class file can be used anywhere on your system with an import statement:

```
//: ToolTest.java
// Uses the tools library
import com.bruceeckel.tools.*;
public class ToolTest {
    public static void main(String[] args) {
        P.rintln("Available from now on!");
    }
} ///:~
```

So from now on, whenever you come up with a useful new utility, you can add it to the tools directory. (Or to your own personal util or tools directory.)

7.36 Classpath Pitfall

The P.java file brought up an interesting pitfall. Especially with early implementations of Java, setting the classpath correctly is generally quite a headache. During the development of this book, the P.java file was introduced and seemed to work fine, but at some point it began breaking. For a long time I was certain that this was the fault of one implementation of Java or another, but finally I discovered that at one point I had introduced a program that used a different class P. Because it was used as a tool, it was sometimes placed in the classpath, and other times it wasn't. When it was, the P in CodePackager.java was found first by Java when executing a program in which it was looking for the class in com.bruceeckel.tools, and the compiler would say that a particular method couldn't be found.

This was frustrating because you can see the method in the above class P and no further diagnostics were reported to give you a clue that it was finding a completely different class. (That wasn't even public.)

At first this could seem like a compiler bug, but if you look at the import statement it says only "here's where you might find P." However, the compiler is supposed to look anywhere in its classpath, so if it finds a P there it will use it, and if it finds the "wrong" one first during a search then it will stop looking. If you're having an experience like this, check to make sure that there's only one class of each name anywhere in your classpath.

7.37 Using Imports to Change Behavior

A feature that is missing from Java is C's conditional compilation , which allows you to change a switch and get different behavior without changing any other code. The reason such a feature was left out of Java is probably because it is most often used in C to solve cross-platform issues: different portions of the code are compiled depending on the platform that the code is being compiled for. Since Java is intended to be automatically cross-platform, such a feature should not be necessary.

However, there are other valuable uses for conditional compilation. A very common use is for debugging code. The debugging features are enabled during development, and disabled for a shipping product. Allen Holub (www.holub.com) came up with the idea of using packages to mimic conditional compilation. He used this to create a Java version of C's very useful assertion mechanism , whereby you can say "this should be true" or "this should be false" and if the statement doesn't agree with your assertion you'll find out about it. Such a tool is quite helpful during debugging.

Here is the class that you'll use for debugging:

```
//: Assert.java
// Assertion tool for debugging
package com.bruceeckel.tools.debug;
public class Assert {
    private static void perr(String msg) {
        System.err.println(msg);
}

public final static void is_true(boolean exp) {
    if(!exp) perr("Assertion failed");
}
public final static void is_false(boolean exp){
    if(exp) perr("Assertion failed");
}
public final static void
    is_true(boolean exp, String msg) {
        if(!exp) perr("Assertion failed:" + msg);
}
public final static void
is_false(boolean exp, String msg) {
    if(exp) perr("Assertion failed: " + msg);
}
} ///:~
```

This class simply encapsulates boolean tests, which print error messages if they fail. In Chapter 9, you'll learn about a more sophisticated tool for dealing with errors called exception handling , but the perr( ) method will work fine in the meantime.

When you want to use this class, you add a line in your program:

```
import com.bruceeckel.tools.debug.*;
```

To remove the assertions so you can ship the code, a second Assert class is created, but in a different package:

```
//: Assert.java
// Turning off the assertion output
// so you can ship the program.
package com.bruceeckel.tools;
public class Assert {
    public final static void is_true(boolean exp){}
public final static void is_false(boolean exp){}
public final static void
is_true(boolean exp, String msg) {}
public final static void
is_false(boolean exp, String msg) {}
} ///:~
```

Now if you change the previous import statement to:

```
import com.bruceeckel.tools.*;
```

The program will no longer print out assertions. Here's an example:

```
//: TestAssert.java
// Demonstrating the assertion tool
package c05;
// Comment the following, and uncomment the
// subsequent line to change assertion behavior:
import com.bruceeckel.tools.debug.*;
// import com.bruceeckel.tools.*;
public class TestAssert {
    public static void main(String[] args) {
        Assert.is_true((2 + 2) == 5);
        Assert.is_false((1 + 1) == 2);
        Assert.is_true((2 + 2) == 5, "2 + 2 == 5");
        Assert.is_false((1 + 1) == 2, "1 +1 != 2");
    }
} ///:~
```

By changing the package that's imported, you change your code from the debug version to the production version. This technique can be used for any kind of conditional code.

7.38 Package Caveat

It's worth remembering that anytime you create a package, you implicitly specify a directory structure when you give the package a name. The package must live in the directory indicated by its name, which must be a directory that is searchable starting from the CLASSPATH. Experimenting with the package keyword can be a bit frustrating at first, because unless you adhere to the package-name to directory-path rule, you'll get a lot of mysterious run-time messages about not being able to find a particular class, even if that class is sitting there in the same directory. If you get a message like this, try commenting out the package statement, and if it runs you'll know where the problem lies.

7.39 Remote Methods

Traditional approaches to executing code on other machines across a network have been confusing as well as tedious and error-prone to implement. The nicest way to think about this problem is that some object happens to live on another machine, and you can send a message to that object and get a result as if the object lived on your local machine. This simplification is exactly what Java 1.1 Remote Method Invocation (RMI) allows you to do. This section walks you through the steps necessary to create your own RMI objects.

7.40 Remote Interfaces

RMI makes heavy use of interfaces. When you want to create a remote object, you mask the underlying implementation by passing around an interface. Thus, when the client gets a handle to a remote object, what they really get is an interface handle, which happens to connect to some local stub code that talks across the network. But you don't think about this, you just send messages via your interface handle.

When you create a remote interface, you must follow these guidelines:

The remote interface must be public (it cannot have "package access," that is, it cannot be "friendly"). Otherwise, a client will get an error when attempting to load a remote object that implements the remote interface.

The remote interface must extend the interface java.rmi.Remote.

Each method in the remote interface must declare java.rmi.RemoteException in its throws clause in addition to any application-specific exceptions.

A remote object passed as an argument or return value (either directly or embedded within a local object) must be declared as the remote interface, not the implementation class.

Here's a simple remote interface that represents an accurate time service:

```
//: PerfectTimeI.java
// The PerfectTime remote interface
package c15.ptime;
import java.rmi.*;
interface PerfectTimeI extends Remote {
long getPerfectTime() throws RemoteException;
} ///:~
```

It looks like any other interface except that it extends Remote and all of its methods throw RemoteException. Remember that an interface and all of its methods are automatically public.

7.41 Implementing the Remote Interface

The server must contain a class that extends UnicastRemoteObject and implements the remote interface. This class can also have additional methods, but only the methods in the remote interface will be available to the client, of course, since the client will get only a handle to the interface, not the class that implements it.

You must explicitly define the constructor for the remote object even if you're only defining a default constructor that calls the base-class constructor. You must write it out since it must throw RemoteException.

Here's the implementation of the remote interface PerfectTimeI:

```
//: PerfectTime.java
// The implementation of the PerfectTime
// remote object
package c15.ptime;
import java.rmi.*;
import java.rmi.server.*;
import java.rmi.registry.*;
import java.net.*;

public class PerfectTime
extends UnicastRemoteObject
implements PerfectTimeI {
// Implementation of the interface:
public long getPerfectTime()
throws RemoteException {
return System.currentTimeMillis();
}
// Must implement constructor to throw
// RemoteException:
public PerfectTime() throws RemoteException {
// super(); // Called automatically
}
// Registration for RMI serving:
public static void main(String[] args) {
System.setSecurityManager(
new RMISecurityManager());
try {
PerfectTime pt = new PerfectTime();
Naming.bind(
"//colossus:2005/PerfectTime", pt);
System.out.println("Ready to do time");
} catch(Exception e) {
e.printStackTrace();
}
}
} ///:~
```

Here, main( ) handles all the details of setting up the server. When you're serving RMI objects, at some point in your program you must:

- Create and install a security manager that supports RMI. The only one available for RMI as part of the Java distribution is RMISecurityManager.
- Create one or more instances of a remote object. Here, you can see the creation of the PerfectTime object.
- Register at least one of the remote objects with the RMI remote object registry for bootstrapping purposes. One remote object can have methods that produce handles to other remote objects. This allows you to set it up so the client must go to the registry only once, to get the first remote object.

7.42 Setting up the Registry

Here, you see a call to the static method Naming.bind( ). However, this call requires that the registry be running as a separate process on the computer. The name of the registry server is rmiregistry, and under 32-bit Windows you say:

```
start rmiregistry
```

to start it in the background. On Unix, it is:

```
rmiregistry &
```

Like many network programs, the rmiregistry is located at the IP address of whatever machine started it up, but it must also be listening at a port. If you invoke the rmiregistry as above, with no argument, the registry's port will default to 1099. If you want it to be at some other port, you add an argument on the command line to specify the port. For this example, the port will be located at 2005, so the rmiregistry should be started like this under 32-bit Windows:

```
start rmiregistry 2005
```

or for Unix:

```
rmiregistry 2005 &
```

The information about the port must also be given to the bind( ) command, as well as the IP address of the machine where the registry is located. But this brings up what can be a frustrating problem if you're expecting to test RMI programs locally the way the network programs have been tested so far in this chapter. In the JDK 1.1.1 release, there are a couple of problems:

localhost does not work with RMI. Thus, to experiment with RMI on a single machine, you must provide the name of the machine. To find out the name of your machine under 32-bit Windows, go to the control panel and select "Network." Select the "Identification" tab, and you'll see your computer name. In my case, I called my computer "Colossus" (for all the hard disks I've had to put on to hold all the different development systems). It appears that capitalization is ignored.

RMI will not work unless your computer has an active TCP/IP connection, even if all your components are just talking to each other on the local machine. This means that you must connect to your Internet service provider before trying to run the program or you'll get some obscure exception messages.

Will all this in mind, the bind( ) command becomes:

```
Naming.bind("//colossus:2005/PerfectTime", pt);
```

If you are using the default port 1099, you don't need to specify a port, so you could say:

```
Naming.bind("//colossus/PerfectTime", pt);
```

In a future release of the JDK (after 1.1) when the localhost bug is fixed, you will be able to perform local testing by leaving off the IP address and using only the identifier:

```
Naming.bind("PerfectTime", pt);
```

The name for the service is arbitrary; it happens to be PerfectTime here, just like the name of the class, but you could call it anything you want. The important thing is that it's a unique name in the registry that the client knows to look for to procure the remote object. If the name is already in the registry, you'll get an AlreadyBoundException. To prevent this, you can always use rebind( ) instead of bind( ), since rebind( ) either adds a new entry or replaces the one that's already there.

Even though main( ) exits, your object has been created and registered so it's kept alive by the registry, waiting for a client to come along and request it. As long as the rmiregistry is running and you don't call Naming.unbind( ) on your name, the object will be there. For this reason, when you're developing your code you need to shut down the rmiregistry and restart it when you compile a new version of your remote object.

You aren't forced to start up rmiregistry as an external process. If you know that your application is the only one that's going to use the registry, you can start it up inside your program with the line:

```
LocateRegistry.createRegistry(2005);
```

Like before, 2005 is the port number we happen to be using in this example. This is the equivalent of running rmiregistry 2005 from a command line, but it can often be more convenient when you're developing RMI code since it eliminates the extra steps of starting and stopping the registry. Once you've executed this code, you can bind( ) using Naming as before.

7.43 Creating Stubs and Skeletons

If you compile and run PerfectTime.java, it won't work even if you have the rmiregistry running correctly. That's because the framework for RMI isn't all there yet. You must first create the stubs and skeletons that provide the network connection operations and allow you to pretend that the remote object is just another local object on your machine.

What's going on behind the scenes is complex. Any objects that you pass into or return from a remote object must implement Serializable (if you want to pass remote references instead of the entire objects, the object arguments can implement Remote), so you can imagine that the stubs and skeletons are automatically performing serialization and deserialization as they "marshal" all of the arguments across the network and return the result. Fortunately, you don't have to know any of this, but you do have to create the stubs and skeletons. This is a simple process: you invoke the rmic tool on your compiled code, and it creates the necessary files. So the only requirement is that another step be added to your compilation process.

The rmic tool is particular about packages and classpaths, however. PerfectTime.java is in the package c15.Ptime, and even if you invoke rmic in the same directory in which PerfectTime.class is located, rmic won't find the file, since it searches the classpath. So you must specify the location off the class path, like so:

```
rmic c15.PTime.PerfectTime
```

You don't have to be in the directory containing PerfectTime.class when you execute this command, but the results will be placed in the current directory.

When rmic runs successfully, you'll have two new classes in the directory:

```
PerfectTime_Stub.class
PerfectTime_Skel.class
```

corresponding to the stub and skeleton. Now you're ready to get the server and client to talk to each other.

7.44 Using the Remote Object

The whole point of RMI is to make the use of remote objects simple. The only extra thing that you must do in your client program is to look up and fetch the remote interface from the server. From then on, it's just regular Java programming: sending messages to objects. Here's the program that uses PerfectTime:

```
//: DisplayPerfectTime.java
// Uses remote object PerfectTime
```

```
package c15.ptime;
import java.rmi.*;
import java.rmi.registry.*;
public class DisplayPerfectTime {
public static void main(String[] args) {
System.setSecurityManager(
new RMISecurityManager());
try {
PerfectTimeI t =
(PerfectTimeI)Naming.lookup(
"//colossus:2005/PerfectTime");
for(int i = 0; i < 10; i++)
System.out.println("Perfect time = "+
t.getPerfectTime());
} catch(Exception e) {
e.printStackTrace();
}
}
} ///:~
```

The ID string is the same as the one used to register the object with Naming, and the first part represents the URL and port number. Since you're using a URL, you can also specify a machine on the Internet.

What comes back from Naming.lookup( ) must be cast to the remote interface, not to the class. If you use the class instead, you'll get an exception.

You can see in the method call

```
t.getPerfectTime( )
```

that once you have a handle to the remote object, programming with it is indistinguishable from programming with a local object (with one difference: remote methods throw RemoteException).

7.45 Alternatives to RMI

RMI is just one way to create objects that can be distributed across a network. It has the advantage of being a "pure Java" solution, but if you have a lot of code written in some other language, it might not meet your needs. The two most compelling alternatives are Microsoft's DCOM (which, according to Microsoft's plan, will eventually be hosted on platforms other than Windows) and CORBA, which is supported in Java 1.1 and was designed from the start to be cross-platform.

7.46 Package Imports

Instead of importing each class you need individually, you can import an entire package by replacing the class name with an asterisk (*) like this:

```
import java.net.*;
public class URLSplitter {
public static void main(String[] args) {
for (int i = 0; i < args.length; i++) {
try {
URL u = new URL(args[i]);
```

```
System.out.println("Protocol: " + u.getProtocol());
System.out.println("Host: " + u.getHost());
System.out.println("Port: " + u.getPort());
System.out.println("File: " + u.getFile());
System.out.println("Ref:  " + u.getRef());
}
catch (MalformedURLException e) {
System.err.println(args[i] + "is not a valid URL");
}
}
}
}
```

This does not affect the final compiled code at all. However compilation will take a little longer. In general the time you save in not having to recover from error messages about missing classes more than makes up for the time you lose in compilation.

7.47 Name Conflicts When Importing Packages

It is possible that you will try to import a package that contains classes that have the same name as a class in your own source code. In general you should try to avoid this, especially when the conflict is with a class in the java packages.

The two classes may or may not mean the same thing. In general you should probably rename the class in your own source code rather than in the package. However if the two classes with conflicting names are related functionally, it may make sense to implement your class as a subclass of the class in the package.

EXERCISES

1. *Compile and run the JabberServer and JabberClient programs in this chapter. Now edit the files to remove all of the buffering for the input and output, then compile and run them again to observe the results.*
2. *Create a server that asks for a password, then opens a file and sends the file over the network connection. Create a client that connects to this server, gives the appropriate password, then captures and saves the file. Test the pair of programs on your machine using the localhost (the local loopback IP address 127.0.0.1 produced by calling InetAddress.getByName(null)).*
3. *Modify the server in Exercise 2 so that it uses multithreading to handle multiple clients.*

   Modify JabberClient so that output flushing doesn't occur and observe the effect.

   Build on ShowHTML.java to produce an applet that is a password-protected gateway to a particular portion of your Web site.
4. *Create a client/server pair of programs that use datagrams to transmit a file from one machine to the other. (See the description at the end of the datagram section of this chapter.)*
5. *Take the VLookup.java program and modify it so that when you click on the resulting name it automatically takes that name and copies it to the clipboard (so you can simply paste it into your email).*
6. *Create an inheritance hierarchy of Rodent: Mouse, Gerbil, Hamster, etc. In the base class, provide methods that are common to all Rodents, and override these in the derived classes to perform different behaviors depending on the specific type of Rodent. Create an array of Rodent, fill it with different specific types of Rodents, and call your base-class methods to see what happens.*
7. *Change Exercise 1 so that Rodent is an interface.*
8. *Repair the problem in WindError.java.*

9. *In GreenhouseControls.java, add Event inner classes that turn fans on and off.*
10. *Create a class with public, private, protected, and "friendly" data members and method members. Create an object of this class and see what kind of compiler messages you get when you try to access all the class members. Be aware that classes in the same directory are part of the "default" package.*
11. *Create a class with protected data. Create a second class in the same file with a method that manipulates the protected data in the first class.*
12. *Create a new directory and edit your CLASSPATH to include that new directory. Copy the P.class file to your new directory and then change the names of the file, the P class inside and the method names. (You might also want to add additional output to watch how it works.) Create another program in a different directory that uses your new class.*
13. *Create the following file in the c05 directory (presumably in your CLASSPATH):*

```
//: PackagedClass.java
package c05;
class PackagedClass {
public PackagedClass() {
System.out.println(
"Creating a packaged class");
}
} ///:~
```

Then create the following file in a directory other than c05:

```
//: Foreign.java
package c05.foreign;
import c05.*;
public class Foreign {
public static void main (String[] args) {
PackagedClass pc = new PackagedClass();
}
} ///:~
```

13. *Explain why the compiler generates an error. Would making the Foreign class part of the c05 package change anything?*

8

Exception Handling

8.1 Exception Handling Statements

The Java programming language provides a mechanism known as exceptions to help programs report and handle errors. When an error occurs, the program throws an exception. What does this mean? It means that the normal flow of the program is interrupted and that the runtime environment attempts to find an exception handler—a block of code that can handle a particular type of error. The exception handler can attempt to recover from the error or, if it determines that the error is unrecoverable, provide a gentle exit from the program.

If there's a golden rule of programming it's this: Errors occur in software programs. This we know. But what really matters is what happens after the error occurs. How is the error handled? Who handles it? Can the program recover, or should it just die?

What's an Exception and Why Do I Care?

The Java language uses exceptions to provide error-handling capabilities for its programs. An exception is an event that occurs during the execution of a program that disrupts the normal flow of instructions.

8.1.1 Your First Encounter with Java Exceptions

If you have done any amount of Java programming at all, you have undoubtedly already encountered exceptions. Your first encounter with Java exceptions was probably in the form of an error message from the compiler like this one:

InputFile.java:11: Exception java.io.FileNotFoundException must be caught, or it must be declared in the throws clause of this method.

```
in = new FileReader(filename);
^
```

This message indicates that the compiler found an exception that is not being handled. The Java language requires that a method either catch all "checked" exceptions (those that are checked by the runtime system) or specify that it can throw that type of exception.

8.1.2 What's an Exception and Why Do I Care?

The term exception is shorthand for the phrase "exceptional event". It can be defined as follows:

Definition: An exception is an event that occurs during the execution of a program that disrupts the normal flow of instructions.

Many kinds of errors can cause exceptions—problems ranging from serious hardware errors, such as a hard disk crash, to simple programming errors, such as trying to access an out-of-bounds array element. When such an error occurs within a Java method, the method creates an exception object and hands it off to the runtime system. The exception object contains information about the exception, including its type and the state of the program when the error occurred. The runtime system is then responsible for finding some code to handle the error. In Java terminology, creating an exception object and handing it to the runtime system is called throwing an exception.

After a method throws an exception, the runtime system leaps into action to find someone to handle the exception. The set of possible "someones" to handle the exception is the set of methods in the call stack of the method where the error occurred. The runtime system searches backwards through the call stack, beginning with the method in which the error occurred, until it finds a method that contains an appropriate exception handler. An exception handler is considered appropriate if the type of the exception thrown is the same as the type of exception handled by the handler. Thus the exception bubbles up through the call stack until an appropriate handler is found and one of the calling methods handles the exception. The exception handler chosen is said to catch the exception.

If the runtime system exhaustively searches all of the methods on the call stack without finding an appropriate exception handler, the runtime system (and consequently the Java program) terminates.

8.2 Advatages of Using Exception Methods

By using exceptions to manage errors, Java programs have the following advantages over traditional error management techniques:

1. Separating Error Handling Code from "Regular" Code
2. Propagating Errors Up the Call Stack
3. Grouping Error Types and Error Differentiation

Advantage 1: Separating Error Handling Code from "Regular" Code

In traditional programming, error detection, reporting, and handling often lead to confusing spaghetti code. For example, suppose that you have a function that reads an entire file into memory. In pseudo-code, your function might look something like this:

```
readFile {
    open the file;
    determine its size;
    allocate that much memory;
    read the file into memory;
    close the file;
}
```

At first glance this function seems simple enough, but it ignores all of these potential errors:

- What happens if the file can't be opened?
- What happens if the length of the file can't be determined?
- What happens if enough memory can't be allocated?
- What happens if the read fails?
- What happens if the file can't be closed?

To answer these questions within your read_file function, you'd have to add a lot of code to do error detection, reporting and handling. Your function would end up looking something like this:

```
errorCodeType readFile {
    initialize errorCode = 0;
    open the file;
if (theFileIsOpen) {
```

```
    determine the length of the file;
    if (gotTheFileLength) {
     allocate that much memory;
     if (gotEnoughMemory) {
        read the file into memory;
        if (readFailed) {
    errorCode = -1;
    }
        } else {
        errorCode = -2;
    }
} else {
errorCode = -3;
}
close the file;
if (theFileDidntClose && errorCode == 0) {
errorCode = -4;
} else {
errorCode = errorCode and -4;
}
} else {
errorCode = -5;
}
return errorCode;
}
```

With error detection built in, your original 7 lines (in bold) have been inflated to 29 lines of code—a bloat factor of almost 400 percent. Worse, there's so much error detection, reporting, and returning that the original 7 lines of code are lost in the clutter. And worse yet, the logical flow of the code has also been lost in the clutter, making it difficult to tell if the code is doing the right thing: Is the file really being closed if the function fails to allocate enough memory? It's even more difficult to ensure that the code continues to do the right thing after you modify the function three months after writing it. Many programmers "solve" this problem by simply ignoring it—errors are "reported" when their programs crash.

Java provides an elegant solution to the problem of error management: exceptions. Exceptions enable you to write the main flow of your code and deal with the, well, exceptional cases elsewhere. If your read_file function used exceptions instead of traditional error management techniques, it would look something like this:

```
readFile {
    try {
        open the file;
        determine its size;
        allocate that much memory;
        read the file into memory;
        close the file;
} catch (fileOpenFailed) {
    doSomething;
} catch (sizeDeterminationFailed) {
```

```
        doSomething;
} catch (memoryAllocationFailed) {
        doSomething;
} catch (readFailed) {
        doSomething;
} catch (fileCloseFailed) {
        doSomething;
    }
}
```

Note that exceptions don't spare you the effort of doing the work of detecting, reporting, and handling errors. What exceptions do provide for you is the means to separate all the grungy details of what to do when something out-of-the-ordinary happens from the main logic of your program.

In addition, the bloat factor for error management code in this program is about 250 percent—compared to 400 percent in the previous example.

Advantage 2: Propagating Errors Up the Call Stack

A second advantage of exceptions is the ability to propagate error reporting up the call stack of methods. Suppose that the readFile method is the fourth method in a series of nested method calls made by your main program: method1 calls method2, which calls method3, which finally calls readFile.

```
method1 {
    call method2;
}
method2 {
    call method3;
}
method3 {
    call readFile;
}
```

Suppose also that method1 is the only method interested in the errors that occur within readFile. Traditional error notification techniques force method2 and method3 to propagate the error codes returned by readFile up the call stack until the error codes finally reach method1—the only method that is interested in them.

```
method1 {
    errorCodeType error;
    error = call method2;
    if (error)
        doErrorProcessing;
    else
    proceed;
}
    errorCodeType method2 {
    errorCodeType error;
    error = call method3;
    if (error)
        return error;
else
```

```
        proceed;
    }
    errorCodeType method3 {
        errorCodeType error;
        error = call readFile;
        if (error)
            return error;
    else
        proceed;
    }
```

As you learned earlier, the Java runtime system searches backwards through the call stack to find any methods that are interested in handling a particular exception. A Java method can "duck" any exceptions thrown within it, thereby allowing a method further up the call stack to catch it. Thus only the methods that care about errors have to worry about detecting errors.

```
    method1 {
        try {
            call method2;
        } catch (exception) {
    doErrorProcessing;
    }
    }
    method2 throws exception {
        call method3;
    }
    method3 throws exception {
        call readFile;
    }
```

However, as you can see from the pseudo-code, ducking an exception does require some effort on the part of the "middleman" methods. Any checked exceptions that can be thrown within a method are part of that method's public programming interface and must be specified in the throws clause of the method. Thus a method informs its callers about the exceptions that it can throw, so that the callers can intelligently and consciously decide what to do about those exceptions.

Note again the difference in the bloat factor and code obfuscation factor of these two error management techniques. The code that uses exceptions is more compact and easier to understand.

Advantage 3: Grouping Error Types and Error Differentiation

Often exceptions fall into categories or groups. For example, you could imagine a group of exceptions, each of which represents a specific type of error that can occur when manipulating an array: the index is out of range for the size of the array, the element being inserted into the array is of the wrong type, or the element being searched for is not in the array. Furthermore, you can imagine that some methods would like to handle all exceptions that fall within a category (all array exceptions), and other methods would like to handle specific exceptions (just the invalid index exceptions, please).

Because all exceptions that are thrown within a Java program are first-class objects, grouping or categorization of exceptions is a natural outcome of the class hierarchy. Java exceptions must be instances of Throwable or any Throwable descendant. As for other Java classes, you can create subclasses of the Throwable class and subclasses of your subclasses. Each "leaf" class (a class with no subclasses) represents a specific type of exception and each "node" class (a class with one or more subclasses) represents a group of related exceptions.

For example, in the following diagram, ArrayException is a subclass of Exception (a subclass of Throwable) and has three subclasses.

InvalidIndexException, ElementTypeException, and NoSuchElementException are all leaf classes. Each one represents a specific type of error that can occur when manipulating an array. One way a method can exceptions is to catch only those that are instances of a leaf class. For example, an exception handler that handles only invalid index exceptions has a catch statement like this:

```
catch (InvalidIndexException e) {
. . .
}
```

ArrayException is a node class and represents any error that can occur when manipulating an array object, including those errors specifically represented by one of its subclasses. A method can catch an exception based on its group or general type by specifying any of the exception's superclasses in the catch statement. For example, to catch all array exceptions regardless of their specific type, an exception handler would specify an ArrayException argument:

```
catch (ArrayException e) {
. . .
}
```

This handler would catch all array exceptions including InvalidIndexException, ElementTypeException, and NoSuchElementException. You can find out precisely which type of exception occurred by querying the exception handler parameter e. You could even set up an exception handler that handles any Exception with this handler:

```
catch (Exception e) {
. . .
}
```

Exception handlers that are too general, such as the one shown here, can make your code more error prone by catching and handling exceptions that you didn't anticipate and therefore are not correctly handled within the handler. We don't recommend writing general exception handlers as a rule.

As you've seen, you can create groups of exceptions and handle exceptions in a general fashion, or you can use the specific exception type to differentiate exceptions and handle exceptions in an exact fashion.

8.3 Basic Exceptions

An exceptional condition is a problem that prevents the continuation of the method or scope that you're in. It's important to distinguish an exceptional condition from a normal problem, in which you have enough information in the current context to somehow cope with the difficulty. With an exceptional condition, you cannot continue processing because you don't have the information necessary to deal with the problem in the current context . All you can do is jump out of the current context and relegate that problem to a higher context. This is what happens when you throw an exception.

A simple example is a divide. If you're about to divide by zero, it's worth checking to make sure you don't go ahead and perform the divide. But what does it mean that the denominator is zero? Maybe you know, in the context of the problem you're trying to solve in that particular method, how to deal with a zero denominator. But if it's an unexpected value, you can't deal with it and so must throw an exception rather than continuing along that path.

When you throw an exception, several things happen. First, the exception object is created in the same way that any Java object is created: on the heap, with new. Then the current path of execution (the one you couldn't continue, remember) is stopped and the handle for the exception object is ejected from the current context. At this point the exception-handling mechanism takes over and begins to look for an appropriate place to continue executing the program. This appropriate place is the exception handler , whose job is to recover from the problem so the program can either try another tack or simply continue.

As a simple example of throwing an exception, consider an object handle called t. It's possible that you might be passed a handle that hasn't been initialized, so you might want to check before trying to call a method using that object handle. You can send information about the error into a larger context by creating an object representing your information and "throwing" it out of your current context. This is called throwing an exception . Here's what it looks like:

```
if(t == null)
throw new NullPointerException();
```

This throws the exception, which allows you - in the current context - to abdicate responsibility for thinking about the issue further. It's just magically handled somewhere else. Precisely where will be shown shortly.

8.4 Exception Arguments

Like any object in Java, you always create exceptions on the heap using new and a constructor gets called. There are two constructors in all the standard exceptions; the first is the default constructor, and the second takes a string argument so you can place pertinent information in the exception:

```
if(t == null)
throw new NullPointerException("t = null");
```

This string can later be extracted using various methods, as will be shown later.

The keyword throw causes a number of relatively magical things to happen. First it executes the new-expression to create an object that isn't there under normal program execution, and of course, the constructor is called for that object. Then the object is, in effect, "returned" from the method, even though that object type isn't normally what the method is designed to return. A simplistic way to think about exception handling is as an alternate return mechanism, although you get into trouble if you take that analogy too far. You can also exit from ordinary scopes by throwing an exception. But a value is returned, and the method or scope exits.

Any similarity to an ordinary return from a method ends here, because where you return is someplace completely different from where you return for a normal method call. (You end up in an appropriate exception handler that might be miles away - many levels lower on the call stack - from where the exception was thrown.)

In addition, you can throw any type of Throwable object that you want. Typically, you'll throw a different class of exception for each different type of error. The idea is to store the information in the exception object and in the type of exception object chosen, so someone in the bigger context can figure out what to do with your exception. (Often, the only information is the type of exception object, and nothing meaningful is stored within the exception object.)

8.5 Catching an Exception

If a method throws an exception, it must assume that exception is caught and dealt with. One of the advantages of Java exception handling is that it allows you to concentrate on the problem you're trying to solve in one place, and then deal with the errors from that code in another place.

To see how an exception is caught, you must first understand the concept of a guarded region, which is a section of code that might produce exceptions, and is followed by the code to handle those exceptions.

8.6 The Try Block

If you're inside a method and you throw an exception (or another method you call within this method throws an exception), that method will exit in the process of throwing. If you don't want a throw to leave a method, you can set up a special block within that method to capture the exception. This is called the try block because you "try" your various method calls there. The try block is an ordinary scope, preceded by the keyword try:

```
try {
// Code that might generate exceptions
}
```

If you were checking for errors carefully in a programming language that didn't support exception handling, you'd have to surround every method call with setup and error testing code, even if you call the same method several times. With exception handling, you put everything in a try block and capture all the exceptions in one place. This means your code is a lot easier to write and easier to read because the goal of the code is not confused with the error checking.

8.7 Exception Handlers

Of course, the thrown exception must end up someplace. This "place" is the exception handler, and there's one for every exception type you want to catch. Exception handlers immediately follow the try block and are denoted by the keyword catch:

```
try {
// Code that might generate exceptions
} catch(Type1 id1) {
// Handle exceptions of Type1
} catch(Type2 id2) {
// Handle exceptions of Type2
} catch(Type3 id3) {
// Handle exceptions of Type3
}
// etc...
```

Each catch clause (exception handler) is like a little method that takes one and only one argument of a particular type. The identifier (id1, id2, and so on) can be used inside the handler, just like a method argument. Sometimes you never use the identifier because the type of the exception gives you enough information to deal with the exception, but the identifier must still be there.

The handlers must appear directly after the try block. If an exception is thrown, the exception-handling mechanism goes hunting for the first handler with an argument that matches the type of the exception. Then it enters that catch clause, and the exception is considered handled. (The search for handlers stops once the catch clause is finished.) Only the matching catch clause executes; it's not like a switch statement in which you need a break after each case to prevent the remaining ones from executing.

Note that, within the try block, a number of different method calls might generate the same exception, but you need only one handler.

8.8 Using Exceptions

The following error message is one of two similar error messages you will see if you try to compile the class InputFile, because the InputFile class contains calls to methods that throw exceptions when an error occurs:

InputFile.java:8:

Warning: Exception java.io.FileNotFoundException must be caught, or it must be declared in throws clause of this method.

```
in = new FileReader(filename);
^
```

The Java language requires that methods either catch or specify all checked exceptions that can be thrown within the scope of that method. (Details about what this actually means are covered in the next section, Java's Catch or Specify Requirement.) If the compiler detects a method, such as those in InputFile, that doesn't meet this requirement, it issues an error message like the one shown above and refuses to compile the program.

Let's look at InputFile in more detail and see what's going on.

The InputFile class wraps a FileReader and provides a method, getWord, for reading a word from the current position in the reader.

```
// Note: This class won't compile by design!
import java.io.*;
public class InputFile {
private FileReader in;
public InputFile(String filename) {
in = new FileReader(filename);
}
public String getWord() {
int c;
StringBuffer buf = new StringBuffer();
do {
c = in.read();
if (Character.isWhitespace((char)c))
return buf.toString();
else {
buf.append((char)c);
} while (c != -1);

return buf.toString();
}
}
```

The compiler prints the first error message because of the bold line in the above code listing. The bold line creates a new FileReader object and uses it to open a file whose name is passed into the **FileReader constructor.**

So what should the FileReader do if the named file does not exist on the file system? Well, that depends on what the program using the FileReader wants to do. The implementers of FileReader have no idea what the InputFile class wants to do if the file does not exist. Should the FileReader kill the program? Should it try an alternate filename? Should it just create a file of the indicated name? There's no possible way the FileReader implementers could choose a solution that would suit every user of FileReader. So, they punted, or rather, threw, an exception. If the file named in the argument to the FileReader constructor does not exist on the file system, the constructor throws a java.io.FileNotFoundException. By throwing an exception, FileReader allows the calling method to handle the error in whatever way is most appropriate for it.

As you can see from the code, the InputFile class completely ignores the fact that the FileReader constructor can throw an exception. However, as stated previously, the Java language requires that a method either catch or specify all checked exceptions that can be thrown within the scope of that method. Because the InputFile class does neither, the compiler refuses to compile the program and prints an error message.

In addition to the first error message shown above, you also see the following similar error message when you compile the InputFile class:

InputFile.java:15: Warning: Exception java.io.IOException must be caught, or it must be declared in throws clause of this method.

```
while ((c = in.read()) != -1) {
^
```

The InputFile class's getWord method reads from the FileReader that was opened in InputFile's constructor. The FileReader read method throws a java.io.IOException if for some reason it can't read from the file. Again, the InputFile class makes no attempt to catch or specify this exception. Thus you see the second error message.

At this point, you have two options. You can either arrange to catch the exceptions within the appropriate methods in the InputFile class, or the InputFile methods can "duck" and allow other methods further up the call stack to catch them. Either way, the InputFile methods must do something, either catch or specify the exceptions, before the InputFile class can be compiled. For the diligent, there's a class, InputFileDeclared, that fixes the bugs in InputFile by specifying the exceptions.

8.9 Java's Catch or Specify Requirement

As stated previously, Java requires that a method either catch or specify all checked exceptions that can be thrown within the scope of the method. This requirement has several components that need further description: "catch", "specify," "checked exceptions," and "exceptions that can be thrown within the scope of the method."

- **Catch**

A method can catch an exception by providing an exception handler for that type of exception. The next page, Dealing with Exceptions, introduces an example program, talks about catching exceptions, and shows you how to write an exception handler for the example program.

- **Specify**

If a method chooses not to catch an exception, the method must specify that it can throw that exception. Why did the Java designers make this requirement? Because any exception that can be thrown by a method is really part of the method's public programming interface: callers of a method must know about the exceptions that a method can throw in order to intelligently and consciously decide what to do about those exceptions. Thus, in the method signature you specify the exceptions that the method can throw.

The next page, Dealing with Exceptions, talks about specifying exceptions that a method throws and shows you how to do it.

- **Checked Exceptions**

Java has different types of exceptions, including I/O Exceptions, runtime exceptions, and exceptions of your own creation, to name a few. Of interest to us in this discussion are runtime exceptions. Runtime exceptions are those exceptions that occur within the Java runtime system. This includes arithmetic exceptions (such as when dividing by zero), pointer exceptions (such as trying to access an object through a null reference), and indexing exceptions (such as attempting to access an array element through an index that is too large or too small).

Runtime exceptions can occur anywhere in a program and in a typical program can be very numerous. The cost of checking for runtime exceptions often exceeds the benefit of catching or specifying them. Thus the compiler does not require that you catch or specify runtime exceptions, although you can. Checked exceptions are exceptions that are not runtime exceptions and are checked by the compiler; the compiler checks that these exceptions are caught or specified.

Some consider this a loophole in Java's exception handling mechanism, and programmers are tempted to make all exceptions runtime exceptions. In general, this is not recommended. Runtime Exceptions—The Controversy contains a thorough discussion about when and how to use runtime exceptions.

8.9.1 Exceptions that can be thrown within the Scope of the Method

The statement "exceptions that can be thrown within the scope of the method" may seem obvious at first: just look for the throw statement. However, this statement includes more than just the exceptions that can be thrown directly by the method: the key is in the phrase within the scope of. This phrase includes any exception that can be thrown while the flow of control remains within the method. This statement includes both

- Exceptions that are thrown directly by the method with Java's throw statement.
- Exceptions that are thrown indirectly by the method through calls to other methods

8.10 Dealing with Exceptions

Your First Encounter with Java Exceptions briefly described how you were (probably) first introduced to Java exceptions: a compiler error complaining that you must either catch or specify exceptions. Then, Java's Catch or Specify Requirement discussed what exactly the error message means and why the Java language designers decided to make this requirement. We're now going to show you both how to catch an exception and how to specify one.

8.10.1 The List of Numbers Example

The sections below, both the one on catching an exception and the one on specifying an exception, use the same example. This example defines and implements a class named ListOfNumbers. The ListOfNumbers class calls two methods from classes in the Java packages that can throw exceptions. Catching and Handling Exceptions will show you how to write exception handlers for both exceptions, and Specifying the Exceptions Thrown by a Method will show you how to specify those exceptions instead of catching them.

8.10.2 Catching and Handling Exceptions

Once you've familiarized yourself with the ListOfNumbers class and where the exceptions can be thrown, you can learn how to write exception handlers to catch and handle those exceptions.

This section covers the three components of an exception handler—the try, catch, and finally blocks—by showing you how to use them to write an exception handler for the ListOfNumbers class's writeList method. In addition, this section contains a page that walks through the writeList method and analyzes what occurs within the method during various scenarios.

8.10.3 Specifying the Exceptions Thrown by a Method

If it is not appropriate for your method to catch and handle an exception thrown by a method that it calls, or if your method itself throws its own exception, you must specify in the method signature that the method throws the exception. Using the ListOfNumbers class, this section shows you how to specify exceptions that a method throws.

Example 8.1 The ListOfNumbers Example

The following example defines and implements a class named ListOfNumbers. The ListOfNumbers class calls two methods from classes in the Java packages that can throw exceptions.

```
// Note: This class won't compile by design!
// See ListOfNumbersDeclared.java or ListOfNumbers.java
// for a version of this  class that will compile.

import java.io.*;
import java.util.Vector;

public class ListOfNumbers {
    private Vector victor;
    private static final int size = 10;

    public ListOfNumbers () {
        victor = new Vector(size);
        for (int i = 0; i < size; i++)
        victor.addElement(new Integer(i));
}
public void writeList() {
    PrintWriter out = new PrintWriter(new FileWriter("OutFile.txt"));

    for (int i = 0; i < size; i++)
        out.println("Value at: " + i + "= " + victor.elementAt(i));
        out.close();
    }
}
```

Upon construction, ListOfNumbers creates a Vector that contains ten Integer elements with sequential values 0 through 9. The ListOfNumbers class also defines a method named writeList that writes the list of numbers into a text file called OutFile.txt.

The writeList method calls two methods that can throw exceptions. First, the following line invokes the constructor for FileWriter, which throws an IOException if the file cannot be opened for any reason:

```
out = new PrintWriter(new FileWriter("OutFile.txt"));
```

Second, the Vector class's elementAt method throws an ArrayIndexOutOfBoundsException if you pass in an index whose value is too small (a negative number) or too large (larger than the number of elements currently contained by the Vector). Here's how ListOfNumbers invokes elementAt:

```
out.println("Value at: "+ i + "= "+ victor.elementAt(i));
```

If you try to compile the ListOfNumbers class, the compiler prints an error message about the exception thrown by the FileWriter constructor, but does not display an error message about the exception thrown by elementAt. This is because the exception thrown by the FileWriter constructor, IOException, is a checked exception and the exception thrown by the elementAt method, ArrayIndexOutOfBoundsException, is a runtime exception. Java requires that you catch or specify only checked exceptions. For more information, refer to Java's Catch or Specify Requirement.

The next section, Catching and Handling Exceptions, will show you how to write an exception handler for the ListOfNumbers' writeList method.

Following that, a section named Specifying the Exceptions Thrown By a Method will show you how to specify that the ListOfNumbers' writeList method throws the exceptions instead of catching them.

8.11 Three Exception Handling Staements

Three statements play a part in handling exceptions:

- The try statement identifies a block of statements within which an exception might be thrown.
- The catch statement must be associated with a try statement and identifies a block of statements that can handle a particular type of exception. The statements are executed if an exception of a particular type occurs within the try block.
- The finally statement must be associated with a try statement and identifies a block of statements that are executed regardless of whether or not an error occurs within the try block.

Here's the general form of these statements:

```
try {
statement(s)
} catch (exceptiontype name) {
statement(s)
} finally {
statement(s)
}
```

This has been a brief overview of the statements provided by the Java programming language used in reporting and handling errors. However, other factors and considerations, such as the difference between runtime and checked exceptions and the hierarchy of exceptions classes, which represent various types of exceptions, play a role in using the exception mechanism. The Handling Errors with Exceptions lesson provides a complete discussion on this subject.

Traditional programming languages set flags or return bad values like -1 to indicate problems. Programmers often don't check these values. Java throws Exception objects to indicate a problem. These cannot be ignored.

```
try-catch-finally
public class HelloThere {
public static void main(String[] args) {
try {
System.out.println("Hello "+ args[0]);
}
catch (ArrayIndexOutOfBoundsException e) {
System.out.println("Hello Whoever you are.");
}
```

```
finally {
System.out.println("How are you?");
}
}
}
```

Checked exceptions must be caught at compile time. Runtime exceptions do not need to be. Errors often cannot be.

8.11.1 The try Block

The first step in constructing an exception handler is to enclose the statements that might throw an exception within a try block. In general, a try block looks like this:

```
try {
   Java statements
}
```

The segment of code labelled Java statements is composed of one or more legal Java statements that could throw an exception.

To construct an exception handler for the writeList method from the ListOfNumbers class, you need to enclose the exception-throwing statements of the writeList method within a try block. There is more than one way to accomplish this task. You could put each statement that might potentially throw an exception within its own try statement, and provide separate exception handlers for each try. Or you could put all of the writeList statements within a single try statement and associate multiple handlers with it. The following listing uses one try statement for the entire method because the code tends to be easier to read.

```
PrintWriter out = null;
try {
    System.out.println("Entering try statement");
    out = new PrintWriter(
        new FileWriter("OutFile.txt"));
    for (int i = 0; i < size; i++)
    out.println("Value at: " + i + " = " + victor.elementAt(i));
}
```

The try statement governs the statements enclosed within it and defines the scope of any exception handlers associated with it. In other words, if an exception occurs within the try statement, that exception is handled by the appropriate exception handler associated with this try statement.

A try statement must be accompanied by at least one catch block or one finally block.

8.11.2 The catch Block(s)

As you learned on the previous page, the try statement defines the scope of its associated exception handlers. You associate exception handlers with a try statement by providing one or more catch blocks directly after the try block:

```
try {
. . .
} cat0ch ( . . . ) {
. . .
} catch ( . . . ) {
. . .
}
```

There can be no intervening code between the end of the try statement and the beginning of the first catch statement. The general form of Java's catch statement is:

```
catch (SomeThrowableObject variableName) {
Java statements
}
```

As you can see, the catch statement requires a single formal argument. The argument to the catch statement looks like an argument declaration for a method. The argument type, SomeThrowableObject, declares the type of exception that the handler can handle and must be the name of a class that inherits from the Throwable class defined in the java.lang package. When Java programs throw an exception they are really just throwing an object, and only objects that derive from Throwable can be thrown. You'll learn more about throwing exceptions in How to Throw Exceptions.

variableName is the name by which the handler can refer to the exception caught by the handler. For example, the exception handlers for the writeList method (shown later) each call the exception's getMessage method using the exception's declared name e:

```
e.getMessage()
```

You access the instance variables and methods of exceptions in the same manner that you access the instance variables and methods of other objects. getMessage is a method provided by the Throwable class that prints additional information about the error that occurred. The Throwable class also implements two methods for filling in and printing the contents of the execution stack when the exception occurred. Subclasses of Throwable can add other methods or instance variables. To find out what methods an exception implements, check its class definition and definitions for any of its ancestor classes.

The catch block contains a series of legal Java statements. These statements are executed if and when the exception handler is invoked. The runtime system invokes the exception handler when the handler is the first one in the call stack whose type matches that of the exception thrown.

The writeList method from the ListOfNumbers class uses two exception handlers for its try statement, with one handler for each of the two types of exceptions that can be thrown within the try block — ArrayIndexOutOfBoundsException and IOException.

```
try {
. . .
} catch (ArrayIndexOutOfBoundsException e) {
System.err.println("Caught ArrayIndexOutOfBoundsException: " +
e.getMessage());
} catch (IOException e) {
System.err.println("Caught IOException: " +
e.getMessage());
}
```

8.11.3 Catching Multiple Exception Types with One Handler

The two exception handlers used by the writeList method are very specialized. Each handles only one type of exception. The Java language allows you to write general exception handlers that handle multiple types of exceptions.

As you know, Java exceptions are Throwable objects; they are instances of Throwable or a subclass of Throwable. The Java packages contain numerous classes that derive from Throwable and thus, build a hierarchy of Throwable classes.

Your exception handler can be written to handle any class that inherits from Throwable. If you write a handler for a "leaf" class (a class with no subclasses), you've written a specialized handler: it will only handle exceptions of that specific type. If you write a handler for a "node" class (a class with subclasses), you've written a general handler: it will handle any exception whose type is the node class or any of its subclasses.

Let's modify the writeList method once again. Only this time, let's write it so that it handles both IOExceptions and ArrayIndexOutOfBoundsExceptions. The closest common ancester of IOException and ArrayIndexOutOfBoundsException is the Exception class. An exception handler that handles both types of exceptions looks like this:

```
try {
. . .
} catch (Exception e) {
System.err.println("Exception caught: " + e.getMessage());
}
```

The class is pretty high in the Throwable class hierarchy. So in addition to the IOException and ArrayIndexOutOfBoundsException types that this exception handler is intended to catch, it will catch numerous other types. Generally speaking, your exception handlers should be more specialized. Handlers that can catch most or all exceptions are typically useless for error recovery because the handler has to determine what type of exception occurred anyway to determine the best recovery strategy. Also, exception handlers that are too general can make code more error prone by catching and handling exceptions that weren't anticipated by the programmer and for which the handler was not intended.

8.11.4 The finally Block

The final step in setting up an exception handler is providing a mechanism for cleaning up the state of the method before (possibly) allowing control to be passed to a different part of the program. You do this by enclosing the cleanup code within a finally block.

The try block of the writeList method that you've been working with opens a PrintWriter. The program should close that stream before allowing control to pass out of the writeList method. This poses a somewhat complicated problem because writeList's try block has three different exit possibilities:

- The new FileWriter statement failed and threw an IOException.
- The victor.elementAt(i) statement failed and threw an ArrayIndexOutOfBoundsException.
- Everything succeeded and the try block exited normally.

The runtime system always executes the statements within the finally block regardless of what happens within the try block. Regardless of whether control exits the writeList method's try block due to one of the three scenarios listed previously, the code within the finally block will be executed.

This is the finally block for the writeList method. It cleans up and closes the PrintWriter.

```
finally {
    if (out != null) {
        System.out.println("Closing PrintWriter");
        out.close();
    } else {
        System.out.println("PrintWriter not open");
    }
}
```

8.11.5 Is the finally Statement Really Necessary?

At first the need for a finally statement may not be immediately apparent. Programmers often ask "Is the finally statement really necessary or is it just sugar for my Java?" In particular, C++ programmers doubt the need for a finally statement because C++ doesn't have one.

The need for a finally statement is not apparent until you consider the following: how does the PrintWriter in the writeList method get closed if you don't provide an exception handler for the ArrayIndexOutOfBoundsException and an ArrayIndexOutOfBoundsException occurs? (It's easy and legal to omit an exception handler for ArrayIndexOutOfBoundsException because it's a runtime exception and the compiler won't alert you that the writeList contains a method call that might throw one.) The answer is that the PrintWriter does not get closed if an ArrayIndexOutOfBoundsException occurs and writeList does not provide a handler for it—unless the writeList provides a finally statement.

There are other benefits to using the finally statement. In the writeList example it is possible to provide for cleanup without the intervention of a finally statement. For example, you could put the code to close the PrintWriter at the end of the try block and again within the exception handler for ArrayIndexOutOfBoundsException, as shown here:

```
try {
    . . .
    out.close();          // don't do this; it duplicates code
} catch (ArrayIndexOutOfBoundsException e) {
    out.close();          // don't do this; it duplicates code
    System.err.println("Caught ArrayIndexOutOfBoundsException:"+
                                          e.getMessage());
} catch (IOException e) {
    System.err.println("Caught IOException: "+ e.getMessage());
}
```

However, this duplicates code, making the code hard to read and prone to errors if you modify the code later. For example, if you add code to the try block that may throw a new type of exception, you will have to remember to close the PrintWriter within the new exception handler (which if you're anything like me, you are bound to forget).

8.11.6 Putting It All Together

The previous sections describe how to construct the try, catch, and finally code blocks for the writeList example. Now, let's walk through the code and investigate what happens during three scenarios.

When all of the components are put together, the writeList method looks like this:

```
public void writeList() {
PrintWriter out = null;
try {
System.out.println("Entering try statement");
out = new PrintWriter(
new FileWriter("OutFile.txt"));
for (int i = 0; i < size; i++)
out.println("Value at: "+ i + "= " + victor.elementAt(i));
} catch (ArrayIndexOutOfBoundsException e) {
System.err.println("Caught ArrayIndexOutOfBoundsException: "+
```

```
e.getMessage());
} catch (IOException e) {
System.err.println("Caught IOException: "+ e.getMessage());
} finally {
if (out != null) {
System.out.println("Closing PrintWriter");
out.close();
} else {
System.out.println("PrintWriter not open");
}
}
}
```

This try block in this method has three different exit possibilities:

- The new FileWriter statement fails and throws an IOException.
- The victor.elementAt(i) statement fails and throws an ArrayIndexOutOfBoundsException.

Everything succeeds and the try statement exits normally.

This section investigates in detail what happens in the writeList method during each of those exit possibilities.

Scenario 1: An IOException Occurs

The new FileWriter("OutFile.txt") statement can fail for any number of reasons: the user doesn't have write permission on the file or directory, the file system is full, or the directory for the file doesn't exist. If any of these situations is true, then the constructor for FileWriter throws an IOException.

When the IOException is thrown, the runtime system immediately stops execution of the try block. Then the runtime system attempts to locate an exception handler appropriate for handling an IOException.

The runtime system begins its search at the top of the method call stack. When the exception occurred, the FileWriter constructor was at the top of the call stack. However, the FileWriter constructor doesn't have an appropriate exception handler so the runtime system checks the next method in the method call stack—the writeList method. The writeList method has two exception handlers: one for ArrayIndexOutofBoundsException and one for IOException.

The runtime system checks writeList's handlers in the order that they appear following the try statement. The argument to the first exception handler is ArrayIndexOutofBoundsException, but the exception that was thrown is an IOException. An IOException cannot legally be assigned to an ArrayIndexOutofBoundsException, so the runtime system continues its search for an appropriate exception handler.

The argument to writeList's second exception handler is an IOException. The exception thrown by the FileWriter constructor is also an IOException and can be legally assigned to the handler's IOException argument. Thus, this handler is deemed appropriate and the runtime system executes this handler, which prints this statement:

Caught IOException: OutFile.txt

After the exception handler has run, the runtime system passes control to the finally block. In this particular scenario, the PrintWriter never was opened, and thus out is null and won't get closed. After the finally block has completed executing, the program continues with the first statement after the finally block.

The complete output that you see from the ListOfNumbers program when an IOException is thrown is this:

- Entering try statement
- Caught IOException: OutFile.txt
- PrintWriter not open

Scenario 2: An ArrayIndexOutofBoundsException Occurs

This scenario is the same as the first except that a different error occurs during the try block. In this scenario, the argument passed to the Vector's elementAt method is out of bounds. That is, the argument is either less than 0 or is larger than the size of the array. (The way the code is written, this is actually impossible, but let's suppose a bug is introduced into the code when someone modifies it.)

As in to scenario 1, when the exception occurs the runtime system stops execution of the try block and attempts to locate an exception handler suitable for an ArrayIndexOutofBoundsException. The runtime system searches for an appropriate exception handler as it did before. It comes upon the catch statement in the writeList method that handles exceptions of the type ArrayIndexOutofBoundsException. Since the type of the thrown exception matches the type of the exception handler, the runtime system executes this exception handler.

After the exception handler has run, the runtime system passes control to the finally block. In this particular scenario, the PrintWriter did get opened, thus the finally statement closes it. After the finally block has completed executing, the program continues with the first statement after the finally block.

The complete output that you see from the ListOfNumbers program when an ArrayIndexOutofBoundsException is thrown is something like this:

- Entering try statement
- Caught ArrayIndexOutOfBoundsException: 10 >= 10
- Closing PrintWriter

Scenario 3: The try block exits normally

In this scenario, all the statements within the scope of the try block execute successfully and throw no exceptions. Execution falls off the end of the try block, and then the runtime system passes control to the finally block. Since everything was successful, the PrintWriter is open when control reaches the finally block, which closes the PrintWriter. Again, after the finally block has completed executing, the program continues with the first statement after the finally block.

Thus, the output that you see from the ListOfNumbers program when no exceptions are thrown is:

- Entering try statement
- Closing PrintWriter

Specifying the Exceptions Thrown by a Method

The previous section showed you how to write an exception handler for the writeList method in the ListOfNumbers class. Sometimes, it's appropriate for your code to catch exceptions that can occur within it. In other cases, however, it's better to let a method further up the call stack handle the exception. For example, if you were providing the ListOfNumbers class as part of a package of classes, you probably couldn't anticipate the needs of all of the users of your package. In this case, it's better to not catch the exception and to allow someone further up the call stack to handle it.

If the writeList method doesn't catch the exceptions that can occur within it, then the writeList method must specify that it can throw them. Let's modify the writeList method to specify the methods that it can throw. To remind you, here's the original version of the writeList method:

```
public void writeList() {
PrintWriter out = new PrintWriter(
new FileWriter("OutFile.txt"));
for (int i = 0; i < size; i++)
out.println("Value at: "+ i + "= " + victor.elementAt(i));
}
```

As you recall, the new FileWriter("OutFile.txt") statement might throw an IOException (which is not a runtime exception). The victor.elementAt(i) statement can throw an ArrayIndexOutofBoundsException (which, as a subclass of RuntimeException, is a runtime exception).

To specify that writeList throws these two exceptions, you add a throws clause to the method signature for the writeList method. The throws clause is composed of the throws keyword followed by a comma-separated list of all the exceptions thrown by that method. The throws clause goes after the method name and argument list and before the curly bracket that defines the scope of the method. Here's an example:

public void writeList throws IOException, ArrayIndexOutOfBoundsException {

Remember that ArrayIndexOutofBoundsException is a runtime exception, so you don't have to specify it in the throws clause, although you can.

8.12 Why use Exceptions Instead of Return Values?

- Forces error checking
- Low overhead for non-exceptional case
- Traditional programming languages set flags or return bad values like -1 to indicate problems. Programmers often don't check these values.
- Java throws Exception objects to indicate a problem. These cannot be ignored.

```
try-catch
try-catch
public class HelloThere {
public static void main(String[] args) {
try {
System.out.println("Hello "+ args[0]);
}
catch (ArrayIndexOutOfBoundsException e) {
System.out.println("Hello Whoever you are.");
}
}
}
```

8.13 The Different Kinds of Exceptions

- Checked Exceptions
- Errors
- Runtime Exceptions

Checked exceptions must be caught at compile time. Runtime exceptions do not need to be. Errors often cannot be.

The Throwable class hierarchy

Almost all the code is in the java.lang.Throwable class. Almost all of its subclasses only provide new constructors that change the message of the exception.

8.14 Writing Exception Subclasses

Most exception subclasses will inherit all their functionality from the superclass. Each subclass mainly serves as a marker for a different kind of exception. However it only rarely provides new methods or fields. Thus most of the time the only methods you need to implement are the constructors. There should be one noargs constructor and one constructor that takes a String message as an argument. These will mostly just invoke the matching superclass constructor.

8.15 Error Handling with Exceptions

The basic philosophy of Java is that "badly-formed code will not be run."

As with C++, the ideal time to catch the error is at compile time, before you even try to run the program. However, not all errors can be detected at compile time. The rest of the problems must be handled at run-time through some formality that allows the originator of the error to pass appropriate information to a recipient who will know how to handle the difficulty properly.

In C and other earlier languages, there could be several of these formalities, and they were generally established by convention and not as part of the programming language. Typically, you returned a special value or set a flag, and the recipient was supposed to look at the value or the flag and determine that something was amiss. However, as the years passed, it was discovered that programmers who use a library tend to think of themselves as invincible, as in, "Yes, errors might happen to others but not in my code." So, not too surprisingly, they wouldn't check for the error conditions (and sometimes the error conditions were too silly to check for [41]). If you were thorough enough to check for an error every time you called a method, your code could turn into an unreadable nightmare. Because programmers could still coax systems out of these languages they were resistant to admitting the truth: This approach to handling errors was a major limitation to creating large, robust, maintainable programs.

The solution is to take the casual nature out of error handling and to enforce formality. This actually has a long history, since implementations of exception handling go back to operating systems in the 1960s and even to BASIC's on error goto . But C++ exception handling was based on Ada, and Java's is based primarily on C++ (although it looks even more like Object Pascal).

The word "exception" is meant in the sense of "I take exception to that." At the point where the problem occurs you might not know what to do with it, but you do know that you can't just continue on merrily; you must stop and somebody, somewhere, must figure out what to do. But you don't have enough information in the current context to fix the problem. So you hand the problem out to a higher context where someone is qualified to make the proper decision (much like a chain of command).

The other rather significant benefit of exceptions is that they clean up error handling code. Instead of checking for a particular error and dealing with it at multiple places in your program, you no longer need to check at the point of the method call (since the exception will guarantee that someone catches it). And, you need to handle the problem in only one place, the so-called exception handler . This saves you code and it separates the code that describes what you want to do from the code that is executed when things go awry. In general, reading, writing, and debugging code becomes much clearer with exceptions than when using the old way.

Because exception handling is enforced by the Java compiler, there are only so many examples that can be written in this book without learning about exception handling. This chapter introduces you to the code you need to write to properly handle the exceptions, and the way you can generate your own exceptions if one of your methods gets into trouble.

The C programmer can look up the return value of printf( ) for an example of this.

8.16 Termination v/s Resumption

There are two basic models in exception-handling theory. In termination (which is what Java and C++ support), you assume the error is so critical there's no way to get back to where the exception occurred. Whoever threw the exception decided that there was no way to salvage the situation, and they don't want to come back.

The alternative is called resumption. It means that the exception handler is expected to do something to rectify the situation, and then the faulting method is retried, presuming success the second time. If you want resumption, it means you still hope to continue execution after the exception is handled. In this case, your exception is more like a method call - which is how you should set up situations in Java in which you want resumption-like behavior. (That is, don't throw an exception; call a method that fixes the problem.) Alternatively, place your try block inside a while loop that keeps reentering the try block until the result is satisfactory.

Historically, programmers using operating systems that supported resumptive exception handling eventually ended up using termination-like code and skipping resumption. So although resumption sounds attractive at first, it seems it isn't quite so useful in practice. The dominant reason is probably the coupling that results: your handler must often be aware of where the exception is thrown from and contain non-generic code specific to the throwing location. This makes the code difficult to write and maintain, especially for large systems where the exception can be generated from many points.

8.17 The Exception Specification

In Java, you're required to inform the client programmer, who calls your method, of the exceptions that might be thrown from your method. This is civilized because the caller can know exactly what code to write to catch all potential exceptions. Of course, if source code is available, the client programmer could hunt through and look for throw statements, but often a library doesn't come with sources. To prevent this from being a problem, Java provides syntax (and forces you to use that syntax) to allow you to politely tell the client programmer what exceptions this method throws, so the client programmer can handle them. This is the exception specification and it's part of the method declaration, appearing after the argument list.

The exception specification uses an additional keyword, throws, followed by a list of all the potential exception types. So your method definition might look like this:

```
void f() throws tooBig, tooSmall, divZero { //...
If you say
void f() { // ...
```

it means that no exceptions are thrown from the method. (Except for the exceptions of type RuntimeException, which can reasonably be thrown anywhere - this will be described later.)

You can't lie about an exception specification - if your method causes exceptions and doesn't handle them, the compiler will detect this and tell you that you must either handle the exception or indicate with an exception specification that it may be thrown from your method. By enforcing exception specifications from top to bottom, Java guarantees that exception correctness can be ensured at compile time .[42]

There is one place you can lie: you can claim to throw an exception that you don't. The compiler takes your word for it and forces the users of your method to treat it as if it really does throw that exception. This has the beneficial effect of being a placeholder for that exception, so you can actually start throwing the exception later without requiring changes to existing code.

8.18 Catching any Exception

It is possible to create a handler that catches any type of exception. You do this by catching the base-class exception type Exception (there are other types of base exceptions, but Exception is the base that's pertinent to virtually all programming activities):

```
catch(Exception e) {
System.out.println("caught an exception");
}
```

This will catch any exception, so if you use it you'll want to put it at the end of your list of handlers to avoid pre-empting any exception handlers that might otherwise follow it.

Since the Exception class is the base of all the exception classes that are important to the programmer, you don't get much specific information about the exception, but you can call the methods that come from its base type Throwable:

```
String getMessage( )
Gets the detail message.
String toString( )
Returns a short description of the Throwable, including the detail
message if there is one.
void printStackTrace( )
void printStackTrace(PrintStream)
```

Prints the Throwable and the Throwable's call stack trace. The call stack shows the sequence of method calls that brought you to the point at which the exception was thrown.

The first version prints to standard error, the second prints to a stream of your choice. If you're working under Windows, you can't redirect standard error so you might want to use the second version and send the results to System.out; that way the output can be redirected any way you want.

In addition, you get some other methods from Throwable's base type Object (everybody's base type). The one that might come in handy for exceptions is getClass( ), which returns an object representing the class of this object. You can in turn query this Class object for its name with getName( ) or toString( ). You can also do more sophisticated things with Class objects that aren't necessary in exception handling. Class objects will be studied later in the book.

Here's an example that shows the use of the Exception methods: (See page 97 if you have trouble executing this program.)

```
//: ExceptionMethods.java
// Demonstrating the Exception Methods
package c09;
public class ExceptionMethods {
public static void main(String[] args) {
try {
throw new Exception("Here's my Exception");
} catch(Exception e) {
System.out.println("Caught Exception");
```

```
System.out.println(
"e.getMessage(): " + e.getMessage());
System.out.println(
"e.toString(): " + e.toString());
System.out.println("e.printStackTrace():");
e.printStackTrace();
}
}
} ///:~
```

The output for this program is:

```
Caught Exception
e.getMessage(): Here's my Exception
e.toString(): java.lang.Exception: Here's my Exception
e.printStackTrace():
java.lang.Exception: Here's my Exception
at ExceptionMethods.main
```

You can see that the methods provide successively more information - each is effectively a superset of the previous one.

8.19 Creating Your Own Exception Classes

As you have undoubtedly noticed in your travels (travails?) through the Java language, the packages that ship with the Java development environment provide numerous exception classes. All of these classes are descendants of the Throwable class and allow programs to differentiate between the various types of exceptions that can occur during the execution of a Java program

You can create your own exception classes, as well, to represent problems that can occur within the classes that you write. Indeed, if you are a package developer you will find that you must create your own set of exception classes to allow your users to differentiate an error that can occur in your package versus those errors that occur in the Java development environment or other packages.

8.19.1 The throw Statement

All Java methods use the throw statement to throw an exception. The throw statement requires a single argument: a throwable object. In the Java system, throwable objects are instances of any subclass of the Throwable class. Here's an example of a throw statement:

throw someThrowableObject;

If you attempt to throw an object that is not throwable, the compiler refuses to compile your program and displays an error message similar to the following:

testing.java:10: Cannot throw class java.lang.Integer; it must be a subclass of class java.lang.Throwable.

```
throw new Integer(4);
^
```

The next page, The Throwable Class and Its Subclasses, talks more about the Throwable class.

Let's look at the throw statement in context. The following method is taken from a class that implements a common stack object. The pop method removes the top element from the stack and returns it:

```
public Object pop() throws EmptyStackException {
```

```
Object obj;
if (size == 0)
throw new EmptyStackException();
obj = objectAt(size - 1);
setObjectAt(size - 1, null);
size—;
return obj;
}
```

The pop method checks to see if there are any elements on the stack. If the stack is empty (its size is equal to 0), then pop instantiates a new EmptyStackException object and throws it. The EmptyStackException class is defined in the java.util package. Later pages in this lesson describe how you can create your own exception classes. For now, all you really need to remember is that you can throw only objects that inherit from the java.lang.Throwable class.

You'll notice that the declaration of the pop method contains this clause:

throws EmptyStackException

The throws clause specifies that the method can throw an EmptyStackException. As you know, the Java language requires that methods either catch or specify all checked exceptions that can be thrown within the scope of that method. You do this with the throws clause of the method declaration. For more information about this requirement see Java's Catch or Specify Requirement. Also, Specifying the Exceptions Thrown by a Method shows you in more detail how a method can specify the exceptions it can throw.

8.19.2 The Throwable Class and Its Subclasses

As you learned on the previous page, you can throw only objects that derive from the Throwable class. This includes direct descendants (that is, objects that derive directly from the Throwable class) as well as indirect descendants (objects that derive from children or grandchildren of the Throwable class).

This diagram illustrates the class hierarchy of the Throwable class and its most significant subclasses.

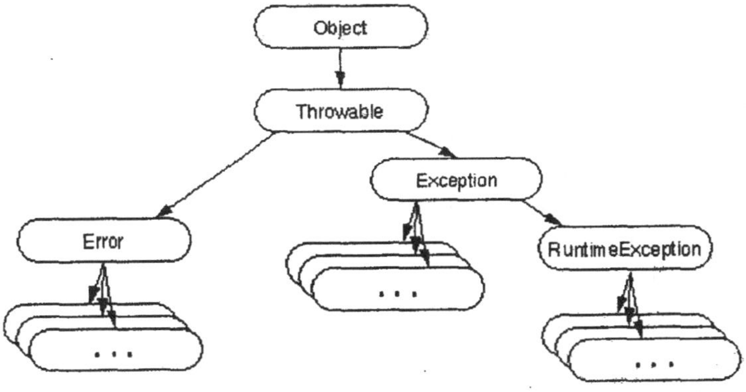

Fig. 8.1 :

As you can see from the diagram, Throwable has two direct descendants: Error and Exception.

8.19.3 Errors

When a dynamic linking failure or some other "hard" failure in the virtual machine occurs, the virtual machine throws an Error. Typical Java programs should not catch Errors. In addition, it's unlikely that typical Java programs will ever throw Errors either.

8.19.4 Exceptions

Most programs throw and catch objects that derive from the Exception class. Exceptions indicate that a problem occurred but that the problem is not a serious systemic problem. Most programs you write will throw and catch Exceptions.

The Exception class has many descendants defined in the Java packages. These descendants indicate various types of exceptions that can occur. For example, IllegalAccessException signals that a particular method could not be found, and NegativeArraySizeException indicates that a program attempted to create an array with a negative size.

One Exception subclass has special meaning in the Java language: RuntimeException.

8.20 Rethrowing an Exception

Sometimes you'll want to rethrow the exception that you just caught, particularly when you use Exception to catch any exception. Since you already have the handle to the current exception, you can simply re-throw that handle:

```
catch(Exception e) {
System.out.println("An exception was thrown");
throw e;
}
```

Rethrowing an exception causes the exception to go to the exception handlers in the next-higher context. Any further catch clauses for the same try block are still ignored. In addition, everything about the exception object is preserved, so the handler at the higher context that catches the specific exception type can extract all the information from that object.

If you simply re-throw the current exception, the information that you print about that exception in printStackTrace( ) will pertain to the exception's origin, not the place where you re-throw it. If you want to install new stack trace information, you can do so by calling fillInStackTrace( ), which returns an exception object that it creates by stuffing the current stack information into the old exception object. Here's what it looks like:

```
//: Rethrowing.java
// Demonstrating fillInStackTrace()
public class Rethrowing {
public static void f() throws Exception {
System.out.println(
"originating the exception in f()");
throw new Exception("thrown from f()");
}
public static void g() throws Throwable {
try {
f();
} catch(Exception e) {
System.out.println(
```

```
"Inside g(), e.printStackTrace()");
e.printStackTrace();
throw e; // 17
// throw e.fillInStackTrace(); // 18
}
}
public static void
main(String[] args) throws Throwable {
try {
g();
} catch(Exception e) {
System.out.println(
"Caught in main, e.printStackTrace()");
e.printStackTrace();
}
}
} ///:~
```

The important line numbers are marked inside of comments. With line 17 un-commented (as shown), the output is:

```
originating the exception in f()
Inside g(), e.printStackTrace()
java.lang.Exception: thrown from f()
at Rethrowing.f(Rethrowing.java:8)
at Rethrowing.g(Rethrowing.java:12)
at Rethrowing.main(Rethrowing.java:24)
Caught in main, e.printStackTrace()
java.lang.Exception: thrown from f()
at Rethrowing.f(Rethrowing.java:8)
at Rethrowing.g(Rethrowing.java:12)
at Rethrowing.main(Rethrowing.java:24)
```

So the exception stack trace always remembers its true point of origin, no matter how many times it gets rethrown.

With line 17 commented and line 18 un-commented, fillInStackTrace( ) is used instead, and the result is:

```
originating the exception in f()
Inside g(), e.printStackTrace()
java.lang.Exception: thrown from f()
at Rethrowing.f(Rethrowing.java:8)
at Rethrowing.g(Rethrowing.java:12)
at Rethrowing.main(Rethrowing.java:24)
Caught in main, e.printStackTrace()
java.lang.Exception: thrown from f()
at Rethrowing.g(Rethrowing.java:18)
at Rethrowing.main(Rethrowing.java:24)
```

Because of fillInStackTrace( ), line 18 becomes the new point of origin of the exception.

The class Throwable must appear in the exception specification for g( ) and main( ) because fillInStackTrace( ) produces a handle to a Throwable object. Since Throwable is a base class of

Exception, it's possible to get an object that's a Throwable but not an Exception, so the handler for Exception in main( ) might miss it. To make sure everything is in order, the compiler forces an exception specification for Throwable. For example, the exception in the following program is not caught in main( ):

```
//: ThrowOut.java
public class ThrowOut {
public static void
main(String[] args) throws Throwable {
try {
throw new Throwable();
} catch(Exception e) {
System.out.println("Caught in main()");
}
}
} ///:~
```

It's also possible to rethrow a different exception from the one you caught. If you do this, you get a similar effect as when you use fillInStackTrace( ): the information about the original site of the exception is lost, and what you're left with is the information pertaining to the new throw:

```
//: RethrowNew.java
// Rethrow a different object from the one that
// was caught

public class RethrowNew {
public static void f() throws Exception {
System.out.println(
"originating the exception in f()");
throw new Exception("thrown from f()");
}
public static void main(String[] args) {
try {
f();
} catch(Exception e) {
System.out.println(
"Caught in main, e.printStackTrace()");
e.printStackTrace();
throw new NullPointerException("from main");
}
}
} ///:~
```

The output is:

```
originating the exception in f()
Caught in main, e.printStackTrace()
java.lang.Exception: thrown from f()
at RethrowNew.f(RethrowNew.java:8)
at RethrowNew.main(RethrowNew.java:13)
java.lang.NullPointerException: from main
at RethrowNew.main(RethrowNew.java:18)
```

The final exception knows only that it came from main( ), and not from f( ). Note that Throwable isn't necessary in any of the exception specifications.

You never have to worry about cleaning up the previous exception, or any exceptions for that matter. They're all heap-based objects created with new, so the garbage collector automatically cleans them all up.

This is a significant improvement over C++ exception handling, which doesn't catch violations of exception specifications until run time, when it's not very useful.

8.21 Standard Java Exceptions

Java contains a class called Throwable that describes anything that can be thrown as an exception. There are two general types of Throwable objects ("types of" = "inherited from"). Error represents compile-time and system errors that you don't worry about catching (except in special cases). Exception is the basic type that can be thrown from any of the standard Java library class methods and from your methods and run-time accidents.

The best way to get an overview of the exceptions is to browse online Java documentation from http://java.sun.com. (Of course, it's easier to download it first.) It's worth doing this once just to get a feel for the various exceptions, but you'll soon see that there isn't anything special between one exception and the next except for the name. Also, the number of exceptions in Java keeps expanding; basically it's pointless to print them in a book. Any new library you get from a third-party vendor will probably have its own exceptions as well. The important thing to understand is the concept and what you should do with the exceptions.

8.22 Java.lang.Exception

This is the basic exception class your program can catch. Other exceptions are derived from this. The basic idea is that the name of the exception represents the problem that occurred and the exception name is intended to be relatively self-explanatory. The exceptions are not all defined in java.lang; some are created to support other libraries such as util, net, and io, which you can see from their full class names or what they are inherited from. For example, all IO exceptions are inherited from java.io.IOException.

The special case of RuntimeException

The first example in this chapter was

```
if(t == null)
throw new NullPointerException();
```

It can be a bit horrifying to think that you must check for null on every handle that is passed into a method (since you can't know if the caller has passed you a valid handle). Fortunately, you don't - this is part of the standard run-time checking that Java performs for you, and if any call is made to a null handle, Java will automatically throw a NullPointerException. So the above bit of code is always superfluous.

There's a whole group of exception types that are in this category. They're always thrown automatically by Java and you don't need to include them in your exception specifications. Conveniently enough, they're all grouped together by putting them under a single base class called RuntimeException, which is a perfect example of inheritance: it establishes a family of types that have some characteristics and behaviors in common. Also, you never need to write an exception specification saying that a method might throw a RuntimeException, since that's just assumed. Because they indicate bugs, you virtually never catch a RuntimeException - it's dealt with automatically.

If you were forced to check for RuntimeExceptions your code could get messy. Even though you don't typically catch RuntimeExceptions, in your own packages you might choose to throw some of the RuntimeExceptions.

What happens when you don't catch such exceptions? Since the compiler doesn't enforce exception specifications for these, it's quite plausible that a RuntimeException could percolate all the way out to your main( ) method without being caught. To see what happens in this case, try the following example:

```
//: NeverCaught.java
// Ignoring RuntimeExceptions
public class NeverCaught {
static void f() {
throw new RuntimeException("From f()");
}
static void g() {
f();
}
public static void main(String[] args) {
g();
}
} ///:~
```

You can already see that a RuntimeException (or anything inherited from it) is a special case, since the compiler doesn't require an exception specification for these types.

The output is:

```
java.lang.RuntimeException: From f()
at NeverCaught.f(NeverCaught.java:9)
at NeverCaught.g(NeverCaught.java:12)
at NeverCaught.main(NeverCaught.java:15)
```

So the answer is: If a RuntimeException gets all the way out to main( ) without being caught, printStackTrace( ) is called for that exception as the program exits.

Keep in mind that it's possible to ignore only RuntimeExceptions in your coding, since all other handling is carefully enforced by the compiler. The reasoning is that a RuntimeException represents a programming error:

An error you cannot catch (receiving a null handle handed to your method by a client programmer, for example)

An error that you, as a programmer, should have checked for in your code (such as ArrayIndexOutOfBoundsException where you should have paid attention to the size of the array).

You can see what a tremendous benefit it is to have exceptions in this case, since they help in the debugging process.

It's interesting to notice that you cannot classify Java exception handling as a single-purpose tool. Yes, it is designed to handle those pesky run-time errors that will occur because of forces outside your code's control, but it's also essential for certain types of programming bugs that the compiler cannot detect.

8.23 Runtime Exceptions

The RuntimeException class represents exceptions that occur within the Java virtual machine (during runtime). An example of a runtime exception is NullPointerException, which occurs when a method tries to access a member of an object through a null reference. A NullPointerException can occur anywhere a program tries to dereference a reference to an object. The cost of checking for the exception often outweighs the benefit of catching it.

Because runtime exceptions are so ubiquitous and attempting to catch or specify all of them all the time would be a fruitless exercise (and a fruitful source of unreadable and unmaintainable code), the compiler allows runtime exceptions to go uncaught and unspecified.

The Java packages define several RuntimeException classes. You can catch these exceptions just like other exceptions. However, a method is not required to specify that it throws RuntimeExceptions. In addition, you can create your own RuntimeException subclasses. Runtime Exceptions—The Controversy contains a thorough discussion of when and how to use runtime exceptions.

8.24 Creating Your Own Exception Classes

When you design a package of Java classes that collaborate to provide some useful function to your users, you work hard to ensure that your classes interact well together and that their interfaces are easy to understand and use. You should spend just as much time thinking about and designing the exceptions that your classes throw.

Suppose you are writing a linked list class that you're planning to distribute as freeware. Among other methods, your linked list class supports these methods:

objectAt(int n) : Returns the object in the nth position in the list.

firstObject : Returns the first object in the list.

indexOf(Object n) : Searches the list for the specified Object and returns its position in the list.

8.24.1 What Can Go Wrong?

Because many programmers will be using your linked list class, you can be assured that many will misuse or abuse your class and its methods. Also, some legitimate calls to your linked list's methods may result in an undefined result. Regardless, in the face of errors, you want your linked list class to be as robust as possible, to do something reasonable about errors, and to communicate errors back to the calling program. However, you can't anticipate how each user of your linked list class will want the object to behave under adversity. So, often the best thing to do when an error occurs is to throw an exception.

Each of the methods supported by your linked list might throw an exception under certain conditions, and each method might throw a different type of exception than the others. For example,

objectAt : Throws an exception if the integer passed into the method is less than 0 or larger than the number of objects currently in the list.

firstObject : Throws an exception if the list contains no objects.

indexOf : Throws an exception if the object passed into the method is not in the list.

But what type of exception should each method throw? Should it be an exception provided with the Java development environment? Or should you roll your own?

8.24.2 Choosing the Exception Type to Throw

When faced with choosing the type of exception to throw, you have two choices:

- Use one written by someone else. The Java development environment provides a lot of exception classes that you could use.

- Write one of your own.

You should go to the trouble of writing your own exception classes if you answer "yes" to any of the following questions. Otherwise, you can probably get away with using someone else's:

Do you need an exception type that isn't represented by those in the Java development environment?

Would it help your users if they could differentiate your exceptions from those thrown by classes written by other vendors?

Does your code throw more than one related exception?

If you use someone else's exceptions, will your users have access to those exceptions? A similar question is: Should your package be independent and self-contained?

Your linked list class can throw multiple exceptions, and it would be convenient to be able to catch all exceptions thrown by the linked list with one exception handler. Also, if you plan to distribute your linked list in a package, all related code should be packaged together. Thus for the linked list, you should roll your own exception class hierarchy.

The following diagram illustrates one possible exception class hierarchy for your linked list:

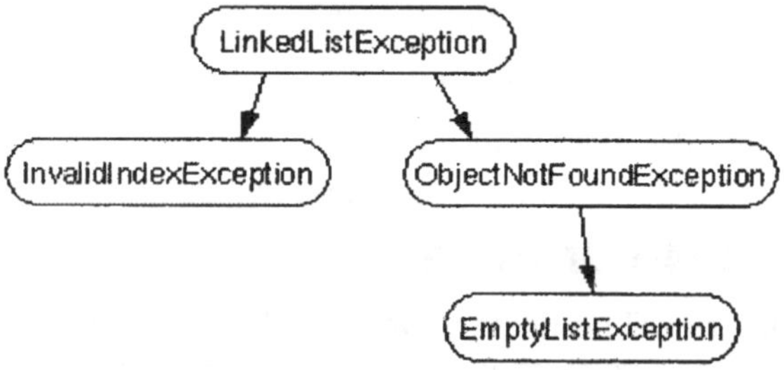

Fig. 8.2 :

LinkedListException is the parent class of all the possible exceptions that can be thrown by the linked list class. Users of your linked list class can write a single exception handler to handle all linked list exceptions with a catch statement like this:

```
catch (LinkedListException) {
. . .
}
```

Or, users could write more specialized handlers for each subclass of LinkedListException.

8.24.3 Choosing a Superclass

The diagram above does not indicate the superclass of the LinkedListException class. As you know, Java exceptions must be Throwable objects (they must be instances of Throwable or a subclass of Throwable). So, your temptation might be to make LinkedListExceptiona subclass of Throwable. However, the java.lang package provides two Throwable subclasses that further divide the type of problems that can occur within a Java program: Errors and Exceptions. Most of the applets and applications that you write will throw objects that are Exceptions. (Errors are reserved for serious hard errors that occur deep in the system.)

Theoretically, any Exception subclass could be used as the parent class of LinkedListException. However, a quick perusal of those classes show that they are either too specialized or completely unrelated to LinkedListException to be appropriate. Thus, the parent class of LinkedListException should be Exception.

Because runtime exceptions don't have to be specified in the throws clause of a method, many packages developers ask: "Isn't it just easier if I make all of my exception inherit from RuntimeException?" The answer to this question is covered in detail on Runtime Exceptions—The Controversy. The bottom line is that you shouldn't subclass RuntimeException unless your class really is a runtime exception! For most of you, this means "No, your exceptions shouldn't inherit from RuntimeException."

8.24.4 Naming Conventions

It's good practice to append the word "Exception" to the end of all classes that inherit (directly or indirectly) from the Exception class. Similarly, classes that inherit from the Error class should end with the string "Error".

8.25 Runtime Exceptions—The Controversy

Because the Java language does not require methods to catch or specify runtime exceptions, it's tempting for programmers to write code that throws only runtime exceptions or to make all of their exception subclasses inherit from RuntimeException. Both of these programming shortcuts allow programmers to write Java code without bothering with all of the nagging errors from the compiler and without bothering to specify or catch any exceptions. While this may seem convenient to the programmer, it sidesteps the intent of Java's catch or specify requirement and can cause problems for the programmers using your classes.

```
InputFile.java:8: Warning: Exception
java.io.FileNotFoundException must be caught, or it must be
declared in throws clause of this method.
fis = new FileInputStream(filename);
^
```

Why did the Java designers decide to force a method to specify all uncaught checked exceptions that can be thrown within its scope? Because any exception that can be thrown by a method is really part of the method's public programming interface: callers of a method must know about the exceptions that a method can throw in order to intelligently and conciously decide what to do about those exceptions. The exceptions that a method can throw are as much a part of that method's programming interface as its parameters and return value.

Your next question might be: "Well then, if it's so good to document a method's API including the exceptions that it can throw, why not specify runtime exceptions, too?"

Runtime exceptions represent problems that are detected by the runtime system. This includes arithmetic exceptions (such as when dividing by zero), pointer exceptions (such as trying to access an object through a null reference), and indexing exceptions (such as attempting to access an array element through an index that is too large or too small).

Runtime exceptions can occur anywhere in a program and in a typical program can be very numerous. Typically, the cost of checking for runtime exceptions exceeds the benefit of catching or specifying them. Thus the compiler does not require that you catch or specify runtime exceptions, although you can.

Checked exceptions represent useful information about the operation of a legally specified request that the caller may have had no control over and that the caller needs to be informed about—for example, the file system is now full, or the remote end has closed the connection, or the access privileges don't allow this action.

What does it buy you if you throw a RuntimeException or create a subclass of RuntimeException just because you don't want to deal with specifying it? Simply, you get the ability to throw an exception without specifying that you do so. In other words, it is a way to avoid documenting the exceptions that a method can throw. When is this good? Well, when is it ever good to avoid documenting a method's behavior? The answer is "hardly ever."

Rules of Thumb:

A method can detect and throw a RuntimeException when it's encountered an error in the virtual machine runtime. However, it's typically easier to just let the virtual machine detect and throw it. Normally, the methods you write should throw Exceptions, not RuntimeException.

Similarly, you create a subclass of RuntimeException when you are creating an error in the virtual machine runtime (which you probably aren't). Otherwise you should subclass Exception.

Do not throw a runtime exception or create a subclass of RuntimeException simply because you don't want to be bothered with specifying the exceptions your methods can throw.

8.26 The throw Statement

All Java methods use the throw statement to throw an exception. The throw statement requires a single argument: a throwable object. In the Java system, throwable objects are instances of any subclass of the Throwable class. Here's an example of a throw statement:

throw someThrowableObject;

If you attempt to throw an object that is not throwable, the compiler refuses to compile your program and displays an error message similar to the following:

testing.java:10: Cannot throw class java.lang.Integer;

it must be a subclass of class java.lang.Throwable.

```
throw new Integer(4);
^
```

The next page, The Throwable Class and Its Subclasses, talks more about the Throwable class.

EmptyStackException is not a checked exception, so technically pop doesn't have to use the throws clause]

Let's look at the throw statement in context. The following method is taken from a class that implements a common stack object. The pop method removes the top element from the stack and returns it:

```
public Object pop() throws EmptyStackException {
Object obj;
if (size == 0)
throw new EmptyStackException();
obj = objectAt(size - 1);
setObjectAt(size - 1, null);
size—;
return obj;
}
```

The pop method checks to see if there are any elements on the stack. If the stack is empty (its size is equal to 0), then pop instantiates a new EmptyStackException object and throws it. The EmptyStackException class is defined in the java.util package. Later pages in this lesson describe how you can create your own exception classes. For now, all you really need to remember is that you can throw only objects that inherit from the java.lang.Throwable class. The throws Clause You'll notice that the declaration of the pop method contains this clause:

throws EmptyStackException

The throws clause specifies that the method can throw an EmptyStackException. As you know, the Java language requires that methods either catch or specify all checked exceptions that can be thrown within the scope of that method. You do this with the throws clause of the method declaration. For more information about this requirement see Java's Catch or Specify Requirement. Also, Specifying the Exceptions Thrown by a Method shows you in more detail how a method can specify the exceptions it can throw.

You're not stuck using the Java exceptions. This is important because you'll often need to create your own exceptions to denote a special error that your library is capable of creating, but which was not foreseen when the Java hierarchy was created.

To create your own exception class, you're forced to inherit from an existing type of exception, preferably one that is close in meaning to your new exception. Inheriting an exception is quite simple:

```
//: Inheriting.java
// Inheriting your own exceptions
class MyException extends Exception {
public MyException() {}
public MyException(String msg) {
super(msg);
}
}
public class Inheriting {
public static void f() throws MyException {
System.out.println(
"Throwing MyException from f()");
throw new MyException();
}
public static void g() throws MyException {
System.out.println(
"Throwing MyException from g()");
throw new MyException("Originated in g()");
}
public static void main(String[] args) {
try {
f();
} catch(MyException e) {
e.printStackTrace();
}
try {
g();
} catch(MyException e) {
e.printStackTrace();
```

```
}
}
} ///:~
```

The inheritance occurs in the creation of the new class:

```
class MyException extends Exception {
public MyException() {}
public MyException(String msg) {
super(msg);
}
}
```

The key phrase here is extends Exception , which says "it's everything an Exception is and more." The added code is small - the addition of two constructors that define the way MyException is created. Remember that the compiler automatically calls the base-class default constructor if you don't explicitly call a base-class constructor, as in the MyException( ) default constructor. In the second constructor, the base-class constructor with a String argument is explicitly invoked by using the super keyword.

The output of the program is:

```
Throwing MyException from f()
MyException
at Inheriting.f(Inheriting.java:16)
at Inheriting.main(Inheriting.java:24)
Throwing MyException from g()
MyException: Originated in g()
at Inheriting.g(Inheriting.java:20)
at Inheriting.main(Inheriting.java:29)
```

You can see the absence of the detail message in the MyException thrown from f( ).

The process of creating your own exceptions can be taken further. You can add extra constructors and members:

```
//: Inheriting2.java
// Inheriting your own exceptions
class MyException2 extends Exception {
public MyException2() {}
public MyException2(String msg) {
super(msg);
}
public MyException2(String msg, int x) {
super(msg);
i = x;
}
public int val() { return i; }
private int i;
}
public class Inheriting2 {
public static void f() throws MyException2 {
System.out.println(
```

```
"Throwing MyException2 from f()");
throw new MyException2();
}
public static void g() throws MyException2 {
System.out.println(
"Throwing MyException2 from g()");
throw new MyException2("Originated in g()");
}
public static void h() throws MyException2 {
System.out.println(
"Throwing MyException2 from h()");
throw new MyException2(
"Originated in h()", 47);
}
public static void main(String[] args) {
try {
f();
} catch(MyException2 e) {
e.printStackTrace();
}
try {
g();
} catch(MyException2 e) {
e.printStackTrace();
}
try {
h();
} catch(MyException2 e) {
e.printStackTrace();
System.out.println("e.val() = " + e.val());
}
}
} ///:~
```

A data member i has been added, along with a method that reads that value and an additional constructor that sets it. The output is:

```
Throwing MyException2 from f()
MyException2
at Inheriting2.f(Inheriting2.java:22)
at Inheriting2.main(Inheriting2.java:34)
Throwing MyException2 from g()
MyException2: Originated in g()
at Inheriting2.g(Inheriting2.java:26)
at Inheriting2.main(Inheriting2.java:39)
Throwing MyException2 from h()
MyException2: Originated in h()
at Inheriting2.h(Inheriting2.java:30)
at Inheriting2.main(Inheriting2.java:44)
```

```
e.val() = 47
```

Since an exception is just another kind of object, you can continue this process of embellishing the power of your exception classes. Keep in mind, however, that all this dressing up might be lost on the client programmers using your packages, since they might simply look for the exception to be thrown and nothing more. (That's the way most of the Java library exceptions are used.) If this is the case, it's possible to create a new exception type with almost no code at all:

```
//: SimpleException.java
class SimpleException extends Exception {
} ///:~
```

This relies on the compiler to create the default constructor (which automatically calls the base-class default constructor). Of course, in this case you don't get a SimpleException(String) constructor, but in practice that isn't used much.

8.27 Exception Restrictions

When you override a method, you can throw only the exceptions that have been specified in the base-class version of the method. This is a useful restriction, since it means that code that works with the base class will automatically work with any object derived from the base class (a fundamental OOP concept, of course), including exceptions.

This example demonstrates the kinds of restrictions imposed (at compile time) for exceptions:

```
//: StormyInning.java
// Overridden methods may throw only the
// exceptions specified in their base-class
// versions, or exceptions derived from the
// base-class exceptions.

class BaseballException extends Exception {}
class Foul extends BaseballException {}
class Strike extends BaseballException {}

abstract class Inning {
Inning() throws BaseballException {}
void event () throws BaseballException {
// Doesn't actually have to throw anything
}
abstract void atBat() throws Strike, Foul;
void walk() {} // Throws nothing
}

class StormException extends Exception {}
class RainedOut extends StormException {}
class PopFoul extends Foul {}

interface Storm {
void event() throws RainedOut;
void rainHard() throws RainedOut;
}
```

```
public class StormyInning extends Inning
implements Storm {
// OK to add new exceptions for constructors,
// but you must deal with the base constructor
// exceptions:
StormyInning() throws RainedOut,
BaseballException {}
StormyInning(String s) throws Foul,
BaseballException {}
// Regular methods must conform to base class:
//! void walk() throws PopFoul {} //Compile error
// Interface CANNOT add exceptions to existing
// methods from the base class:
//! public void event() throws RainedOut {}
// If the method doesn't already exist in the
// base class, the exception is OK:
public void rainHard() throws RainedOut {}
// You can choose to not throw any exceptions,
// even if base version does:
public void event() {}
// Overridden methods can throw
// inherited exceptions:
void atBat() throws PopFoul {}
public static void main(String[] args) {
try {
StormyInning si = new StormyInning();
si.atBat();
} catch(PopFoul e) {
} catch(RainedOut e) {
} catch(BaseballException e) {}
// Strike not thrown in derived version.
try {
// What happens if you upcast?
Inning i = new StormyInning();
i.atBat();
// You must catch the exceptions from the
// base-class version of the method:
} catch(Strike e) {
} catch(Foul e) {
} catch(RainedOut e) {
} catch(BaseballException e) {}
}
} ///:~
```

In Inning, you can see that both the constructor and the event( ) method say they will throw an exception, but they never do. This is legal because it allows you to force the user to catch any exceptions that you might add in overridden versions of event( ). The same idea holds for abstract methods, as seen in atBat( ).

The interface Storm is interesting because it contains one method (event( ))that is defined in Inning, and one method that isn't. Both methods throw a new type of exception, RainedOut. When StormyInning extends Inning and implements Storm , you'll see that the event( ) method in Storm cannot change the exception interface of event( ) in Inning. Again, this makes sense because otherwise you'd never know if you were catching the correct thing when working with the base class. Of course, if a method described in an interface is not in the base class, such as rainHard( ), then there's no problem if it throws exceptions.

The restriction on exceptions does not apply to constructors. You can see in StormyInning that a constructor can throw anything it wants, regardless of what the base-class constructor throws. However, since a base-class constructor must always be called one way or another (here, the default constructor is called automatically), the derived-class constructor must declare any base-class constructor exceptions in its exception specification.

The reason StormyInning.walk( ) will not compile is that it throws an exception, while Inning.walk( ) does not. If this was allowed, then you could write code that called Inning.walk( ) and that didn't have to handle any exceptions, but then when you substituted an object of a class derived from Inning, exceptions would be thrown so your code would break. By forcing the derived-class methods to conform to the exception specifications of the base-class methods, substitutability of objects is maintained.

The overridden event( ) method shows that a derived-class version of a method may choose to not throw any exceptions, even if the base-class version does. Again, this is fine since it doesn't break any code that is written assuming the base-class version throws exceptions. Similar logic applies to atBat( ), which throws PopFoul, an exception that is derived from Foul thrown by the base-class version of atBat( ). This way, if someone writes code that works with Inning and calls atBat( ), they must catch the Foul exception. Since PopFoul is derived from Foul, the exception handler will also catch PopFoul.

The last point of interest is in main( ). Here you can see that if you're dealing with exactly a StormyInning object, the compiler forces you to catch only the exceptions that are specific to that class, but if you upcast to the base type then the compiler (correctly) forces you to catch the exceptions for the base type. All these constraints produce much more robust exception-handling code. [43]

It's useful to realize that although exception specifications are enforced by the compiler during inheritance, the exception specifications are not part of the type of a method, which is comprised of only the method name and argument types. Therefore, you cannot overload methods based on exception specifications. In addition, because an exception specification exists in a base-class version of a method doesn't mean that it must exist in the derived-class version of the method, and this is quite different from inheriting the methods (that is, a method in the base class must also exist in the derived class). Put another way, the "exception specification interface" for a particular method may narrow during inheritance and overriding, but it may not widen - this is precisely the opposite of the rule for the class interface during inheritance.

8.28 Performing Cleanup with Finally

There's often some piece of code that you want to execute whether or not an exception occurs in a try block. This usually pertains to some operation other than memory recovery (since that's taken care of by the garbage collector). To achieve this effect, you use a finally clause [44] at the end of all the exception handlers. The full picture of an exception-handling section is thus:

```
try {
// The guarded region:
```

```
// Dangerous stuff that might throw A, B, or C
} catch (A a1) {
// Handle A
} catch (B b1) {
// Handle B
} catch (C c1) {
// Handle C
} finally {
// Stuff that happens every time
}
```

To demonstrate that the finally clause always runs, try this program:

```
//: FinallyWorks.java
// The finally clause is always executed
public class FinallyWorks {
static int count = 0;
public static void main(String[] args) {
while(true) {
try {
// post-increment is zero first time:
if(count++ == 0)
throw new Exception();
System.out.println("No exception");
} catch(Exception e) {
System.out.println("Exception thrown");
} finally {
System.out.println("in finally clause");
if(count == 2) break; // out of "while"
}
}
}
} ///:~
```

This program also gives a hint for how you can deal with the tact that exceptions in Java (like exceptions in C++) do not allow you to resume back to where the exception was thrown, as discussed earlier. If you place your try block in a loop, you can establish a condition that must be met before you continue the program. You can also add a static counter or some other device to allow the loop to try several different approaches before giving up. This way you can build a greater level of robustness into your programs.

The output is:

Exception thrown
in finally clause
No exception
in finally clause

Whether an exception is thrown or not, the finally clause is always executed.

8.28.1 What's Finally For?

In a language without garbage collection and without automatic destructor calls, [45] finally is important because it allows the programmer to guarantee the release of memory regardless of what happens in the try block. But Java has garbage collection, so releasing memory is virtually never a problem. Also, it has no destructors to call. So when do you need to use finally in Java?

finally is necessary when you need to set something other than memory back to its original state. This is usually something like an open file or network connection, something you've drawn on the screen or even a switch in the outside world, as modeled in the following example:

```
//: OnOffSwitch.java
// Why use finally?
class Switch {
boolean state = false;
boolean read() { return state; }
void on() { state = true; }
void off() { state = false; }
}
public class OnOffSwitch {
static Switch sw = new Switch();
public static void main(String[] args) {
try {
sw.on();
// Code that can throw exceptions...
sw.off();
} catch(NullPointerException e) {
System.out.println("NullPointerException");
sw.off();
} catch(IllegalArgumentException e) {
System.out.println("IOException");
sw.off();
}
}
} ///:~
```

The goal here is to make sure that the switch is off when main( ) is completed, so sw.off( ) is placed at the end of the try block and at the end of each exception handler. But it's possible that an exception could be thrown that isn't caught here, so sw.off( ) would be missed. However, with finally you can place the closure code from a try block in just one place:

```
//: WithFinally.java
// Finally Guarantees cleanup
class Switch2 {
boolean state = false;
boolean read() { return state; }
void on() { state = true; }
void off() { state = false; }
}

public class WithFinally {
static Switch2 sw = new Switch2();
public static void main(String[] args) {
```

```
try {
sw.on();
// Code that can throw exceptions...
} catch(NullPointerException e) {
System.out.println("NullPointerException");
} catch(IllegalArgumentException e) {
System.out.println("IOException");
} finally {
sw.off();
}
}
} ///:~
```

Here the sw.off( ) has been moved to just one place, where it's guaranteed to run no matter what happens.

Even in cases in which the exception is not caught in the current set of catch clauses, finally will be executed before the exception-handling mechanism continues its search for a handler at the next higher level:

```
//: AlwaysFinally.java
// Finally is always executed
class Ex extends Exception {}
public class AlwaysFinally {
public static void main(String[] args) {
System.out.println(
"Entering first try block");
try {
System.out.println(
"Entering second try block");
try {
throw new Ex();
} finally {
System.out.println(
"finally in 2nd try block");
}
} catch(Ex e) {
System.out.println(
"Caught Ex in first try block");
} finally {
System.out.println(
"finally in 1st try block");
}
}
} ///:~
```

The output for this program shows you what happens:

Entering first try block
Entering second try block

finally in 2nd try block
Caught Ex in first try block
finally in 1st try block

The finally statement will also be executed in situations in which break and continue statements are involved. Note that, along with the labeled break and labeled continue, finally eliminates the need for a goto statement in Java.

8.28.2 Pitfall: the Lost Exception

In general, Java's exception implementation is quite outstanding, but unfortunately there's a flaw. Although exceptions are an indication of a crisis in your program and should never be ignored, it's possible for an exception to simply be lost. This happens with a particular configuration using a finally clause:

```
//: LostMessage.java
// How an exception can be lost
class VeryImportantException extends Exception {
public String toString() {
return "A very important exception!";
}
}

class HoHumException extends Exception {
public String toString() {
return "A trivial exception";
}
}

public class LostMessage {
void f() throws VeryImportantException {
throw new VeryImportantException();
}
void dispose() throws HoHumException {
throw new HoHumException();
}
public static void main(String[] args)
throws Exception {
LostMessage lm = new LostMessage();
try {
lm.f();
} finally {
lm.dispose();
}
}
} ///:~
```

The output is:

A trivial exception

```
at LostMessage.dispose(LostMessage.java:21)
at LostMessage.main(LostMessage.java:29)
```

You can see that there's no evidence of the VeryImportantException, which is simply replaced by the HoHumException in the finally clause. This is a rather serious pitfall, since it means that an exception can be completely lost, and in a far more subtle and difficult-to-detect fashion than the example above. In contrast, C++ treats the situation in which a second exception is thrown before the first one is handled as a dire programming error. Perhaps a future version of Java will repair the problem. (The above results were produced with Java 1.1.)

C++ exception handling does not have the finally clause because it relies on destructors to accomplish this sort of cleanup. A destructor is a function that's always called when an object becomes unused. You always know exactly where and when the destructor gets called. C++ has automatic destructor calls, but Delphi's Object Pascal versions 1 and 2 do not (which changes the meaning and use of the concept of a destructor for that language).

8.29 Exception Matching

When an exception is thrown, the exception-handling system looks through the "nearest" handlers in the order they are written. When it finds a match, the exception is considered handled, and no further searching occurs.

Matching an exception doesn't require a perfect match between the exception and its handler. A derived-class object will match a handler for the base class, as shown in this example:

```
//: Human.java
// Catching Exception Hierarchies
class Annoyance extends Exception {}
class Sneeze extends Annoyance {}
public class Human {
public static void main(String[] args) {
try {
throw new Sneeze();
} catch(Sneeze s) {
System.out.println("Caught Sneeze");
} catch(Annoyance a) {
System.out.println("Caught Annoyance");
}
}
} ///:~
```

The Sneeze exception will be caught by the first catch clause that it matches, which is the first one, of course. However, if you remove the first catch clause:

```
try {
throw new Sneeze();
} catch(Annoyance a) {
System.out.println("Caught Annoyance");
}
```

The remaining catch clause will still work because it's catching the base class of Sneeze. Put another way, catch(Annoyance e) will catch a Annoyance or any class derived from it . This is useful because if you decide to add more exceptions to a method, if they're all inherited from the same base class then the client programmer's code will not need changing, assuming they catch the base class, at the very least.

If you try to "mask" the derived-class exceptions by putting the base-class catch clause first, like this:

```
try {
throw new Sneeze();
} catch(Annoyance a) {
System.out.println("Caught Annoyance");
} catch(Sneeze s) {
System.out.println("Caught Sneeze");
}
```

the compiler will give you an error message, since it sees that the Sneeze catch-clause can never be reached.

8.30 Exception Guidelines

Use exceptions to:

1. Fix the problem and call the method (which caused the exception) again.
2. Patch things up and continue without retrying the method.
3. Calculate some alternative result instead of what the method was supposed to produce.
4. Do whatever you can in the current context and rethrow the same exception to a higher context.
5. Do whatever you can in the current context and throw a different exception to a higher context.
6. Terminate the program.
7. Simplify. If your exception scheme makes things more complicated, then it is painful and annoying to use.
8. Make your library and program safer. This is a short-term investment (for debugging) and a long-term investment (for application robustness).

EXERCISES

1. *Create a class with a main( ) that throws an object of class Exception inside a try block. Give the constructor for Exception a string argument. Catch the exception inside a catch clause and print out the string argument. Add a finally clause and print a message to prove you were there.*
2. *Create your own exception class using the extends keyword. Write a constructor for this class that takes a String argument and stores it inside the object with a String handle. Write a method that prints out the stored String. Create a try-catch clause to exercise your new exception.*
3. *Write a class with a method that throws an exception of the type created in Exercise 2. Try compiling it without an exception specification to see what the compiler says. Add the appropriate exception specification. Try out your class and its exception inside a try-catch clause.*
5. *Define a reasonably named package for financial classes. Place last week's Money class in this package.*
6. *Add an overloaded constructor to the Money class that only takes the number of dollars.*
7. *Add an overloaded constructor to the Money class that takes no arguments and initializes the object to $0.00.*
8. *Add an equals() method to the Money class.*
9. *Define an exception class called MoneyOverflowException which can be thrown when an operation with Money results in an over flow. Place this class in the same finance package.*
10. *Rewrite the methods in the Money class so that they recognize overflow and throw a MoneyOverFlowException if it occurs.*
11. *Use the classes in the java.math package to eliminate the possibility of overflow in the Money class,*
12. *Rewrite the two logistic equation problems from Week 2 using the java.math.BigDecimal class to pro-*

vide 20 decimal digits of precision. Some hints:

Invocation of the setScale() method with every iteration is necessary to keep the value of population from overflawing the memory of the computer.

You may need to use compareTo() and the Comparable interface instead of either == or equals().

9

Multithreaded Programming

9.1 What is a Thread?

All programmers are familiar with writing sequential programs. You've probably written a program that displays "Hello World!", or sorts a list of names, or computes a list of prime numbers. These are sequential programs: each has a beginning, an execution sequence, and an end. At any given time during the runtime of the program there is a single point of execution.

A thread is similar to the sequential programs described above: a single thread also has a beginning, an end, a sequence, and at any given time during the runtime of the thread there is a single point of execution. However, a thread itself is not a program. It cannot run on its own, but runs within a program. The following figure shows the relationship.

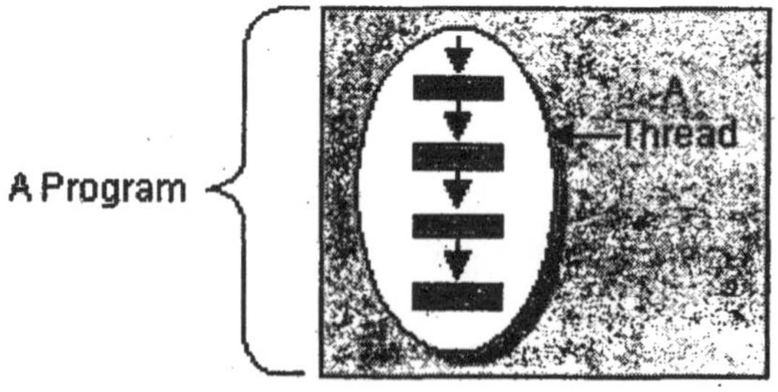

Fig. 9.1

Definition: A thread is a single sequential flow of control within a program.

A thread can be loosely defined as a separate stream of execution that takes place simultaneously with and independently of everything else that might be happening. A thread is like a classic program that starts at point A and executes until it reaches point B. It does not have an event loop. A thread runs independently of anything else happening in the computer. Without threads an entire program can be held up by one CPU intensive task or one infinite loop, intentional or otherwise. With threads the other tasks that don't get stuck in the loop can continue processing without waiting for the stuck task to finish.

It turns out that implementing threading is harder than implementing multitasking in an operating system. The reason it's relatively easy to implement multitasking is that individual programs are isolated from each other. Individual threads, however, are not. To return to the printing example, suppose that while the printing is happening in one thread, the user deletes a large chunk of text in another thread. What's printed? The document as it was before the deletion? The document as it was after the deletion? The document with some but not all of the deleted text? Or does the whole system go down in flames? Most often in a non-threaded or poorly threaded system it's the latter.

Threaded environments like Java allow a thread to put locks on shared resources so that while one thread is using data no other thread can touch that data. This is done with synchronization. Synchronization should be used sparingly since the purpose of threading is defeated if the entire system gets stopped waiting for a lock to be released. The proper choice of objects and methods to synchronize is one of the more difficult things to learn about threaded programming.

There is nothing new in the concept of a single thread. The real hoopla surrounding threads is not about a single sequential thread, but rather about the use of multiple threads in a single program all running at the same time and performing different tasks.

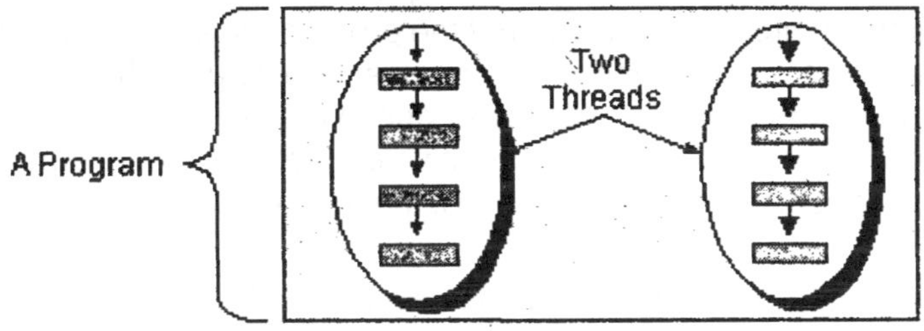

Fig. 9.2

The HotJava Web browser is an example of a multithreaded application. Within the HotJava browser you can scroll a page while it's downloading an applet or image, play animation and sound concurrently, print a page in the background while you download a new page, or watch three sorting algorithms race to the finish. You are used to life operating in a concurrent fashion...so why not your browser?

Some texts use the name lightweight process instead of thread. A thread is similar to a real process in that a thread and a running program are both a single sequential flow of control. However, a thread is considered lightweight because it runs within the context of a full-blown program and takes advantage of the resources allocated for that program and the program's environment.

As a sequential flow of control, a thread must carve out some of its own resources within a running program. (It must have its own execution stack and program counter for example.) The code running within the thread works only within that context. Thus, some other texts use execution context as a synonym for thread.

9.2 How Java Uses Threads

Java applications and applets are naturally threaded. The runtime environment starts execution of the program with the main() method in one thread. Garbage collection takes place in another thread. Screen updating occurs in a third thread. There may be other threads running as well, mostly related to the behavior of the applet viewer or web browser. All of this happens invisibly to the programmer. Some of the time you're only concerned with what happens in the primary thread which includes the main() method of a program. If this is the case you may not need to worry about threading at all.

Sometimes, however, you need to add your own threads to an applet or application. The simplest reason for adding a separate thread is to perform a long calculation. For instance if you're trying to find the ten millionth prime number, you probably don't want to make users twiddle their thumbs while you search. Or you may be waiting for a resource that isn't available yet, a large graphic to download from the Internet, for example. Once again you shouldn't make the user wait while your program waits. Any operation that is going to take a noticeable period of time should be placed in its own thread.

The other reason to use threading is to more evenly divide the computer's power among different tasks. If you want to draw random rectangles on the display, you would still like the applet to respond to user input. If all the CPU time is spent drawing rectangles, there's nothing left over for the user. On a preemptively multitasking operating system like Solaris or Windows NT, the user may at least be able to kill the application. On a cooperatively multitasking operating system like the MacOS or Windows, the user may have to reboot their machine. This is a bad thing. With threads you can set the priority of different processes, so that user input receives a high priority and drawing pretty pictures receives a low priority. Then the user can stop the applet without flipping the power switch on their machine.

A fundamental concept in computer programming is the idea of handling more than one task at a time. Many programming problems require that the program be able to stop what it's doing, deal with some other problem and return to the main process. The solution has been approached in many ways. Initially, programmers with low-level knowledge of the machine wrote interrupt service routines and the suspension of the main process was initiated through a hardware interrupt. Although this worked well, it was difficult and non-portable, so it made moving a program to a new type of machine slow and expensive.

Sometimes interrupts are necessary for handling time-critical tasks, but there's a large class of problems in which you're simply trying to partition the problem into separately-running pieces so that the whole program can be more responsive. Within a program, these separately-running pieces are called threads and the general concept is called multithreading. A common example of multithreading is the user interface. By using threads, a user can press a button and get a quick response rather than being forced to wait until the program finishes its current task.

Ordinarily, threads are just a way to allocate the time of a single processor. But if the operating system supports multiple processors, each thread can be assigned to a different processor and they can truly run in parallel. One of the convenient features of multithreading at the language level is that the programmer doesn't need to worry about whether there are many processors or just one. The program is logically divided into threads and if the machine has more than one processor then the program runs faster, without any special adjustments.

All this makes threading sound pretty simple. There is a catch: shared resources. If you have more than one thread running that's expecting to access the same resource you have a problem. For example, two processes can't simultaneously send information to a printer. To solve the problem, resources that can be shared, such as the printer, must be locked while they are being used. So a thread locks a resource, completes its task and then releases the lock so that someone else can use the resource.

Java's threading is built into the language, which makes a complicated subject much simpler. The threading is supported on an object level, so one thread of execution is represented by one object. Java also provides limited resource locking. It can lock the memory of any object (which is, after all, one kind of shared resource) so that only one thread can use it at a time. This is accomplished with the synchronized keyword. Other types of resources must be locked explicitly by the programmer, typically by creating an object to represent the lock that all threads must check before accessing that resource.

9.3 Multiple Threads

Objects provide a way to divide a program up into independent sections. Often, you also need to turn a program into separate, independently-running subtasks.

Each of these independent subtasks is called a thread, and you program as if each thread runs by itself and has the CPU to itself. Some underlying mechanism is actually dividing up the CPU time for you, but in general, you don't have to think about it, which makes programming with multiple threads a much easier task.

Some definitions are useful at this point. A process is a self-contained running program with its own address space. A multitasking operating system is capable of running more than one process (program) at a time, while making it look like each one is chugging along by periodically providing CPU cycles to each process. A thread is a single sequential flow of control within a process. A single process can thus have multiple concurrently executing threads.

There are many possible uses for multithreading, but in general, you'll have some part of your program tied to a particular event or resource, and you don't want to hang up the rest of your program because of that. So you create a thread associated with that event or resource and let it run independently of the main program. A good example is a "quit" button - you don't want to be forced to poll the quit button in every piece of code you write in your program and yet you want the quit button to be responsive, as if you were checking it regularly. In fact, one of the most immediately compelling reasons for multithreading is to produce a responsive user interface.

9.4 Multitasking vs. Multithreading

The earliest computers did one thing at a time. A lab computer might calculate detonation waves for one of the physicists. Next it would calculate mixing ratios for a chemist. All programs were run sequentially, one at a time; and each had full run of the computer. However two programs couldn't be run at once. This is called batch processing, and it's a very efficient way to get maximum usage out of a very expensive computer because almost all the computer's time is spent actually calculating jobs and not switching between one program and another. However batch processing can be very annoying when your differential equation integration program that would take all of two seconds of CPU time gets stuck in line behind the physics department's nuclear structure modeling project that's going run for the next three days.

Time sharing operating systems were invented to allow multiple people to use one then very expensive computer at the same time. On a time sharing system many people can run programs at the same time. The operating system is responsible for splitting the time among the different programs that are running. That way you can finish integrating your differential equation while the physics department's nuclear modeling program is still churning away. The physics department nuclear modeling program might take two weeks to run instead of three days, but everyone with the shorter programs is happy (at least until the physicists figured out how to hack the computer so that it only ran their program).

Once systems allowed different users to run programs at the same time it was a short step to letting the same user run multiple programs simultaneously. Each running program (generally caled a process) had its own memory space, its own set of variables, its own stack and heap, and so on. One process could spawn another process, but once that occurred the two processes behaved more or less independently. Mechanisms like remote procedure calls (RPC) were developed to allow processes to interact with each other, but such interaction was expensive and difficult. And this is where matters stopped for about twenty years.

However it's not just users that want to do different things at the same time. Many programs also need to do several things at once. A web browser, for instance, can print a file in the background while it downloads a page in one window and formats the page as it downloads. The ability of an individual program to do more than one thing at the same time is most efficiently implemented through threads.

9.5 The Thread Classes

Java has two ways a program can implement threading. One is to create a subclass of java.lang.Thread. However sometimes you'll want to thread an object that's already a subclass of another class. Then you use the java.lang.Runnable interface.

The Thread class has three primary methods that are used to control a thread:

public native synchronized void start()

```
public void run()
public final void stop()
```

The start() method prepares a thread to be run; the run() method actually performs the work of the thread; and the stop() method halts the thread. The thread dies when the the run() method terminates or when the thread's stop() method is invoked.

You never call run() explicitly. It is called automatically by the runtime as necessary once you've called start(). There are also methods to supend and resume threads, to put threads to sleep and wake them up, to yield control to other threads, and many more. I'll discuss these later.

The Runnable interface allows you to add threading to a class which, for one reason or another, cannot conveniently extend Thread. It declares a single method, run():

```
public abstract void run()
```

By passing an object which implements Runnable to a Thread() constructor, you can substitute the Runnable's run() method for the Thread's own run() method. (More properly the Thread object's run() method simply calls the Runnable's run() method.)

9.5.1 A Simple Thread

When writing a threaded program you can pretend that you're writing many different programs, each with its own run() method. Each thread is a subclass of java.lang.Thread. The following program is a thread that prints the numbers between -128 and 127.

```
public class BytePrinter extends Thread {
public void run() {
for (int b = -128; b < 128; b++) {
System.out.println(b);
}
}
}
```

You launch this thread from another method, probably in another class, by instantiating an object of this class using new and calling its start() method. To create a thread just call the default constructor for your subclass of Thread. For instance

```
BytePrinter bp = new BytePrinter();
```

This class only has the default, noargs constructor; but there's absolutely no reason you can't add other constructors to your Thread subclass.

Constructing a thread object puts it at the starting line. The bell goes off and the thread starts running when you call the thread's start() method like this:

```
bp.start();
```

```
Once the start() method is called program execution splits in two.
```

```
Some CPU time goes into whatever statements follow bp.start() and
some goes into the bp thread. It is unpredictable which statements
will run first. Most likely they will be intermixed. The bp thread
will now continue running until one of seven things happens
bp's run() method completes.
bp's stop() method is called.
bp's suspend() method is called.
bp's sleep() method is called.
bp's yield() method is called.
bp blocks waiting for an unavailable resource
Another thread preempts this thread.
```

Once program control reaches the end of bp's run() method the thread dies, though you can restart it from the beginning by calling its start() method again.

For example, the following program launches a single BytePrinter thread:

```
public class ThreadTest {
public static void main(String args[])      {
System.out.println("Constructing the thread...");
BytePrinter bp = new BytePrinter();
System.out.println("Starting the thread...");
bp.start();
System.out.println("The thread has been started.");
System.out.println("The main() method is finishing.");
return;
}
}
```

Here's some sample output:

% java ThreadTest
Constructing the thread...
Starting the thread...
The thread has been started.
The main() method is finishing.

```
-128
-127
-126
-125
-124
-123
-122
-121
-120
```

Of course this continues for a couple hundred more lines.

9.5.2 Multiple Threads

The following program launches three BytePrinter threads:

```
public class ThreadsTest {
public static void main(String args[]) {
```

```
BytePrinter bp1 = new BytePrinter();
BytePrinter bp2 = new BytePrinter();
BytePrinter bp3 = new BytePrinter();
bp1.start();
bp2.start();
bp3.start();
}
}
```

The order of the output you see from this program is implementation dependent, and mostly unpredictable. It may look something like this:

```
-128
-127
-126
 125
 126
 127
-128
-127
-126
 125
 126
 127
-128
-127
-126
 125
 126
 127
```

In this case the three threads run sequentially, one after the other. However on a few systems you may see something different

9.5.3 Multiple Preemptive Threads

However on a few systems you may see something like this:

```
-128
-127
-126
-125
-124
-123
-128
-127
-126
-125
-128
-127
-126
-125
```

```
-124
-123
-122
-121
-120
-119
-124
-123
 125
 126
 127
```

In this case output from the three different threads is intermixed. Some systems use cooperative threads that require a thread to explicitly yield control before other, equal priority threads get a chance to run. Other systems use preemptive threading in which the virtual machine guarantees that all threads of the same priority get time in which to run. However, even on preemptive VMs this thread takes so little time to run it's unlikely any intermixing will occur.

9.5.4 Customizing a Thread's run Method

The run method gives a thread something to do. Its code implements the thread's running behavior. It can do anything that can be encoded in Java statements: compute a list of prime's, sort some data, perform some animation.

The Thread class implements a generic thread that, by default, does nothing. That is, the implementation of its run method is empty. This is not particularly useful, so the Thread class defines API that lets a Runnable object provide a more interesting run method for a thread.

There are two techniques for providing a run method for a thread:

- Subclassing Thread and Overriding run
- Implementing the Runnable Interface

Subclassing Thread and Overriding run

The first way to customize what a thread does when it is running is to subclass Thread (itself a Runnable object) and override its empty run method so that it does something. Let's look at the SimpleThread class, the first of two classes in this example, which does just that:

```
public class SimpleThread extends Thread {
public SimpleThread(String str) {
super(str);
}
public void run() {
for (int i = 0; i < 10; i++) {
System.out.println(i + " " + getName());
try {
sleep((int)(Math.random() * 1000));
} catch (InterruptedException e) {}
}
System.out.println("DONE! " + getName());
}
}
```

The first method in the SimpleThread class is a constructor that takes a String as its only argument. This constructor is implemented by calling a superclass constructor and is interesting to us only because it sets the Thread's name, which is used later in the program.

The next method in the SimpleThread class is the run method. The run method is the heart of any Thread and where the action of the Thread takes place. The run method of the SimpleThread class contains a for loop that iterates ten times. In each iteration the method displays the iteration number and the name of the Thread, then sleeps for a random interval of up to 1 second. After the loop has finished, the run method prints DONE! along with the name of the thread. That's it for the SimpleThread class.

The TwoThreadsTest class provides a main method that creates two SimpleThread threads: one is named "Jamaica" and the other is named "Fiji". (If you can't decide on where to go for vacation you can use this program to help you decide—go to the island whose thread prints "DONE!" first.)

```
public class TwoThreadsTest {
public static void main (String[] args) {
new SimpleThread("Jamaica").start();
new SimpleThread("Fiji").start();
}
}
```

The main method also starts each thread immediately following its construction by calling the start method. To save you from typing in this program, click here for the source code to the SimpleThread class and here for the source code to the TwoThreadsTest program. Compile and run the program and watch your vacation fate unfold. You should see output similar to the following:

```
0 Jamaica
0 Fiji
1 Fiji
1 Jamaica
2 Jamaica
2 Fiji
3 Fiji
3 Jamaica
4 Jamaica
4 Fiji
5 Jamaica
5 Fiji
6 Fiji
6 Jamaica
7 Jamaica
7 Fiji
8 Fiji
9 Fiji
8 Jamaica
DONE! Fiji
9 Jamaica
DONE! Jamaica
```

(Looks like I'm going to Fiji!!) Notice how the output from each thread is intermingled with the output from the other. This is because both SimpleThread threads are running concurrently. Thus, both run methods are running at the same time and each thread is displaying its output at the same time as the other.

Try This: Change the main program so that it creates a third thread with the name "Bora Bora". Compile and run the program again. Does this change the island of choice for your vacation? Here's the code for the new main program, which is now named ThreeThreadsTest.

Now, let's look at another example, the Clock applet, that uses the other technique for providing a run method to a Thread.

9.6 Naming Threads

It's often useful to give different threads in the same class names so you can tell them apart. The following constructor allows you to do that:

public Thread(String name)

This is normally called from the constructor of a subclass, like this:

```
public class NamedBytePrinter extends Thread {
public NamedBytePrinter(String name) {
super(name);
}
public void run() {
for (int b = -128; b < 128; b++) {
System.out.println(this.getName() + ": " + b);
}
}
}
```

The getName() method of the Thread class returns this value.

The following program now distinguishes the output of different threads:

```
public class NamedThreadsTest {
public static void main(String[] args) {
NamedBytePrinter frank = new NamedBytePrinter("Frank");
NamedBytePrinter mary = new NamedBytePrinter("Mary");
NamedBytePrinter chris = new NamedBytePrinter("Chris");
frank.start();
mary.start();
chris.start();
}
}
```

Named Threads Output

For example,

```
Frank: -128
Mary: -128
Mary: -127
Mary: -126
Mary: -125
Mary: -124
Mary: -123
```

```
Mary: -122
Mary: -121
Chris: -128
Chris: -127
Chris: -126
Chris: -125
Chris: -124
Chris: -123
Chris: -122
Chris: -121
Chris: -120
Mary: -120
Mary: -119
Chris: -119
Chris: -118
Frank: -127
Frank: -126
Frank: -125
Mary: 121
Mary: 122
Mary: 123
Chris: 127
Frank: 123
Frank: 124
Frank: 125
Mary: 124
Mary: 125
Frank: 126
Frank: 127
Mary: 126
Mary: 127
```

Again, the exact ordering and even whether the thread output is intermixed, can vary from system to system and run to run.

9.7 Responsive user interfaces

As a starting point, consider a program that performs some CPU-intensive operation and thus ends up ignoring user input and being unresponsive. This one, a combined applet/application, will simply display the result of a running counter:

```
//: Counter1.java
// A non-responsive user interface
package c14;
import java.awt.*;
import java.awt.event.*;
import java.applet.*;

public class Counter1 extends Applet {
private int count = 0;
```

```
private Button
onOff = new Button("Toggle"),
start = new Button("Start");
private TextField t = new TextField(10);
private boolean runFlag = true;
public void init() {
add(t);
start.addActionListener(new StartL());
add(start);
onOff.addActionListener(new OnOffL());
add(onOff);
}
public void go() {
while (true) {
try {
Thread.currentThread().sleep(100);
} catch (InterruptedException e){}
if(runFlag)
t.setText(Integer.toString(count++));
}
}
class StartL implements ActionListener {
public void actionPerformed(ActionEvent e) {
go();
}
}
class OnOffL implements ActionListener {
public void actionPerformed(ActionEvent e) {
runFlag = !runFlag;
}
}
public static void main(String[] args) {
Counter1 applet = new Counter1();
Frame aFrame = new Frame("Counter1");
aFrame.addWindowListener(
new WindowAdapter() {
public void windowClosing(WindowEvent e) {
System.exit(0);
}
});
aFrame.add(applet, BorderLayout.CENTER);
aFrame.setSize(300,200);
applet.init();
applet.start();
aFrame.setVisible(true);
}
} ///:~
```

At this point, the AWT and applet code should be reasonably familiar from Chapter 13. The go( ) method is where the program stays busy: it puts the current value of count into the TextField t , then increments count.

Part of the infinite loop inside go( ) is to call sleep( ). sleep( ) must be associated with a Thread object, and it turns out that every application has some thread associated with it. (Indeed, Java is based on threads and there are always some running along with your application.) So regardless of whether you're explicitly using threads, you can produce the current thread used by your program with Thread. currentThread() (a static method of the Thread class) and then call sleep( ) for that thread.

Note that sleep( ) can throw InterruptedException, although throwing such an exception is considered a hostile way to break from a thread and should be discouraged. (Once again, exceptions are for exceptional conditions, not normal flow of control.) Interrupting a sleeping thread is included to support a future language feature.

When the start button is pressed, go( ) is invoked. And upon examining go( ), you might naively think (as I did) that it should allow multithreading because it goes to sleep. That is, while the method is asleep, it seems like the CPU could be busy monitoring other button presses. But it turns out that the real problem is that go( ) never returns, since it's in an infinite loop, and this means that actionPerformed( ) never returns. Since you're stuck inside actionPerformed( ) for the first keypress, the program can't handle any other events. (To get out, you must somehow kill the process; the easiest way to do this is to press Control-C in the console window.)

The basic problem here is that go( ) needs to continue performing its operations, and at the same time it needs to return so actionPerformed( ) can complete and the user interface can continue responding to the user. But in a conventional method like go( ) it cannot continue and at the same time return control to the rest of the program. This sounds like an impossible thing to accomplish, as if the CPU must be in two places at once, but this is precisely the illusion that threading provides. The thread model (and programming support in Java) is a programming convenience to simplify juggling several operations at the same time within a single program. With threads, the CPU will pop around and give each thread some of its time. Each thread has the consciousness of constantly having the CPU to itself, but the CPU's time is actually sliced between all the threads.

Threading reduces computing efficiency somewhat, but the net improvement in program design, resource balancing, and user convenience is often quite valuable. Of course, if you have more than one CPU, then the operating system can dedicate each CPU to a set of threads or even a single thread and the whole program can run much faster. Multitasking and multithreading tend to be the most reasonable ways to utilize multiprocessor systems.

9.8 Inheriting from Thread

The simplest way to create a thread is to inherit from class Thread, which has all the wiring necessary to create and run threads. The most important method for Thread is run( ), which you must override to make the thread do your bidding. Thus, run( ) is the code that will be executed "simultaneously" with the other threads in a program.

The following example creates any number of threads that it keeps track of by assigning each thread a unique number, generated with a static variable. The Thread's run( ) method is overridden to count down each time it passes through its loop and to finish when the count is zero (at the point when run( ) returns, the thread is terminated).

```
//: SimpleThread.java
// Very simple Threading example
public class SimpleThread extends Thread {
```

```
private int countDown = 5;
private int threadNumber;
private static int threadCount = 0;
public SimpleThread() {
threadNumber = ++threadCount;
System.out.println("Making " + threadNumber);
}
public void run() {
while(true) {
System.out.println("Thread " +
threadNumber + "(" + countDown + ")");
if(—countDown == 0) return;
}
}
public static void main(String[] args) {
for(int i = 0; i < 5; i++)
new SimpleThread().start();
System.out.println("All Threads Started");
}
} ///:~
```

A run( ) method virtually always has some kind of loop that continues until the thread is no longer necessary, so you must establish the condition on which to break out of this loop (or, in the case above, simply return from run( )). Often, run( ) is cast in the form of an infinite loop, which means that, barring some external call to stop( ) or destroy( ) for that thread, it will run forever (until the program completes).

In main( ) you can see a number of threads being created and run. The special method that comes with the Thread class is start( ), which performs special initialization for the thread and then calls run( ). So the steps are: the constructor is called to build the object, then start( ) configures the thread and calls run( ). If you don't call start( ) (which you can do in the constructor, if that's appropriate) the thread will never be started.

The output for one run of this program (it will be different every time) is:

```
Making 1
Making 2
Making 3
Making 4
Making 5
Thread 1(5)
Thread 1(4)
Thread 1(3)
Thread 1(2)
Thread 2(5)
Thread 2(4)
Thread 2(3)
Thread 2(2)
Thread 2(1)
Thread 1(1)
```

```
All Threads Started
Thread 3(5)
Thread 4(5)
Thread 4(4)
Thread 4(3)
Thread 4(2)
Thread 4(1)
Thread 5(5)
Thread 5(4)
Thread 5(3)
Thread 5(2)
Thread 5(1)
Thread 3(4)
Thread 3(3)
Thread 3(2)
Thread 3(1)
```

You'll notice that nowhere in this example is sleep( ) called, and yet the output indicates that each thread gets a portion of the CPU's time in which to execute. This shows that sleep( ), while it relies on the existence of a thread in order to execute, is not involved with either enabling or disabling threading. It's simply another method.

You can also see that the threads are not run in the order that they're created. In fact, the order that the CPU attends to an existing set of threads is indeterminate, unless you go in and adjust the priorities using Thread's setPriority( ) method.

When main( ) creates the Thread objects it isn't capturing the handles for any of them. An ordinary object would be fair game for garbage collection, but not a Thread. Each Thread "registers" itself so there is actually a reference to it someplace and the garbage collector can't clean it up.

9.9 Threading for a Responsive Interface

Now it's possible to solve the problem in Counter1.java with a thread. The trick is to place the subtask - that is, the loop that's inside go( ) - inside the run( ) method of a thread. When the user presses the start button, the thread is started, but then the creation of the thread completes, so even though the thread is running, the main job of the program (watching for and responding to user-interface events) can continue. Here's the solution:

```
//: Counter2.java
// A responsive user interface with threads
import java.awt.*;
import java.awt.event.*;
import java.applet.*;

class SeparateSubTask extends Thread {
private int count = 0;
private Counter2 c2;
private boolean runFlag = true;
public SeparateSubTask(Counter2 c2) {
this.c2 = c2;
start();
```

```
}
public void invertFlag() { runFlag = !runFlag;}
public void run() {
while (true) {
try {
sleep(100);
} catch (InterruptedException e){}
if(runFlag)
c2.t.setText(Integer.toString(count++));
}
}
}
public class Counter2 extends Applet {
TextField t = new TextField(10);
private SeparateSubTask sp = null;
private Button
onOff = new Button("Toggle"),
start = new Button("Start");
public void init() {
add(t);
start.addActionListener(new StartL());
add(start);
onOff.addActionListener(new OnOffL());
add(onOff);
}
class StartL implements ActionListener {
public void actionPerformed(ActionEvent e) {
if(sp == null)
sp = new SeparateSubTask(Counter2.this);
}
}
class OnOffL implements ActionListener {
public void actionPerformed(ActionEvent e) {
if(sp != null)
sp.invertFlag();
}
}
public static void main(String[] args) {
Counter2 applet = new Counter2();
Frame aFrame = new Frame("Counter2");
aFrame.addWindowListener(
new WindowAdapter() {
public void windowClosing(WindowEvent e) {
System.exit(0);
}
});
aFrame.add(applet, BorderLayout.CENTER);
```

```
aFrame.setSize(300,200);
applet.init();
applet.start();
aFrame.setVisible(true);
}
} ///:~
```

Counter2 is now a straightforward program, whose job is only to set up and maintain the user interface. But now, when the user presses the start button, a method is not called. Instead a thread of class SeparateSubTask is created (the constructor starts it, in this case), and then the Counter2 event loop continues. Note that the handle to the SeparateSubTask is stored so that when you press the onOff button it can toggle the runFlag inside the SeparateSubTask object. That thread (when it looks at the flag) can then start and stop itself. (This could also have been accomplished by making SeparateSubTask an inner class.)

The class SeparateSubTask is a simple extension of Thread with a constructor (that stores the Counter2 handle and then runs the thread by calling start( )) and a run( ) that essentially contains the code from inside go( ) in Counter1.java. Because SeparateSubTask knows that it holds a handle to a Counter2, it can reach in and access Counter2's TextField when it needs to.

When you press the onOff button, you'll see a virtually instant response. Of course, the response isn't really instant, not like that of a system that's driven by interrupts. The counter stops only when the thread has the CPU and notices that the flag has changed.

Improving the code with an inner class

As an aside, look at the coupling that occurs between the SeparateSubTask and Counter2 classes. The SeparateSubTask is intimately tied to Counter2 - it must keep a handle to its "parent" Counter2 object so it can call back and manipulate it. And yet the two classes shouldn't really merge together into a single class (although in the next section you'll see that Java provides a way to combine them) because they're doing separate things and are created at different times. They are tightly connected (what I call a "couplet") and this makes the coding awkward. This is a situation in which an inner class can improve the code significantly:

```
//: Counter2i.java
// Counter2 using an inner class for the thread
import java.awt.*;
import java.awt.event.*;
import java.applet.*;
public class Counter2i extends Applet {
private class SeparateSubTask extends Thread {
int count = 0;
boolean runFlag = true;
SeparateSubTask() { start(); }
public void run() {
while (true) {
try {
sleep(100);
} catch (InterruptedException e){}
if(runFlag)
t.setText(Integer.toString(count++));
}
```

```
}
}
private SeparateSubTask sp = null;
private TextField t = new TextField(10);
private Button
onOff = new Button("Toggle"),
start = new Button("Start");
public void init() {
add(t);
start.addActionListener(new StartL());
add(start);
onOff.addActionListener(new OnOffL());
add(onOff);
}
class StartL implements ActionListener {
public void actionPerformed(ActionEvent e) {
if(sp == null)
sp = new SeparateSubTask();
}
}
class OnOffL implements ActionListener {
public void actionPerformed(ActionEvent e) {
if(sp != null)
sp.runFlag = !sp.runFlag; // invertFlag();
}
}
public static void main(String[] args) {
Counter2i applet = new Counter2i();
Frame aFrame = new Frame("Counter2i");
aFrame.addWindowListener(
new WindowAdapter() {
public void windowClosing(WindowEvent e) {
System.exit(0);
}
});
aFrame.add(applet, BorderLayout.CENTER);
aFrame.setSize(300,200);
applet.init();
applet.start();
aFrame.setVisible(true);
}
} ///:~
```

This SeparateSubTask name will not collide with the SeparateSubTask in the previous example even though they're in the same directory, since it's hidden as an inner class. You can also see that the inner class is private, which means that its fields and methods can be given default access (except for run( ), which must be public since it is public in the base class). The private inner class is not accessible to anyone but Counter2i, and since the two classes are tightly coupled it's convenient to loosen the access restrictions between them. In SeparateSubTask you can see that the invertFlag( ) method has been removed since Counter2i can now directly access runFlag.

Also, notice that SeparateSubTask's constructor has been simplified - now it only starts the thread. The handle to the Counter2i object is still being captured as in the previous version, but instead of doing it by hand and referencing the outer object by hand, the inner class mechanism takes care of it automatically. In run( ), you can see that t is simply accessed, as if it were a field of SeparateSubTask. The t field in the parent class can now be made private since SeparateSubTask can access it without getting any special permission - and it's always good to make fields "as private as possible" so they cannot be accidentally changed by forces outside your class.

Anytime you notice classes that appear to have high coupling with each other, consider the coding and maintenance improvements you might get by using inner classes.

9.10 Combining the Thread with the Main Class

In the example above you can see that the thread class is separate from the program's main class. This makes a lot of sense and is relatively easy to understand. There is, however, an alternate form that you will often see used that is not so clear but is usually more concise (which probably accounts for its popularity). This form combines the main program class with the thread class by making the main program class a thread. Since for a GUI program the main program class must be inherited from either Frame or Applet, an interface must be used to paste on the additional functionality. This interface is called Runnable, and it contains the same basic method that Thread does. In fact, Thread also implements Runnable, which specifies only that there be a run( ) method.

The use of the combined program/thread is not quite so obvious. When you start the program, you create an object that's Runnable, but you don't start the thread. This must be done explicitly. You can see this in the following program, which reproduces the functionality of Counter2:

```
//: Counter3.java
// Using the Runnable interface to turn the
// main class into a thread.
import java.awt.*;
import java.awt.event.*;
import java.applet.*;
public class Counter3
extends Applet implements Runnable {
private int count = 0;
private boolean runFlag = true;
private Thread selfThread = null;
private Button
onOff = new Button("Toggle"),
start = new Button("Start");
private TextField t = new TextField(10);
public void init() {
add(t);
start.addActionListener(new StartL());
add(start);
onOff.addActionListener(new OnOffL());
add(onOff);
}
```

```
public void run() {
while (true) {
try {
selfThread.sleep(100);
} catch (InterruptedException e){}
if(runFlag)
t.setText(Integer.toString(count++));
}
}
class StartL implements ActionListener {
public void actionPerformed(ActionEvent e) {
if(selfThread == null) {
selfThread = new Thread(Counter3.this);
selfThread.start();
}
}
}
class OnOffL implements ActionListener {
public void actionPerformed(ActionEvent e) {
runFlag = !runFlag;
}
}
public static void main(String[] args) {
Counter3 applet = new Counter3();
Frame aFrame = new Frame("Counter3");
aFrame.addWindowListener(
new WindowAdapter() {
public void windowClosing(WindowEvent e) {
System.exit(0);
}
});
aFrame.add(applet, BorderLayout.CENTER);
aFrame.setSize(300,200);
applet.init();
applet.start();
aFrame.setVisible(true);
}
} ///:~
```

Now the run( ) is inside the class, but it's still dormant after init( ) completes. When you press the start button, the thread is created (if it doesn't already exist) in the somewhat obscure expression:

```
new Thread(Counter3.this);
```

When something has a Runnable interface, it simply means that it has a run( ) method, but there's nothing special about that - it doesn't produce any innate threading abilities, like those of a class inherited from Thread. So to produce a thread from a Runnable object, you must create a thread separately and hand it the Runnable object; there's a special constructor for this that takes a Runnable as its argument. You can then call start( ) for that thread:

```
selfThread.start();
```

This performs the usual initialization and then calls run( ).

The convenient aspect about the Runnable interface is that everything belongs to the same class. If you need to access something, you simply do it without going through a separate object. The penalty for this convenience is strict, though - you can have only a single thread running for that particular object (although you can create more objects of that type, or create other threads in different classes).

Note that the Runnable interface is not what imposes this restriction. It's the combination of Runnable and your main class that does it, since you can have only one object of your main class per application.

9.11 Making many Threads

Consider the creation of many different threads. You can't do this with the previous example, so you must go back to having separate classes inherited from Thread to encapsulate the run( ). But this is a more general solution and easier to understand, so while the previous example shows a coding style you'll often see, I can't recommend it for most cases because it's just a little bit more confusing and less flexible.

The following example repeats the form of the examples above with counters and toggle buttons. But now all the information for a particular counter, including the button and text field, is inside its own object that is inherited from Thread. All the fields in Ticker are private, which means that the Ticker implementation can be changed at will, including the quantity and type of data components to acquire and display information. When a Ticker object is created, the constructor requires a handle to an AWT Container, which Ticker fills with its visual components. This way, if you change the visual components, the code that uses Ticker doesn't need to be modified.

```
//: Counter4.java
// If you separate your thread from the main
// class, you can have as many threads as you
// want.
import java.awt.*;
import java.awt.event.*;
import java.applet.*;

class Ticker extends Thread {
private Button b = new Button("Toggle");
private TextField t = new TextField(10);
private int count = 0;
private boolean runFlag = true;
public Ticker(Container c) {
b.addActionListener(new ToggleL());
Panel p = new Panel();
p.add(t);
p.add(b);
c.add(p);
}
class ToggleL implements ActionListener {
public void actionPerformed(ActionEvent e) {
runFlag = !runFlag;
```

```
}
}
public void run() {
while (true) {
if(runFlag)
t.setText(Integer.toString(count++));
try {
sleep(100);
} catch (InterruptedException e){}
}
}
}

public class Counter4 extends Applet {
private Button start = new Button("Start");
private boolean started = false;
private Ticker[] s;
private boolean isApplet = true;
private int size;
public void init() {
// Get parameter "size" from Web page:
if(isApplet)
size =
Integer.parseInt(getParameter("size"));
s = new Ticker[size];
for(int i = 0; i < s.length; i++)
s[i] = new Ticker(this);
start.addActionListener(new StartL());
add(start);
}
class StartL implements ActionListener {
public void actionPerformed(ActionEvent e) {
if(!started) {
started = true;
for(int i = 0; i < s.length; i++)
s[i].start();
}
}
}
public static void main(String[] args) {
Counter4 applet = new Counter4();
// This isn't an applet, so set the flag and
// produce the parameter values from args:
applet.isApplet = false;
applet.size =
(args.length == 0 ? 5 :
Integer.parseInt(args[0]));
Frame aFrame = new Frame("Counter4");
```

```
aFrame.addWindowListener(
new WindowAdapter() {
public void windowClosing(WindowEvent e) {
System.exit(0);
}
});
aFrame.add(applet, BorderLayout.CENTER);
aFrame.setSize(200, applet.size * 50);
applet.init();
applet.start();
aFrame.setVisible(true);
}
} ///:~
```

Ticker contains not only its threading equipment but also the way to control and display the thread. You can create as many threads as you want without explicitly creating the windowing components.

In Counter4 there's an array of Ticker objects called s. For maximum flexibility, the size of this array is initialized by reaching out into the Web page using applet parameters. Here's what the size parameter looks like on the page, embedded inside the applet description:

```
<applet code=Counter4 width=600 height=600>
<param name=size value="20">
</applet>
```

The param, name, and value are all Web-page keywords. name is what you'll be referring to in your program, and value can be any string, not just something that resolves to a number.

You'll notice that the determination of the size of the array s is done inside init( ), and not as part of an inline definition of s. That is, you cannot say as part of the class definition (outside of any methods):

```
int size = Integer.parseInt(getParameter("size"));
Ticker[] s = new Ticker[size];
```

You can compile this, but you'll get a strange null-pointer exception at run time. It works fine if you move the getParameter( ) initialization inside of init( ). The applet framework performs the necessary startup to grab the parameters before entering init( ).

In addition, this code is set up to be either an applet or an application. When it's an application the size argument is extracted from the command line (or a default value is provided).

Once the size of the array is established, new Ticker objects are created; as part of the Ticker constructor the button and text field for each Ticker is added to the applet.

Pressing the start button means looping through the entire array of Tickers and calling start( ) for each one. Remember, start( ) performs necessary thread initialization and then calls run( ) for that thread.

The ToggleL listener simply inverts the flag in Ticker and when the associated thread next takes note it can react accordingly.

One value of this example is that it allows you to easily create large sets of independent subtasks and to monitor their behavior. In this case, you'll see that as the number of subtasks gets larger, your machine will probably show more divergence in the displayed numbers because of the way that the threads are served.

You can also experiment to discover how important the sleep(100) is inside Ticker.run( ). If you remove the sleep( ), things will work fine until you press a toggle button. Then that particular thread has a false runFlag and the run( ) is just tied up in a tight infinite loop, which appears difficult to break during multithreading, so the responsiveness and speed of the program really bogs down.

9.12 Daemon Threads

A "daemon" thread is one that is supposed to provide a general service in the background as long as the program is running, but is not part of the essence of the program. Thus, when all of the non-daemon threads complete the program is terminated. Conversely, if there are any non-daemon threads still running the program doesn't terminate. (There is, for instance, a thread that runs main( ).)

You can find out if a thread is a daemon by calling isDaemon( ), and you can turn the daemonhood of a thread on and off with setDaemon( ). If a thread is a daemon, then any threads it creates will automatically be daemons.

The following example demonstrates daemon threads:

```
//: Daemons.java
// Daemonic behavior
import java.io.*;

class Daemon extends Thread {
private static final int SIZE = 10;
private Thread[] t = new Thread[SIZE];
public Daemon() {
setDaemon(true);
start();
}
public void run() {
for(int i = 0; i < SIZE; i++)
t[i] = new DaemonSpawn(i);
for(int i = 0; i < SIZE; i++)
System.out.println(
"t[" + i + "].isDaemon() = "
+ t[i].isDaemon());
while(true)
yield();
}
}

class DaemonSpawn extends Thread {
public DaemonSpawn(int i) {
System.out.println(
"DaemonSpawn "+ i + "started");
start();
}
public void run() {
while(true)
yield();
}
```

```
}

public class Daemons {
public static void main(String[] args) {
Thread d = new Daemon();
System.out.println(
"d.isDaemon() = "+ d.isDaemon());
// Allow the daemon threads to finish
// their startup processes:
BufferedReader stdin =
new BufferedReader(
new InputStreamReader(System.in));
System.out.println("Waiting for CR");
try {
stdin.readLine();
} catch(IOException e) {}
}
} ///:~
```

The Daemon thread sets its daemon flag to "true" and then spawns a bunch of other threads to show that they are also daemons. Then it goes into an infinite loop that calls yield( ) to give up control to the other processes. In an earlier version of this program, the infinite loops would increment int counters, but this seemed to bring the whole program to a stop. Using yield( ) makes the program quite peppy.

There's nothing to keep the program from terminating once main( ) finishes its job since there are nothing but daemon threads running. So that you can see the results of starting all the daemon threads, System.in is set up to read so the program waits for a carriage return before terminating. Without this you see only some of the results from the creation of the daemon threads. (Try replacing the readLine( ) code with sleep( ) calls of various lengths to see this behavior.)

9.13 Sharing Limited Resources

You can think of a single-threaded program as one lonely entity moving around through your problem space and doing one thing at a time. Because there's only one entity, you never have to think about the problem of two entities trying to use the same resource at the same time, like two people trying to park in the same space, walk through a door at the same time, or even talk at the same time.

With multithreading, things aren't lonely anymore, but you now have the possibility of two or more threads trying to use the same limited resource at once. Colliding over a resource must be prevented or else you'll have two threads trying to access the same bank account at the same time, print to the same printer, or adjust the same valve, etc.

9.14 Improperly Accessing Resources

Consider a variation on the counters that have been used so far in this chapter. In the following example, each thread contains two counters that are incremented and displayed inside run( ). In addition, there's another thread of class Watcher that is watching the counters to see if they're always equivalent. This seems like a needless activity, since looking at the code it appears obvious that the counters will always be the same. But that's where the surprise comes in. Here's the first version of the program:

```
//: Sharing1.java
```

```
// Problems with resource sharing while threading
import java.awt.*;
import java.awt.event.*;
import java.applet.*;

class TwoCounter extends Thread {
private boolean started = false;
private TextField
t1 = new TextField(5),
t2 = new TextField(5);
private Label l =
new Label("count1 == count2");
private int count1 = 0, count2 = 0;
// Add the display components as a panel
// to the given container:
public TwoCounter(Container c) {
Panel p = new Panel();
p.add(t1);
p.add(t2);
p.add(l);
c.add(p);
}
public void start() {
if(!started) {
started = true;
super.start();
}
}
public void run() {
while (true) {
t1.setText(Integer.toString(count1++));
t2.setText(Integer.toString(count2++));
try {
sleep(500);
} catch (InterruptedException e){}
}
}
public void synchTest() {
Sharing1.incrementAccess();
if(count1 != count2)
l.setText("Unsynched");
}
}

class Watcher extends Thread {
private Sharing1 p;
public Watcher(Sharing1 p) {
this.p = p;
```

```
start();
}
public void run() {
while(true) {
for(int i = 0; i < p.s.length; i++)
p.s[i].synchTest();
try {
sleep(500);
} catch (InterruptedException e){}
}
}
}

public class Sharing1 extends Applet {
TwoCounter[] s;
private static int accessCount = 0;
private static TextField aCount =
new TextField("0", 10);
public static void incrementAccess() {
accessCount++;
aCount.setText(Integer.toString(accessCount));
}
private Button
start = new Button("Start"),
observer = new Button("Observe");
private boolean isApplet = true;
private int numCounters = 0;
private int numObservers = 0;
public void init() {
if(isApplet) {
numCounters =
Integer.parseInt(getParameter("size"));
numObservers =
Integer.parseInt(
getParameter("observers"));
}
s = new TwoCounter[numCounters];
for(int i = 0; i < s.length; i++)
s[i] = new TwoCounter(this);
Panel p = new Panel();
start.addActionListener(new StartL());
p.add(start);
observer.addActionListener(new ObserverL());
p.add(observer);
p.add(new Label("Access Count"));
p.add(aCount);
add(p);
}
```

```
class StartL implements ActionListener {
public void actionPerformed(ActionEvent e) {
for(int i = 0; i < s.length; i++)
s[i].start();
}
}
class ObserverL implements ActionListener {
public void actionPerformed(ActionEvent e) {
for(int i = 0; i < numObservers; i++)
new Watcher(Sharing1.this);
}
}
public static void main(String[] args) {
Sharing1 applet = new Sharing1();
// This isn't an applet, so set the flag and
// produce the parameter values from args:
applet.isApplet = false;
applet.numCounters =
(args.length == 0 ? 5 :
Integer.parseInt(args[0]));
applet.numObservers =
(args.length < 2 ? 5 :
Integer.parseInt(args[1]));
Frame aFrame = new Frame("Sharing1");
aFrame.addWindowListener(
new WindowAdapter() {
public void windowClosing(WindowEvent e){
System.exit(0);
}
});
aFrame.add(applet, BorderLayout.CENTER);
aFrame.setSize(350, applet.numCounters *100);
applet.init();
applet.start();
aFrame.setVisible(true);
}
} ///:~
```

As before, each counter contains its own display components: two text fields and a label that initially indicates that the counts are equivalent. These components are added to the Container in the TwoCounter constructor. Because this thread is started via a button press by the user, it's possible that start( ) could be called more than once. It's illegal for Thread.start( ) to be called more than once for a thread (an exception is thrown). You can see that the machinery to prevent this in the started flag and the overridden start( ) method.

In run( ), count1 and count2 are incremented and displayed in a manner that would seem to keep them identical. Then sleep( ) is called; without this call the program balks because it becomes hard for the CPU to swap tasks.

The synchTest( ) method performs the apparently useless activity of checking to see if count1 is equivalent to count2; if they are not equivalent it sets the label to "Unsynched" to indicate this. But first, it calls a static member of the class Sharing1 that increments and displays an access counter to show how many times this check has occurred successfully. (The reason for this will become apparent in future variations of this example.)

The Watcher class is a thread whose job is to call synchTest( ) for all of the TwoCounter objects that are active. It does this by stepping through the array that's kept in the Sharing1 object. You can think of the Watcher as constantly peeking over the shoulders of the TwoCounter objects.

Sharing1 contains an array of TwoCounter objects that it initializes in init( ) and starts as threads when you press the "start" button. Later, when you press the "Observe" button, one or more observers are created and freed upon the unsuspecting TwoCounter threads.

Note that to run this as an applet in a browser, your Web page will need to contain the lines:

```
<applet code=Sharing1 width=650 height=500>
<param name=size value="20">
<param name=observers value="1">
</applet>
```

You can change the width, height, and parameters to suit your experimental tastes. By changing the size and observers you'll change the behavior of the program. You can also see that this program is set up to run as a stand-alone application by pulling the arguments from the command line (or providing defaults).

Here's the surprising part. In TwoCounter.run( ), the infinite loop is just repeatedly passing over the adjacent lines:

```
t1.setText(Integer.toString(count1++));
t2.setText(Integer.toString(count2++));
```

(as well as sleeping, but that's not important here). When you run the program, however, you'll discover that count1 and count2 will be observed (by the Watcher) to be unequal at times! This is because of the nature of threads - they can be suspended at any time. So at times, the suspension occurs between the execution of the above two lines, and the Watcher thread happens to come along and perform the comparison at just this moment, thus finding the two counters to be different.

This example shows a fundamental problem with using threads. You never know when a thread might be run. Imagine sitting at a table with a fork, about to spear the last piece of food on your plate and as your fork reaches for it, the food suddenly vanishes (because your thread was suspended and another thread came in and stole the food). That's the problem that you're dealing with.

Sometimes you don't care if a resource is being accessed at the same time you're trying to use it (the food is on some other plate). But for multithreading to work, you need some way to prevent two threads from accessing the same resource, at least during critical periods.

Preventing this kind of collision is simply a matter of putting a lock on a resource when one thread is using it. The first thread that accesses a resource locks it, and then the other threads cannot access that resource until it is unlocked, at which time another thread locks and uses it, etc. If the front seat of the car is the limited resource, the child who shouts "Dibs!" asserts the lock.

9.15 How Java Shares Resources

Java has built-in support to prevent collisions over one kind of resource: the memory in an object. Since you typically make the data elements of a class private and access that memory only through methods, you can prevent collisions by making a particular method synchronized. Only one thread at a time can call a synchronized method for a particular object (although that thread can call more than one of the object's synchronized methods). Here are simple synchronized methods:

```
synchronized void f() { /* ... */ }
synchronized void g(){ /* ... */ }
```

Each object contains a single lock (also called a monitor) that is automatically part of the object (you don't have to write any special code). When you call any synchronized method, that object is locked and no other synchronized method of that object can be called until the first one finishes and releases the lock. In the example above, if f( ) is called for an object, g( ) cannot be called for the same object until f( ) is completed and releases the lock. Thus, there's a single lock that's shared by all the synchronized methods of a particular object, and this lock prevents common memory from being written by more than one method at a time (i.e. more than one thread at a time).

There's also a single lock per class (as part of the Class object for the class), so that synchronized static methods can lock each other out from static data on a class-wide basis.

Note that if you want to guard some other resource from simultaneous access by multiple threads, you can do so by forcing access to that resource through synchronized methods.

9.16 Synchronizing the Counters

Armed with this new keyword it appears that the solution is at hand: we'll simply use the synchronized keyword for the methods in TwoCounter. The following example is the same as the previous one, with the addition of the new keyword:

```
//: Sharing2.java
// Using the synchronized keyword to prevent
// multiple access to a particular resource.
import java.awt.*;
import java.awt.event.*;
import java.applet.*;

class TwoCounter2 extends Thread {
private boolean started = false;
private TextField
t1 = new TextField(5),
t2 = new TextField(5);
private Label l =
new Label("count1 == count2");
private int count1 = 0, count2 = 0;
public TwoCounter2(Container c) {
Panel p = new Panel();
p.add(t1);
p.add(t2);
p.add(l);
c.add(p);
}
public void start() {
if(!started) {
started = true;
super.start();
```

```
}
}
public synchronized void run() {
while (true) {
t1.setText(Integer.toString(count1++));
t2.setText(Integer.toString(count2++));
try {
sleep(500);
} catch (InterruptedException e){}
}
}
public synchronized void synchTest() {
Sharing2.incrementAccess();
if(count1 != count2)
l.setText("Unsynched");
}
}

class Watcher2 extends Thread {
private Sharing2 p;
public Watcher2(Sharing2 p) {
this.p = p;
start();
}
public void run() {
while(true) {
for(int i = 0; i < p.s.length; i++)
p.s[i].synchTest();
try {
sleep(500);
} catch (InterruptedException e){}
}
}
}

public class Sharing2 extends Applet {
TwoCounter2[] s;
private static int accessCount = 0;
private static TextField aCount =
new TextField("0", 10);
public static void incrementAccess() {
accessCount++;
aCount.setText(Integer.toString(accessCount));
}
private Button
start = new Button("Start"),
observer = new Button("Observe");
private boolean isApplet = true;
```

```
private int numCounters = 0;
private int numObservers = 0;
public void init() {
if(isApplet) {
numCounters =
Integer.parseInt(getParameter("size"));
numObservers =
Integer.parseInt(
getParameter("observers"));
}
s = new TwoCounter2[numCounters];
for(int i = 0; i < s.length; i++)
s[i] = new TwoCounter2(this);
Panel p = new Panel();
start.addActionListener(new StartL());
p.add(start);
observer.addActionListener(new ObserverL());
p.add(observer);
p.add(new Label("Access Count"));
p.add(aCount);
add(p);
}
class StartL implements ActionListener {
public void actionPerformed(ActionEvent e) {
for(int i = 0; i < s.length; i++)
s[i].start();
}
}
class ObserverL implements ActionListener {
public void actionPerformed(ActionEvent e) {
for(int i = 0; i < numObservers; i++)
new Watcher2(Sharing2.this);
}
}
public static void main(String[] args) {
Sharing2 applet = new Sharing2();
// This isn't an applet, so set the flag and
// produce the parameter values from args:
applet.isApplet = false;
applet.numCounters =
(args.length == 0 ? 5 :
Integer.parseInt(args[0]));
applet.numObservers =
(args.length < 2 ? 5 :
Integer.parseInt(args[1]));
Frame aFrame = new Frame("Sharing2");
aFrame.addWindowListener(
new WindowAdapter() {
```

```
public void windowClosing(WindowEvent e){
System.exit(0);
}
});
aFrame.add(applet, BorderLayout.CENTER);
aFrame.setSize(350, applet.numCounters *100);
applet.init();
applet.start();
aFrame.setVisible(true);
}
} ///:~
```

You'll notice that both run( ) and synchTest( ) are synchronized. If you synchronize only one of the methods, then the other is free to ignore the object lock and can be called with impunity. This is an important point: Every method that accesses a critical shared resource must be synchronized or it won't work right.

Now a new issue arises. The Watcher2 can never get a peek at what's going on because the entire run( ) method has been synchronized, and since run( ) is always running for each object the lock is always tied up and synchTest( ) can never be called. You can see this because the accessCount never changes.

What we'd like for this example is a way to isolate only part of the code inside run( ). The section of code you want to isolate this way is called a critical section and you use the synchronized keyword in a different way to set up a critical section. Java supports critical sections with the synchronized block; this time synchronized is used to specify the object whose lock is being used to synchronize the enclosed code:

```
synchronized(syncObject) {
// This code can be accessed by only
// one thread at a time, assuming all
// threads respect syncObject's lock
}
```

Before the synchronized block can be entered, the lock must be acquired on syncObject. If some other thread already has this lock, then the block cannot be entered until the lock is given up.

The Sharing2 example can be modified by removing the synchronized keyword from the entire run( ) method and instead putting a synchronized block around the two critical lines. But what object should be used as the lock? The one that is already respected by synchTest( ), which is the current object (this)! So the modified run( ) looks like this:

```
public void run() {
while (true) {
synchronized(this) {
t1.setText(Integer.toString(count1++));
t2.setText(Integer.toString(count2++));
}
try {
sleep(500);
} catch (InterruptedException e){}
}
}
```

This is the only change that must be made to Sharing2.java, and you'll see that while the two counters are never out of synch (according to when the Watcher is allowed to look at them), there is still adequate access provided to the Watcher during the execution of run( ).

Of course, all synchronization depends on programmer diligence: every piece of code that can access a shared resource must be wrapped in an appropriate synchronized block.

9.17 Synchronized Efficiency

Since having two methods write to the same piece of data never sounds like a particularly good idea, it might seem to make sense for all methods to be automatically synchronized and eliminate the synchronized keyword altogether. (Of course, the example with a synchronized run( ) shows that this wouldn't work either.) But it turns out that acquiring a lock is not a cheap operation - it multiplies the cost of a method call (that is, entering and exiting from the method, not executing the body of the method) by a minimum of four times, and could be more depending on your implementation. So if you know that a particular method will not cause contention problems it is expedient to leave off the synchronized keyword.

9.18 Sleep

Sometimes the computer may run too fast for the human beings. If this is the case you need to slow it down. You can make a particular Thread slow down by interspersing it with calls to the sleep(long ms) method. ms is the number of milliseconds you want the thread to wait before proceeding on. There are one thousand milliseconds in a second.

The sleep() method throws InterruptedExceptions. Therefore when you put a thread to sleep, you need to catch InterruptedExceptions. Thus every call to sleep() should be wrapped in a try catch block like this:

```
try {
this.sleep(1000);
}
catch (InterruptedException e) {
}
To delay a program for a fixed amount of time you often do something
like this:
try {
Thread.currentThread.sleep(1000);
}
catch (InterruptedException e) {
}
```

9.19 Synchronization: the Problem. Part 1

So far all the threads have run independently of each other. One thread did not need to know what another thread was doing. Sometimes, however, threads need to share data. In this case it is important to ensure that one thread doesn't change the data while the other thread is executing. The classic example is file access. If one thread is writing to a file while another thread is reading the file, it's likely that the thread that's reading the file will get corrupt data.

For example, consider the following toy problem:

```
public class Counter {
int i = 0;
```

```
public void count() {
int limit = i + 100;
while (i++ != limit)  System.out.println(i);
}
}
public class CounterThread extends Thread {
Counter c;
public static void main(String[] args) {
Counter c = new Counter();
CounterThread ct1 = new CounterThread(c);
CounterThread ct2 = new CounterThread(c);
ct1.start();
ct2.start();
}
public CounterThread(Counter c) {
this.c = c;
}
public void run() {
c.count();
}
}
```

Given these two classes what do you expect the output will be?

If you're reading this on the web before class, I really want you to think about this problem before moving on to the next page. Give it some real thought; then run the program and see if that is indeed what happens.

9.20 Synchronization: the Problem, part 2

The fact is there's no guarantee what the output will be. The Roaster DR3 VM gave me the following output the first time I ran this program:

```
1
3
4
5
6
7
8
9
10
11
90
91
92
93
94
```

```
95
96
97
98
99
100
101
102
```

Synchronization: the problem, part 3

The second time I ran it on the same VM it appeared to be caught in an infinite loop. The output looked like this:

```
1
3
4
5
6
7
8
9
10
11
90
91
92
93
94
95
96
97
98
99
100
101
102
103
104
105
342
343
344
345
```

I didn't run it long enough to be sure, but my best guess is that it would have continued to run until it wrapped around into the negative numbers, then counted back up to 100, and then stopped.

Synchronization: the problem, part 4

Sun's JDK for the Mac 1.0.2 behaved similarly. However it skipped 7 and stopped at 107:

```
1
```

```
2
3
4
5
6
8
9
10
11
98
99
100
101
102
103
104
105
106
107
```

Can you explain this behavior? How do you get an infinite loop one run, and termination the next with no external input to the program? Why do different VMs give different results? Why is this program non-deterministic? There are no calls to Math.random(). There's no user input. Nothing reads anything from the host machine such as the number of active processes running or the current time. It's just a simple counting program!

9.21 Synchronization: Some Solutions

The fundamental problem in the previous program was that there were two threads modifying the fields of the same object. Furthermore the order in which the fields were modified is indeterminate.

There are a number of possible solutions to this problem. Not all solutions are valid in all situations. For example, one of the simplest and most direct is to make the object immutable, that is not to allow it to change after it's been constructed. You can guarantee this by making all fields private, not providing any setter methods, and not allowing any non-constructor method in the class to change the value of a field. However, this solution is inappropriate for this problem because the count() method must change the field i.

You can do a similar thing by declaring fields to be final. This way they can't be changed after the object is constructed. This isn't always practical, however.

In this example, it would be simple to make i a local variable instead of a field. This is a relatively uncommon solution (why?), but it does work for this case, primarily because this is a toy example.

```
public class Counter {
public void count() {
int i = 0;
int limit = 100;
while (i++ != limit)  System.out.println(i);
}
}
```

By making i a local variable instead of a field, each thread that invokes the count() method on this object gets a separate and different i. Each time a method is called, a separate stack frame is set up for its variables and arguments. Different invocations of a method do not share variables. However this has changed the meaning of the program. Now each thread counts from 0 to 100. If this is what was originally intended this is fine. However if the intention was for the first thread to count from 0 to 100 and the second thread to count from 101 to 200, then this solution's no good.

9.22 Synchronization: Another Solution

A somewhat more general solution that combines the previous two is to copy the value of the field into a local variable, then change only the local variable. The field remains unchanged inside the method. For example,

```
public class Counter {
int i = 0;
public void count() {
int i = this.i;
int limit = i + 100;
while (i++ != limit) System.out.println(i);
}
}
```

Note how the local variable i shadows the field i, and how the this keyword is used to refer to the field i outside the shadow.

This trick is primarily useful when you don't need to save the changed variable back into the field when the method is done. The following saves the state, but is still subject to less obvious synchronization problems.

```
public class Counter {
int i = 0;
public void count() {
int i = this.i;
int limit = i + 100;
while (i++ != limit) System.out.println(i);
this.i = i;
}
}
```

In fact, this is probably even worse than the original example because it will work 99 times out of a 100. The bug here is extremely hard to pin down if you don't spot it in the source code.

9.23 The Synchronized Keyword

Java does allow you to guarantee that no more than one thread at a time will run a method. Other threads will have to wait for the first thread to finish running. In the meantime they block, that is stop executing.

You do this by applying the synchronized keyword to the method, like this:

public class SychronizedCounter extends Counter {

```
public synchronized void count() {
int limit = i + 100;
while (i++ != limit) System.out.println(i);
```

```
}
}
```

However you don't want to synchronize lightly. This solution severely impacts performance. In general synchronized methods run three to ten times slower that the equivalent non-synchronized method.

Synchronization is not a panacea, either. There can still be thread related bugs in classes that have synchronized methods. There can also be non-thread related bugs. In fact there's one in this very class. Can you find it?

9.24 Synchronizing on Objects

Magic Feather example.

Each object has a magic feather called a monitor. When you use the synchronized keyword on a method, you're gaining the monitor of the current object or locking it. As long as a thread possesses the monitor or lock of an object no other thread can get the lock for that object. (Another thread may be able to lock a different object in the same class, however.)

When you use the synchronized modifier to specify that a method is synchronized, you are locking on the particular object whose method is invoked. (Static methods can also be synchronized. In this case, the lock is placed on the java.lang.Class object associated with the object's class.) Since there's only one lock per object, it's not just the synchronized method that can't be invoked by other threads. It's any other synchronized method or block of code in that object.

You can synchronize at a lower level than a method. For example the following program had problems if another thread changed the value of i or this.i while the assignment was taking place.

```
public class Counter {
int i = 0;
public void count() {
int i = this.i;
int limit = i + 100;
while (i++ != limit)  System.out.println(i);
this.i = i;
}
}
```

You can fix this by synchronizing the lines of code that refer to the field:

```
public void count() {
synchronized (this) {
int i = this.i;
}
int limit = i + 100;
while (i++ != limit) System.out.println(i);
synchronized (this) {
this.i = i;
}
}
```

9.25 Synchronizing on Arbitrary Objects

In the previous example, I synchronized on the object itself, i.e. this. You can synchronize on other objects too. For example, the following static method uses a simple bubble sort to sort an array of ints. The sorting code synchronizes on the array to make sure that no other thread modifies the array while it's being sorted:

```
public static void bubbleSort(int[] n) {
boolean sorted = false;
synchronized(n) {
while (!sorted) {
sorted = true;
for (int i=0; i < n.length - 1; i++) {
if (n[i] > n[i+1]) {
int temp = n[i];
n[i] = n[i+1];
n[i+1] = temp;
sorted = false;
} // end if
} // end for
} // end while
} // end synchronized
} // end sort
```

Here you're not worried about this object being changed by a different thread. After all, the method is static. You're worried that the array may be changed by a different thread, so that's what you synchronize.

You can synchronize arrays because they are objects, albeit a funny sort of object. You cannot synchronize primitive data types like int, float, or char.

You can synchronize strings because they're objects, but you don't need to because strings are immutable.

Also note that you don't know anything about what else is going on in the program. There may only be one thread that has access to this array. Then again, there might be dozens. Whether or not you need to synchronize a method like this requires you to know lots of details about where this method is going to be used. When you're writing general utility classes and methods, that may be used by many different programs, you must assume that different threads will call the method at the same time. The Java class library makes this assumption and is thread safe.

9.26 How Many Threads are There?

As a general rule, there are at least three threads executing in any Java program. First of all there's the main thread into which your program is running. This is the thread that includes the main() method that started your application. In an applet this will be the thread into which the applet viewer or web browser was launched.

Next, there's a low priority thread that handles garbage collection and runs finalizers.

In programs that use the AWT, there's also a screen updater thread that checks to see if anything needs to be repainted about 100 times a second.

Finally there are any threads your program has explicitly spawned. However you're program is always running in one thread or another. You're never outside the thread system. You can determine the currently executing thread with the static Thread.currentThread() method:

public static native Thread currentThread()

For example, the following program prints the name of the primary thread of execution:

```
public class PrimaryThread {
public static void main(String[] args) {
System.out.println(Thread.currentThread());
}
}
```

You use the currentThread() method to get a reference to the current thread so you can manipulate it.

9.27 Thread Groups

Threads are organized into thread groups. A thread group is simply a related collection of threads. For instance, for security reasons all the threads an applet spawns are members of a particular thread group. The applet is allowed to manipulate threads in its own group but not in others. Thus an applet can't turn off the system's garbage collection thread, for example.

Thread groups are organized into a hierarchy of parents and children.

The following program prints all active threads by using the getThreadGroup() method of java.lang.Thread and getParent() method of java.lang.ThreadGroup to walk up to the top level thread group; then using enumerate to list all the threads in the main thread group and its children (which covers all thread groups).

```
public class AllThreads {
public static void main(String[] args) {
ThreadGroup top = Thread.currentThread().getThreadGroup();
while(true) {
if (top.getParent() != null) top = top.getParent();
else break;
}
Thread[] theThreads = new Thread[top.activeCount()];
top.enumerate(theThreads);
for (int i = 0; i < theThreads.length; i++) {
System.out.println(theThreads[i]);
}
}
}
```

The exact list of threads varies from system to system, but it should look something like this:

```
Thread[clock handler,11,system]
Thread[idle thread,0,system]
Thread[Async Garbage Collector,1,system]
Thread[Finalizer thread,1,system]
Thread[main,1,main]
Thread[Thread-0,5,main]
```

9.28 Daemon Threads

Threads that work in the background to support the runtime environment are called daemon threads. For example, the clock handler thread, the idle thread, the garbage collector thread, the screen updater thread, and the garbage collector thread are all daemon threads. The virtual machine exits whenever all non-daemon threads have completed.

```
public final void setDaemon(boolean isDaemon)
public final boolean isDaemon()
```

By default a thread you create is not a daemon thread. However you can use the setDaemon(true) method to turn it into one.

9.29 Cooperative vs. Preemptive Threading

In cooperative models, once a thread is given control it continues to run until it explicitly yields control or it blocks. In a preemptive model, the virtual machine is allowed to step in and hand control from one thread to another at any time. Both models have their advantages and disadvantages.

Java threads are generally preemptive between priorities. A higher priority thread takes precedence over a lower priority thread. If a higher priority thread goes to sleep or blocks, then a lower priority thread can be run (assuming one is available and ready to be run). However, as soon as the higher priority thread wakes up or unblocks, it will interrupt the lower priority thread and run until it finishes, it or blocks again, or until it is preempted by an even higher priority thread.

The Java Language Specification allows VMs to occasionally run a lower priority thread instead of a runnable higher priority thread, but in practice this is unusual.

However, nothing in the Java Language Specification specifies what is supposed to happen with equal priority threads. On some systems these threads will be time-sliced, and the runtime will allot a certain amount of time to a thread. When that time is up, the runtime preempts the running thread and switches to the next thread with the same priority. On other systems, a running thread will not be preempted in favor of a thread with the same priority. It will continue to run until it blocks, explicitly yields control, or is preempted by a higher priority thread.

9.30 Cooperating

Since you can't be sure whether you'll be working with a cooperative or preemptive model, it's important not to assume preemption is available. CPU- intensive threads should yield control at periodic intervals. There are four different ways a thread can give up control and allow other threads to run.

- It can block.
- It can call Thread.yield().
- It can go to sleep.
- It can be suspended.

Blocking occurs when a thread has to wait for an operation to complete. Most commonly this is an I/O operation, particularly one involving a network connection. It's also possible for a call to block while waiting for user input. Placing I/O and user input in separate, high priority threads is often a good idea because it allows the computer to be used more efficiently. Other CPU intensive threads can get a lot of work done while waiting for data to come in over the network or the user to type a character or two.

When a program calls Thread.yield(), it's signifying that the current thread, the one which called Thread.yield(), is willing to step aside in favor of another thread. The VM looks to see if any other threads of the same priority are ready to run. If any are, it pauses the currently executing thread and passes control to the next thread in line. If no other threads of the same or higher priority are ready to run, control returns to the thread that yielded. Thus Thread.yield() only signals a willingness to give up control. It does not guarantee that the thread will actually stop. That depends completely on what other threads exist and what their status is.

If a thread definitely wants to give up control for a period of time, whether or not there are any other threads of equal or higher priority ready to run, then it can call sleep(). The sleep() methods put a thread to sleep for a certain amount of time during which even lower priority threads may have an opportunity to run.

```
public static void sleep(long milliseconds) throws InterruptedException
```

public static void sleep(long milliseconds, int nanoseconds) throws InterruptedException

Finally, a thread can be suspended. When a thread calls suspend() (or more commonly when a different thread invokes the thread's suspend() method), it is paused indefinitely until some other thread starts it running again by invoking its resume() method.

public final void suspend()
public final void resume()

9.31 Suspend and Resume

The suspend() method temporarily halts a running thread. The resume() method picks up execution of the thread where it left off.

```
public final void suspend()
public final void resume()
The three overloaded join() methods block the calling thread until
the thread whose join() method is invoked dies.
public final void join() throws InterruptedException
public final void join(long milliseconds) throws InterruptedException
public final void join(long milliseconds, int nanoseconds)
throws InterruptedException
```

For example, t.join() waits for the Thread t to finish before continuing. t.join(1000) waits at most one second for t to finish before continuing.

You would generally use this when one thread depends on another, for example for a file to be read or an image to be loaded from the net.

9.32 The Runnable Interface

So far all the threads you've seen have been subclasses of java.lang.Thread. Sometimes, however, you want to add threading to a class that already inherits from a class other than Thread. The most common such occurrence is when you want to add threading to an applet. The easiest way to improve the perceived performance of an applet is to implement the java.lang.Runnable interface.

The Runnable interface declares just one method, run().

```
public void run()
```

Your class needs to implement this method just as it would if it were a subclass of Thread and declare that it implements the Runnable interface like this:

public class MyThreadedClass extends SomeClass implements Runnable {

```
.
.
public void run() {
.
.
.
}
}
```

To start the threaded object create a new Thread and pass the Runnable object to the Thread constructor. Then call the Thread's start() method like this:

```
MyThreadedClass mtc = new MyThreadedClass();
Thread t = new Thread(mtc);
t.start();
```

9.33 Animation

Animation is one of the primary uses of the Runnable interface. To animate objects in Java, you create a thread that calculates successive frames and then calls repaint() to paint the screen. You could just stick an infinite loop in your paint() method, but that is quite dangerous, especially on non-preemptive systems like the Mac. It also doesn't provide any support for timing.

Let's begin with a simple animation that bounces a red ball around in a box. The red ball will just be a big red circle. Its coordinates will be stored in a java.awt.Rectangle field called ball. The paint() method will do nothing but look at this field and then draw it.

The run() method of this applet is where the action will take place. Here you'll increment the coordinates of the ball, then check to see if the ball has moved to the edge of the visible area. If it has reverse the direction of the ball. The applet's really quite simple. Here it is:

```
import java.awt.*;
import java.applet.*;
public class Bounce extends Applet implements Runnable {
Rectangle r;
int x_increment = 1;
int y_increment = 1;
public void init () {
r = new Rectangle( 30, 40, 20, 20);
Thread t = new Thread(this);
t.start();
}
public void paint (Graphics g) {
g.setColor(Color.red);
g.fillOval(r.x, r.y, r.width, r.height);
}
public void run() {
while (true) {  // infinite loop
r.x += x_increment;
r.y += y_increment;
```

```
if (r.x >= size().width || r.x < 0) x_increment *= -1;
if (r.y >= size().height || r.y < 0) y_increment *= -1;
this.repaint();
}
}
}
```

9.34 Timing

True animation should provide a timing engine. This ball is rather fast on some platforms, rather slow on others. You'd like it's performance to be more uniform.

Think of a movie. It plays at 30 frames per second, and movies are shot at that frame rate. You wouldn't want the speed of a movie to be dependent on the speed of the projector, especially if different projectors had different speeds. (In fact this is exactly why old silent movies look so ridiculously speeded up. The silent movies were shot at about 15 frames per second, but modern projectors play everything at 30 frames per second.)

Although you can't speed up an animation beyond what a virtual machine is capable of playing, you can slow it down using sleep(). The following applet limits the movement of the ball to 100 pixels (both vertically and horizontally) per second.

```
import java.awt.*;
import java.applet.*;
import java.util.*;
```

public class SleepyBounce extends Applet implements Runnable {

```
Rectangle r;
int x_increment = 1;
int y_increment = 1;
int speed = 50;

public void init () {
r = new Rectangle(37, 17, 20, 20);
Thread t = new Thread(this);
t.start();
}

public void paint (Graphics g) {
g.setColor(Color.red);
g.fillOval(r.x, r.y, r.width, r.height);
}

public void run() {

while (true) {  // infinite loop
long t1 = (new Date()).getTime();
r.x += x_increment;
r.y += y_increment;
if (r.x >= size().width || r.x < 0) x_increment *= -1;
if (r.y >= size().height || r.y < 0) y_increment *= -1;
this.repaint();
```

```
long t2 = (new Date()).getTime();
long sleepTime = speed - (t2 - t1);
if (sleepTime > 0) {
try {
Thread.currentThread().sleep(sleepTime);
}
catch (InterruptedException ie) {
}
}
}
}
}
```

9.35 Flicker

You may or may not have noticed some flickering in the last applet. It's quite common for animation applets to flicker. The problem has to do with a failure to sync between when the physical display wants to redraw and when the applet wants to redraw. If they don't match up there's flicker.

There are two ways to solve this problem. The simplest solution is a clipping region. A clipping region is a rectangular area inside of which you can draw and outside of which you can't. By setting the clipping region you limit the area which is drawn into. This means first of all that nothing outside that region flickers. Secondly the smaller area can be drawn more quickly so there's less likelihood of flicker.

To set a clipping rectangle call g.clipRect(Rect r) inside your paint() method where r is the rectangle you want to clip to. The bounce applet is perfect for this since you have a convenient rectangle to which to clip. Here's a revised ClipBounce applet that clips the region to be drawn.

```
import java.awt.*;
import java.applet.*;
import java.util.*;
```

public class ClipBounce extends Applet implements Runnable {

```
Rectangle r;
int x_increment = 1;
int y_increment = 1;
int speed = 30;
public void init () {
r = new Rectangle(37, 17, 20, 20);
Thread t = new Thread(this);
t.start();
}
public void paint (Graphics g) {
g.setColor(Color.red);
g.clipRect(r.x, r.y, r.width, r.height);
g.fillOval(r.x, r.y, r.width, r.height);
}
public void run() {
while (true) {  // infinite loop
long t1 = (new Date()).getTime();
```

```
r.x += x_increment;
r.y += y_increment;
if (r.x >= size().width || r.x < 0) x_increment *= -1;
if (r.y >= size().height || r.y < 0) y_increment *= -1;
this.repaint();
long t2 = (new Date()).getTime();
try {
Thread.currentThread().sleep(speed - (t2 - t1));
}
catch (InterruptedException ie) {
}
}
}
}
```

The second and often more effective method to avoid flicker is to use offscreen images and the update() method. By overriding the update() method you can do all your painting in an offscreen Image, and then just copy the final Image onto the screen. Copying an image happens much more quickly and evenly than painting individual elements so there's no visible flicker.

The cookbook approach is simple. Add the following three private fields to your applet and the public update() method. Flicker will magically disappear.

```
private Image offScreenImage;
private Dimension offScreenSize;
private Graphics offScreenGraphics;
public final synchronized void update (Graphics g) {
Dimension d = this.getSize();
if((this.offScreenImage == null) || (d.width != 
this.offScreenSize.width)
|| (d.height != this.offScreenSize.height)) {
this.offScreenImage = this.createImage(d.width, d.height);
this.offScreenSize = d;
this.offScreenGraphics = this.offScreenImage.getGraphics();
}
this.offScreenGraphics.clearRect(0, 0, d.width, d.height);
this.paint(this.offScreenGraphics);
g.drawImage(this.offScreenImage, 0, 0, null);
}
```

9.36 Stopping Animations

It's a good idea to give the user a way to stop a thread from running. With simple animation threads like this, the custom is that a mouse click stops the animation if it's running and restarts it if it isn't.

To implement this add a boolean field bouncing that is true if and only if the thread is running. Then add a MouseListener method which stops the thread if it's started and starts it if it's stopped. Here's the revised applet.

```
import java.awt.*;
import java.awt.event.*;
import java.applet.*;
```

```
import java.util.*;
public class FlickBounce extends Applet
implements Runnable, MouseListener {
Rectangle r;
int x_increment = 1;
int y_increment = 1;
int speed = 30;
boolean bouncing = false;
Thread bounce;
public void init () {
r = new Rectangle(37, 17, 20, 20);
addMouseListener(this);
bounce = new Thread(this);
}
public void start() {
bounce.start();
bouncing = true;
}
private Image offScreenImage;
private Dimension offScreenSize;
private Graphics offScreenGraphics;
public final synchronized void update (Graphics g) {
Dimension d = this.getSize();
if((this.offScreenImage ==null)||(d.width != this.offScreenSize.width)
||  (d.height != this.offScreenSize.height)) {
this.offScreenImage = this.createImage(d.width, d.height);
this.offScreenSize = d;
this.offScreenGraphics = this.offScreenImage.getGraphics();
}
offScreenGraphics.clearRect(0, 0, d.width, d.height);
this.paint(this.offScreenGraphics);
g.drawImage(this.offScreenImage, 0, 0, null);

}

public void paint (Graphics g) {
g.setColor(Color.red);
g.fillOval(r.x, r.y, r.width, r.height);
}

public void run() {

while (true) {  // infinite loop
long t1 = (new Date()).getTime();
r.x += x_increment;
r.y += y_increment;
if (r.x >= size().width || r.x < 0) x_increment *= -1;
if (r.y >= size().height || r.y < 0) y_increment *= -1;
```

```
this.repaint();
long t2 = (new Date()).getTime();
try {
Thread.currentThread().sleep(speed - (t2 - t1));
}
catch (InterruptedException ie) {
}
}
}
public void mouseClicked(MouseEvent e) {
if (bouncing) {
bounce.suspend();
bouncing = false;
}
else {
bounce.resume();
bouncing = true;
}
}
public void mousePressed(MouseEvent e) {}
public void mouseReleased(MouseEvent e) {}
public void mouseEntered(MouseEvent e) {}
public void mouseExited(MouseEvent e) {}
}
```

9.37 Multiple Independent Animations

There are times when it makes sense to have multiple animations running at once. In this case rather than implementing Runnable, you should subclass Thread. The following program demonstrates this with an applet that bounces two balls independently of each other.

```
import java.awt.*;
import java.applet.*;
public class TwoBall extends Applet implements Runnable {
Ball b1, b2;
Thread t;

public void init () {

b1 = new Ball(10, 32, size());
b1.start();
b2 = new Ball(155, 75, size());
b2.start();
t = new Thread(this);
t.start();

}

public void paint (Graphics g) {
```

```
g.fillOval(b1.getX(), b1.getY(), b1.getWidth(), b1.getHeight());
g.fillOval(b2.getX(), b2.getY(), b2.getWidth(), b2.getHeight());
}
public void run() {
Thread.currentThread().setPriority(Thread.MIN_PRIORITY);
while (true) {  // infinite loop
this.repaint();
try {
Thread.currentThread().sleep(10);
}
catch (InterruptedException e) {
}
}

}


}

class Ball extends Thread {

private Rectangle r;
private int x_increment = 1;
private int y_increment = 1;
private Dimension bounds;

public Ball(int x, int y, Dimension d) {
r = new Rectangle(x, y, 20, 20);
bounds = d;
}
public int getX() {
return r.x;
}

public int getY() {
return r.y;
}

public int getHeight() {
return r.height;
}

public int getWidth() {
return r.width;
}
public void run() {
Thread.currentThread().setPriority(Thread.MIN_PRIORITY);
while (true) {  // infinite loop
```

```
r.x += x_increment;
r.y += y_increment;
if (r.x + r.width >= bounds.width || r.x < 0) {
x_increment *= -1;
}
if (r.y + r.height >= bounds.height || r.y < 0) {
y_increment *= -1;
}
try {
Thread.currentThread().sleep(30);
}
catch (InterruptedException e) {
}
}
}
}
```

9.38 Java Beans Revisited

Now that you understand synchronization you can take another look at Java Beans. Whenever you create a Bean, you must assume that it will run in a multithreaded environment. This means that:

Whenever possible, all the public methods of a Bean should be synchronized. Of course, this incurs the synchronized runtime overhead. If that's a problem, methods that will not cause problems in critical sections can be left un- synchronized, but keep in mind that this is not always obvious. Methods that qualify tend to be small (such as getCircleSize( ) in the following example) and/or "atomic," that is, the method call executes in such a short amount of code that the object cannot be changed during execution. Making such methods un- synchronized might not have a significant effect on the execution speed of your program. You might as well make all public methods of a Bean synchronized and remove the synchronized keyword only when you know for sure that it's necessary and that it makes a difference.

When firing a multicast event to a bunch of listeners interested in that event, you must assume that listeners might be added or removed while moving through the list.

The first point is fairly easy to deal with, but the second point requires a little more thought. Consider the BangBean.java example presented in the last chapter. That ducked out of the multithreading question by ignoring the synchronized keyword (which hadn't been introduced yet) and making the event unicast. Here's that example modified to work in a multithreaded environment and to use multicasting for events:

```
//: BangBean2.java
// You should write your Beans this way so they
// can run in a multithreaded environment.
import java.awt.*;
import java.awt.event.*;
import java.util.*;
import java.io.*;

public class BangBean2 extends Canvas
implements Serializable {
private int xm, ym;
```

```
private int cSize = 20; // Circle size
private String text = "Bang!";
private int fontSize = 48;
private Color tColor = Color.red;
private Vector actionListeners = new Vector();
public BangBean2() {
addMouseListener(new ML());
addMouseMotionListener(new MM());
}
public synchronized int getCircleSize() {
return cSize;
}
public synchronized void
setCircleSize(int newSize) {
cSize = newSize;
}
public synchronized String getBangText() {
return text;
}
public synchronized void
setBangText(String newText) {
text = newText;
}
public synchronized int getFontSize() {
return fontSize;
}
public synchronized void
setFontSize(int newSize) {
fontSize = newSize;
}
public synchronized Color getTextColor() {
return tColor;
}
public synchronized void
setTextColor(Color newColor) {
tColor = newColor;
}
public void paint(Graphics g) {
g.setColor(Color.black);
g.drawOval(xm - cSize/2, ym - cSize/2,
cSize, cSize);
}
// This is a multicast listener, which is
// more typically used than the unicast
// approach taken in BangBean.java:
public synchronized void addActionListener (
ActionListener l) {
actionListeners.addElement(l);
```

```
}
public synchronized void removeActionListener(
ActionListener l) {
actionListeners.removeElement(l);
}
// Notice this isn't synchronized:
public void notifyListeners() {
ActionEvent a =
new ActionEvent(BangBean2.this,
ActionEvent.ACTION_PERFORMED, null);
Vector lv = null;
// Make a copy of the vector in case someone
// adds a listener while we're
// calling listeners:
synchronized(this) {
lv = (Vector)actionListeners.clone();
}
// Call all the listener methods:
for(int i = 0; i < lv.size(); i++) {
ActionListener al =
(ActionListener)lv.elementAt(i);
al.actionPerformed(a);
}
}
class ML extends MouseAdapter {
public void mousePressed(MouseEvent e) {
Graphics g = getGraphics();
g.setColor(tColor);
g.setFont(
new Font(
"TimesRoman", Font.BOLD, fontSize));
int width =
g.getFontMetrics().stringWidth(text);
g.drawString(text,
(getSize().width - width) /2,
getSize().height/2);
g.dispose();
notifyListeners();
}
}
class MM extends MouseMotionAdapter {
public void mouseMoved(MouseEvent e) {
xm = e.getX();
ym = e.getY();
repaint();
}
}
// Testing the BangBean2:
```

```
public static void main(String[] args) {
BangBean2 bb = new BangBean2();
bb.addActionListener(new ActionListener() {
public void actionPerformed(ActionEvent e){
System.out.println("ActionEvent" + e);
}
});
bb.addActionListener(new ActionListener() {
public void actionPerformed(ActionEvent e){
System.out.println("BangBean2 action");
}
});
bb.addActionListener(new ActionListener() {
public void actionPerformed(ActionEvent e){
System.out.println("More action");
}
});
Frame aFrame = new Frame("BangBean2 Test");
aFrame.addWindowListener(new WindowAdapter(){
public void windowClosing(WindowEvent e) {
System.exit(0);
}
});
aFrame.add(bb, BorderLayout.CENTER);
aFrame.setSize(300,300);
aFrame.setVisible(true);
}
} ///:~
```

Adding synchronized to the methods is an easy change. However, notice in addActionListener( ) and removeActionListener( ) that the ActionListeners are now added to and removed from a Vector, so you can have as many as you want.

You can see that the method notifyListeners( ) is not synchronized. It can be called from more than one thread at a time. It's also possible for addActionListener( ) or removeActionListener( ) to be called in the middle of a call to notifyListeners( ), which is a problem since it traverses the Vector actionListeners . To alleviate the problem, the Vector is cloned inside a synchronized clause and the clone is traversed. This way the original Vector can be manipulated without impact on notifyListeners( ).

The paint( ) method is also not synchronized. Deciding whether to synchronize overridden methods is not as clear as when you're just adding your own methods. In this example it turns out that paint( ) seems to work OK whether it's synchronized or not. But the issues you must consider are:

Does the method modify the state of "critical" variables within the object? To discover whether the variables are "critical" you must determine whether they will be read or set by other threads in the program. (In this case, the reading or setting is virtually always accomplished via synchronized methods, so you can just examine those.) In the case of paint( ), no modification takes place.

Does the method depend on the state of these "critical" variables? If a synchronized method modifies a variable that your method uses, then you might very well want to make your method synchronized as well. Based on this, you might observe that cSize is changed by synchronized methods and therefore paint( ) should be synchronized. Here, however, you can ask "What's the worst thing that will happen if cSize is changed during a paint( )?" When you see that it's nothing too bad, and a transient effect at that, it's best to leave paint( ) un- synchronized to prevent the extra overhead from the synchronized method call.

A third clue is to notice whether the base-class version of paint( ) is synchronized, which it isn't. This isn't an airtight argument, just a clue. In this case, for example, a field that is changed via synchronized methods (that is cSize) has been mixed into the paint( ) formula and might have changed the situation. Notice, however, that synchronized doesn't inherit - that is, if a method is synchronized in the base class then it is not automatically synchronized in the derived class overridden version.

The test code in TestBangBean2 has been modified from that in the previous chapter to demonstrate the multicast ability of BangBean2 by adding extra listeners.

9.39 Blocking

A thread can be in any one of four states:

New: the thread object has been created but it hasn't been started yet so it cannot run.

Runnable: This means that a thread can be run when the time-slicing mechanism has CPU cycles available for the thread. Thus, the thread might or might not be running, but there's nothing to prevent it from being run if the scheduler can arrange it; it's not dead or blocked.

Dead: the normal way for a thread to die is by returning from its run( ) method. You can also call stop( ), but this throws an exception that's a subclass of Error (which means you usually don't catch it). Remember that throwing an exception should be a special event and not part of normal program execution; thus the use of stop( ) is discouraged (and it's deprecated in Java 1.2). There's also a destroy( ) method (which has never been implemented) that you should never call if you can avoid it since it's drastic and doesn't release object locks.

Blocked: the thread could be run but there's something that prevents it. While a thread is in the blocked state the scheduler will simply skip over it and not give it any CPU time. Until a thread re-enters the runnable state it won't perform any operations.

9.39.1 Becoming blocked

The blocked state is the most interesting and is worth further examination. A thread can become blocked for five reasons:

- You've put the thread to sleep by calling sleep(milliseconds), in which case it will not be run for the specified time.
- You've suspended the execution of the thread with suspend( ). It will not become runnable again until the thread gets the resume( ) message.
- You've suspended the execution of the thread with wait( ). It will not become runnable again until the thread gets the notify( ) or notifyAll( ) message. (Yes, this looks just like number 2, but there's a distinct difference that will be revealed.)
- The thread is waiting for some IO to complete.
- The thread is trying to call a synchronized method on another object and that object's lock is not available.

You can also call yield( ) (a method of the Thread class) to voluntarily give up the CPU so that other threads can run. However, the same thing happens if the scheduler decides that your thread has had enough time and jumps to another thread. That is, nothing prevents the scheduler from re-starting your thread. When a thread is blocked, there's some reason that it cannot continue running.

The following example shows all five ways of becoming blocked. It all exists in a single file called

Blocking.java, but it will be examined here in discrete pieces. (You'll notice the "Continued" and "Continuing" tags that allow the tool shown in Chapter 17 to piece everything together.) First, the basic framework:

```
//: Blocking.java
// Demonstrates the various ways a thread
// can be blocked.
import java.awt.*;
import java.awt.event.*;
import java.applet.*;
import java.io.*;
//////////// The basic framework ///////////
class Blockable extends Thread {
private Peeker peeker;
protected TextField state = new TextField(40);
protected int i;
public Blockable(Container c) {
c.add(state);
peeker = new Peeker(this, c);
}
public synchronized int read() { return i; }
protected synchronized void update() {
state.setText(getClass().getName()
+ " state: i = " + i);
}
public void stopPeeker() {
// peeker.stop(); Deprecated in Java 1.2
peeker.terminate(); // The preferred approach
}
}
class Peeker extends Thread {
private Blockable b;
private int session;
private TextField status = new TextField(40);
private boolean stop = false;
public Peeker(Blockable b, Container c) {
c.add(status);
this.b = b;
start();
}
public void terminate() { stop = true; }
public void run() {
while (!stop) {
status.setText(b.getClass().getName()
+ " Peeker " + (++session)
+ "; value = " + b.read());
try {
sleep(100);
} catch (InterruptedException e){}
```

```
}
}
} ///:Continued
```

The Blockable class is meant to be a base class for all the classes in this example that demonstrate blocking. A Blockable object contains a TextField called state that is used to display information about the object. The method that displays this information is update( ). You can see it uses getClass( ).getName( ) to produce the name of the class instead of just printing it out; this is because update( ) cannot know the exact name of the class it is called for, since it will be a class derived from Blockable.

The indicator of change in Blockable is an int i, which will be incremented by the run( ) method of the derived class.

There's a thread of class Peeker that is started for each Blockable object, and the Peeker's job is to watch its associated Blockable object to see changes in i by calling read( ) and reporting them in its status TextField . This is important: Note that read( ) and update( ) are both synchronized, which means they require that the object lock be free.

9.39.2 Sleeping

The first test in this program is with sleep( ):

```
///:Continuing
////////////// Blocking via sleep() ///////////
class Sleeper1 extends Blockable {
public Sleeper1(Container c) { super(c); }
public synchronized void run() {
while(true) {
i++;
update();
try {
sleep(1000);
} catch (InterruptedException e){}
}
}
}
class Sleeper2 extends Blockable {
public Sleeper2(Container c) { super(c); }
public void run() {
while(true) {
change();
try {
sleep(1000);
} catch (InterruptedException e){}
}
}
public synchronized void change() {
i++;
update();
}
} ///:Continued
```

In Sleeper1 the entire run( ) method is synchronized. You'll see that the Peeker associated with this object will run along merrily until you start the thread, and then the Peeker stops cold. This is one form of blocking: since Sleeper1.run( ) is synchronized, and once the thread starts it's always inside run( ), the method never gives up the object lock and the Peeker is blocked.

Sleeper2 provides a solution by making run un- synchronized. Only the change( ) method is synchronized, which means that while run( ) is in sleep( ), the Peeker can access the synchronized method it needs, namely read( ). Here you'll see that the Peeker continues running when you start the Sleeper2 thread.

9.39.3 Suspending and Resuming

The next part of the example introduces the concept of suspension. The Thread class has a method suspend( ) to temporarily halt the thread and resume( ) that re-starts it at the point it was halted. Presumably, resume( ) is called by some thread outside the suspended one, and in this case there's a separate class called Resumer that does just that. Each of the classes demonstrating suspend/ resume has an associated resumer:

```
///:Continuing
///////////// Blocking via suspend() ///////////
class SuspendResume extends Blockable {
public SuspendResume(Container c) {
super(c);
new Resumer(this);
}
}
class SuspendResume1 extends SuspendResume {
public SuspendResume1(Container c) { super(c);}
public synchronized void run() {
while(true) {
i++;
update();
suspend(); // Deprecated in Java 1.2
}
}
}
class SuspendResume2 extends SuspendResume {
public SuspendResume2(Container c) { super(c);}
public void run() {
while(true) {
change();
suspend(); // Deprecated in Java 1.2
}
}
public synchronized void change() {
i++;
update();
}
}
class Resumer extends Thread {
private SuspendResume sr;
public Resumer(SuspendResume sr) {
this.sr = sr;
```

```
start();
}
public void run() {
while(true) {
try {
sleep(1000);
} catch (InterruptedException e){}
sr.resume(); // Deprecated in Java 1.2
}
}
} ///:Continued
```

SuspendResume1 also has a synchronized run( ) method. Again, when you start this thread you'll see that its associated Peeker gets blocked waiting for the lock to become available, which never happens. This is fixed as before in SuspendResume2, which does not synchronize the entire run( ) method but instead uses a separate synchronized change( ) method.

You should be aware that Java 1.2 deprecates the use of suspend( ) and resume( ), because suspend( ) holds the object's lock and is thus deadlock-prone. That is, you can easily get a number of locked objects waiting on each other, and this will cause your program to freeze. Although you might see them used in older programs you should not use suspend( ) and resume( ). The proper solution is described later in this chapter.

9.39.4 Wait and Notify

The point with the first two examples is that both sleep( ) and suspend( ) do not release the lock as they are called. You must be aware of this when working with locks. On the other hand, the method wait( ) does release the lock when it is called, which means that other synchronized methods in the thread object could be called during a wait( ). In the following two classes, you'll see that the run( ) method is fully synchronized in both cases, however, the Peeker still has full access to the synchronized methods during a wait( ). This is because wait( ) releases the lock on the object as it suspends the method it's called within.

You'll also see that there are two forms of wait( ). The first takes an argument in milliseconds that has the same meaning as in sleep( ): pause for this period of time. The difference is that in wait( ), the object lock is released and you can come out of the wait( ) because of a notify( ) as well as having the clock run out.

The second form takes no arguments, and means that the wait( ) will continue until a notify( ) comes along and will not automatically terminate after a time.

One fairly unique aspect of wait( ) and notify( ) is that both methods are part of the base class Object and not part of Thread as are sleep( ), suspend( ), and resume( ). Although this seems a bit strange at first - to have something that's exclusively for threading as part of the universal base class - it's essential because they manipulate the lock that's also part of every object. As a result, you can put a wait( ) inside any synchronized method, regardless of whether there's any threading going on inside that particular class. In fact, the only place you can call wait( ) is within a synchronized method or block. If you call wait( ) or notify( ) within a method that's not synchronized, the program will compile, but when you run it you'll get an IllegalMonitorStateException with the somewhat non-intuitive message "current thread not owner." Note that sleep( ), suspend( ), and resume( ) can all be called within non- synchronized methods since they don't manipulate the lock.

You can call wait( ) or notify( ) only for your own lock. Again, you can compile code that tries to use the wrong lock, but it will produce the same IllegalMonitorStateException message as before. You can't fool with someone else's lock, but you can ask another object to perform an operation that manipulates its own lock. So one approach is to create a synchronized method that calls notify( ) for its own object. However, in Notifier you'll see the notify( ) call inside a synchronized block:

```
synchronized(wn2) {
wn2.notify();
}
```

where wn2 is the object of type WaitNotify2. This method, which is not part of WaitNotify2, acquires the lock on the wn2 object, at which point it's legal for it to call notify( ) for wn2 and you won't get the IllegalMonitorStateException.

```
///:Continuing
/////////// Blocking via wait() ///////////
class WaitNotify1 extends Blockable {
public WaitNotify1(Container c) { super(c); }
public synchronized void run() {
while(true) {
i++;
update();
try {
wait(1000);
} catch (InterruptedException e){}
}
}
}
class WaitNotify2 extends Blockable {
public WaitNotify2(Container c) {
super(c);
new Notifier(this);
}
public synchronized void run() {
while(true) {
i++;
update();
try {
wait();
} catch (InterruptedException e){}
}
}
}
class Notifier extends Thread {
private WaitNotify2 wn2;
public Notifier(WaitNotify2 wn2) {
this.wn2 = wn2;
start();
}
public void run() {
while(true) {
try {
```

```
sleep(2000);
} catch (InterruptedException e){}
synchronized(wn2) {
wn2.notify();
}
}
}
} ///:Continued
```

wait( ) is typically used when you've gotten to the point where you're waiting for some other condition, under the control of forces outside your thread, to change and you don't want to idly wait by inside the thread. So wait( ) allows you to put the thread to sleep while waiting for the world to change, and only when a notify( ) or notifyAll( ) occurs does the thread wake up and check for changes. Thus, it provides a way to synchronize between threads.

9.39.5 Blocking on IO

If a stream is waiting for some IO activity, it will automatically block. In the following portion of the example, the two classes work with generic Reader and Writer objects (using the Java 1.1 Streams), but in the test framework a piped stream will be set up to allow the two threads to safely pass data to each other (which is the purpose of piped streams).

The Sender puts data into the Writer and sleeps for a random amount of time. However, Receiver has no sleep( ), suspend( ), or wait( ). But when it does a read( ) it automatically blocks when there is no more data.

```
///:Continuing
class Sender extends Blockable { // send
private Writer out;
public Sender(Container c, Writer out) {
super(c);
this.out = out;
}
public void run() {
while(true) {
for(char c = 'A'; c <= 'z'; c++) {
try {
i++;
out.write(c);
state.setText("Sender sent: "
+ (char)c);
sleep((int)(3000 * Math.random()));
} catch (InterruptedException e){}
catch (IOException e) {}
}
}
}
}
class Receiver extends Blockable {
private Reader in;
public Receiver(Container c, Reader in) {
```

```
super(c);
this.in = in;
}
public void run() {
try {
while(true) {
i++; // Show peeker it's alive
// Blocks until characters are there:
state.setText("Receiver read: "
+ (char)in.read());
}
} catch(IOException e) { e.printStackTrace();}
}
} ///:Continued
```

Both classes also put information into their state fields and change i so the Peeker can see that the thread is running.

9.39.6 Testing

The main applet class is surprisingly simple because most of the work has been put into the Blockable framework. Basically, an array of Blockable objects is created, and since each one is a thread, they perform their own activities when you press the "start" button. There's also a button and actionPerformed( ) clause to stop all of the Peeker objects, which provides a demonstration of the alternative to the deprecated (in Java 1.2) stop( ) method of Thread.

To set up a connection between the Sender and Receiver objects, a PipedWriter and PipedReader are created. Note that the PipedReader in must be connected to the PipedWriter out via a constructor argument. After that, anything that's placed in out can later be extracted from in, as if it passed through a pipe (hence the name). The in and out objects are then passed to the Receiver and Sender constructors, respectively, which treat them as Reader and Writer objects of any type (that is, they are upcast).

The array of Blockable handles b is not initialized at its point of definition because the piped streams cannot be set up before that definition takes place (the need for the try block prevents this).

```
///:Continuing
/////////// Testing Everything ///////////
public class Blocking extends Applet {
private Button
start = new Button("Start"),
stopPeekers = new Button("Stop Peekers");
private boolean started = false;
private Blockable[] b;
private PipedWriter out;
private PipedReader in;
public void init() {
out = new PipedWriter();
try {
in = new PipedReader(out);
} catch(IOException e) {}
```

```
b = new Blockable[] {
new Sleeper1(this),
new Sleeper2(this),
new SuspendResume1(this),
new SuspendResume2(this),
new WaitNotify1(this),
new WaitNotify2(this),
new Sender(this, out),
new Receiver(this, in)
};
start.addActionListener(new StartL());
add(start);
stopPeekers.addActionListener(
new StopPeekersL());
add(stopPeekers);
}
class StartL implements ActionListener {
public void actionPerformed(ActionEvent e) {
if(!started) {
started = true;
for(int i = 0; i < b.length; i++)
b[i].start();
}
}
}
class StopPeekersL implements ActionListener {
public void actionPerformed(ActionEvent e) {
// Demonstration of the preferred
// alternative to Thread.stop():
for(int i = 0; i < b.length; i++)
b[i].stopPeeker();
}
}
public static void main(String[] args) {
Blocking applet = new Blocking();
Frame aFrame = new Frame("Blocking");
aFrame.addWindowListener(
new WindowAdapter() {
public void windowClosing(WindowEvent e) {
System.exit(0);
}
});
aFrame.add(applet, BorderLayout.CENTER);
aFrame.setSize(350,550);
applet.init();
applet.start();
aFrame.setVisible(true);
}
```

```
} ///:~
```

In init( ), notice the loop that moves through the entire array and adds the state and peeker.status text fields to the page.

When the Blockable threads are initially created, each one automatically creates and starts its own Peeker. So you'll see the Peekers running before the Blockable threads are started. This is essential, as some of the Peekers will get blocked and stop when the Blockable threads start, and it's essential to see this to understand that particular aspect of blocking.

9.39.7 Deadlock

Because threads can become blocked and because objects can have synchronized methods that prevent threads from accessing that object until the synchronization lock is released, it's possible for one thread to get stuck waiting for another thread, which in turn waits for another thread, etc., until the chain leads back to a thread waiting on the first one. Thus, there's a continuous loop of threads waiting on each other and no one can move. This is called deadlock. The claim is that it doesn't happen that often, but when it happens to you it's frustrating to debug.

There is no language support to help prevent deadlock; it's up to you to avoid it by careful design. These are not comforting words to the person who's trying to debug a deadlocking program.

The deprecation of stop( ), suspend( ), resume( ), and destroy( ) in Java 1.2

One change that has been made in Java 1.2 to reduce the possibility of deadlock is the deprecation of Thread's stop( ), suspend( ), resume( ), and destroy( ) methods.

The reason that the stop( ) method is deprecated is because it is unsafe. It releases all the locks that the thread had acquired, and if the objects are in an inconsistent state ("damaged") other threads can view and modify them in that state. The resulting problems can be subtle and difficult to detect. Instead of using stop( ), you should follow the example in Blocking.java and use a flag to tell the thread when to terminate itself by exiting its run( ) method.

There are times when a thread blocks, such as when it is waiting for input, and it cannot poll a flag as it does in Blocking.java. In these cases, you still shouldn't use stop( ), but instead you can use the interrupt( ) method in Thread to break out of the blocked code:

```
//: Interrupt.java
// The alternative approach to using stop()
// when a thread is blocked
import java.awt.*;
import java.awt.event.*;
import java.applet.*;

class Blocked extends Thread {
public synchronized void run() {
try {
wait(); // Blocks
} catch(InterruptedException e) {
System.out.println("InterruptedException");
}
System.out.println("Exiting run()");
}
```

```
}
public class Interrupt extends Applet {
private Button
interrupt = new Button("Interrupt");
private Blocked blocked = new Blocked();
public void init() {
add(interrupt);
interrupt.addActionListener(
new ActionListener() {
public
void actionPerformed(ActionEvent e) {
System.out.println("Button pressed");
if(blocked == null) return;
Thread remove = blocked;
blocked = null; // to release it
remove.interrupt();
}
});
blocked.start();
}
public static void main(String[] args) {
Interrupt applet = new Interrupt();
Frame aFrame = new Frame("Interrupt");
aFrame.addWindowListener(
new WindowAdapter() {
public void windowClosing(WindowEvent e) {
System.exit(0);
}
});
aFrame.add(applet, BorderLayout.CENTER);
aFrame.setSize(200,100);
applet.init();
applet.start();
aFrame.setVisible(true);
}
} ///:~
```

The wait( ) inside Blocked.run( ) produces the blocked thread. When you press the button, the blocked handle is set to null so the garbage collector will clean it up, and then the object's interrupt( ) method is called. The first time you press the button you'll see that the thread quits, but after that there's no thread to kill so you just see that the button has been pressed.

The suspend( ) and resume( ) methods turn out to be inherently deadlock-prone. When you call suspend( ), the target thread stops but it still holds any locks that it has acquired up to that point. So no other thread can access the locked resources until the thread is resumed. Any thread that wants to resume the target thread and also tries to use any of the locked resources produces deadlock. You should not use suspend( ) and resume( ), but instead put a flag in your Thread class to indicate whether the thread should be active or suspended. If the flag indicates that the thread is suspended, the thread goes into a wait using wait( ). When the flag indicates that the thread should be resumed the thread is restarted with notify( ). An example can be produced by modifying Counter2.java. Although the effect is similar, you'll notice that the code organization is quite different - anonymous inner classes are used for all of the listeners and the Thread is an inner class, which makes programming slightly more convenient since it eliminates some of the extra bookkeeping necessary in Counter2.java:

```
//: Suspend.java
// The alternative approach to using suspend()
// and resume(), which have been deprecated
// in Java 1.2.
import java.awt.*;
import java.awt.event.*;
import java.applet.*;

public class Suspend extends Applet {
private TextField t = new TextField(10);
private Button
suspend = new Button("Suspend"),
resume = new Button("Resume");
class Suspendable extends Thread {
private int count = 0;
private boolean suspended = false;
public Suspendable() { start(); }
public void fauxSuspend() {
suspended = true;
}
public synchronized void fauxResume() {
suspended = false;
notify();
}
public void run() {
while (true) {
try {
sleep(100);
synchronized(this) {
while(suspended)
wait();
}
} catch (InterruptedException e){}
t.setText(Integer.toString(count++));
}
}
}
private Suspendable ss = new Suspendable();
public void init() {
add(t);
suspend.addActionListener(
new ActionListener() {
```

```
public
void actionPerformed(ActionEvent e) {
ss.fauxSuspend();
}
});
add(suspend);
resume.addActionListener(
new ActionListener() {
public
void actionPerformed(ActionEvent e) {
ss.fauxResume();
}
});
add(resume);
}
public static void main(String[] args) {
Suspend applet = new Suspend();
Frame aFrame = new Frame("Suspend");
aFrame.addWindowListener(
new WindowAdapter() {
public void windowClosing(WindowEvent e){
System.exit(0);
}
});
aFrame.add(applet, BorderLayout.CENTER);
aFrame.setSize(300,100);
applet.init();
applet.start();
aFrame.setVisible(true);
}
} ///:~
```

The flag suspended inside Suspendable is used to turn suspension on and off. To suspend, the flag is set to true by calling fauxSuspend( ) and this is detected inside run( ). The wait( ), as described earlier in this chapter, must be synchronized so that it has the object lock. In fauxResume( ), the suspended flag is set to false and notify( ) is called - since this wakes up wait( ) inside a synchronized clause the fauxResume( ) method must also be synchronized so that it acquires the lock before calling notify( ) (thus the lock is available for the wait( ) to wake up with). If you follow the style shown in this program you can avoid using wait( ) and notify( ).

The destroy( ) method of Thread has never been implemented; it's like a suspend( ) that cannot resume, so it has the same deadlock issues as suspend( ). However, this is not a deprecated method and it might be implemented in a future version of Java (after 1.2) for special situations in which the risk of a deadlock is acceptable.

You might wonder why these methods, now deprecated, were included in Java in the first place. It seems a clear admission of a rather significant mistake to simply remove them outright (and pokes yet another hole in the arguments for Java's exceptional design and infallibility touted by Sun marketing people). The heartening part about the change is that it clearly indicates that the technical people and not the marketing people are running the show - they discovered a problem and they are fixing it.

I find this much more promising and hopeful than leaving the problem in because fixing it would admit an error. It means that Java will continue to improve, even if it means a little discomfort on the part of Java programmers. I'd rather deal with the discomfort than watch the language stagnate.

9.40 Priorities

The priority of a thread tells the scheduler how important this thread is. If there are a number of threads blocked and waiting to be run, the scheduler will run the one with the highest priority first. However, this doesn't mean that threads with lower priority don't get run (that is, you can't get deadlocked because of priorities). Lower priority threads just tend to run less often.

You can read the priority of a thread with getPriority( ) and change it with setPriority( ). The form of the prior "counter" examples can be used to show the effect of changing the priorities. In this applet you'll see that the counters slow down as the associated threads have their priorities lowered:

```
//: Counter5.java
// Adjusting the priorities of threads
import java.awt.*;
import java.awt.event.*;
import java.applet.*;

class Ticker2 extends Thread {
private Button
b = new Button("Toggle"),
incPriority = new Button("up"),
decPriority = new Button("down");
private TextField
t = new TextField(10),
pr = new TextField(3); // Display priority
private int count = 0;
private boolean runFlag = true;
public Ticker2(Container c) {
b.addActionListener(new ToggleL());
incPriority.addActionListener(new UpL());
decPriority.addActionListener(new DownL());
Panel p = new Panel();
p.add(t);
p.add(pr);
p.add(b);
p.add(incPriority);
p.add(decPriority);
c.add(p);
}
class ToggleL implements ActionListener {
public void actionPerformed(ActionEvent e) {
runFlag = !runFlag;
}
}
class UpL implements ActionListener {
public void actionPerformed(ActionEvent e) {
```

```
int newPriority = getPriority() + 1;
if(newPriority > Thread.MAX_PRIORITY)
newPriority = Thread.MAX_PRIORITY;
setPriority(newPriority);
}
}
class DownL implements ActionListener {
public void actionPerformed(ActionEvent e) {
int newPriority = getPriority() - 1;
if(newPriority < Thread.MIN_PRIORITY)
newPriority = Thread.MIN_PRIORITY;
setPriority(newPriority);
}
}
public void run() {
while (true) {
if(runFlag) {
t.setText(Integer.toString(count++));
pr.setText(
Integer.toString(getPriority()));
}
yield();
}
}
}
public class Counter5 extends Applet
{
private Button
start = new Button("Start"),
upMax = new Button("Inc Max Priority"),
downMax = new Button("Dec Max Priority");
private boolean started = false;
private static final int SIZE = 10;
private Ticker2[] s = new Ticker2[SIZE];
private TextField mp = new TextField(3);
public void init() {
for(int i = 0; i < s.length; i++)
s[i] = new Ticker2(this);
add(new Label("MAX_PRIORITY = "
+ Thread.MAX_PRIORITY));
add(new Label("MIN_PRIORITY = "
+ Thread.MIN_PRIORITY));
add(new Label("Group Max Priority = "));
add(mp);
add(start);
add(upMax); add(downMax);
start.addActionListener(new StartL());
upMax.addActionListener(new UpMaxL());
```

```
downMax.addActionListener(new DownMaxL());
showMaxPriority();
// Recursively display parent thread groups:
ThreadGroup parent =
s[0].getThreadGroup().getParent();
while(parent != null) {
add(new Label(
"Parent threadgroup max priority = "
+ parent.getMaxPriority()));
parent = parent.getParent();
}
}
public void showMaxPriority() {
mp.setText(Integer.toString(
s[0].getThreadGroup().getMaxPriority()));
}
class StartL implements ActionListener {
public void actionPerformed(ActionEvent e) {
if(!started) {
started = true;
for(int i = 0; i < s.length; i++)
s[i].start();
}
}
}
class UpMaxL implements ActionListener {
public void actionPerformed(ActionEvent e) {
int maxp =
s[0].getThreadGroup().getMaxPriority();
if(++maxp > Thread.MAX_PRIORITY)
maxp = Thread.MAX_PRIORITY;
s[0].getThreadGroup().setMaxPriority(maxp);
showMaxPriority();
}
}
class DownMaxL implements ActionListener {
public void actionPerformed(ActionEvent e) {
int maxp =
s[0].getThreadGroup().getMaxPriority();
if(—maxp < Thread.MIN_PRIORITY)
maxp = Thread.MIN_PRIORITY;
s[0].getThreadGroup().setMaxPriority(maxp);
showMaxPriority();
}
}
public static void main(String[] args) {
Counter5 applet = new Counter5();
Frame aFrame = new Frame("Counter5");
```

```
aFrame.addWindowListener(
new WindowAdapter() {
public void windowClosing(WindowEvent e) {
System.exit(0);
}
});
aFrame.add(applet, BorderLayout.CENTER);
aFrame.setSize(300, 600);
applet.init();
applet.start();
aFrame.setVisible(true);
}
} ///:~
```

Ticker2 follows the form established earlier in this chapter, but there's an extra TextField for displaying the priority of the thread and two more buttons for incrementing and decrementing the priority.

Also notice the use of yield( ), which voluntarily hands control back to the scheduler. Without this the multithreading mechanism still works, but you'll notice it runs slowly (try removing the call to yield( )!). You could also call sleep( ), but then the rate of counting would be controlled by the sleep( ) duration instead of the priority.

The init( ) in Counter5 creates an array of 10 Ticker2s; their buttons and fields are placed on the form by the Ticker2 constructor. Counter5 adds buttons to start everything up as well as increment and decrement the maximum priority of the threadgroup. In addition, there are labels that display the maximum and minimum priorities possible for a thread and a TextField to show the thread group's maximum priority. (The next section will fully describe thread groups.) Finally, the priorities of the parent thread groups are also displayed as labels.

When you press an "up" or "down" button, that Ticker2's priority is fetched and incremented or decremented accordingly.

When you run this program, you'll notice several things. First of all, the thread group's default priority is 5. Even if you decrement the maximum priority below 5 before starting the threads (or before creating the threads, which requires a code change), each thread will have a default priority of 5.

The simple test is to take one counter and decrement its priority to one, and observe that it counts much slower. But now try to increment it again. You can get it back up to the thread group's priority, but no higher. Now decrement the thread group's priority a couple of times. The thread priorities are unchanged, but if you try to modify them either up or down you'll see that they'll automatically pop to the priority of the thread group. Also, new threads will still be given a default priority, even if that's higher than the group priority. (Thus the group priority is not a way to prevent new threads from having higher priorities than existing ones.)

Finally, try to increment the group maximum priority. It can't be done. You can only reduce thread group maximum priorities, not increase them.

9.41 Thread Groups

All threads belong to a thread group. This can be either the default thread group or a group you explicitly specify when you create the thread. At creation, the thread is bound to a group and cannot change to a different group. Each application has at least one thread that belongs to the system thread group. If you create more threads without specifying a group, they will also belong to the system thread group.

Thread groups must also belong to other thread groups. The thread group that a new one belongs to must be specified in the constructor. If you create a thread group without specifying a thread group for it to belong to, it will be placed under the system thread group. Thus, all thread groups in your application will ultimately have the system thread group as the parent.

The reason for the existence of thread groups is hard to determine from the literature, which tends to be confusing on this subject. It's often cited as "security reasons." According to Arnold & Gosling, [62] "Threads within a thread group can modify the other threads in the group, including any farther down the hierarchy. A thread cannot modify threads outside of its own group or contained groups." It's hard to know what "modify" is supposed to mean here. The following example shows a thread in a "leaf" subgroup modifying the priorities of all the threads in its tree of thread groups as well as calling a method for all the threads in its tree.

```
//: TestAccess.java
// How threads can access other threads
// in a parent thread group
public class TestAccess {
public static void main(String[] args) {
ThreadGroup
x = new ThreadGroup("x"),
y = new ThreadGroup(x, "y"),
z = new ThreadGroup(y, "z");
Thread
one = new TestThread1(x, "one"),
two = new TestThread2(z, "two");
}
}
class TestThread1 extends Thread {
private int i;
TestThread1(ThreadGroup g, String name) {
super(g, name);
}
void f() {
i++; // modify this thread
System.out.println(getName() + " f()");
}
}

class TestThread2 extends TestThread1 {
TestThread2(ThreadGroup g, String name) {
super(g, name);
start();
}
public void run() {
ThreadGroup g =
getThreadGroup().getParent().getParent();
g.list();
Thread[] gAll = new Thread[g.activeCount()];
g.enumerate(gAll);
```

```
for(int i = 0; i < gAll.length; i++) {
gAll[i].setPriority(Thread.MIN_PRIORITY);
((TestThread1)gAll[i]).f();
}
g.list();
}
} ///:~
```

In main( ), several ThreadGroups are created, leafing off from each other: x has no argument but its name (a String), so it is automatically placed in the "system" thread group, while y is under x and z is under y. Note that initialization happens in textual order so this code is legal.

Two threads are created and placed in different thread groups. TestThread1 doesn't have a run( ) method but it does have an f( ) that modifies the thread and prints something so you can see it was called. TestThread2 is a subclass of TestThread1 and its run( ) is fairly elaborate. It first gets the thread group of the current thread, then moves up the heritage tree by two levels using getParent( ). (This is contrived since I purposely place the TestThread2 object two levels down in the hierarchy.) At this point, an array of handles to Threads is created using the method activeCount( ) to ask how many threads are in this thread group and all the child thread groups. The enumerate( ) method places handles to all of these threads in the array gAll, then I simply move through the entire array calling the f( ) method for each thread, as well as modifying the priority. Thus, a thread in a "leaf" thread group modifies threads in parent thread groups.

The debugging method list( ) prints all the information about a thread group to standard output and is helpful when investigating thread group behavior. Here's the output of the program:

```
java.lang.ThreadGroup[name=x,maxpri=10]
Thread[one,5,x]
java.lang.ThreadGroup[name=y,maxpri=10]
java.lang.ThreadGroup[name=z,maxpri=10]
Thread[two,5,z]
one f()
two f()
java.lang.ThreadGroup[name=x,maxpri=10]
Thread[one,1,x]
java.lang.ThreadGroup[name=y,maxpri=10]
java.lang.ThreadGroup[name=z,maxpri=10]
Thread[two,1,z]
```

Not only does list( ) print the class name of ThreadGroup or Thread, but it also prints the thread group name and its maximum priority. For threads, the thread name is printed, followed by the thread priority and the group that it belongs to. Note that list( ) indents the threads and thread groups to indicate that they are children of the un-indented thread group.

You can see that f( ) is called by the TestThread2 run( ) method, so it's obvious that all threads in a group are vulnerable. However, you can access only the threads that branch off from your own system thread group tree, and perhaps this is what is meant by "safety." You cannot access anyone else's system thread group tree.

9.41.1 Controlling Thread Groups

Putting aside the safety issue, one thing thread groups do seem to be useful for is control: you can perform certain operations on an entire thread group with a single command. The following example demonstrates this and the restrictions on priorities within thread groups. The commented numbers in parentheses provide a reference to compare to the output.

```
//: ThreadGroup1.java
// How thread groups control priorities
// of the threads inside them.
public class ThreadGroup1 {
public static void main(String[] args) {
// Get the system thread & print its Info:
ThreadGroup sys =
Thread.currentThread().getThreadGroup();
sys.list(); // (1)
// Reduce the system thread group priority:
sys.setMaxPriority(Thread.MAX_PRIORITY - 1);
// Increase the main thread priority:
Thread curr = Thread.currentThread();
curr.setPriority(curr.getPriority() + 1);
sys.list(); // (2)
// Attempt to set a new group to the max:
ThreadGroup g1 = new ThreadGroup("g1");
g1.setMaxPriority(Thread.MAX_PRIORITY);
// Attempt to set a new thread to the max:
Thread t = new Thread(g1, "A");
t.setPriority(Thread.MAX_PRIORITY);
g1.list(); // (3)
// Reduce g1's max priority, then attempt
// to increase it:
g1.setMaxPriority(Thread.MAX_PRIORITY - 2);
g1.setMaxPriority(Thread.MAX_PRIORITY);
g1.list(); // (4)
// Attempt to set a new thread to the max:
t = new Thread(g1, "B");
t.setPriority(Thread.MAX_PRIORITY);
g1.list(); // (5)
// Lower the max priority below the default
// thread priority:
g1.setMaxPriority(Thread.MIN_PRIORITY + 2);
// Look at a new thread's priority before
// and after changing it:
t = new Thread(g1, "C");
g1.list(); // (6)
t.setPriority(t.getPriority() -1);
g1.list(); // (7)
// Make g2 a child Threadgroup of g1 and
// try to increase its priority:
ThreadGroup g2 = new ThreadGroup(g1, "g2");
g2.list(); // (8)
g2.setMaxPriority(Thread.MAX_PRIORITY);
g2.list(); // (9)
```

```
// Add a bunch of new threads to g2:
for (int i = 0; i < 5; i++)
new Thread(g2, Integer.toString(i));
// Show information about all threadgroups
// and threads:
sys.list(); // (10)
System.out.println("Starting all threads:");
Thread[] all = new Thread[sys.activeCount()];
sys.enumerate(all);
for(int i = 0; i < all.length; i++)
if(!all[i].isAlive())
all[i].start();
// Suspends & Stops all threads in
// this group and its subgroups:
System.out.println("All threads started");
sys.suspend(); // Deprecated in Java 1.2
// Never gets here...
System.out.println("All threads suspended");
sys.stop(); // Deprecated in Java 1.2
System.out.println("All threads stopped");
}
} ///:~
```

The output that follows has been edited to allow it to fit on the page (the java.lang. has been removed) and to add numbers to correspond to the commented numbers in the listing above.

```
(1) ThreadGroup[name=system,maxpri=10]
Thread[main,5,system]
(2) ThreadGroup[name=system,maxpri=9]
Thread[main,6,system]
(3) ThreadGroup[name=g1,maxpri=9]
Thread[A,9,g1]
(4) ThreadGroup[name=g1,maxpri=8]
Thread[A,9,g1]
(5) ThreadGroup[name=g1,maxpri=8]
Thread[A,9,g1]
Thread[B,8,g1]
(6) ThreadGroup[name=g1,maxpri=3]
Thread[A,9,g1]
Thread[B,8,g1]
Thread[C,6,g1]
(7) ThreadGroup[name=g1,maxpri=3]
Thread[A,9,g1]
Thread[B,8,g1]
Thread[C,3,g1]
(8) ThreadGroup[name=g2,maxpri=3]
(9) ThreadGroup[name=g2,maxpri=3]
(10)ThreadGroup[name=system,maxpri=9]
Thread[main,6,system]
ThreadGroup[name=g1,maxpri=3]
```

```
Thread[A,9,g1]
Thread[B,8,g1]
Thread[C,3,g1]
ThreadGroup[name=g2,maxpri=3]
Thread[0,6,g2]
Thread[1,6,g2]
Thread[2,6,g2]
Thread[3,6,g2]
Thread[4,6,g2]
Starting all threads:
All threads started
```

All programs have at least one thread running, and the first action in main( ) is to call the static method of Thread called currentThread( ). From this thread, the thread group is produced and list( ) is called for the result. The output is:

(1) ThreadGroup[name=system,maxpri=10]

Thread[main,5,system]

You can see that the name of the main thread group is system, and the name of the main thread is main, and it belongs to the system thread group.

The second exercise shows that the system group's maximum priority can be reduced and the main thread can have its priority increased:

(2) ThreadGroup[name=system,maxpri=9]

Thread[main,6,system]

The third exercise creates a new thread group, g1, which automatically belongs to the system thread group since it isn't otherwise specified. A new thread A is placed in g1. After attempting to set this group's maximum priority to the highest level and A's priority to the highest level, the result is:

(3) ThreadGroup[name=g1,maxpri=9]

Thread[A,9,g1]

Thus, it's not possible to change the thread group's maximum priority to be higher than its parent thread group.

The fourth exercise reduces g1's maximum priority by two and then tries to increase it up to Thread.MAX_PRIORITY. The result is:

(4) ThreadGroup[name=g1,maxpri=8]

Thread[A,9,g1]

You can see that the increase in maximum priority didn't work. You can only decrease a thread group's maximum priority, not increase it. Also, notice that thread A's priority didn't change, and now it is higher than the thread group's maximum priority. Changing a thread group's maximum priority doesn't affect existing threads.

The fifth exercise attempts to set a new thread to maximum priority:

(5) ThreadGroup[name=g1,maxpri=8]

Thread[A,9,g1]

Thread[B,8,g1]

The new thread cannot be changed to anything higher than the maximum thread group priority.

The default thread priority for this program is 6; that's the priority a new thread will be created at and where it will stay if you don't manipulate the priority. Exercise six lowers the maximum thread group priority below the default thread priority to see what happens when you create a new thread under this condition:

(6) ThreadGroup[name=g1,maxpri=3]

Thread[A,9,g1]

Thread[B,8,g1]

Thread[C,6,g1]

Even though the maximum priority of the thread group is 3, the new thread is still created using the default priority of 6. Thus, maximum thread group priority does not affect default priority. (In fact, there appears to be no way to set the default priority for new threads.)

After changing the priority, attempting to decrement it by one, the result is:

(7) ThreadGroup[name=g1,maxpri=3]

Thread[A,9,g1]

Thread[B,8,g1]

Thread[C,3,g1]

Only when you attempt to change the priority is the thread group's maximum priority enforced.

A similar experiment is performed in (8) and (9), in which a new thread group g2 is created as a child of g1 and its maximum priority is changed. You can see that it's impossible for g2's maximum to go higher than g1's:

(8) ThreadGroup[name=g2,maxpri=3]

(9) ThreadGroup[name=g2,maxpri=3]

Also notice that g2 is automatically set to the thread group maximum priority of g1 as g2 is created.

After all of these experiments, the entire system of thread groups and threads is printed out:

(10)ThreadGroup[name=system,maxpri=9]

Thread[main,6,system]

ThreadGroup[name=g1,maxpri=3]

Thread[A,9,g1]

Thread[B,8,g1]

Thread[C,3,g1]

ThreadGroup[name=g2,maxpri=3]

Thread[0,6,g2]

Thread[1,6,g2]

Thread[2,6,g2]

Thread[3,6,g2]

Thread[4,6,g2]

So because of the rules of thread groups, a child group must always have a maximum priority that's less than or equal to its parent's maximum priority.

The last part of this program demonstrates methods for an entire group of threads. First the program moves through the entire tree of threads and starts each one that hasn't been started. For drama, the system group is then suspended and finally stopped. (Although it's interesting to see that suspend( ) and stop( ) work on entire thread groups, you should keep in mind that these methods are deprecated in Java 1.2.) But when you suspend the system group you also suspend the main thread and the whole program shuts down, so it never gets to the point where the threads are stopped. Actually, if you do stop the main thread it throws a ThreadDeath exception, so this is not a typical thing to do. Since ThreadGroup is inherited from Object, which contains the wait( ) method, you can also choose to suspend the program for any number of seconds by calling wait(seconds * 1000) . This must acquire the lock inside a synchronized block, of course.

The ThreadGroup class also has suspend( ) and resume( ) methods so you can stop and start an entire thread group and all of its threads and subgroups with a single command. (Again, suspend( ) and resume( ) are deprecated in Java 1.2.)

Thread groups can seem a bit mysterious at first, but keep in mind that you probably won't be using them directly very often.

9.42 Runnable Revisited

Earlier in this chapter, I suggested that you think carefully before making an applet or main Frame as an implementation of Runnable. If you take that approach, you can make only one of those threads in your program. This limits your flexibility if you decide that you want to have more than one thread of that type.

Of course, if you must inherit from a class and you want to add threading behavior to the class, Runnable is the correct solution. The final example in this chapter exploits this by making a Runnable Canvas class that paints different colors on itself. This application is set up to take values from the command line to determine how big the grid of colors is and how long to sleep( ) between color changes. By playing with these values you'll discover some interesting and possibly inexplicable features of threads:

```
//: ColorBoxes.java
// Using the Runnable interface
import java.awt.*;
import java.awt.event.*;
class CBox extends Canvas implements Runnable {
private Thread t;
private int pause;
private static final Color[] colors = {
Color.black, Color.blue, Color.cyan,
Color.darkGray, Color.gray, Color.green,
Color.lightGray, Color.magenta,
Color.orange, Color.pink, Color.red,
Color.white, Color.yellow
};
private Color cColor = newColor();
private static final Color newColor() {
return colors[
(int)(Math.random() * colors.length)
];
}
public void paint(Graphics  g) {
```

```
g.setColor(cColor);
Dimension s = getSize();
g.fillRect(0, 0, s.width, s.height);
}
public CBox(int pause) {
this.pause = pause;
t = new Thread(this);
t.start();
}
public void run() {
while(true) {
cColor = newColor();
repaint();
try {
t.sleep(pause);
} catch(InterruptedException e) {}
}
}
}
public class ColorBoxes extends Frame {
public ColorBoxes(int pause, int grid) {
setTitle("ColorBoxes");
setLayout(new GridLayout(grid, grid));
for (int i = 0; i < grid * grid; i++)
add(new CBox(pause));
addWindowListener(new WindowAdapter() {
public void windowClosing(WindowEvent e) {
System.exit(0);
}
});
}
public static void main(String[] args) {
int pause = 50;
int grid = 8;
if(args.length > 0)
pause = Integer.parseInt(args[0]);
if(args.length > 1)
grid = Integer.parseInt(args[1]);
Frame f = new ColorBoxes(pause, grid);
f.setSize(500, 400);
f.setVisible(true);
}
} ///:~
```

ColorBoxes is a typical application with a constructor that sets up the GUI. This constructor takes an argument of int grid to set up the GridLayout so that it has grid cells in each dimension. Then it adds the appropriate number of CBox objects to fill the grid, passing the pause value to each one. In main( ) you can see how pause and grid have default values that can be changed if you pass in command-line arguments.

CBox is where all the work takes place. This is inherited from Canvas and it implements the Runnable interface so each Canvas can also be a Thread. Remember that when you implement Runnable, you don't make a Thread object, just a class that has a run( ) method. Thus, you must explicitly create a Thread object and hand the Runnable object to the constructor, then call start( ) (this happens in the constructor). In CBox this thread is called t.

Notice the array colors, which is an enumeration of all the colors in class Color. This is used in newColor( ) to produce a randomly-selected color. The current cell color is cColor.

paint( ) is quite simple - it just sets the color to cColor and fills the entire canvas with that color.

In run( ), you see the infinite loop that sets the cColor to a new random color and then calls repaint( ) to show it. Then the thread goes to sleep( ) for the amount of time specified on the command line.

Precisely because this design is flexible and threading is tied to each Canvas element, you can experiment by making as many threads as you want. (In reality, there is a restriction imposed by the number of threads your JVM can comfortably handle.)

This program also makes an interesting benchmark, since it can show dramatic speed differences between one JVM implementation and another.

9.43 Too Many Threads

At some point, you'll find that ColorBoxes bogs down. On my machine, this occurred somewhere after a 10 x 10 grid. Why does this happen? You're naturally suspicious that the AWT might have something to do with it, so here's an example that tests that premise by making fewer threads. The code is reorganized so that a Vector implements Runnable and that Vector holds a number of color blocks and randomly chooses ones to update. Then a number of these Vector objects are created, depending roughly on the grid dimension you choose. As a result, you have far fewer threads than color blocks, so if there's a speedup we'll know it was because there were too many threads in the previous example:

```
//: ColorBoxes2.java
// Balancing thread use
import java.awt.*;
import java.awt.event.*;
import java.util.*;

class CBox2 extends Canvas {
private static final Color[] colors = {
Color.black, Color.blue, Color.cyan,
Color.darkGray, Color.gray, Color.green,
Color.lightGray, Color.magenta,
Color.orange, Color.pink, Color.red,
Color.white, Color.yellow
};
private Color cColor = newColor();
private static final Color newColor() {
return colors[
(int)(Math.random() * colors.length)
];
}
void nextColor() {
```

```
cColor = newColor();
repaint();
}
public void paint(Graphics g) {
g.setColor(cColor);
Dimension s = getSize();
g.fillRect(0, 0, s.width, s.height);
}
}

class CBoxVector
extends Vector implements Runnable {
private Thread t;
private int pause;
public CBoxVector(int pause) {
this.pause = pause;
t = new Thread(this);
}
public void go() { t.start(); }
public void run() {
while(true) {
int i = (int)(Math.random() * size());
((CBox2)elementAt(i)).nextColor();
try {
t.sleep(pause);
} catch(InterruptedException e) {}
}
}
}

public class ColorBoxes2 extends Frame {
private CBoxVector[] v;
public ColorBoxes2(int pause, int grid) {
setTitle("ColorBoxes2");
setLayout(new GridLayout(grid, grid));
v = new CBoxVector[grid];
for(int i = 0; i < grid; i++)
v[i] = new CBoxVector(pause);
for (int i = 0; i < grid * grid; i++) {
v[i % grid].addElement(new CBox2());
add((CBox2)v[i % grid].lastElement());
}
for(int i = 0; i < grid; i++)
v[i].go();
addWindowListener(new WindowAdapter() {
public void windowClosing(WindowEvent e) {
System.exit(0);
}
```

```
});
}
public static void main(String[] args) {
// Shorter default pause than ColorBoxes:
int pause = 5;
int grid = 8;
if(args.length > 0)
pause = Integer.parseInt(args[0]);
if(args.length > 1)
grid = Integer.parseInt(args[1]);
Frame f = new ColorBoxes2(pause, grid);
f.setSize(500, 400);
f.setVisible(true);
}
} ///:~
```

In ColorBoxes2 an array of CBoxVector is created and initialized to hold grid CBoxVectors, each of which knows how long to sleep. An equal number of Cbox2 objects is then added to each CBoxVector, and each vector is told to go( ), which starts its thread.

CBox2 is similar to CBox: it paints itself with a randomly-chosen color. But that's all a CBox2 does. All of the threading has been moved into CBoxVector.

The CBoxVector could also have inherited Thread and had a member object of type Vector. That design has the advantage that the addElement( ) and elementAt( ) methods could then be given specific argument and return value types instead of generic Objects. (Their names could also be changed to something shorter.) However, the design used here seemed at first glance to require less code. In addition, it automatically retains all the other behaviors of a Vector. With all the casting and parentheses necessary for elementAt( ), this might not be the case as your body of code grows.

As before, when you implement Runnable you don't get all of the equipment that comes with Thread, so you have to create a new Thread and hand yourself to its constructor in order to have something to start( ), as you can see in the CBoxVector constructor and in go( ). The run( ) method simply chooses a random element number within the vector and calls nextColor( ) for that element to cause it to choose a new randomly-selected color.

Upon running this program, you see that it does indeed run faster and respond more quickly (for instance, when you interrupt it, it stops more quickly), and it doesn't seem to bog down as much at higher grid sizes. Thus, a new factor is added into the threading equation: you must watch to see that you don't have "too many threads" (whatever that turns out to mean for your particular program and platform). If you do, you must try to use techniques like the one above to "balance" the number of threads in your program. If you see performance problems in a multithreaded program you now have a number of issues to examine:

- Do you have enough calls to sleep( ), yield( ), and/or wait( )?
- Are calls to sleep( ) long enough?
- Are you running too many threads?
- Have you tried different platforms and JVMs?

Issues like this are one reason that multithreaded programming is often considered an art.

9.44 Implementing the Runnable Interface

The Clock applet shown below displays the current time and updates its display every second. You can scroll this page and perform other tasks while the clock continues to update because the code that updates the clock's display runs within its own thread.

Note: Because some old browsers don't support 1.1, the above applet is a 1.0 version (here is the 1.0 code; here's the 1.1 code). To run the 1.1 version of the applet, go to example-1dot1/Clock.html.

The Clock applet uses a different technique than SimpleThread for providing the run method for its thread. Instead of subclassing Thread, Clock implements the Runnable interface (and therefore implements the run method defined in it). Clock then creates a thread with itself as the Thread's target. When created in this way, the Thread gets its run method from its target. The code that accomplishes this is shown in bold here:

```
import java.awt.Graphics;
import java.util.*;
import java.text.DateFormat;
import java.applet.Applet;
public class Clock extends Applet implements Runnable {
private Thread clockThread = null;
public void start() {
if (clockThread == null) {
clockThread = new Thread(this, "Clock");
clockThread.start();
}
}
public void run() {
Thread myThread = Thread.currentThread()
while (clockThread == myThread) {
repaint();
try {
Thread.sleep(1000);
} catch (InterruptedException e){
// the VM doesn't want us to sleep anymore,
// so get back to work
}
}
}
public void paint(Graphics g) {
// get the time and convert it to a date
Calendar cal = Calendar.getInstance();
Date date = cal.getTime();
// format it and display it
DateFormat dateFormatter = DateFormat.getTimeInstance();
g.drawString(dateFormatter.format(date), 5, 10);
}
// overrides Applet's stop method, not Thread's
public void stop() {
clockThread = null;
}
}
```

The Clock applet's run method loops until the browser asks it to stop. During each iteration of the loop, the clock repaints its display. The paint method figures out what time it is, formats it in a localized way, and displays it. You'll see more of the Clock applet in The Life Cycle of a Thread which uses it to teach you about the life of a thread.

9.44.1 Deciding to Use the Runnable Interface

You have now seen two ways to provide the run method for a Java thread:

- Subclass the Thread class defined in the java.lang package and override the run method.

Example: See the SimpleThread class described in Subclassing Thread and Overriding run.

Provide a class that implements the Runnable interface (also defined in the java.lang package) and therefore implements the run method. In this case, a Runnable object provides the run method to the thread.

Example: See the Clock applet just shown.

There are good reasons for choosing either of these options over the other However, for most cases, including that of the Clock applet, the following rule of thumb will guide you to the best option.

Rule of Thumb: If your class must subclass some other class (the most common example being Applet), you should use Runnable as described in option #2.

To run in a Java-enabled browser, the Clock class has to be a subclass of the Applet class. Also, the Clock applet needs a thread so that it can continuously update its display without taking over the process in which it is running. (Some browsers might create a new thread for each applet so as to prevent a misbehaved applet from taking over the main browser thread. However, you should not count on this when writing your applets; your applets should create their own threads when doing computer-intensive work.) But since the Java language does not support multiple class inheritance, the Clock class cannot be a subclass of both Thread and Applet. Thus the Clock class must use the Runnable interface to provide its threaded behavior.

9.45 The Life Cycle of a Thread

Now that you've seen how to give a thread something to do, we'll review some details that were glossed over in the previous section. In particular, we look at the life cycle of a thread: how to create and start a thread, some of the special things it can do while it's running, and how to stop it.

The following diagram shows the states that a Java thread can be in during its life. It also illustrates which method calls cause a transition to another state. This figure is not a complete finite state diagram, but rather an overview of the more interesting and common facets of a thread's life. The remainder of this section uses the Clock applet previously introduced to discuss a thread's life cycle in terms of its state.

9.45.1 Creating a Thread

The application in which an applet is running calls the applet's start method when the user visits the applet's page. The Clock applet creates a Thread, clockThread, in its start with the bold code shown here:

```
public void start() {
if (clockThread == null) {
clockThread = new Thread(this, "Clock");
clockThread.start();
}
```

```
}
```

After the bold statement has been executed, clockThread is in the New Thread state. When a thread is a New Thread, it is merely an empty Thread object; no system resources have been allocated for it yet. When a thread is in this state, you can only start the thread. Calling any method besides start when a thread is in this state makes no sense and causes an IllegalThreadStateException. (In fact, the runtime system throws an IllegalThreadStateException any time a method is called on a thread and that thread's state does not allow for that method call.)

Notice that this—the Clock instance— is the first argument to the thread constructor. The first argument to this thread constructor must implement the Runnable interface and becomes the thread's target. The clock thread gets its run method from its target Runnable object—in this case, the Clock instance. The second argument is just a name for the thread.

9.45.2 Starting a Thread

Now consider the next line of code in Clock's start method shown here in bold:

```
public void start() {
if (clockThread == null) {
clockThread = new Thread(this, "Clock");
clockThread.start();
}
}
```

The start method creates the system resources necessary to run the thread, schedules the thread to run, and calls the thread's run method. ClockThread's run method is the one defined in the Clock class.

After the start method has returned, the thread is "running". Yet, it's somewhat more complex than that. As the previous figure shows, a thread that has been started is actually in the Runnable state. Many computers have a single processor, thus making it impossible to run all "running" threads at the same time. The Java runtime system must implement a scheduling scheme that shares the processor between all "running" threads. (See Understanding Thread Priority for more information about scheduling.) So at any given time, a "running" thread actually may be waiting for its turn in the CPU.

Here's another look at Clock's run method:

```
public void run() {
Thread myThread = Thread.currentThread();
while (clockThread == myThread) {
repaint();
try {
Thread.sleep(1000);
} catch (InterruptedException e){
// the VM doesn't want us to sleep anymore,
// so get back to work
}
}
}
```

Clock's run method loops while the condition clockThread == myThread is true. This exit condition is explained in more detail in Stopping a Thread. However, for now, know that it allows the thread, and thus the applet, to exit gracefully.

Within the loop, the applet repaints itself and then tells the thread to sleep for one second (1000 milliseconds). An applet's repaint method ultimately calls the applet's paint method, which does the actual update of the applet's display area. The Clock paint method gets the current time, formats, and displays it:

```
public void paint(Graphics g) {
// get the time and convert it to a date
Calendar cal = Calendar.getInstance();
Date date = cal.getTime();
// format it and display it
DateFormat dateFormatter = DateFormat.getTimeInstance();
g.drawString(dateFormatter.format(date), 5, 10);
}
```

9.45.3 Making a Thread Not Runnable

A thread becomes Not Runnable when one of these events occurs:

Its sleep method is invoked.

The thread calls the wait method to wait for a specific condition to be satisifed.

The thread is blocking on I/O.

The clockThread in the Clock applet becomes Not Runnable when the run method calls sleep on the current thread:

```
public void run() {
Thead myThread = Thead.currentThread();
while (clockThread == myThread) {
repaint();
try {
Thread.sleep(1000);
} catch (InterruptedException e){
// the VM doesn't want us to sleep anymore,
// so get back to work
}
}
}
```

During the second that the clockThread is asleep, the thread does not run, even if the processor becomes available. After the second has elapsed, the thread becomes Runnable again and, if the processor becomes available, the thread begins running again.

For each entrance into the Not Runnable state, there is a specific and distinct escape route that returns the thread to the Runnable state. An escape route works only for its corresponding entrance. For example, if a thread has been put to sleep, then the specified number of milliseconds must elapse before the thread becomes Runnable again. The following list describes the escape route for every entrance into the Not Runnable state:

If a thread has been put to sleep, then the specified number of milliseconds must elapse.

If a thread is waiting for a condition, then another object must notify the waiting thread of a change in condition by calling notify or notifyAll. More information is available in Synchronizing Threads.

If a thread is blocked on I/O, then the I/O must complete.

9.45.4 Stopping a Thread

A program doesn't stop a thread like it stops an applet (by calling a method). Rather, a thread arranges for its own death by having a run method that terminates naturally. For example, the while loop in this run method is a finite loop— it will iterate 100 times and then exit:

```
public void run() {
int i = 0;
while (i < 100) {
i++;
System.out.println("i = " + i);
}
}
```

A thread with this run method dies naturally when the loop completes and the run method exits.

Let's look at how the Clock applet thread arranges for its own death. You might want to use this technique with your applets. Recall Clock's run method:

```
public void run() {
Thead myThread = Thread.currentThread();
while (clockThread == myThread) {
repaint();
try {
Thread.sleep(1000);
} catch (InterruptedException e){
// the VM doesn't want us to sleep anymore,
// so get back to work
}
}
}
```

The exit condition for this run method is the exit condition for the while loop because there is no code after the while loop:

while (clockThread == myThread) {

This condition indicates that the loop will exit when the currently exiting thread is not equal to clockThread. When would this ever be the case?

When you leave the page, the application in which the applet is running calls the applet's stop method. This method then sets the clockThread to null, thereby telling the main loop in the run method to terminate:

```
public void stop() {     // applets' stop method
clockThread = null;
}
```

If you revisit the page, the start method is called again and the clock starts up again with a new thread. Even if you stop and start the applet faster than one iteration of the loop, clockThread will be a different thread than myThread and the loop will still terminate.

The isAlive Method

A final word about thread state: The API for the Thread class includes a method called isAlive. The isAlive method returns true if the thread has been started and not stopped. If the isAlive method returns false, you know that the thread either is a New Thread or is Dead. If the isAlive method returns true, you know that the thread is either Runnable or Not Runnable. You cannot differentiate between a New Thread or a Dead thread. Nor can you differentiate between a Runnable thread and a Not Runnable thread.

9.46 Understanding Thread Priority

Previously, this lesson claimed that threads run concurrently. While conceptually this is true, in practice it usually isn't. Most computer configurations have a single CPU, so threads actually run one at a time in such a way as to provide an illusion of concurrency. Execution of multiple threads on a single CPU, in some order, is called scheduling. The Java runtime supports a very simple, deterministic scheduling algorithm known as fixed priority scheduling. This algorithm schedules threads based on their priority relative to other runnable threads.

When a Java thread is created, it inherits its priority from the thread that created it. You can also modify a thread's priority at any time after its creation using the setPriority method. Thread priorities are integers ranging between MIN_PRIORITY and MAX_PRIORITY (constants defined in the Thread class). The higher the integer, the higher the priority. At any given time, when multiple threads are ready to be executed, the runtime system chooses the runnable thread with the highest priority for execution. Only when that thread stops, yields, or becomes not runnable for some reason will a lower priority thread start executing. If two threads of the same priority are waiting for the CPU, the scheduler chooses one of them to run in a round-robin fashion. The chosen thread will run until one of the following conditions is true:

- A higher priority thread becomes runnable.
- It yields, or its run method exits.
- On systems that support time-slicing, its time allotment has expired.
- Then the second thread is given a chance to run, and so on, until the interpreter exits.

The Java runtime system's thread scheduling algorithm is also preemptive. If at any time a thread with a higher priority than all other runnable threads becomes runnable, the runtime system chooses the new higher priority thread for execution. The new higher priority thread is said to preempt the other threads.

Rule of thumb: At any given time, the highest priority thread is running. However, this is not guaranteed. The thread scheduler may choose to run a lower priority thread to avoid starvation. For this reason, use priority only to affect scheduling policy for efficiency purposes. Do not rely on thread priority for algorithm correctness.

9.47 The 400,000 Micron Thread Race

This Java source code implements an applet that animates a race between two "runner" threads with different priorities. When you click the mouse down over the applet, it starts the two runners. The top runner, labelled "2", has a priority of 2. The second runner, labelled "3", has a priority of 3.

Try this: Click the applet below to start the race.

Note: Because some old browsers don't support 1.1, the above applet is a 1.0 version (here is the 1.0 code; here's the 1.1 code). To run the 1.1 version of the applet, go to example-1dot1/RaceApplet.html.

This is the run method for both runners.

```
public int tick = 1;
public void run() {
while (tick < 400000)
tick++;
}
```

This run method simply counts from 1 to 400,000. The instance variable tick is public because the applet uses this value to determine how far the runner has progressed (how long its line is).

In addition to the two runner threads, this applet also has a third thread that handles the drawing. The drawing thread's run method contains an infinite loop; during each iteration of the loop it draws a line for each runner (whose length is computed from the runner's tick variable), and then sleeps for 10 milliseconds. The drawing thread has a thread priority of 4—higher than either runner. So, whenever the drawing thread wakes up after 10 milliseconds, it becomes the highest priority thread, preempting whichever runner is currently running, and draws the lines. You can see the lines inch their way across the page

This is not a fair race because one runner has a higher priority than the other. Each time the drawing thread yields the CPU by going to sleep for 10 milliseconds, the scheduler chooses the highest priority runnable thread to run; in this case, it's always runner 3. Here is another version of the applet that implements a fair race, that is, both of the runners have the same priority and they have an equal chance of being chosen to run.

Note: Because some old browsers don't support 1.1, the above applet is a 1.0 version (here is the 1.0 code; here's the 1.1 code). To run the 1.1 version of the applet, go to example-1dot1/ RaceApplet.html.

In this race, each time the drawing thread yields the CPU by going to sleep, there are two runnable threads of equal priority—the runners—waiting for the CPU; the scheduler must choose one of the threads to run. In this situation, the scheduler chooses the next thread to run in a round-robin fashion.

9.47.1 Selfish Threads

The Runner class used in the races above actually implements "socially-impaired" thread behavior. Recall the run method from the Runner class used in the races above:

```
public int tick = 1;
public void run() {
while (tick < 400000)
tick++;
}
```

The while loop in the run method is in a tight loop. Once the scheduler chooses a thread with this thread body for execution, the thread never voluntarily relinquishes control of the CPU—the thread continues to run until the while loop terminates naturally or until the thread is preempted by a higher priority thread. This thread is called a selfish thread.

In some situations, having selfish threads doesn't cause any problems because a higher priority thread preempts the selfish one (just as the drawing thread in the RaceApplet preempts the selfish runners). However, in other situations, threads with CPU-greedy run methods, such as the Runner class, can take over the CPU and cause other threads to wait for a long time before getting a chance to run.

9.47.2 Time-Slicing

Some systems, such as Windows 95/NT, fight selfish thread behavior with a strategy known as time-slicing. Time-slicing comes into play when there are multiple "Runnable" threads of equal priority and those threads are the highest priority threads competing for the CPU. For example, this stand-alone Java program (which is based on the RaceApplet above) creates two equal priority selfish threads that have the following run method.

```
public void run() {
while (tick < 400000) {
tick++;
if ((tick % 50000) == 0)
System.out.println("Thread #" + num + ", tick = "+ tick);
}
}
```

This run contains a tight loop that increments the integer tick and every 50,000 ticks prints out the thread's identifier and its tick count.

When running this program on a time-sliced system, you will see messages from both threads intermingled with one another. Like this:

```
Thread #1, tick = 50000
Thread #0, tick = 50000
Thread #0, tick = 100000
Thread #1, tick = 100000
Thread #1, tick = 150000
Thread #1, tick = 200000
Thread #0, tick = 150000
Thread #0, tick = 200000
Thread #1, tick = 250000
Thread #0, tick = 250000
Thread #0, tick = 300000
Thread #1, tick = 300000
Thread #1, tick = 350000
Thread #0, tick = 350000
Thread #0, tick = 400000
Thread #1, tick = 400000
```

This output is produced because a time-sliced system divides the CPU into time slots and iteratively gives each of the equal-and-highest priority threads a time slot in which to run. The time-sliced system iterates through the equal-and-highest priority threads, allowing each one a bit of time to run, until one or more of them finishes or until a higher priority thread preempts them. Notice that time-slicing makes no guarantees as to how often or in what order threads are scheduled to run.

When running this program on a non-time-sliced system, however, you will see messages from one thread finish printing before the other thread ever gets a chance to print one message. Like this:

```
Thread #0, tick = 50000
Thread #0, tick = 100000
Thread #0, tick = 150000
Thread #0, tick = 200000
Thread #0, tick = 250000
Thread #0, tick = 300000
Thread #0, tick = 350000
Thread #0, tick = 400000
Thread #1, tick = 50000
Thread #1, tick = 100000
Thread #1, tick = 150000
```

```
Thread #1, tick = 200000
Thread #1, tick = 250000
Thread #1, tick = 300000
Thread #1, tick = 350000
Thread #1, tick = 400000
```

This is because a non-time-sliced system chooses one of the equal-and-highest priority threads to run and allows that thread to run until it relinquishes the CPU (by sleeping, yielding, finishing its job) or until a higher priority preempts it.

Note: The Java runtime does not implement (and therefore does not guarantee) time-slicing. However, some systems on which you can run Java do support time-slicing. Your Java programs should not rely on time-slicing as it may produce different results on different systems.

Try this: Compile and run the RaceTest and SelfishRunner classes on your computer. Can you tell if you have a time-sliced system?

As you can imagine, writing CPU-intensive code can have negative repercussions on other threads running in the same process. In general, you should try to write "well-behaved" threads that voluntarily relinquish the CPU periodically and give other threads an opportunity to run. In particular, you should never write Java code that relies on time-sharing—this will practically guarantee that your program will give different results on different computer systems.

A thread can voluntarily yield the CPU without going to sleep or some other drastic means by calling the yield method. The yield method gives other threads of the same priority a chance to run. If there are no equal priority threads that are runnable, then the yield is ignored.

Try this: Rewrite the SelfishRunner class to be a PoliteRunner by calling the yield method from the run method. Be sure to modify the main program to create PoliteRunners instead of SelfishRunners. Compile and run the new classes on your computer. Now isn't that better?

9.48 Synchronizing Threads

So far, this lesson has contained examples with independent, asynchronous threads. That is, each thread contained all of the data and methods required for its execution and didn't require any outside resources or methods. In addition, the threads in those examples ran at their own pace without concern over the state or activities of any other concurrently running threads.

However, there are many interesting situations where separate, concurrently running threads do share data and must consider the state and activities of other threads. One such set of programming situations are known as producer/consumer scenarios where the producer generates a stream of data which then is consumed by a consumer.

For example, imagine a Java application where one thread (the producer) writes data to a file while a second thread (the consumer) reads data from the same file. Or, as you type characters on the keyboard, the producer thread places key events in an event queue and the consumer thread reads the events from the same queue. Both of these examples use concurrent threads that share a common resource: the first shares a file, the second shares an event queue. Because the threads share a common resource, they must be synchronized in some way.

The Producer generates an integer between 0 and 9 (inclusive), stores it in a CubbyHole object, and prints the generated number. To make the synchronization problem more interesting, the Producer sleeps for a random amount of time between 0 and 100 milliseconds before repeating the number generating cycle:

```
public class Producer extends Thread {
private CubbyHole cubbyhole;
private int number;
public Producer(CubbyHole c, int number) {
cubbyhole = c;
this.number = number;
}
public void run() {
for (int i = 0; i < 10; i++) {
cubbyhole.put(i);
System.out.println("Producer #" + this.number + "put: "+ i);
try {
sleep((int)(Math.random() * 100));
} catch (InterruptedException e) { }
}
}
}
```

The Consumer, being ravenous, consumes all integers from the CubbyHole (the exact same object into which the Producer put the integers in the first place) as quickly as they become available.

```
public class Consumer extends Thread {
private CubbyHole cubbyhole;
private int number;

public Consumer(CubbyHole c, int number) {
cubbyhole = c;
this.number = number;
}

public void run() {
int value = 0;
for (int i = 0; i < 10; i++) {
value = cubbyhole.get();
System.out.println("Consumer #" + this.number + "got: "+ value);
}
}
}
```

The Producer and Consumer in this example share data through a common CubbyHole object. And you will note that neither the Producer nor the Consumer makes any effort whatsoever to ensure that the Consumer is getting each value produced once and only once. The synchronization between these two threads actually occurs at a lower level, within the get and put methods of the CubbyHole object. However, let's assume for a moment that these two threads make no arrangements for synchronization and talk about the potential problems that might arise in that situation.

One problem arises when the Producer is quicker than the Consumer and generates two numbers before the Consumer has a chance to consume the first one. Thus the Consumer would skip a number. Part of the output might look like this:

```
Consumer #1 got: 3
Producer #1 put: 4
Producer #1 put: 5
Consumer #1 got: 5
. . .
```

Another problem that might arise is when the Consumer is quicker than the Producer and consumes the same value twice. In this situation, the Consumer would print the same value twice and might produce output that looked like this:

```
. . .
Producer #1 put: 4
Consumer #1 got: 4
Consumer #1 got: 4
Producer #1 put: 5
. . .
```

Either way, the result is wrong. You want the Consumer to get each integer produced by the Producer exactly once. Problems such as those just described are called race conditions. They arise from multiple, asynchronously executing threads trying to access a single object at the same time and getting the wrong result.

Race conditions in the producer/consumer example are prevented by having the storage of a new integer into the CubbyHole by the Producer be synchronized with the retrieval of an integer from the CubbyHole by the Consumer. The Consumer must consume each integer exactly once.

The activities of the Producer and Consumer must be synchronized in two ways. First, the two threads must not simultaneously access the CubbyHole. A Java thread can prevent this from happening by locking an object. When an object is locked by one thread and another thread tries to call a synchronized method on the same object, the second thread will block until the object is unlocked. Locking an Object discusses this.

And second, the two threads must do some simple coordination. That is, the Producer must have some way to indicate to the Consumer that the value is ready and the Consumer must have some way to indicate that the value has been retrieved. The Thread class provides a collection of methods—wait, notify, and notifyAll—to help threads wait for a condition and notify other threads of when that condition changes. Using the notifyAll and wait Methods has more information.

The Main Program

Here's a small stand-alone Java application that creates a CubbyHole object, a Producer, a Consumer, and then starts both the Producer and the Consumer.

```
public class ProducerConsumerTest {
public static void main(String[] args) {
CubbyHole c = new CubbyHole();
Producer p1 = new Producer(c, 1);
Consumer c1 = new Consumer(c, 1);

p1.start();
c1.start();
}
}
```

The Output

Here's the output of ProducerConsumerTest.

```
Producer #1 put: 0
Consumer #1 got: 0
Producer #1 put: 1
Consumer #1 got: 1
Producer #1 put: 2
Consumer #1 got: 2
Producer #1 put: 3
Consumer #1 got: 3
Producer #1 put: 4
Consumer #1 got: 4
Producer #1 put: 5
Consumer #1 got: 5
Producer #1 put: 6
Consumer #1 got: 6
Producer #1 put: 7
Consumer #1 got: 7
Producer #1 put: 8
Consumer #1 got: 8
Producer #1 put: 9
Consumer #1 got: 9
```

9.49 Locking an Object

The code segments within a program that access the same object from separate, concurrent threads are called critical sections. In the Java language, a critical section can be a block or a method and are identified with the synchronized keyword. The Java platform then associates a lock with every object that has synchronized code.

In the producer/consumer example, the put and get methods of the CubbyHole (page 645) are the critical sections. The Consumer should not access the CubbyHole when the Producer is changing it, and the Producer should not modify it when the Consumer is getting the value. So put and get in the CubbyHole class should be marked with the synchronized keyword.

Here's a code skeleton for the CubbyHole class:

```
public class CubbyHole {
private int contents;
private boolean available = false;
public synchronized int get() {
...
}
public synchronized void put(int value) {
...
}
}
```

Note that the method declarations for both put and get contain the synchronized keyword. Hence, the system associates a unique lock with every instance of CubbyHole (including the one shared by the Producer and the Consumer). Whenever control enters a synchronized method, the thread that called the method locks the object whose method has been called. Other threads cannot call a synchronized method on the same object until the object is unlocked.

So, when the Producer calls CubbyHole's put method, it locks the CubbyHole, thereby preventing the Consumer from calling the CubbyHole's get method:

```
public synchronized void put(int value) {
// CubbyHole locked by the Producer
..
// CubbyHole unlocked by the Producer
}
```

When the put method returns, the Producer unlocks the CubbyHole.

Similarly, when the Consumer calls CubbyHole's get method, it locks the CubbyHole, thereby preventing the Producer from calling put:

```
public synchronized int get() {
// CubbyHole locked by the Consumer
...
// CubbyHole unlocked by the Consumer
}
```

The acquisition and release of a lock is done automatically and atomically by the Java runtime system. This ensures that race conditions cannot occur in the underlying implementation of the threads, thus ensuring data integrity. Synchronization isn't the whole story. The two threads must also be able to notify one another when they've done their job. Learn more about that after a brief foray into reentrant locks.

9.49.1 Reaquiring a Lock

The Java runtime system allows a thread to re-acquire a monitor that it already holds because Java monitors are reentrant. Reentrant monitors are important because they eliminate the possibility of a single thread deadlocking itself on a monitor that it already holds.

Consider this class:

```
public class Reentrant {
public synchronized void a() {
b();
System.out.println("here I am, in a()");
}
public synchronized void b() {
System.out.println("here I am, in b()");
}
}
```

Reentrant contains two synchronized methods: a and b. The first synchronized method, a, calls the other synchronized method, b.

When control enters method a, the current thread acquires the monitor for the Reentrant object. Now, a calls b and because b is also synchronized the thread attempts to acquire the same monitor again. Because Java supports reentrant monitors, this works. The current thread can acquire the Reentrant object's monitor again and both a and b execute to conclusion as is evidenced by the output:

```
here I am, in b()
here I am, in a()
```

In systems that don't support reentrant monitors, this sequence of method calls would cause deadlock.

9.49.2 Using the Notify All and Wait Methods

The CubbyHole stores its value in a private member variable called contents. CubbyHole has another private member variable, available, that is a boolean. available is true when the value has just been put but not yet gotten and is false when the value has been gotten but not yet put. So, here's one possible implementation for the put and get methods:

```
public synchronized int get() {     // won't work!
if (available == true) {
available = false;
return contents;
}
}
public synchronized int put(int value) {     // won't work!
if (available == false) {
available = true;
value = ;
}
}
```

As implemented, these two methods won't work. Look at the get method. What happens if the Producer hasn't put anything in the CubbyHole and available isn't true? get does nothing. Similarly, if the Producer calls put before the Consumer got the value, put doesn't do anything.

You really want the Consumer to wait until the Producer puts something in the CubbyHole and the Producer must notify the Consumer when it's done so. Similarly, the Producer must wait until the Consumer takes a value (and notifies the Producer of its activities) before replacing it with a new value. The two threads must coordinate more fully and can use Object's wait and notifyAll methods to do so.

Here are the new implementations of get and put that wait on and notify each other of their activities:

```
public synchronized int get() {
while (available == false) {
try {
// wait for Producer to put value
wait();
} catch (InterruptedException e) {
}
}
available = false;
// notify Producer that value has been retrieved
notifyAll();
return contents;
}
public synchronized void put(int value) {
while (available == true) {
try {
// wait for Consumer to get value
wait();
```

```
        } catch (InterruptedException e) {
        }
        }
        contents = value;
        available = true;
        // notify Consumer that value has been set
        notifyAll();
        }
```

The code in the get method loops until the Producer has produced a new value. Each time through the loop, get calls the wait method. The wait method relinquishes the lock held by the Consumer on the CubbyHole (thereby allowing the Producer to get the lock and update the CubbyHole) and then waits for notification from the Producer. When the Producer puts something in the CubbyHole, it notifies the Consumer by calling notifyAll. The Consumer then comes out of the wait state, available is now true, the loop exits, and the get method returns the value in the CubbyHole.

The put method works in a similar fashion, waiting for the Consumer thread to consume the current value before allowing the Producer to produce a new one.

The notifyAll method wakes up all threads waiting on the object in question (in this case, the CubbyHole). The awakened threads compete for the lock. One thread gets it, and the others go back to waiting. The Object class also defines the notify method, which arbitrarily wakes up one of the threads waiting on this object.

The Object class contains not only the version of wait that is used in the producer/consumer example and which waits indefinitely for notification, but also two other versions of the wait method:

wait(long timeout)

Waits for notification or until the timeout period has elapsed. timeout is measured in milliseconds.

wait(long timeout, int nanos)

Waits for notification or until timeout milliseconds plus nanos nanoseconds have elapsed.

Note: Besides using these timed wait methods to synchronize threads, you also can use them in place of sleep. Both wait and sleep delay for the requested amount of time, but you can easily wake up wait with a notify but a sleeping thread cannot be awoken prematurely. This doesn't matter too much for threads that don't sleep for long, but it could be important for threads that sleep for minutes at a time.

9.49.3 Avoiding Starvation and Deadlock

The dining philosophers are often used to illustrate various problems that can occur when many synchronized threads are competing for limited resources.

The story goes like this: Five philosophers are sitting at a round table. In front of each philosopher is a bowl of rice. Between each pair of philosophers is one chopstick. Before an individual philosopher can take a bite of rice he must have two chopsticks—one taken from the left, and one taken from the right. The philosophers must find some way to share chopsticks such that they all get to eat.

The following applet does a rough animation using an image of Duke for the dining philosophers. This particular algorithm works as follows: Duke always reaches for the chopstick on his right first. If the chopstick is there, Duke takes it and raises his right hand. Next, Duke tries for the left chopstick. If the chopstick is available, Duke picks it up and raises his other hand. Now that Duke has both chopsticks, he takes a bite of rice and says "Mmm!" He then puts both chopsticks down, allowing either of his two neighbors to get the chopsticks. Duke then starts all over again by trying for the right chopstick. Between each attempt to grab a chopstick, each Duke pauses for a random period of time.

The slider controls the amount of time that each philosopher will wait before attempting to pick up a chopstick. When the slider is set to 0, the philosophers don't wait—they just grab—and the applet ends up in deadlock: all the philosophers are frozen with their right hand in the air. Why? Because each philosopher immediately has one chopstick and is waiting on a condition that cannot be satisfied—they are all waiting for the left chopstick, which is held by the philosopher to their left.

When you move the slider so that the waiting period is longer, the applet may proceed for a while without deadlocking. However, deadlock is always possible with this particular implementation of the dining philosophers problem because it is possible for all five philosophers to be holding their right chopsticks. Rather than rely on luck to prevent deadlock, you must either prevent it or detect it.

For most Java programmers, the best choice is to prevent deadlock rather than to try and detect it. Deadlock detection is complicated and beyond the scope of this tutorial. The simplest approach to to preventing deadlock is to impose ordering on the condition variables. In the dining philosopher applet, there is no ordering imposed on the condition variables because the philosophers and the chopsticks are arranged in a circle. All chopsticks are equal.

However, we can change the rules in the applet by numbering the chopsticks 1 through 5 and insisting that the philosophers pick up the chopstick with the lower number first. The philosopher who is sitting between chopsticks 1 and 2 and the philosopher who is sitting between chopsticks 1 and 5 must now reach for the same chopstick first (chopstick 1) rather than picking up the one on the right. Whoever gets chopstick 1 first is now free to take another one. Whoever doesn't get chopstick 1 must now wait for the first philosopher to release it. Deadlock is not possible.

9.49.4 The ThreadGroup Class

The ThreadGroup class manages groups of threads for Java applications. A ThreadGroup can contain any number of threads. The threads in a group are generally related in some way, such as who created them, what function they perform, or when they should be started and stopped.

ThreadGroups can contain not only threads but also other ThreadGroups. The top-most thread group in a Java application is the thread group named main. You can create threads and thread groups in the main group. You can also create threads and thread groups in subgroups of main. The result is a root-like hierarchy of threads and thread groups:

The ThreadGroup class has methods that can be categorized as follows:

Collection Management Methods—Methods that manage the collection of threads and subgroups contained in the thread group.

Methods That Operate on the Group—These methods set or get attributes of the ThreadGroup object.

Methods That Operate on All Threads within a Group—This is a set of methods that perform some operation, such as start or resume, on all the threads and subgroups within the ThreadGroup.

Access Restriction Methods—ThreadGroup and Thread allow the security manager to restrict access to threads based on group membership.

9.49.5 Collection Management Methods

The ThreadGroup provides a set of methods that manage the threads and subgroups within the group and allow other objects to query the ThreadGroup for information about its contents. For example, you can call ThreadGroup's activeCount method to find out the number of active threads currently in the group. The activeCount method is often used with the enumerate method to get an array filled with references to all the active threads in a ThreadGroup. For example, the listCurrentThreads method in the following example fills an array with all of the active threads in the current thread group and prints their names:

```
public class EnumerateTest {
public void listCurrentThreads() {
ThreadGroup currentGroup = Thread.currentThread().getThreadGroup();
int numThreads = currentGroup.activeCount();
Thread[] listOfThreads = new Thread[numThreads];
currentGroup.enumerate(listOfThreads);
for (int i = 0; i < numThreads; i++)
System.out.println("Thread #" + i + " = " +
listOfThreads[i].getName());
}
}
```

Other collection management methods provided by the ThreadGroup class include activeGroupCount and list.

9.49.6 Methods that Operate on the Group

The ThreadGroup class supports several attributes that are set and retrieved from the group as a whole. These attributes include the maximum priority that any thread within the group can have, whether the group is a "daemon" group, the name of the group, and the parent of the group.

The methods that get and set ThreadGroup attributes operate at the group level. They inspect or change the attribute on the ThreadGroup object, but do not affect any of the threads within the group. The following is a list of ThreadGroup methods that operate at the group level:

- getMaxPriority and setMaxPriority
- getDaemon and setDaemon
- getName
- getParent and parentOf
- toString

For example, when you use setMaxPriority to change a group's maximum priority, you are only changing the attribute on the group object; you are not changing the priority of any of the threads within the group. Consider the following program that creates a group and a thread within that group:

```
public class MaxPriorityTest {
public static void main(String[] args) {
ThreadGroup groupNORM = new ThreadGroup(
"A group with normal priority");
Thread priorityMAX = new Thread(groupNORM,
"A thread with maximum priority");
// set Thread's priority to max (10)
priorityMAX.setPriority(Thread.MAX_PRIORITY);
// set ThreadGroup's max priority to normal (5)
groupNORM.setMaxPriority(Thread.NORM_PRIORITY);
System.out.println("Group's maximum priority = " +
groupNORM.getMaxPriority());
System.out.println("Thread's priority = " +
```

```
priorityMAX.getPriority());
}
}
```

When the ThreadGroup groupNORM is created, it inherits its maximum priority attribute from its parent thread group. In this case, the parent group priority is the maximum (MAX_PRIORITY) allowed by the Java runtime system. Next the program sets the priority of the priorityMAX thread to the maximum allowed by the Java runtime system. Then the program lowers the group's maximum to the normal priority (NORM_PRIORITY). The setMaxPriority method does not affect the priority of the priorityMAX thread, so that at this point, the priorityMAX thread has a priority of 10, which is greater than the maximum priority of its group, groupNORM. This is the output from the program:

- Group's maximum priority = 5
- Thread's priority = 10

As you can see a thread can have a higher priority than the maximum allowed by its group as long as the thread's priority is set before the group's maximum priority is lowered. A thread group's maximum priority is used to limit a thread's priority when the thread is first created within a group or when you use setPriority to change the thread's priority. Note that setMaxPriority does change the maximum priority of all of its descendant-threadgroups.

Similarly, a group's daemon status applies only to the group. Changing a group's daemon status does not affect the daemon status of any of the threads in the group. Furthermore, a group's daemon status does not in any way imply the daemon status of its threads—you can put any thread within a daemon thread group. The daemon status of a thread group simply indicates that the group will be destroyed when all of its threads have been terminated.

9.49.7 Methods that Operate on All Threads within a Group

The ThreadGroup class has three methods that allow you to modify the current state of all the threads within that group:

- resume
- stop
- suspend

These methods apply the appropriate state change to every thread in the thread group and its subgroups.

9.49.8 Access Restriction Methods

The ThreadGroup class itself does not impose any access restrictions, such as allowing threads from one group to inspect or modify threads in a different group. Rather the Thread and ThreadGroup classes cooperate with security managers (subclasses of the SecurityManager class), which can impose access restrictions based on thread group membership.

The Thread and ThreadGroup class both have a method, checkAccess, which calls the current security manager's checkAccess method. The security manager decides whether to allow the access based on the group membership of the threads involved. If access is not allowed, the checkAccess method throws a SecurityException. Otherwise, checkAccess simply returns.

The following is a list of ThreadGroup methods that call ThreadGroup's checkAccess before performing the action of the method. These are what are known as regulated accesses, that is, accesses that must be approved by the security manager before they can be completed.

```
ThreadGroup(ThreadGroup parent, String name)
```

```
setDaemon(boolean isDaemon)
setMaxPriority(int maxPriority)
stop
suspend
resume
destroy
```

This is a list of the methods in the Thread class that call checkAccess before proceeding:
constructors that specify a thread group

```
stop
suspend
resume
setPriority(int priority)
setName(String name)
setDaemon(boolean isDaemon)
```

A stand-alone Java application does not have a security manager by default; no restrictions are imposed and any thread can inspect or modify any other thread, regardless of the group they are in. You can define and implement your own access restrictions for thread groups by subclassing SecurityManager, overriding the appropriate methods, and installing the SecurityManager as the current security manager in your application. For information about implementing a security manager, see the lesson Providing Your Own Security Manager.

The HotJava Web browser is an example of an application that implements its own security manager. HotJava needs to ensure that applets are well-behaved and don't do nasty things to other applets running at the same time (such as lowering the priority of another applet's threads). HotJava's security manager does not allow threads in different groups to modify one another. Please note that access restrictions based on thread groups may vary from browser to browser and thus applets may behave differently in different browsers. For more information about access restrictions on thread groups within applets, see Security Restrictions.

EXERCISES

1. *Write a multiball applet where the number of balls is a PARAM that is defined in HTML. Allow a broader range of behavior for the balls. Specfically allow the size, color, starting positions, starting directions, and speed of each ball to be given in a PARAM tag.*

2. *Inherit a class from Thread and override the run( ) method. Inside run( ), print a message, then call sleep( ). Repeat this three times, then return from run( ). Put a start-up message in the constructor and override finalize( ) to print a shut-down message. Make a separate thread class that calls System.gc( ) and System.runFinalization( ) inside run( ), printing a message as it does so. Make several thread objects of both types and run them to see what happens.*

3. *Modify Counter2.java so that the thread is an inner class and doesn't need to explicitly store a handle to a Counter2.*

   Modify Sharing2.java to add a synchronized block inside the run( ) method of TwoCounter instead of synchronizing the entire run( ) method.

4. *Create two Thread subclasses, one with a run( ) that starts up, captures the handle of the second Thread object and then calls wait( ). The other class' run( ) should call notifyAll( ) for the first thread after some number of seconds have passed, so the first thread can print out a message.*

5. *In Counter5.java inside Ticker2, remove the yield( ) and explain the results. Replace the yield( ) with a sleep( ) and explain the results.*

6. *In ThreadGroup1.java, replace the call to sys.suspend( ) with a call to wait( ) for the thread group, causing it to wait for two seconds. For this to work correctly you must acquire the lock for sys inside a synchronized block.*
7. *Change Daemons.java so that main( ) has a sleep( ) instead of a readLine( ). Experiment with different sleep times to see what happens.*

10 Input and Output with Streams

10.1 Streams

Sometimes data is written to a file instead of the computer screen. Under Unix and DOS you can sometimes do this using the redirection operators < and >. However sometimes you need a more fine-grained approach that writes only certain data to a file while still putting other data on the screen. Or you may need access to multiple files simultaneously. Or maybe you want to query the user for input rather than accepting it all on the command line. Or maybe you want to read data out of a file that's in a particular format. Or perhaps you want to send data to or read data from a network socket or a URL. In Java all these methods require streams. In fact the System.out object you've been using since class 1 is a stream.

10.1.1 What is a Stream?

A stream is a sequence of data of undetermined length. It's called a stream because it's like a stream of water that continues to flow. There's no definite end to it.

A better analogy might be a queue of people waiting to get on a ride at an amusement park. As people are processed at the front (i.e. get on the roller coaster) more are added at the back of the line. If it's a slow day the roller coaster may catch up with the end of the line and have to wait for people to board. Other days there may always be people in line until the park closes. Each person is a discrete individual and must be put on the roller coaster or not put on the roller coaster. There are no half-people. There's always a definite number of people in line though this number may change from moment to moment as people enter at the back of the line and exit from the front of the line. Although all the people are discrete, you'll sometimes have a family that must be put together in the same car. Thus although the individuals are discrete, they aren't necessarily unrelated.

In Java a stream is composed of discrete bytes. The bytes may represent chars or other kinds of data. They may come faster than you can handle them, or your thread may block while waiting for the next one to arrive. It often doesn't matter.

The key to processing the stream is a while loop that processes each piece of data, until you encounter the end-of-stream character or some other exceptional condition occurs. In Unix you type end-of-stream with Control-D. On Windows, you type end-of-stream with Control-Z.

10.2 The Stream Classes

Almost all the classes that work directly with streams are part of the `java.io` package. (There are also a few more in the sun.io and sun.net packages, but those are deliberately hidden from you. There are also a couple in java.util.zip.) The two main classes are java.io.InputStream and java.io.OutputStream. These are abstract base classes for many different subclasses with more specialized abilities, including:

- BufferedInputStream
- BufferedOutputStream
- ByteArrayInputStream
- ByteArrayOutputStream
- DataInputStream
- DataOutputStream
- FileInputStream
- FileOutputStream
- FilterInputStream
- FilterOutputStream
- LineNumberInputStream
- ObjectInputStream
- ObjectOutputStream
- PipedInputStream
- PipedOutputStream
- PrintStream
- PushbackInputStream
- SequenceInputStream
- StringBufferInputStream

10.2.1 Origin of Streams

System.out is an OutputStream; specifically it's a PrintStream. There's a corresponding System.in which is an InputStream used to read data from the console.

Data for streams can also come from files. Later you'll see how to use the File class and the FileInputStream and FileOutputStream classes to read and write data from files.

Network connections commonly provide streams. We'll talk about this in a couple of weeks.When you connect to a web or ftp or some other kind of server, you read the data it sends from an InputStream connected from that server and write data onto an OutputStream connected to that server.

Java programs themselves produce streams. ByteArrayInputStreams, ByteArrayOutputStreams, StringBufferInputStreams, Piped InputStreams, and PipedOutputStreams all use the stream metaphor to move data from one part of a Java program to another.

Perhaps a little surprisingly, components like TextArea do not produce streams. However you can always use the strings they do produce to create a ByteArrayInputStream or a StringBufferInputStream.

10.3 The InputStream Class

java.io.InputStream is an abstract class that contains the basic methods for reading raw bytes of data from a stream. Although InputStream is an abstract class many methods in the class library are only specified to return an InputStream, so you'll often have to deal directly with only the methods declared in this class.

```
public abstract int read() throws IOException
public int read(byte b[]) throws IOException
public int read(byte b[], int offset, int length) throws IOException
public long skip(long n) throws IOException
public int available() throws IOException
public void close() throws IOException
public synchronized void mark(int readlimit)
```

```
public synchronized void reset() throws IOException
public boolean markSupported()
```

Notice that almost all these methods can throw an IOException. This is true of pretty much anything to do with input and output. The only exception is the PrintStream class which eats all exceptions.

10.3.1 Reading bytes of data

The basic read() method of the InputStream class reads a single unsigned byte of data and returns the int value of the unsigned byte. This is a number between 0 and 255. If the end of stream is encountered it returns -1 instead, and you can use this as a flag to watch for the end of stream.

public abstract int read() throws IOException

Here's a simple program that echoes back what the user types at the command line. The byte is cast to its equivalent in the ISO Latin-1 character set before being printed. This program does not properly handle Unicode. In general, input and output streams do not properly handle Unicode data. Therefore you should use them only for raw data and use the java.io.Reader and java.io.Writer classes for text data, especially non-ASCII data.

```
/* Note that as a general rule on most platforms characters
are only sent to System.in a line at a time, not as each character
is typed. This allows the user to backspace over mistakes and
correct them.  Java does not allow you to put the console into
"raw" mode.
*/
import java.io.*;
public class Echo {
public static void main(String[] args) {
echo(System.in);
}
public static void echo(InputStream is) {
try {
while (true) {
// Notice that although a byte is read, an int
// with value between 0 and 255 is returned.
// Then this is converted to an ISO Latin-1 char
// in the same range before being printed.
int i = is.read();
// -1 is returned to indicate the end of stream
if (i == -1) break;
// without the cast a numeric string like "65"
// would be printed instead of the character "A"
char c = (char) i;
System.out.print(c);
}
}
catch (IOException e) {
System.err.println(e);
}
System.out.println();
```

```
}
}
```

10.3.2 Reading many bytes of data

The basic read() method reads a byte at a time. This is less than perfectly efficient. The following two polymorphic variants read multiple bytes into an array of bytes.

```
public int read(byte b[]) throws IOException
public int read(byte b[], int offset, int length) throws IOException
```

The first method tries to read enough bytes to fill the array b. The second method reads length bytes from the input stream and stores them into the array b starting at position offset.

These methods block until there is some data available. Then they read as many bytes as they can into b, or until they've read length bytes.

These methods then return the number of bytes actually read. You should not assume that the array will be filled or that length bytes will actually have been read. If the end of stream is encountered, -1 is returned.

10.3.3 Counting the available bytes

The available() method tests how many bytes are ready to be read from the stream without blocking.

```
public int available() throws IOException
```

For example, the following program is a more efficient version of Echo that uses available() to test how many bytes are ready to be read, creates an array of exactly that size, reads the bytes into the array, then converts the array to a String and prints the String.

```
import java.io.*;
public class EfficientEcho {
public static void main(String[] args) {
echo(System.in);
}
public static void echo(InputStream is) {
try {
while (true) {
int n = is.available();
if (n > 0) {
byte[] b = new byte[n];
int result = is.read(b);
if (result == -1) break;
String s = new String(b);
System.out.print(s);
} // end if
} // end while
} // end try
catch (IOException e) {
System.err.println(e);
}
}
}
```

10.3.4 Skipping Bytes

The skip() method reads a specified number of bytes and throws them away.

```
public int skip(long n) throws IOException
```

You might use this, for example, if you want to quickly move past a standard header or prefix to some data. For example, in the following code fragment skip() is used to move past some padding included in Java byte code to make sure that a jump table entry for a switch statement is aligned on a four byte boundary:

```
case 171: // lookupswitch
pad = 3 - (position % 4);
dis.skip(pad);
defaultByte = dis.readInt();
int npairs = dis.readInt();
result = position + "lookupswitch " + defaultByte + "" + npairs;
for (int i = 0; i < npairs; i++) {
int newPosition = position + pad + 12 + i*8;
result += "\n" + newPosition + "    "
+ dis.readInt() + "  " + dis.readInt();
}
```

10.3.5 Marking and Resetting

It's often useful to be able to read a few bytes, and then back up and reread them. For example, in the design of a Java compiler you don't know for sure whether you've read <, <<, or <<= until you've read one two many characters. It would be useful to be able to back up and reread the token once you know which token you've read. Compiler design and other parsing problems provide many more examples, but this need occurs elsewhere as well.

Some but not all input streams allow you to mark a particular position in the stream, and then return to it. There are three methods that allow this:

```
public synchronized void mark(int readlimit)
public synchronized void reset() throws IOException
public boolean markSupported()
```

The boolean markSupported() method returns true if this stream supports marking and false if it doesn't.

Assuming the stream does support marking, the mark() method places a bookmark in the stream which you can return to later using the reset() method. There can be only one mark() in the stream at any given time. Marking a second location erases the first mark. If marking is not supported, these methods throw IOExceptions.

10.3.6 Closing Streams

When you're done with a stream, you may want to close it to release any resources associated with the stream. Once the stream is closed attempts to read from it, will throw IOExceptions.

```
You close a stream with the close() method:
public void close() throws IOException
An IOException is thrown if the stream can't be closed.
```

10.4 Output Streams

The java.io.OutputStream class sends raw bytes of data to a target such as the console or a network server. Like InputStream, OutputStream is an abstract class. However, many methods in the class library are only specified to return OutputStream rather than the more specific subclass. Furthermore, many of the methods of OutputStream are generally useful. These are:

```
public abstract void write(int b) throws IOException
public void write(byte b[]) throws IOException
public void write(byte b[], int offset, int len) throws IOException
public void flush() throws IOException
public void close() throws IOException
```

The write() methods send raw bytes of data to whomever is listening to this stream.

Sometimes output streams are buffered by the operating system for performance. In other words, rather than writing each byte as it's written the bytes are accumulated in a buffer ranging from several bytes to several thousand bytes. Then, when the buffer fills up, all the data is written at once. The flush() method forces the data to be written whether or not the buffer is full.

This is not the same as the buffering performed by a BufferedOutputStream. That buffering is handled by the Java runtime. This buffering is at the native OS level. However, a call to flush() should empty both buffers

The close() method closes the stream and releases any resources associated with the stream. Once the stream is closed attempts to write to it throw IOExceptions.

10.4.1 Output Stream Example

The only output streams you've seen so far are System.out and System.err. The following example uses the write() and flush() methods of the OutputStream class to write the String "Hello World" on System.out.

```
import java.io.*;
public class HelloOutputStream {
public static void main(String[] args) {
String s = "Hello World\r\n";
// Convert s to a byte array
byte[] b = new byte[s.length()];
s.getBytes(0, s.length()-1, b, 0);
try {
System.out.write(b);
System.out.flush();
}
catch (IOException e) {
System.err.println(e);
}

}
}
```

What's wrong with this program?

10.5 Input from Files

The java.io.FileInputStream class represents an InputStream that reads bytes from a file. It has the following public methods:

```
public FileInputStream(String name) throws FileNotFoundException
public FileInputStream(File file) throws FileNotFoundException
public FileInputStream(FileDescriptor fdObj)
public native int read() throws IOException
public int read(byte b[]) throws IOException
public int read(byte b[], int offset, int length) throws IOException
public native long skip(long n) throws IOException
public native int available() throws IOException
public native void close() throws IOException
public final FileDescriptor getFD() throws IOException
```

Except for the constructors and getFD(), these methods merely override the methods of the same name in java.io.InputStream. You use them exactly like you use those methods, only you'll end up reading data from a file.

10.5.1 Examples of Input from Files

You create a new FileInputStream object by passing the name of the file to the constructor, like this:

FileInputStream fis = new FileInputStream("14");

This throws a FileNotFoundException, a subclass of IOException, if the named file can't be located. Generally Java looks for files in the current working directory. This is not necessarily the same directory where the .class file is located.

The following simple application reads the files named on the command line and prints them on System.out.

```
import java.io.*;
public class Type {
public static void main(String[] args) {
for (int i = 0; i < args.length; i++) {
try {
FileInputStream fis = new FileInputStream(args[i]);
int n;
while ((n = fis.available()) > 0) {
byte[] b = new byte[n];
int result = fis.read(b);
if (result == -1) break;
String s = new String(b);
System.out.print(s);
} // end while
} // end try
// Is this catch strictly necessary?
catch (FileNotFoundException e) {
System.err.println("Could not find file " + args[i]);
}
catch (IOException e) {
```

```
System.err.println(e);
}
System.out.println();
} // end for
} // end main
}
```

10.5.2 Writing Data to Files

The java.io.FileOutputStream class represents an OutputStream that writes bytes to a file. It has the following public methods:

```
public FileOutputStream(String name) throws IOException
public FileOutputStream(String name, boolean append) throws IOException
public FileOutputStream(File file) throws IOException
public FileOutputStream(FileDescriptor fdObj)
public native void write(int b) throws IOException
public void write(byte b[]) throws IOException
public void write(byte b[], int offset, int length) throws IOException
public native void close() throws IOException
public final FileDescriptor getFD() throws IOException
```

Except for the constructors and getFD(), these methods merely override the methods of the same name in java.io.OutputStream. You use them exactly like you use those methods, only the output is written into a file.

10.5.3 Example of Output to Files

You create a new FileOutputStream object by passing the name of the file to the constructor, like this:

```
FileOutputStream fos = new FileOutputStream("16");
```

If the file exists in the current directory, it will be overwritten by the new data. If the file doesn't exist it will be created in the current directory.

The following example reads user input from System.in and writes it into the files specified on the command line.

```
import java.io.*;
public class MultiType {
public static void main(String[] args) {
FileOutputStream[] fos = new FileOutputStream[args.length];
for (int i = 0; i < args.length; i++) {
try {
fos[i] = new FileOutputStream(args[i]);
}
catch (IOException e) {
System.err.println(e);
}
} // end for
try {
while (true) {
int n = System.in.available();
if (n > 0) {
```

```
byte[] b = new byte[n];
int result = System.in.read(b);
if (result == -1) break;
for (int i = 0; i < args.length; i++) {
try {
fos[i].write(b, 0, result);
}
catch (IOException e) {
System.err.println(e);
}
} // end for
} // end if
} // end while
} // end try
catch (IOException e) {
System.err.println(e);
}
} // end main
}
```

10.5.4 Appending Data to Files

It's often useful to be able to append data to an existing file rather than overwriting it. To do this just pass the boolean value true as the second argument to the FileOutputStream() constructor. For example,

```
FileOutputStream fos = new FileOutputStream("16", true);
The following example reads user input from System.in and appends it
to the files specified on the command line.
import java.io.*;
public class Append {
public static void main(String[] args) {
FileOutputStream[] fos = new FileOutputStream[args.length];
for (int i = 0; i < args.length; i++) {
try {
fos[i] = new FileOutputStream(args[i], true);
}
catch (IOException e) {
System.err.println(e);
}
} // end for
try {
while (true) {
int n = System.in.available();
if (n > 0) {
byte[] b = new byte[n];
int result = System.in.read(b);
if (result == -1) break;
for (int i = 0; i < args.length; i++) {
```

```
try {
fos[i].write(b, 0, result);
}
catch (IOException e) {
System.err.println(e);
}
} // end for
} // end if
} // end while
} // end try
catch (IOException e) {
System.err.println(e);
}
} // end main
}
```

10.6 Filter Streams

The java.io.FilterInputStream and java.io.FilterOutputStream classes are concrete subclasses of InputStream and OutputStream that somehow modify data read from an underlying stream. You rarely use these classes directly, but their subclasses are extremely important, especially DataInputStream and DataOutputStream.

You connect filter streams to an underlying stream that supplies the actual bytes of data by passing the original stream to the filter stream's constructor. For example, to create a new DataOutputStream from a FileOutputStream you might do this:

```
FileOutputStream fos = new FileOutputStream("ln.txt");
DataOutputStream dos = new DataOutputStream(fos);
It's not uncommon to combine these into one line like this:
DataOutputStream dos = new DataOutputStream(new File Output Stream
("ln.txt"));
```

Once two streams are chained together like this you can call the methods of any of the underlying streams on the resulting stream.

10.6.1 Filter Stream Classes

- **BufferedInputStream and BufferedOutputStream**

These classes buffer reads and writes by reading data first into a buffer (an internal array of bytes). Thus an application can read bytes from the stream without necessarily calling the underlying native method. The data is read from or written into the buffer in blocks; subsequent accesses go straight to the buffer.

- **DataInputStream and DataOutputStream**

These classes read and write primitive Java data types and Strings in a machine-independent way. (Big-endian for integer types, IEEE-754 for floats and doubles, UTF-8 for Unicode)

- **PrintStream**

The print stream class is implemented by System.out and System.err. It allows very simple printing of both primitive values, objects, and string literals. It uses the platform's default character encoding to convert characters into bytes. This class traps all IOExceptions. This class is primarily intended for debugging.

- **PushbackInputStream**

This input stream has a one byte pushback buffer so a program can unread the last character read. The next time data is read from the stream, the "unread" character is re-read.

You can also create your own subclasses of FilterInputStream and FilterOutputStream that perform custom filtering.

10.7 Buffered Streams

The java.io.BufferedInputStream and java.io.BufferedOutputStream classes buffer reads and writes by first storing the in a buffer (an internal array of bytes). Then the program reads bytes from the stream without calling the underlying native method until the buffer is empty. The data is read from or written into the buffer in blocks; subsequent accesses go straight to the buffer.

The only real difference to the programmer between a regular stream and a buffered stream are the constructors:

```
public BufferedInputStream(InputStream in)
public BufferedInputStream(InputStream in, int size)
public BufferedOutputStream(OutputStream out)
public BufferedOutputStream(OutputStream out, int size)
```

The size argument is the number of bytes in the buffer. If a size isn't specified, a 512 byte buffer is used.

The best size for the buffer is highly platform dependent and generally related to the block size of the disk, at least for file streams. Less than 512 bytes is probably too little and more than 4096 bytes is probably too much. Ideally you want an integral multiple of the block size of the disk. However, you should use smaller buffer sizes for unreliable network connections.

For example,

```
URL u = new URL("http://java.developer.com");
BufferedInputStream bis = new BufferedInputStream(u.openStream(),
256);
```

10.8 Data Stream Classes

The java.io.DataInputStream and java.io.DataOutputStream classes read and write primitive Java data types and Strings in a machine-independent way. Generally you use a DataInputStream to read data written by a DataOutputStream. This format uses IEEE 754 for floating point data, big-endian format for integer data, and a modified UTF-8 for Unicode data.

DataOutputStream declares these methods:

```
public DataOutputStream(OutputStream out)
public synchronized void write(int b) throws IOException
public synchronized void write(byte b[], int offset, int length)
throws IOException
public final void writeBoolean(boolean v) throws IOException
public final void writeByte(int v) throws IOException
public final void writeShort(int v) throws IOException
public final void writeChar(int v) throws IOException
public final void writeInt(int v) throws IOException
```

```
public final void writeFloat(float v) throws IOException
public final void writeDouble(double v) throws IOException
public final void writeBytes(String s) throws IOException
public final void writeChars(String s) throws IOException
public final void writeUTF(String str) throws IOException
public final int size()
public void flush() throws IOException
```

The size() method returns the number of bytes written to this data output stream.

10.8.1 DataInputStream

Generally you use a DataInputStream to read data written by a DataOutputStream. This format uses IEEE 754 for floating point data, big-endian format for integer data, and a modified UTF-8 for Unicode data.

```
DataInputStream has these methods:
public DataInputStream(InputStream in)
public final int read(byte b[]) throws IOException
public final int read(byte b[], int offset, int length) throws
IOException
public final void readFully(byte b[]) throws IOException
public final void readFully(byte b[], int offset, int length) throws
IOException
public final int skipBytes(int n) throws IOException
public final boolean readBoolean() throws IOException
public final byte readByte() throws IOException
public final int readUnsignedByte() throws IOException
public final short readShort() throws IOException
public final int readUnsignedShort() throws IOException
public final char readChar() throws IOException
public final int readInt() throws IOException
public final long readLong() throws IOException
public final float readFloat() throws IOException
public final double readDouble() throws IOException
public final String readUTF() throws IOException
public static final String readUTF(DataInput in) throws IOException
```

The readFully() methods read repeatedly from the underlying stream until the byte array is filled. This contrasts with the regular read() methods which only read as many bytes as are available at the moment.

There's also a fairly common readLine() method that was used quite commonly in Java 1.0. However it's deprecated in favor of BufferedReader in Java 1.1

10.9 Print Streams

The java.io.PrintStream class is a subclass of FilterOutputStream. It is implemented by System.out and System.err. It allows very simple printing of both primitive values, objects, and string literals. It uses the platform's default character encoding to convert characters into bytes.

This class traps all IOExceptions. However you can test the error status with checkError(). This returns true if an error has occurred, false otherwise.

public boolean checkError()

The main use of the class is the exceptionally overloaded print() and println() methods. They differ in that println() adds an end-of-line character to whatever it prints while print() does not.

```
public void print(boolean b)
public void print(int i)
public void print(long l)
public void print(float f)
public void print(double d)
public void print(char s[])
public void print(String s)
public void print(Object obj)
public void println()
public void println(boolean x)
public void println(char x)
public void println(int x)
public void println(long x)
public void println(float x)
public void println(double x)
public void println(char x[])
public void println(String x)
public void println(Object x)
```

PrintStream is primarily intended for debugging. Otherwise it's unofficially deprecated in Java 1.1. You should use the PrintWriter class instead.

10.10 Pushback Input Stream

The PushbackInputStream class provides a pushback buffer so a program can unread the last character read. The next time data is read from the stream, the "unread" characters are re-read.

```
public void unread(int b) throws IOException
public void unread(byte b[], int offset, int length) throws IOException
public void unread(byte b[]) throws IOException
```

By default the buffer is only one byte long, and trying to unread more than that throws an IOException. However you can change the default buffer size with the second constructor below:

public PushbackInputStream(InputStream in)

```
public PushbackInputStream(InputStream in, int size)
```

Although both PushbackInputStream and BufferedInputStream use buffers, only a PushbackInputStream allows unreading and only a BufferedInputStream allows marking and resetting. In a PushbackInputStream markSupported() returns false.

```
public boolean markSupported()
```

The read() and available() methods work exactly as with normal input streams. However, they first attempt to read from the pushback buffer.

```
public int read() throws IOException
public int read(byte b[], int offset, int length) throws IOException
public int available() throws IOException
```

10.11 The File Class

The java.io.File class represents a file name on the host system. It attempts to abstract system-dependent file name features like the path separator character.

There are two ways to reference a file, relative and absolute. Absolute addressing gives a complete path to a file, starting with the disk and working its way down. How this is represented varies from operating system to operating system. Here are some examples:

```
Unix:    "/home/users/elharo/file1"
DOS:     "C:\home\users\elharo\file1"
MacOS:   "Macintosh HD:home:users:elharo:file1"
```

All three Strings reference a file called file1 on the primary hard drive in the elharo directory which is itself in the users directory which is in the home directory. One obvious difference is the path separator character. Unix uses a / to separate directories, DOS and Windows based file systems use a \. The MacOS uses a :. Other OS's may use something completely different.

Worse yet there's no guarantee that the Mac's primary hard drive is called "Macintosh HD" or that it even has such a disk. On Unix /home and /home/users may be on completely different disks, perhaps even on different machines. For these and more reasons absolute pathnames are a royal pain to work with and should be avoided whenever possible.

Relative addressing, which should be used if possible, doesn't give the complete path to the file. Instead it gives the path relative to some other known file. A relative pathname may point to a file in the same directory as a known file by only giving its name. Other times it may point to a file in a subdirectory of a known directory.

Generally one directory is set as the current directory. This is where methods that look for files are relative to. Normally this is the directory in which you started running the application.

java.io.File can hold a directory name equally as well as a filename.

10.12 Note to C Programmers

A File object is not a file handle. Just because you have a File object does not mean that the equivalent file actually exists on the disk. There are methods you can use to determine whether a File object refers to a real file or not (specifically exists()).

10.13 File Constructors

There are three constructor methods in java.io.File. Each takes some variation of a filename as an argument(s). The simplest is

```
public File(String path)
```

path is simply a String with either a full or relative pathname to the file which can be understood by the host operating system. For example,

```
File f1 = new File("25");
File f2 = new File("/etc/passwd");
```

If you like you can separate the path and the filename using the

```
public File(String path, String name)
```

constructor. Here name is the filename and path is the name of the directory that contains the file. For example,

```
File f2 = new File("/etc", "passwd");
Finally there's
public File(File dir, String name)
```

which is like the previous constructor except that now dir is a File object itself instead of a String.

Some methods in other classes also return File objects, most notably the java.awt.FileDialog methods. The File objects returned by these methods will conform to the conventions of the host operating system.

10.14 File Methods

Given that you have a File object in place there are a number of questions you can ask about it and things you can do with it.

public String getName()

`The most basic question you can ask a file is "What is your name?" You do this with the getName() method which takes no arguments and returns a String. The String returned is just the name of the file. It does not include any piece of the directory or directories that contain this file. In other words you get back "file1" instead of "/home/users/elharo/file1."`

`public String getPath()`

`getPath() returns a String that contains the path being used for this File. It will be relative or absolute depending on how the File object was created.`

`public String getAbsolutePath()`

`getAbsolutePath() returns the complete, non-relative path to the file.`

`public String getCanonicalPath() throws IOException`

`getCanonicalPath() returns the canonical form of this File object's pathname. This is system-dependent.`

`public String getParent()`

getParent() returns a String that contains the name of the single directory which contains this file in the hierarchy. It does not return a full path all the way back up to the root. If the file is at the top level of the disk then it has no parent directory and null is returned.

`public boolean exists()`

The exists() method indicates whether or not a particular file exists where you expect it to be.

`public boolean canWrite()`

The canWrite() method indicates whether you have write access to this file. It's not a bad idea to check canWrite() before trying to put data in a file.

`public boolean canRead()`

The canRead() method indicates whether you have read access to this file. It's not a bad idea to check canRead() before trying to read data out of a file.

`public boolean isFile()`

The isFile() method indicates whether this is file exists and is a normal file, in other words not a directory.

```
public boolean isDirectory()
```

The isDirectory() returns true if this file exists and is a directory.

```
public boolean isAbsolute()
```

isAbsolute() returns true if the file name is an absolute path and false if it's a relative path.

```
public long lastModified()
```

lastModified() returns the last modification time. Since the conversion between this long and a real date is platform dependent, you should only use this to compare modification dates of different files.

```
public long length()
```

f.length() is the length of the file in bytes.

```
public boolean mkdir()
```

f.mkdir() tries to create a directory with the given name. If the directory is created, the method returns true. Otherwise it returns false.

```
public boolean mkdirs()
```

mkdirs() is a command I've wanted in other languages for years. Given a filename it creates not just one but every directory in the path as necessary, permissions permitting. mkdirs() returns true if all directories in this path are created, and false if only some or none of them are created. You may need to manually test the existence of each directory in the path if the method returns false because it could have been partially successful.

```
public boolean renameTo(File dest)
```

f1.renameTo(f2) tries to change the name of f1 to f2. This may involve a move to a different directory if the filenames so indicate. If f2 already exists, then it is overwritten by f1 (permissions permitting). If f1 is renamed, the method returns true. Otherwise it returns false.

```
public String[] list()
```

The list() method returns an array of Strings initialized to the names of each file in directory f. It's useful for processing all the files in a directory.

```
public String[] list(FilenameFilter filter)
```

This is the same as the previous method except you can use a FilenameFilter object (discussed in the next section) to restrict which files are added to the list.

```
public boolean delete()
```

f.delete() tries to delete the file f. This method returns true if the file existed and was deleted. (You can't delete a file that doesn't exist). Otherwise it returns false.

The File class also contains the usual equals(), hashCode() and toString() methods which behave exactly as you would expect. It does not contain a clone() method.

10.14.1 Examples of the File Methods

The following program reads filenames from the command line and returns various information about those files using the methods of the File class.

```
import java.io.*;
public class FileInfo {
public static void main(String[] args) {
for (int i = 0; i < args.length; i++) {
```

```
File f = new File(args[i]);
if (f.exists()) {
System.out.println("getName: " + f.getName());
System.out.println("getPath: " + f.getPath());
System.out.println("getAbsolutePath: " + f.getAbsolutePath());
System.out.println("getCanonicalPath: " + f.getCanonicalPath());
System.out.println("getParent: " + f.getParent());
if (f.canWrite()) System.out.println(f.getName() + " is writable.");
if (f.canRead()) System.out.println(f.getName() + " is readable.");
if (f.isFile()) {
System.out.println(f.getName() +" is a file.");
}
else if (f.isDirectory()) {
System.out.println(f.getName() + "is a directory.");
}
else {
System.out.println("What is this?");
}
if (f.isAbsolute()) {
System.out.println(f.getName() + "is an absolute path.");
}
else {
System.out.println(f.getName() + "is not an absolute path.");
}
try {
System.out.println("Last Modified" + f.lastModified());
System.out.println(f.getName() + " is " + f.length() + " bytes.");
System.out.println(f.getName() + " is " + f.length() + " bytes.");
}
catch (IOException e) {
}
}
else {
System.out.println("I'm sorry. I can't find the file " + args[i]);
}
}
}
}
```

10.15 File Dialogs

Many times you'll want some control over the FileDialog. You may want to specify that it should start looking in a particular directory, or that only text files should be shown. Java lets you do this. To start the FileDialog off in a particular directory call the FileDialog's setDirectory(String dir) method where dir is the path to the directory. That is

```
fd.setDirectory("/usr/tmp");
```

You can even set the FileDialog to point at a particular file using setFile(String filename). However if you already know the file name why do you need to bring up a FileDialog? More likely is that you'll want to look for a particular type of file, for instance text files. To make this happen you need to use a FilenameFilter to specify which files you'll accept. The key method is

```
setFilenameFilter(FilenameFilter fnf).
```

10.16 Filename Filters

java.io.FilenameFilter is an interface that declares single method,

boolean accept(File dir, String name)

File dir is a directory and String name is a filename. The method should return true if the file passes through the filter and false if it doesn't.

Since FilenameFilter is an interface, you must implement it in a class. Here is an example class which filters out everything that is not a java source code file.

```
import java.io.*;
public class javaFilter implements FilenameFilter {
public boolean accept(File dir, String name) {
if (name.endsWith(".java")) return true;
return false;
}
}
```

Files do not need to be filtered by filename only. You can test modification date, permissions, filesize and more. For example this accept method tests whether the file ends with .java and is in a directory to which you have write permission.

public boolean accept(File dir, String name) {

```
if (name.endsWith(".java") && dir.canWrite()) return true;
return false;
}
```

10.17 Random Access Files

Random access files can be read from or written to or both from a particular byte position in the file. The position in the file is indicated by a file pointer.

There are two constructors in this class:

```
public RandomAccessFile(String name, String mode) throws IOException
public RandomAccessFile(File file, String mode) throws IOException
```

The first argument to the constructor is the file you want to access. The second argument is the mode for access. This should either be the String "r" for read-only access or the string "rw" for read and write access. Java does not support write only access. For example,

RandomAccessFile raf = new RandomAccessFile("29", "r");

The getFilePointer(), length(), and seek() methods allow you to determine and modify the point in the file at which reads and writes occur. Attempts to seek (position the file pointer) past the end of the file just move the file pointer to the end of the file. Attempts to write from the end of the file extend the file. Attempts to read from the end of the file throw EOFExceptions.

```
public native long getFilePointer() throws IOException
public native void seek(long pos) throws IOException
public native long length() throws IOException
```

Reads and writes use methods that work identically to the methods of the DataInputStream and DataOutputStream classes, except that you can set the position at which the read or write occurs between calls to the read and write methods.

```
public native int read() throws IOException
public int read(byte b[], int offset, int length) throws IOException
public int read(byte b[]) throws IOException
public final void readFully(byte b[]) throws IOException
public final void readFully(byte b[], int offset, int length) throws
IOException
public native void write(int b) throws IOException
public void write(byte b[]) throws IOException
public void write(byte b[], int offset, int length) throws IOException
public final boolean readBoolean() throws IOException
public final byte readByte() throws IOException
public final int readUnsignedByte() throws IOException
public final short readShort() throws IOException
public final int readUnsignedShort() throws IOException
public final char readChar() throws IOException
public final int readInt() throws IOException
public final long readLong() throws IOException
public final float readFloat() throws IOException
public final double readDouble() throws IOException
public final String readLine() throws IOException
public final String readUTF() throws IOException
public final void writeBoolean(boolean v) throws IOException
public final void writeByte(int v) throws IOException
public final void writeShort(int v) throws IOException
public final void writeChar(int v) throws IOException
public final void writeInt(int v) throws IOException
public final void writeLong(long v) throws IOException
public final void writeFloat(float v) throws IOException
public final void writeDouble(double v) throws IOException
public final void writeBytes(String s) throws IOException
public final void writeChars(String s) throws IOException
public final void writeUTF(String str) throws IOException
Finally, they're a few miscellaneous methods:
public final FileDescriptor getFD() throws IOException
public int skipBytes(int n) throws IOException
public native void close() throws IOException
```

10.18 Readers and Writers

The java.io.Reader and java.io.Writer classes are abstract superclasses for classes that read and write character based data. The subclasses are notable for handling the conversion between different character sets.

Input and output streams are fundamentally byte based. However readers and writers are based on characters, which can have varying widths depending on the character set being used. For example, ASCII and ISO Latin-1 use one byte characters. Unicode uses two byte characters. UTF-8 uses characters of varying width between one and three bytes. Readers and writers know how to handle all these character sets and many more seamlessly.

10.18.1 The java.io.Reader class

The methods of the java.io.Reader class are deliberately similar to the methods of the java.io.InputStream class. However rather than working with bytes, they work with chars.

The basic read() method reads a single character (which may may take between one and four bytes depending on the character set) and returns the character as an int between 0 and 65535. It returns -1 if the end of stream is seen.

```
public int read() throws IOException
```

You can also read many characters into an array of chars. These methods return the number of bytes successfully read or -1 if the end of stream occurs.

```
public int read(char cbuf[]) throws IOException
```

public abstract int read(char cbuf[], int offset, int length) throws IOException

All the read() methods block until some input is available, an I/O error occurs, or the end of the stream is reached.

You can skip a certain number of characters. This method also blocks until some characters are available. It returns the number of characters skipped or -1 if the end of stream is reached.

```
public long skip(long n) throws IOException
```

The ready() method returns true if the Reader is ready to be read from, false if it isn't. Generally this means the underying stream has available data.

```
public boolean ready() throws IOException
```

Readers may or may not support marking and resetting, like input streams. The markSupported() method returns true if the underlying streams supports marking and resetting, false if it doesn't

```
public boolean markSupported()
```

public void mark(int readAheadLimit) throws IOException

```
public void reset() throws IOException
```

Finally the close() method closes the Reader and releases any resources associated with it.

```
public abstract void close() throws IOException
```

10.18.2 The java.io.Writer class

The methods of the java.io.Writer class are deliberately similar to the methods of the java.io.OutputStream class. However rather than working with bytes, they work with chars.

The basic write() method writes a single two-byte character with a value between 0 and 65535. The value is taken from the two low-order bytes of the argument c.

public void write(int c) throws IOException

You can also write an array of characters, a sub-array of characters, a String, or a substring.

```
public void write(char c[]) throws IOException
public abstract void write(char c[], int offset, int length) throws
IOException
public void write(String s) throws IOException
public void write(String s, int offset, int length) throws IOException
```

Like OutputStreams, Writers may be buffered. To force the write to take place, call flush():

```
public abstract void flush() throws IOException
```

Finally the close() method closes the Writer and releases any resources associated with it.

```
public abstract void close() throws IOException
```

10.18.3 The Input Stream Reader Class

The java.io.InputStreamReader class serves as a bridge between byte streams and character streams: It reads bytes from the input stream and translates them into characters according to a specified character encoding.

The encoding can be set in the constructor, or you can accept the platform's default encoding.

```
public InputStreamReader(InputStream in)
public InputStreamReader(InputStream in, String encoding)
throws UnsupportedEncodingException
```

For example, to attach an InputStreamReader to System.in with the default encoding, (generally ISO Latin-1):

```
InputStreamReader isr = new InputStreamReader(System.in);
```

On the other hand if you wanted to read a file that had been encoded using the Macintosh Symbol font, you might do this:

FileInputStream fis = new FileInputStream("symbol.txt");

InputStreamReader isr = new InputStreamReader(fis, "MacSymbol");

```
public String getEncoding()
```

The getEncoding() method returns a string containing the name of the encoding used by this reader.

The other methods just override methods from java.io.Reader, but behave identically from the perspective of the programmer.

```
public int read() throws IOException
public int read(char c[], int off, int length) throws IOException
public boolean ready() throws IOException
public void close() throws IOException
```

10.18.4 Available Encodings

Name Character Set

```
8859_3   ISO 8859-3 (Latin Extended-B) Pinyin, Sami, Croatian, and a
few others
8859_4   ISO 8859-4 (Latin Extended-C)
8859_5   ISO 8859-5 Latin/Cyrillic
8859_6   ISO 8859-6 Latin/Arabic
8859_7   ISO 8859-7 Latin/Greek
8859_8   ISO 8859-8 Latin/Hebrew
8859_9   ISO 8859-9 Latin/Turkish
Big5         The Big 5 encoding for Chinese
CNS11643Chinese

Cp037    EBCDIC American English

Cp273    IBM273
```

Cp277	EBCDIC Danish/Norwegian
Cp278	EBCDIC Finnish/Swedish
Cp280	EBCDIC Italian
Cp284	EBCDIC Spanish
Cp285	EBCDIC UK English
Cp297	EBCDIC French
Cp420	EBCDIC Arabic 1
Cp424	EBCDIC Hebrew
Cp437	the original DOS IBM PC character set, essentially ASCII with a few extra characters for drawing lines and boxes
Cp500	EBCDIC Flemish/Romulsch
Cp737	DOS Greek
Cp775	DOS Baltic
Cp850	DOS Latin-1
Cp852	DOS Latin-2
Cp855	DOS Cyrillic
Cp856	IBM856
Cp857	DOS Turkish
Cp860	DOS Portuguese
Cp861	DOS Icelandic
Cp862	DOS Hebrew
Cp863	DOS Canadian French
Cp864	DOS Arabic
Cp865	IBM865
Cp866	IBM866
Cp868	EBCDIC Arabic
Cp869	DOS modern Greek
Cp870	EBCDIC Serbian
Cp871	EBCDIC Icelandic
Cp874	Windows Thai
Cp875	IBM875
Cp918	EBCDIC Arabic 2
Cp921	IBM921
Cp922	IBM922
Cp1006	IBM1006
Cp1025	IBM1025
Cp1026	IBM1026
Cp1046	IBM1046
Cp1097	IBM1097
Cp1098	IBM1098
Cp1112	IBM1112
Cp1122	IBM1122
Cp1123	IBM1123
Cp1124	IBM1124
Cp1250	Windows Eastern European (essentially ISO Latin-2)
Cp1251	Windows Cyrillic
Cp1252	Windows Western European (essentially ISO-Latin-1)
Cp1253	Windows Greek

```
Cp1254  Windows Turkish
Cp1255  Windows Hebrew
Cp1256  Windows Arabic
Cp1257  Windows Baltic
Cp1258  Windows Vietnamese
EUCJIS  Japanese EUC
GB2312  Chinese
JIS Japanese Hiragana
JIS0208 Japanese
KSC5601 Korean
MacArabic    The Macintosh Arabic character set
MacCentralEurope  The Macintosh Central European character set
MacCroatian  The Macintosh Croatian character set
MacCyrillic  The Macintosh Cyrillic character set
MacDingbat   Zapf Dingbats
MacGreek The Macintosh modern Greek character set
MacHebrew    The Macintosh Hebrew character set
MacIceland   The Macintosh Icelandic character set
MacRoman The Macintosh Roman character set
MacRomania   The Macintosh Romanian character set
MacSymbol    The Symbol font (includes a complete Greek alphabet in
place of the usual Roman letters)
MacThai The Macintosh Thai character set
MacTurkish   The Macintosh Turkish character set
MacUkraine   The Macintosh Ukrainian character set
SJIS    Windows Japanese
UTF8    UCS Transformation Format, 8-bit form
Unicode Normal Unicode
UnicodeBig   Unicode with big-endian byte order
```

Note that just because Java can read and write the appropriate bytes for a character set does not mean the host platform has the fonts needed to display that character set.

10.18.5 The Output Stream Writer Class

The java.io.OutputStreamWriter class connects byte streams and character streams: It writes bytes onto the underlying output stream after translating characters according to a specified character encoding.

The encoding can be set in the constructor, or you can accept the platform's default encoding.

```
public OutputStreamWriter(OutputStream out, String enc)
throws UnsupportedEncodingException
public OutputStreamWriter(OutputStream out)
```

For example, to attach an OutputStreamWriter to System.out with the default encoding, (generally ISO Latin-1):

```
OutputStreamWriter osw = new OutputStreamWriter(System.out);
```

On the other hand if you wanted to write a file encoded in the Macintosh Symbol font, you might do this:

```
FileOutputStream fos = new FileOutputStream("symbol.txt");
```

```
OutputStreamWriter osw = new OutputStreamWriter(fos, "MacSymbol");
public String getEncoding()
```

The getEncoding() method returns a string containing the name of the encoding used by this writer.

The other methods just override methods from java.io.Writer, but behave identically from the perspective of the programmer.

```
public void write(int c) throws IOException
public void write(char c[], int offset, int length) throws IOException
public void write(String s, int offset, int length) throws IOException
public void flush() throws IOException
public void close() throws IOException
```

10.19 Reading Files

The FileReader class reads text files using the platform's default character encoding and the buffer size. If you need to change these values, construct an InputStreamReader on a FileInputStream instead.

```
public FileReader(String fileName) throws FileNotFoundException
public FileReader(File file) throws FileNotFoundException
public FileReader(FileDescriptor fd)
Only the constructors are declared in this class. For example,
FileReader fr = new FileReader("36");
```

10.20 Writing Text Files

The java.io.FileWriter class writes text files using the platform's default character encoding and the buffer size. If you need to change these values, construct an OutputStreamReader on a FileOutputStream instead.

```
public FileWriter(String fileName) throws IOException
public FileWriter(String fileName, boolean append) throws IOException
public FileWriter(File file) throws IOException
public FileWriter(FileDescriptor fd)
Only the constructors are declared in this class. For example,
FileWriter fw = new FileWriter("36");
```

10.20.1 Buffering Reads for Better Performance

The java.io.BufferedReader class is a subclass of java.io.Reader that you chain to another Reader class to buffer characters. This allows more efficient reading of characters and lines.

The BufferedReader is also notable for its readLine() method that allows you to read text a line at a time.

Each time you read from an unbuffered Reader, there's a matching read from the underlying input stream. Therefore it's a good idea to wrap a BufferedReader around each Reader whose read() operations are expensive, such as a FileReader. For example,

```
BufferedReader br = new BufferedReader(new FileReader("37"));
```

There are two constructors, one with a default buffer size of 8192 characters, and one that lets you specify the buffer size:

```
public BufferedReader(Reader in, int sz)
```

```
public BufferedReader(Reader in)
```

The one new method in this class is readLine().
public String readLine() throws IOException
This method returns a String that contains a line of text from a text file. \r, \n, and \r\n are assumed to be line breaks and are not included in the returned String. The following example reads a text file, line by line, and prints it to System.out:

```
// Implement the Unix cat utility in java
import java.io.*;
class cat {
public static void main (String args[]) {
String thisLine;
//Loop across the arguments
for (int i=0; i < args.length; i++) {
//Open the file for reading
try {
BufferedReader br = new BufferedReader(new FileReader(args[i]));
while ((thisLine = br.readLine()) != null) { // while loop begins
here
System.out.println(thisLine);
} // end while
} // end try
catch (IOException e) {
System.err.println("Error: " + e);
}
} // end for
} // end main
}
```

BufferedReaders do support marking and resetting, at least up to the length of the buffer.

```
public boolean markSupported()
public void mark(int readAheadLimit) throws IOException
public void reset() throws IOException
```

Finally, BufferedReader overrides several methods from the superclass Reader; but how you use them does not change at all:

```
public int read() throws IOException
public int read(char c[], int off, int length) throws IOException
public long skip(long n) throws IOException
public boolean ready() throws IOException
public void close() throws IOException
```

10.20.2 Line Numbering

The java.io.LineNumberReader class is a subclass of java.io.BufferedReader that keeps track of which line you're currently reading. It has all the methods of BufferedReader including readLine(). It also has two constructors, getLineNumber(), and setLineNumber() methods:

```
public LineNumberReader(Reader in)
public LineNumberReader(Reader in, int size)
public void setLineNumber(int lineNumber)
```

```
public int getLineNumber()
```

The setLineNumber() method does not change the file pointer. It just changes the value getLineNumber() returns. For example, it would allow you to start counting from -5 if you knew there were six lines of header data you didn't want to count.

The following example reads a text file, line by line, and prints it to System.out but prefixes each line with a line number:

```
import java.io.*;
class linecat  {
public static void main (String args[]) {
String thisLine;
//Loop across the arguments
for (int i=0; i < args.length; i++) {
//Open the file for reading
try {
LineNumberReader br = new LineNumberReader(new FileReader(args[i]));
while ((thisLine = br.readLine()) != null) { // while loop begins
here
System.out.println(br.getLineNumber() + ": " + thisLine);
} // end while
} // end try
catch (IOException e) {
System.err.println("Error: " + e);
}
} // end for
} // end main
}
```

10.20.3 Buffering Writes for Better Performance

The java.io.BufferedWriter class is a subclass of java.io.Writer that you chain to another Writer class to buffer characters. This allows more efficient writing of text.

Each time you write to an unbuffered Writer, there's a matching write to the underlying output stream. Therefore it's a good idea to wrap a BufferedWriter around each Writer whose write() operations are expensive and that does not require immediate response, such as a FileWriter. For example,

```
BufferedWriter bw = new BufferedWriter(new FileWriter("37"));
```

There are two constructors, one with a default buffer size of 8192 characters, and one that lets you specify the buffer size:

```
public BufferedWriter(Writer out)
public BufferedWriter(Writer out, int size)
```

The one new method in this class is newLine(). This method that writes a platform dependent line terminator string, \n on Unix, \r on the Mac, \r\n on Windows.

```
public String newLine() throws IOException
```

Finally, BufferedWriter overrides several methods from the superclass Writer; but how you use them does not change at all:

```
public void write(int c) throws IOException
```

```
public void write(char c[], int off, int length) throws IOException
public void write(String s, int offset, int length) throws IOException
public void flush() throws IOException
public void close() throws IOException
```

10.21 Print Writers

The java.io.PrintWriter class is a subclass of java.io.Writer allows you to use the familiar print() and println() methods. It's very similar to the java.io.PrintStream class. The main difference is that it properly handles multiple byte and other non ISO Latin-1 character sets. The other, more minor difference, is that automatic flushing is performed only when println() is invoked, not every time a newline character is seen.

Javasoft would like to deprecate PrintStream and use PrintWriter instead, but that would break too much existing code.

```
public PrintWriter(Writer out)
public PrintWriter(Writer out, boolean autoFlush)
public PrintWriter(OutputStream out)
public PrintWriter(OutputStream out, boolean autoFlush)
public void flush()
public void close()
public boolean checkError()
protected void setError()
public void write(int c)
public void write(char buf[], int offset, int length)
public void write(char buf[])
public void write(String s,
public void write(String s)
public void print(boolean b)
public void print(char c)
public void print(int i)
public void print(long l)
public void print(float f)
public void print(double d)
public void print(char s[])
public void print(String s)
public void print(Object obj)
public void println()
public void println(boolean x)
public void println(char x)
public void println(int x)
public void println(long x)
public void println(float x)
public void println(double x)
public void println(char x[])
public void println(String x)
public void println(Object x)
```

10.22 Java Streams

At this point you might be scratching your head, wondering if there is another design for IO streams that could require more typing. Could someone have come up with an odder design?" Prepare yourself: Java 1.1 makes some significant modifications to the IO stream library. When you see the Reader and Writer classes your first thought (like mine) might be that these were meant to replace the InputStream and OutputStream classes. But that's not the case. Although some aspects of the original streams library are deprecated (if you use them you will receive a warning from the compiler), the old streams have been left in for backwards compatibility and:

New classes have been put into the old hierarchy, so it's obvious that Sun is not abandoning the old streams.

There are times when you're supposed to use classes in the old hierarchy in combination with classes in the new hierarchy and to accomplish this there are "bridge" classes: InputStreamReader converts an InputStream to a Reader and OutputStreamWriter converts an OutputStream to a Writer.

As a result there are situations in which you have more layers of wrapping with the new IO stream library than with the old. Again, this is a drawback of the decorator pattern - the price you pay for added flexibility.

The most important reason for adding the Reader and Writer hierarchies in Java 1.1 is for internationalization. The old IO stream hierarchy supports only 8-bit byte streams and doesn't handle the 16-bit Unicode characters well. Since Unicode is used for internationalization (and Java's native char is 16-bit Unicode), the Reader and Writer hierarchies were added to support Unicode in all IO operations. In addition, the new libraries are designed for faster operations than the old.

As is the practice in this book, I will attempt to provide an overview of the classes but assume that you will use online documentation to determine all the details, such as the exhaustive list of methods.

10.22.1 Sources and Sinks of Data

Almost all of the Java 1.0 IO stream classes have corresponding Java 1.1 classes to provide native Unicode manipulation. It would be easiest to say "Always use the new classes, never use the old ones," but things are not that simple. Sometimes you are forced into using the Java 1.0 IO stream classes because of the library design; in particular, the java.util.zip libraries are new additions to the old stream library and they rely on old stream components. So the most sensible approach to take is to try to use the Reader and Writer classes whenever you can, and you'll discover the situations when you have to drop back into the old libraries because your code won't compile.

Here is a table that shows the correspondence between the sources and sinks of information (that is, where the data physically comes from or goes to) in the old and new libraries.

Sources & Sinks:

```
Java 1.0 class
Corresponding Java 1.1 class
InputStream
Reader
converter: InputStreamReader
OutputStream
Writer
converter: OutputStreamWriter
FileInputStream
FileReader
```

```
FileOutputStream
FileWriter
StringBufferInputStream
StringReader
(no corresponding class)
StringWriter
ByteArrayInputStream
CharArrayReader
ByteArrayOutputStream
CharArrayWriter
PipedInputStream
PipedReader
PipedOutputStream
PipedWriter
```

In general, you'll find that the interfaces in the old library components and the new ones are similar if not identical.

10.22.2 Modifying Stream Behavior

In Java 1.0, streams were adapted for particular needs using "decorator" subclasses of FilterInputStream and FilterOutputStream. Java 1.1 IO streams continues the use of this idea, but the model of deriving all of the decorators from the same "filter" base class is not followed. This can make it a bit confusing if you're trying to understand it by looking at the class hierarchy.

In the following table, the correspondence is a rougher approximation than in the previous table. The difference is because of the class organization: while BufferedOutputStream is a subclass of FilterOutputStream, BufferedWriter is not a subclass of FilterWriter (which, even though it is abstract, has no subclasses and so appears to have been put in either as a placeholder or simply so you wouldn't wonder where it was). However, the interfaces to the classes are quite a close match and it's apparent that you're supposed to use the new versions instead of the old whenever possible (that is, except in cases where you're forced to produce a Stream instead of a Reader or Writer).

```
Filters:
Java 1.0 class
Corresponding Java 1.1 class
FilterInputStream
FilterReader
FilterOutputStream
FilterWriter ( abstract class with no subclasses)
BufferedInputStream
BufferedReader
(also has readLine( ))
BufferedOutputStream
BufferedWriter
DataInputStream
use DataInputStream
(Except when you need to use readLine( ), when you should use a
BufferedReader)
PrintStream
PrintWriter
```

```
LineNumberInputStream
LineNumberReader
StreamTokenizer
StreamTokenizer
(use constructor that takes a Reader instead)
PushBackInputStream
```

PushBackReader

There's one direction that's quite clear: Whenever you want to use readLine( ), you shouldn't do it with a DataInputStream any more (this is met with a deprecation message at compile time), but instead use a BufferedReader. Other than this, DataInputStream is still a "preferred" member of the Java 1.1 IO library.

To make the transition to using a PrintWriter easier, it has constructors that take any OutputStream object. However, PrintWriter has no more support for formatting than PrintStream does; the interfaces are virtually the same.

Unchanged Classes

Apparently, the Java library designers felt that they got some of the classes right the first time so there were no changes to these and you can go on using them as they are:

```
Java 1.0 classes without corresponding Java 1.1 classes
DataOutputStream
File
RandomAccessFile
```

SequenceInputStream

The DataOutputStream, in particular, is used without change, so for storing and retrieving data in a transportable format you're forced to stay in the InputStream and OutputStream hierarchies.

An example

To see the effect of the new classes, let's look at the appropriate portion of the IOStreamDemo.java example modified to use the Reader and Writer classes:

```
//: NewIODemo.java
// Java 1.1 IO typical usage
import java.io.*;

public class NewIODemo {
public static void main(String[] args) {
try {
// 1. Reading input by lines:
BufferedReader in =
new BufferedReader(
new FileReader(args[0]));
String s, s2 = new String();
while((s = in.readLine())!= null)
s2 += s + "\n";
in.close();

// 1b. Reading standard input:
```

```
BufferedReader stdin =
new BufferedReader(
new InputStreamReader(System.in));
System.out.print("Enter a line:");
System.out.println(stdin.readLine());

// 2. Input from memory
StringReader in2 = new StringReader(s2);
int c;
while((c = in2.read()) != -1)
System.out.print((char)c);

// 3. Formatted memory input
try {
DataInputStream in3 =
new DataInputStream(
// Oops: must use deprecated class:
new StringBufferInputStream(s2));
while(true)
System.out.print((char)in3.readByte());
} catch(EOFException e) {
System.out.println("End of stream");
}

// 4. Line numbering & file output
try {
LineNumberReader li =
new LineNumberReader(
new StringReader(s2));
BufferedReader in4 =
new BufferedReader(li);
PrintWriter out1 =
new PrintWriter(
new BufferedWriter(
new FileWriter("IODemo.out")));
while((s = in4.readLine()) != null )
out1.println(
"Line "+ li.getLineNumber() + s);
out1.close();
} catch(EOFException e) {
System.out.println("End of stream");
}

// 5. Storing & recovering data
try {
DataOutputStream out2 =
new DataOutputStream(
new BufferedOutputStream(
```

```
new FileOutputStream("Data.txt")));
out2.writeDouble(3.14159);
out2.writeBytes("That was pi");
out2.close();
DataInputStream in5 =
new DataInputStream(
new BufferedInputStream(
new FileInputStream("Data.txt")));
BufferedReader in5br =
new BufferedReader(
new InputStreamReader(in5));
// Must use DataInputStream for data:
System.out.println(in5.readDouble());
// Can now use the "proper" readLine():
System.out.println(in5br.readLine());
} catch(EOFException e) {
System.out.println("End of stream");
}

// 6. Reading and writing random access
// files is the same as before.
// (not repeated here)

} catch(FileNotFoundException e) {
System.out.println(
"File Not Found:" + args[1]);
} catch(IOException e) {
System.out.println("IO Exception");
}
}
} ///:~
```

In general, you'll see that the conversion is fairly straightforward and the code looks quite similar. There are some important differences, though. First of all, since random access files have not changed, section 6 is not repeated.

Section 1 shrinks a bit because if all you're doing is reading line input you need only to wrap a BufferedReader around a FileReader. Section 1b shows the new way to wrap System.in for reading console input, and this expands because System.in is a DataInputStream and BufferedReader needs a Reader argument, so InputStreamReader is brought in to perform the translation.

In section 2 you can see that if you have a String and want to read from it you just use a StringReader instead of a StringBufferInputStream and the rest of the code is identical.

Section 3 shows a bug in the design of the new IO stream library. If you have a String and you want to read from it, you're not supposed to use a StringBufferInputStream any more. When you compile code involving a StringBufferInputStream constructor, you get a deprecation message telling you to not use it. Instead, you're supposed to use a StringReader. However, if you want to do formatted memory input as in section 3, you're forced to use a DataInputStream - there is no "DataReader" to replace it - and a DataInputStream constructor requires an InputStream argument. So you have no choice but to use the deprecated StringBufferInputStream class. The compiler will give you a deprecation message but there's nothing you can do about it. [48]

Section 4 is a reasonably straightforward translation from the old streams to the new, with no surprises. In section 5, you're forced to use all the old streams classes because DataOutputStream and DataInputStream require them and there are no alternatives. However, you don't get any deprecation messages at compile time. If a stream is deprecated, typically its constructor produces a deprecation message to prevent you from using the entire class, but in the case of DataInputStream only the readLine( ) method is deprecated since you're supposed to use a BufferedReader for readLine( ) (but a DataInputStream for all other formatted input).

If you compare section 5 with that section in IOStreamDemo.java, you'll notice that in this version, the data is written before the text. That's because a bug was introduced in Java 1.1, which is shown in the following code:

```
//: IOBug.java
// Java 1.1 (and higher?) IO Bug
import java.io.*;
public class IOBug {
public static void main(String[] args)
throws Exception {
DataOutputStream out =
new DataOutputStream(
new BufferedOutputStream(
new FileOutputStream("Data.txt")));
out.writeDouble(3.14159);
out.writeBytes("That was the value of pi\n");
out.writeBytes("This is pi/2:\n");
out.writeDouble(3.14159/2);
out.close();
DataInputStream in =
new DataInputStream(
new BufferedInputStream(
new FileInputStream("Data.txt")));
BufferedReader inbr =
new BufferedReader(
new InputStreamReader(in));
// The doubles written BEFORE the line of text
// read back correctly:
System.out.println(in.readDouble());
// Read the lines of text:
System.out.println(inbr.readLine());
System.out.println(inbr.readLine());
// Trying to read the doubles after the line
// produces an end-of-file exception:
System.out.println(in.readDouble());
}
} ///:~
```

It appears that anything you write after a call to writeBytes( ) is not recoverable. This is a rather limiting bug, and we can hope that it will be fixed by the time you read this. You should run the above program to test it; if you don't get an exception and the values print correctly then you're out of the woods.

10.22.3 Redirecting Standard IO

Java 1.1 has added methods in class System that allow you to redirect the standard input, output, and error IO streams using simple static method calls:

```
setIn(InputStream)
setOut(PrintStream)
setErr(PrintStream)
```

Redirecting output is especially useful if you suddenly start creating a large amount of output on your screen and it's scrolling past faster than you can read it. Redirecting input is valuable for a command-line program in which you want to test a particular user-input sequence repeatedly. Here's a simple example that shows the use of these methods:

```
//: Redirecting.java
// Demonstrates the use of redirection for
// standard IO in Java 1.1
import java.io.*;
class Redirecting {
public static void main(String[] args) {
try {
BufferedInputStream in =
new BufferedInputStream(
new FileInputStream(
"Redirecting.java"));
// Produces deprecation message:
PrintStream out =
new PrintStream(
new BufferedOutputStream(
new FileOutputStream("test.out")));
System.setIn(in);
System.setOut(out);
System.setErr(out);

BufferedReader br =
new BufferedReader(
new InputStreamReader(System.in));
String s;
while((s = br.readLine()) != null)
System.out.println(s);
out.close(); // Remember this!
} catch(IOException e) {
e.printStackTrace();
}
}
} ///:~
```

This program attaches standard input to a file, and redirects standard output and standard error to another file.

This is another example in which a deprecation message is inevitable. The message you can get when compiling with the -deprecation flag is:

Note: The constructor java.io.PrintStream(java.io.OutputStream) has been deprecated.

However, both System.setOut( ) and System.setErr( ) require a PrintStream object as an argument, so you are forced to call the PrintStream constructor. You might wonder, if Java 1.1 deprecates the entire PrintStream class by deprecating the constructor, why the library designers, at the same time as they added this deprecation, also add new methods to System that required a PrintStream rather than a PrintWriter, which is the new and preferred replacement. It's a mystery.

10.23 Compression

Java 1.1 has also added some classes to support reading and writing streams in a compressed format. These are wrapped around existing IO classes to provide compression functionality.

One aspect of these Java 1.1 classes stands out: They are not derived from the new Reader and Writer classes, but instead are part of the InputStream and OutputStream hierarchies. So you might be forced to mix the two types of streams. (Remember that you can use InputStreamReader and OutputStreamWriter to provide easy conversion between one type and another.)

Java 1.1 Compression class

```
Function
CheckedInputStream
GetCheckSum( ) produces checksum for any InputStream (not just decompression)
CheckedOutputStream
GetCheckSum( ) produces checksum for any OutputStream (not just compression)
DeflaterOutputStream
Base class for compression classes
ZipOutputStream
A DeflaterOutputStream that compresses data into the Zip file format
GZIPOutputStream
A DeflaterOutputStream that compresses data into the GZIP file format
InflaterInputStream
Base class for decompression classes
ZipInputStream
A DeflaterInputStream that Decompresses data that has been stored in the Zip file format
GZIPInputStream
```

A DeflaterInputStream that decompresses data that has been stored in the GZIP file format

Although there are many compression algorithms, Zip and GZIP are possibly the most commonly used. Thus you can easily manipulate your compressed data with the many tools available for reading and writing these formats.

Simple compression with GZIP

The GZIP interface is simple and thus is probably more appropriate when you have a single stream of data that you want to compress (rather than a collection of dissimilar pieces of data). Here's an example that compresses a single file:

```
//: GZIPcompress.java
// Uses Java 1.1 GZIP compression to compress
// a file whose name is passed on the command
// line.
import java.io.*;
import java.util.zip.*;

public class GZIPcompress {
public static void main(String[] args) {
try {
BufferedReader in =
new BufferedReader(
new FileReader(args[0]));
BufferedOutputStream out =
new BufferedOutputStream(
new GZIPOutputStream(
new FileOutputStream("test.gz")));
System.out.println("Writing file");
int c;
while((c = in.read()) != -1)
out.write(c);
in.close();
out.close();
System.out.println("Reading file");
BufferedReader in2 =
new BufferedReader(
new InputStreamReader(
new GZIPInputStream(
new FileInputStream("test.gz"))));
String s;
while((s = in2.readLine()) != null)
System.out.println(s);
} catch(Exception e) {
e.printStackTrace();
}
}
} ///:~
```

The use of the compression classes is straightforward - you simply wrap your output stream in a GZIPOutputStream or ZipOutputStream and your input stream in a GZIPInputStream or ZipInputStream. All else is ordinary IO reading and writing. This is, however, a good example of when you're forced to mix the old IO streams with the new: in uses the Reader classes, whereas GZIPOutputStream's constructor can accept only an OutputStream object, not a Writer object.

10.24 Multi-File Storage with Zip

The Java 1.1 library that supports the Zip format is much more extensive. With it you can easily store multiple files, and there's even a separate class to make the process of reading a Zip file easy. The library uses the standard Zip format so that it works seamlessly with all the tools currently downloadable on the Internet. The following example has the same form as the previous example, but it handles as many command-line arguments as you want. In addition, it shows the use of the Checksum classes to calculate and verify the checksum for the file. There are two Checksum types: Adler32 (which is faster) and CRC32 (which is slower but slightly more accurate).

```
//: ZipCompress.java
// Uses Java 1.1 Zip compression to compress
// any number of files whose names are passed
// on the command line.
import java.io.*;
import java.util.*;
import java.util.zip.*;

public class ZipCompress {
public static void main(String[] args) {
try {
FileOutputStream f =
new FileOutputStream("test.zip");
CheckedOutputStream csum =
new CheckedOutputStream(
f, new Adler32());
ZipOutputStream out =
new ZipOutputStream(
new BufferedOutputStream(csum));
out.setComment("A test of Java Zipping");
// Can't read the above comment, though
for(int i = 0; i < args.length; i++) {
System.out.println(
"Writing file " + args[i]);
BufferedReader in =
new BufferedReader(
new FileReader(args[i]));
out.putNextEntry(new ZipEntry(args[i]));
int c;
while((c = in.read()) != -1)
out.write(c);
in.close();
}
out.close();
// Checksum valid only after the file
// has been closed!
System.out.println("Checksum: " +
csum.getChecksum().getValue());
// Now extract the files:
System.out.println("Reading file");
FileInputStream fi =
new FileInputStream("test.zip");
CheckedInputStream csumi =
```

```
new CheckedInputStream(
fi, new Adler32());
ZipInputStream in2 =
new ZipInputStream(
new BufferedInputStream(csumi));
ZipEntry ze;
System.out.println("Checksum: " +
csumi.getChecksum().getValue());
while((ze = in2.getNextEntry()) != null) {
System.out.println("Reading file " + ze);
int x;
while((x = in2.read()) != -1)
System.out.write(x);
}
in2.close();
// Alternative way to open and read
// zip files:
ZipFile zf = new ZipFile("test.zip");
Enumeration e = zf.entries();
while(e.hasMoreElements()) {
ZipEntry ze2 = (ZipEntry)e.nextElement();
System.out.println("File: "+ ze2);
// ... and extract the data as before
}
} catch(Exception e) {
e.printStackTrace();
}
}
} ///:~
```

For each file to add to the archive, you must call putNextEntry( ) and pass it a ZipEntry object. The ZipEntry object contains an extensive interface that allows you to get and set all the data available on that particular entry in your Zip file: name, compressed and uncompressed sizes, date, CRC checksum, extra field data, comment, compression method, and whether it's a directory entry. However, even though the Zip format has a way to set a password, this is not supported in Java's Zip library. And although CheckedInputStream and CheckedOutputStream support both Adler32 and CRC32 checksums, the ZipEntry class supports only an interface for CRC. This is a restriction of the underlying Zip format, but it might limit you from using the faster Adler32.

To extract files, ZipInputStream has a getNextEntry( ) method that returns the next ZipEntry if there is one. As a more succinct alternative, you can read the file using a ZipFile object, which has a method entries( ) to return an Enumeration to the ZipEntries.

In order to read the checksum you must somehow have access to the associated Checksum object. Here, a handle to the CheckedOutputStream and CheckedInputStream objects is retained, but you could also just hold onto a handle to the Checksum object.

A baffling method in Zip streams is setComment( ). As shown above, you can set a comment when you're writing a file, but there's no way to recover the comment in the ZipInputStream. Comments appear to be supported fully on an entry-by-entry basis only via ZipEntry.

Of course, you are not limited to files when using the GZIP or Zip libraries - you can compress anything, including data to be sent through a network connection.

10.25 The Java Archive (jar) Utility

The Zip format is also used in the Java 1.1 JAR (Java ARchive) file format, which is a way to collect a group of files into a single compressed file, just like Zip. However, like everything else in Java, JAR files are cross-platform so you don't need to worry about platform issues. You can also include audio and image files as well as class files.

JAR files are particularly helpful when you deal with the Internet. Before JAR files, your Web browser would have to make repeated requests of a Web server in order to download all of the files that make up an applet. In addition, each of these files was uncompressed. By combining all of the files for a particular applet into a single JAR file, only one server request is necessary and the transfer is faster because of compression. And each entry in a JAR file can be digitally signed for security (refer to the Java documentation for details).

A JAR file consists of a single file containing a collection of zipped files along with a "manifest" that describes them. (You can create your own manifest file; otherwise the jar program will do it for you.) You can find out more about JAR manifests in the online documentation.

The jar utility that comes with Sun's JDK automatically compresses the files of your choice. You invoke it on the command line:

jar [options] destination [manifest] inputfile(s)

The options are simply a collection of letters (no hyphen or any other indicator is necessary). These are:

c

Creates a new or empty archive.

t

Lists the table of contents.

x

Extracts all files

x file

Extracts the named file

f

Says: "I'm going to give you the name of the file." If you don't use this, jar assumes that its input will come from standard input, or, if it is creating a file, its output will go to standard output.

m

Says that the first argument will be the name of the user-created manifest file

v

Generates verbose output describing what jar is doing

O

Only store the files; doesn't compress the files (use to create a JAR file that you can put in your classpath)

M

Don't automatically create a manifest file

If a subdirectory is included in the files to be put into the JAR file, that subdirectory is automatically added, including all of its subdirectories, etc. Path information is also preserved.

Here are some typical ways to invoke jar:

```
jar cf myJarFile.jar *.class
```

This creates a JAR file called myJarFile.jar that contains all of the class files in the current directory, along with an automatically-generated manifest file.

```
jar cmf myJarFile.jar myManifestFile.mf *.class
```

Like the previous example, but adding a user-created manifest file called myManifestFile.mf.

```
jar tf myJarFile.jar
```

Produces a table of contents of the files in myJarFile.jar.

```
jar tvf myJarFile.jar
```

Adds the "verbose" flag to give more detailed information about the files in myJarFile.jar.

```
jar cvf myApp.jar audio classes image
```

Assuming audio, classes, and image are subdirectories, this combines all of the subdirectories into the file myApp.jar. The "verbose" flag is also included to give extra feedback while the jar program is working.

If you create a JAR file using the O option, that file can be placed in your CLASSPATH:

```
CLASSPATH="lib1.jar;lib2.jar;"
```

Then Java can search lib1.jar and lib2.jar for class files.

The jar tool isn't as useful as a zip utility. For example, you can't add or update files to an existing JAR file; you can create JAR files only from scratch. Also, you can't move files into a JAR file, erasing them as they are moved. However, a JAR file created on one platform will be transparently readable by the jar tool on any other platform (a problem that sometimes plagues zip utilities).

Java 1.1 UI APIs

Java 1.1 has also added some important new functionality, including focus traversal, desktop color access, printing "inside the sandbox," and the beginnings of clipboard support.

Focus traversal is quite easy, since it's transparently present in the AWT library components and you don't have to do anything to make it work. If you make your own components and want them to handle focus traversal, you override isFocusTraversable( ) to return true. If you want to capture the keyboard focus on a mouse click, you catch the mouse down event and call requestFocus( ).

10.26 Desktop Colors

The desktop colors provide a way for you to know what the various color choices are on the current user's desktop. This way, you can use those colors in your program if you desire. The colors are automatically initialized and placed in static members of class SystemColor, so all you need to do is read the member you're interested in. The names are intentionally self-explanatory: desktop, activeCaption, activeCaptionText, activeCaptionBorder, inactiveCaption, inactiveCaptionText, inactiveCaptionBorder, window, windowBorder, windowText, menu, menuText, text, textText, textHighlight, textHighlightText, textInactiveText, control, controlText, controlHighlight, controlLtHighlight, controlShadow, controlDkShadow, scrollbar, info (for help), and infoText (for help text).

10.27 Printing

Unfortunately, there isn't much that's automatic with printing. Instead you must go through a number of mechanical, non-OO steps in order to print. Printing a component graphically can be slightly more automatic: by default, the print( ) method calls paint( ) to do its work. There are times when this is satisfactory, but if you want to do anything more specialized you must know that you're printing so you can in particular find out the page dimensions.

The following example demonstrates the printing of both text and graphics, and the different approaches you can use for printing graphics. In addition, it tests the printing support:

```
//: PrintDemo.java
// Printing with Java 1.1
import java.awt.*;
import java.awt.event.*;

public class PrintDemo extends Frame {
Button
printText = new Button("Print Text"),
printGraphics = new Button("Print Graphics");
TextField ringNum = new TextField(3);
Choice faces = new Choice();
Graphics g = null;
Plot plot = new Plot3(); // Try different plots
Toolkit tk = Toolkit.getDefaultToolkit();
public PrintDemo() {
ringNum.setText("3");
ringNum.addTextListener(new RingL());
Panel p = new Panel();
p.setLayout(new FlowLayout());
printText.addActionListener(new TBL());
p.add(printText);
p.add(new Label("Font:"));
p.add(faces);
printGraphics.addActionListener(new GBL());
p.add(printGraphics);
p.add(new Label("Rings:"));
p.add(ringNum);
setLayout(new BorderLayout());
add(p, BorderLayout.NORTH);
add(plot, BorderLayout.CENTER);
String[] fontList = tk.getFontList();
for(int i = 0; i < fontList.length; i++)
faces.add(fontList[i]);
faces.select("Serif");
}
class PrintData {
public PrintJob pj;
public int pageWidth, pageHeight;
```

```
PrintData(String jobName) {
pj = getToolkit().getPrintJob(
PrintDemo.this, jobName, null);
if(pj != null) {
pageWidth = pj.getPageDimension().width;
pageHeight= pj.getPageDimension().height;
g = pj.getGraphics();
}
}
void end() { pj.end(); }
}
class ChangeFont {
private int stringHeight;
ChangeFont(String face, int style,int point){
if(g != null) {
g.setFont(new Font(face, style, point));
stringHeight =
g.getFontMetrics().getHeight();
}
}
int stringWidth(String s) {
return g.getFontMetrics().stringWidth(s);
}
int stringHeight() { return stringHeight; }
}
class TBL implements ActionListener {
public void actionPerformed(ActionEvent e) {
PrintData pd =
new PrintData("Print Text Test");
// Null means print job canceled:
if(pd == null) return;
String s = "PrintDemo";
ChangeFont cf = new ChangeFont(
faces.getSelectedItem(), Font.ITALIC,72);
g.drawString(s,
(pd.pageWidth - cf.stringWidth(s)) / 2,
(pd.pageHeight - cf.stringHeight()) / 3);

s = "A smaller point size";
cf = new ChangeFont(
faces.getSelectedItem(), Font.BOLD, 48);
g.drawString(s,
(pd.pageWidth - cf.stringWidth(s)) / 2,
(int)((pd.pageHeight -
cf.stringHeight())/1.5));
g.dispose();
pd.end();
}
```

```
}
class GBL implements ActionListener {
public void actionPerformed(ActionEvent e) {
PrintData pd =
new PrintData("Print Graphics Test");
if(pd == null) return;
plot.print(g);
g.dispose();
pd.end();
}
}
class RingL implements TextListener {
public void textValueChanged(TextEvent e) {
int i = 1;
try {
i = Integer.parseInt(ringNum.getText());
} catch(NumberFormatException ex) {
i = 1;
}
plot.rings = i;
plot.repaint();
}
}
public static void main(String[] args) {
Frame pdemo = new PrintDemo();
pdemo.setTitle("Print Demo");
pdemo.addWindowListener(
new WindowAdapter() {
public void windowClosing(WindowEvent e) {
System.exit(0);
}
});
pdemo.setSize(500, 500);
pdemo.setVisible(true);
}
}

class Plot extends Canvas {
public int rings = 3;
}

class Plot1 extends Plot {
// Default print() calls paint():
public void paint(Graphics g) {
int w = getSize().width;
int h = getSize().height;
int xc = w / 2;
int yc = w / 2;
```

```
int x = 0, y = 0;
for(int i = 0; i < rings; i++) {
if(x < xc && y < yc) {
g.drawOval(x, y, w, h);
x += 10; y += 10;
w -= 20; h -= 20;
}
}
}
}
class Plot2 extends Plot {
// To fit the picture to the page, you must
// know whether you're printing or painting:
public void paint(Graphics g) {
int w, h;
if(g instanceof PrintGraphics) {
PrintJob pj =
((PrintGraphics)g).getPrintJob();
w = pj.getPageDimension().width;
h = pj.getPageDimension().height;
}
else {
w = getSize().width;
h = getSize().height;
}
int xc = w / 2;
int yc = w / 2;
int x = 0, y = 0;
for(int i = 0; i < rings; i++) {
if(x < xc && y < yc) {
g.drawOval(x, y, w, h);
x += 10; y += 10;
w -= 20; h -= 20;
}
}
}
}

class Plot3 extends Plot {
// Somewhat better. Separate
// printing from painting:
public void print(Graphics g) {
// Assume it's a PrintGraphics object:
PrintJob pj =
((PrintGraphics)g).getPrintJob();
int w = pj.getPageDimension().width;
int h = pj.getPageDimension().height;
```

```
doGraphics(g, w, h);
}
public void paint(Graphics g) {
int w = getSize().width;
int h = getSize().height;
doGraphics(g, w, h);
}
private void doGraphics(
Graphics g, int w, int h) {
int xc = w / 2;
int yc = w / 2;
int x = 0, y = 0;
for(int i = 0; i < rings; i++) {
if(x < xc && y < yc) {
g.drawOval(x, y, w, h);
x += 10; y += 10;
w -= 20; h -= 20;
}
}
}
} ///:~
```

The program allows you to select fonts from a Choice list (and you'll see that the number of fonts available in Java 1.1 is still extremely limited, and has nothing to do with any extra fonts you install on your machine). It uses these to print out text in bold, italic, and in different sizes. In addition, a new type of component called a Plot is created to demonstrate graphics. A Plot has rings that it will display on the screen and print onto paper, and the three derived classes Plot1, Plot2, and Plot3 perform these tasks in different ways so that you can see your alternatives when printing graphics. Also, you can change the number of rings in a plot - this is interesting because it shows the printing fragility in Java 1.1. On my system, the printer gave error messages and didn't print correctly when the ring count got "too high" (whatever that means), but worked fine when the count was "low enough." You will notice, too, that the page dimensions produced when printing do not seem to correspond to the actual dimensions of the page. This might be fixed in a future release of Java, and you can use this program to test it.

This program encapsulates functionality inside inner classes whenever possible, to facilitate reuse. For example, whenever you want to begin a print job (whether for graphics or text), you must create a PrintJob object, which has its own Graphics object along with the width and height of the page. The creation of a PrintJob and extraction of page dimensions is encapsulated in the PrintData class.

10.27.1 Printing Text

Conceptually, printing text is straightforward: you choose a typeface and size, decide where the string should go on the page, and draw it with Graphics.drawString( ). This means, however, that you must perform the calculations of exactly where each line will go on the page to make sure it doesn't run off the end of the page or collide with other lines. If you want to make a word processor, your work is cut out for you.

ChangeFont encapsulates a little of the process of changing from one font to another by automatically creating a new Font object with your desired typeface, style (Font.BOLD or Font.ITALIC - there's no support for underline, strikethrough, etc.), and point size. It also simplifies the calculation of the width and height of a string.

When you press the "Print text" button, the TBL listener is activated. You can see that it goes through two iterations of creating a ChangeFont object and calling drawString( ) to print out the string in a calculated position, centered, one-third, and two-thirds down the page, respectively. Notice whether these calculations produce the expected results. (They didn't with the version I used.)

10.27.2 Printing Graphics

W

hen you press the "Print graphics" button the GBL listener is activated. The creation of a PrintData object initializes g, and then you simply call print( ) for the component you want to print. To force printing you must call dispose( ) for the Graphics object and end( ) for the PrintData object (which turns around and calls end( ) for the PrintJob).

The work is going on inside the Plot object. You can see that the base-class Plot is simple - it extends Canvas and contains an int called rings to indicate how many concentric rings to draw on this particular Canvas. The three derived classes show different approaches to accomplishing the same goal: drawing on both the screen and on the printed page.

Plot1 takes the simplest approach to coding: ignore the fact that there are differences in painting and printing, and just override paint( ). The reason this works is that the default print( ) method simply turns around and calls paint( ). However, you'll notice that the size of the output depends on the size of the on-screen canvas, which makes sense since the width and height are determined by calling Canvas.getSize( ). The other situation in which this is acceptable is if your image is always a fixed size.

When the size of the drawing surface is important, then you must discover the dimensions. Unfortunately, this turns out to be awkward, as you can see in Plot2. For some possibly good reason that I don't know, you cannot simply ask the Graphics object the dimensions of its drawing surface. This would have made the whole process quite elegant. Instead, to see if you're printing rather than painting, you must detect the PrintGraphics using the RTTI instanceof keyword (described in Chapter 11), then downcast and call the sole PrintGraphics method: getPrintJob( ). Now you have a handle to the PrintJob and you can find out the width and height of the paper. This is a hacky approach, but perhaps there is some rational reason for it. (On the other hand, you've seen some of the other library designs by now so you might get the impression that the designers were, in fact, just hacking around...)

You can see that paint( ) in Plot2 goes through both possibilities of printing or painting. But since the print( ) method should be called when printing, why not use that? This approach is used in Plot3, and it eliminates the need to use instanceof since inside print( ) you can assume that you can cast to a PrintGraphics object. This is a little better. The situation is improved by placing the common drawing code (once the dimensions have been detected) inside a separate method doGraphics( ).

10.28 Running Frames within Applets

What if you'd like to print from within an applet? Well, to print anything you must get a PrintJob object through a Toolkit object's getPrintJob( ) method, which takes only a Frame object and not an Applet. Thus it would seem that it's possible to print from within an application, but not an applet. However, it turns out that you can create a Frame from within an applet (which is the reverse of what I've been doing for the applet/application examples so far, which has been making an applet and putting inside a Frame). This is a useful technique since it allows you to use many applications within applets (as long as they don't violate applet security). When the application window comes up within an applet, however, you'll notice that the Web browser sticks a little caveat on it, something to the effect of "Warning: Applet Window."

You can see that it's quite straightforward to put a Frame inside an applet. The only thing that you must add is code to dispose( ) of the Frame when the user closes it (instead of calling System.exit( )):

```
//: PrintDemoApplet.java
// Creating a Frame from within an Applet
import java.applet.*;
import java.awt.*;
import java.awt.event.*;

public class PrintDemoApplet extends Applet {
public void init() {
Button b = new Button("Run PrintDemo");
b.addActionListener(new PDL());
add(b);
}
class PDL implements ActionListener {
public void actionPerformed(ActionEvent e) {
final PrintDemo pd = new PrintDemo();
pd.addWindowListener(new WindowAdapter() {
public void windowClosing(WindowEvent e){
pd.dispose();
}
});
pd.setSize(500, 500);
pd.show();
}
}
} ///:~
```

There's some confusion involved with Java 1.1 printing support. Some of the publicity seemed to claim that you'd be able to print from within an applet. However, the Java security system contains a feature that could lock out an applet from initiating its own print job, requiring that the initiation be done via a Web browser or applet viewer. At the time of this writing, this seemed to remain an unresolved issue. When I ran this program from within a Web browser, the PrintDemo window came up just fine, but it wouldn't print from the browser.

10.29 The Clipboard

Java 1.1 supports limited operations with the system clipboard (in the java.awt.datatransfer package). You can copy String objects to the clipboard as text, and you can paste text from the clipboard into String objects. Of course, the clipboard is designed to hold any type of data, but how this data is represented on the clipboard is up to the program doing the cutting and pasting. Although it currently supports only string data, the Java clipboard API provides for extensibility through the concept of a "flavor." When data comes off the clipboard, it has an associated set of flavors that it can be converted to (for example, a graph might be represented as a string of numbers or as an image) and you can see if that particular clipboard data supports the flavor you're interested in.

The following program is a simple demonstration of cut, copy, and paste with String data in a TextArea. One thing you'll notice is that the keyboard sequences you normally use for cutting, copying, and pasting also work. But if you look at any TextField or TextArea in any other program you'll find that they also automatically support the clipboard key sequences. This example simply adds programmatic control of the clipboard, and you could use these techniques if you want to capture clipboard text into some non- TextComponent.

```
//: CutAndPaste.java
// Using the clipboard from Java 1.1
import java.awt.*;
import java.awt.event.*;
import java.awt.datatransfer.*;

public class CutAndPaste extends Frame {
MenuBar mb = new MenuBar();
Menu edit = new Menu("Edit");
MenuItem
cut = new MenuItem("Cut"),
copy = new MenuItem("Copy"),
paste = new MenuItem("Paste");
TextArea text = new TextArea(20,20);
Clipboard clipbd =
getToolkit().getSystemClipboard();
public CutAndPaste() {
cut.addActionListener(new CutL());
copy.addActionListener(new CopyL());
paste.addActionListener(new PasteL());
edit.add(cut);
edit.add(copy);
edit.add(paste);
mb.add(edit);
setMenuBar(mb);
add(text, BorderLayout.CENTER);
}
class CopyL implements ActionListener {
public void actionPerformed(ActionEvent e) {
String selection = text.getSelectedText();
StringSelection clipString =
new StringSelection(selection);
clipbd.setContents(clipString, clipString);
}
}
class CutL implements ActionListener {
public void actionPerformed(ActionEvent e) {
String selection = text.getSelectedText();
StringSelection clipString =
new StringSelection(selection);
clipbd.setContents(clipString, clipString);
text.replaceRange("",
text.getSelectionStart(),
text.getSelectionEnd());
```

```
}
}
class PasteL implements ActionListener {
public void actionPerformed(ActionEvent e) {
Transferable clipData =
clipbd.getContents(CutAndPaste.this);
try {
String clipString =
(String)clipData.
getTransferData(
DataFlavor.stringFlavor);
text.replaceRange(clipString,
text.getSelectionStart(),
text.getSelectionEnd());
} catch(Exception ex) {
System.out.println("not String flavor");
}
}
}
public static void main(String[] args) {
CutAndPaste cp = new CutAndPaste();
cp.addWindowListener(
new WindowAdapter() {
public void windowClosing(WindowEvent e) {
System.exit(0);
}
});
cp.setSize(300,200);
cp.setVisible(true);
}
} ///:~
```

The creation and addition of the menu and TextArea should by now seem a pedestrian activity. What's different is the creation of the Clipboard field clipbd, which is done through the Toolkit.

All the action takes place in the listeners. The CopyL and CutL listeners are the same except for the last line of CutL, which erases the line that's been copied. The special two lines are the creation of a StringSelection object from the String and the call to setContents( ) with this StringSelection. That's all there is to putting a String on the clipboard.

In PasteL, data is pulled off the clipboard using getContents( ). What comes back is a fairly anonymous Transferable object, and you don't really know what it contains. One way to find out is to call getTransferDataFlavors( ), which returns an array of DataFlavor objects indicating which flavors are supported by this particular object. You can also ask it directly with isDataFlavorSupported( ), passing in the flavor you're interested in. Here, however, the bold approach is taken: getTransferData( ) is called assuming that the contents supports the String flavor, and if it doesn't the problem is sorted out in the exception handler.

In the future you can expect more data flavors to be supported.

EXERCISES

1. *Open a text file so that you can read the file one line at a time. Read each line as a String and place that String object into a Vector. Print out all of the lines in the Vector in reverse order.*
2. *Modify Exercise 1 so that the name of the file you read is provided as a command-line argument.*
3. *Modify Exercise 2 to also open a text file so you can write text into it. Write the lines in the Vector, along with line numbers, out to the file.*
4. *Modify Exercise 2 to force all the lines in the Vector to upper case and send the results to System.out.*
5. *Modify Exercise 2 to take additional arguments of words to find in the file. Print out any lines in which the words match.*
6. *In Blips.java, copy the file and rename it to BlipCheck.java and rename the class Blip2 to BlipCheck (making it public in the process). Remove the //! marks in the file and execute the program including the offending lines. Next, comment out the default constructor for BlipCheck. Run it and explain why it works.*
7. *In Blip3.java, comment out the two lines after the phrases "You must do this:" and run the program. Explain the result and why it differs from when the two lines are in the program.*
8. *Convert the SortedWordCount.java program to use the Java 1.1 IO Streams.*
9. *Repair the program CADState.java as described in the text.*

   (Intermediate) In Chapter 7, locate the GreenhouseControls.java example, which consists of three files. In GreenhouseControls.java, the Restart( ) inner class has a hard-coded set of events. Change the program so that it reads the events and their relative times from a text file. (Challenging: Use a factory method from Chapter 16 to build the events.)
10. *Use the java.awt.FileDialog class and the appropriate OutputStream, InputStream, and Reader and Writer classes to make the Open, Save, and Save As commands of last week's text editing program functional. Also rename each window to the name of the file being edited (or Untitled if a new file has not yet been saved.) Finally, keep track of whether or not each window has been modified since being opened. If it has, and the user attempts to close it, then prompt them with the Yes-No-Cancel dialog box from two weeks ago to see if they want to save the file. If they answer yes, you should save the file. If they answer no, just close the window. If they answer cancel, you should not close the window or quit the program.*

Java

Object Oriented Programming in

Vol-2

V.K. Jain
BE, M.TECH, FIE FIETE, MISHRAE
CHARTERED ENGINEER
&
HEMLATA

CYBER TECH PUBLICATIONS
4230/1, First Floor, Ansari Road, Darya Ganj
New Delhi 110002 Ph. : 3244078

JAVA OBJECT ORINTED PROGRAMMING

First Edition 2026

Published by :
Parikshit Rawat for Cyber Tech Publication
4230/1, Ansari Road, Daryaganj,
New Delhi-110 002

Printed at :
Tanwar Printers, Maujpur, Delhi-110053. Ph. : 2195710

FROM AUTHOR'S DESK

Java is a network-oriented programming language invented by Sun Microsystems that is specifically designed for writing programs that can be safely downloaded to your computer through the Internet and immediately run without fear of viruses or other harm to your computer or files. Using small Java programs (called "Applets"), Web pages can include functions such as animations, calculators, and other fancy tricks.

You can expect to see a huge variety of features added to the Web using Java, since you can write a Java program to do almost anything a regular computer program can do, and then include that Java program in a Web page. Therfore learning Java is a must for all students. Java is a need and craze in present day programming environment and is straight forward in the sense that no previous experience is required.

A vast amount of curriculum exists at different levels. Contents have been included in such a manner that needs of almost are available syllabee are fulfilled.

Department of electronics and Computer Society of India together has done a great service to nation by way of accrediting the courses and thus prescribing the syllabi for different levels. This book has been written exactly as per syllabus of DOEACC syllabus for "A" level Examination.Keeping in view the diversified syllabus prescribed by DOEACC every possible efforts have been made to present entire textware in concised form and allout effrts had been made by the author to present the contents commensurate with latest available knowledge on this subjectware. The authors have tried to make the textware as simple as possible. The book is full of Examples and illustrations including real life examples.

The various facaades of computer science are changing its attributes with such a fast speed that its very difficult to keep track of latest development and its a great task to get aware with the latest happenings in the field. Therefore in presenting the state-of-the art textware, immense help had been sought by the authors from various literature forms who in turn expresses his gratitude to the authors of the works from where information has been derived.

We are to acknowledge with great sense of gratitude to Mrs. Heera Jain, Consultant Engineer Amitabh Bajaj BE and Naveena Bajaj M.Sc., Anurag Jain Director NICT (Vikas Marg Branch) and Shree TP Gupta of Compographic for the great help provided in manuscripting and in preperation of the figures etc.

Any suugestions in direction of improving the textware may be forwarded at following address and shall be highly welcome and acknowledged.

Ms. Hemlata
B.A.
Java Programmer
24.3.2001

Er. V.K.Jain
B.E., M.Tech, FIE, FIETE
MISHRAE
Chartered Engineer
11 LF Tansen Marg, N. Delhi.
Tel. 3316697, 3711906

11

String Operations in the Java Library

11.1 Characters and Strings

The Java platform contains three classes that you can use when working with character data:

- Character—A class whose instances can hold a single character value. This class also defines handy methods that can manipulate or inspect single-character data.
- String— A class for working with immutable (unchanging) data composed of multiple characters.
- StringBuffer—A class for storing and manipulating mutable data composed of multiple characters.

11.2 Characters

An object of Character type contains a single character value. You use a Character object instead of a primitive char variable when an object is required-for example, when passing a character value into a method that changes the value or when placing a character value into a data structure, such as a vector, that requires objects. The following sample program, CharacterDemo, creates a few character objects and displays some information about them. The code that is related to the Character class is shown in boldface:

```
public class CharacterDemo {
public static void main(String args[]) {
Character a = new Character('a');
Character a2 = new Character('a');
Character b = new Character('b');
int difference = a.compareTo(b);
if (difference == 0) {
System.out.println("a is equal to b.");
} else if (difference < 0) {
System.out.println("a is less than b.");
} else if (difference > 0) {
System.out.println("a is greater than b.");
}
System.out.println("a is "
+ ((a.equals(a2)) ? "equal" : "not equal")
+ "to a2.");
System.out.println("The character "+ a.toString() + "is "
+ (Character.isUpperCase(a.charValue()) ? "upper" : "lower")
+ "case.");
}
}
```

The following is the output from this program:

a is less than b.
a is equal to a2.
The character a is lowercase.

The CharacterDemo program calls the following constructors and methods provided by the Character class:

Character(char)

The Character class's only constructor, which creates a Character object containing the value provided by the argument. Once a Character object has been created, the value it contains cannot be changed.

compareTo(Character)

An instance method that compares the values held by two character objects: the object on which the method is called (a in the example) and the argument to the method (b in the example). This method returns an integer indicating whether the value in the current object is greater than, equal to, or less than the value held by the argument. A letter is greater than another letter if its numeric value is greater.

equals(Object)

An instance method that compares the value held by the current object with the value held by another. This method returns true if the values held by both objects are equal.

toString()

An instance method that converts the object to a string. The resulting string is one character in length and contains the value held by the character object.

charValue()

An instance method that returns the value held by the character object as a primitive char value.

isUpperCase(char)

A class method that determines whether a primitive char value is uppercase. This is one of many Character class methods that inspect or manipulate character data.

11.3 String and String Buffer

The Java platform provides two classes, String and StringBuffer, that store and manipulate strings-character data consisting of more than one character. The String class provides for strings whose value will not change. For example, if you write a method that requires string data and the method is not going to modify the string in any way, pass a String object into the method. The StringBuffer class provides for strings that will be modified; you use string buffers when you know that the value of the character data will change. You typically use string buffers for constructing character data dynamically: for example, when reading text data from a file. Because strings are constants, they are more efficient to use than are string buffers and can be shared. So it's important to use strings when you can.

Following is a sample program called StringsDemo, which reverses the characters of a string. This program uses both a string and a string buffer.

```
public class StringsDemo {
public static void main(String[] args) {
String palindrome = "Dot saw I was Tod";
int len = palindrome.length();
```

```
StringBuffer dest = new StringBuffer(len);
for (int i = (len - 1); i >= 0; i—) {
dest.append(palindrome.charAt(i));
}
System.out.println(dest.toString());
}
}
```

The output from this program is:

doT saw I was toD

In addition to highlighting the differences between strings and string buffers, this section discusses several features of the String and StringBuffer classes: creating strings and string buffers, using accessor methods to get information about a string or string buffer, and modifying a string buffer.

11.3.1 Creating Strings and StringBuffers

A string is often created from a string literal—a series of characters enclosed in double quotes. For example, when it encounters the following string literal, the Java platform creates a String object whose value is Gobbledygook.

"Gobbledygook"

The StringsDemo program uses this technique to create the string referred to by the palindrome variable:

String palindrome = "Dot saw I was Tod";

You can also create String objects as you would any other Java object: using the new keyword and a constructor. The String class provides several constructors that allow you to provide the initial value of the string, using different sources, such as an array of characters, an array of bytes, or a string buffer.

Here's an example of creating a string from a character array:

```
char[] helloArray = { 'h', 'e', 'l', 'l', 'o' };
helloString = new String(helloArray);
System.out.println(helloString);
```

The last line of this code snippet displays: hello.

You must always use new to create a string buffer. The StringsDemo program creates the string buffer referred to by dest, using the constructor that sets the buffer's capacity:

```
String palindrome = "Dot saw I was Tod";
int len = palindrome.length();
StringBuffer dest = new StringBuffer(len);
```

This code creates the string buffer with an initial capacity equal to the length of the string referred to by the name palindrome. This ensures only one memory allocation for dest because it's just big enough to contain the characters that will be copied to it. By initializing the string buffer's capacity to a reasonable first guess, you minimize the number of times memory must be allocated for it. This makes your code more efficient because memory allocation is a relatively expensive operation.

11.4 Accessor Methods

Getting the Length of a String or a String Buffer

Methods used to obtain information about an object are known as accessor methods. One accessor method that you can use with both strings and string buffers is the length method, which returns the number of characters contained in the string or the string buffer. After the following two lines of code have been executed, len equals 17:

```
String palindrome = "Dot saw I was Tod";
int len = palindrome.length();
```

In addition to length, the StringBuffer class has a method called capacity, which returns the amount of space allocated for the string buffer rather than the amount of space used. For example, the capacity of the string buffer referred to by dest in the StringsDemo program never changes, although its length increases by 1 for each iteration of the loop. The following figure shows the capacity and the length of dest after nine characters have been appended to it.

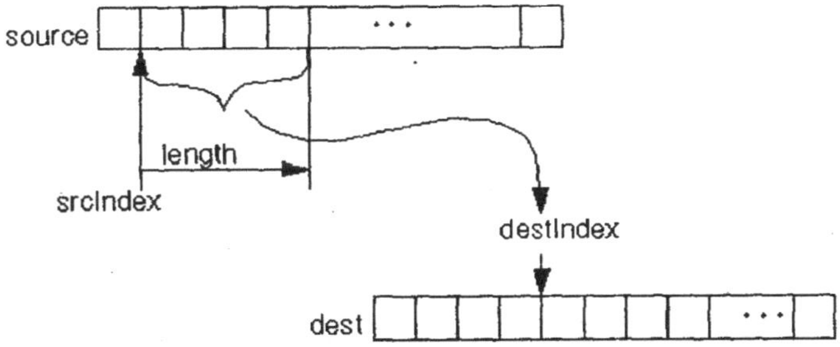

A string buffer's length is the number of characters it contains; a string buffer's capacity is the number of character spaces that have been allocated. The String class doesn't have a capacity method, because a string cannot change.

Getting Characters by Index from a String or a String Buffer

You can get the character at a particular index within a string or a string buffer by using the charAt accessor. The index of the first character is 0; the index of the last is length()-1. For example, the following code gets the character at index 9 in a string:

```
String anotherPalindrome = "Niagara. O roar again!";
char aChar = anotherPalindrome.charAt(9);
```

Indices begin at 0, so the character at index 9 is 'O', as illustrated in the following figure:

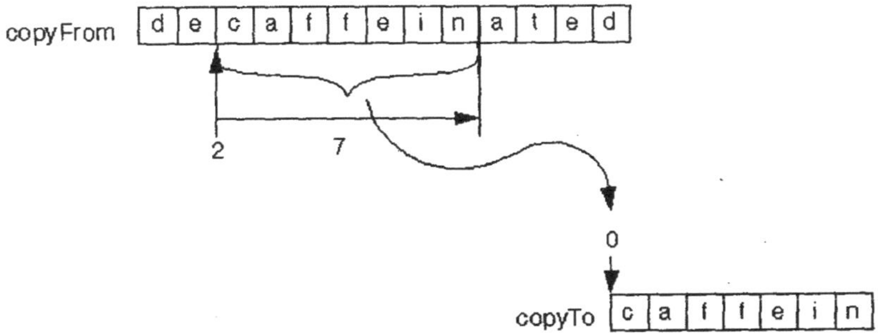

Use the charAt method to get a character at a particular index. The figure also shows that to compute the index of the last character of a string, you have to subtract 1 from the value returned by the length method.

If you want to get more than one character from a string or a string buffer, you can use the substring method. The substring method has two versions, as shown in the following table:

The following code gets from the Niagara palindrome the substring that extends from index 11 to index 15, which is the word "roar":

```
String anotherPalindrome = "Niagara. O roar again!";
String roar = anotherPalindrome.substring(11, 15);
```

Use the substring method to get part of a string or string buffer. Remember that indices begin at 0.

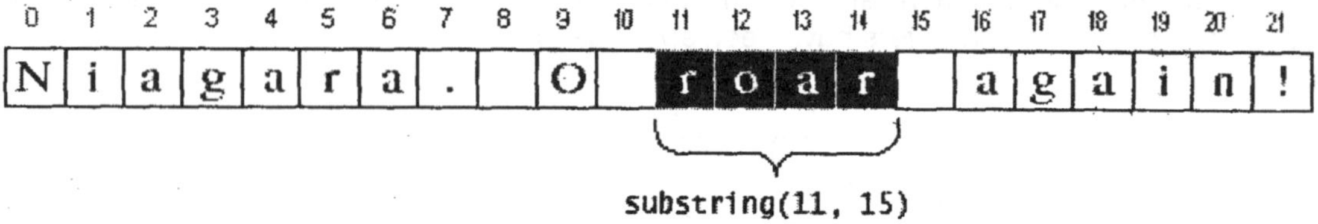

11.4.1 More Accessor Methods For the String Class

In addition to the length and charAt accessors you saw on the previous page, the String class provides two accessors that return the position within the string of a specific character or string: indexOf and lastIndexOf. The indexOf method searches forward from the beginning of the string, and lastIndexOf searches backward from the end of the string.

The indexOf and lastIndexOf methods are frequently used with substring, which returns a substring of the string. The following class illustrates the use of lastIndexOf and substring to isolate different parts of a filename.

Note: The methods in the following Filename class don't do any error checking and assume that their argument contains a full directory path and a filename with an extension. If these methods were production code they would verify that their arguments were properly constructed.

```
// This class assumes that the string used to initialize
// fullPath has a directory path, filename, and extension.
// The methods won't work if it doesn't.
public class Filename {
private String fullPath;
private char pathSeparator, extensionSeparator;

public Filename(String str, char sep, char ext) {
fullPath = str;
pathSeparator = sep;
extensionSeparator = ext;
}
public String extension() {
int dot = fullPath.lastIndexOf(extensionSeparator);
return fullPath.substring(dot + 1);
}

public String filename() {
int dot = fullPath.lastIndexOf(extensionSeparator);
```

```
int sep = fullPath.lastIndexOf(pathSeparator);
return fullPath.substring(sep + 1, dot);
}

public String path() {
int sep = fullPath.lastIndexOf(pathSeparator);
return fullPath.substring(0, sep);
}
}

Here's a small program that constructs a Filename object and calls
all of its methods:
public class FilenameDemo {
public static void main(String[] args) {
Filename myHomePage = new Filename("/home/mem/index.html",
'/', '.');
System.out.println("Extension = " + myHomePage.extension());
System.out.println("Filename = " + myHomePage.filename());
System.out.println("Path = " + myHomePage.path());
}
}
```

And here's the output from the program:

```
Extension = html
Filename = index
Path = /home/mem
```

The extension method uses lastIndexOf to locate the last occurrence of the period (.) in the filename. Then substring uses the return value of lastIndexOf to extract the filename extension—that is, the substring from the period to the end of the string. This code assumes that the filename actually has a period in it; if the filename does not have a period , then lastIndexOf returns -1, and the substring method throws a StringIndexOutOfBoundsException.

Also, notice that extension uses dot + 1 as the argument to substring. If the period character is the last character of the string, then dot + 1 is equal to the length of the string which is one larger than the largest index into the string (because indices start at 0). However, substring accepts an index equal to but not greater than the length of the string and interprets it to mean "the end of the string."

Try this: Inspect the other methods in the Filename class and notice how the lastIndexOf and substring methods work together to isolate different parts of a filename.

While the methods in the example above use only one version of the lastIndexOf method, the String class actually supports four different versions of both the indexOf and lastIndexOf methods. The four versions work as follows:

```
indexOf(int character)
lastIndexOf(int character)
Return the index of the first (last) occurrence of the specified
character.
indexOf(int character, int from)
lastIndexOf(int character, int from)
```

Return the index of the first (last) occurrence of the specified character, searching forward (backward) from the specified index.

```
indexOf(String string)
lastIndexOf(String string)
Return the index of the first (last) occurrence of the specified
String.
indexOf(String string, int from)
lastIndexOf(String string, int from)
```

Return the index of the first (last) occurrence of the specified String, searching forward (backward) from the specified index.

For the StringBuffer Class

Like String, StringBuffer provides length and charAt accessor methods. In addition to these two accessors, StringBuffer also has a method called capacity. The capacity method differs from length in that it returns the amount of space currently allocated for the StringBuffer, rather than the amount of space used. For example, the capacity of the StringBuffer in the reverseIt method shown here never changes, while the length of the StringBuffer increases by one for each iteration of the loop:

```
public class ReverseString {
public static String reverseIt(String source) {
int i, len = source.length();
StringBuffer dest = new StringBuffer(len);
for (i = (len - 1); i >= 0; i–)
dest.append(source.charAt(i));
return dest.toString();
}
}
```

Modifying StringBuffers

The reverseIt method uses StringBuffer's append method to add a character to the end of the destination string: dest.

```
class ReverseString {
public static String reverseIt(String source) {
int i, len = source.length();
StringBuffer dest = new StringBuffer(len);

for (i = (len - 1); i >= 0; i–) {
dest.append(source.charAt(i));
}
return dest.toString();
}
}
```

If the appended character causes the size of the StringBuffer to grow beyond its current capacity, the StringBuffer allocates more memory. Because memory allocation is a relatively expensive operation, you can make your code more efficient by initializing a StringBuffer's capacity to a reasonable first guess, thereby minimizing the number of times memory must be allocated for it. For example, the reverseIt method constructs the StringBuffer with an initial capacity equal to the length of the source string, ensuring only one memory allocation for dest.

The version of the append method used in reverseIt is only one of the StringBuffer methods that appends data to the end of a StringBuffer. There are several append methods that append data of various types, such as float, int, boolean, and even Object, to the end of the StringBuffer. The data is converted to a string before the append operation takes place.

11.5 Inserting Characters

At times, you may want to insert data into the middle of a StringBuffer. You do this with one of StringBufffer's insert methods. This example illustrates how you would insert a string into a StringBuffer:

```
StringBuffer sb = new StringBuffer("Drink Java!");
sb.insert(6, "Hot ");
System.out.println(sb.toString());
```

This code snippet prints:

Drink Hot Java!

With StringBuffer's many insert methods, you specify the index before which you want the data inserted. In the example, "Hot " needed to be inserted before the 'J' in "Java". Indices begin at 0, so the index for 'J' is 6. To insert data at the beginning of a StringBuffer, use an index of 0. To add data at the end of a StringBuffer, use an index equal to the current length of the StringBuffer or use append.

Setting Characters

Another useful StringBuffer modifier is setCharAt, which replaces the character at a specific location in the StringBuffer with the character specified in the argument list.. setCharAt is useful when you want to reuse a StringBuffer.

11.6 Converting Objects to Strings

11.6.1 The to String Method

It's often convenient or necessary to convert an object to a String because you need to pass it to a method that accepts only String values. The reverseIt method used earlier in this lesson uses StringBuffer's toString method to convert the StringBuffer to a String object before returning the String.

```
class ReverseString {
public static String reverseIt(String source) {
int i, len = source.length();
StringBuffer dest = new StringBuffer(len);
for (i = (len - 1); i >= 0; i—) {
dest.append(source.charAt(i));
}
return dest.toString();
}
}
```

All classes inherit toString from the Object class and many classes in the java.lang package override this method to provide an implementation that is meaningful to that class. For example, the "type wrapper" classes—Character, Integer, Boolean, and the others—all override toString to provide a String representation of the object.

11.6.2 The valueOf Method

As a convenience, the String class provides the class method valueOf, You can use valueOf to convert variables of different types to Strings. For example, to print the value of pi:

System.out.println(String.valueOf(Math.PI));

11.7 Converting Strings to Numbers

The String class itself does not provide any methods for converting a String to a floating point, integer, or other numerical type. However, four of the "type wrapper" classes (Integer, Double, Float, and Long) provide a class method named valueOf that converts a String to an object of that type. Here's a small, contrived example of the Float class's valueOf:

```
String piStr = "3.14159";
Float pi = Float.valueOf(piStr);
```

11.7.1 Strings and the Java Compiler

The Java compiler uses the String and StringBuffer classes behind the scenes to handle literal strings and concatenation.

```
Literal Strings
In Java, you specify literal strings between double quotes:
"Hello World!"
```

You can use literal strings anywhere you would use a String object. For example, System.out.println accepts a String argument, so you could use a literal string in place of a String there.

System.out.println("Might I add that you look lovely today.");

You can also use String methods directly from a literal string.

```
int len = "Goodbye Cruel World".length();
```

Because the compiler automatically creates a new String object for every literal string it encounters, you can use a literal string to initialize a String.

```
String s = "Hola Mundo";
```

The above construct is equivalent to, but more efficient than, this one, which ends up creating two Strings instead of one:

```
String s = new String("Hola Mundo");
```

The compiler creates the first string when it encounters the literal string "Hola Mundo!", and the second one when it encounters new String.

```
Concatenation and the + Operator
```

In Java, you can use + to concatenate Strings together:

```
String cat = "cat";

System.out.println("con" + cat + "enation");
```

This is a little deceptive because, as you know, Strings can't be changed. However, behind the scenes the compiler uses StringBuffers to implement concatenation. The above example compiles to:

```
String cat = "cat";
```

System.out.println(new StringBuffer().append("con").

```
append(cat).append("enation").toString());
```

You can also use the + operator to append values to a String that are not themselves Strings:

```
System.out.println("Java's Number " + 1);
```

The compiler converts the non-String value (the integer 1 in the example) to a String object before performing the concatenation operation.

11.7.2 Summary of Strings

The following table summarizes the methods found in the String and StringBuffer classes.

Summary of the String Class

Method or Constructor Purpose

```
String()
String (byte[])
String (byte[], int, int)
String (byte[], int, int, String)
String (byte[], String)
String (char[])
String (char[], int, int)
String (String)
```

String (StringBuffer) Creates a new string object. For all constructors that take arguments, the first argument provides the value for the string.

11.8 Other Interesting Features

String and StringBuffer provide several other useful ways to manipul ate string data, including concatenation, comparison, substitution, and conversion to upper and lower case. java.lang.String and java.lang.StringBuffer summarize and list all of the methods and variables supported by these two classes.

Here's a fun program, Palindrome, that determines whether a string is a palindrome. This program uses many methods from the String and the StringBuffer classes:

```
public class Palindrome {
public static boolean isPalindrome(String stringToTest) {
String workingCopy = removeJunk(stringToTest);
String reversedCopy = reverse(workingCopy);
return reversedCopy.equalsIgnoreCase(workingCopy);
}
protected static String removeJunk(String string) {
int i, len = string.length();
StringBuffer dest = new StringBuffer(len);
char c;

for (i = (len - 1); i >= 0; i--) {
c = string.charAt(i);
if (Character.isLetterOrDigit(c)) {
dest.append(c);
}
}
return dest.toString();
```

```
}
protected static String reverse(String string) {
StringBuffer sb = new StringBuffer(string);
return sb.reverse().toString();
}
public static void main(String[] args) {
String string = "Madam, I'm Adam.";
System.out.println();
System.out.println("Testing whether the following"
+ "string is a palindrome:");
System.out.println("    "+ string);
System.out.println();
if (isPalindrome(string)) {
System.out.println("It IS a palindrome!");
} else {
System.out.println("It is NOT a palindrome!");
}
System.out.println();
}
}
```

The output from this program is:

Testing whether the following string is a palindrome:

```
Madam, I'm Adam.
It IS a palindrome!
```

11.9 Arrays and Strings

Like other programming languages, Java allows you to collect and manage multiple values through an array object. You manage data comprised of multiple characters through a String object.

As you already know a sequence of character data is called a string and is implemented in the Java environment by the String class (a member of the java.lang package). Count's main method uses Strings in its the declaration of the args array:

String[] args

This code explicitly declares an array named args that contains String objects. The empty brackets indicate that the length of the array is unknown at compilation time because the array is passed in at runtime. The countChars method also uses two Strings both in the form of a literal string (a string of characters between double quotation marks):

```
"Counted "
. . .
" chars."
```

The program implicitly allocates two String objects, one for each of the two literal strings shown previously. String objects are immutable—that is, they cannot be changed once they've been created. The java.lang package provides a different class, StringBuffer, which you can use to create and manipulate character data on the fly. Using String and StringBuffer covers thoroughly the use of both the String and StringBuffer classes.

11.10 String Concatenation

Java lets you concatenate strings together easily using the + operator. The countChars method uses this feature of the Java language to print its output. The following code snippet concatenates three strings together to produce its output:

"Counted " + count + " chars."

Two of the strings concatenated together are literal strings: "Counted " and " chars." The third string—the one in the middle—is actually an integer that first gets converted to a string and then is concatenated to the others.

11.11 I/O Library

Creating a good input/output (IO) system is one of the more difficult tasks for the language designer.

This is evidenced by the number of different approaches. The challenge seems to be in covering all eventualities. Not only are there different kinds of IO that you want to communicate with (files, the console, network connections), but you need to talk to them in a wide variety of ways (sequential, random-access, binary, character, by lines, by words, etc.).

The Java library designers attacked the problem by creating lots of classes. In fact, there are so many classes for Java's IO system that it can be intimidating at first (ironically, the Java IO design actually prevents an explosion of classes). There has also been a significant change in the IO library between Java 1.0 and Java 1.1. Instead of simply replacing the old library with a new one, the designers at Sun extended the old library and added the new one alongside it. As a result you can sometimes end up mixing the old and new libraries and creating even more intimidating code.

This chapter will help you understand the variety of IO classes in the standard Java library and how to use them. The first portion of the chapter will introduce the "old" Java 1.0 IO stream library, since there is a significant amount of existing code that uses that library. The remainder of the chapter will introduce the new features in the Java 1.1 IO library. Note that when you compile some of the code in the first part of the chapter with a Java 1.1 compiler you can get a "deprecated feature" warning message at compile time. The code still works; the compiler is just suggesting that you use certain new features that are described in the latter part of this chapter. It is valuable, however, to see the difference between the old and new way of doing things and that's why it was left in - to increase your understanding (and to allow you to read code written for Java 1.0).

11.12 Input and Output

The Java library classes for IO are divided by input and output, as you can see by looking at the online Java class hierarchy with your Web browser. By inheritance, all classes derived from InputStream have basic methods called read( ) for reading a single byte or array of bytes. Likewise, all classes derived from OutputStream have basic methods called write( ) for writing a single byte or array of bytes. However, you won't generally use these methods; they exist so more sophisticated classes can use them as they provide a more useful interface. Thus, you'll rarely create your stream object by using a single class, but instead will layer multiple objects together to provide your desired functionality. The fact that you create more than one object to create a single resulting stream is the primary reason that Java's stream library is confusing.

It's helpful to categorize the classes by their functionality. The library designers started by deciding that all classes that had anything to do with input would be inherited from InputStream and all classes that were associated with output would be inherited from OutputStream.

QUESTIONS

1. What is the initial capacity of the following string buffer?

   StringBuffer sb = new StringBuffer("Able was I ere I saw Elba.");

2. Consider the following string:

   String hannah = "Did Hannah see bees? Hannah did.";

   (a) What is the value displayed by the expression hannah.length()?
   (b) What is the value returned by the method call hannah.charAt(12)?
   (c) Write an expression that refers to the letter b in the string referred to by hannah.

3. How long is the string returned by the following expression? What is the string?

   "Was it a car or a cat I saw?".substring(9, 12)

4. In the following program, called ComputeResult, what is the value of result after each numbered line executes?

```
public class ComputeResult {
public static void main(String[] args) {
String original = "software";
StringBuffer result = new StringBuffer("hi");
int index = original.indexOf('a');
/*1*/    result.setCharAt(0, original.charAt(0));
/*2*/    result.setCharAt(1, original.charAt(original.length()-1));
/*3*/    result.insert(1, original.charAt(4));
/*4*/    result.append(original.substring(1,4));
/*5*/    result.insert(3, (original.substring(index, index+2) + " "));
System.out.println(result);
}
}
```

EXERCISES

5. Show two ways to concatenate the following two strings together to get the string "Hi, mom.":

   String hi = "Hi, ";
   String mom = "mom.";

6. Write a program that computes your initials from your full name and displays them.

7. An anagram is a word or a phrase made by transposing the letters of another word or phrase; for example, "parliament" is an anagram of "partial men," and "software" is an anagram of "swear oft." Write a program that figures out whether one string is an anagram of another string. The program should ignore white space and punctuation.

12 Exploring Java Lang

12.1 Simple Wrappers

12.1.1 Numbers

This section begins with a discussion of the Number class in java.lang and its subclasses. In particular, this section talks about why you might need these classes, points out the common methods and class variables they have in common, and shows you how to convert instances to strings.

Additionally, this section talks about other classes you might need to work with numbers. For instance, if you need to display a number in a particular format, you can use the NumberFormat and DecimalFormat classes in java.text to format them. Also, the Math class in java.lang contains class methods that perform mathematical functions beyond those provided by the language. This class has methods for the trigonometric functions, exponential functions, and so on.

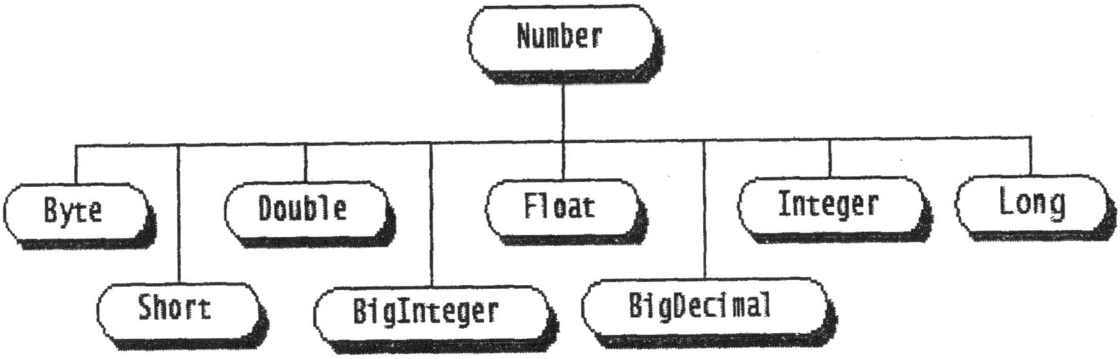

Fig. 12.1

12.1.2 Formatting Numbers

Programs store and operate on numbers in a locale-independent way. Before displaying or printing a number, a program must convert it to a String that is in a locale-sensitive format. For example, in France the number 123456.78 should be formatted as 123 456,78, and in Germany it should appear as 123.456,78. In this section, you will learn how to make your programs independent of the locale conventions for decimal points, thousands-separators, and other formatting properties.

12.1.3 Using Predefined Formats

By invoking the methods provided by the NumberFormat class, you can format numbers, currencies, and percentages according to Locale. The material that follows demonstrates formatting techniques with a sample program called NumberFormatDemo.

(1) Numbers

You can use the NumberFormat methods to format primitive-type numbers, such as double, and their corresponding wrapper objects, such as Double.

The following code example formats a Double according to Locale. Invoking the getNumberInstance method returns a locale-specific instance of NumberFormat. The format method accepts the Double as an argument and returns the formatted number in a String.

```
Double amount = new Double(345987.246);
NumberFormat numberFormatter;
String amountOut;
numberFormatter = NumberFormat.getNumberInstance(currentLocale);
amountOut = numberFormatter.format(amount);
System.out.println(amountOut + " " +
currentLocale.toString());
```

The output from this example shows how the format of the same number varies with Locale:

```
345 987,246     fr_FR
345.987,246     de_DE
345,987.246     en_US
```

(2) Currencies

If you're writing business applications, you'll probably need to format and to display currencies. You format currencies in the same manner as numbers, except that you call getCurrencyInstance to create a formatter. When you invoke the format method, it returns a String that includes the formatted number and the appropriate currency sign.

This code example shows how to format currency in a locale-specific manner:

```
Double currency = new Double(9876543.21);
NumberFormat currencyFormatter;
String currencyOut;
currencyFormatter = NumberFormat.getCurrencyInstance(currentLocale);
currencyOut = currencyFormatter.format(currency);
System.out.println(currencyOut + " " +
currentLocale.toString());
The output generated by the preceding lines of code is as follows:
9 876 543,21 F  fr_FR
9.876.543,21 DM      de_DE
$9,876,543.21   en_US
```

At first glance this output may look wrong to you, because the numeric values are all the same. Of course, 9 876 543,21 F is not equivalent to 9.876.543,21 DM. However, bear in mind that the NumberFormat class is unaware of exchange rates. The methods belonging to the NumberFormat class format currencies but do not convert them.

(3) Percentages

You can also use the methods of the NumberFormat class to format percentages. To get the locale-specific formatter, invoke the getPercentInstance method. With this formatter, a decimal fraction such as 0.75 is displayed as 75%.

The following code sample shows how to format a percentage.

```
Double percent = new Double(0.75);
NumberFormat percentFormatter;
String percentOut;
percentFormatter = NumberFormat.getPercentInstance(currentLocale);
percentOut = percentFormatter.format(percent);
```

12.1.4 Customizing Formats

You can use the DecimalFormat class to format decimal numbers into locale-specific strings. This class allows you to control the display of leading and trailing zeros, prefixes and suffixes, grouping (thousands) separators, and the decimal separator. If you want to change formatting symbols, such as the decimal separator, you can use the DecimalFormatSymbols in conjunction with the DecimalFormat class. These classes offer a great deal of flexibility in the formatting of numbers, but they can make your code more complex.

The text that follows uses examples that demonstrate the DecimalFormat and DecimalFormatSymbols classes. The code examples in this material are from a sample program called DecimalFormatDemo.

12.2 Constructing Patterns

You specify the formatting properties of DecimalFormat with a pattern String. The pattern determines what the formatted number looks like. For a full description of the pattern syntax, see Number Format Pattern Syntax.

The example that follows creates a formatter by passing a pattern String to the DecimalFormat constructor. The format method accepts a double value as an argument and returns the formatted number in a String:

```
DecimalFormat myFormatter = new DecimalFormat(pattern);
String output = myFormatter.format(value);
System.out.println(value + "" + pattern + " " + output);
```

The output for the preceding lines of code is described in the following table. The value is the number, a double , that is to be formatted. The pattern is the String that specifies the formatting properties. The output, which is a String, represents the formatted number.

Output from DecimalFormatDemo Program value pattern output Explanation

123456.789 ###,###.### 123,456.789 The pound sign (#) denotes a digit, the comma is a placeholder for the grouping separator, and the period is a placeholder for the decimal separator.

123456.789 ###.## 123456.79 The value has three digits to the right of the decimal point, but the pattern has only two. The format method handles this by rounding up.

123.78 000000.000 000123.780 The pattern specifies leading and trailing zeros, because the 0 character is used instead of the pound sign (#).

12345.67 $###,###.### $12,345.67 The first character in the pattern is the dollar sign ($). Note that it immediately precedes the leftmost digit in the formatted output.

12345.67 \u00A5###,###.### c member of Class (to which all Class objects belong). A Class object is like any other object and so you can get and manipulate a handle to it. (That's what the loader does.) One of the ways to get a handle to the Class object is forName( ), which takes a String containing the textual name (watch the spelling and capitalization!) of the particular class you want a handle for. It returns a Class handle.

The output of this program for one JVM is:

```
inside main
Loading Candy
After creating Candy
Loading Gum
After Class.forName("Gum")
Loading Cookie
After creating Cookie
```

You can see that each Class object is loaded only when it's needed, and the static initialization is performed upon class loading.

Interestingly enough, a different JVM yielded:

Loading Candy

```
Loading Cookie
inside main
After creating Candy
Loading Gum
After Class.forName("Gum")
After creating Cookie
```

It appears that this JVM anticipated the need for Candy and Cookie by examining the code in main( ), but could not see Gum because it was created by a call to forName( ) and not through a more typical call to new. While this JVM produces the desired effect because it does get the classes loaded before they're needed, it's uncertain whether the behavior shown is precisely correct.

Class literals

In Java 1.1 you have a second way to produce the handle to the Class object: use the class literal . In the above program this would look like:

Gum.class;

which is not only simpler, but also safer since it's checked at compile time. Because it eliminates the method call, it's also more efficient.

Class literals work with regular classes as well as interfaces, arrays, and primitive types. In addition, there's a standard field called TYPE that exists for each of the primitive wrapper classes. The TYPE field produces a handle to the Class object for the associated primitive type, such that:

```
boolean.class
Boolean.TYPE
char.class
Character.TYPE
byte.class
Byte.TYPE
short.class
Short.TYPE
int.class
Integer.TYPE
long.class
Long.TYPE
float.class
Float.TYPE
double.class
```

```
Double.TYPE
void.class
Void.TYPE
```

12.2.1 Checking before a cast

So far, you've seen RTTI forms including:

The classic cast, e.g. " (Shape)," which uses RTTI to make sure the cast is correct and throws a ClassCastException if you've performed a bad cast.

The Class object representing the type of your object. The Class object can be queried for useful runtime information.

In C++, the classic cast " (Shape)" does not perform RTTI. It simply tells the compiler to treat the object as the new type. In Java, which does perform the type check, this cast is often called a "type safe downcast." The reason for the term "downcast" is the historical arrangement of the class hierarchy diagram. If casting a Circle to a Shape is an upcast, then casting a Shape to a Circle is a downcast. However, you know a Circle is also a Shape, and the compiler freely allows an upcast assignment, but you don't know that a Shape is necessarily a Circle, so the compiler doesn't allow you to perform a downcast assignment without using an explicit cast.

There's a third form of RTTI in Java. This is the keyword instanceof that tells you if an object is an instance of a particular type. It returns a boolean so you use it in the form of a question, like this:

if(x instanceof Dog)
((Dog)x).bark();

The above if statement checks to see if the object x belongs to the class Dog before casting x to a Dog. It's important to use instanceof before a downcast when you don't have other information that tells you the type of the object; otherwise you'll end up with a ClassCastException.

Ordinarily, you might be hunting for one type (triangles to turn purple, for example), but the following program shows how to tally all of the objects using instanceof.

```
//: PetCount.java
// Using instanceof
package c11.petcount;
import java.util.*;

class Pet {}
class Dog extends Pet {}
class Pug extends Dog {}
class Cat extends Pet {}
class Rodent extends Pet {}
class Gerbil extends Rodent {}
class Hamster extends Rodent {}

class Counter { int i; }

public class PetCount {
static String[] typenames = {
"Pet", "Dog", "Pug", "Cat",
"Rodent", "Gerbil", "Hamster",
};
```

```
public static void main(String[] args) {
Vector pets = new Vector();
try {
Class[] petTypes = {
Class.forName("c11.petcount.Dog"),
Class.forName("c11.petcount.Pug"),
Class.forName("c11.petcount.Cat"),
Class.forName("c11.petcount.Rodent"),
Class.forName("c11.petcount.Gerbil"),
Class.forName("c11.petcount.Hamster"),
};
for(int i = 0; i < 15; i++)
pets.addElement(
petTypes[
(int)(Math.random()*petTypes.length)]
.newInstance());
} catch(InstantiationException e) {}
catch(IllegalAccessException e) {}
catch(ClassNotFoundException e) {}
Hashtable h = new Hashtable();
for(int i = 0; i < typenames.length; i++)
h.put(typenames[i], new Counter());
for(int i = 0; i < pets.size(); i++) {
Object o = pets.elementAt(i);
if(o instanceof Pet)
((Counter)h.get("Pet")).i++;
if(o instanceof Dog)
((Counter)h.get("Dog")).i++;
if(o instanceof Pug)
((Counter)h.get("Pug")).i++;
if(o instanceof Cat)
((Counter)h.get("Cat")).i++;
if(o instanceof Rodent)
((Counter)h.get("Rodent")).i++;
if(o instanceof Gerbil)
((Counter)h.get("Gerbil")).i++;
if(o instanceof Hamster)
((Counter)h.get("Hamster")).i++;
}
for(int i = 0; i < pets.size(); i++)
System.out.println(
pets.elementAt(i).getClass().toString());
for(int i = 0; i < typenames.length; i++)
System.out.println(
typenames[i] + "quantity: "+
((Counter)h.get(typenames[i])).i);
}
} ///:~
```

There's a rather narrow restriction on instanceof in Java 1.0: You can compare it to a named type only, and not to a Class object. In the example above you might feel that it's tedious to write out all of those instanceof expressions, and you're right. But in Java 1.0 there is no way to cleverly automate it by creating a Vector of Class objects and comparing it to those instead. This isn't as great a restriction as you might think, because you'll eventually understand that your design is probably flawed if you end up writing a lot of instanceof expressions.

Of course this example is contrived - you'd probably put a static data member in each type and increment it in the constructor to keep track of the counts. You would do something like that if you had control of the source code for the class and could change it. Since this is not always the case, RTTI can come in handy.

12.2.2 Using class literals

It's interesting to see how the PetCount.java example can be rewritten using Java 1.1 class literals. The result is cleaner in many ways:

```
//: PetCount2.java
// Using Java 1.1 class literals
package c11.petcount2;
import java.util.*;

class Pet {}
class Dog extends Pet {}
class Pug extends Dog {}
class Cat extends Pet {}
class Rodent extends Pet {}
class Gerbil extends Rodent {}
class Hamster extends Rodent {}

class Counter { int i; }

public class PetCount2 {
public static void main(String[] args) {
Vector pets = new Vector();
Class[] petTypes = {
// Class literals work in Java 1.1+ only:
Pet.class,
Dog.class,
Pug.class,
Cat.class,
Rodent.class,
Gerbil.class,
Hamster.class,
};
try {
for(int i = 0; i < 15; i++) {
// Offset by one to eliminate Pet.class:
int rnd = 1 + (int)(
Math.random() * (petTypes.length - 1));
pets.addElement(
```

```
petTypes[rnd].newInstance());
}
} catch(InstantiationException e) {}
catch(IllegalAccessException e) {}
Hashtable h = new Hashtable();
for(int i = 0; i < petTypes.length; i++)
h.put(petTypes[i].toString(),
new Counter());
for(int i = 0; i < pets.size(); i++) {
Object o = pets.elementAt(i);
if(o instanceof Pet)
((Counter)h.get(
"class c11.petcount2.Pet")).i++;
if(o instanceof Dog)
((Counter)h.get(
"class c11.petcount2.Dog")).i++;
if(o instanceof Pug)
((Counter)h.get(
"class c11.petcount2.Pug")).i++;
if(o instanceof Cat)
((Counter)h.get(
"class c11.petcount2.Cat")).i++;
if(o instanceof Rodent)
((Counter)h.get(
"class c11.petcount2.Rodent")).i++;
if(o instanceof Gerbil)
((Counter)h.get(
"class c11.petcount2.Gerbil")).i++;
if(o instanceof Hamster)
((Counter)h.get(
"class c11.petcount2.Hamster")).i++;
}
for(int i = 0; i < pets.size(); i++)
System.out.println(
pets.elementAt(i).getClass().toString());
Enumeration keys = h.keys();
while(keys.hasMoreElements()) {
String nm = (String)keys.nextElement();
Counter cnt = (Counter)h.get(nm);
System.out.println(
nm.substring(nm.lastIndexOf('.') + 1) +
"quantity: "+ cnt.i);
}
}
} ///:~
```

Here, the typenames array has been removed in favor of getting the type name strings from the Class object. Notice the extra work for this: the class name is not, for example, Gerbil, but instead c11.petcount2.Gerbil since the package name is included. Notice also that the system can distinguish between classes and interfaces.

You can also see that the creation of petTypes does not need to be surrounded by a try block since it's evaluated at compile time and thus won't throw any exceptions, unlike Class.forName( ).

When the Pet objects are dynamically created, you can see that the random number is restricted so it is between 1 and petTypes.length and does not include zero. That's because zero refers to Pet.class, and presumably a generic Pet object is not interesting. However, since Pet.class is part of petTypes the result is that all of the pets get counted.

12.2.3 A Dynamic Instanceof

Java 1.1 has added the isInstance method to the class Class. This allows you to dynamically call the instanceof operator, which you could do only statically in Java 1.0 (as previously shown). Thus, all those tedious instanceof statements can be removed in the PetCount example:

```
//: PetCount3.java
// Using Java 1.1 isInstance()
package c11.petcount3;
import java.util.*;

class Pet {}
class Dog extends Pet {}
class Pug extends Dog {}
class Cat extends Pet {}
class Rodent extends Pet {}
class Gerbil extends Rodent {}
class Hamster extends Rodent {}

class Counter { int i; }

public class PetCount3 {
public static void main(String[] args) {
Vector pets = new Vector();
Class[] petTypes = {
Pet.class,
Dog.class,
Pug.class,
Cat.class,
Rodent.class,
Gerbil.class,
Hamster.class,
};
try {
for(int i = 0; i < 15; i++) {
// Offset by one to eliminate Pet.class:
int rnd = 1 + (int)(
Math.random() * (petTypes.length - 1));
pets.addElement(
petTypes[rnd].newInstance());
}
```

```
} catch(InstantiationException e) {}
catch(IllegalAccessException e) {}
Hashtable h = new Hashtable();
for(int i = 0; i < petTypes.length; i++)
h.put(petTypes[i].toString(),
new Counter());
for(int i = 0; i < pets.size(); i++) {
Object o = pets.elementAt(i);
// Using isInstance to eliminate individual
// instanceof expressions:
for (int j = 0; j < petTypes.length; ++j)
if (petTypes[j].isInstance(o)) {
String key = petTypes[j].toString();
((Counter)h.get(key)).i++;
}
}
for(int i = 0; i < pets.size(); i++)
System.out.println(
pets.elementAt(i).getClass().toString());
Enumeration keys = h.keys();
while(keys.hasMoreElements()) {
String nm = (String)keys.nextElement();
Counter cnt = (Counter)h.get(nm);
System.out.println(
nm.substring(nm.lastIndexOf('.') + 1) +
"quantity: " + cnt.i);
}
}
} ///:~
```

You can see that the Java 1.1 isInstance( ) method has eliminated the need for the instanceof expressions. In addition, this means that you can add new types of pets simply by changing the petTypes array; the rest of the program does not need modification (as it did when using the instanceof expressions).

12.3 RTTI Syntax

Java performs its RTTI using the Class object, even if you're doing something like a cast. The class Class also has a number of other ways you can use RTTI.

First, you must get a handle to the appropriate Class object. One way to do this, as shown in the previous example, is to use a string and the Class.forName( ) method. This is convenient because you don't need an object of that type in order to get the Class handle. However, if you do already have an object of the type you're interested in, you can fetch the Class handle by calling a method that's part of the Object root class: getClass( ). This returns the Class handle representing the actual type of the object. Class has several interesting and sometimes useful methods, demonstrated in the following example:

```
//: ToyTest.java
// Testing class Class
interface HasBatteries {}
```

```
interface Waterproof {}
interface ShootsThings {}
class Toy {
// Comment out the following default
// constructor to see
// NoSuchMethodError from (*1*)
Toy() {}
Toy(int i) {}
}

class FancyToy extends Toy
implements HasBatteries,
Waterproof, ShootsThings {
FancyToy() { super(1); }
}

public class ToyTest {
public static void main(String[] args) {
Class c = null;
try {
c = Class.forName("FancyToy");
} catch(ClassNotFoundException e) {}
printInfo(c);
Class[] faces = c.getInterfaces();
for(int i = 0; i < faces.length; i++)
printInfo(faces[i]);
Class cy = c.getSuperclass();
Object o = null;
try {
// Requires default constructor:
o = cy.newInstance(); // (*1*)
} catch(InstantiationException e) {}
catch(IllegalAccessException e) {}
printInfo(o.getClass());
}
static void printInfo(Class cc) {
System.out.println(
"Class name: " + cc.getName() +
" is interface? [" +
cc.isInterface() + "]");
}
} ///:~
```

You can see that class FancyToy is quite complicated, since it inherits from Toy and implements the interfaces of HasBatteries, Waterproof, and ShootsThings. In main( ), a Class handle is created and initialized to the FancyToy Class using forName( ) inside an appropriate try block.

The Class.getInterfaces( ) method returns an array of Class objects representing the interfaces that are contained in the Class object of interest.

If you have a Class object you can also ask it for its direct base class using getSuperclass( ). This, of course, returns a Class handle that you can further query. This means that, at run time, you can discover an object's entire class hierarchy.

The newInstance( ) method of Class can, at first, seem like just another way to clone( ) an object. However, you can create a new object with newInstance( ) without an existing object, as seen here, because there is no Toy object, only cy, which is a handle to y's Class object. This is a way to implement a "virtual constructor," which allows you to say "I don't know exactly what type you are, but create yourself properly anyway." In the example above, cy is just a Class handle with no further type information known at compile time. And when you create a new instance, you get back an Object handle. But that handle is pointing to a Toy object. Of course, before you can send any messages other than those accepted by Object, you have to investigate it a bit and do some casting. In addition, the class that's being created with newInstance( ) must have a default constructor. There's no way to use newInstance( ) to create objects that have non-default constructors, so this can be a bit limiting in Java 1. However, the reflection API in Java 1.1 (discussed in the next section) allows you to dynamically use any constructor in a class.

The final method in the listing is printInfo( ), which takes a Class handle and gets its name with getName( ), and finds out whether it's an interface with isInterface( ).

The output from this program is:

```
Class name: FancyToy is interface? [false]
Class name: HasBatteries is interface? [true]
Class name: Waterproof is interface? [true]
Class name: ShootsThings is interface? [true]
Class name: Toy is interface? [false]
```

Thus, with the Class object you can find out just about everything you want to know about an object.

12.4 Reflection: Run-Time Class Information

If you don't know the precise type of an object, RTTI will tell you. However, there's a limitation: the type must be known at compile time in order for you to be able to detect it using RTTI and do something useful with the information. Put another way, the compiler must know about all the classes you're working with for RTTI.

This doesn't seem like that much of a limitation at first, but suppose you're given a handle to an object that's not in your program space. In fact, the class of the object isn't even available to your program at compile time. For example, suppose you get a bunch of bytes from a disk file or from a network connection and you're told that those bytes represent a class. Since the compiler can't know about the class while it's compiling the code, how can you possibly use such a class?

In a traditional programming environment this seems like a far-fetched scenario. But as we move into a larger programming world there are important cases in which this happens. The first is component-based programming in which you build projects using Rapid Application Development (RAD) in an application builder tool. This is a visual approach to creating a program (which you see on the screen as a form) by moving icons that represent components onto the form. These components are then configured by setting some of their values at program time. This design-time configuration requires that any component be instantiable and that it expose some part of itself and allow its values to be read and set. In addition, components that handle GUI events must expose information about appropriate methods so that the RAD environment can assist the programmer in overriding these event-handling methods. Reflection provides the mechanism to detect the available methods and produce the method names. Java 1.1 provides a structure for component-based programming through Java.

Another compelling motivation for discovering class information at run-time is to provide the ability to create and execute objects on remote platforms across a network. This is called Remote Method Invocation (RMI) and it allows a Java program (version 1.1 and higher) to have objects distributed across many machines. This distribution can happen for a number of reasons: perhaps you're doing a computation-intensive task and you want to break it up and put pieces on machines that are idle in order to speed things up. In some situations you might want to place code that handles particular types of tasks (e.g. "Business Rules" in a multi-tier client/server architecture) on a particular machine so that machine becomes a common repository describing those actions and it can be easily changed to affect everyone in the system. (This is an interesting development since the machine exists solely to make software changes easy!) Along these lines, distributed computing also supports specialized hardware that might be good at a particular task - matrix inversions, for example - but inappropriate or too expensive for general purpose programming.

In Java 1.1, the class Class (described previously in this chapter) is extended to support the concept of reflection, and there's an additional library, java.lang.reflect, with classes Field, Method, and Constructor (each of which implement the Member interface). Objects of these types are created by the JVM at run-time to represent the corresponding member in the unknown class. You can then use the Constructors to create new objects, the get( ) and set( ) methods to read and modify the fields associated with Field objects, and the invoke( ) method to call a method associated with a Method object. In addition, you can call the convenience methods getFields( ), getMethods( ), getConstructors( ), etc., to return arrays of the objects representing the fields, methods, and constructors. (You can find out more by looking up the class Class in your online documentation.) Thus, the class information for anonymous objects can be completely determined at run time, and nothing need be known at compile time.

It's important to realize that there's nothing magic about reflection. When you're using reflection to interact with an object of an unknown type, the JVM will simply look at the object and see that it belongs to a particular class (just like ordinary RTTI) but then, before it can do anything else, the Class object must be loaded. Thus, the .class file for that particular type must still be available to the JVM, either on the local machine or across the network. So the true difference between RTTI and reflection is that with RTTI, the compiler opens and examines the .class file at compile time. Put another way, you can call all the methods of an object in the "normal" way. With reflection, the .class file is unavailable at compile time; it is opened and examined by the run-time environment.

12.5 A Class Method Extractor

You'll rarely need to use the reflection tools directly; they're in the language to support the other Java features such as object serialization (described in Chapter 10), Java Beans, and RMI (described later in the book). However, there are times when it's quite useful to be able to dynamically extract information about a class. One extremely useful tool is a class method extractor. As mentioned before, looking at a class definition source code or online documentation shows only the methods that are defined or overridden within that class definition . But there could be dozens more available to you that have come from base classes. To locate these is both tedious and time consuming. Fortunately, reflection provides a way to write a simple tool that will automatically show you the entire interface. Here's the way it works:

```
//: ShowMethods.java
// Using Java 1.1 reflection to show all the
// methods of a class, even if the methods are
// defined in the base class.
import java.lang.reflect.*;
```

```
public class ShowMethods {
static final String usage =
"usage: \n" +
"ShowMethods qualified.class.name\n" +
"To show all methods in class or: \n" +
"ShowMethods qualified.class.name word\n" +
"To search for methods involving 'word' ";
public static void main(String[] args) {
if(args.length < 1) {
System.out.println(usage);
System.exit(0);
}
try {
Class c = Class.forName(args[0]);
Method[] m = c.getMethods();
Constructor[] ctor = c.getConstructors();
if(args.length == 1) {
for (int i = 0; i < m.length; i++)
System.out.println(m[i].toString());
for (int i = 0; i < ctor.length; i++)
System.out.println(ctor[i].toString());
}
else {
for (int i = 0; i < m.length; i++)
if(m[i].toString()
.indexOf(args[1])!= -1)
System.out.println(m[i].toString());
for (int i = 0; i < ctor.length; i++)
if(ctor[i].toString()
.indexOf(args[1])!= -1)
System.out.println(ctor[i].toString());
}
} catch (ClassNotFoundException e) {
System.out.println("No such class: " + e);
}
}
} ///:~
```

The Class methods getMethods( ) and getConstructors( ) return an array of Method and Constructor, respectively. Each of these classes has further methods to dissect the names, arguments, and return values of the methods they represent. But you can also just use toString( ), as is done here, to produce a String with the entire method signature. The rest of the code is just for extracting command line information, determining if a particular signature matches with your target string (using indexOf( )), and printing the results.

This shows reflection in action, since the result produced by Class.forName( ) cannot be known at compile-time, and therefore all the method signature information is being extracted at run-time. If you investigate your online documentation on reflection, you'll see that there is enough support to actually set up and make a method call on an object that's totally unknown at compile-time. Again, this is something you'll probably never need to do yourself - the support is there for Java and so a programming environment can manipulate Java Beans - but it's interesting.

An interesting experiment is to run java ShowMethods ShowMethods . This produces a listing that includes a public default constructor, even though you can see from the code that no constructor was defined. The constructor you see is the one that's automatically synthesized by the compiler. If you then make ShowMethods a non- public class (that is, friendly), the synthesized default constructor no longer shows up in the output. The synthesized default constructor is automatically given the same access as the class.

The output for ShowMethods is still a little tedious. For example, here's a portion of the output produced by invoking java ShowMethods java.lang.String :

```
public boolean
java.lang.String.startsWith(java.lang.String,int)
public boolean
java.lang.String.startsWith(java.lang.String)
public boolean java.lang.String.endsWith(java.lang.String)
```

It would be even nicer if the qualifiers like java.lang could be stripped off. The StreamTokenizer class introduced in the previous chapter can help solve this problem:

```
//: ShowMethodsClean.java
// ShowMethods with the qualifiers stripped
// to make the results easier to read
import java.lang.reflect.*;
import java.io.*;
public class ShowMethodsClean {
static final String usage =
"usage: \n" +
"ShowMethodsClean qualified.class.name\n" +
"To show all methods in class or: \n" +
"ShowMethodsClean qualif.class.name word\n" +
"To search for methods involving 'word' ";
public static void main(String[] args) {
if(args.length < 1) {
System.out.println(usage);
System.exit(0);
}
try {
Class c = Class.forName(args[0]);
Method[] m = c.getMethods();
Constructor[] ctor = c.getConstructors();
// Convert to an array of cleaned Strings:
String[] n =
new String[m.length + ctor.length];
for(int i = 0; i < m.length; i++) {
String s = m[i].toString();
n[i] = StripQualifiers.strip(s);
}
for(int i = 0; i < ctor.length; i++) {
String s = ctor[i].toString();
```

```
n[i + m.length] =
StripQualifiers.strip(s);
}
if(args.length == 1)
for (int i = 0; i < n.length; i++)
System.out.println(n[i]);
else
for (int i = 0; i < n.length; i++)
if(n[i].indexOf(args[1])!= -1)
System.out.println(n[i]);
} catch (ClassNotFoundException e) {
System.out.println("No such class: " + e);
}
}
}
class StripQualifiers {
private StreamTokenizer st;
public StripQualifiers(String qualified) {
st = new StreamTokenizer(
new StringReader(qualified));
st.ordinaryChar(' '); // Keep the spaces
}
public String getNext() {
String s = null;
try {
if(st.nextToken() !=
StreamTokenizer.TT_EOF) {
switch(st.ttype) {
case StreamTokenizer.TT_EOL:
s = null;
break;
case StreamTokenizer.TT_NUMBER:
s = Double.toString(st.nval);
break;
case StreamTokenizer.TT_WORD:
s = new String(st.sval);
break;
default: // single character in ttype
s = String.valueOf((char)st.ttype);
}
}
} catch(IOException e) {
System.out.println(e);
}
return s;
}
public static String strip(String qualified) {
StripQualifiers sq =
```

```
new StripQualifiers(qualified);
String s = "", si;
while((si = sq.getNext()) != null) {
int lastDot = si.lastIndexOf('.');
if(lastDot != -1)
si = si.substring(lastDot + 1);
s += si;
}
return s;
}
} ///:~
```

The class ShowMethodsClean is quite similar to the previous ShowMethods, except that it takes the arrays of Method and Constructor and converts them into a single array of String. Each of these String objects is then passed through StripQualifiers.Strip( ) to remove all the method qualification. As you can see, this uses the StreamTokenizer and String manipulation to do its work.

This tool can be a real time-saver while you're programming, when you can't remember if a class has a particular method and you don't want to go walking through the class hierarchy in the online documentation, or if you don't know whether that class can do anything with, for example, Color objects.

12.6 Accessing System Resources

12.6.1 The Runtime Object

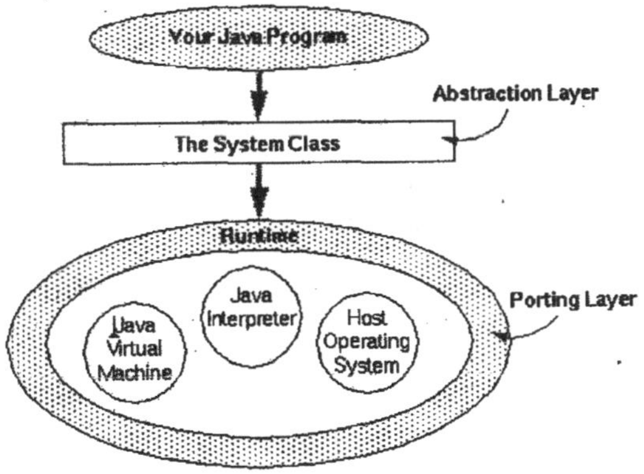

Fig. 12.2

At the core of the Java runtime environment are the Java virtual machine, the Java interpreter, and the host operating system.

The oval labelled Runtime in the diagram represents the current runtime environment and is an instance of the Runtime class. The current runtime environment could be anything from Sun's implementation of the Java virtual machine and interpreter running on Solaris to ACME Company's implementation of the virtual machine and interpreter running on the ACME toaster.

Runtime objects provide two services. First, they communicate with the components of the runtime environment—getting information and invoking functions. Second, Runtime objects are also the interface to system-dependent capabilities. For example, UNIX Runtime objects might support the getenv and setenv functions. Other Runtime objects, such as for Mac OS, might not support getenv and setenv because the host operating system doesn't support these functions, but they might support others.

Because the Runtime class is tightly integrated with the implementation of the Java interpreter, the Java virtual machine, and the host operating system, it is system-dependent. If objects in your program message the Runtime object directly, you sacrifice the system indepedent nature of you Java program. In general, this is not a good idea (particularly for applets).

12.6.2 Controlling Cloneability

You might suggest that, to remove clonability, the clone( ) method simply be made private, but this won't work since you cannot take a base-class method and make it more private in a derived class. So it's not that simple. And yet, it's necessary to be able to control whether an object can be cloned. There are actually a number of attitudes you can take to this in a class that you design:

Indifference. You don't do anything about cloning, which means that your class can't be cloned but a class that inherits from you can add cloning if it wants. This works only if the default Object.clone( ) will do something reasonable with all the fields in your class.

Support clone( ). Follow the standard practice of implementing Cloneable and overriding clone( ). In the overridden clone( ), you call super.clone( ) and catch all exceptions (so your overridden clone( ) doesn't throw any exceptions).

Support cloning conditionally. If your class holds handles to other objects that might or might not be cloneable (an example of this is a collection class), you can try to clone all of the objects that you have handles to as part of your cloning, and if they throw exceptions just pass them through. For example, consider a special sort of Vector that tries to clone all the objects it holds. When you write such a Vector, you don't know what sort of objects the client programmer might put into your Vector, so you don't know whether they can be cloned.

Don't implement Cloneable but override clone( ) as protected, producing the correct copying behavior for any fields. This way, anyone inheriting from this class can override clone( ) and call super.clone( ) to produce the correct copying behavior. Note that your implementation can and should invoke super.clone( ) even though that method expects a Cloneable object (it will throw an exception otherwise), because no one will directly invoke it on an object of your type. It will get invoked only through a derived class, which, if it is to work successfully, implements Cloneable.

Try to prevent cloning by not implementing Cloneable and overriding clone( ) to throw an exception. This is successful only if any class derived from this calls super.clone( ) in its redefinition of clone( ). Otherwise, a programmer may be able to get around it.

Prevent cloning by making your class final. If clone( ) has not been overridden by any of your ancestor classes, then it can't be. If it has, then override it again and throw CloneNotSupportedException. Making the class final is the only way to guarantee that cloning is prevented. In addition, when dealing with security objects or other situations in which you want to control the number of objects created you should make all constructors private and provide one or more special methods for creating objects. That way, these methods can restrict the number of objects created and the conditions in which they're created. Here's an example that shows the various ways cloning can be implemented and then, later in the hierarchy, "turned off:"

```
//: CheckCloneable.java
// Checking to see if a handle can be cloned
// Can't clone this because it doesn't
// override clone():
class Ordinary {}
```

```
// Overrides clone, but doesn't implement
// Cloneable:
class WrongClone extends Ordinary {
public Object clone()
throws CloneNotSupportedException {
return super.clone(); // Throws exception
}
}
// Does all the right things for cloning:
class IsCloneable extends Ordinary
implements Cloneable {
public Object clone()
throws CloneNotSupportedException {
return super.clone();
}
}
// Turn off cloning by throwing the exception:
class NoMore extends IsCloneable {
public Object clone()
throws CloneNotSupportedException {
throw new CloneNotSupportedException();
}
}
class TryMore extends NoMore {
public Object clone()
throws CloneNotSupportedException {
// Calls NoMore.clone(), throws exception:
return super.clone();
}
}

class BackOn extends NoMore {
private BackOn duplicate(BackOn b) {
// Somehow make a copy of b
// and return that copy. This is a dummy
// copy, just to make the point:
return new BackOn();
}
public Object clone() {
// Doesn't call NoMore.clone():
return duplicate(this);
}
}
// Can't inherit from this, so can't override
// the clone method like in BackOn:
final class ReallyNoMore extends NoMore {}

public class CheckCloneable {
static Ordinary tryToClone(Ordinary ord) {
```

```
String id = ord.getClass().getName();
Ordinary x = null;
if(ord instanceof Cloneable) {
try {
System.out.println("Attempting " + id);
x = (Ordinary)((IsCloneable)ord).clone();
System.out.println("Cloned " + id);
} catch(CloneNotSupportedException e) {
System.out.println(
"Could not clone " + id);
}
}
return x;
}
public static void main(String[] args) {
// Upcasting:
Ordinary[] ord = {
new IsCloneable(),
new WrongClone(),
new NoMore(),
new TryMore(),
new BackOn(),
new ReallyNoMore(),
};
Ordinary x = new Ordinary();
// This won't compile, since clone() is
// protected in Object:
//! x = (Ordinary)x.clone();
// tryToClone() checks first to see if
// a class implements Cloneable:
for(int i = 0; i < ord.length; i++)
tryToClone(ord[i]);
}
} ///:~
```

The first class, Ordinary, represents the kinds of classes we've seen throughout the book: no support for cloning, but as it turns out, no prevention of cloning either. But if you have a handle to an Ordinary object that might have been upcast from a more derived class, you can't tell if it can be cloned or not.

The class WrongClone shows an incorrect way to implement cloning. It does override Object.clone( ) and makes that method public, but it doesn't implement Cloneable, so when super.clone( ) is called (which results in a call to Object.clone( )), CloneNotSupportedException is thrown so the cloning doesn't work.

In IsCloneable you can see all the right actions performed for cloning: clone( ) is overridden and Cloneable is implemented. However, this clone( ) method and several others that follow in this example do not catch CloneNotSupportedException, but instead pass it through to the caller, who must then put a try-catch block around it. In your own clone( ) methods you will typically catch CloneNotSupportedException inside clone( ) rather than passing it through. As you'll see, in this example it's more informative to pass the exceptions through.

Class NoMore attempts to "turn off" cloning in the way that the Java designers intended: in the derived class clone( ), you throw CloneNotSupportedException. The clone( ) method in class TryMore properly calls super.clone( ), and this resolves to NoMore.clone( ), which throws an exception and prevents cloning.

But what if the programmer doesn't follow the "proper" path of calling super.clone( ) inside the overridden clone( ) method? In BackOn, you can see how this can happen. This class uses a separate method duplicate( ) to make a copy of the current object and calls this method inside clone( ) instead of calling super.clone( ). The exception is never thrown and the new class is cloneable. You can't rely on throwing an exception to prevent making a cloneable class. The only sure-fire solution is shown in ReallyNoMore, which is final and thus cannot be inherited. That means if clone( ) throws an exception in the final class, it cannot be modified with inheritance and the prevention of cloning is assured. (You cannot explicitly call Object.clone( ) from a class that has an arbitrary level of inheritance; you are limited to calling super.clone( ), which has access to only the direct base class.) Thus, if you make any objects that involve security issues, you'll want to make those classes final.

The first method you see in class CheckCloneable is tryToClone( ), which takes any Ordinary object and checks to see whether it's cloneable with instanceof. If so, it casts the object to an IsCloneable, calls clone( ) and casts the result back to Ordinary, catching any exceptions that are thrown. Notice the use of run-time type identification (see Chapter 11) to print out the class name so you can see what's happening.

In main( ), different types of Ordinary objects are created and upcast to Ordinary in the array definition. The first two lines of code after that create a plain Ordinary object and try to clone it. However, this code will not compile because clone( ) is a protected method in Object. The remainder of the code steps through the array and tries to clone each object, reporting the success or failure of each. The output is:

12.6.3 Attempting IsCloneable

```
Cloned IsCloneable
Attempting NoMore
Could not clone NoMore
Attempting TryMore
Could not clone TryMore
Attempting BackOn
Cloned BackOn
Attempting ReallyNoMore
Could not clone ReallyNoMore
So to summarize, if you want a class to be cloneable:
Implement the Cloneable interface.
Override clone( ).
Call super.clone( ) inside your clone( ).
Capture exceptions inside your clone( ).
This will produce the most convenient effects.
```

12.7 The Copy-Constructor

Cloning can seem to be a complicated process to set up. It might seem like there should be an alternative. One approach that might occur to you (especially if you're a C++ programmer) is to make a special constructor whose job it is to duplicate an object. In C++, this is called the copy constructor At first, this seems like the obvious solution. Here's an example:

```
//: CopyConstr
// To allow derived constructors (or other
// methods) to put in different qualities:
protected void addQualities(FruitQualities q) {
fq = q;
}
protected FruitQualities getQualities() {
return fq;
}
}

class Tomato extends Fruit {
Tomato() {
super(new FruitQualities(), 100);
}
Tomato(Tomato t) { // Copy-constructor
super(t); // Upcast for base copy-constructor
// Other copy-construction activities...
}
}

class ZebraQualities extends FruitQualities {
private int stripedness;
ZebraQualities() { // Default constructor
// do something meaningful...
}
ZebraQualities(ZebraQualities z) {
super(z);
stripedness = z.stripedness;
}
}

class GreenZebra extends Tomato {
GreenZebra() {
addQualities(new ZebraQualities());
}
GreenZebra(GreenZebra g) {
super(g); // Calls Tomato(Tomato)
// Restore the right qualities:
addQualities(new ZebraQualities());
}
void evaluate() {
ZebraQualities zq =
(ZebraQualities)getQualities();
// Do something with the qualities
// ...
}
}
```

```
public class CopyConstructor {
public static void ripen(Tomato t) {
// Use the "copy constructor":
t = new Tomato(t);
System.out.println("In ripen, t is a " +
t.getClass().getName());
}
public static void slice(Fruit f) {
f = new Fruit(f); // Hmmm... will this work?
System.out.println("In slice, f is a " +
f.getClass().getName());
}
public static void main(String[] args) {
Tomato tomato = new Tomato();
ripen(tomato); // OK
slice(tomato); // OOPS!
GreenZebra g = new GreenZebra();
ripen(g); // OOPS!
slice(g); // OOPS!
g.evaluate();
}
} ///:~
```

This seems a bit strange at first. Sure, fruit has qualities, but why not just put data members representing those qualities directly into the Fruit class? There are two potential reasons. The first is that you might want to easily insert or change the qualities. Note that Fruit has a protected addQualities( ) method to allow derived classes to do this. (You might think the logical thing to do is to have a protected constructor in Fruit that takes a FruitQualities argument, but constructors don't inherit so it wouldn't be available in second or greater level classes.) By making the fruit qualities into a separate class, you have greater flexibility, including the ability to change the qualities midway through the lifetime of a particular Fruit object.

The second reason for making FruitQualities a separate object is in case you want to add new qualities or to change the behavior via inheritance and polymorphism. Note that for GreenZebra (which really is a type of tomato - I've grown them and they're fabulous), the constructor calls addQualities( ) and passes it a ZebraQualities object, which is derived from FruitQualities so it can be attached to the FruitQualities handle in the base class. Of course, when GreenZebra uses the FruitQualities it must downcast it to the correct type (as seen in evaluate( )), but it always knows that type is ZebraQualities.

You'll also see that there's a Seed class, and that Fruit (which by definition carries its own seeds) contains an array of Seeds.

Finally, notice that each class has a copy constructor, and that each copy constructor must take care to call the copy constructors for the base class and member objects to produce a deep copy. The copy constructor is tested inside the class CopyConstructor. The method ripen( ) takes a Tomato argument and performs copy-construction on it in order to duplicate the object:

t = new Tomato(t);

while slice( ) takes a more generic Fruit object and also duplicates it:

f = new Fruit(f);

These are tested with different kinds of Fruit in main( ). Here's the output:

```
In ripen, t is a Tomato
In slice, f is a Fruit
In ripen, t is a Tomato
In slice, f is a Fruit
```

This is where the problem shows up. After the copy-construction that happens to the Tomato inside slice( ), the result is no longer a Tomato object, but just a Fruit. It has lost all of its tomato-ness. Further, when you take a GreenZebra, both ripen( ) and slice( ) turn it into a Tomato and a Fruit, respectively. Thus, unfortunately, the copy constructor scheme is no good to us in Java when attempting to make a local copy of an object.

12.7.1 Why does it work in C++ and not Java?

The copy constructor is a fundamental part of C++, since it automatically makes a local copy of an object. Yet the example above proves that it does not work for Java. Why? In Java everything that we manipulate is a handle, while in C++ you can have handle-like entities and you can also pass around the objects directly. That's what the C++ copy constructor is for: when you want to take an object and pass it in by value, thus duplicating the object. So it works fine in C++, but you should keep in mind that this scheme fails in Java, so don't use it.

12.8 Using the System Class

Unlike most other classes, you don't instantiate the System class to use it. To be more precise, you cannot instantiate the System class—it's a final class and all of its constructors are private. All of System's variables and methods are class variables and class methods—they are declared static.

To use a class variable, you use it directly from the name of the class using Java's dot (.) notation. For example, to reference the System's class variable out, you append the variable name to the class name separated by a period, like this:

12.8.1 System.out

You call class methods in a similar fashion. For example, to call System's getProperty method, you append the method name to the end of the class name separated by a period:

System.getProperty(argument);

The following small Java program uses the System class twice, first to retrieve the current user's name and then to display it.

```
class UserNameTest {
public static void main(String[] args) {
String name;
name = System.getProperty("user.name");
System.out.println(name);
}
}
```

You'll notice that the program never instantiates a System object. It just references the getProperty method and the out variable directly from the class. The code sample use System's getProperty method to search the properties database for the property called "user.name." System Properties later in this lesson talks more about system properties and the getProperty method.

The code sample also uses System.out, a PrintStream that implements the standard output stream. The println method prints its argument to the standard output stream. The next page of this lesson discusses the standard output stream and the other two standard I/O streams provided by the System class.

Sometimes, a program requires access to system resources such as system properties, standard input and output, or the current time. Your program could make system calls directly to the window or operating system, but then your program would be able to run only in that particular environment. Each time you want to run the program in a new environment, you'd have to port your program by rewriting the system-dependent sections of code. The Java platform lets your program access system resources through a (relatively) system-independent API implemented by the System class and through a system-dependent API implemented by the Runtime class.

Purity Tip: Some of the system resources available through the System and Runtime classes cannot be used in 100% Pure Java programs. These resources are noted throughout this lesson. Most system programming needs are met through the System class. However, in rare cases, a program might have to access the system through the Runtime object that represents the current runtime environment. The last section of this lesson, The Runtime Object explains how to do this and talks about the trade-offs of accessing the system directly via the Runtime object.

The following diagram shows that the System class allows your Java programs to use system resources but insulates them from system-specific details. If you've experimented with other lessons in this tutorial, you've no doubt already seen the System class's standard output stream used in several examples to display text. This and other resources available through System are briefly described here and covered in the sections indicated.

12.8.2 Using the System Class

All of System's methods and variables are class methods and class variables. You don't instantiate the System class to use it; you use the System class's methods and variables directly from a reference to the System class.

(1) The Standard I/O Streams

Probably the most frequently used items from the System class are the streams used for reading and writing text. The System class provides one stream for reading text—the standard input stream—and two streams for writing text—the standard output and standard error streams.

(2) System Properties

Properties are key/value pairs that your Java programs can use to set up various attributes or parameters between invocations. The Java platform itself maintains a set of system properties that contain information about the current platform. You can access the system properties through the System class.

(3) Forcing Finalization and Garbage Collection

In Java, you don't have to free an object when you're done with it-the garbage collector runs periodically in the background and cleans up unreferenced objects. Or you can force the garbage collector to run using System's gc method. Also, you can request that the runtime system perform object finalization using System's runFinalization method.

(4) Providing Your Own Security Manager

The security manager is an application-wide object that determines whether potentially threatening operations should be allowed. You use the System class to set and get the security manager for an application. Subclasses of java.lang.SecurityManager implement a specific management policy.

(5) Miscellaneous System Methods

The System class includes several miscellaneous methods that let you get the current time in milliseconds, exit the interpreter, and copy arrays.

12.8.3 The Runtime Object

Most system programming needs are met through the programming interface provided by the System class. However, in rare cases, a program must bypass the system-independent interface of the System class and use system resources directly from the runtime environment. The Java environment provides a Runtimeobject, which represents the current runtime environment. You can use a Runtime object to access system resources directly.

Note: Messaging the Runtime object directly compromises your ability to run your program on different systems. You should do this only in special situations.

12.9 Command-Line Arguments

A Java application can accept any number of arguments from the command line. Command-line arguments allow the user to affect the operation of an application for one invocation. For example, an application might allow the user to specify verbose mode—that is, specify that the application display a lot of trace information. This is done using the command-line argument -verbose. Purity Tip: Programs that use command-line arguments are not 100% Pure Java because some systems, like the Mac OS, don't normally have a command line or command-line arguments. Consider using properties instead so that your programs fit more naturally into the environment. If you really must use command-line arguments, have them comply with the POSIX conventions.

The user enters command-line arguments when invoking the application and specifies them after the name of the class to run. For example, suppose you have a Java application, called Sort, that sorts lines in a file. To sort the data in a file named friends.txt, you would run it like this:

```
java Sort friends.txt
```

In the Java language, when you invoke an application, the runtime system passes the command-line arguments to the application's main method via an array of Strings. Each String in the array contains one of the command-line arguments. In the previous example, the command-line arguments passed to the Sort application is an array that contains a single String: "friends.txt".

Note to C and C++ Programmers: The command-line arguments passed to a Java application differ in number and in type than those passed to a C or C++ program. When you invoke a Java application, the system passes only one parameter to it:

```
args: An array of strings that contains the arguments
```

You can derive the number of command-line arguments with the array's length attribute:

```
numberOfArgs = args.length;
```

In Java, you always know the name of the application because it's the name of the class in which the main method is defined. So the Java runtime system does not pass the class name you invoke to the main method. Rather, it passes only the items on the command line that appear after the class name. For example, consider the following statement, which is used to invoke a Java application:

```
java diff file1 file2
```

The command-line arguments are in a different font.

Echoing Command-Line Arguments

The following simple application displays each of its command-line arguments on a line by itself:

```
public class Echo {
public static void main (String[] args) {
for (int i = 0; i < args.length; i++)
System.out.println(args[i]);
}
}
```

Here's an example of how to invoke the application using Windows 95/NT. You enter the words that are shown here in a different font:

```
java Echo Drink Hot Java
Drink
Hot
Java
```

Note that the application displays each word—Drink, Hot, and Java—on a line by itself. This is because the space character separates command-line arguments. If you want Drink, Hot, and Java to be interpreted as a single argument, you would join them by enclosing them within double quotation marks. On Windows 95/NT, you run it like this:

```
java Echo "Drink Hot Java"
Drink Hot Java
```

12.9.1 Parsing Numeric Command-Line Arguments

If your program needs to support a numeric command-line argument, it must convert a String argument that represents a number, such as "34", to a number. Here's a code snippet that converts a command-line argument to an int:

```
int firstArg;
if (args.length > 0)
firstArg = Integer.parseInt(args[0]);
```

parseInt throws a NumberFormatException if the format of args[0] isn't valid. All of the Number classes—Integer, Float, Double, and so on—have parseXXX methods that convert a String representing a number to an object of their type.

12.9.2 Setting Program Attributes

Java programs run within an environment that contains system attributes: a host machine, a user, a current directory, and an operating system. A Java program also can set up its own configurable attributes, called program attributes. Program attributes allow the user to configure various startup options, preferred window size, and so on for the program. Sometimes the term preferences is used instead of program attributes. System attributes are maintained by the System class and are covered later in System Properties. Java programs can set their own set of program attributes through three mechanisms: properties, command-line arguments, and applet parameters.

12.10 Using Properties to Manage Program Attributes

A property defines attributes on a persistent basis. That is, you use properties when attribute values need to persist between invocations of a program. This section shows you how to do this in your programs.

(1) Command-Line Arguments

A command-line argument defines attributes for Java applications on a nonpersistent basis. You use command-line arguments to set one or more attributes for a single invocation of an application. This section shows how to accept and process command-line arguments in a Java program.

(2) Applet Parameters

An applet parameter is similar to a command-line argument, except that it is used with applets, not applications. Use applet parameters to set one or more attributes for a single invocation of an applet. For information about applet parameters, see Defining and Using Applet Parameters.

12.11 Solving Common Coding Problems

This section covers some common problems that you might encounter when learning the Java language. After each problem is a list of possible solutions.

Problem: The compiler complains that it can't find a class.

Make sure you've imported the class or its package.

Unset the CLASSPATH environment variable, if it's set.

Make sure you're spelling the class name exactly the same way as it is declared. Case matters!

If your classes are in packages, make sure that they appear in the correct subdirectory as outlined in Managing Source and Class Files. Also, some programmers use different names for the class name from the .java filename. Make sure you're using the class name and not the filename. In fact, make the names the same and you won't run into this problem for this reason.

Problem: The interpreter says it can't find one of my classes.

Make sure you specified the class name—not the class file name—to the interpreter.

Unset the CLASSPATH environment variable, if it's set.

If your classes are in packages, make sure that they appear in the correct subdirectory as outlined in Managing Source and Class Files. Make sure you're invoking the interpreter from the directory in which the .class file is located.

Problem: My program doesn't work! What's wrong with it?

The following is a list of common programming mistakes by novice Java programmers. Make sure one of these isn't what's holding you back.

Did you forget to use break after each case statement in a switch statement? Did you use the assignment operator = when you really wanted to use the comparison operator ==?

Are the termination conditions on your loops correct? Make sure you're not terminating loops one iteration too early or too late. That is, make sure you are using < or <= and > or >= as appropriate for your situation. Remember that array indices begin at 0, so iterating over an array looks like this:

```
for (int i = 0; i < array.length; i++)
. . .
```

Are you comparing floating-point numbers using ==? Remember that floats are approximations of the real thing. The greater than and less than (> and <) operators are more appropriate when conditional logic is performed on floating-point numbers. Are you having trouble with encapsulation, inheritance, or other object-oriented programming and design concepts? Review the information in Object-Oriented Programming Concepts. Make sure that blocks of statements are enclosed in curly brackets { }. The following code looks right because of indentation, but it doesn't do what the indents imply because the brackets are missing:

```
for (int i = 0; i < arrayOfInts.length; i++)
arrayOfInts[i] = i;
System.out.println("[i] = " + arrayOfInts[i]);
```

Are you using the correct conditional operator? Make sure you understand && and || and are using them appropriately. Do you use the negation operator ! a lot? Try to express conditions without it. Doing so is less confusing and error-prone. Are you using a do-while? If so, do you know that a do-while executes at least once, but a similar while loop may not be executed at all? Are you trying to change the value of an argument from a method? Arguments in Java are passed by value and can't be changed in a method. Did you inadvertently add an extra semicolon (;), thereby terminating a statement prematurely? Notice the extra semicolon at the end of this for statement:

```
for (int i = 0; i < arrayOfInts.length; i++) ;
arrayOfInts[i] = i;
```

12.11.1 Managing Source and Class Files

The JDK relies on hierarchical file systems to manage source and class files for Java programs, although The Java Language Specification does not require this. The strategy is as follows.

You put the source code for a class or interface in a text file whose name is the short name of the class or interface and whose extension is .java (the JDK requires this extension for public classes and it's a good idea for other classes). Then, you put the source file in a directory whose name reflects the name of the package to which the class or interface belongs. For example, the source code for the Rectangle class would be in a file named Rectangle.java and the file would be in a directory named graphics. The graphics directory may be anywhere on the file system. The following diagram shows how this works.

The long name of the package member and the pathname to the file are parallel (assuming the UNIX filename separator slash /):

```
graphics.Rectangle         class name
graphics/Rectangle.java pathname to file
```

Furthermore, by convention, each company uses its reversed Internet domain name in its package names. (However, some companies now choose to drop "com" from their package names.) The fictional company called Taranis Interactive whose Internet domain name is taranis.com would precede all of its package names with com.taranis. Each component of the package name corresponds to a subdirectory. So, if Taranis had a graphics package that contained a Rectangle.java source file, it would be contained in a series of subdirectories, as shown here:

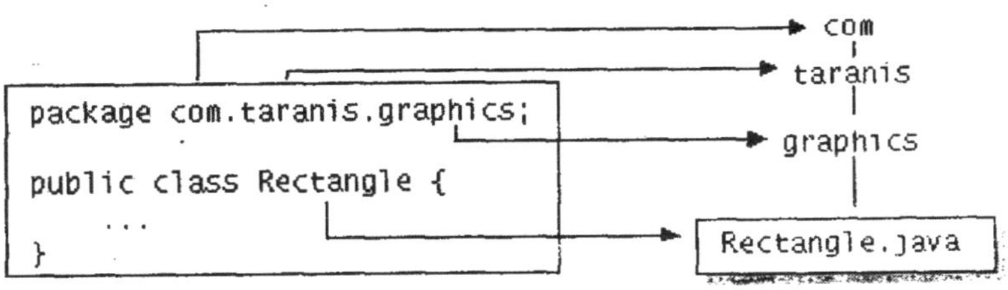

Fig. 12.3

When you compile a source file, the compiler creates a different output file for each class and interface defined in it. The basename of the output file is the name of the class or interface, and its extension is .class:

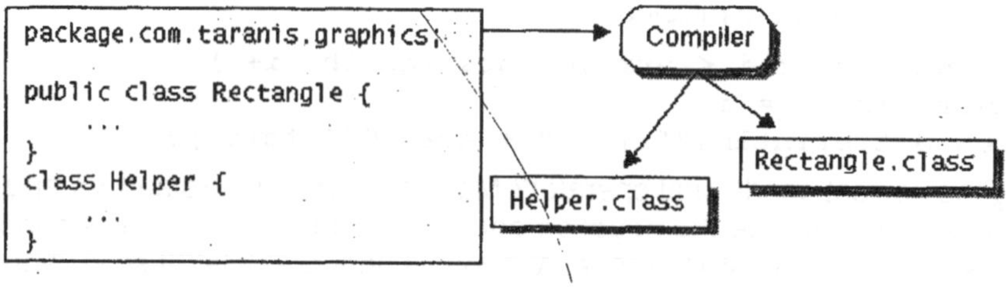

Fig. 12.4

Like a .java file, a .class file should also be in a series of directories that reflect the package name. However, it does not have to be in the same directory as its source. You could arrange your source and class directories separately, like this:

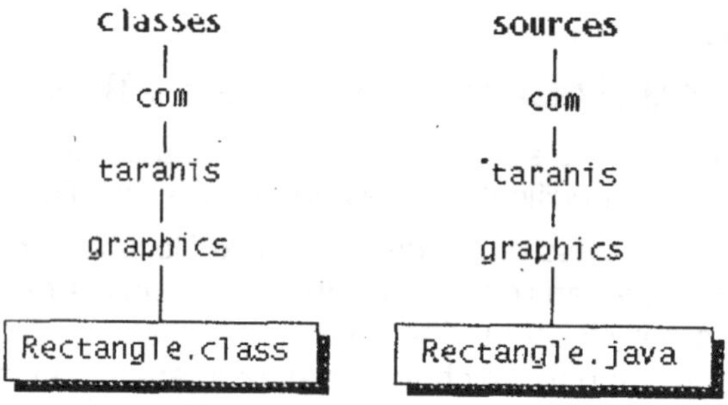

Fig. 12.5

By doing this, you can give the classes directory to other programmers without revealing your sources. Why all the bother about directories and filenames? You need to manage your source and class files in this manner so that the compiler and the interpreter can find all of the classes and interfaces used by your program. When the compiler encounters a new class as it's compiling your program, it must be able to find the class so as to resolve names, do type checking, and so on. Similarly, when the interpreter encounters a new class as it's running your program, it must be able to find the class to invoke its methods, and so on. Both the compiler and the interpreter search for classes in each directory or zip file listed in your class path. Definition: A class path is a list of directories or zip files to search for class files.

Each directory listed in the class path is a top-level directory in which package directories appear. From the top-level directory, the compiler and the interpreter can construct the rest of the path based on the package and class name for the class. For example, the class path entry for the directory structure shown in the previous diagram page would include classes, but not com or any of the directories below com. Both the compiler and the interpreter construct the path name to a .class file with its full package name. By default, the compiler and the interpreter search the current directory and the zip file containing the JDK class files. In other words, the current directory and the JDK class files are automatically in your class path. Most, if not all, classes can be found in these two locations. So it's likely that you don't have to worry about your class path. In some cases, however, you may have to set your class path.

12.11.2 Setting the Class Path

If you must, you can change your class path. This can be done in either of two ways:

- Set the CLASSPATH environment variable (not recommended).

- Use the -classpath runtime option when you invoke the compiler or the interpreter.

We don't recommend setting the CLASSPATH environment variable because it can be long-lived (particularly if you set it in a login or startup script). It's also easy to forget about, and then one day, your programs won't work because the compiler or interpreter loads a crusty old class file instead of the one you want. An old, out-of-date CLASSPATH variable is a fruitful source of confusing problems. The second option, setting the class path with the runtime option, is preferable because it sets the class path only for the current invocation of the compiler or the interpreter. Here's how to use the runtime option -classpath to set your class path.

Platform-specific Details: Using the -classpath Runtime Option:

UNIX:

```
javac -classpath .:~/classes:/JDK/lib/classes.zip
DOS shell (Windows 95/NT):
javac -classpath .;C:\classes;C:\JDK\lib\classes.zip
```

When you specify a class path in this manner, you completely override the current class path. Thus you must include the classes.zip file from the JDK in the class path. It's a good idea to include the current directory as well. The order of the entries in the class path is important. When the Java interpreter is looking for a class, it searches the entries in your class path, in order, until it finds a class with the correct name. The Java interpreter runs the first class with the correct name that it encounters and does not search the remaining entries.

Note: If you load an applet into a Java application such as HotJava or the Applet Viewer and the loaded class is in the class path, the applet doesn't have the restrictions that applets loaded over the network do, so it can never be reloaded. We recommend never starting an application such as HotJava in the same directory as an Applet class because the current directory "." is usually part of the class path.

import graphics.A*; // does not work

Instead, it generates a compiler error. With the import statement, you can import only a single package member or an entire package. For your convenience, the Java runtime system automatically imports three packages for you:

```
The default package (the package with no name)
The java.lang package
The current package
Disambiguating a Name
```

If by some chance a member in one package shares the same name with a member in another package and both packages are imported, you must refer to the member by its long name. For example, the previous example defined a class named Rectangle in the graphics package. The java.awt package also contains a Rectangle class. If both graphics and java.awt have been imported, then the following is ambiguous:

Rectangle rect;

In such a situation, you have to be more specific and indicate exactly which Rectangle class you want by using the member's long name:

graphics.Rectangle rect;

12.12 Miscellaneous System Methods

The System class provides several methods that provide miscellaneous functionality including copying arrays and getting the current time.

12.12.1 Copying Arrays

Use System's arraycopy method to efficiently copy data from one array into another. The arraycopy method requires five arguments:

```
public static
void arraycopy(Object source,
        int srcIndex,
        Object dest,
        int destIndex,
        int length,
```

The two Object arguments indicate the array to copy from and the array to copy to. The three integer arguments indicate the starting location in each the source and the destination array, and the number of elements to copy. This diagram illustrates how the copy takes place:

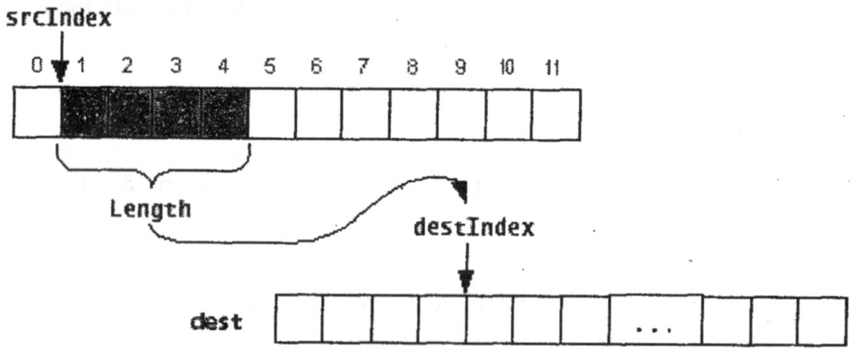

Fig. 12.6

The following program uses arraycopy to copy some elements from the copyFrom array to the copyTo array.

```
public class ArrayCopyTest {
public static void main(String[] args) {
char[] copyFrom = { 'd', 'e', 'c', 'a', 'f', 'f', 'e',
'i', 'n', 'a', 't', 'e', 'd' };
char[] copyTo = new char[7];
System.arraycopy(copyFrom, 2, copyTo, 0, 7);
System.out.println(new String(copyTo));
}
}
```

The arraycopy method call in this example program begins the copy at element number 2 in the source array. Recall that array indices start at 0, so that the copy begins at the array element 'c'. The arraycopy method call puts the copied elements into the destination array beginning at the first element (element 0) in the destination array copyTo. The copy copies 7 elements: 'c', 'a', 'f', 'f', 'e', 'i', and 'n'. Effectively, the arraycopy method takes the "caffein" out of "decaffeinated", like this:

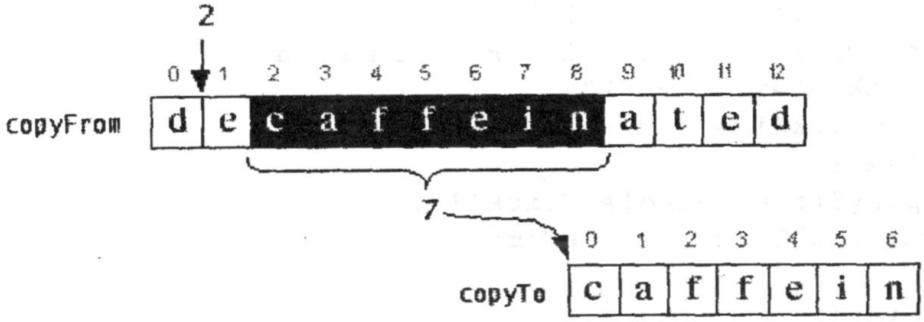

Fig. 12.7

Note that the destination array must be allocated before you call arraycopy and must be large enough to contain the data being copied.

12.12.2 Getting the Current Time

The currentTimeMillis method returns the current time in milliseconds since 00:00:00, January 1, 1970. The currentTimeMillis method is commonly used during performance tests: get the current time, perform the operation that you want to time, get the current time again—the difference in the two time samples is roughly the amount of time that the operation took to perform. Often in graphical user interfaces the time difference between mouse clicks is used to determine whether a user double clicked. The following applet uses currentTimeMillis to compute the number of milliseconds between two mouse clicks. If the time period between the clicks is smaller than 200 milliseconds, the two mouse clicks are interpreted as a double mouse click.

Note: Because some old browsers don't support 1.1, the above applet is a 1.0 version (here is the 1.0 code; here's the 1.1 code). To run the 1.1 version of the applet, go to example-1dot1/TimingIsEverything.html. For more information about running applets, refer to About Our Examples.

Here's the source for the TimingIsEverything applet:

```
import java.awt.Graphics;
import java.awt.Dimension;
import java.awt.event.MouseAdapter;
import java.awt.event.MouseEvent;
public class TimingIsEverything extends java.applet.Applet {
public long firstClickTime = 0;
public String displayStr;
public void init() {
displayStr = "Double Click Me";
addMouseListener(new MyAdapter());
}
public void paint(Graphics g) {
g.drawRect(0, 0, getSize().width-1, getSize().height-1);
g.drawString(displayStr, 40, 30);
}
class MyAdapter extends MouseAdapter {
public void mouseClicked(MouseEvent evt) {
long clickTime = System.currentTimeMillis();
```

```
long clickInterval = clickTime - firstClickTime;
if (clickInterval < 300) {
displayStr = "Double Click!! (Interval = "
+ clickInterval + ")";
firstClickTime = 0;
} else {
displayStr = "Single Click!!";
firstClickTime = clickTime;
}
repaint();
}
}
}
```

You could use the return value from this method to compute the current date and time. However, you'll probably find that it's more convenient to get the current date and time from the Date class.

Note: Previous versions of the System class support two other time-related methods besides the currentTimeMillis method: currentTime and nowMillis. These two methods are now obsolete—you should use currentTimeMillis instead.

12.12.3 Exiting the Runtime Environment

To exit the Java interpreter, call the System.exit method. The interpreter exits with the integer exit code that you specify to the exit method.

System.exit(-1);

Note: The exit method causes the Java interpreter to exit, not just your Java program. Use this function with caution.

Security consideration: Invocation of the exit method is subject to security restrictions. Depending on the browser that an applet is running in, a call to exit from within an applet will likely result in a SecurityException. See Security Restrictions for information about the security restrictions placed on applets.

12.13 Introducing the Security Manager

Each Java application can have its own security manager object that acts as a full-time security guard. The SecurityManager class in the java.lang package is an abstract class that provides the programming interface and partial implementation for all Java security managers. By default an application does not have a security manager. That is, the Java runtime system does not automatically create a security manager for every Java application. So by default an application allows all operations that are subject to security restrictions. To change this default lenient behavior, an application must create and install its own security manager. You will learn how to create a security manager in Writing a Security Manager, and how to install it in Installing Your Security Manager.

Note: The existing browsers and applet viewers do create their own security manager when starting up. Thus an applet is subject to whatever access restrictions are imposed on it by the security manager for the particular application in which the applet is running. You can get the current security manager for an application using the System class's getSecurityManager() method:

```
SecurityManager appsm = System.getSecurityManager();
```

Note that getSecurityManager() returns null if there is no current security manager for the application so you should check to make sure that you have a valid object before calling any of its methods. Once you have the security manager, you can request permission to allow or disallow certain operations. Indeed many of the classes in the Java packages do just this. For example, the System.exit() method, which terminates the Java interpreter, uses the security manager's checkExit() method to approve the exit operation:

```
SecurityManager security = System.getSecurityManager();
if (security != null) {
security.checkExit(status);}
// code continues here if checkedExit() returns
```

If the security manager approves the exit operation, the checkExit() returns normally. If the security manager disallows the operation, the checkExit() method throws a SecurityException. In this manner, the security manager allows or disallows a potentially threatening operation before it can be completed. The SecurityManager class defines many other methods used to verify other kinds of operations. For example, SecurityManager's checkAccess() method verifies thread accesses, and checkPropertyAccess() verifies access to the specified property. Each operation or group of operations has its own checkXXX() method.

In addition, the set of checkXXX() methods represent the set of operations in the Java package classes and the Java runtime that are already subject to the protection of the security manager. So, typically, your code will not have to invoke any of SecurityManager's checkXXX() methods—the Java package classes and the Java runtime already do this for you at a low enough level that any operation represented by a checkXXX() method is already protected. However, when writing your own security manager, you may have to override SecurityManager's checkXXX() methods to tighten or modify the security policy for specific operations, or you may have to add a few of your own to put other kinds of operations under the scrutiny of the security manager. Deciding What SecurityManager Methods to Override explains which operation or group of operations each checkXXX() method in the SecurityManager class is designed to protect.

12.13.1 Setting and Getting the Security Manager

The security manager is an object that enforces a certain security policy for a Java application. You can set the current security manager for your applications using System's setSecurityManager method, and you can retrieve the current security manager using System's getSecurityManager method. An application's security manager is a java.lang.SecurityManager object. Providing Your Own Security Manager discusses security managers in detail and shows you how to create and install your own security manager using these two System methods.

Security consideration: The security manager for an application can be set only once. Typically, a browser sets its security manager during its startup procedure. Thus, most of the time, applets cannot set the security manager because it's already been set. A SecurityException will result if your applet attempts to do so. See Security Restrictions for information about the security restrictions placed on applets.

12.13.2 Deciding What SecurityManager Methods to Override

You may have to override several of SecurityManager's checkXXX() methods depending on which operations you want your security manager to impose restrictions on. The first column in the following table are objects on which you can perform various operations. The second column lists the SecurityManager methods that approve the operations on the objects in the first column.

Table - 12.1

Operations On	Approved By
sockets	checkAccept(String host, int port)
checkConnect	(String host, int port)
checkConnect	(String host, int port, Object executionContext)
checkListen	(int port)
threads	checkAccess(Thread thread)
checkAccess	(ThreadGroup threadgroup)
class loader	checkCreateClassLoader()
file system	checkDelete(String filename)
checkLink	(String library)
checkRead	(FileDescriptor filedescriptor)
checkRead	(String filename)
checkRead	(String filename, Object executionContext)
checkWrite	(FileDescriptor filedescriptor)
checkWrite	(String filename)
system commands	checkExec(String command)
interpreter	checkExit(int status)
package	checkPackageAccess(String packageName)
checkPackageDefinition	(String packageName)
properties	checkPropertiesAccess()
checkPropertyAccess	(String key)
checkPropertyAccess	(String key, String def)
networking	checkSetFactory()
windows	checkTopLevelWindow(Object window)

Depending on your security policy, you can override some or all of these methods. For example, suppose you are writing a Web browser or applet viewer and want to disallow applets from using sockets altogether. To do this you override the four methods that affect socket access. Many of the checkXXX() methods are called in multiple situations. For example, the checkAccess(ThreadGroup g) method is invoked when you create a ThreadGroup, set its daemon status, stop it, and so on. When overriding a checkXXX() method make sure that you understand all the situations in which it can be invoked.

The default implementation provided by the SecurityManager class for all checkXXX() methods is:

```
public void checkXXX(. . .) {
throw new SecurityException();
}
```

Most security policies that you want to implement will likely be more selective than disallowing everything! So you may find that you have to override all SecurityManager's checkXXX() methods.

12.13.3 Installing Your Security Manager

Once you've completed writing your SecurityManager subclass, you can install it as the current security manager for your Java application. You do this with the setSecurityManager() method from the System class. Here's a small test application, SecurityManagerTest, that installs the PasswordSecurityManager class from the previous page as the current security manager. Then to verify that the security manager is in place and operational, the SecurityManagerTest application opens two files—one for reading and one for writing—and copies the contents of the first file into the second.

The main() method begins by installing a new security manager:

```
try {
System.setSecurityManager(new PasswordSecurityManager("Booga Booga"));
} catch (SecurityException se) {
System.out.println("SecurityManager already set!");
}
```

The bold line in the previous code snippet creates a new instance of the PasswordSecurityManager class with the password "Booga Booga". This instance is passed to System's setSecurityManager() method, which installs the object as the current security manager for the running application. This security manager will remain in effect for the duration of the execution of this application. You can set the security manager for your application only once. In other words, your Java application can invoke System.setSecurityManager() only one time during its lifetime. Any subsequent attempt to install a security manager within a Java application will result in a SecurityException.

The rest of the program copies the contents of this file inputtext.txt into an output file named outputtext.txt. This is a simple test to verify that the PasswordSecurityManager has been properly installed.

```
try {
DataInputStream fis = new DataInputStream(
new FileInputStream("inputtext.txt"));
DataOutputStream fos = new DataOutputStream(
new FileOutputStream("outputtext.txt"));
String inputString;
while ((inputString = fis.readLine()) != null) {
fos.writeBytes(inputString);
fos.writeByte('\n');
}
fis.close();
fos.close();
} catch (IOException ioe) {
System.err.println("I/O failed for SecurityManagerTest.");
}
```

The bold lines in the previous code snippet are restricted file system accesses. These method calls will result in a call to PasswordSecurityManager's checkAccess() method.

12.13.4 Running the Test Program

When you run the SecurityManagerTest application, you are prompted twice for a password: once when the application opens the input file and once when the application opens the output file. If you type in the correct password, the access is granted—the file object—and the application proceeds to the next statement. If you type in an incorrect password, checkXXX() throws a SecurityException, which the test application makes no attempt to catch so the application terminates. This is an example of the output from the application when you type in the password correctly the first time, but incorrectly the second:

What's the secret password?

```
Booga Booga
What's the secret password?
Wrong password
java.lang.SecurityException: Not Even!
```

```
a                                                                    t
PasswordSecurityManager.checkWrite(PasswordSecurityManager.java:46)
at java.io.FileOutputStream.(FileOutputStream.java)
at SecurityManagerTest.main(SecurityManagerTest.java:15)
```

Notice that the error message that the application prints is the error message for the checkWrite(String) method.

12.13.5 Writing a Security Manager

To write your own security manager, you must create a subclass of the SecurityManager class. Your SecurityManager subclass overrides various methods from SecurityManager to customize the verifications and approvals needed in your Java application. This page walks through an example security manager that restricts reading and writing to the file system. To get approval from the security manager, a method that opens a file for reading invokes one of SecurityManager's checkRead() methods. Similarly, a method that opens a file for writing invokes one of SecurityManager's checkWrite() methods. If the security manager approves the operation then the checkXXX() method returns, otherwise checkXXX() throws a SecurityException.

To impose a stricter policy on file system accesses, our example SecurityManager subclass must override SecurityManager's checkRead() and checkWrite() methods. SecurityManager provides three versions of checkRead() and two versions of checkWrite(). Each of which should verify whether the application is allowed to open a file for I/O. A policy frequently implemented by browsers is that applets loaded over the network cannot read from or write to the local file system unless the user approves it. The policy implemented by our example prompts the user for a password when the application attempts to open a file for reading or for writing. If the password is correct then the access is allowed. All security managers must be a subclass of SecurityManager. Thus, our PasswordSecurityManager class extends SecurityManager.

```
class PasswordSecurityManager extends SecurityManager
{
. . .
}
```

Next, PasswordSecurityManager declares a private instance variable password to contain the password that the user must enter in order to allow the restricted file system accesses. The password is set upon construction:

```
PasswordSecurityManager(String password) {
super();
this.password = password;}
```

The next method in the PasswordSecurityManager class is a private helper method named accessOK(). This method prompts the user for a password and verifies it. If the user enters a valid password, the method returns true; otherwise, it returns false.

```
private boolean accessOK() {
int c;
DataInputStream dis = new DataInputStream(System.in);
String response;
System.out.println("What's the secret password?");
try {
response = dis.readLine();
```

```
if (response.equals(password))
return true;
else
return false;
} catch (IOException e) {
return false;}
}
```

Finally at the end of the PasswordSecurityManager class are the three overridden checkRead() methods and the two overridden checkWrite() methods:

```
public void checkRead(FileDescriptor filedescriptor) {
if (!accessOK())
throw new SecurityException("Not a Chance!");}
public void checkRead(String filename) {
if (!accessOK())
throw new SecurityException("No Way!");}
public void checkRead(String filename, Object executionContext) {
if (!accessOK())
throw new SecurityException("Forget It!");}
public void checkWrite(FileDescriptor filedescriptor) {
if (!accessOK())
throw new SecurityException("Not!");}
public void checkWrite(String filename) {
if (!accessOK())
throw new SecurityException("Not Even!");
}
```

All the checkXXX() methods call accessOK() to prompt the user for a password. If access is not OK, then checkXXX() throws a SecurityException. Otherwise, checkXXX() returns normally. Note that SecurityException is a runtime exception, and as such does not need to be declared in the throws clause of these methods. checkRead() and checkWrite() are just a few of the many of SecurityManager's checkXXX() methods that verify various kinds of operations. You can override or add any number of checkXXX() methods to implement your security policy. You do not need to override all of SecurityManager's checkXXX() methods, just the ones that you want to customize. However, the default implementation provided by the SecurityManager class for all checkXXX() methods throws a SecurityException. In other words, by default the SecurityManager class disallows all operations that are subject to security restrictions. So you may find that you have to override many of SecurityManager's checkXXX() methods to get the behavior you want. All of SecurityManager's checkXXX() methods operate in the same way:

- If access is allowed, the method returns.
- If access is not allowed, the method throws a SecurityException.

Make sure that you implement your overridden checkXXX() methods in this manner.

Well, that's it for our SecurityManager subclass. As you can see implementing a SecurityManager is simple. You just:

- Create a SecurityManager subclass.
- Override a few methods.

The tricky part is determining which methods to override and implementing your security policy. Deciding What SecurityManager Methods to Override will help you figure out which methods you should override depending on what types of operations you'd like to protect. The next page shows you how to install the PasswordSecurityManager class as the on-duty security manager for your Java application.

12.13.6 Providing Your Own Security Manager

Security becomes a major concern when writing and using programs that interact with the Internet. Will you download something that corrupts your file system? Will you be open for a virus attack? It's unlikely that computers on the Internet will ever be completely safe from attack from the few evil-doers out there. However, you can take steps to provide a significant level of protection and security for your computers and data. One of the ways that Java provides protection from attack is through the use of security managers. A security manager implements and imposes the security policy for an application.

12.14 Forcing Finalization and Garbage Collection

The Java runtime system performs memory management tasks for you. When your program has finished using an object, that is, when there are no more references to an object, the object is finalized and is then garbage collected. These tasks happen asynchronously in the background. However, you can force object finalization and garbage collection using the appropriate method in the System class.

12.14.1 Finalizing Objects

Before an object is garbage collected, the Java runtime system gives the object a chance to clean up after itself. This step is known as finalization and is achieved through a call to the object's finalize method. You can force object finalization to occur by calling System's runFinalization method.

System.runFinalization();

This method calls the finalize methods on all objects that are waiting to be garbage collected.

12.14.2 Running the Garbage Collector

You can ask the garbage collector to run at any time by calling System's gc method:

System.gc();

You might want to run the garbage collector to ensure that it runs at the best time for your program rather than when it's most convenient for the runtime system to run it. For example, your program may wish to run the garbage collector right before it enters a compute or memory intensive section of code or when it knows there will be some idle time. Note that the garbage collector requires time to complete its task. The amount of time that gc requires to complete varies depending on certain factors: How big your heap is and how fast your processor is, for example. Your program should only run the garbage collector when doing so will have no performance impact on your program. For general information about Java's garbage collection scheme, see Cleaning Up Unused Objects.

12.15 System Properties

The System class maintains a set of properties, key/value pairs, that define traits or attributes of the current working environment. When the runtime system first starts up, the system properties are initialized to contain information about the runtime environment. including information about the current user, the current version of the Java runtime, and even the character used to separate components of a filename. Here is a complete list of the system properties you get when the runtime system first starts up and what they mean:

Key Meaning

```
"file.separator" File separator (for example, "/")
"java.class.path" Java classpath
"java.class.version" Java class version number
"java.home" Java installation directory
"java.vendor" Java vendor-specific string
"java.vendor.url" Java vendor URL
"java.version" Java version number
"line.separator" Line separator
"os.arch" Operating system architecture
"os.name" Operating system name
"os.version" Operating system version
"path.separator" Path separator (for example, ":")
"user.dir" User's current working directory
"user.home" User home directory
"user.name" User account name
```

Your Java programs can read or write system properties through several methods in the System class. You can use a key to look up one property in the properties list, or you can get the whole set of properties all at once. You can also change the set of system properties completely.

Security consideration: Applets can access some, but not all system properties. For a complete list of the system properties that can and cannot be used by applets, refer to Getting System Properties. Applets cannot write system properties.

12.15.1 Reading System Propertie

The System class has two methods that you can use to read the system properties: getProperty and getProperties.

The System class has two different versions of getProperty. Both retrieve the value of the property named in the argument list. The simpler of the two getProperty methods takes a single argument: the key for the property you want to search for. For example, to get the value of path.separator, use the following statement:

System.getProperty("path.separator");

The getProperty method returns a string containing the value of the property. If the property does not exist, this version of getProperty returns null. Which brings us to the next version of getProperty method. This version requires two String arguments: the first argument is the key to look up and the second argument is a default value to return if the key cannot be found or if it has no value. For example, this call to getProperty looks up the System property called subliminal.message. This is not a valid system property, so instead of returning null, this method returns the default value provided as a second argument: "Buy Java Now!"

System.getProperty("subliminal.message", "Buy Java Now!");

You should use this version of getProperty if you don't want to risk a NullPointerException, or if you really want to provide a default value for a property that doesn't have value or that cannot be found. The last method provided by the System class to access properties values is the getProperties method, which returns a Properties object that contains the complete set of system property key/ value pairs. You can use the various Properties class methods to query the Properties objects for specific values or to list the entire set of properties. For information about the Properties class, see

Using Properties to Manage Program Attributes.

12.15.2 Writing System Properties

You can modify the existing set of system properties using System's setProperties method. This method takes a Properties object that has been initialized to contain the key/value pairs for the properties that you want to set. Thus this method replaces the entire set of system properties with the new set represented by the Properties object. The next example is a Java program that creates a Properties object and initializes it from this file: myProperties.txt.

subliminal.message=Buy Java Now!

The example program then uses System.setProperties to install the new Properties objects as the current set of system properties.

```
import java.io.FileInputStream;
import java.util.Properties;
public class PropertiesTest {
public static void main(String[] args) throws Exception {
// set up new properties object
// from file "myProperties.txt"
FileInputStream propFile = new FileInputStream(
"myProperties.txt");
Properties p = new Properties(System.getProperties());
p.load(propFile);
// set the system properties
System.setProperties(p);
// display new properties
System.getProperties().list(System.out);
}
}
```

Note how the example program creates the Properties object, p, which is used as the argument to setProperties:

Properties p = new Properties(System.getProperties());

This statement initializes the new properties object, p with the current set of system properties, which in the case of this small program, is the set of properties initialized by the runtime system. Then the program loads additional properties into p from the file myProperties.txt and sets the system properties to p. This has the effect of adding the properties listed in myProperties.txt to the set of properties created by the runtime system at startup. Note that you can create p without any default Properties object like this:

Properties p = new Properties();

If you do this then your application won't have access to the system properties. Also note that the value of system properties can be overwritten! For example, if myProperties.txt contains the following line, the java.vendor system property wil be overwritten:

java.vendor=Acme Software Company

In general, you should be careful not to overwrite system properties. The setProperties method changes the set of system properties for the current running application. These changes are not persistent. That is, changing the system properties within an application will not effect future invocations of the Java interpreter for this or any other application. The runtime system re-initializes the system properties each time its starts up. If you want your changes to the system properties to be persistent, then your application must write the values to some file before exiting and read them in again upon startup.

12.16 You don't need to import java.lang.*

There is one exception to the import rule. All classes in the java.lang package are imported by default. Thus you do not need to import java.lang.*; to use them without fully qualifed names.

Consider the System.out.println() method we've been using since the first day of class.

System is really the java.lang.System class. This class has a public static field called out which is an instance of the java.io.PrintStream class. So when you write System.out.println(), you're really calling the println() method of the out field of the java.lang.System class.

12.17 The java.lang package

Each package defines a number of classes, interfaces, exceptions, and errors. For example, the java.lang package contains these:

Interfaces in java.lang

```
Cloneable
Runnable
Classes in java.lang
Boolean
Byte
Character
Class
ClassLoader
Compiler
Double
Float
Integer
Long
Math
Number
Object
Process
Runtime
SecurityManager
Short
String
StringBuffer
System
Thread
ThreadGroup
Throwable
Void
Exceptions in java.lang
ArithmeticException
ArrayIndexOutOfBoundsException
```

```
ArrayStoreException
ClassCastException
ClassNotFoundException
CloneNotSupportedException
Exception
IllegalAccessException
IllegalArgumentException
IllegalMonitorStateException
IllegalStateException
IllegalThreadStateException
IndexOutOfBoundsException
InstantiationException
InterruptedException
NegativeArraySizeException
NoSuchFieldException
NoSuchMethodException
NullPointerException
NumberFormatException
RuntimeException
SecurityException
StringIndexOutOfBoundsException
Errors in java.lang
AbstractMethodError
ClassCircularityError
ClassFormatError
Error
ExceptionInInitializerError
IllegalAccessError
IncompatibleClassChangeError
InstantiationError
InternalError
LinkageError
NoClassDefFoundError
NoSuchFieldError
NoSuchMethodError
OutOfMemoryError
StackOverflowError
ThreadDeath
UnknownError
UnsatisfiedLinkError
VerifyError
VirtualMachineError
```

12.18 java.lang.Object

The java.lang.Object class is the ultimate superclass of all objects If a class does not explicitly extend a class, then the compiler assumes it extends java.lang.Object.

There is one exception. Guesses?

The Methods of java.lang.Object

java.lang.Object provides a number of methods that are common to all objects. toString() is the most common such method. Since the default toString() method only produces the name of the class, you should override it in all classes you define.

```
public Object()
public final Class getClass()
public int hashCode()
public boolean equals(Object obj)
protected Object clone() throws CloneNotSupportedException
public String toString()
public final void notify()
public final void notifyAll()
public final void wait(long timeout) throws InterruptedException
public final void wait(long timeout, int nanos) throws
InterruptedException
public final void wait() throws InterruptedException
protected void finalize() throws Throwable
```

12.19 The Equals() Method

The equals() of java.lang.Object acts the same as the == operator; that is, it tests for object identity rather than object equality. The implicit contract of the equals() method, however, is that it tests for equality rather than identity. Thus most classes will override equals() with a version that does field by field comparisons before deciding whether to return true or false.

To elaborate, an object created by a clone() method (that is a copy of the object) should pass the equals() test if neither the original nor the clone has changed since the clone was created. However the clone will fail to be == to the original object.

For example, here is an equals() method you could use for the Car class. Two car are equal if and only if their license plates are equal, and that's what this method tests for.

```
public boolean equals(Object o) {
if ( o instanceof Car) {
Car c = (Car) o;
if (this.licensePlate.equals(c.licensePlate)) return true;
}
return false;
}
```

This example is particularly interesting because it demonstrates the impossibility of writing a useful generic equals() method that tests equality for any object. It is not sufficient to simply test for equality of all the fields of two objects. It is entirely possible that some of the fields may not be relevant to the test for equality as in this example where changing the speed of a car does not change the actual car that's referred to.

Be careful to avoid this common mistake when writing equals() methods:

```
public boolean equals(Car c) {
if ( o instanceof Car) {
Car c = (Car) o;
if (this.licensePlate.equals(c.licensePlate)) return true;
```

```
}
return false;
}
```

The equals() method must allow tests against any object of any class, not simply against other objects of the same class (Car in this example.)

12.20 The hashCode() method of java.lang.Object

Anytime you override equals() you should also override hashCode(). The hashCode() method should ideally return the same int for any two objects that compace equal and a different int for any two objects that don't compare equal, where equality is defined by the equals() method. This is used as an index by the java.util.Hashtable class.

In the Car example equality is determined exclusively by comparing license plates; therefore only the licesePlate field is used to determine the hash code. Since licensePlate is a String, and since the String class has its own hashCode() method, we can sponge off of that.

```
public int hashCode()
{
return this.licensePlate.hashCode();
}
```

Other times you may need to use the bitwise operators to merge hash codes for multiple fields. There are also a variety of useful methods in the type wrapper classes (java.lang.Double, java.lang.Float, etc.) that convert primitive data types to integers that share the same bit string. These can be used to hash primitive data types.

12.21 java.lang.Math

The Java class library is huge. We will not cover it all today. In fact, the remaining eight classes will focus mostly on the class library. However, I do want to take this opportunity to look briefly at one useful class in the library, java.lang.Math. This is a class which contains static methods for performing many standard mathematical operations like square roots and cosines. You will need it for many of this weeks exercises.

The Math class contains several dozen static methods. Recall that to use a static method from a class, you just prefix its name with the name of the class followed by a period. For instance

double x = Math.sqrt(9.0);

You never need to instantiate the Math class directly. (In fact you can't. The Math() constructor is declared private.)

12.21.1 Examples of java.lang.Math Methods

Here is an example program that exercises most of the routines in java.lang.Math. If your high school math is a little rusty, don't worry if you don't remember the exact meaning of logarithms or cosines. Just know that they're here in Java if you need them.

public class MathLibraryExample

```
{
public static void main(String args[]) {
int i = 7;
int j = -9;
double x = 72.3;
```

```
double y = 0.34;

System.out.println("i is " + i);
System.out.println("j is " + j);
System.out.println("x is " + x);
System.out.println("y is " + y);

// The absolute value of a number is equal to
// the number if the number is positive or
// zero and equal to the negative of the number
// if the number is negative.

System.out.println("|" + i + "| is " + Math.abs(i));
System.out.println("|" + j + "| is " + Math.abs(j));
System.out.println("|" + x + "| is " + Math.abs(x));
System.out.println("|" + y + "| is " + Math.abs(y));

// Truncating and Rounding functions

// You can round off a floating point number
// to the nearest integer with round()
System.out.println(x + " is approximately " + Math.round(x));
System.out.println(y + " is approximately " + Math.round(y));
// The "ceiling" of a number is the
// smallest integer greater than or equal to
// the number. Every integer is its own
// ceiling.
System.out.println("The ceiling of " + i + " is " + Math.ceil(i));
System.out.println("The ceiling of " + j + " is " + Math.ceil(j));
System.out.println("The ceiling of " + x + " is " + Math.ceil(x));
System.out.println("The ceiling of " + y + " is "+ Math.ceil(y));

// The "floor" of a number is the largest
// integer less than or equal to the number.
// Every integer is its own floor.
System.out.println("The floor of " + i + " is " + Math.floor(i));
System.out.println("The floor of " + j + " is " + Math.floor(j));
System.out.println("The floor of " + x + " is " + Math.floor(x));
System.out.println("The floor of " + y + " is " + Math.floor(y));

// Comparison operators

// min() returns the smaller of the two arguments you pass it
System.out.println("min(" + i + "," + j + ") is " + Math.min(i,j));
System.out.println("min(" + x + "," + y + ") is " + Math.min(x,y));
System.out.println("min(" + i + "," + x + ") is " + Math.min(i,x));
System.out.println("min(" + y + "," + j + ") is " + Math.min(y,j));
```

```
// There's a corresponding max() method
// that returns the larger of two numbers
System.out.println("max(" + i + "," + j + ") is " + Math.max(i,j));
System.out.println("max(" + x + "," + y + ") is " + Math.max(x,y));
System.out.println("max(" + i + "," + x + ") is " + Math.max(i,x));
System.out.println("max(" + y + "," + j + ") is " + Math.max(y,j));

// The Math library defines a couple
// of useful constants:
System.out.println("Pi is " + Math.PI);
System.out.println("e is " + Math.E);
// Trigonometric methods
// All arguments are given in radians

// Convert a 45 degree angle to radians
double angle = 45.0 * 2.0 * Math.PI/360.0;
System.out.println("cos(" + angle + ") is " + Math.cos(angle));
System.out.println("sin(" + angle + ") is " + Math.sin(angle));

// Inverse Trigonometric methods
// All values are returned as radians

double value = 0.707;
System.out.println("acos(" + value + ") is " + Math.acos(value));
System.out.println("asin(" + value + ") is " + Math.asin(value));
System.out.println("atan(" + value + ") is " + Math.atan(value));

// Exponential and Logarithmic Methods

// exp(a) returns e (2.71828...) raised
// to the power of a.
System.out.println("exp(1.0) is " + Math.exp(1.0));
System.out.println("exp(10.0) is " + Math.exp(10.0));
System.out.println("exp(0.0) is " +  Math.exp(0.0));

// log(a) returns  the natural
// logarithm (base e) of a.
System.out.println("log(1.0) is " + Math.log(1.0));
System.out.println("log(10.0) is " + Math.log(10.0));
System.out.println("log(Math.E) is " + Math.log(Math.E));

// pow(x, y) returns the x raised
// to the yth power.
System.out.println("pow(2.0, 2.0) is " + Math.pow(2.0,2.0));
System.out.println("pow(10.0, 3.5) is " + Math.pow(10.0,3.5));
System.out.println("pow(8, -1) is " + Math.pow(8,-1));

// sqrt(x) returns the square root of x.
```

```
for (i=0; i < 10; i++) {
System.out.println("The square root of " + i + " is " + Math.sqrt(i));
}


// Finally there's one Random method
// that returns a pseudo-random number
// between 0.0 and 1.0;

System.out.println("Here's one random number: " + Math.random());
System.out.println("Here's another random number: " + Math.random());
}
}
java.lang.Math
```

Here's the output from the math library example

```
i is 7
j is -9
x is 72.3
y is 0.34
|7| is 7
|-9| is 9
|72.3| is 72.3
|0.34| is 0.34
72.3 is approximately 72
0.34 is approximately 0
The ceiling of 7 is 7
The ceiling of -9 is -9
The ceiling of 72.3 is 73
The ceiling of 0.34 is 1
The floor of 7 is 7
The floor of -9 is -9
The floor of 72.3 is 72
The floor of 0.34 is 0
min(7,-9) is -9
min(72.3,0.34) is 0.34
min(7,72.3) is 7
min(0.34,-9) is -9
max(7,-9) is 7
max(72.3,0.34) is 72.3
max(7,72.3) is 72.3
max(0.34,-9) is 0.34
Pi is 3.14159
e is 2.71828
cos(0.785398) is 0.707107
sin(0.785398) is 0.707107
acos(0.707) is 0.785549
asin(0.707) is 0.785247
```

```
atan(0.707) is 0.615409
exp(1.0) is 2.71828
exp(10.0) is 22026.5
exp(0.0) is 1
log(1.0) is 0
log(10.0) is 2.30259
log(Math.E) is 1
pow(2.0, 2.0) is 4
pow(10.0, 3.5) is 3162.28
pow(8, -1) is 0.125
The square root of 0 is 0
The square root of 1 is 1
The square root of 2 is 1.41421
The square root of 3 is 1.73205
The square root of 4 is 2
The square root of 5 is 2.23607
The square root of 6 is 2.44949
The square root of 7 is 2.64575
The square root of 8 is 2.82843
The square root of 9 is 3
Here's one random number: 0.820582
Here's another random number: 0.866157
```

12.22 java.util.Date

A Date object represents a precise moment in time, down to the millisecond. Dates are represented as a long that counts the number of milliseconds since midnight, January 1, 1970, Greenwich Meantime.

Does this have a year 2000 problem? If so in what year?

To create a Date object for the current date and time use the noargs Date() constructor like this:

```
Date now = new Date();
```

To create a Date object for a specific time, pass the number of milliseconds since midnight, January 1, 1970, Greenwich Meantime to the constructor, like this:

```
Date midnight_jan2_1970 = new Date(24L*60L*60L*1000L);
```

You can return the number of milliseconds in the Date as a long, using the getTime() method. For example, to time a block of code, you might do this

```
Date d1 = new Date();
// timed code goes here
Date d2 = new Date();
long elapsed_time = d2.getTime() - d1.getTime();
```

System.out.println("That took " + elapsed_time + " milliseconds");

You can change a Date by passing the new date as a number of milliseconds since midnight, January 1, 1970, GMT, to the setTime() method, like this:

```
Date midnight_jan2_1970 = new Date();
midnight_jan2_1970.setTime(24L*60L*60L*1000L);
```

The before() method returns true if this Date is before the Date argument, false if it's not. For example

```
if (midnight_jan2_1970.before(new Date())) {
```

The after() method returns true if this Date is after the Date argument, false if it's not. For example

```
if (midnight_jan2_1970.after(new Date())) {
```

The Date class also has the usual hashCode(), equals(), and toString() methods.

12.23 java.util.Calendar

The Calendar class converts a time in milliseconds since midnight, January 1, 1970, Greenwich Mean Time, (that is a Date object), into days, minutes, hours, and seconds according to the local calendar.

12.24 java.util.Random

The java.util.Random class allows you to create objects that produce pseudo-random numbers with uniform or gaussian distributions according to a linear congruential formula with a 48-bit seed.

The algorithm used is good enough for games. I wouldn't use it for cryptography.

You can choose the seed or you can let Java pick one based on the current time.

```
Random r = new Random(109876L);
int i = r.nextInt();
int j = r.nextInt();
long l = r.nextLong();
float f = r.nextFloat();
double d = r.nextDouble();
int k = r.nextGaussian();
```

The nextInt(), nextLong(), and nextBytes() methods all cover their respective ranges with equal likelihood. For example, to simulate a six-sided die; that is to generate a random integer between 1 and 6, you might write

```
Random r = new Random();
int die = r.nextInt();
die = Math.abs(die);
die = die % 6;
die += 1;
System.out.println(die);
```

The nextGaussian() method returns a pseudo-random, Gaussian distributed, double value with mean 0.0 and standard deviation 1.0.

The nextBytes() method fills a byte[] array with random bytes. For example,

```
byte[] ba = new byte[1024];
Random r = new Random();
r.nextBytes(ba);
for (int i = 0; i < ba.length; i++) {
System.out.println(ba[i]);
}
```

12.25 java.lang.String

Strings are objects. Specifically they're instances of the class java.lang.String. This class has many methods that are useful for working with strings.

Internally Java Strings are arrays of Unicode characters. For example the String "Hello" is a five element array. Like arrays, Strings begin counting at 0. Thus in the String "Hello" 'H' is character 0, 'e' is character 1, and so on.

```
0  1  2  3  4
H  e  l  l  o
Constructors
public String()
public String(String value)
public String(char value[])
public String(char value[], int offset, int count)
public String(byte bytes[], int offset, int length, String enc)
throws UnsupportedEncodingException
public String(byte bytes[], String enc) throws
UnsupportedEncodingException
public String(byte bytes[], int offset, int length)
public String(byte bytes[])
public String(StringBuffer buffer)
index methods
public int length()
public int indexOf(int ch)
public int indexOf(int ch, int fromIndex)
public int lastIndexOf(int ch)
public int lastIndexOf(int ch, int fromIndex)
public int indexOf(String str)
public int indexOf(String str, int fromIndex)
public int lastIndexOf(String str)
public int lastIndexOf(String str, int fromIndex)
valueOf() methods
public static String valueOf(char data[])
public static String valueOf(char data[], int offset, int count)
public static String copyValueOf(char data[], int offset, int count)
public static String copyValueOf(char data[])
public static String valueOf(boolean b)
public static String valueOf(char c)
public static String valueOf(int i)
public static String valueOf(long l)
public static String valueOf(float f)
public static String valueOf(double d)
substring() methods
public char charAt(int index)
public void getChars(int srcBegin, int srcEnd, char dst[], int
dstBegin)
public byte[] getBytes(String enc) throws UnsupportedEncodingException
public byte[] getBytes()
public String substring(int beginIndex)
```

```
public String substring(int beginIndex, int endIndex)
public String concat(String str)
public char[] toCharArray()
Beginnings are inclusive. Ends are exclusive.
comparisons
public boolean equals(Object anObject)
public boolean equalsIgnoreCase(String anotherString)
public int compareTo(String anotherString)
public boolean regionMatches(int toffset, String other, int ooffset,
int len)
public boolean regionMatches(boolean ignoreCase, int toffset,
String other, int ooffset, int len)
public boolean startsWith(String prefix, int toffset)
public boolean startsWith(String prefix)
public boolean endsWith(String suffix)
Modifying Strings
public String replace(char oldChar, char newChar)
public String toLowerCase(Locale locale)
public String toLowerCase()
public String toUpperCase(Locale locale)
public String toUpperCase()
public String trim()
```

12.26 Abstract

Java allows methods and classes to be declared abstract. An abstract method is not actually implemented in the class. It is merely declared there. The body of the method is then implemented in subclasses of that class. An abstract method must be part of an abstract class. You create abstract classes by adding the keyword abstract after the access specifier, e.g.

```
public abstract class MotorVehicle
```

Abstract classes cannot be instantiated. It is a compile-time error to try something like

```
MotorVehicle m = new MotorVehicle();
```

when MotorVehicle has been declared to be abstract. MotorVehicle is actually a pretty good example of the sort of class that might be abstract. You're unlikely to be interested in a generic motor vehicle. Rather you'll have trucks, motorcycles, cars, go-carts and other subclasses of MotorVehicle, but nothing that is only a MotorVehicle.

An abstract method provides a declaration but no implementation. In other words, it has no method body. Abstract methods can only exist inside abstract classes and interfaces. For example, the MotorVehicle class might have an abstract fuel() method:

```
public abstract void fuel();
```

Car would override/implement this method with a fuel() method that filled the gas tank with gasoline. EighteenWheelerTruck might override this method with a fuel() method that filled its gas tank with diesel. ElectricCar would override/implement this method with a fuel() method that plugged into the wall socket.

13

Networking

13.1 Network Programming

Historically, network programming has been error-prone, difficult, and complex.

The programmer had to know many details about the network and sometimes even the hardware. You usually needed to understand the various "layers" of the networking protocol, and there were a lot of different functions in each different networking library concerned with connecting, packing, and unpacking blocks of information; shipping those blocks back and forth; and handshaking. It was a daunting task.

However, the concept of networking is not so difficult. You want to get some information from that machine over there and move it to this machine here, or vice versa. It's quite similar to reading and writing files, except that the file exists on a remote machine and the remote machine can decide exactly what it wants to do about the information you're requesting or sending.

One of Java's great strengths is painless networking. As much as possible, the underlying details of networking have been abstracted away and taken care of within the JVM and local machine installation of Java. The programming model you use is that of a file; in fact, you actually wrap the network connection (a "socket") with stream objects, so you end up using the same method calls as you do with all other streams. In addition, Java's built-in multithreading is exceptionally handy when dealing with another networking issue: handling multiple connections at once.

13.2 Identifying a Machine

Of course, in order to tell one machine from another and to make sure that you are connected with the machine you want, there must be some way of uniquely identifying machines on a network. Early networks were satisfied to provide unique names for machines within the local network. However, Java works within the Internet, which requires a way to uniquely identify a machine from all the others in the world . This is accomplished with the IP (Internet Protocol) address that can exist in two forms:

The familiar DNS (Domain Name Service) form. My domain name is bruceeckel.com, so suppose I have a computer called Opus in my domain. Its domain name would be Opus.bruceeckel.com. This is exactly the kind of name that you use when you send email to people, and is often incorporated into a World-Wide-Web address.

Alternatively, you can use the "dotted quad" form, which is four numbers separated by dots, such as 123.255.28.120.

In both cases, the IP address is represented internally as a 32-bit number [63] (so each of the quad numbers cannot exceed 255), and you can get a special Java object to represent this number from either of the forms above by using the static InetAddress.getByName( ) method that's in java.net. The result is an object of type InetAddress that you can use to build a "socket" as you will see later.

As a simple example of using InetAddress.getByName( ), consider what happens if you have a dial-up Internet service provider (ISP). Each time you dial up, you are assigned a temporary IP address. But while you're connected, your IP address has the same validity as any other IP address on the Internet. If someone connects to your machine using your IP address then they can connect to a Web server or FTP server that you have running on your machine. Of course, they need to know your IP address, and since it's assigned each time you dial up, how can you find out what it is?

The following program uses InetAddress.getByName( ) to produce your IP address. To use it, you must know the name of your computer. It has been tested only on Windows 95, but there you can go to "Settings," "Control Panel," "Network," and then select the "Identification" tab. "Computer name" is the name to put on the command line.

```
//: WhoAmI.java
// Finds out your network address when you're
// connected to the Internet.
package c15;
import java.net.*;

public class WhoAmI {
public static void main(String[] args)
throws Exception {
if(args.length != 1) {
System.err.println(
"Usage: WhoAmI MachineName");
System.exit(1);
}
InetAddress a =
InetAddress.getByName(args[0]);
System.out.println(a);
}
} ///:~
```

In my case, the machine is called "Colossus" (from the movie of the same name, because I keep putting bigger disks on it). So, once I've connected to my ISP I run the program:

java WhoAmI Colossus

I get back a message like this (of course, the address is different each time):

Colossus/199.190.87.75

If I tell my friend this address, he can log onto my personal Web server by going to the URL http://199.190.87.75 (only as long as I continue to stay connected during that session). This can sometimes be a handy way to distribute information to someone else or to test out a Web site configuration before posting it to a "real" server.

13.3 Servers and Clients

The whole point of a network is to allow two machines to connect and talk to each other. Once the two machines have found each other they can have a nice, two-way conversation. But how do they find each other? It's like getting lost in an amusement park: one machine has to stay in one place and listen while the other machine says, "Hey, where are you?"

The machine that "stays in one place" is called the server, and the one that seeks is called the client.

This distinction is important only while the client is trying to connect to the server. Once they've connected, it becomes a two-way communication process and it doesn't matter anymore that one happened to take the role of server and the other happened to take the role of the client.

So the job of the server is to listen for a connection, and that's performed by the special server object that you create. The job of the client is to try to make a connection to a server, and this is performed by the special client object you create. Once the connection is made, you'll see that at both server and client ends, the connection is just magically turned into an IO stream object, and from then on you can treat the connection as if you were reading from and writing to a file. Thus, after the connection is made you will just use the familiar IO commands from Chapter 10. This is one of the nice features of Java networking.

13.4 Testing Programs Without a Network

For many reasons, you might not have a client machine, a server machine, and a network available to test your programs. You might be performing exercises in a classroom situation, or you could be writing programs that aren't yet stable enough to put onto the network. The creators of the Internet Protocol were aware of this issue, and they created a special address called localhost to be the "local loopback" IP address for testing without a network. The generic way to produce this address in Java is:

```
InetAddress addr = InetAddress.getByName(null);
```

If you hand getByName( ) a null, it defaults to using the localhost. The InetAddress is what you use to refer to the particular machine, and you must produce this before you can go any further. You can't manipulate the contents of an InetAddress (but you can print them out, as you'll see in the next example). The only way you can create an InetAddress is through one of that class's static member methods getByName( ) (which is what you'll usually use), getAllByName( ), or getLocalHost( ).

You can also produce the local loopback address by handing it the string localhost:

```
InetAddress.getByName("localhost");
```

or by using its dotted quad form to name the reserved IP number for the loopback:

```
InetAddress.getByName("127.0.0.1");
```

All three forms produce the same result.

13.5 Port: a Unique Place Within the Machine

An IP address isn't enough to identify a unique server, since many servers can exist on one machine. Each IP machine also contains ports, and when you're setting up a client or a server you must choose a port where both client and server agree to connect; if you're meeting someone, the IP address is the neighborhood and the port is the bar.

The port is not a physical location in a machine, but a software abstraction (mainly for bookkeeping purposes). The client program knows how to connect to the machine via its IP address, but how does it connect to a desired service (potentially one of many on that machine)? That's where the port numbers come in as second level of addressing. The idea is that if you ask for a particular port, you're requesting the service that's associated with the port number. The time of day is a simple example of a service. Typically, each service is associated with a unique port number on a given server machine. It's up to the client to know ahead of time which port number the desired service is running on.

The system services reserve the use of ports 1 through 1024, so you shouldn't use those or any other port that you know to be in use. The first choice for examples in this book will be port 8080 (in memory of the venerable old 8-bit Intel 8080 chip in my first computer, a CP/M machine).

13.6 Sockets

The socket is the software abstraction used to represent the "terminals" of a connection between two machines. For a given connection, there's a socket on each machine, and you can imagine a hypothetical "cable" running between the two machines with each end of the "cable" plugged into a socket. Of course, the physical hardware and cabling between machines is completely unknown. The whole point of the abstraction is that we don't have to know more than is necessary.

In Java, you create a socket to make the connection to the other machine, then you get an InputStream and OutputStream (or, with the appropriate converters, Reader and Writer) from the socket in order to be able to treat the connection as an IO stream object. There are two stream-based socket classes: a ServerSocket that a server uses to "listen" for incoming connections and a Socket that a client uses in order to initiate a connection. Once a client makes a socket connection, the ServerSocket returns (via the accept( ) method) a corresponding server side Socket through which direct communications will take place. From then on, you have a true Socket to Socket connection and you treat both ends the same way because they are the same. At this point, you use the methods getInputStream( ) and getOutputStream( ) to produce the corresponding InputStream and OutputStream objects from each Socket. These must be wrapped inside buffers and formatting classes.

The use of the term ServerSocket would seem to be another example of a confusing name scheme in the Java libraries. You might think ServerSocket would be better named "ServerConnector" or something without the word "Socket" in it. You might also think that ServerSocket and Socket should both be inherited from some common base class. Indeed, the two classes do have several methods in common but not enough to give them a common base class. Instead, ServerSocket's job is to wait until some other machine connects to it, then to return an actual Socket. This is why ServerSocket seems to be a bit misnamed, since its job isn't really to be a socket but instead to make a Socket object when someone else connects to it.

However, the ServerSocket does create a physical "server" or listening socket on the host machine. This socket listens for incoming connections and then returns an "established" socket (with the local and remote endpoints defined) via the accept( ) method. The confusing part is that both of these sockets (listening and established) are associated with the same server socket. The listening socket can accept only new connection requests and not data packets. So while ServerSocket doesn't make much sense programmatically, it does "physically."

When you create a ServerSocket, you give it only a port number. You don't have to give it an IP address because it's already on the machine it represents. When you create a Socket, however, you must give both the IP address and the port number where you're trying to connect. (On the other hand, the Socket that comes back from ServerSocket.accept( ) already contains all this information.)

13.7 A Simple Server and Client

This example makes the simplest use of servers and clients using sockets. All the server does is wait for a connection, then uses the Socket produced by that connection to create an InputStream and OutputStream. After that, everything it reads from the InputStream it echoes to the OutputStream until it receives the line END, at which time it closes the connection.

The client makes the connection to the server, then creates an OutputStream. Lines of text are sent through the OutputStream. The client also creates an InputStream to hear what the server is saying (which, in this case, is just the words echoed back).

Both the server and client use the same port number and the client uses the local loopback address to connect to the server on the same machine so you don't have to test it over a network. (For some configurations, you might need to be connected to a network for the programs to work, even if you aren't communicating over that network.)

Here is the server:

```
//: JabberServer.java
// Very simple server that just
// echoes whatever the client sends.
import java.io.*;
import java.net.*;
public class JabberServer {
// Choose a port outside of the range 1-1024:
public static final int PORT = 8080;
public static void main(String[] args)
throws IOException {
ServerSocket s = new ServerSocket(PORT);
System.out.println("Started: " + s);
try {
// Blocks until a connection occurs:
Socket socket = s.accept();
try {
System.out.println(
"Connection accepted: "+ socket);
BufferedReader in =
new BufferedReader(
new InputStreamReader(
socket.getInputStream()));
// Output is automatically flushed
// by PrintWriter:
PrintWriter out =
new PrintWriter(
new BufferedWriter(
new OutputStreamWriter(
socket.getOutputStream())),true);
while (true) {
String str = in.readLine();
if (str.equals("END")) break;
System.out.println("Echoing: "+ str);
out.println(str);
}
// Always close the two sockets...
} finally {
System.out.println("closing...");
socket.close();
}
} finally {
s.close();
}
}
} ///:~
```

You can see that the ServerSocket just needs a port number, not an IP address (since it's running on this machine!). When you call accept( ), the method blocks until some client tries to connect to it. That is, it's there waiting for a connection but other processes can run (see Chapter 14). When a connection is made, accept( ) returns with a Socket object representing that connection.

The responsibility for cleaning up the sockets is crafted carefully here. If the ServerSocket constructor fails, the program just quits (notice we must assume that the constructor for ServerSocket doesn't leave any open network sockets lying around if it fails). For this case, main( ) throws IOException so a try block is not necessary. If the ServerSocket constructor is successful then all other method calls must be guarded in a try-finally block to ensure that, no matter how the block is left, the ServerSocket is properly closed.

The same logic is used for the Socket returned by accept( ). If accept( ) fails, then we must assume that the Socket doesn't exist or hold any resources, so it doesn't need to be cleaned up. If it's successful, however, the following statements must be in a try-finally block so that if they fail the Socket will still be cleaned up. Care is required here because sockets use important non-memory resources, so you must be diligent in order to clean them up (since there is no destructor in Java to do it for you).

Both the ServerSocket and the Socket produced by accept( ) are printed to System.out. This means that their toString( ) methods are automatically called. These produce:

ServerSocket[addr=0.0.0.0,PORT=0,localport=8080]
Socket[addr=127.0.0.1,PORT=1077,localport=8080]

Shortly, you'll see how these fit together with what the client is doing.

The next part of the program looks just like opening files for reading and writing except that the InputStream and OutputStream are created from the Socket object. Both the InputStream and OutputStream objects are converted to Java 1.1 Reader and Writer objects using the "converter" classes InputStreamReader and OutputStreamWriter, respectively. You could also have used the Java 1.0 InputStream and OutputStream classes directly, but with output there's a distinct advantage to using the Writer approach. This appears with PrintWriter, which has an overloaded constructor that takes a second argument, a boolean flag that indicates whether to automatically flush the output at the end of each println( ) (but not print( )) statement. Every time you write to out, its buffer must be flushed so the information goes out over the network. Flushing is important for this particular example because the client and server each wait for a line from the other party before proceeding. If flushing doesn't occur, the information will not be put onto the network until the buffer is full, which causes lots of problems in this example.

When writing network programs you need to be careful about using automatic flushing. Every time you flush the buffer a packet must be created and sent. In this case, that's exactly what we want, since if the packet containing the line isn't sent then the handshaking back and forth between server and client will stop. Put another way, the end of a line is the end of a message. But in many cases messages aren't delimited by lines so it's much more efficient to not use auto flushing and instead let the built-in buffering decide when to build and send a packet. This way, larger packets can be sent and the process will be faster.

Note that, like virtually all streams you open, these are buffered. There's an exercise at the end of the chapter to show you what happens if you don't buffer the streams (things get slow).

The infinite while loop reads lines from the BufferedReader in and writes information to System.out and to the PrintWriter out. Note that these could be any streams, they just happen to be connected to the network.

When the client sends the line consisting of "END" the program breaks out of the loop and closes the Socket.

Here's the client:

```
//: JabberClient.java
// Very simple client that just sends
// lines to the server and reads lines
// that the server sends.
import java.net.*;
import java.io.*;

public class JabberClient {
public static void main(String[] args)
throws IOException {
// Passing null to getByName() produces the
// special "Local Loopback" IP address, for
// testing on one machine w/o a network:
InetAddress addr =
InetAddress.getByName(null);
// Alternatively, you can use
// the address or name:
// InetAddress addr =
//    InetAddress.getByName("127.0.0.1");
// InetAddress addr =
//    InetAddress.getByName("localhost");
System.out.println("addr = " + addr);
Socket socket =
new Socket(addr, JabberServer.PORT);
// Guard everything in a try-finally to make
// sure that the socket is closed:
try {
System.out.println("socket = " + socket);
BufferedReader in =
new BufferedReader(
new InputStreamReader(
socket.getInputStream()));
// Output is automatically flushed
// by PrintWriter:
PrintWriter out =
new PrintWriter(
new BufferedWriter(
new OutputStreamWriter(
socket.getOutputStream())),true);
for(int i = 0; i < 10; i ++) {
out.println("howdy "+ i);
String str = in.readLine();
System.out.println(str);
}
out.println("END");
} finally {
System.out.println("closing...");
```

```
socket.close();
}
}
} ///:~
```

In main( ) you can see all three ways to produce the InetAddress of the local loopback IP address: using null, localhost, or the explicit reserved address 127.0.0.1. Of course, if you want to connect to a machine across a network you substitute that machine's IP address. When the InetAddress addr is printed (via the automatic call to its toString( ) method) the result is:

localhost/127.0.0.1

By handing getByName( ) a null, it defaulted to finding the localhost, and that produced the special address 127.0.0.1.

Note that the Socket called socket is created with both the InetAddress and the port number. To understand what it means when you print out one of these Socket objects, remember that an Internet connection is determined uniquely by these four pieces of data: clientHost, clientPortNumber, serverHost, and serverPortNumber. When the server comes up, it takes up its assigned port (8080) on the localhost (127.0.0.1). When the client comes up, it is allocated to the next available port on its machine, 1077 in this case, which also happens to be on the same machine (127.0.0.1) as the server. Now, in order for data to move between the client and server, each side has to know where to send it. Therefore, during the process of connecting to the "known" server, the client sends a "return address" so the server knows where to send its data. This is what you see in the example output for the server side:

Socket[addr=127.0.0.1,port=1077,localport=8080]

This means that the server just accepted a connection from 127.0.0.1 on port 1077 while listening on its local port (8080). On the client side:

Socket[addr=localhost/127.0.0.1,PORT=8080,localport=1077]

which means that the client made a connection to 127.0.0.1 on port 8080 using the local port 1077.

You'll notice that every time you start up the client anew, the local port number is incremented. It starts at 1025 (one past the reserved block of ports) and keeps going up until you reboot the machine, at which point it starts at 1025 again. (On UNIX machines, once the upper limit of the socket range is reached, the numbers will wrap around to the lowest available number again.)

Once the Socket object has been created, the process of turning it into a BufferedReader and PrintWriter is the same as in the server (again, in both cases you start with a Socket). Here, the client initiates the conversation by sending the string "howdy" followed by a number. Note that the buffer must again be flushed (which happens automatically via the second argument to the PrintWriter constructor). If the buffer isn't flushed, the whole conversation will hang because the initial "howdy" will never get sent (the buffer isn't full enough to cause the send to happen automatically). Each line that is sent back from the server is written to System.out to verify that everything is working correctly. To terminate the conversation, the agreed-upon "END" is sent. If the client simply hangs up, then the server throws an exception.

You can see that the same care is taken here to ensure that the network resources represented by the Socket are properly cleaned up, using a try-finally block.

Sockets produce a "dedicated" connection that persists until it is explicitly disconnected. (The dedicated connection can still be disconnected un-explicitly if one side, or an intermediary link, of the connection crashes.) This means the two parties are locked in communication and the connection is constantly open. This seems like a logical approach to networking, but it puts an extra load on the network. Later in the chapter you'll see a different approach to networking, in which the connections are only temporary.

13.8 Serving multiple clients

The JabberServer works, but it can handle only one client at a time. In a typical server, you'll want to be able to deal with many clients at once. The answer is multithreading, and in languages that don't directly support multithreading this means all sorts of complications. In Chapter 14 you saw that multithreading in Java is about as simple as possible, considering that multithreading is a rather complex topic. Because threading in Java is reasonably straightforward, making a server that handles multiple clients is relatively easy.

The basic scheme is to make a single ServerSocket in the server and call accept( ) to wait for a new connection. When accept( ) returns, you take the resulting Socket and use it to create a new thread whose job is to serve that particular client. Then you call accept( ) again to wait for a new client.

In the following server code, you can see that it looks similar to the JabberServer.java example except that all of the operations to serve a particular client have been moved inside a separate thread class:

```
//: MultiJabberServer.java
// A server that uses multithreading to handle
// any number of clients.
import java.io.*;
import java.net.*;

class ServeOneJabber extends Thread {
private Socket socket;
private BufferedReader in;
private PrintWriter out;
public ServeOneJabber(Socket s)
throws IOException {
socket = s;
in =
new BufferedReader(
new InputStreamReader(
socket.getInputStream()));
// Enable auto-flush:
out =
new PrintWriter(
new BufferedWriter(
new OutputStreamWriter(
socket.getOutputStream())), true);
// If any of the above calls throw an
// exception, the caller is responsible for
// closing the socket. Otherwise the thread
// will close it.
start(); // Calls run()
}
public void run() {
try {
```

```
while (true) {
String str = in.readLine();
if (str.equals("END")) break;
System.out.println("Echoing: " + str);
out.println(str);
}
System.out.println("closing...");
} catch (IOException e) {
} finally {
try {
socket.close();
} catch(IOException e) {}
}
}
}

public class MultiJabberServer {
static final int PORT = 8080;
public static void main(String[] args)
throws IOException {
ServerSocket s = new ServerSocket(PORT);
System.out.println("Server Started");
try {
while(true) {
// Blocks until a connection occurs:
Socket socket = s.accept();
try {
new ServeOneJabber(socket);
} catch(IOException e) {
// If it fails, close the socket,
// otherwise the thread will close it:
socket.close();
}
}
} finally {
s.close();
}
}
} ///:~
```

The ServeOneJabber thread takes the Socket object that's produced by accept( ) in main( ) every time a new client makes a connection. Then, as before, it creates a BufferedReader and auto-flushed PrintWriter object using the Socket. Finally, it calls the special Thread method start( ), which performs thread initialization and then calls run( ). This performs the same kind of action as in the previous example: reading something from the socket and then echoing it back until it reads the special "END" signal.

The responsibility for cleaning up the socket must again be carefully designed. In this case, the socket is created outside of the ServeOneJabber so the responsibility can be shared. If the ServeOneJabber constructor fails, it will just throw the exception to the caller, who will then clean up the thread. But if the constructor succeeds, then the ServeOneJabber object takes over responsibility for cleaning up the thread, in its run( ).

Notice the simplicity of the MultiJabberServer. As before, a ServerSocket is created and accept( ) is called to allow a new connection. But this time, the return value of accept( ) (a Socket) is passed to the constructor for ServeOneJabber, which creates a new thread to handle that connection. When the connection is terminated, the thread simply goes away.

If the creation of the ServerSocket fails, the exception is again thrown through main( ). But if it succeeds, the outer try-finally guarantees its cleanup. The inner try-catch guards only against the failure of the ServeOneJabber constructor; if the constructor succeeds, then the ServeOneJabber thread will close the associated socket.

To test that the server really does handle multiple clients, the following program creates many clients (using threads) that connect to the same server. Each thread has a limited lifetime, and when it goes away, that leaves space for the creation of a new thread. The maximum number of threads allowed is determined by the final int maxthreads . You'll notice that this value is rather critical, since if you make it too high the threads seem to run out of resources and the program mysteriously fails.

```
//: MultiJabberClient.java
// Client that tests the MultiJabberServer
// by starting up multiple clients.
import java.net.*;
import java.io.*;

class JabberClientThread extends Thread {
private Socket socket;
private BufferedReader in;
private PrintWriter out;
private static int counter = 0;
private int id = counter++;
private static int threadcount = 0;
public static int threadCount() {
return threadcount;
}
public JabberClientThread(InetAddress addr) {
System.out.println("Making client " + id);
threadcount++;
try {
socket =
new Socket(addr, MultiJabberServer.PORT);
} catch(IOException e) {
// If the creation of the socket fails,
// nothing needs to be cleaned up.
}
try {
in =
new BufferedReader(
new InputStreamReader(
socket.getInputStream()));
```

```
// Enable auto-flush:
out =
new PrintWriter(
new BufferedWriter(
new OutputStreamWriter(
socket.getOutputStream())), true);
start();
} catch(IOException e) {
// The socket should be closed on any
// failures other than the socket
// constructor:
try {
socket.close();
} catch(IOException e2) {}
}
// Otherwise the socket will be closed by
// the run() method of the thread.
}
public void run() {
try {
for(int i = 0; i < 25; i++) {
out.println("Client " + id + ": " + i);
String str = in.readLine();
System.out.println(str);
}
out.println("END");
} catch(IOException e) {
} finally {
// Always close it:
try {
socket.close();
} catch(IOException e) {}
threadcount—; // Ending this thread
}
}
}

public class MultiJabberClient {
static final int MAX_THREADS = 40;
public static void main(String[] args)
throws IOException, InterruptedException {
InetAddress addr =
InetAddress.getByName(null);
while(true) {
if(JabberClientThread.threadCount()
< MAX_THREADS)
new JabberClientThread(addr);
Thread.currentThread().sleep(100);
```

```
    }
  }
} ///:~
```

The JabberClientThread constructor takes an InetAddress and uses it to open a Socket. You're probably starting to see the pattern: the Socket is always used to create some kind of Reader and/or Writer (or InputStream and/or OutputStream) object, which is the only way that the Socket can be used. (You can, of course, write a class or two to automate this process instead of doing all the typing if it becomes painful.) Again, start( ) performs thread initialization and calls run( ). Here, messages are sent to the server and information from the server is echoed to the screen. However, the thread has a limited lifetime and eventually completes. Note that the socket is cleaned up if the constructor fails after the socket is created but before the constructor completes. Otherwise the responsibility for calling close( ) for the socket is relegated to the run( ) method.

The threadcount keeps track of how many JabberClientThread objects currently exist. It is incremented as part of the constructor and decremented as run( ) exits (which means the thread is terminating). In MultiJabberClient.main( ), you can see that the number of threads is tested, and if there are too many, no more are created. Then the method sleeps. This way, some threads will eventually terminate and more can be created. You can experiment with MAX_THREADS to see where your particular system begins to have trouble with too many connections.

13.9 Datagrams

The examples you've seen so far use the Transmission Control Protocol (TCP, also known as stream-based sockets), which is designed for ultimate reliability and guarantees that the data will get there. It allows retransmission of lost data, it provides multiple paths through different routers in case one goes down, and bytes are delivered in the order they are sent. All this control and reliability comes at a cost: TCP has a high overhead.

There's a second protocol, called User Datagram Protocol (UDP), which doesn't guarantee that the packets will be delivered and doesn't guarantee that they will arrive in the order they were sent. It's called an "unreliable protocol" (TCP is a "reliable protocol"), which sounds bad, but because it's much faster it can be useful. There are some applications, such as an audio signal, in which it isn't so critical if a few packets are dropped here or there but speed is vital. Or consider a time-of-day server, where it really doesn't matter if one of the messages is lost. Also, some applications might be able to fire off a UDP message to a server and can then assume, if there is no response in a reasonable period of time, that the message was lost.

The support for datagrams in Java has the same feel as its support for TCP sockets, but there are significant differences. With datagrams, you put a DatagramSocket on both the client and server, but there is no analogy to the ServerSocket that waits around for a connection. That's because there is no "connection," but instead a datagram just shows up. Another fundamental difference is that with TCP sockets, once you've made the connection you don't need to worry about who's talking to whom anymore; you just send the data back and forth through conventional streams. However, with datagrams, the datagram packet must know where it came from and where it's supposed to go. That means you must know these things for each datagram packet that you load up and ship off.

A DatagramSocket sends and receives the packets, and the DatagramPacket contains the information. When you're receiving a datagram, you need only provide a buffer in which the data will be placed; the information about the Internet address and port number where the information came from will be automatically initialized when the packet arrives through the DatagramSocket. So the constructor for a DatagramPacket to receive datagrams is:

DatagramPacket(buf, buf.length)

in which buf is an array of byte. Since buf is an array, you might wonder why the constructor couldn't figure out the length of the array on its own. I wondered this, and can only guess that it's a throwback to C-style programming, in which of course arrays can't tell you how big they are.

You can reuse a receiving datagram; you don't have to make a new one each time. Every time you reuse it, the data in the buffer is overwritten.

The maximum size of the buffer is restricted only by the allowable datagram packet size, which limits it to slightly less than 64Kbytes. However, in many applications you'll want it to be much smaller, certainly when you're sending data. Your chosen packet size depends on what you need for your particular application.

When you send a datagram, the DatagramPacket must contain not only the data, but also the Internet address and port where it will be sent. So the constructor for an outgoing DatagramPacket is:

DatagramPacket(buf, length, inetAddress, port)

This time, buf (which is a byte array) already contains the data that you want to send out. The length might be the length of buf, but it can also be shorter, indicating that you want to send only that many bytes. The other two arguments are the Internet address where the packet is going and the destination port within that machine.

You might think that the two constructors create two different objects: one for receiving datagrams and one for sending them. Good OO design would suggest that these should be two different classes, rather than one class with different behavior depending on how you construct the object. This is probably true, but fortunately the use of DatagramPackets is simple enough that you're not tripped up by the problem, as you can see in the following example. This example is similar to the MultiJabberServer and MultiJabberClient example for TCP sockets. Multiple clients will send datagrams to a server, which will echo them back to the same client that sent the message.

To simplify the creation of a DatagramPacket from a String and vice-versa, the example begins with a utility class, Dgram, to do the work for you:

```
//: Dgram.java
// A utility class to convert back and forth
// Between Strings and DataGramPackets.
import java.net.*;

public class Dgram {
public static DatagramPacket toDatagram(
String s, InetAddress destIA, int destPort) {
// Deprecated in Java 1.1, but it works:
byte[] buf = new byte[s.length() + 1];
s.getBytes(0, s.length(), buf, 0);
// The correct Java 1.1 approach, but it's
// Broken (it truncates the String):
// byte[] buf = s.getBytes();
return new DatagramPacket(buf, buf.length,
destIA, destPort);
}
public static String toString(DatagramPacket p){
// The Java 1.0 approach:
```

```
// return new String(p.getData(),
//  0, 0, p.getLength());
// The Java 1.1 approach:
return
new String(p.getData(), 0, p.getLength());
}
} ///:~
```

The first method of Dgram takes a String, an InetAddress, and a port number and builds a DatagramPacket by copying the contents of the String into a byte buffer and passing the buffer into the DatagramPacket constructor. Notice the "+1" in the buffer allocation - this was necessary to prevent truncation. The getBytes( ) method of String is a special operation that copies the chars of a String into a byte buffer. This method is now deprecated; Java 1.1 has a "better" way to do this but it's commented out here because it truncates the String. So you'll get a deprecation message when you compile it under Java 1.1, but the behavior will be correct. (This bug might be fixed by the time you read this.)

The Dgram.toString( ) method shows both the Java 1.0 approach and the Java 1.1 approach (which is different because there's a new kind of String constructor).

Here is the server for the datagram demonstration:

```
//: ChatterServer.java
// A server that echoes datagrams
import java.net.*;
import java.io.*;
import java.util.*;

public class ChatterServer {
static final int INPORT = 1711;
private byte[] buf = new byte[1000];
private DatagramPacket dp =
new DatagramPacket(buf, buf.length);
// Can listen & send on the same socket:
private DatagramSocket socket;

public ChatterServer() {
try {
socket = new DatagramSocket(INPORT);
System.out.println("Server started");
while(true) {
// Block until a datagram appears:
socket.receive(dp);
String rcvd = Dgram.toString(dp) +
", from address: " + dp.getAddress() +
", port: " + dp.getPort();
System.out.println(rcvd);
String echoString =
"Echoed: " + rcvd;
// Extract the address and port from the
```

```
// received datagram to find out where to
// send it back:
DatagramPacket echo =
Dgram.toDatagram(echoString,
dp.getAddress(), dp.getPort());
socket.send(echo);
}
} catch(SocketException e) {
System.err.println("Can't open socket");
System.exit(1);
} catch(IOException e) {
System.err.println("Communication error");
e.printStackTrace();
}
}
public static void main(String[] args) {
new ChatterServer();
}
} ///:~
```

The ChatterServer contains a single DatagramSocket for receiving messages, instead of creating one each time you're ready to receive a new message. The single DatagramSocket can be used repeatedly. This DatagramSocket has a port number because this is the server and the client must have an exact address where it wants to send the datagram. It is given a port number but not an Internet address because it resides on "this" machine so it knows what its Internet address is (in this case, the default localhost). In the infinite while loop, the socket is told to receive( ), whereupon it blocks until a datagram shows up, and then sticks it into our designated receiver, the DatagramPacket dp . The packet is converted to a String along with information about the Internet address and socket where the packet came from. This information is displayed, and then an extra string is added to indicate that it is being echoed back from the server.

Now there's a bit of a quandary. As you will see, there are potentially many different Internet addresses and port numbers that the messages might come from - that is, the clients can reside on any machine. (In this demonstration they all reside on the localhost, but the port number for each client is different.) To send a message back to the client that originated it, you need to know that client's Internet address and port number. Fortunately, this information is conveniently packaged inside the DatagramPacket that sent the message, so all you have to do is pull it out using getAddress( ) and getPort( ), which are used to build the DatagramPacket echo that is sent back through the same socket that's doing the receiving. In addition, when the socket sends the datagram, it automatically adds the Internet address and port information of this machine, so that when the client receives the message, it can use getAddress( ) and getPort( ) to find out where the datagram came from. In fact, the only time that getAddress( ) and getPort( ) don't tell you where the datagram came from is if you create a datagram to send and you call getAddress( ) and getPort( ) before you send the datagram (in which case it tells the address and port of this machine, the one the datagram is being sent from). This is an essential part of datagrams: you don't need to keep track of where a message came from because it's always stored inside the datagram. In fact, the most reliable way to program is if you don't try to keep track, but instead always extract the address and port from the datagram in question (as is done here).

To test this server, here's a program that makes a number of clients, all of which fire datagram packets to the server and wait for the server to echo them back.

```
//: ChatterClient.java
// Tests the ChatterServer by starting multiple
// clients, each of which sends datagrams.
import java.lang.Thread;
import java.net.*;
import java.io.*;

public class ChatterClient extends Thread {
// Can listen & send on the same socket:
private DatagramSocket s;
private InetAddress hostAddress;
private byte[] buf = new byte[1000];
private DatagramPacket dp =
new DatagramPacket(buf, buf.length);
private int id;

public ChatterClient(int identifier) {
id = identifier;
try {
// Auto-assign port number:
s = new DatagramSocket();
hostAddress =
InetAddress.getByName("localhost");
} catch(UnknownHostException e) {
System.err.println("Cannot find host");
System.exit(1);
} catch(SocketException e) {
System.err.println("Can't open socket");
e.printStackTrace();
System.exit(1);
}
System.out.println("ChatterClient starting");
}
public void run() {
try {
for(int i = 0; i < 25; i++) {
String outMessage = "Client #" +
id + ", message #" + i;
// Make and send a datagram:
s.send(Dgram.toDatagram(outMessage,
hostAddress,
ChatterServer.INPORT));
// Block until it echoes back:
s.receive(dp);
// Print out the echoed contents:
String rcvd = "Client #" + id +
```

```
", rcvd from " +
dp.getAddress() + ", " +
dp.getPort() + ": " +
Dgram.toString(dp);
System.out.println(rcvd);
}
} catch(IOException e) {
e.printStackTrace();
System.exit(1);
}
}
public static void main(String[] args) {
for(int i = 0; i < 10; i++)
new ChatterClient(i).start();
}
} ///:~
```

ChatterClient is created as a Thread so that multiple clients can be made to bother the server. Here you can see that the receiving DatagramPacket looks just like the one used for ChatterServer. In the constructor, the DatagramSocket is created with no arguments since it doesn't need to advertise itself as being at a particular port number. The Internet address used for this socket will be "this machine" (for the example, localhost) and the port number will be automatically assigned, as you will see from the output. This DatagramSocket, like the one for the server, will be used both for sending and receiving.

The hostAddress is the Internet address of the host machine you want to talk to. The one part of the program in which you must know an exact Internet address and port number is the part in which you make the outgoing DatagramPacket. As is always the case, the host must be at a known address and port number so that clients can originate conversations with the host.

Each thread is given a unique identification number (although the port number automatically assigned to the thread would also provide a unique identifier). In run( ), a message String is created that contains the thread's identification number and the message number this thread is currently sending. This String is used to create a datagram that is sent to the host at its address; the port number is taken directly from a constant in ChatterServer. Once the message is sent, receive( ) blocks until the server replies with an echoing message. All of the information that's shipped around with the message allows you to see that what comes back to this particular thread is derived from the message that originated from it. In this example, even though UDP is an "unreliable" protocol, you'll see that all of the datagrams get where they're supposed to. (This will be true for localhost and LAN situations, but you might begin to see some failures for non-local connections.)

When you run this program, you'll see that each of the threads finishes, which means that each of the datagram packets sent to the server is turned around and echoed to the correct recipient; otherwise one or more threads would hang, blocking until their input shows up.

You might think that the only right way to, for example, transfer a file from one machine to another is through TCP sockets, since they're "reliable." However, because of the speed of datagrams they can actually be a better solution. You simply break the file up into packets and number each packet. The receiving machine takes the packets and reassembles them; a "header packet" tells the machine how many to expect and any other important information. If a packet is lost, the receiving machine sends a datagram back telling the sender to retransmit.

TCP and UDP ports are considered unique. That is, you can simultaneously run a TCP and UDP server on port 8080 without interference.

13.10 A Web Application

Now let's consider creating an application to run on the Web, which will show Java in all its glory. Part of this application will be a Java program running on the Web server, and the other part will be an applet that's downloaded to the browser. The applet collects information from the user and sends it back to the application running on the Web server. The task of the program will be simple: the applet will ask for the email address of the user, and after verifying that this address is reasonably legitimate (it doesn't contain spaces, and it does contain an '@' symbol) the applet will send the email address to the Web server. The application running on the server will capture the data and check a data file in which all of the email addresses are kept. If that address is already in the file, it will send back a message to that effect, which is displayed by the applet. If the address isn't in the file, it is placed in the list and the applet is informed that the address was added successfully.

Traditionally, the way to handle such a problem is to create an HTML page with a text field and a "submit" button. The user can type whatever he or she wants into the text field, and it will be submitted to the server without question. As it submits the data, the Web page also tells the server what to do with the data by mentioning the Common Gateway Interface (CGI) program that the server should run after receiving this data. This CGI program is typically written in either Perl or C (and sometimes C++, if the server supports it), and it must handle everything. First it looks at the data and decides whether it's in the correct format. If not, the CGI program must create an HTML page to describe the problem; this page is handed to the server, which sends it back to the user. The user must then back up a page and try again. If the data is correct, the CGI program opens the data file and either adds the email address to the file or discovers that the address is already in the file. In both cases it must format an appropriate HTML page for the server to return to the user.

As Java programmers, this seems like an awkward way for us to solve the problem, and naturally, we'd like to do the whole thing in Java. First, we'll use a Java applet to take care of data validation at the client site, without all that tedious Web traffic and page formatting. Then let's skip the Perl CGI script in favor of a Java application running on the server. In fact, let's skip the Web server altogether and simply make our own network connection from the applet to the Java application on the server!

As you'll see, there are a number of issues that make this a more complicated problem than it seems. It would be ideal to write the applet using Java 1.1 but that's hardly practical. At this writing, the number of users running Java 1.1-enabled browsers is small, and although such browsers are now commonly available, you'll probably need to take into account that a significant number of users will be slow to upgrade. So to be on the safe side, the applet will be programmed using only Java 1.0 code. With this in mind, there will be no JAR files to combine .class files in the applet, so the applet should be designed to create as few .class files as possible to minimize download time.

Well, it turns out the Web server (the one available to me when I wrote the example) does have Java in it, but only Java 1.0! So the server application must also be written using Java 1.0.

13.10.1 The Server Application

Now consider the server application, which will be called NameCollector. What happens if more than one user at a time tries to submit their email addresses? If NameCollector uses TCP/IP sockets, then it must use the multithreading approach shown earlier to handle more than one client at a time. But all of these threads will try to write to a single file where all the email addresses will be kept. This would require a locking mechanism to make sure that more than one thread doesn't access the file at once. A semaphore will do the trick, but perhaps there's a simpler way.

If we use datagrams instead, multithreading is unnecessary. A single datagram socket will listen for incoming datagrams, and when one appears the program will process the message and send the reply as a datagram back to whomever sent the request. If the datagram gets lost, then the user will notice that no reply comes and can then re-submit the request.

When the server application receives a datagram and unpacks it, it must extract the email address and check the file to see if that address is there already (and if it isn't, add it). And now we run into another problem. It turns out that Java 1.0 doesn't quite have the horsepower to easily manipulate the file containing the email addresses (Java 1.1 does). However, the problem can be solved in C quite readily, and this will provide an excuse to show you the easiest way to connect a non-Java program to a Java program. A Runtime object for a program has a method called exec( ) that will start up a separate program on the machine and return a Process object. You can get an OutputStream that connects to standard input for this separate program and an InputStream that connects to standard output. All you need to do is write a program using any language that takes its input from standard input and writes the output to standard output. This is a convenient trick when you run into a problem that can't be solved easily or quickly enough in Java (or when you have legacy code you don't want to rewrite). You can also use Java's native methods (see Appendix A) but those are much more involved.

13.10.2 The C Program

The job of this non-Java application (written in C because Java wasn't appropriate for CGI programming; if nothing else, the startup time is prohibitive) is to manage the list of email addresses. Standard input will accept an email address and the program will look up the name in the list to see if it's already there. If not, it will add it and report success, but if the name is already there then it will report that. Don't worry if you don't completely understand what the following code means; it's just one example of how you can write a program in another language and use it from Java. The particular programming language doesn't really matter as long as it can read from standard input and write to standard output.

```
//: Listmgr.c
// Used by NameCollector.java to manage
// the email list file on the server
#include <stdio.h>
#include <stdlib.h>
#include <string.h>
#define BSIZE 250

int alreadyInList(FILE* list, char* name) {
char lbuf[BSIZE];
// Go to the beginning of the list:
fseek(list, 0, SEEK_SET);
// Read each line in the list:
while(fgets(lbuf, BSIZE, list)) {
// Strip off the newline:
char * newline = strchr(lbuf, '\n');
if(newline != 0)
*newline = '\0';
if(strcmp(lbuf, name) == 0)
return 1;
```

```
}
return 0;
}
int main() {
char buf[BSIZE];
FILE* list = fopen("emlist.txt", "a+t");
if(list == 0) {
perror("could not open emlist.txt");
exit(1);
}
while(1) {
gets(buf); /* From stdin */
if(alreadyInList(list, buf)) {
printf("Already in list: %s", buf);
fflush(stdout);
}
else {
fseek(list, 0, SEEK_END);
fprintf(list, "%s\n", buf);
fflush(list);
printf("%s added to list", buf);
fflush(stdout);
}
}
} ///:~
```

This assumes that the C compiler accepts '//' style comments. (Many do, and you can also compile this program with a C++ compiler.) If yours doesn't, simply delete those comments.

The first function in the file checks to see whether the name you hand it as a second argument (a pointer to a char) is in the file. Here, the file is passed as a FILE pointer to an already-opened file (the file is opened inside main( )). The function fseek( ) moves around in the file; here it is used to move to the top of the file. fgets( ) reads a line from the file list into the buffer lbuf, not exceeding the buffer size BSIZE. This is inside a while loop so that each line in the file is read. Next, strchr( ) is used to locate the newline character so that it can be stripped off. Finally, strcmp( ) is used to compare the name you've passed into the function to the current line int the file. strcmp( ) returns zero if it finds a match. In this case the function exits and a one is returned to indicate that yes, the name was already in the list. (Note that the function returns as soon as it discovers the match, so it doesn't waste time looking at the rest of the list.) If you get all the way through the list without a match, the function returns zero.

In main( ), the file is opened using fopen( ). The first argument is the file name and the second is the way to open the file; a+ means "Append, and open (or create if the file does not exist) for update at the end of the file." The fopen( ) function returns a FILE pointer which, if it's zero, means that the open was unsuccessful. This is dealt with by printing an error message with perror( ) and terminating the program with exit( ).

Assuming that the file was opened successfully, the program enters an infinite loop. The function call gets(buf) gets a line from standard input (which will be connected to the Java program, remember) and places it in the buffer buf. This is simply passed to the alreadyInList( ) function, and if it's already in the list, printf( ) sends that message to standard output (where the Java program is listening). fflush( ) is a way to flush the output buffer.

If the name is not already in the list, fseek( ) is used to move to the end of the list and fprintf( ) "prints" the name to the end of the list. Then printf( ) is used to indicate that the name was added to the list (again flushing standard output) and the infinite loop goes back to waiting for a new name.

Remember that you usually cannot compile this program on your computer and load it onto the Web server machine, since that machine might use a different processor and operating system. For example, my Web server runs on an Intel processor but it uses Linux, so I must download the source code and compile using remote commands (via telnet) with the C compiler that comes with the Linux distribution.

The Java Program

This program will first start the C program above and make the necessary connections to talk to it. Then it will create a datagram socket that will be used to listen for datagram packets from the applet.

```
//: NameCollector.java
// Extracts email names from datagrams and stores
// them inside a file, using Java 1.02.
import java.net.*;
import java.io.*;
import java.util.*;

public class NameCollector {
final static int COLLECTOR_PORT = 8080;
final static int BUFFER_SIZE = 1000;
byte[] buf = new byte[BUFFER_SIZE];
DatagramPacket dp =
new DatagramPacket(buf, buf.length);
// Can listen & send on the same socket:
DatagramSocket socket;
Process listmgr;
PrintStream nameList;
DataInputStream addResult;
public NameCollector() {
try {
listmgr =
Runtime.getRuntime().exec("listmgr.exe");
nameList = new PrintStream(
new BufferedOutputStream(
listmgr.getOutputStream()));
addResult = new DataInputStream(
new BufferedInputStream(
listmgr.getInputStream()));

} catch(IOException e) {
System.err.println(
"Cannot start listmgr.exe");
System.exit(1);
}
try {
socket =
```

```
new DatagramSocket(COLLECTOR_PORT);
System.out.println(
"NameCollector Server started");
while(true) {
// Block until a datagram appears:
socket.receive(dp);
String rcvd = new String(dp.getData(),
0, 0, dp.getLength());
// Send to listmgr.exe standard input:
nameList.println(rcvd.trim());
nameList.flush();
byte[] resultBuf = new byte[BUFFER_SIZE];
int byteCount =
addResult.read(resultBuf);
if(byteCount != -1) {
String result =
new String(resultBuf, 0).trim();
// Extract the address and port from
// the received datagram to find out
// where to send the reply:
InetAddress senderAddress =
dp.getAddress();
int senderPort = dp.getPort();
byte[] echoBuf = new byte[BUFFER_SIZE];
result.getBytes(
0, byteCount, echoBuf, 0);
DatagramPacket echo =
new DatagramPacket(
echoBuf, echoBuf.length,
senderAddress, senderPort);
socket.send(echo);
}
else
System.out.println(
"Unexpected lack of result from " +
"listmgr.exe");
}
} catch(SocketException e) {
System.err.println("Can't open socket");
System.exit(1);
} catch(IOException e) {
System.err.println("Communication error");
e.printStackTrace();
}
}
public static void main(String[] args) {
new NameCollector();
}
```

```
} ///:~
```

The first definitions in NameCollector should look familiar: the port is chosen, a datagram packet is created, and there's a handle to a DatagramSocket. The next three definitions concern the connection to the C program: a Process object is what comes back when the C program is fired up by the Java program, and that Process object produces the InputStream and OutputStream objects representing, respectively, the standard output and standard input of the C program. These must of course be "wrapped" as is usual with Java IO, so we end up with a PrintStream and DataInputStream.

All the work for this program happens inside the constructor. To start up the C program, the current Runtime object is procured. This is used to call exec( ), which returns the Process object. You can see that there are simple calls to produce the streams from the Process object: getOutputStream( ) and getInputStream( ). From this point on, all you need to consider is sending data to the stream nameList and getting the results from addResult.

As before, a DatagramSocket is connected to a port. Inside the infinite while loop, the program calls receive( ), which blocks until a datagram shows up. When the datagram appears, its contents are extracted into the String rcvd . This is trimmed to remove white space at each end and sent to the C program in the line:

```
nameList.println(rcvd.trim());
```

This is only possible because Java's exec( ) provides access to any executable that reads from standard input and writes to standard output. There are other ways to talk to non-Java code, which are discussed in Appendix A.

Capturing the result from the C program is slightly more complicated. You must call read( ) and provide a buffer where the results will be placed. The return value for read( ) is the number of bytes that came from the C program, and if this value is -1 it means that something is wrong. Otherwise, the resultBuf is turned into a String and the spaces are trimmed off. This string is then placed into a DatagramPacket as before and shipped back to the same address that sent the request in the first place. Note that the sender's address is part of the DatagramPacket we received.

Remember that although the C program must be compiled on the Web server, the Java program can be compiled anywhere since the resulting byte codes will be the same regardless of the platform on which the program will be running.

13.10.3 The NameSender Applet

As mentioned earlier, the applet must be written with Java 1.0 so that it will run on the largest number of browsers, so it's best if the number of classes produced is minimized. Thus, instead of using the Dgram class developed earlier, all of the datagram manipulations will be placed in line. In addition, the applet needs a thread to listen for the reply from the server, and instead of making this a separate thread it's integrated into the applet by implementing the Runnable interface. This isn't as easy to read, but it produces a one-class (and one-server-hit) applet:

```
//: NameSender.java
// An applet that sends an email address
// as a datagram, using Java 1.02.
import java.awt.*;
import java.applet.*;
import java.net.*;
import java.io.*;

public class NameSender extends Applet
```

```
implements Runnable {
private Thread pl = null;
private Button send = new Button(
"Add email address to mailing list");
private TextField t = new TextField(
"type your email address here", 40);
private String str = new String();
private Label
l = new Label(), l2 = new Label();
private DatagramSocket s;
private InetAddress hostAddress;
private byte[] buf =
new byte[NameCollector.BUFFER_SIZE];
private DatagramPacket dp =
new DatagramPacket(buf, buf.length);
private int vcount = 0;
public void init() {
setLayout(new BorderLayout());
Panel p = new Panel();
p.setLayout(new GridLayout(2, 1));
p.add(t);
p.add(send);
add("North", p);
Panel labels = new Panel();
labels.setLayout(new GridLayout(2, 1));
labels.add(l);
labels.add(l2);
add("Center", labels);
try {
// Auto-assign port number:
s = new DatagramSocket();
hostAddress = InetAddress.getByName(
getCodeBase().getHost());
} catch(UnknownHostException e) {
l.setText("Cannot find host");
} catch(SocketException e) {
l.setText("Can't open socket");
}
l.setText("Ready to send your email address");
}
public boolean action (Event evt, Object arg) {
if(evt.target.equals(send)) {
if(pl != null) {
// pl.stop(); Deprecated in Java 1.2
Thread remove = pl;
pl = null;
remove.interrupt();
}
```

```
l2.setText("");
// Check for errors in email name:
str = t.getText().toLowerCase().trim();
if(str.indexOf(' ') != -1) {
l.setText("Spaces not allowed in name");
return true;
}
if(str.indexOf(',') != -1) {
l.setText("Commas not allowed in name");
return true;
}
if(str.indexOf('@') == -1) {
l.setText("Name must include '@'");
l2.setText("");
return true;
}
if(str.indexOf('@') == 0) {
l.setText("Name must preceed '@'");
l2.setText("");
return true;
}
String end =
str.substring(str.indexOf('@'));
if(end.indexOf('.') == -1) {
l.setText("Portion after '@' must " +
"have an extension, such as '.com'");
l2.setText("");
return true;
}
// Everything's OK, so send the name. Get a
// fresh buffer, so it's zeroed. For some
// reason you must use a fixed size rather
// than calculating the size dynamically:
byte[] sbuf =
new byte[NameCollector.BUFFER_SIZE];
str.getBytes(0, str.length(), sbuf, 0);
DatagramPacket toSend =
new DatagramPacket(
sbuf, 100, hostAddress,
NameCollector.COLLECTOR_PORT);
try {
s.send(toSend);
} catch(Exception e) {
l.setText("Couldn't send datagram");
return true;
}
l.setText("Sent: " + str);
send.setLabel("Re-send");
```

```
pl = new Thread(this);
pl.start();
l2.setText(
"Waiting for verification " + ++vcount);
}
else return super.action(evt, arg);
return true;
}
// The thread portion of the applet watches for
// the reply to come back from the server:
public void run() {
try {
s.receive(dp);
} catch(Exception e) {
l2.setText("Couldn't receive datagram");
return;
}
l2.setText(new String(dp.getData(),
0, 0, dp.getLength()));
}
} ///:~
```

The UI for the applet is quite simple. There's a TextField in which you type your email address, and a Button to send the email address to the server. Two Labels are used to report status back to the user.

By now you can recognize the DatagramSocket, InetAddress, buffer, and DatagramPacket as trappings of the network connection. Lastly, you can see the run( ) method that implements the thread portion so the applet can listen for the reply sent back by the server.

The init( ) method sets up the GUI with the familiar layout tools, then creates the DatagramSocket that will be used both for sending and receiving datagrams.

The action( ) method (remember, we're confined to Java 1.0 now, so we can't use any slick inner listener classes) watches only to see if you press the "send" button. When the button is pressed, the first action is to check the Thread pl to see if it's null. If it's not null, there's a live thread running. The first time the message is sent a thread is started up to watch for the reply. Thus, if a thread is running, it means this is not the first time the user has tried to send the message. The pl handle is set to null and the old listener is interrupted. (This is the preferred approach, since stop( ) is deprecated in Java 1.2.

Regardless of whether this is the first time the button was pressed, the text in l2 is erased.

The next group of statements checks the email name for errors. The String.indexOf( ) method is used to search for illegal characters, and if one is found it is reported to the user. Note that all of this happens without any network activity, so it's fast and it doesn't bog down the Internet.

Once the name is verified, it is packaged into a datagram and sent to the host address and port number in the same way that was described in the earlier datagram example. The first label is changed to show you that the send has occurred, and the button text is changed so that it reads "re-send." At this point, the thread is started up and the second label informs you that the applet is waiting for a reply from the server.

The run( ) method for the thread uses the DatagramSocket that lives in NameSender to receive( ), which blocks until the datagram packet comes from the server. The resulting packet is placed into NameSender's DatagramPacket dp . The data is retrieved from the packet and placed into the second label in NameSender. At this point, the thread terminates and becomes dead. If the reply doesn't come back from the server in a reasonable amount of time, the user might become impatient and press the button again, thus terminating the current thread (and, after re-sending the data, starting a new one). Because a thread is used to listen for the reply, the user still has full use of the UI.

13.10.4 The Web Page

Of course, the applet must go inside a Web page. Here is the complete Web page; you can see that it's intended to be used to automatically collect names for my mailing list:

```
<HTML>
<HEAD>
<META CONTENT="text/html">
<TITLE>
Add Yourself to Bruce Eckel's Java Mailing List
</TITLE>
</HEAD>
<BODY LINK="#0000ff" VLINK="#800080" BGCOLOR="#ffffff">
<FONT SIZE=6><P>
Add Yourself to Bruce Eckel's Java Mailing List
</P></FONT>
```

The applet on this page will automatically add your email address to the mailing list, so you will receive update information about changes to the online version of "Thinking in Java," notification when the book is in print, information about upcoming Java seminars, and notification about the "Hands-on Java Seminar" Multimedia CD. Type in your email address and press the button to automatically add yourself to this mailing list.

```
<HR>
<applet code=NameSender width=400 height=100>
</applet>
<HR>
```

If after several tries, you do not get verification it means that the Java application on the server is having problems. In this case, you can add yourself to the list by sending email to

```
<A HREF="mailto:Bruce@EckelObjects.com">
Bruce@EckelObjects.com</A>
</BODY>
</HTML>
```

13.10.5 Problems with this approach

This certainly seems like an elegant approach. There's no CGI programming and so there are no delays while the server starts up a CGI program. The datagram approach seems to produce a nice quick response. In addition, when Java 1.1 is available everywhere, the server portion can be written entirely in Java. (Although it's quite interesting to see how easy it is to connect to a non-Java program using standard input and output.)

There are problems, however. One problem is rather subtle: since the Java application is running constantly on the server and it spends most of its time blocked in the Datagram.receive( ) method, there might be some CPU hogging going on. At least, that's the way it appeared on the server where

I was experimenting. On the other hand, there wasn't much else happening on that server, and starting the program using "nice" (a Unix program to prevent a process from hogging the CPU) or its equivalent could solve the problem if you have a more heavily-loaded server. In any event, it's worth keeping your eye on an application like this - a blocked receive( ) could hog the CPU.

The second problem is a show stopper. It concerns firewalls. A firewall is a machine that sits between your network and the Internet. It monitors all traffic coming in from the Internet and going out to the Internet, and makes sure that traffic conforms to what it expects.

Firewalls are conservative little beasts. They demand strict conformance to all the rules, and if you're not conforming they assume that you're doing something sinful and shut you out (not quite so bad as the Spanish Inquisition, but close). For example, if you are on a network behind a firewall and you start connecting to the Internet using a Web browser, the firewall expects that all your transactions will connect to the server using the accepted http port, which is 80. Now along comes this Java applet NameSender, which is trying to send a datagram to port 8080, which is way outside the range of the "protected" ports 0-1024. The firewall naturally assumes the worst - that someone has a virus - and it doesn't allow the transaction to happen.

As long as your customers have raw connections to the Internet (for example, using a typical Internet service provider) there's no problem, but you might have some important customers dwelling behind firewalls, and they won't be able to use your program.

This is rather disheartening after learning so much Java, because it would seem that you must give up Java on the server and learn how to write CGI scripts in C or Perl. But as it turns out, despair is not in order.

One scenario is part of Sun's grand scheme. If everything goes as planned, Web servers will be equipped with servlet servers . These will take a request from the client (going through the firewall-accepted port 80) and instead of starting up a CGI program they will start up a Java program called a servlet. This is a little application that's designed to run only on the server. A servlet server will automatically start up the servlet to handle the client request, which means you can write all your programs in Java (further enabling the "100 percent pure Java initiative"). It is admittedly an appealing idea: once you're comfortable with Java, you don't have to switch to a more primitive language to handle requests on the server.

Since it's only for handling requests on the server, the servlet API has no GUI abilities. This fits quite well with NameCollector.java, which doesn't have a GUI anyway.

At this writing, a low-cost servlet server was available from java.sun.com. In addition, Sun is encouraging other Web server manufacturers to add servlet capabilities to their servers.

14

Java Applets

14.1 What is an Applet?

According to Sun "An applet is a small program that is intended not to be run on its own, but rather to be embedded inside another application....The Applet class provides a standard interface between applets and their environment."

Four definitions of applet:

- A small application
- A secure program that runs inside a web browser
- A subclass of java.applet.Applet
- An instance of a subclass of java.applet.Applet

```
public class Applet extends Panel
```

java.lang.Object

```
|
+—java.awt.Component
|
+—java.awt.Container
|
+—java.awt.Panel
|
+—java.applet.Applet
```

14.2 What Can an Applet Do?

An applet can:

- Draw pictures on a web page
- Create a new window and draw in it.
- Play sounds.
- Receive input from the user through the keyboard or the mouse.
- Make a network connection to the server from which it came and can send to and receive arbitrary data from that server.
- Anything you can do with these abilities you can do in an applet.

An applet cannot:

- Write data on any of the host's disks.
- Read any data from the host's disks without the user's permission. In some environments, notably Netscape, an applet cannot read data from the user's disks even with permission.
- Delete files
- Read from or write to arbitrary blocks of memory, even on a non-memory-protected operating

system like the MacOS. All memory access is strictly controlled.

- Make a network connection to a host on the Internet other than the one from which it was downloaded.
- Call the native API directly (though Java API calls may eventually lead back to native API calls).
- Introduce a virus or trojan horse into the host system.
- An applet is not supposed to be able to crash the host system. However in practice Java isn't quite stable enough to make this claim yet.

14.3 Who Can an Applet Talk To?

By default an applet can only open network connections to the system from which the applet was downloaded. This system is called the codebase. An applet cannot talk to an arbitrary system on the Internet. Any communication between different client systems must be mediated through the server.

The concern is that if connections to arbitrary hosts were allowed, then a malicious applet might be able to make connections to other systems and launch network based attacks on other machines in an organization's internal network. This would be an especially large problem because the machine's inside a firewall may be configured to trust each other more than they would trust any random machine from the Internet. If the internal network is properly protected by a firewall, this might be the only way an external machine could even talk to an internal machine. Furthermore arbitrary network connections would allow crackers to more easily hide their true location by passing their attacks through several applet intermediaries.

HotJava, Sun's applet viewer, and Internet Explorer (but not Netscape) let you grant applets permission to open connections to any system on the Internet, though this is not enabled by default.

14.4 Applet Arcitecture

Applets adopt following architecture

public class Applet extends Panel

```
java.lang.Object
|
+—java.awt.Component
|
+—java.awt.Container
|
+—java.awt.Panel
|
+—java.applet.Applet
```

14.5 How much CPU time does an Applet Get?

One of the few legitimate concerns about hostile applets is excessive use of CPU time. It is possible on a non-preemptively multitasking system (specifically the Mac) to write an applet that uses so much CPU time in a tight loop that it effectively locks up the host system. This is not a problem on preemptively multitasking systems like Solaris and Windows NT. Even on those platforms, though, it is possible for an applet to force the user to kill their web browser, possibly losing accumulated bookmarks, email and other work.

It's also possible for an applet to use CPU time for purposes other than the apparent intent of the applet. For instance, a popular applet could launch a Chinese lottery attack on a Unix password file. A popular game applet could launch a thread in the background which tried a random assortment of keys to break a DES encrypted file. If the key was found, then a network connection could be opened to the applet server to send the decrypted key back. The more popular the applet was the faster the key would be found. The ease with which Java applets are decompiled would probably mean that any such applet would be discovered, but there really isn't a way to prevent it from running in the first place.

14.6 The Basic Applet Life Cycle

- The browser reads the HTML page and finds any <APPLET> tags.
- The browser parses the <APPLET> tag to find the CODE and possibly CODEBASE parameter.
- The browser downloads the .class file for the applet from the URL found in the last step.
- The browser converts the raw bytes downloaded into a Java class, that is a java.lang.Class object.
- The browser instantiates the applet class to form an applet object. This requires the applet to have a noargs constructor.
- The browser calls the applet's init() method.
- The browser calls the applet's start() method.
- While the applet is running, the browser passes any events intended for the applet, e.g. mouse clicks, key presses, etc., to the applet's handleEvent() method. Update events are used to tell the applet that it needs to repaint itself.
- The browser calls the applet's stop() method.
- The browser calls the applet's destroy() method.

14.6.1 The Life Cycle of an Applet

Below is the Simple applet.

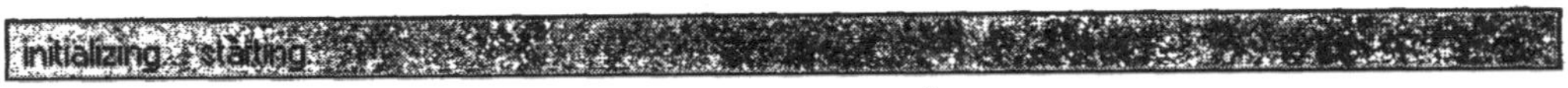

Fig14.1

Note: Because some old browsers don't support 1.1, the above applet is a 1.0 version (here is the 1.0 code; here's the 1.1 code). To run the 1.1 version of the applet, go to example-1dot1/Simple.html. For more information about running applets, refer to About Our Examples.

(1) Loading the Applet

You should see "initializing... starting..." above, as the result of the applet being loaded. When an applet is loaded, here's what happens:

- An instance of the applet's controlling class (an Applet subclass) is created.
- The applet initializes itself.
- The applet starts running.
- Leaving and Returning to the Applet's Page

When the user leaves the page — for example, to go to another page — the applet has the option of stopping itself. When the user returns to the page, the applet can start itself again. The same sequence occurs when the user iconifies and then reopens the window that contains the applet. (Other terms used instead of iconify are minaturize, minimize, and close.)

Try this: Leave and then return to this page. You'll see "stopping..." added to the applet output above, as the applet is given the chance to stop itself. You'll also see "starting...", when the applet is told to start itself again. Next, iconify this window, and then open it again. Many window systems provide a button in the title bar that lets you iconify the window. You should see "stopping...." and then "starting...." added to the applet output.

Browser note: Some browsers reload the applet when you return to its page. In at least one browser, a bug exists where an applet can initialize itself more than once without being reloaded.

(2) Reloading the Applet

Some browsers let the user reload applets, which consists of unloading the applet and then loading it again. Before an applet is unloaded, it's given the chance to stop itself and then to perform a final cleanup, so that the applet can release any resources it holds. After that, the applet is unloaded and then loaded again, as described in Loading the Applet, above.

Try this: If your browser or other applet viewer lets you easily reload applets, reload the applet. Look at the standard output to see what happens when you reload the applet. (See Displaying Short Status Stringsfor information about the standard output.) You should see "stopping..." and "preparing for unloading..." when the applet is unloaded. You can't see this in the applet GUI because the applet is unloaded before the text can be displayed. When the applet is reloaded, you should see "initializing..." and "starting...", just like when you loaded the applet for the first time.

(3) Quitting the Browser

When the user quits the browser (or whatever application is displaying the applet), the applet has the chance to stop itself and do final cleanup before the browser exits.

An applet can react to major events in the following ways:

It can initialize itself.
It can start running.
It can stop running.
It can perform a final cleanup, in preparation for being unloaded.

14.6.2 The Basic Applet Methods

All applets have the following four methods:

- public void init();
- public void start();
- public void stop();
- public void destroy();

They have these methods because their superclass, java.applet.Applet, has these methods. (It has others too, but right now I just want to talk about these four.)

In the superclass, these are simply do-nothing methods. For example,

public void init() {}

Subclasses may override these methods to accomplish certain tasks at certain times. For instance, the init() method is a good place to read parameters that were passed to the applet via <PARAM> tags because it's called exactly once when the applet starts up. However, they do not have to override them. Since they're declared in the superclass, the web browser can invoke them when it needs to without knowing in advance whether the method is implemented in the superclass or the subclass. This is a good example of polymorphism.

14.6.3 init(), start(), stop(), and destroy()

The init() method is called exactly once in an applet's life, when the applet is first loaded. It's normally used to read PARAM tags, start downloading any other images or media files you need, and set up the user interface. Most applets have init() methods.

The start() method is called at least once in an applet's life, when the applet is started or restarted. In some cases it may be called more than once. Many applets you write will not have explicit start()methods and will merely inherit one from their superclass. A start() method is often used to start any threads the applet will need while it runs.

The stop() method is called at least once in an applet's life, when the browser leaves the page in which the applet is embedded. The applet's start() method will be called if at some later point the browser returns to the page containing the applet. In some cases the stop() method may be called multiple times in an applet's life. Many applets you write will not have explicit stop()methods and will merely inherit one from their superclass. Your applet should use the stop() method to pause any running threads. When your applet is stopped, it should not use any CPU cycles.

The destroy() method is called exactly once in an applet's life, just before the browser unloads the applet. This method is generally used to perform any final clean-up. For example, an applet that stores state on the server might send some data back to the server before it's terminated. many applets will not have explicit destroy() methods and just inherit one from their superclass.

For example, in a video applet, the init() method might draw the controls and start loading the video file. The start() method would wait until the file was loaded, and then start playing it. The stop() method would pause the video, but not rewind it. If the start() method were called again, the video would pick up where it left off; it would not start over from the beginning. However, if destroy() were called and then init(), the video would start over from the beginning.

In the JDK's appletviewer, selecting the Restart menu item calls stop() and then start(). Selecting the Reload menu item calls stop(), destroy(), and init(), in that order. (Normally the byte codes will also be reloaded and the HTML file reread though Netscape has a problem with this.)

The applet start() and stop() methods are not related to the similarly named methods in the java.lang.Thread class.

Your own code may occasionally invoke start() and stop(). For example, it's customary to stop playing an animation when the user clicks the mouse in the applet and restart it when they click the mouse again.

Your own code can also invoke init() and destroy(), but this is normally a bad idea. Only the environment should call init() and destroy().

14.7 Overview of Applets

This section discusses the parts of an applet. If you haven't yet compiled an applet and included it in an HTML page, you might want to do so now. Step by step instructions are in The "Hello World" Applet.

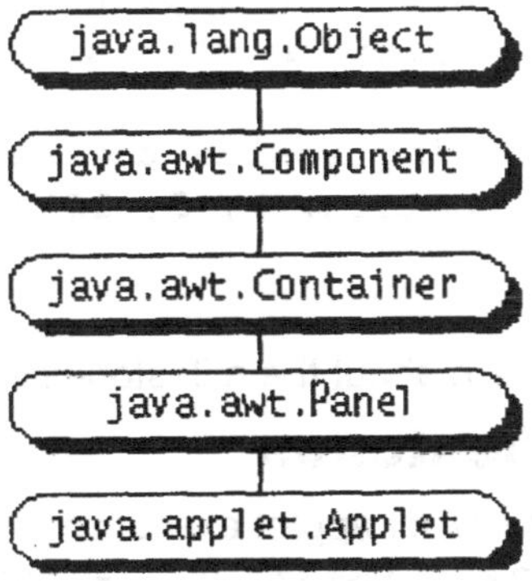

Fig 14.2

Every applet is implemented by creating a subclass of the Applet class. The following figure shows the inheritance hierarchy of the Applet class. This hierarchy determines much of what an applet can do and how, as you'll see on the next few pages.

14.7.1 A Simple Applet

Below is the source code for an applet called Simple. The Simple applet displays a descriptive string whenever it encounters a major milestone in its life, such as when the user first visits the page the applet's on. The pages that follow use the Simple applet and build upon it to illustrate concepts that are common to many applets. If you find yourself baffled by the Java source code, you might want to go to Learning the Java Language to learn about the language.

```
/* * 1.0 code. */
import java.applet.Applet;
import java.awt.Graphics;
public class Simple extends Applet {
StringBuffer buffer;
public void init() {
buffer = new StringBuffer();
addItem("initializing... ");
}
public void start() {
addItem("starting... ");
}
public void stop() {
addItem("stopping... ");
}
public void destroy() {
addItem("preparing for unloading...");
}
void addItem(String newWord) {
System.out.println(newWord);
buffer.append(newWord);
repaint();
}

public void paint(Graphics g) {
//Draw a Rectangle around the applet's display area.
g.drawRect(0, 0, size().width - 1, size().height - 1);

//Draw the current string inside the rectangle.
g.drawString(buffer.toString(), 5, 15);
}
}
```

You can use the Simple applet to learn about the milestones in every applet's life.

14.7.2 Methods for Milestones

The Applet class provides a framework for applet execution, defining methods that the system calls when milestones — major events in an applet's life cycle — occur. Most applets override some or all of these methods to respond appropriately to milestones.

14.7.3 Methods for Drawing and Event Handling

Applets inherit the drawing and event handling methods of the AWT Component class. (AWT stands for Abstract Windowing Toolkit; applets and applications use its classes to produce user interfaces.) Drawing refers to anything related to representing an applet on-screen — drawing images, presenting user interface components such as buttons, or using graphics primitives. Event handling refers to detecting and processing user input such as mouse clicks and key presses, as well as more abstract events such as saving files and iconifying windows.

Methods for Adding UI Components

Applets inherit from the AWT Container class. This means that they are designed to hold Components — user interface objects such as buttons, labels, pop-up lists, and scrollbars. Like other Containers, applets use layout managers to control the positioning of Components.

14.7.4 What Applets Can and Can't Do

For security reasons, applets that are loaded over the network have several restrictions. One is that an applet can't ordinarily read or write files on the computer that it's executing on. Another is that an applet can't make network connections except to the host that it came from. Despite these restrictions, applets can do some things that you might not expect. For example, applets can invoke the public methods of other applets on the same page.

14.7.5 Test Driving an Applet

Once you've written an applet, you'll need to add it to an HTML page so that you can try it out. This section tells you how to use the <APPLET> HTML tag to add an applet to an HTML page.

```
Methods for Milestones
public class Simple extends Applet {
. . .
public void init() { . . . }
public void start() { . . . }
public void stop() { . . . }
public void destroy() { . . . }
. . .
}
```

The Simple applet, like every other applet, features a subclass of the Applet class. The Simple class overrides four Applet methods so that it can respond to major events:

init

To initialize the applet each time it's loaded (or reloaded).

start

To start the applet's execution, such as when the applet's loaded or when the user revisits a page that contains the applet.

stop

To stop the applet's execution, such as when the user leaves the applet's page or quits the browser.

destroy

To perform a final cleanup in preparation for unloading.

Not every applet needs to override every one of these methods. Some very simple applets override none of them. For example, the Writing Applets doesn't override any of these methods, since it doesn't do anything except draw itself. The "Hello World" applet just displays a string once, using its paint method. (The paint method is described on the following page.) Most applets, however, do more.

The init method is useful for one-time initialization that doesn't take very long. In general, the init method should contain the code that you would normally put into a constructor. The reason applets shouldn't usually have constructors is that an applet isn't guaranteed to have a full environment until its init method is called. For example, the Applet image loading methods simply don't work inside of a applet constructor. The init method, on the other hand, is a great place to call the image loading methods, since the methods return quickly.

Browser note: Some browsers sometimes call the init method more than once after the applet has been loaded. See the previous page for more details.

Every applet that does something after initialization (except in direct response to user actions) must override the start method. The start method either performs the applet's work or (more likely) starts up one or more threads to perform the work. You'll learn more about threads later in this trail, in Threads in Applets. You'll learn more about handling the events that represent user actions on the next page.

Most applets that override start should also override the stop method. The stop method should suspend the applet's execution, so that it doesn't take up system resources when the user isn't viewing the applet's page. For example, an applet that displays animation should stop trying to draw the animation when the user isn't looking at it.

Many applets don't need to override the destroy method, since their stop method (which is called before destroy) does everything necessary to shut down the applet's execution. However, destroy is available for applets that need to release additional resources.

The init, start, stop, and destroy methods are discussed and used throughout this tutorial. For more information, you can also refer to the Applet API reference page.

14.7.6 Paint Methods for Drawing and Event Handling

The Simple applet defines its onscreen appearance by overriding the paint method:

```
class Simple extends Applet
    {
    . . .
    public void paint(Graphics g) { . . . }
    . . .
    }
```

The paint method is one of two display methods an applet can override:

paint

The basic display method. Many applets implement the paint method to draw the applet's representation within a browser page.

update

A method you can use along with paint to improve drawing performance.

Applets inherit their paint and update methods from the Applet class, which inherits them from the Abstract Window Toolkit (AWT) Component class. For an overview of the Component class, and the AWT in general, see the Overview of the Java UI trail. Within the overview, the architecture of the AWT drawing system is discussed on the Drawing page.

Applets inherit a group of event-handling methods from the Component class. (The architecture of the AWT event system is discussed on the Events page.) The Component class defines several methods, such as action and mouseDown, for handling particular types of events, and then one catch-all method called handleEvent.

To react to an event, an applet must override either the appropriate event-specific method or the handleEvent method. For example, adding the following code to the Simple applet makes it respond to mouse clicks.

```
import java.awt.Event;
. . .
public boolean mouseDown(Event event, int x, int y) {
addItem("click!... ");
return true;
}
```

Below is the resulting applet.

Fig. 14.3

When you click within its rectangle, it displays the word "click!...".

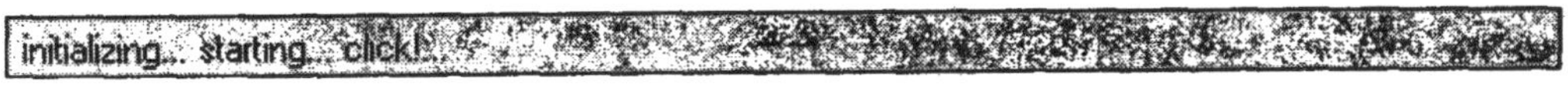

Fig14.4

Note: Because some old browsers don't support 1.1, the above applet is a 1.0 version (here is the 1.0 code; here's the 1.1 code). To run the 1.1 version of the applet, go to example-1dot1/SimpleClick.html. For more information about running applets, refer to About Our Examples.

14.8 Applet Tag

Here's the simplest form of the <APPLET> tag:

<APPLET CODE=AppletSubclass.class WIDTH=anInt HEIGHT=anInt>

</APPLET>

This tag tells the browser to load the applet whose Applet subclass is named AppletSubclass. The following figure shows where the applet class file must be, relative to the HTML document that contains the <APPLET> tag. As the figure shows, unless the applet is declared to be in a package, its class file should be in the same directory as the HTML file that has the <APPLET> tag.

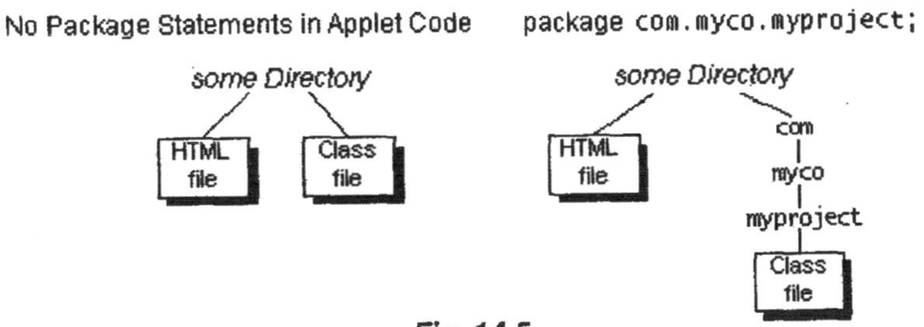

Fig. 14.5

14.8.1 The Applet API

The applet API lets you take advantage of the close relationship that applets have with Web browsers. The API is provided by the java.applet package — mainly by the Applet class and the AppletContext interface. Thanks to the applet API, applets can do the following:

- Be notified by the browser of milestones.
- Load data files specified relative to the URL of the applet or the page in which it is running.
- Display short status strings.
- Make the browser display a document.
- Find other applets running in the same page.
- Play sounds.
- Get parameters specified by the user in the <APPLET> tag.

Further sections discuss each of these topics in turn, except for the milestone methods (init, start, and so on), which are explained in Methods for Milestones. For information about how to use non-applet-specific API in an applet, see the Practical Considerations when Writing Applets lesson.

The Applet getCodeBase and getDocumentBase methods get information from the browser about where the applet and its HTML page came from. Finding and Loading Data Files describes how to use these methods to help you load your applet's data files, such as images.

Displaying Short Status Strings describes how to make an applet display a string on the status line of the application in which it is running.

Displaying Documents in the Browser tells you how to use the two showDocument methods to request that the browser visit a particular URL.

Using the AppletContext getApplet and getApplets methods, an applet can get the Applet objects for other applets running on the same page. Once an applet has another's Applet object, the applet can send messages to it. Sending Messages to Other Applets provides details and example applets that communicate with each other.

The Applet class and AudioClip interface provide support for playing sounds. The Playing Sounds section tells you about this support and includes an example of using sound in an applet.

You can improve the versatility of your applet by providing parameters. Defining and Using Applet Parameters describes how to decide which parameters to provide, how to implement them, and how to inform the user about them.

Finally, Using the <APPLET> Tag tells you how to customize an applet by editing its HTML tag.

14.8.2 Finding and Loading Data Files

Whenever an applet needs to load some data from a file that's specified with a relative URL (a URL that doesn't completely specify the file's location), the applet usually uses either the code base or the document base to form the complete URL. The code base, returned by the Applet getCodeBase method, is a URL that specifies the directory from which the applet's classes were loaded. The document base, returned by the Applet getDocumentBase method, specifies the directory of the HTML page that contains the applet.

Unless the <APPLET> tag specifies a code base, both the code base and document base refer to the same directory on the same server. For example, in the figure in Test Driving an Applet, the code and document bases would both specify the someDirectory directory.

Data that the applet always needs, or needs to rely on as a backup, is usually specified relative to the code base. Data that the applet user specifies, often by using parameters, is usually specified relative to the document base.

Note: For security reasons, browsers limit the URLs from which untrusted applets can read. For example, most browsers don't allow untrusted applets to use ".." to get to directories above the code base or document base. Also, since untrusted applets can't read files except those on the applet's originating host, the document base isn't generally useful if the document and the untrusted applet are on different servers.

The Applet class defines convenient forms of image-loading and sound-loading methods that let you specify images and sounds relative to a base URL. For example, assume an applet is set up with one of the directory structures shown in the following figure.

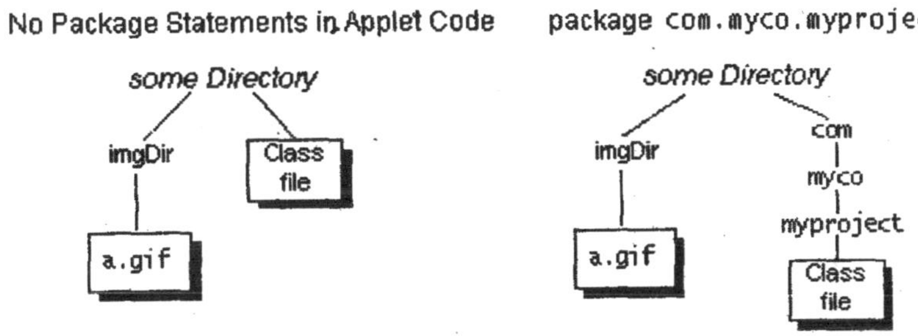

Fig 14.6

To create an Image object using the a.gif image file under imgDir, the applet can use the following code:

Image image = getImage(getCodeBase(), "imgDir/a.gif");

When a Java-enabled browser encounters an <APPLET> tag, it reserves a display area of the specified width and height for the applet, loads the bytecodes for the specified Applet subclass, creates an instance of the subclass, and then calls the instance's init and start methods.

The <APPLET> tag has many options that you can use to customize your applet's execution. For example, you can put your applet's files into an archive. You can also specify parameters to be passed to the applet. These options are described in Using the APPLET Tag.

14.8.3 Taking Advantage of the Applet API

(1) Displaying Short Status Strings

All applet viewers — from the Applet Viewer to Java-compatible browsers — allow applets to display a short status string. In current implementations, this string appears on the status line at the bottom of the applet viewer window. In browsers, all applets on the page, as well as the browser itself, generally share the same status line.

You should never put crucial information in the status line. If many users might need the information, it should instead be displayed within the applet area. If only a few, sophisticated users might need the information, consider displaying the information on the standard output (see Displaying Diagnostics to the Standard Output and Error Streams).

The status line is not usually very prominent, and it can be overwritten by other applets or by the browser. For these reasons, it's best used for incidental, transitory information. For example, an applet that loads several image files might display the name of the image file it's currently loading.

Applets display status lines with the showStatus method. Here's an example of its use:

```
showStatus("MyApplet: Loading image file " + file);
```

Note: Please don't put scrolling text in the status line. Browser users find such status line abuse highly annoying!

(2) Displaying Documents in the Browser

Have you ever wanted an applet to display formatted HTML text? Here's the easy way to do it: Ask the browser to display the text for you.

With the AppletContext showDocument methods, an applet can tell the browser which URL to show and in which browser window. (By the way, the JDK Applet Viewer ignores these methods, since it can't display documents.) Here are the two forms of show Document:

public void showDocument(java.net.URL url)
public void showDocument(java.net.URL url, String targetWindow)

The one-argument form of showDocument simply tells the browser to display the document at the specified URL, without specifying the window to display the document in.

Terminology Note: In this discussion, frame refers not to an AWT Frame but to an HTML frame within a browser window.

The two-argument form of showDocument lets you specify which window or HTML frame to display the document in. The second argument can have the values listed below.

- "_blank" : Display the document in a new, nameless window.
- "windowName" : Display the document in a window named windowName. This window is created if necessary.
- "_self": Display the document in the window and frame that contain the applet.
- "_parent" : Display the document in the applet's window but in the parent frame of the applet's frame. If the applet frame has no parent frame, this acts the same as "_self".
- "_top" : Display the document in the applet's window but in the top-level frame. If the applet's frame is the top-level frame, this acts the same as "_self".

The following applet lets you try every option of both forms of showDocument. The applet brings up a window that lets you type in a URL and choose any of the showDocument options. When you press Return or click the Show document button, the applet calls showDocument.

Fig14.7

Note: Because some old browsers don't support 1.1, the above applet is a 1.0 version (here is the 1.0 code; here's the 1.1 code). To run the 1.1 version of the applet, go to example-1dot1/ShowDocument.html. For more information about running applets, refer to About Our Examples.

Following is the applet code that calls showDocument. (Here's the whole program.)

```
...//In an Applet subclass:
urlWindow = new URLWindow(getAppletContext());
. . .
class URLWindow extends Frame {
. . .
public URLWindow(AppletContext appletContext) {
. . .
```

```
this.appletContext = appletContext;
. . .
}
. . .
public boolean action(Event event, Object o) {
. . .
String urlString = /* user-entered string */;
URL url = null;
try {
url = new URL(urlString);
} catch (MalformedURLException e) {
...//Inform the user and return...
}
if (url != null) {
if (/* user doesn't want to specify the window */) {
appletContext.showDocument(url);
} else {
appletContext.showDocument(url,
/* user-specified window */);
}
}
. . .
```

14.8.4 Sending Messages to Other Applets

Applets can find other applets and send messages to them, with the following security restrictions:

Many browsers require that the applets originate from the same server.

Many browsers further require that the applets originate from the same directory on the server (the same code base).

The Java API requires that the applets be running on the same page, in the same browser window.

Note: Some browsers let applets invoke methods on other applets — even applets on different pages in the same browser — as long as all of the applets come from the same code base. This method of interapplet communication isn't supported by the Java API, so it's possible that it will not be supported by all browsers.

An applet can find another applet either by looking it up by name (using the AppletContext getApplet method) or by finding all the applets on the page (using the AppletContext getApplets method). Both methods, if successful, give the caller one or more Applet objects. Once the caller finds an Applet object, the caller can invoke methods on the object.

14.9 Finding an Applet by Name: The getApplet Method

The getApplet method looks through all of the applets on the current page to see if one of them has the specified name. If so, getApplet returns the applet's Applet object.

By default, an applet has no name. For an applet to have a name, one must be specified in the HTML code that adds the applet to a page. You can specify an applet's name in two ways:

By specifying a NAME attribute within the applet's <APPLET> tag. For example:

```
<APPLET CODEBASE=example/ CODE=Sender.class
WIDTH=450
HEIGHT=200
NAME="buddy">
</applet>
```

By specifying a NAME parameter with a <PARAM> tag. For example:

```
<APPLET CODEBASE=example/ CODE=Receiver.class
WIDTH=450
HEIGHT=35>
<PARAM NAME="name" value="old pal">
</applet>
```

Browser Note: Although at least one Java-enabled browser conducts a case-sensitive search, the expected behavior is for the getApplet method to perform a case-insensitive search. For example, getApplet("old pal") and getApplet("OLD PAL") should both find an applet named "Old Pal".

Below are two applets that illustrate lookup by name. The first, the Sender, looks up the second, the Receiver. When the Sender finds the Receiver, the Sender sends a message to the Receiver by invoking one of the Receiver's methods (passing the Sender's name as an argument). The Receiver reacts to this method call by changing its leftmost text string to "Received message from sender-name!".

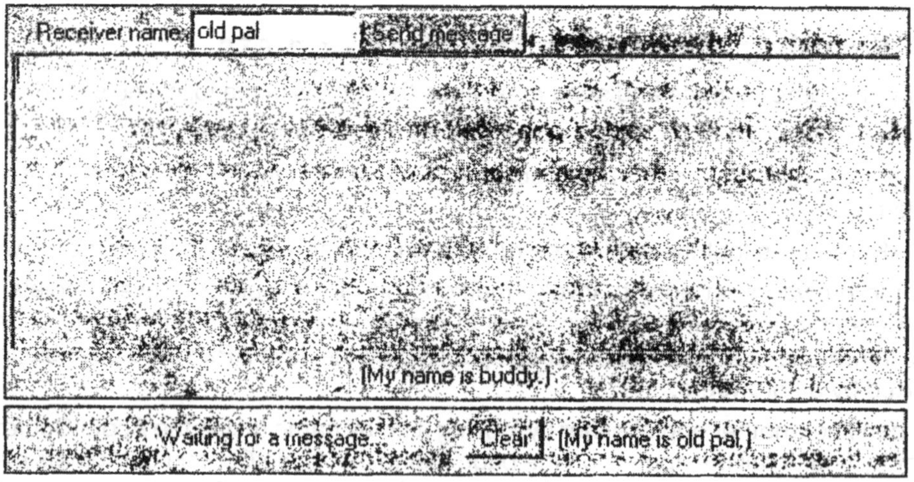

Fig14.8

Note: Because some old browsers don't support 1.1, the above applets are 1.0 versions. Here are links to the 1.0 code for the Sender and Receiver classes. To run the 1.1 versions of the applets, go to example-1dot1/iac.html.

Try this: Click the Send message button of the top applet (the Sender). Some status information will appear in the Sender's window, and the Receiver will confirm (with its own status string) that it received a message, After you've read the Receiver status string, press the Receiver's Clear button to reset the Receiver. In the Sender's text field labeled "Receiver name:," type in buddy and press Return. Since "buddy" is the Sender's own name, the Sender will find an applet named buddy but won't send it a message, since it isn't a Receiver instance.

Here's the whole Sender program. The code it uses to look up and communicate with the Receiver is listed below. Code that you can use without change in your own applet is in bold font.

```
Applet receiver = null;
String receiverName = nameField.getText(); //Get name to search for.
receiver = getAppletContext().getApplet(receiverName);
```

The Sender goes on to make sure that the Receiver was found and that it's an instance of the correct class (Receiver). If all goes well, the Sender sends a message to the Receiver. (Here's the Receiver program.)

```
if (receiver != null)
{
//Use the instanceof operator to make sure the applet
//we found is a Receiver object.
if (!(receiver instanceof Receiver)) {
status.appendText("Found applet named "
+ receiverName + ", "
+ "but it's not a Receiver object.\n");
} else {
status.appendText("Found applet named "
+ receiverName + ".\n"
+ "  Sending message to it.\n");
//Cast the receiver to be a Receiver object
//(instead of just an Applet object) so that the
//compiler will let us call a Receiver method.
((Receiver)receiver).processRequestFrom(myName);
}
} . . .
```

From an applet's point of view, its name is stored in a parameter named NAME. It can get the value of the parameter using the Applet getParameter method. For example, Sender gets its own name with the following code:

myName = getParameter("NAME");

The example applets in this page perform one-way communication — from the Sender to the Receiver. If you want your receiver to be able to send messages to the sender, then you just need to have the sender give a reference to itself (this) to the receiver. For example:

((Receiver)receiver).startCommunicating(this);

Finding All the Applets on a Page: The getApplets Method

The getApplets method returns a list (an Enumeration, to be precise) of all the applets on the page. For security reasons, many browsers and applet viewers implement getApplets so that it returns only those applets that originated from the same host as the applet calling getApplets. Here's an applet that simply lists all the applets it can find on this page:

Note: Because some old browsers don't support 1.1, the above applet is a 1.0 version (here is the 1.0 code; here's the 1.1 code). To run the 1.1 version of the applet, go to example-1dot1/iac.html. For more information about running applets, refer to About Our Examples.

Fig 14.9

Below are the relevant parts of the method that calls getApplets. (Here's the whole program.)

```
public void printApplets()
{
//Enumeration will contain all applets on this page (including
//this one) that we can send messages to.
Enumeration e = getAppletContext().getApplets();
. . .
while (e.hasMoreElements()) {
Applet applet = (Applet)e.nextElement();
String info = ((Applet)applet).getAppletInfo();
if (info != null) {
textArea.appendText("- " + info + "\n");
} else {
textArea.appendText("- "
+ applet.getClass().getName()
+ "\n");
}
}
. . .
}
```

14.10 Defining and Using Applet Parameters

Parameters are to applets what command-line arguments are to applications. They allow the user to customize the applet's operation. By defining parameters, you can increase your applet's flexibility, making your applet work in multiple situations without recoding and recompiling it.

The next few pages discuss parameters from the applet programmer's point of view.

14.10.1 Deciding Which Parameters to Support

When implementing parameters, you must answer four questions:

- What should the applet let the user configure?
- What should the parameters be named?
- What kind of value should each parameter take?
- What should the default value of each parameter be?
- Writing the Code to Support Parameters

Applets get the user-defined values of parameters by calling the Applet getParameter method.

- Giving Information about Parameters

By implementing the getParameterInfo method, applets provide information that browsers can use to help the user set parameter values.

14.10.2 What Should the Applet Let the User Configure?

The parameters your applet should support depend on what your applet does and on how flexible you want it to be. Applets that display images might have parameters to specify the image locations. Similarly, applets that play sounds might have parameters to specify the sounds.

Besides parameters that specify resource locations (such as image and sound files), applets sometimes provide parameters for specifying details of the applet's appearance or operation. For example, an animation applet might let the user specify the number of images shown per second. Or an applet might let the user change the strings the applet displays. Anything is possible.

14.10.3 What Should the Parameters Be Named?

Once you decide what parameters your applet will support, you need to figure out their names. Here are some typical parameter names:

- **SOURCE or SRC**

For a data file such as an image file.

XXXSOURCE (for example, IMAGESOURCE)

Used in applets that let the user specify more than one type of data file.

* XXXS

For a parameter that takes a list of XXXs (where XXX might be IMAGE, again).

- **NAME**

Used only for an applet's name. Applet names are used for interapplet communication, as described in Sending Messages to Other Applets.) .

Clarity of names is more important than keeping the name length short. Do not use names of <APPLET> tag attributes, which are documented in The <APPLET> Tag.

Note: Although this tutorial usually refers to parameter names using ALL UPPERCASE, parameter names are case-insensitive. For example, IMAGESOURCE and imageSource both refer to the same parameter. Parameter values, on the other hand, are case-sensitive unless you take steps interpret them otherwise, such as by using the String toLowerCase method before interpreting the parameter's value.

14.10.4 What Kind of Value Should Each Parameter Take?

Parameter values are all strings. Whether or not the user puts quotation marks around a parameter value, that value is passed to your applet as a string. However, your applet can interpret the string in many ways.

Applets typically interpret a parameter value as one of the following types:

- A URL
- An integer
- A floating-point number
- A boolean value — typically "true"/"false" or "yes"/"no"
- A string — for example, the string to use as a window title

- A list of any of the above

14.10.5 What Should the Default Value of Each Parameter Be?

Applets should attempt to provide useful default values for each parameter, so that the applet will execute even if the user doesn't specify a parameter or specifies it incorrectly. For example, an animation applet should provide a reasonable setting for the number of images it displays per second. This way, if the user doesn't specify the relevant parameter, the applet will still work well.

An Example: AppletButton

Throughout this tutorial, applets that need to bring up windows use the highly configurable AppletButton class.

Note: If you're using 1.1 or 1.2, you should look at the Swing version of AppletButton.java.

One page alone — Using Layout Managers — uses AppletButton five times for five different examples, one per layout manager the AWT provides. AppletButton's GUI is simple, consisting of a button and a label that displays status. When the user clicks the button, the applet brings up a window.

The AppletButton class is so flexible because it defines parameters that let the user specify any or all of the following:

The type of window to bring up

The window's title
The window's height
The window's width
The label of the button that brings up the window

Here's what a typical <APPLET> tag for AppletButton looks like. You can see this applet running at the URL Using Layout Managers.

```
<APPLET CODE=AppletButton.class CODEBASE=example
WIDTH=350 HEIGHT=60>
<PARAM NAME=windowClass VALUE=BorderWindow>
<PARAM NAME=windowTitle VALUE="BorderLayout">
<PARAM NAME=buttonText
VALUE="Click here to see a BorderLayout in action">
</APPLET>
```

When the user doesn't specify a value for a parameter, AppletButton uses a reasonable default value. For example, if the user doesn't specify the window's title, AppletButton uses the window's type as the title.

The next page shows you the code AppletButton uses to get its parameter values from the user.

14.11 Writing the Code to Support Parameters

Applets use the Applet getParameter method to get user-specified values for applet parameters. The getParameter method is defined as follows:

public String getParameter(String name)

Your applet might need to convert the string that getParameter returns into another form, such as an integer. The java.lang package provides classes such as Integer that you can use to help with converting strings to primitive types. Here's an example from the AppletButton class of converting a parameter's value into an integer:

```
int requestedWidth = 0;
. . .
String windowWidthString = getParameter("WINDOWWIDTH");
if (windowWidthString != null) {
try {
requestedWidth = Integer.parseInt(windowWidthString);
} catch (NumberFormatException e) {
//Use default width.
}
}
```

Note that if the user doesn't specify a value for the WINDOWWIDTH parameter, the above code uses a default value of 0, which the applet interprets as "use the window's natural size." It's important that you supply default values wherever possible.

Besides using the getParameter method to get values of applet-specific parameters, you can also use getParameter to get the values of attributes of the applet's <APPLET> tag. See The <APPLET> Tag for a list of <APPLET> tag attributes.

An Example: AppletButton

Below is the AppletButton code that gets the applet's parameters. For more information on AppletButton, see the previous page.

```
String windowClass;
String buttonText;
String windowTitle;
int requestedWidth = 0;
int requestedHeight = 0;
public void init() {
windowClass = getParameter("WINDOWCLASS");
if (windowClass == null) {
windowClass = "TestWindow";
}
buttonText = getParameter("BUTTONTEXT");
if (buttonText == null) {
buttonText = "Click here to bring up a " + windowClass;
}

windowTitle = getParameter("WINDOWTITLE");
if (windowTitle == null) {
windowTitle = windowClass;
}

String windowWidthString = getParameter("WINDOWWIDTH");
if (windowWidthString != null) {
try {
requestedWidth = Integer.parseInt(windowWidthString);
} catch (NumberFormatException e) {
//Use default width.
}
```

```
}

String windowHeightString = getParameter("WINDOWHEIGHT");
if (windowHeightString != null) {
try {
requestedHeight = Integer.parseInt(windowHeightString);
} catch (NumberFormatException e) {
//Use default height.
}
}
```

14.11.1 Giving Information about Parameters

Now that you've provided all those nice parameters to the user, you need to help the user set the parameter values correctly. Of course, your applet's documentation should describe each parameter and give the user examples and hints of setting them. Your job doesn't stop there, though. You should also implement the getParameterInfo method so that it returns information about your applet's parameters. Browsers can use this information to help the user set your applet's parameter values.

Below is an example of implementing the getParameterInfo method. This example is from the Animator applet, a wonderfully flexible applet that provides 13 parameters for users to customize their animation.

```
public String[][] getParameterInfo() {
String[][] info = {
// Parameter Name      Kind of Value   Description
{"imagesource",      "URL",           "a directory"},
{"startup",          "URL",           "displayed at startup"},
{"background",       "URL",           "displayed as background"},
{"startimage",       "int"",           "start index"},
{"endimage",         "int",           "end index"},
{"namepattern",      "URL",           "used to generate indexed names"},
{"pause",            "int",           "milliseconds"},
{"pauses",           "ints",          "milliseconds"},
{"repeat",           "boolean",       "repeat or not"},
{"positions",        "coordinates",   "path"},
{"soundsource",      "URL",           "audio directory"},
{"soundtrack",       "URL",           "background music"},
{"sounds",           "URLs",          "audio samples"},
};
return info;
}
```

As you can see, the getParameterInfo method must return an array of three-String arrays. In each three-String array, the first string is the parameter name. The second string gives the user a hint about what general kind of value the applet needs for the parameter. The third string describes the meaning of the parameter.

14.12 Procedural Programs

Traditional, procedural programs have a single order of execution. Control moves in a linear fashion from the first statement to the second statement to the third statement and so forth with occasional loops and branches. User input occurs at precisely defined points in the program. A user cannot input data excet when the computer is ready to receive it.

This doesn't work well with GUI programs. Users can often select menu items, type text, click the mouse, or otherwise provide input at almost any time. They have many, many choices at any one point about what to do.

14.12.1 The Event Queue

Instead GUI models require an event approach. Each user action, be it a mouse click, a key press, or something else is placed in an event queue as it occurs. Normally this takes place at the operating system level. The program removes events from the queue and processes them, one at a time. Generally an infinite while loop reads from the queue, and a big switch statement dispatches each different event to the appropriate code to handle it.

Depending on the architecture of the system, there may be only one system event queue or each application may have its own event queue. The operating system is responsible for making sure the right events get to the right programs.

In the applications we're concerned with, that is Java programs, each virtual machine has one main AWT event queue. There's almost certainly a native, event queue as well, but from here on out I'll only talk about the Java event queue. Your Java program will only see events that are sent to it by the native user interface.

14.12.2 Low Level Events

Low level events represent direct communication from the user. A Low level event is a key press or a key release, a mouse click, drag, move, or release, and so on.

These include:

```
java.awt.event.ComponentEvent
component resized, moved, etc.
java.awt.event.FocusEvent
component got focus, lost focus
java.awt.event.KeyEvent
key press, key release, etc.
java.awt.event.MouseEvent
mouse down, mouse move, mouse drag, mouse up
java.awt.event.ContainerEvent
a component was added to or removed from the container
java.awt.event.WindowEvent
```

the window was activated, deactivated, opened, closed, inconified, or deiconified

java.lang.Object

```
|
+-java.util.EventObject
|
+-java.awt.AWTEvent
|
+-java.awt.event.ComponentEvent
|
```

```
+—java.awt.event.InputEvent
|        |
|        +—java.awt.event.KeyEvent
|        |
|        +—java.awt.event.MouseEvent
|
+—java.awt.event.FocusEvent
|
+—java.awt.event.ContainerEvent
|
+—java.awt.event.WindowEvent
```

14.12.3 High Level Events

High level or semantic events encapsulate the meaning of a user interface component. These include:

```
java.awt.event.ActionEvent
do a command
java.awt.event.AdjustmentEvent
value was adjusted
java.awt.event.ItemEvent
item state has changed
java.awt.event.TextEvent
the value of the text object changed
```

For example, when the user clicks the mouse on a Button, then releases it, the Button gets two or three separate, low-level, MouseEvents. (One for mouse down, one for mouse up, and possibly one for mouse drag if the user moves the mouse while the button is pressed.) However, the Button then fires one high level ActionEvent.

If the user clicks the mouse on a Button, moves the mouse off the Button, then releases it, the Button gets two separate, low-level, MouseEvents. (One for mouse down, one for for mouse drag.) However, the Button eats these events and does nothing.

Processing Events

The Java runtime is responsible for handling the event queue. In particular it makes sure that each low-level event is directed to the proper component. You do not need to worry about deciding which component the event is meant for. The runtime handles this for you. In particular the runtime passes the event to the component's processEvent() method:

- protected void processEvent(AWTEvent e)

The processEvent() method determines the type of the event and passes it on to one of five other methods in the java.awt.Component class:

```
protected void processComponentEvent(ComponentEvent e)
protected void processFocusEvent(FocusEvent e)
protected void processKeyEvent(KeyEvent e)
protected void processMouseEvent(MouseEvent e)
protected void processMouseMotionEvent(MouseEvent e)
```

Each of these methods looks to see if any listener objects of the right type are registered for this component. If so, the event is passed to each of those listener objects in an unpredictable order.

Internally, these methods use a java.awt.AWTEventMulticaster object to track the registration of listeners with a component.

❑ EventListeners

To respond to an event a component receives you register an event listener for the event type with the component. Event listeners are objects which implement a java.util.EventListener interface. The AWT defines eleven sub-interfaces of java.util.EventListener, one for each type of event:

```
java.awt.event.ComponentListener
java.awt.event.ContainerListener
java.awt.event.FocusListener
java.awt.event.KeyListener
java.awt.event.MouseListener
java.awt.event.MouseMotionListener
java.awt.event.WindowListener
java.awt.event.ActionListener
java.awt.event.AdjustmentListener
java.awt.event.ItemListener
java.awt.event.TextListener
```

Each of these interfaces defines the events an event listener of that type must be prepared to respond to. For example, MouseListener declares these methods,

```
public abstract void mouseClicked(MouseEvent e)
public abstract void mousePressed(MouseEvent e)
public abstract void mouseReleased(MouseEvent e)
public abstract void mouseEntered(MouseEvent e)
public abstract void mouseExited(MouseEvent e)
```

When a component receives a mouse event, its processMouseEvent() method checks the ID of the mouse event to determine whether this is a mouse pressed, mouse released, mouse entered, or mouse exited event. Then it calls the corresponding method in each registered MouseListener object.

14.12.4 Mouse Events

A java.awt.event.MouseEvent is sent to a component when the mouse state changes over the component. There are seven types of mouse events, each represented by an integer constant:

MouseEvent.MOUSE_CLICKED	A mouse button was pressed, then released
MouseEvent.MOUSE_DRAGGED	The mouse was moved over the component while a mouse button was held down
MouseEvent.MOUSE_ENTERED	The cursor entered the component's space
MouseEvent.MOUSE_EXITED	The cursor left the component's space
MouseEvent.MOUSE_MOVED	The mouse moved in the component's space
MouseEvent.MOUSE_PRESSED	The mouse button was pressed (but not re leased) over the component
MouseEvent.MOUSE_RELEASED	The mouse button was released ever the component.

Besides its type, the main thing you want to know about a MouseEvent is the location; that is, where the mouse was clicked. You can either request the x and y locations separately, or together as a java.awt.Point object.

```
public int getX()
```

```
public int getY()
public Point getPoint()
```

14.12.5 Mouse Listeners and and Mouse Motion Listeners

Generally you respond to mouse events directed at your component, by registering a MouseListener object with the component.

public interface MouseListener extends EventListener

For reasons of efficiency, the MouseListener interface only declares five methods:

```
public abstract void mouseClicked(MouseEvent e)
public abstract void mousePressed(MouseEvent e)
public abstract void mouseReleased(MouseEvent e)
public abstract void mouseEntered(MouseEvent e)
public abstract void mouseExited(MouseEvent e)
```

A mouse listener does not respond to mouse dragged or mouse moved events because these are too common. Responding to each of them, even with a noop method, would result in many unnecessary method calls. Instead, mouse moved and mouse dragged events are responded to by the MouseMotionListener interface.

```
public interface MouseMotionListener extends EventListener
```

The MouseMotionListener interface declares these two methods that are missing from MouseListener:

```
public abstract void mouseDragged(MouseEvent e)
public abstract void mouseMoved(MouseEvent e)
```

If you don't care about mouse dragged and mouse moved events, then you simply don't register a MouseMotionListener on the component and the component won't bother to report such events.

14.12.6 Dots

For example, let's suppose you want an applet that draws a red circle wherever the user clicks the mouse. Recall that applet's are subclasses of java.awt.Component. Therefore you need to install a MouseListener on your applet that responds to mouse clicked events. In an applets of this nature it's simplest just to make the applet itself the MouseListener.

In this case, since you need to store the points clicked in a Vector, it's most convenient to use getPoint(). The coordinates are relative to the component to which this event is directed, not necessarily the global coordinate system of the applet (though in this case they're the same thing).

```
import java.applet.*;
import java.awt.*;
import java.awt.event.*;
import java.util.*;
public class Dots extends Applet implements MouseListener {
Vector theDots = new Vector();
public void init() {
this.addMouseListener(this);
}

public void mouseClicked(MouseEvent e)
{
theDots.addElement(e.getPoint());
```

```
this.repaint();
}
// You have to implement these methods, but they don't need
// to do anything.
public void mousePressed(MouseEvent e) {}
public void mouseReleased(MouseEvent e) {}
public void mouseEntered(MouseEvent e) {}
public void mouseExited(MouseEvent e) {}
// paint the dots
public void paint(Graphics g) {
g.setColor(Color.red);
Enumeration e = theDots.elements();
while (e.hasMoreElements()) {
Point p = (Point) e.nextElement();
g.drawOval(p.x, p.y, 5, 5);
}
}
}
```

14.12.7 KeyEvents

A java.awt.event.KeyEvent is sent to a component when a key is pressed while the component has the focus. There are three types of key events, each represented by an integer constant:

KeyEvent.KEY_PRESSED	A key was pressed
KeyEvent.KEY_RELEASED	A key was released
KeyEvent.KEY_TYPED	A key press followed by a key release.

Most of the time you'll only respond to the last event, KeyEvent.KEY_TYPED.

The main thing you want to know about a KeyEvent is what key was pressed. You get this with the getKeyChar() method.

```
public char getKeyChar()
```

This returns the Unicode character corresponding to the pressed key.

A KEY_PRESSED or KEY_RELEASED event doesn't just have a character. It also has a key code. (KEY_TYPED events do not have key codes. More precisely the key code is undefined.) If you're concerned about the key that was pressed, rather than the character that was typed, you'll ask the key event for its key code rather than its key char. You get the code for a KeyEvent by calling getKeyCode():

public int getKeyCode()

You can convert this into a localized string such as "END", "F4" or "Q" by passing it to the static method, KeyEvent.getKeyText():

public static String getKeyText(int keyCode)

Generally you respond to key events directed at your component, by registering a KeyListener object with the component. The KeyListener interface defines the following methods, one for each type of KeyEvent.

```
public abstract void keyTyped(KeyEvent e)
public abstract void keyPressed(KeyEvent e)
public abstract void keyReleased(KeyEvent e)
```

14.12.8 Key Codes

Not all keyboards are created alike. Macs have Command and option keys. PCs have Alt keys. Some PCs have a Windows 95 key. Some don't. Some keyboards have numeric keypads, but many don't. Emacs expects there to be a Meta key which I for one have never actually seen on any keyboard in existence, but which is often mapped to the Escape key (which is again a key some keyboards don't have). Keyboard inconsistency is one of the problems a truly cross-platform environment has to deal with.

The KeyEvent class defines a little more than one hundred virtual key codes that map to different, common, keyboard keys. KeyEvent.VK_0 thru KeyEvent.VK_9 are the same as ASCII '0' thru '9' (0x30 - 0x39)

```
KeyEvent.VK_0
KeyEvent.VK_1
KeyEvent.VK_2
KeyEvent.VK_3
KeyEvent.VK_4
KeyEvent.VK_5
KeyEvent.VK_6
KeyEvent.VK_7
KeyEvent.VK_8
KeyEvent.VK_9
```

KeyEvent.VK_A thru KeyEvent.VK_Z are the same as ASCII 'A' thru 'Z'; that is, KeyEvent.VK_A, KeyEvent.VK_B, KeyEvent.VK_C, KeyEvent.VK_D, KeyEvent.VK_E, KeyEvent.VK_F, and so on.

14.12.9 Funky Key Codes

The remaining keys are the interesting ones:

```
KeyEvent.VK_ACCEPT   KeyEvent.VK_ADD   KeyEvent.VK_ALT
KeyEvent.VK_BACK_QUOTE KeyEvent.VK_BACK_SLASH KeyEvent.VK_BACK_SPACE
KeyEvent.VK_CANCEL   KeyEvent.VK_CAPS_LOCK   KeyEvent.VK_CLEAR
KeyEvent.VK_CLOSE_BRACKET KeyEvent.VK_COMMA   KeyEvent.VK_CONTROL
KeyEvent.VK_CONVERT   KeyEvent.VK_DECIMAL   KeyEvent.VK_DELETE
KeyEvent.VK_DIVIDE   KeyEvent.VK_DOWN   KeyEvent.VK_END
KeyEvent.VK_ENTER   KeyEvent.VK_EQUALS   KeyEvent.VK_ESCAPE
KeyEvent.VK_F1   KeyEvent.VK_F2   KeyEvent.VK_F3
  KeyEvent.VK_F4   KeyEvent.VK_F5   KeyEvent.VK_F6   KeyEvent.VK_F7
KeyEvent.VK_F8   KeyEvent.VK_F9   KeyEvent.VK_F10   KeyEvent.VK_F11
KeyEvent.VK_F12 KeyEvent.VK_FINAL KeyEvent.VK_HELP KeyEvent.VK_HOME
KeyEvent.VK_INSERT   KeyEvent.VK_KANA   KeyEvent.VK_KANJI
KeyEvent.VK_LEFT   KeyEvent.VK_META   KeyEvent.VK_MODECHANGE
KeyEvent.VK_MULTIPLY  KeyEvent.VK_NONCONVERT  KeyEvent.VK_NUM_LOCK
KeyEvent.VK_NUMPAD0   KeyEvent.VK_NUMPAD1   KeyEvent.VK_NUMPAD2
KeyEvent.VK_NUMPAD3   KeyEvent.VK_NUMPAD4   KeyEvent.VK_NUMPAD5
KeyEvent.VK_NUMPAD6   KeyEvent.VK_NUMPAD7   KeyEvent.VK_NUMPAD8
KeyEvent.VK_NUMPAD9 KeyEvent.VK_OPEN_BRACKET KeyEvent.VK_PAGE_DOWN
KeyEvent.VK_PAGE_UP   KeyEvent.VK_PAUSE   KeyEvent.VK_PERIOD
KeyEvent.VK_PRINTSCREEN   KeyEvent.VK_QUOTE   KeyEvent.VK_RIGHT
KeyEvent.VK_SCROLL_LOCK KeyEvent.VK_SEMICOLON KeyEvent.VK_SEPARATER
```

```
KeyEvent.VK_SHIFT    KeyEvent.VK_SLASH    KeyEvent.VK_SPACE
KeyEvent.VK_SUBTRACT    KeyEvent.VK_TAB    KeyEvent.VK_UNDEFINED
KeyEvent.VK_UP
```

14.12.10 Modifier Keys

Both KeyEvent and MouseEvent are subclasses of java.awt.event.InputEvent. The primary feature InputEvent adds is the ability to test for additional conditions on the event such as whether the ALT key was pressed at the same time as another key, or whether the option key was held while the mouse was dragged. For example, when the shift key is held down, many drawing programs constrain lines to be vertical or horizontal, rectangles to be squares, ovals to be circles, and so on.

The following four methods tell you whether or not the specified key was pressed when this event was sent.

```
public boolean isShiftDown()
public boolean isControlDown()
public boolean isMetaDown()
public boolean isAltDown()
```

All may be invoked on either MouseEvent objects or KeyEvent objects.

There is also a getWhen() method which returns the time the event occurred. This is given as the number of milliseconds since midnight, January 1, 1970, Greenwich Mean Time.

public long getWhen()

The java.util.Date and java.util.Calendar classes have methods you can use to convert this to a date and time. However, most of the time you'll only be concerned with differences in the time between one event and another.

14.12.11 Mouse Button Modifiers

An InputEvent's modifiers are stored as an int value. Each bit in the int is a flag corresponding to a particular modifier. The corresponding values for these flags are given as public final static ints in the InputEvent class:

```
InputEvent.SHIFT_MASK
InputEvent.CTRL_MASK
InputEvent.META_MASK
InputEvent.ALT_MASK
InputEvent.BUTTON1_MASK
InputEvent.BUTTON2_MASK
InputEvent.BUTTON3_MASK
You can retrieve the modifiers for an event with the getModifiers()
method:
public int getModifiers()
Use the bitwise & operator to test whether a particular flag is set.
For example,
if (e.getModifiers() & InputEvent.BUTTON2_MASK != 0) {
System.out.println("Button 2 was pressed");
}
```

14.12.12 Focus Events

At any given time exactly one component in an applet should have the focus. The component that possesses the focus receives user input from the keyboard and the mouse. In other words it is the component to which low-level events are directed.

The focus can be adjusted in a number of ways. For example, if the user hits the tab key, the focus will generally shift from one component to the next. If the user hits Shift-Tab, the focus will move back one component. When the user selects a component with the mouse, that component gets the focus.

Through whatever means it gets it, when a component gains or loses the focus, it gets a FocusEvent. A change in the focus can be permanent or temporary. Permanent focus change occurs when the focus is directly moved from one component to another, either by calling requestFocus() or by direct user action such as the Tab key. Temporary focus change occurs when a component gains or loses focus focus as an indirect result of another operation, such as a window deactivation. In this case, the original focus state is automatically restored once the operation is finished, or the window is reactivated.

This is a bad choice of terms. Even a component that has the focus permanently can lose it.

The isTemporary() method returns true if the focus change is temporary, false if it's permanent.

```
public boolean isTemporary()
```

You respond to changes in focus by installing a FocusListener in the component. This interface declares two methods:

```
public abstract void focusGained(FocusEvent e)
public abstract void focusLost(FocusEvent e)
```

14.12.13 Component Events

java.awt.event.ComponentEvent is the superclass of all the events we've discussed so far. It also has a few events of its own that allow you to react when a component is shown, hidden, moved, or resized. These are

```
ComponentEvent.COMPONENT_MOVED
ComponentEvent.COMPONENT_RESIZED
ComponentEvent.COMPONENT_SHOWN
ComponentEvent.COMPONENT_HIDDEN
```

As you might guess, you respond to these events by registering a java.awt.event.ComponentListener with your component. This interface declares four methods:

```
public abstract void componentResized(ComponentEvent e)
public abstract void componentMoved(ComponentEvent e)
public abstract void componentShown(ComponentEvent e)
public abstract void componentHidden(ComponentEvent e)
```

The ComponentEvent class doesn't have any particularly useful methods of its own, but you can use the various methods of the java.awt.Component class to determine where a component was moved or to what size it was resized.

14.13 HTML in 10 minutes

HTML is the HyperText Markup Language.
HTML files are text files featuring semantically tagged elements.
HTML filenames are suffixed with .htm or .html.

Here's a simple HTML file:

```
<html>
```

```
<head>
<title>My First HTML Document</title>
</head>
<body>
<h1>A level one heading</h1>
Hello there. This is <STRONG>very</STRONG> important.
</body>
</html>
```

Look at this file in your web browser <examplehtml.html>.

Elements that are enclosed in angle brackets like <html>, <head>, and <title> are called tags. Tags are case insensitive. <html> means the same thing as <HTML> as <Html> <HtMl>.

Most tags are matched with closing tags, and affect the text contained between them. The closing tag is the same as the opening tag except for a / after the opening angle bracket. For example, </html>, </head>, and </title> are closing tags. The text in between <title> and </title>, My First HTML Document in the above example, is the title of the page.

As you can see from the above example tags may, in general, nest. However they may not overlap (though some browsers can handle this).

Some tags have attributes. An attribute is a name, followed by an = sign, followed by the string value of the parameter. For example, to make a centered H1 heading, use the ALIGN parameter with value center; i.e.

<h1 align="center">A level one heading</h1>

Attributes are also case-insensitive. The double quotes around the value are optional unless the value contains embedded white space.

A Level one Heading

Hello there. This is very important.

14.13.1 Learning URLs

URL stands for uniform resource locator. A URL is a pointer to a particular resource on the Internet at a particular location. For example

http://metalab.unc.edu/javafaq/course/week5/exercises.html and ftp://ftp.macfaq.com/pub/macfaq/ are both URLs.

A URL specifies the protocol used to access a server (e.g., ftp, http), the name of the server, and the location of a file on that server. A typical URL looks like http://metalab.unc.edu/javafaq/books.html. This specifies that there is a file called books.html in a directory called javafaq on the server metalab.unc.edu, and that this file can be accessed via the http protocol. The full syntax is:

protocol://hostname[:port]/path/filename#section

The protocol, also sometimes called the scheme, is generally one of these

```
file   a file on your local disk
ftp    an FTP server
http   a World Wide Web server
gopher a Gopher server
mailto an email address
news a Usenet newsgroup
```

```
telnet   a connection to a Telnet-based service
WAIS     a WAIS server
```

A few other protocols are occasionally encountered including rmi (remote method invocation) and https (secure http).

14.13.2 Hypertext Links

To make a hypertext link, you surround the text you want to be linked with <A></A> tags. Inside the <A> tag place an HREF parameter whose value is the URL you want to link too. For example, make sure you get the

```
<A>  HREF="http://metalab.unc.edu/javafaq/course/week5/
exercises.html">
exercises
</A>
```

from the web site.

Most browsers will underline the linked text, and color it blue or purple, but this is a presentation decision left up to the browser. The browser also provides the user with a means to activate the link (normally by clicking on the linked text). When the user activates the link, the browsers attempts to load the page specified in the link. If the URL in the anchor is not an HTTP URL, then the browser will take wnatever action is appropriate, perhaps saving a file for an ftp URL or launching an email program for a mailto URL.

14.13.3 Relative URLs

When a web browser reads an HTML document, it has a great deal of information about the document. This includes the protocol used to retrieve the document, the name of the host where the document lives, and the path to that document on the host. Most of this is likely to be the same for many of the URLs in that document. Relative URLs inherit the protocol, hostname, and path of their parent document rather than respecifying it in each <A HREF> tag. Thus if any piece of the URL is missing, it is assumed to be the same as that of the document in which the URL is found. Such a URL is called a relative URL. In contrast, a completely specified URL is called an absolute URL. For example, suppose while browsing http://metalab.unc.edu/javafaq/books.html you click on this hyperlink:

<a href="javafaq.html">the FAQ</A>

Your browser cuts books.html off the end of

```
http://metalab.unc.edu/javafaq/books.html
```

to get

```
http://metalab.unc.edu/javafaq/
```

Then it attaches javafaq.html onto the end of

```
http://metalab.unc.edu/javafaq/ to get
http://metalab.unc.edu/javafaq/javafaq.html
```

If the relative link begins with a /, then it is relative to the document root instead of relative to the current file. Thus if while browsing http://metalab.unc.edu/javafaq/books.html you clicked on this hyperlink:

```
<a href="/boutell/faq/www_faq.html">
```

Your browser would throw away /javafaq/javafaq.html and attach /boutell/faq/www_faq.html to the end of http://metalab.unc.edu to get http://metalab.unc.edu/boutell/faq/www_faq.html.

Relative URLs have a number of advantages. First and least they save a little typing. More importantly relative URLs allow entire trees of HTML documents to be moved or copied from one site to another without breaking all the internal links.

14.14 The APPLET HTML Tag

Applets are embedded in web pages using the <APPLET> and </APPLET> tags. The <APPLET> tag is similar to the <IMG> tag. Like <IMG> <APPLET> references a source file that is not part of the HTML page on which it is embedded. IMGs do this with the SRC attribute. APPLETs do this with the CODE attribute. The CODE attribute tells the browser where to look for the compiled .class file. It is relative to the location of the source document. Thus if you're browsing http://metalab.unc.edu/javafaq/index.html and that page references an applet with CODE="animation.class", then the file animation.class should be at the URL http://metalab.unc.edu/javafaq/animation.class.

For reasons that remain a mystery to HTML authors everywhere if the applet resides somewhere other than the same directory as the page it lives on, you don't just give a URL to its location. Rather you point at the CODEBASE. The CODEBASE attribute is a URL that points at the directory where the .class file is. The CODE attribute is the name of the .class file itself. For instance if on the HTML page of the previous section you had written

```
<applet code="HelloWorldApplet.class" CODEBASE="classes"
width=200 height=200>
</APPLET>
```

then the browser would have tried to find HelloWorldApplet.class in the classes directory in the same directory as the HTML page that included the applet. On the other hand if you had written

```
<applet code="HelloWorldApplet.class"
CODEBASE="http://www.foo.bar.com/classes" width=200 height=200>
</APPLET>
```

then the browser would try to retrieve the applet from http://www.foo.bar.com/classes/HelloWorldApplet.class regardless of where the HTML page was.

In short the applet viewer will try to retrieve the applet from the URL given by the formula (CODEBASE + "/" + code). Once this URL is formed all the usual.rules about relative and absolute URLs apply.

The HEIGHT and WIDTH attributes work exactly as they do with IMG, specifying how big a rectangle the browser should set aside for the applet. These numbers are specified in pixels and are required.

14.14.1 Spacing Preferences

The <APPLET> tag has several attributes to define how it is positioned on the page.

The ALIGN attribute defines how the applet's rectangle is placed on the page relative to other elements. Possible values include LEFT, RIGHT, TOP, TEXTTOP, MIDDLE, ABSMIDDLE, BASELINE, BOTTOM and ABSBOTTOM. This parameter is optional.

You can specify an HSPACE and a VSPACE in pixels to set the amount of blank space between an applet and the surrounding text. The HSPACE and VSPACE parameters are optional.

```
<applet code="HelloWorldApplet.class"
CODEBASE="http://www.foo.bar.com/classes" width=200 height=200
ALIGN=RIGHT HSPACE=5 VSPACE=10>
</APPLET>
```

The ALIGN, HSPACE, and VSPACE attributes are identical to the attributes of the same name used by the <IMG> tag.

14.14.2 Alternate Text

The <APPLET> has an ALT attribute. An ALT attribute is used by a browser that understands the APPLET tag but for some reason cannot play the applet. For instance, if you've turned off Java in Netscape Navigator 3.0, then the browser should display the ALT text. Note that I said it should, not that it does. The ALT tag is optional.

```
<applet code="HelloWorldApplet.class"
CODEBASE="http://www.foo.bar.com/classes" width=200 height=200
ALIGN=RIGHT HSPACE=5 VSPACE=10
ALT="Hello World!">
</APPLET>
```

ALT is not used by browsers that do not understand <APPLET> at all. For that purpose <APPLET> has been defined to require a closing tag, </APPLET>. All raw text between the opening and closing <APPLET> tags is ignored by a Java capable browser. However a non-Java capable browser will ignore the <APPLET> tags instead and read the text between them. For example the following HTML fragment says Hello to people both with and without Java capable browsers.

```
<applet code="HelloWorldApplet.class"
CODEBASE="http://www.foo.bar.com/classes" width=200 height=200
ALIGN=RIGHT HSPACE=5 VSPACE=10
ALT="Hello World!">
Hello World!<P>
</APPLET>
```

14.14.3 Naming Applets

You can give an applet a name by using the NAME attribute of the APPLET tag. This allows communication between different applets on the same Web page.

```
<applet code="HelloWorldApplet.class" Name=Applet1
CODEBASE="http://www.foo.bar.com/classes" width=200 height=200
ALIGN=RIGHT HSPACE=5 VSPACE=10
ALT="Hello World!">
Hello World!<P>
</APPLET>
```

14.14.4 JAR Archives

HTTP 1.0 uses a separate connection for each request. When you're downloading many small files, the time required to set up and tear down the connections can be a significant fraction of the total amount of time needed to load a page. It would be better if you could load all the HTML documents, images, applets, and sounds a page needed in one connection.

One way to do this without changing the HTTP protocol, is to pack all those different files into a single archive file, perhaps a zip archive, and just download that.

We aren't quite there yet. Browsers do not yet understand archive files, but in Java 1.1 applets do. You can pack all the images, sounds, and .class files an applet needs into one JAR archive and load that instead of the individual files. Applet classes do not have to be loaded directly. They can also be stored in JAR archives. To do this you use the ARCHIVES attribute of the APPLET tag

```
<APPLET  CODE=HelloWorldApplet  WIDTH=200  HEIGHT=100
ARCHIVES="HelloWorld.jar">
<hr>
Hello World!
<hr>
</APPLET>
```

In this example, the applet class is still HelloWorldApplet. However, there is no HelloWorldApplet.class file to be downloaded. Instead the class is stored inside the archive file HelloWorld.jar.

Sun provides a tool for creating JAR archives with its JDK 1.1. For example,

% jar cf HelloWorld.jar *.class

This puts all the .class files in the current directory in the file named "HelloWorld.jar". The syntax of the jar command is deliberately similar to the Unix tar command.

14.14.5 The OBJECT Tag

HTML 4.0 deprecates the <APPLET> tag. Instead you are supposed to use the <OBJECT> tag. For the purposes of ewbedding applets, the <OBJECT> tag is used almost exactly like the <APPLET> tag except that the class attribute becomes the classid attribute. For example,

```
<OBJECT classid="MyApplet.class"
CODEBASE="http://www.foo.bar.com/classes" width=200 height=200
ALIGN=RIGHT HSPACE=5 VSPACE=10>
</OBJECT>
```

The <OBJECT> tag is also used to embed ActiveX controls and other kinds of active content, and it has a few additional attributes to allow it to do that. However, for the purposes of Java you don't need to know about these.

The <OBJECT> tag is supported by Netscape ???? and later and Internet Explorer ???? and later. It is not supported by earlier versions of those browsers so <APPLET> is unlikely to disappear anytime soon.

You can support both by placing an <APPLET> element inside an

```
<OBJECT> element like this:
<OBJECT classid="MyApplet.class" width=200 height=200>
<APPLET code="MyApplet.class" width=200 height=200>
</APPLET>
</OBJECT>
```

Browsers that understand <OBJECT> will ignore its content while browsers that don't will display its content.

PARAM elements are the same for <OBJECT> as for <APPLET>.

For the complete story, you can read about the <OBJECT> tag in the HTML 4.0 specification <http://www.w3.org/TR/WD-html40-970708/struct/includes.html>.

14.14.6 Finding an Applet's Size

When running inside a web browser the size of an applet is set by the height and width attributes and cannot be changed by the applet. Many applets need to know their own size. After all you don't want to draw outside the lines. :-)

Retrieving the applet size is straightforward with the getSize() method. java.applet.Applet inherits this method from java.awt.Component. getSize() returns a java.awt.Dimension object. A Dimension object has two public int fields, height and width. Below is a simple applet that prints its own dimensions.

```
import java.applet.*;
import java.awt.*;
public class SizeApplet extends Applet
{
public void paint(Graphics g) {
Dimension appletSize = this.getSize();
int appletHeight = appletSize.height;
int appletWidth = appletSize.width;
g.drawString("This applet is " + appletHeight +
" pixels high by " + appletWidth + " pixels wide.",
15, appletHeight/2);
}
}
```

Note how the applet's height is used to decide where to draw the text. You'll often want to use the applet's dimensions to determine how to place objects on the page. The applet's width wasn't used because it made more sense to left justify the text rather than center it. In other programs you'll have occasion to use the applet width too.

14.14.7 Passing Parameters to Applets

Parameters are passed to applets in NAME=VALUE pairs in <PARAM> tags between the opening and closing APPLET tags. Inside the applet, you read the values passed through the PARAM tags with the getParameter() method of the java.applet.Applet class.

The program below demonstrates this with a generic string drawing applet. The applet parameter "Message" is the string to be drawn.

```
import java.applet.*;
import java.awt.*;
public class DrawStringApplet extends Applet
{
public void paint(Graphics g) {
String inputFromPage = this.getParameter("Message");
g.drawString(inputFromPage, 50, 25);
}
}
```

You also need an HTML file that references your applet. The following simple HTML file will do:

```
<HTML>
<HEAD>
<TITLE> Draw String </TITLE>
</HEAD>
<BODY>
This is the applet:<P>
<APPLET code="DrawStringApplet.class" width="300" height="50">
<PARAM name="Message" value="Howdy, there!">
```

This page will be very boring if your

browser doesn't understand Java.

```
</APPLET>
</BODY>
</HTML>
```

Of course you are free to change "Howdy, there!" to a "message" of your choice. You only need to change the HTML, not the Java source code. PARAMs let you customize applets without changing or recompiling the code.

This applet is very similar to the HelloWorldApplet. However rather than hardcoding the message to be printed it's read into the variable inputFromPage from a PARAM in the HTML.

You pass getParameter() a string that names the parameter you want. This string should match the name of a <PARAM> tag in the HTML page. getParameter() returns the value of the parameter. All values are passed as strings. If you want to get another type like an integer, then you'll need to pass it as a string and convert it to the type you really want.

The <PARAM> HTML tag is also straightforward. It occurs between <APPLET> and </APPLET>. It has two attributes of its own, NAME and VALUE. NAME identifies which PARAM this is. VALUE is the value of the PARAM as a String. Both should be enclosed in double quote marks if they contain white space.

An applet is not limited to one PARAM. You can pass as many named PARAMs to an applet as you like. An applet does not necessarily need to use all the PARAMs that are in the HTML. Additional PARAMs can be safely ignored.

14.14.8 Processing An Unknown Number Of Parameters

Most of the time you have a fairly good idea of what parameters will and won't be passed to your applet. However some of the time there will be an undetermined number of parameters. For instance Sun's imagemap applet passes each "hot button" as a parameter. Different imagemaps have different numbers of hot buttons. Another applet might want to pass a series of URL's to different sounds to be played in sequence. Each URL could be passed as a separate parameter.

Or perhaps you want to write an applet that displays several lines of text. While it would be possible to cram all this information into one long string, that's not too friendly to authors who want to use your applet on their pages. It's much more sensible to give each line its own <PARAM> tag. If this is the case, you should name the tags via some predictable and numeric scheme. For instance in the text example the following set of <PARAM> tags would be sensible:

```
<PARAM name="Line1" value="There once was a man from Japan">
<PARAM name="Line2" value="Whose poetry never would scan">
<PARAM name="Line3" value="When asked reasons why,">
<PARAM name="Line4" value="He replied, with a sigh:">
<PARAM name="Line5" value="I always try to get as many
syllables into the last line as I can.">
```

The program below displays this limerick. Lines are accumulated into an array of Strings called poem. A for loop fills the array with the different lines of poetry. There are 101 spaces in the array, but since you won't normally need that many, an if clause tests to see whether the attempt to get a parameter was successful by checking to see if the line is null. As soon as one fails, the loop is broken. Once the loop is finished num_lines is decremented by one because the last line the loop tried to read wasn't there.

The paint() method loops through the poem array and prints each String on the screen, incrementing the y position by fifteen pixels each step so you don't draw one line on top of the other.

```
import java.applet.*;
import java.awt.*;
public class PoetryApplet extends Applet
{
String[] poem = new String[101];
int numlines;
public void init() {
String nextline;
for (numlines = 1; numlines < poem.length; numlines++)
{
nextline = this.getParameter("Line" + numlines);
if (nextline == null) break;
poem[numlines] = nextline;
}
numlines—;
}
public void paint(Graphics g) {
int y = 15;
for (int i=1; i <= numlines; i++) {
g.drawString(poem[i], 5, y);
y += 15;
}
}
}
```

Here's the applet:

You might think it would be useful to be able to process an arbitrary list of parameters without knowing their names in advance, if nothing else so you could return an error message to the page designer. Unfortunately there's no way to do it in Java 1.0 or 1.1. It may appear in future versions.

14.15 Using the APPLET Tag

This section tells you most of what you need to know to use the <APPLET> tag. It starts by showing you the tag's simplest form. It then discusses some of the most common additions to that simple form: the <PARAM> tag, alternate HTML code and text, the CODEBASE attribute, and the ARCHIVE attribute. For a detailed description of the <APPLET> tag, refer to The <APPLET> Tag.

You should already have seen the simplest form of the <APPLET> tag:

```
<APPLET CODE=AppletSubclass.class WIDTH=anInt HEIGHT=anInt>
</APPLET>
```

This tag tells the browser to load the applet whose Applet subclass is named AppletSubclass, displaying it in an area of the specified width and height.

14.15.1 Specifying Parameters

Some applets let the user customize the applet's configuration with parameters, as described in Defining and Using Applet Parameters. For example, AppletButton (an applet used throughout this tutorial to provide a button that brings up a window) allows the user to set the button's text by specifying the value of a parameter named BUTTONTEXT.

The user specifies the value of a parameter using a <PARAM> tag. The <PARAM> tags should appear just after the <APPLET> tag for the applet they affect:

```
<APPLET CODE=AppletSubclass.class WIDTH=anInt HEIGHT=anInt>
<PARAM NAME=parameter1Name VALUE=aValue>
<PARAM NAME=parameter2Name VALUE=anotherValue>
</APPLET>
```

Here's an example of the <PARAM> tag in use.

```
<APPLET CODE="Animator.class" WIDTH=460 HEIGHT=160>
<PARAM NAME="imageSource" VALUE="images/Beans">
<PARAM NAME="backgroundColor" VALUE="0xc0c0c0">
<PARAM NAME="endImage" VALUE=10>
<PARAM NAME="soundSource" VALUE="audio">
<PARAM NAME="soundtrack" VALUE="spacemusic.au">
<PARAM NAME="sounds"
VALUE="1.au|2.au|3.au|4.au|5.au|6.au|7.au|8au|9.au|0.au">
<PARAM NAME="pause" VALUE=200>
</APPLET>
```

14.15.2 Specifying Alternate HTML Code and Text

Note the ellipsis points (". . .") in the previous HTML example. What did the example leave out? It omitted alternate HTML code — HTML code interpreted only by browsers that don't understand the <APPLET> tag. Alternate HTML code is any text that appears between the <APPLET> and </APPLET> tags, after any <PARAM> tags. Java-enabled browsers ignore alternate HTML code.

To specify alternate text to Java-enabled browsers and other browsers that understand the <APPLET> tag, use the ALT attribute. If the browser can't display an applet for some reason, it can display the applet's ALT text.

We use alternate HTML code throughout the online version of this tutorial to tell readers about the applets they're missing. Often, the alternate HTML code includes one or more pictures of the applet. Here's the complete HTML code for the Animator example shown previously:

```
<APPLET CODE="Animator.class" WIDTH=460 HEIGHT=160
ALT="If you could run this applet, you'd see some animation">
<PARAM NAME="imageSource" VALUE="images/Beans">
<PARAM NAME="backgroundColor" VALUE="0xc0c0c0">
<PARAM NAME="endImage" VALUE=10>
<PARAM NAME="soundSource" VALUE="audio">
<PARAM NAME="soundtrack" VALUE="spacemusic.au">
<PARAM NAME="sounds"
VALUE="1.au|2.au|3.au|4.au|5.au|6.au|7.au|8au|9.au|0.au">
<PARAM NAME="pause" VALUE=200>
Your browser is completely ignoring the &lt;APPLET&gt; tag!
</APPLET>
```

An applet that doesn't understand the <APPLET> tag ignores everything in the previous HTML code except the line that starts with "Your". A browser that does understand the <APPLET> tag ignores everything on that line. If the applet-savvy browser can't run the applet, it might display the ALT text.

Specifying the Applet Directory

By default, a browser looks for an applet's class and archive files in the same directory as the HTML file that has the <APPLET> tag. (If the applet's class is in a package, then the browser uses the package name to construct a directory path underneath the HTML file's directory.) Sometimes, however, it's useful to put the applet's files somewhere else. You can use the CODEBASE attribute to tell the browser in which directory the applet's files are located:

```
<APPLET CODE=AppletSubclass.class CODEBASE=aURL
WIDTH=anInt HEIGHT=anInt>
</APPLET>
```

If aURL is a relative URL, then it's interpreted relative to the HTML document's location. By making aURL an absolute URL, you can load an applet from just about anywhere — even from another HTTP server.

This tutorial uses CODEBASE="someDirectory/" frequently, since we group the examples for each lesson in subdirectories. For example, here's the <APPLET> tag that includes the Simple applet in The Life Cycle of an Applet:

```
<APPLET CODE=Simple.class CODEBASE="example/"
WIDTH=500 HEIGHT=20>
</APPLET>
```

The following figure shows the location of the class file, relative to the HTML file, when CODEBASE is set to "example/".

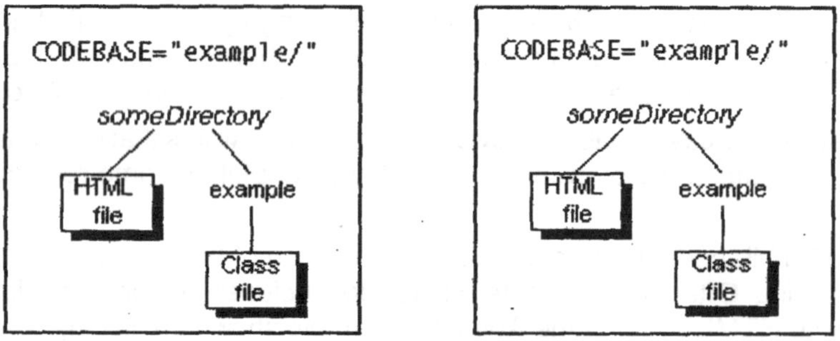

Fig 14.10

The next figure shows where the applet class can be if you specify an absolute URL for the value of CODEBASE.

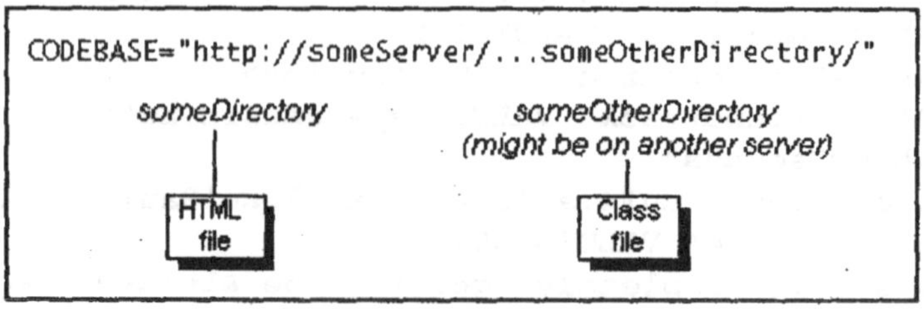

Fig 14.11

14.16 Hello World: The Applet

The reason people are excited about Java as more than just another OOP language is because it allows them to write interactive applets on the web. Hello World isn't a very interactive program, but let's look at a webbed version.

```
import java.applet.Applet;
import java.awt.Graphics;
public class HelloWorldApplet extends Applet
{
public void paint(Graphics g) {
g.drawString("Hello world!", 50, 25);
}
}
```

The applet version of HelloWorld is a little more complicated than the HelloWorld application, and it will take a little more effort to run it as well.

First type in the source code and save it into file called HelloWorldApplet.java. Compile this file in the usual way. If all is well a file called HelloWorldApplet.class will be created. Now you need to create an HTML file that will include your applet. The following simple HTML file will do.

```
<HTML>
<HEAD>
<TITLE> Hello World </TITLE>
</HEAD>

<BODY>
This is the applet:<P>
<applet code="HelloWorldApplet.class" width="150" height="50">
</applet>
</BODY>
</HTML>
```

Save this file as HelloWorldApplet.html in the same directory as the HelloWorldApplet.class file. When you've done that, load the HTML file into a Java enabled browser like Internet Explorer 4.0 or Sun's applet viewer included with the JDK. You should see something like below, though of course the exact details depend on which browser you use.

If you're using the JDK 1.1 to compile your program, you should use the applet viewer, HotJava, Internet Explorer 4.0 or later, or Netscape 4.0.6 or latero Windows and Unix to view the applet. Netscape Navigator 4.0.5 and earlier and 3.x versions of Internet Explorer do not support Java 1.1. Furthermore, no Mac version of Navigator supports Java 1.1.

If the applet compiled without error and produced a HelloWorldApplet.class file, and yet you don't see the string "Hello World" in your browser chances are that the .class file is in the wrong place. Make sure HelloWorldApplet.class is in the same directory as HelloWorld.html. Also make sure that you're using a version of Netscape or Internet Explorer which supports Java. Not all versions do.

In any case Netscape's Java support is less than the perfect so if you have trouble with an applet, the first thing to try is loading it into Sun's Applet Viewer instead. If the Applet Viewer has a problem, then chances are pretty good the problem is with the applet and not with the browser.

14.17 A Web Application

Now let's consider creating an application to run on the Web, which will show Java in all its glory. Part of this application will be a Java program running on the Web server, and the other part will be an applet that's downloaded to the browser. The applet collects information from the user and sends it back to the application running on the Web server. The task of the program will be simple: the applet will ask for the email address of the user, and after verifying that this address is reasonably legitimate (it doesn't contain spaces, and it does contain an '@' symbol) the applet will send the email address to the Web server. The application running on the server will capture the data and check a data file in which all of the email addresses are kept. If that address is already in the file, it will send back a message to that effect, which is displayed by the applet. If the address isn't in the file, it is placed in the list and the applet is informed that the address was added successfully.

Traditionally, the way to handle such a problem is to create an HTML page with a text field and a "submit" button. The user can type whatever he or she wants into the text field, and it will be submitted to the server without question. As it submits the data, the Web page also tells the server what to do with the data by mentioning the Common Gateway Interface (CGI) program that the server should run after receiving this data. This CGI program is typically written in either Perl or C (and sometimes C++, if the server supports it), and it must handle everything. First it looks at the data and decides whether it's in the correct format. If not, the CGI program must create an HTML page to describe the problem; this page is handed to the server, which sends it back to the user. The user must then back up a page and try again. If the data is correct, the CGI program opens the data file and either adds the email address to the file or discovers that the address is already in the file. In both cases it must format an appropriate HTML page for the server to return to the user.

As Java programmers, this seems like an awkward way for us to solve the problem, and naturally, we'd like to do the whole thing in Java. First, we'll use a Java applet to take care of data validation at the client site, without all that tedious Web traffic and page formatting. Then let's skip the Perl CGI script in favor of a Java application running on the server. In fact, let's skip the Web server altogether and simply make our own network connection from the applet to the Java application on the server!

As you'll see, there are a number of issues that make this a more complicated problem than it seems. It would be ideal to write the applet using Java 1.1 but that's hardly practical. At this writing, the number of users running Java 1.1-enabled browsers is small, and although such browsers are now commonly available, you'll probably need to take into account that a significant number of users will be slow to upgrade. So to be on the safe side, the applet will be programmed using only Java 1.0 code. With this in mind, there will be no JAR files to combine .class files in the applet, so the applet should be designed to create as few .class files as possible to minimize download time.

Well, it turns out the Web server (the one available to me when I wrote the example) does have Java in it, but only Java 1.0! So the server application must also be written using Java 1.0.

The first definitions in NameCollector should look familiar: the port is chosen, a datagram packet is created, and there's a handle to a DatagramSocket. The next three definitions concern the connection to the C program: a Process object is what comes back when the C program is fired up by the Java program, and that Process object produces the InputStream and OutputStream objects representing, respectively, the standard output and standard input of the C program. These must of course be "wrapped" as is usual with Java IO, so we end up with a PrintStream and DataInputStream.

All the work for this program happens inside the constructor. To start up the C program, the current Runtime object is procured. This is used to call exec( ), which returns the Process object. You can see that there are simple calls to produce the streams from the Process object: getOutputStream( ) and getInputStream( ). From this point on, all you need to consider is sending data to the stream nameList and getting the results from addResult.

As before, a DatagramSocket is connected to a port. Inside the infinite while loop, the program calls receive( ), which blocks until a datagram shows up. When the datagram appears, its contents are extracted into the String rcvd . This is trimmed to remove white space at each end and sent to the C program in the line:

```
nameList.println(rcvd.trim());
```

This is only possible because Java's exec( ) provides access to any executable that reads from standard input and writes to standard output. There are other ways to talk to non-Java code, which are discussed in Appendix A.

Capturing the result from the C program is slightly more complicated. You must call read( ) and provide a buffer where the results will be placed. The return value for read( ) is the number of bytes that came from the C program, and if this value is -1 it means that something is wrong. Otherwise, the resultBuf is turned into a String and the spaces are trimmed off. This string is then placed into a DatagramPacket as before and shipped back to the same address that sent the request in the first place. Note that the sender's address is part of the DatagramPacket we received.

Remember that although the C program must be compiled on the Web server, the Java program can be compiled anywhere since the resulting byte codes will be the same regardless of the platform on which the program will be running.

The NameSender applet

As mentioned earlier, the applet must be written with Java 1.0 so that it will run on the largest number of browsers, so it's best if the number of classes produced is minimized. Thus, instead of using the Dgram class developed earlier, all of the datagram manipulations will be placed in line. In addition, the applet needs a thread to listen for the reply from the server, and instead of making this a separate thread it's integrated into the applet by implementing the Runnable interface. This isn't as easy to read, but it produces a one-class (and one-server-hit) applet:

```
//: NameSender.java
// An applet that sends an email address
// as a datagram, using Java 1.02.
import java.awt.*;
import java.applet.*;
import java.net.*;
import java.io.*;

public class NameSender extends Applet
implements Runnable {
private Thread pl = null;
private Button send = new Button(
"Add email address to mailing list");
private TextField t = new TextField(
"type your email address here", 40);
private String str = new String();
private Label
l = new Label(), l2 = new Label();
private DatagramSocket s;
private InetAddress hostAddress;
private byte[] buf =
new byte[NameCollector.BUFFER_SIZE];
private DatagramPacket dp =
new DatagramPacket(buf, buf.length);
private int vcount = 0;
public void init() {
```

```
setLayout(new BorderLayout());
Panel p = new Panel();
p.setLayout(new GridLayout(2, 1));
p.add(t);
p.add(send);
add("North", p);
Panel labels = new Panel();
labels.setLayout(new GridLayout(2, 1));
labels.add(l);
labels.add(l2);
add("Center", labels);
try {
// Auto-assign port number:
s = new DatagramSocket();
hostAddress = InetAddress.getByName(
getCodeBase().getHost());
} catch(UnknownHostException e) {
l.setText("Cannot find host");
} catch(SocketException e) {
l.setText("Can't open socket");
}
l.setText("Ready to send your email address");
}
public boolean action (Event evt, Object arg) {
if(evt.target.equals(send)) {
if(pl != null) {
// pl.stop(); Deprecated in Java 1.2
Thread remove = pl;
pl = null;
remove.interrupt();
}
l2.setText("");
// Check for errors in email name:
str = t.getText().toLowerCase().trim();
if(str.indexOf(' ') != -1) {
l.setText("Spaces not allowed in name");
return true;
}
if(str.indexOf(',') != -1) {
l.setText("Commas not allowed in name");
return true;
}
if(str.indexOf('@') == -1) {
l.setText("Name must include '@'");
l2.setText("");
return true;
}
if(str.indexOf('@') == 0) {
```

```
l.setText("Name must preceed '@'");
l2.setText("");
return true;
}
String end =
str.substring(str.indexOf('@'));
if(end.indexOf('.') == -1) {
l.setText("Portion after '@' must " +
"have an extension, such as '.com'");
l2.setText("");
return true;
}
// Everything's OK, so send the name. Get a
// fresh buffer, so it's zeroed. For some
// reason you must use a fixed size rather
// than calculating the size dynamically:
byte[] sbuf =
new byte[NameCollector.BUFFER_SIZE];
str.getBytes(0, str.length(), sbuf, 0);
DatagramPacket toSend =
new DatagramPacket(
sbuf, 100, hostAddress,
NameCollector.COLLECTOR_PORT);
try {
s.send(toSend);
} catch(Exception e) {
l.setText("Couldn't send datagram");
return true;
}
l.setText("Sent: " + str);
send.setLabel("Re-send");
pl = new Thread(this);
pl.start();
l2.setText(
"Waiting for verification " + ++vcount);
}
else return super.action(evt, arg);
return true;
}
// The thread portion of the applet watches for
// the reply to come back from the server:
public void run() {
try {
s.receive(dp);
} catch(Exception e) {
l2.setText("Couldn't receive datagram");
return;
}
```

```
l2.setText(new String(dp.getData(),
0, 0, dp.getLength()));
}
} ///:~
```

The UI for the applet is quite simple. There's a TextField in which you type your email address, and a Button to send the email address to the server. Two Labels are used to report status back to the user.

By now you can recognize the DatagramSocket, InetAddress, buffer, and DatagramPacket as trappings of the network connection. Lastly, you can see the run( ) method that implements the thread portion so the applet can listen for the reply sent back by the server.

The init( ) method sets up the GUI with the familiar layout tools, then creates the DatagramSocket that will be used both for sending and receiving datagrams.

The action( ) method (remember, we're confined to Java 1.0 now, so we can't use any slick inner listener classes) watches only to see if you press the "send" button. When the button is pressed, the first action is to check the Thread pl to see if it's null. If it's not null, there's a live thread running. The first time the message is sent a thread is started up to watch for the reply. Thus, if a thread is running, it means this is not the first time the user has tried to send the message. The pl handle is set to null and the old listener is interrupted. (This is the preferred approach, since stop( ) is deprecated in Java 1.2 as explained in the previous chapter.)

Regardless of whether this is the first time the button was pressed, the text in l2 is erased.

The next group of statements checks the email name for errors. The String.indexOf( ) method is used to search for illegal characters, and if one is found it is reported to the user. Note that all of this happens without any network activity, so it's fast and it doesn't bog down the Internet.

Once the name is verified, it is packaged into a datagram and sent to the host address and port number in the same way that was described in the earlier datagram example. The first label is changed to show you that the send has occurred, and the button text is changed so that it reads "re-send." At this point, the thread is started up and the second label informs you that the applet is waiting for a reply from the server.

The run( ) method for the thread uses the DatagramSocket that lives in NameSender to receive( ), which blocks until the datagram packet comes from the server. The resulting packet is placed into NameSender's DatagramPacket dp . The data is retrieved from the packet and placed into the second label in NameSender. At this point, the thread terminates and becomes dead. If the reply doesn't come back from the server in a reasonable amount of time, the user might become impatient and press the button again, thus terminating the current thread (and, after re-sending the data, starting a new one). Because a thread is used to listen for the reply, the user still has full use of the UI.

14.17.4 The Web page

Of course, the applet must go inside a Web page. Here is the complete Web page; you can see that it's intended to be used to automatically collect names for my mailing list:

```
<HTML>
<HEAD>
<META CONTENT="text/html">
<TITLE>
Add Yourself to Bruce Eckel's Java Mailing List
</TITLE>
</HEAD>
```

```
<BODY LINK="#0000ff" VLINK="#800080" BGCOLOR="#ffffff">
<FONT SIZE=6><P>
Add Yourself to Bruce Eckel's Java Mailing List
</P></FONT>
```

The applet on this page will automatically add your email address to the mailing list, so you will receive update information about changes to the online version of "Thinking in Java," notification when the book is in print, information about upcoming Java seminars, and notification about the "Hands-on Java Seminar" Multimedia CD. Type in your email address and press the button to automatically add yourself to this mailing list.

```
<HR>
<applet code=NameSender width=400 height=100>
</applet>
<HR>
```

If after several tries, you do not get verification it means that the Java application on the server is having problems. In this case, you can add yourself to the list by sending email to

```
<A HREF="mailto:Bruce@EckelObjects.com">
Bruce@EckelObjects.com</A>
</BODY>
</HTML>
```

14.17.5 Problems with this Approach

This certainly seems like an elegant approach. There's no CGI programming and so there are no delays while the server starts up a CGI program. The datagram approach seems to produce a nice quick response. In addition, when Java 1.1 is available everywhere, the server portion can be written entirely in Java. (Although it's quite interesting to see how easy it is to connect to a non-Java program using standard input and output.)

There are problems, however. One problem is rather subtle: since the Java application is running constantly on the server and it spends most of its time blocked in the Datagram.receive( ) method, there might be some CPU hogging going on. At least, that's the way it appeared on the server where I was experimenting. On the other hand, there wasn't much else happening on that server, and starting the program using "nice" (a Unix program to prevent a process from hogging the CPU) or its equivalent could solve the problem if you have a more heavily-loaded server. In any event, it's worth keeping your eye on an application like this - a blocked receive( ) could hog the CPU.

The second problem is a show stopper. It concerns firewalls. A firewall is a machine that sits between your network and the Internet. It monitors all traffic coming in from the Internet and going out to the Internet, and makes sure that traffic conforms to what it expects.

Firewalls are conservative little beasts. They demand strict conformance to all the rules, and if you're not conforming they assume that you're doing something sinful and shut you out (not quite so bad as the Spanish Inquisition, but close). For example, if you are on a network behind a firewall and you start connecting to the Internet using a Web browser, the firewall expects that all your transactions will connect to the server using the accepted http port, which is 80. Now along comes this Java applet NameSender, which is trying to send a datagram to port 8080, which is way outside the range of the "protected" ports 0-1024. The firewall naturally assumes the worst - that someone has a virus - and it doesn't allow the transaction to happen.

As long as your customers have raw connections to the Internet (for example, using a typical Internet service provider) there's no problem, but you might have some important customers dwelling behind firewalls, and they won't be able to use your program.

This is rather disheartening after learning so much Java, because it would seem that you must give up Java on the server and learn how to write CGI scripts in C or Perl. But as it turns out, despair is not in order.

One scenario is part of Sun's grand scheme. If everything goes as planned, Web servers will be equipped with servlet servers . These will take a request from the client (going through the firewall-accepted port 80) and instead of starting up a CGI program they will start up a Java program called a servlet. This is a little application that's designed to run only on the server. A servlet server will automatically, start up the servlet to handle the client request, which means you can write all your programs in Java (further enabling the "100 percent pure Java initiative"). It is admittedly an appealing idea: once you're comfortable with Java, you don't have to switch to a more primitive language to handle requests on the server.

Since it's only for handling requests on the server, the servlet API has no GUI abilities. This fits quite well with NameCollector.java, which doesn't have a GUI anyway.

At this writing, a low-cost servlet server was available from java.sun.com. In addition, Sun is encouraging other Web server manufacturers to add servlet capabilities to their servers.

14.18 Combining an Applet's Files into a Single File

If your applet has more than one file, you should consider providing an archive file that bundles the applet's files into a single file. Whether archive files make sense for your applet depends on several factors, including your applet's size, performance considerations, and the environment you expect your users to have.

Archive files reduce your applet's total download time. Much of the time saved comes from reducing the number of HTTP connections that the browser must make. Each HTTP connection can take several seconds to start. This means that for a multifile applet, connection time can dwarf transfer time. You can further reduce transfer time by compressing the files in your archive file.

If you specify one or more archive files, then the browser looks for the archive files in the same directory that it would search for the applet class file. The browser then looks for the applet's class files in the archive files. If a file isn't in the archive, then the browser generally tries to load it just as it would if the archive file weren't present.

The standard Java archive format, called JAR, was introduced in JDK 1.1 and is based on the ZIP file format. You specify JAR files using the ARCHIVE attribute of the <APPLET> tag. You can specify multiple archive files by separating them with commas:

```
<APPLET CODE="AppletSubclass.class" ARCHIVE="file1, file2"
WIDTH=anInt HEIGHT=anInt>
</APPLET>
```

Unfortunately, not all browsers understand the same archive format or use the same HTML code to specify the applet archive. Watch this page for the latest information about browser support for archives. To learn how to create a JAR file, see Platform-specific Details: Creating a JAR File.

14.19 Security Restrictions

One of the main goals of the Java environment is to make browser users feel secure running any applet. To achieve this goal, we've started out conservatively, restricting capabilities perhaps more than necessary. As time passes, applets will probably get more and more abilities.

Each applet viewer has a SecurityManager object that checks for applet security violations. When a SecurityManager detects a violation, it creates and throws a SecurityException object. Generally, the SecurityException constructor prints a warning message to the standard output. An applet can catch SecurityExceptions and react appropriately, such as by reassuring the user and by resorting to a "safer" (but less ideal) way of accomplishing the task.

Some applet viewers swallow some SecurityExceptions, so that the applet never gets the SecurityException. For example, the JDK Applet Viewer's implementation of the AppletContext getApplet and getApplets methods simply catches and ignores any SecurityExceptions. The user can see an error message in the standard output, but at least the applet gets a valid result from the methods. This makes some sense, since getApplets should be able to return any valid applets it finds, even if it encounters invalid ones. (The Applet Viewer considers an applet valid if it's loaded from the same host as the applet that's calling getApplets.)

14.20 Applet Security

The possibility of surfing the Net, wandering across a random page, playing an applet and catching a virus is a fear that has scared many uninformed people away from Java. This fear has also driven a lot of the development of Java in the direction it's gone. Earlier I discussed various security features of Java including automatic garbage collection, the elimination of pointer arithmetic and the Java interpreter. These serve the dual purpose of making the language simple for programmers and secure for users. You can surf the web without worrying that a Java applet will format your hard disk or introduce a virus into your system.

In fact both Java applets and applications are much safer in practice than code written in traditional languages. This is because even code from trusted sources is likely to have bugs. However Java programs are much less susceptible to common bugs involving memory access than are programs written in traditional languages like C. Furthermore the Java runtime environment provides a fairly robust means of trapping bugs before they bring down your system. Most users have many more problems with bugs than they do with deliberately malicious code. Although users of Java applications aren't protected from out and out malicious code, they are largely protected from programmer errors.

Applets implement additional security restrictions that protect users from malicious code too. This is accomplished through the java.lang.SecurityManager class. This class is subclassed to provide different security environments in different virtual machines. Regrettably implementing this additional level of protection does somewhat restrict the actions an applet can perform. Let's explore exactly what an applet can and cannot do.

14.20.1 User Security Issues and Social Engineering

Contrary to popular belief most computer break-ins by external hackers don't happen because of great knowledge of operating system internals and network protocols. They happen because a hacker went digging through a company's garbage and found a piece of paper with a password written on it, or perhaps because they talked to a low-level bureaucrat on the phone, convinced this person they were from the local data processing department and that they needed him or her to change their password to "DEBUG."

This is sort of attack is called social engineering. Java applets introduce a new path for social engineering. For instance imagine an applet that pops up a dialog box that says, "You have lost your connection to the network. Please enter your username and password to reconnect." How many people would blindly enter their usern ame and password without thinking? Now what if the box didn't really come from a lost network connection but from a hacker's applet? And instead of reconnecting to the network (a connection that was never lost in the first place) the username and password was sent over the Internet to the cracker? See the problem?

EXERCISES

1. *Write an applet that randomly places a designer specified number of rectangles of random sizes and colors at least partially inside the applet's visible area. Be sure to intelligently handle the case where the designer does not provide proper initialization parameters for the applet.*
2. *Make the applet available on a Web page. The Web page should thoroughly test the capabilities of the applet. Include a link to full source code for the applet. Hand in the source code for the applet, sample HTML files for the applet, screenshots of the running applet, and a URL where the applet can be viewed.*
3. *Write an applet that draws a graph of p(n) vs. n where population(n) is the nth iteration of the logistic equation. (You only need to draw the graph. You do not need to draw axes or legends or anything of that nature.) Use PARAM tags to specify the rate, the initial population, the x and y scale factors and the number of iterations to track. Note that it is not necessary to achive convergence. Thus this problem is a little different from previous ones involving the logistic equation.*
4. *ake the applet available on a Web page. Include at least three instances of the applet on the page: one with a rate between 1 and 2, one with a rate between 2 and 3, and one with a rate between 3 and 4. Include a link to full source code for the applet. Hand in the source code for the applet, sample HTML files for the applet, screenshots of the running applet, and a URL where the applet can be viewed.*
5. *Write an applet that reads an indefinite number of strings from PARAM tags and draws them.*
6. *Allow the Web page designer to specify the font face, size, and style of each string in the applet from problem 2. Be sure to handle the case of the font not being available on the client.*

   Also let the designer pick the color of each string. Finally, let the Web page designer specify the position of each string. Thus you should hand in an applet that allows the designer to specify the font, size, style, color, and position of an indefinite number of strings.

Make the applet available on a Web page. The Web page should thoroughly test the capabilities of the applet. Include a link to full source code for the applet. Hand in the source code for the applet, sample HTML files for the applet, screenshots of the running applet, and a URL where the applet can be viewed.

15

Awt : Working With Windows

15.1 What Does AWT Stand For?

You may wonder what does JAVA mean.The word JAVA is not an acronym, althugh I read some where thatt this may mean acronym for Just Another Virtual Acronym.

Similarly so far I've heard it claimed that AWT stands for:

- Abstract Window Toolkit
- Advanced Window Toolkit
- Another Window Toolkit
- Applet Window Toolkit
- Awkward Window Toolkit
- Annoying Window Toolkit

I do not know which if any of these are correct, but Abstract Window Toolkit seems to be the most popular.

15.2 What is a Container?

A container is a component which can contain other components inside itself. It is also an instance of a subclass of java.awt.Container. java.awt.Container extends java.awt.Component so containers are themselves components.

In general components are contained in a container. An applet is a container. Other containers include windows, frames, dialogs, and panels. Containers may contain other containers.

Every container has a LayoutManager that determines how different components [illegible]sitioned within the container.

In short containers contain components. Components are positioned inside the container according to a LayoutManager. Since containers are themselves components, containers may by placed inside other containers. This is really a lot simpler than it sounds. Applets provide a ready-made container and a default LayoutManager, a FlowLayout.

15.3 The Two Kinds of Containers

The AWT defines two different kinds of containers, panels and windows.

Panels are subclasses of java.awt.Panel. A panel is contained inside another container, or perhaps inside the web browser's window. Panels do not stand on their own. Applets are panels.

Windows are subclasses of java.awt.Window. A window is a free-standing, native window. There are two kinds of windows: frames and dialogs. A frame is an instance of a subclass of java.awt.Frame. It represents a normal, native window. A dialog is a subclass of java.awt.Dialog. A dialog is a transitory window that exists merely to impart some information or get some input from the user.

15.3.1 Panels

A Panel is a fairly generic Container whose primary purpose is to subdivide the drawing area into separate rectangular pieces. Since each Panel can have its own LayoutManager, you can do many things with panels that you can't do with a single LayoutManager.

For example, suppose you want a TextArea in the center of an applet with a Button below, like this:

There's no single LayoutManager that will produce this. A BorderLayout will expand the Button to fill the entire width of the applet. A FlowLayout won't make the TextArea big enough.

Panels

Instead of either of these options, we can create the applet with a BorderLayout and put the TextArea in its center. Then we create a Panel, set the LayoutManager of the Panel to FlowLayout, add the button to the panel, and then add the panel to the south part of the applet. Indeed that's exactly what was done to produce the above applet. Here's the code:

```
import java.applet.*;
import java.awt.*;
public class PanelExample extends Applet
{
public void init() {
this.setLayout(new BorderLayout());
this.add("Center", new TextArea());
Panel p = new Panel();
p.setLayout(new FlowLayout());
p.add(new Button("OK"));
this.add("South", p);
}
}
```

It's important in this example to distinguish between adding to the applet (add(...) or this.add(...)) and adding to the panel (p.add(...)).

On the other hand it doesn't matter whether you add the panel to the applet and then add the button to the panel, or first add the button to the panel and then add the panel to the applet.

Another common use for a panel is to align a series of checkboxes in a GridLayout with one column.

Sometimes what's needed is multiple instances of the same LayoutManager. For instance consider the calculator applet again.

On the one hand this looks like it should be simple to implement in Java. After all it's just eighteen buttons and a TextField. On the other hand although most of the keys are the same size, two of the keys and the TextField are oversized. You could almost use a GridLayout, but not quite. Panels are one way to solve this problem.

15.3.2 Nesting Panels

Consider this picture. First a calculator is broken up into a grid of one column and three rows. Put a Panel in each of those cells. Panel A1 will contain the TextField and the top four keys. panel A2 will contain the middle two rows of keys, and panel A3 will contain the bottom two rows of keys.

The eight keys in the middle panel A2 are all the same size. Therefore you can use a GridLayout with two rows and four columns in it. However this isn't true for A1 and A3, so let's continue. Split panel A1 into a grid of two rows and one column. The top cell will be used for the TextField display. However the bottom cell still needs to be split into four pieces so add Panel B1. The bottom is more complex still. Split it into a grid of one row and two columns and put panels B2 and B3 there.

Panel B1 contains four keys, all the same size so put a grid of one row and four columns there, and add those keys. Next split Panel B2 into two rows and one column. Put the oversized zero key in the second cell and Panel C1 in the first. Next split B3 into two columns and one row. Put a panel in the first cell and the oversized equals key in the second.

Finally split C1 into two columns and one row and put the one and two keys there. Then split C2 into two rows and one column for the three and decimal point keys.

15.3.3 A Calculator with Panels

Here's the source code that produces a calculator applet, using only a GridLayout and nested panels. Whether this is easier or harder than using a GridBagLayout is a personal preference.

```
import java.applet.*;
import java.awt.*;
public class Calculator extends Applet
{
TextField screen;
public void init () {
this.setLayout(new GridLayout(3, 1, 3, 3));
Panel A1 = new Panel();
this.add(A1);
Panel A2 = new Panel();
this.add(A2);
Panel A3 = new Panel();
this.add(A3);
A1.setLayout(new GridLayout(2, 1));
screen = new TextField(12);
A1.add(screen);
Panel B1 = new Panel();
B1.setLayout(new GridLayout(1, 4, 3, 3));
B1.add(new Button("C"));
B1.add(new Button("="));
B1.add(new Button("/"));
B1.add(new Button("*"));
A1.add(B1);
A2.setLayout(new GridLayout(2, 4, 3, 3));
A2.add(new Button("7"));
A2.add(new Button("8"));
A2.add(new Button("9"));
A2.add(new Button("-"));
A2.add(new Button("4"));
A2.add(new Button("5"));
A2.add(new Button("6"));
A2.add(new Button("+"));
A3.setLayout(new GridLayout(1, 2, 3, 3));
// 1, 2 and 0
```

```
Panel B2 = new Panel();
B2.setLayout(new GridLayout(2, 1, 3, 3));
// 1 and 2
Panel C1 = new Panel();
C1.setLayout(new GridLayout(1, 2, 3, 3));
C1.add(new Button("1"));
C1.add(new Button("2"));
B2.add(C1);
B2.add(new Button("0"));
// 3, . and =
Panel B3 = new Panel();
B3.setLayout(new GridLayout(1, 2, 3, 3));
// 3 and .
Panel C2 = new Panel();
C2.setLayout(new GridLayout(2, 1, 3, 3));
C2.add(new Button("3"));
C2.add(new Button("."));
B3.add(C2);
B3.add(new Button("="));
A3.add(B2);
A3.add(B3);
}
public Insets insets() {
return new Insets(5, 5, 5, 5);
}
/* Use 1.0 event handling since I need to run this
inside today's web browsers. */
public boolean action(Event e, Object arg) {
if (e.target instanceof Button) {
screen.setText((String) arg);
return true;
}
return false;
}
}
```

15.4 Windows

The java.awt.Window class and its subclasses let you create free-standing windows. Stand-alone windows can also be used to build applications that use the AWT instead of the command-line or to provide additional space for applets.

A Window is a subclass of java.awt.Container that is independent of other containers. That is, a Window is not itself contained. Since Window extends java.awt.Container you can add components like Buttons and TextFields to Windows. You can arrange the Components you add with a LayoutManager. You can draw directly into a Window in a paint() method. Everything you do in an applet panel can also be done in a Window.

Normally you Don't use the Window class directly. Instead you use one of its subclasses, either java.awt.Frame or java.awt.Dialog depending on your need. A Frame is what most people think of as a window in their native environment. It can have a menu bar; it can be independently moved and resized; and it will hang around on the screen as long as the user is interested in the content of the window.

A Dialog will not have a menu bar. It can be moved but often can't be resized. Its purpose is to get some particular information from the user (input) or to impart some particularly important information to the user (output). It is normally visible on the screen only until it gets the input or receives acknowledgement from the user about its output.

15.5 Frames

Frames are very useful in more complex applications. Frames let you separate different functions or data into different windows. For instance a painting application may have several different pictures in varying states of completion open in different windows. Or it may have only one picture but a separate window might contain a tool palette to select different brushes or colors. Each of these windows would be a Frame.

Everything you need to create and work with frames is contained in the java.awt.Frame class. To create a new frame without a title bar use the Frame() constructor with no arguments.

Frame f = new Frame();

More commonly you'll want to name the frame so pass the constructor a string that specifies the window's title.

Frame f = new Frame("My Window");

Frames inherit from java.awt.Container so you can add components to a frame. Unlike panels and applets, the default LayoutManager for a frame is BorderLayout, not FlowLayout. However you can change this using the frame<'s setLayout() method like this:

f.setLayout(new FlowLayout());

Frames inherit from java.awt.Component so they have paint() and update() methods. If you want to draw in the frame and process events manually like you did in applets, just create a subclass of Frame and add listener objects to it. Almost everything you did in those chapters with a user-defined subclass of java.awt.Applet can also be done with a user-defined subclass of java.awt.Frame.

However most of the time you'll prefer to use components. To add a component to a frame call the frame's add() method just as you would call an applet's add() method. The only difference is that you may often call the add() method from outside the Frame class so you'll need to prefix add with a variable that points to the frame and the member operator . In other words given a Frame f, you need to call

```
f.add(new Button("OK");
rather than simply
this.add(new Button("OK"));
```

Of course this depends on what class you're inside of when you call add(). If you're calling add() from one of the Frame subclass's own methods you won't need to do this.

Since the default layout for a frame is BorderLayout, you should specify whether you want the component added to the North, South, East, West or Center. Here's how you'd add a centered label to the center of Frame f:

f.add("Center", new Label("This is a frame", Label.CENTER));

The size and position of any given frame is unpredictable unless you specify it. Specifying the size is easy. Just call the frame's setSize() method like this

f.setSize(150,150);

This size does not include the title bar so you'll need to account for that separately. To determine the height of a Frame's title bar call its insets() method and look at the top member of the resulting java.awt.Insets object. That will be the height of the title bar. That is,

int TitleBarHeight = f.insets().top;

Moving the Frame to the proper place on the screen takes a little more effort. You move a Frame with the setLocation(int x, int y) method. However x and y are relative to the screen, not to the applet.

When a window is first created, it's invisible. Add components to the Frame while it's still invisible. The effect of Buttons, Labels and other widgets popping onto a layout in rapid succession while the window jumps around and changes size can be quite disconcerting. When you're done adding components, resizing and moving the Frame, make it visible by calling its show() method like so:

f.show();

Example 15.4 Frame Example

What follows is a very simple applet that puts up a window. You can move the window and resize it. The window has a single TextArea component that lets you edit some text.

```
import java.awt.*;
import java.applet.*;
public class WindowTester extends Applet
{
public void init() {
Frame myFrame = new Frame("My Applet Window");
myFrame.setSize(250, 250);
myFrame.setLocation(300,200);
myFrame.add("Center", new TextArea(10, 40));
myFrame.show(true);
}
}
```

15.5.1 Window Events

Since java.awt.Window is a subclass of java.awt.Component, a Window, Frame or Dialog can fire events. In particular it fires WindowEvents. There are seven of these:

```
WindowEvent.WINDOW_ACTIVATED
WindowEvent.WINDOW_CLOSED
WindowEvent.WINDOW_CLOSING
WindowEvent.WINDOW_DEACTIVATED
WindowEvent.WINDOW_DEICONIFIED
WindowEvent.WINDOW_ICONIFIED
WindowEvent.WINDOW_OPENED
```

To respond to these events you register a WindowListener object with the window. The object must implement the WindowListener interface and include these methods:

```
public abstract void windowOpened(WindowEvent e)
public abstract void windowClosing(WindowEvent e)
public abstract void windowClosed(WindowEvent e)
public abstract void windowIconified(WindowEvent e)
public abstract void windowDeiconified(WindowEvent e)
```

```
public abstract void windowActivated(WindowEvent e)
public abstract void windowDeactivated(WindowEvent e)
```

Example 15.5 Window Events Example

For example, windows don't close on their own. You have to explicitly close them. The following subclass of Frame puts up a window that responds to efforts to close it by calling setVisible(false) and dispose().

```
import java.awt.*;
import java.awt.event.*;
public class ClosableFrame extends Frame implements WindowListener
{
public ClosableFrame() {
this.addWindowListener(this);
}
public ClosableFrame(String s) {
super(s);
this.addWindowListener(this);
}
public void windowClosing(WindowEvent e) {
this.setVisible(false);
this.dispose();
}
public void windowOpened(WindowEvent e) {}
public void windowClosed(WindowEvent e) {}
public void windowIconified(WindowEvent e) {}
public void windowDeiconified(WindowEvent e) {}
public void windowActivated(WindowEvent e) {}
public void windowDeactivated(WindowEvent e) {}
}
```

15.6 Combining Applets and Applications

An applet needs a frame to run in. Normally the web browser or the applet viewer provides this. However you can create instances of your applet inside a frame of your own creation. This way you can write code that is both an applet and an application.

To convert an applet into an application, add the following main() method to your applet:

```
public static void main(String args[]) {
myApplet a = new myApplet();
a.init();
a.start();
Frame appletFrame = new Frame("Applet Window");
appletFrame.add("Center", a);
appletFrame.setSize(150,150);
appletFrame.setLocation(100,100);
appletFrame.show();
}
```

Line 1 is the standard main() method you're used to from all the command line applications. If the applet is running in a web browser or an applet viewer, this method will not be called. It will only be executed if you start the applet as a stand-alone program.

Line 3 creates a new instance of the applet. This assumes that the applet is called myApplet. You should of course change that to match the name of your applet subclass.

After you create the applet, lines 4 and 5 call the applet's init() and start() methods. Normally the web browser or applet viewer does this for you, but you're not running inside such a program so you need to do it yourself.

After the applet has been created, it's necessary to create a Frame to hold it. Line 7 does this with the normal Frame() constructor. You can change the title of the Frame to suit your application.

Line 8 adds the applet to the Frame. Since the default LayoutManager for a Frame is BorderLayout you add it to the center. Remember that java.applet.Applet is a subclass of java.awt.Component so adding an applet to a Frame is kosher.

Line 9 resizes the Frame. Here the size is arbitrarily set to 150 pixels by 150 pixels. If this program were running as an applet, you'd get those numbers from the height and width parameters; but you're not running in an applet so you have to make something up. If you like you could make it possible to enter the height and width as command line arguments.

Line 10 moves the Frame to (100, 100). If you don't do this the exact location of the Frame is unpredictable, but on some machines it has a distressing tendency to show up not only partially off the screen, but with the title bar completely off the screen so there's no way to move it onto the screen.

Line 11 makes the Frame visible, and the applet is now ready to run, without an applet viewer or a web browser.

Warning: Even with a Frame applets and applications are still different. When you convert an applet to an application in this fashion, you need to make sure your program doesn't rely on methods that only make sense in the context of an applet. For instance you can only read parameters using getParameter() in an applet. Conversely you can only read the command line arguments in an application. Furthermore applications have many fewer security restrictions than applets so code that may run well in an application may throw many security related exceptions in an applet.

15.7 Dialogs

Frames are useful for windows that will stick around for awhile, some text that's being edited for instance. Dialogs are more transitory. They're used for simple user input or for quick alerts to the user.

Like java.awt.Frame, java.awt.Dialog is a subclass of java.awt.Window and hence of java.awt.Container and java.awt.Component. Therefore a lot of what you learned about frames applies to dialogs as well. You move them, resize them and add to them almost exactly as you do frames. There are two differences between dialogs and frames:

- A frame can have a menu bar. A dialog cannot.
- A dialog can be modal. A frame cannot.

Menu bars are covered next class. Right now let's talk about modal versus non-modal dialogs. A modal dialog blocks all other use of the application until the user responds to it. A modal dialog cannot be moved and does not allow the user to switch to another window in the same program. On some platforms the user may not even be able to switch to another program.

In the 1970's a computer virus worked its way into several early timesharing systems. The computer program would periodically break in on a user's session and say "I WANT A COOKIE." The terminal would then refuse to respond to any user input until the user typed the word "COOKIE" at which point the program would say something like "MMM, MMM, THAT WAS GOOD." and return control to the user.

Modal dialogs are a lot like the cookie monster program. They request input from the user and don't let anything else happen until they get it. Non-modal dialogs pop-up but they don't prevent the user from doing other things while they're visible. Because modal dialogs inconvenience users by forcing them to respond when the computer wants them to rather than when they want to, their use should be kept to a minimum.

15.7.1 Methods of Dialogs

Since Dialog and Frame are both subclasses of Window, they share many methods including setLocation() and setSize(). The only methods that are significantly different between a dialog and a frame are the constructors. There are two constructors for Dialog which differ in whether or not the dialog is given a title. This titleless constructor is

Dialog d = new Dialog(new Frame(), false);

The second argument is a boolean which specifies whether or not the dialog should be modal. If it should be, pass true. If it shouldn't be, pass false. Modal dialogs are only modal relative to their parent frame, which is passed as the first argument to the constructor. That is they block input to the parent frame but not to other frames.

Can you pass null instead of a new Frame?

If you create the parent frame one right inside the constructor as done here, the dialog cannot be truly modal.

There are also some common differences between most frames and most dialogs, but these are not written in stone:

Most Frames can be moved and resized by the user. Most Dialogs cannot be.

Most Frames have title bars. Most Dialogs do not.

- You can make a dialog resizable and movable by calling its setResizable() method with a boolean value of true like this:

d.setResizable(true);

You can give a dialog a title bar by adding the title string to the constructor:

Dialog d = new Dialog(new Frame(), "My Dialog Window", false);

All the other methods of the Dialog class are exactly the same as they are for Frames. You resize them the same way. You move them the same way. You make them visible the same way. You add components to them the same way.

Example 15.6 Examples of Dialogs

The following program displays a simple non-modal dialog with an OK Button and no title-bar.

```
import java.applet.*;
import java.awt.*;
public class DialogTester extends Applet
{
public void init() {
Dialog myDialog = new Dialog(new Frame(), false);
myDialog.setSize(250, 250);
myDialog.setLocation(320,240);
```

```
myDialog.add("South", new Button("OK"));
myDialog.show();
}
}
```

❑ Subclassing java.awt.Dialog

The previous example was a little artificial. Normally you create your own subclass of Dialog and instantiate that subclass from the main program. For example one of the simpler common dialogs is a notification dialog that gives the user a message to which they can say OK to signify that they've read it. The following program is such a Dialog class.

```
import java.awt.*;
import java.awt.event.*;
import java.applet.*;
public class Alert extends Dialog implements ActionListener
{
public Alert (String s) {
super(new Frame(), true);
this.add("Center", new Label(s));
Panel p = new Panel();
p.setLayout(new FlowLayout());
Button yes = new Button("Yes");
yes.addActionListener(this);
p.add(yes);
Button no = new Button("No");
no.addActionListener(this);
p.add(no);
this.add("South", p);
this.setSize(300,100);
this.setLocation(100, 200);
}
public void actionPerformed(ActionEvent e) {
this.setVisible(false);
this.dispose();
}
}

class AlertExample extends Applet {
public void init () {
Alert a = new
Alert("Are you sure you want to start global thermonuclear war?");
a.show();
}
}
```

15.8 Creating Windows and Applets

The original design goal of the graphical user interface (GUI) library in Java 1.0 was to allow the programmer to build a GUI that looks good on all platforms.

That goal was not achieved. Instead, the Java 1.0 Abstract Window Toolkit (AWT) produces a GUI that looks equally mediocre on all systems. In addition it's restrictive: you can use only four fonts and you cannot access any of the more sophisticated GUI elements that exist in your operating system (OS). The Java 1.0 AWT programming model is also awkward and non-object-oriented.

Much of this situation has been improved with the Java 1.1 AWT event model, which takes a much clearer, object-oriented approach, along with the introduction of Java Beans, a component programming model that is particularly oriented toward the easy creation of visual programming environments. Java 1.2 finishes the transformation away from the old Java 1.0 AWT by adding the Java Foundation Classes (JFC), the GUI portion of which is called "Swing." These are a rich set of easy-to-use, easy-to-understand Java Beans that can be dragged and dropped (as well as hand programmed) to create a GUI that you can (finally) be satisfied with. The "revision 3" rule of the software industry (a product isn't good until revision 3) seems to hold true with programming languages as well.

One of Java's primary design goals is to create applets, which are little programs that run inside a Web browser. Because they must be safe, applets are limited in what they can accomplish. However, they are a powerful tool in supporting client-side programming, a major issue for the Web.

Programming within an applet is so restrictive that it's often referred to as being "inside the sandbox," since you always have someone - the Java run-time security system - watching over you. Java 1.1 offers digital signing for applets so you can choose to allow trusted applets to have access to your machine. However, you can also step outside the sandbox and write regular applications, in which case you can access the other features of your OS. We've been writing regular applications all along in this book, but they've been console applications without any graphical components. The AWT can also be used to build GUI interfaces for regular applications.

In this section you'll first learn the use of the original "old" AWT, which is still supported and used by many of the code examples that you will come across. Although it's a bit painful to learn the old AWT, it's necessary because you must read and maintain legacy code that uses the old AWT. Sometimes you'll even need to write old AWT code to support environments that haven't upgraded past Java 1.0. In the second part of the chapter you'll learn about the structure of the "new" AWT in Java 1.1 and see how much better the event model is. (If you can, you should use the newest tools when you're creating new programs.) Finally, you'll learn about the new JFC/Swing components, which can be added to Java 1.1 as a library - this means you can use the library without requiring a full upgrade to Java 1.2.

Most of the examples will show the creation of applets, not only because it's easier but also because that's where the AWT's primary usefulness might reside. In addition you'll see how things are different when you want to create a regular application using the AWT, and how to create programs that are both applets and applications so they can be run either inside a browser or from the command line.

Please be aware that this is not a comprehensive glossary of all the methods for the described classes. This chapter will just get you started with the essentials. When you're looking for more sophistication, make sure you go to your information browser to look for the classes and methods that will solve your problem. (If you're using a development environment your information browser might be built in; if you're using the Sun JDK then you use your Web browser and start in the java root directory.) Appendix F lists other resources for learning library details.

15.9 Why use the AWT?

One of the problems with the "old" AWT that you'll learn about in this chapter is that it is a poor example of both object-oriented design and GUI development kit design. It throws us back into the dark ages of programming (some suggest that the 'A' in AWT stands for "awkward," "awful," "abominable," etc.). You must write lines of code to do everything, including tasks that are accomplished much more easily using resources in other environments.

Many of these problems are reduced or eliminated in Java 1.1 because:

- The new AWT in Java 1.1 is a much better programming model and a significant step towards a better library. Java Beans is the framework for that library.

"GUI builders" (visual programming environments) will become de rigeur for all development systems. Java Beans and the new AWT allow the GUI builder to write code for you as you place components onto forms using graphical tools. Other component technologies such as ActiveX will be supported in the same fashion.

So why learn to use the old AWT? "Because it's there." In this case, "there" has a much more ominous meaning and points to a tenet of object-oriented library design: Once you publicize a component in your library, you can never take it out . If you do, you'll wreck somebody's existing code. In addition, there are many existing code examples out there that you'll read as you learn about Java and they all use the old AWT.

The AWT must reach into the GUI components of the native OS, which means that it performs a task that an applet cannot otherwise accomplish. An untrusted applet cannot make any direct calls into an OS because otherwise it could do bad things to the user's machine. The only way an untrusted applet can access important functionality such as "draw a window on the screen" is through calls in the standard Java library that's been specially ported and safety checked for that machine. The original model that Sun created is that this "trusted library" will be provided only by the trusted vendor of the Java system in your Web browser, and the vendor will control what goes into that library.

But what if you want to extend the system by adding a new component that accesses functionality in the OS? Waiting for Sun to decide that your extension should be incorporated into the standard Java library isn't going to solve your problem. The new model in Java 1.1 is "trusted code" or "signed code" whereby a special server verifies that a piece of code that you download is in fact "signed" by the stated author using a public-key encryption system. This way, you'll know for sure where the code comes from, that it's Bob's code and not just someone pretending to be Bob. This doesn't prevent Bob from making mistakes or doing something malicious, but it does prevent Bob from shirking responsibility - anonymity is what makes computer viruses possible. A digitally signed applet - a "trusted applet" - in Java 1.1 can reach into your machine and manipulate it directly, just like any other application you get from a "trusted" vendor and install onto your computer.

But the point of all this is that the old AWT is there. There will always be old AWT code floating around and new Java programmers learning from old books will encounter that code. Also, the old AWT is worth studying as an example of poor library design. The coverage of the old AWT given here will be relatively painless since it won't go into depth and enumerate every single method and class, but instead give you an overview of the old AWT design.

15.10 Graphics Objects

In Java all drawing takes place via a Graphics object. This is an instance of the class java.awt.Graphics.

Initially the Graphics object you use will be the one passed as an argument to an applet's paint() method. Later you'll see other Graphics objects too. Everything you learn today about drawing in an applet transfers directly to drawing in other objects like Panels, Frames, Buttons, Canvases and more.

Each Graphics object has its own coordinate system, and all the methods of Graphics including those for drawing Strings, lines, rectangles, circles, polygons and more. Drawing in Java starts with particular Graphics object. You get access to the Graphics object through the paint(Graphics g) method of your applet. Each draw method call will look like g.drawString("Hello World", 0, 50) where g is the particular Graphics object with which you're drawing.

For convenience's sake in this lecture the variable g will always refer to a preexisting object of the Graphics class. As with any other method you are free to use some other name for the particular Graphics context, myGraphics or appletGraphics perhaps.

15.10.1 Drawing Lines

Drawing straight lines with Java is easy. Just call

```
g.drawLine(x1, y1, x2, y2)
```

where (x1, y1) and (x2, y2) are the endpoints of your lines and g is the Graphics object you're drawing with.

This program draws a line diagonally across the applet.

```
import java.applet.*;
import java.awt.*;
public class SimpleLine extends Applet {
public void paint(Graphics g) {
g.drawLine(0, 0, this.getSize().width, this.getSize().height);
}
}
```

Here's the result

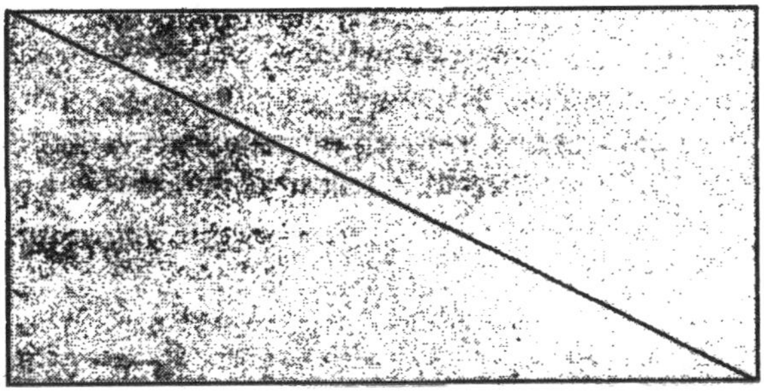

Fig. 15.1

15.10.2 Drawing Rectangles

Drawing rectangles is simple. Start with a Graphics object g and call its drawRect() method:

public void drawRect(int x, int y, int width, int height)

As the variable names suggest, the first int is the left hand side of the rectangle, the second is the top of the rectangle, the third is the width and the fourth is the height. This is in contrast to some APIs where the four sides of the rectangle are given.

This uses drawRect() to draw a rectangle around the sides of an applet.

```
import java.applet.*;
import java.awt.*;
public class RectangleApplet extends Applet {
public void paint(Graphics g) {
```

```
g.drawRect(0, 0, this.getSize().width - 1, this.getSize().height
1);
}
}
```

Remember that getSize().width is the width of the applet and getSize().height is its height.

Why was the rectangle drawn only to getSize().height-1 and getSize().width-1?

Remember that the upper left hand corner of the applet starts at (0, 0), not at (1, 1). This means that a 100 by 200 pixel applet includes the points with x coordinates between 0 and 99, not between 0 and 100. Similarly the y coordinates are between 0 and 199 inclusive, not 0 and 200.

There is no separate drawSquare() method. A square is just a rectangle with equal length sides, so to draw a square call drawRect() and pass the same number for both the height and width arguments.

15.10.3 Filling Rectangles

The drawRect() method draws an open rectangle, a box if you prefer. If you want to draw a filled rectangle, use the fillRect() method. Otherwise the syntax is identical.

This program draws a filled square in the center of the applet. This requires you to separate the applet width and height from the rectangle width and height. Here's the code:

```
import java.applet.*;
import java.awt.*;
public class FillAndCenter extends Applet {
public void paint(Graphics g) {
int appletHeight = this.getSize().height;
int appletWidth = this.getSize().width;
int rectHeight = appletHeight/3;
int rectWidth = appletWidth/3;
int rectTop = (appletHeight - rectHeight)/2;
int rectLeft= (appletWidth - rectWidth)/2;
g.fillRect(rectLeft, rectTop, rectWidth-1, rectHeight-1);
}
}
```

15.10.4 Clearing Rectangles

It is also possible to clear a rectangle that you've drawn. The syntax is exactly what you'd expect:

public abstract void clearRect(int x, int y, int width, int height)

This program uses clearRect() to blink a rectangle on the screen.

```
import java.applet.*;
import java.awt.*;
public class Blink extends Applet {
public void paint(Graphics g) {
int appletHeight = this.getSize().height;
int appletWidth  = this.getSize().width;
int rectHeight   = appletHeight/3;
int rectWidth = appletWidth/3;
int rectTop    = (appletHeight - rectHeight)/2;
int rectLeft   = (appletWidth - rectWidth)/2;
for (int i=0; i < 1000; i++) {
```

```
g.fillRect(rectLeft, rectTop, rectWidth-1, rectHeight-1);
g.clearRect(rectLeft, rectTop, rectWidth-1, rectHeight-1);
}
}
}
```

15.10.5 Ovals and Circles

Java has methods to draw outlined and filled ovals. As you'd probably guess these methods are called drawOval() and fillOval() respectively. As you might not guess they take identical arguments to drawRect() and fillRect(), i.e.

```
public void drawOval(int left, int top, int width, int height)
public void fillOval(int left, int top, int width, int height)
```

Instead of the dimensions of the oval itself, the dimensions of the smallest rectangle which can enclose the oval are specified. The oval is drawn as large as it can be to touch the rectangle's edges at their centers. This picture may help:

The arguments to drawOval() are the same as the arguments to drawRect(). The first int is the left hand side of the enclosing rectangle, the second is the top of the enclosing rectangle, the third is the width and the fourth is the height.

There is no special method to draw a circle. Just draw an oval inside a square.

Java also has methods to draw outlined and filled arcs. They're similar to drawOval() and fillOval() but you must also specify a starting and ending angle for the arc. Angles are given in degrees. The signatures are:

```
public void drawArc(int left, int top, int width, int height,
int startangle, int stopangle)
public void fillArc(int left, int top, int width, int height,
int startangle, int stopangle)
```

The rectangle is filled with an arc of the largest circle that could be enclosed within it. The location of 0 degrees and whether the arc is drawn clockwise or counter-clockwise are currently platform dependent.

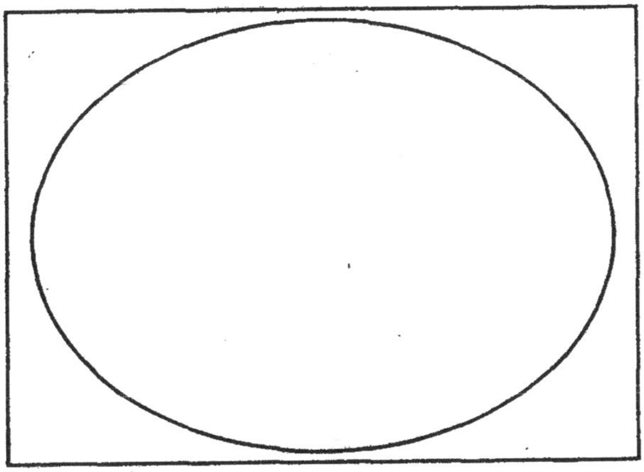

Fig. 15.2

Java has methods to draw outlined and filled ovals. As you'd probably guess these methods are called drawOval() and fillOval() respectively. As you might not guess they take identical arguments to drawRect() and fillRect(), i.e.

```
public void drawOval(int left, int top, int width, int height)
public void fillOval(int left, int top, int width, int height)
```

Instead of the dimensions of the oval itself, the dimensions of the smallest rectangle which can enclose the oval are specified. The oval is drawn as large as it can be to touch the rectangle's edges at their centers. This picture may help:

- The arguments to drawOval() are the same as the arguments to drawRect(). The first int is the left hand side of the enclosing rectangle, the second is the top of the enclosing rectangle, the third is the width and the fourth is the height.
- There is no special method to draw a circle. Just draw an oval inside a square.
- Java also has methods to draw outlined and filled arcs. They're similar to drawOval() and fillOval() but you must also specify a starting and ending angle for the arc. Angles are given in degrees. The signatures are:
- public void drawArc(int left, int top, int width, int height, int startangle, int stopangle)
- public void fillArc(int left, int top, int width, int height, int startangle, int stopangle)

The rectangle is filled with an arc of the largest circle that could be enclosed within it. The location of 0 degrees and whether the arc is drawn clockwise or counter-clockwise are currently platform dependent.

15.10.6 Bullseye

This is a simple applet which draws a series of filled, concentric circles alternating red and white, in other words a bullseye.

```
import java.applet.*;
import java.awt.*;
public class Bullseye extends Applet {
public void paint(Graphics g) {
int rectLeft, rectTop, rectHeight, rectWidth;
int appletHeight = this.getSize().height;
int appletWidth = this.getSize().width;
for (int i=8; i >= 0; i–) {
if ((i % 2) == 0) g.setColor(Color.red);
else g.setColor(Color.white);

// Center the rectangle
rectHeight = appletHeight*i/8;
rectWidth = appletWidth*i/8;
rectLeft = appletWidth/2 - i*appletWidth/16;
rectTop = appletHeight/2 - i*appletHeight/16;
g.fillOval(rectLeft, rectTop, rectWidth, rectHeight);
}
}
}
```

The .class file that draws this image is only 684 bytes. The equivalent GIF image is 1,850 bytes, almost three times larger.

Almost all the work in this applet consists of centering the enclosing rectangles inside the applet. The lines in bold do that. The first two lines just set the height and the width of the rectangle to the appropriate fraction of the applet's height and width. The next two lines set the position of the upper left hand corner. Once the rectangle is positioned, drawing the oval is easy.

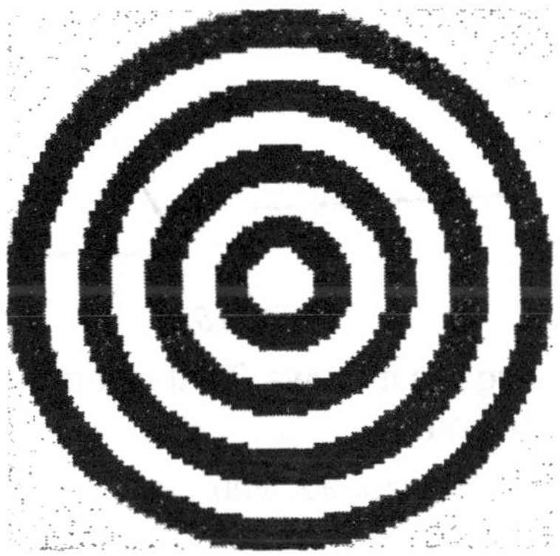

Fig. 15.6

15.10.7 Polygons

In Java rectangles are defined by the position of their upper left hand corner, their height, and their width. However it is implicitly assumed that there is in fact an upper left hand corner. Not all rectangles have an upper left hand corner. For instance consider the rectangle below.

Where is its upper left hand corner? What's been assumed so far is that the sides of the rectangle are parallel to the coordinate axes. You can't yet handle a rectangle that's been rotated at an arbitrary angle.

There are some other things you can't handle either, triangles, stars, rhombuses, kites, octagons and more. To take care of this broad class of shapes Java has a Polygon class.

Polygons are defined by their corners. No assumptions are made about them except that they lie in a 2-D plane. The basic constructor for the Polygon class is

public Polygon(int[] xpoints, int[] ypoints, int npoints)

xpoints is an array that contains the x coordinates of the polygon. ypoints is an array that contains the y coordinates. Both should have the length npoints. Thus to construct a 3-4-5 right triangle with the right angle on the origin you would type

```
int[] xpoints = {0, 3, 0};
int[] ypoints = {0, 0, 4};
Polygon myTriangle = new Polygon(xpoints, ypoints, 3);
```

To actually draw the polygon you use java.awt.Graphics's drawPolygon(Polygon p) method within your paint() method like this:

g.drawPolygon(myTriangle);

You can pass the arrays and number of points directly to the drawPolygon() method if you prefer:

g.drawPolygon(xpoints, ypoints, xpoints.length);

There's also a polymorphic fillPolygon() method. The syntax is exactly as you expect:

```
g.fillPolygon(myTriangle);
g.fillPolygon(xpoints, ypoints, xpoints.length());
```

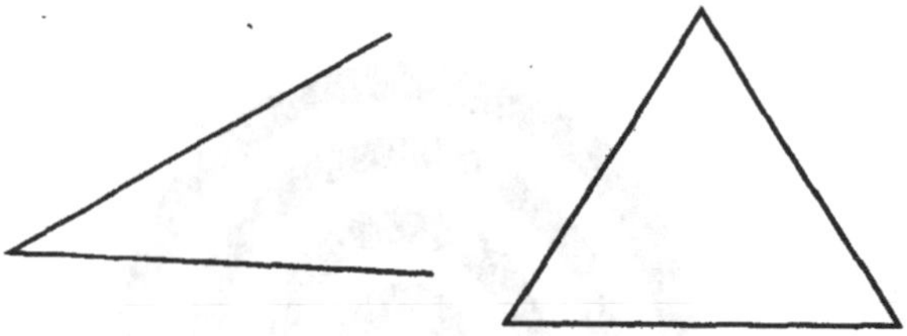

Fig. 15.4

Java automatically closes the polygons it draws. That is it draws polygons that look like the one on the right rather than the one on the left.

If you don't want your polygons to be closed, you can draw a polyline instead with the Graphics class's drawPolyline() method

public abstract void drawPolyline(int xPoints[], int yPoints[], int nPoints)

Example 15.7 Rubik Cube Unbound

This is yet another Java implementation of the classical Rubik's Cube. I tried to make the user interface as simple and obvious as possible. You should be able to figure out how it works. Twist or rotate by pointing and dragging in "natural" directions.

Press s to scramble and r to restore (while positioning the mouse cursor somewhere in the applet region).

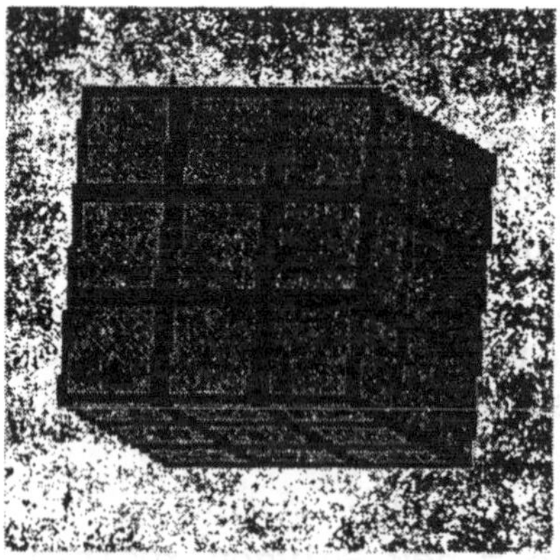

Fig. 15.5

The source code can be found here, but I have hardly documented it at all, so it looks rather cryptic.

(An optional parameter, "bgcolor", has been added. If used, it takes as input a background color as a hexadecimal RGB value, e.g. "25003f" for deep purple. Default is ordinary light gray.)

Example of Cube Applet

```
// Rubik's Cube 3D simulator
// Karl Hrnell, March 11 1996
// Last modified April 17
import java.awt.*;
```

```
import java.lang.Math;
public final class rubik extends java.applet.Applet
{
int i,j,k,n,o,p,q,lastX,lastY,dx,dy;
int rectX[],rectY[];
Color colList[],bgcolor;
final double sideVec[]={0,0,1,0,0,-1,0,-1,0,1,0,0,0,1,0,-1,0,0}; /
/ Normal vectors
final double corners[]={-1,-1,-1,1,-1,-1,1,1,-1,-1,1,-1,
-1,-1,1,1,-1,1,1,1,1,-1,1,1}; // Vertex co-ordinates
double topCorners[],botCorners[];
final int sides[]={4,5,6,7,3,2,1,0,0,1,5,4,1,2,6,5,2,3,7,6,0,4,7,3};
final int nextSide[]={2,3,4,5, 4,3,2,5, 1,3,0,5, 1,4,0,2, 1,5,0,3,
2,0,4,1};
final int mainBlocks [] = {0 ,3 ,0 ,3 ,0 ,3 ,0 ,3 ,0 ,3 ,0 ,3 ,0 ,3
,0 ,3 ,0,3,0,3,0,3,0,3};
final int twistDir[]={-1,1,-1,1, -1,1,-1,1, 1,1,1,1, 1,-1,1,-1,
1,1,1,1, -1,1,-1,1};
final int colDir[]={-1,-1,1,-1,1,-1};
final int circleOrder[]={0,1,2,5,8,7,6,3};
int topBlocks[],botBlocks[];
int sideCols[],sideW,sideH;
int dragReg,twistSide=-1;
int nearSide[],buffer[]; // Which side belongs to dragCorn
double dragCorn[],dragDir[];
double eye[]={0.3651,0.1826,-0.9129}; // Initial observer co-ordi-
nate axes (view)
double eX[]={0.9309,-0.0716,0.3581}; // (sideways)
double eY[]; // (vertical)
double Teye[],TeX[],TeY[];
double light[],temp[]={0,0,0},temp2[]={0,0,0},newCoord[];
double sx,sy,sdxh,sdyh,sdxv,sdyv,d,t1,t2,t3,t4,t5,t6;
double phi,phibase=0,Cphi,Sphi,currDragDir[];
boolean naturalState=true,twisting=false,OKtoDrag=false;
Math m;
Graphics offGraphics;
Image offImage;
public void init()
{
offImage=createImage(120,120); // Double buffer
offGraphics=offImage.getGraphics();
rectX=new int[4];
rectY=new int[4];
newCoord=new double[16]; // Projected co-ordinates (on screen)
dragDir=new double[24];
dragCorn=new double[96];
topCorners=new double[24]; // Vertex co-ordinate storage
botCorners=new double[24]; // for sub-cubes during twist
```

```
topBlocks=new int[24];
botBlocks=new int[24];
buffer=new int[12];
nearSide=new int[12];
light=new double[3];
Teye=new double[3];
TeX=new double[3];
TeY=new double[3];
currDragDir=new double[2];
eY=new double[3];
vecProd(eye,0,eX,0,eY,0); // Fix y axis of observer co-ordinate
system
normalize(eY,0);
colList=new Color[120];
for (i=0;i<20;i++)
{
colList[i]=new Color(103+i*8,103+i*8,103+i*8);
// White
colList[i+20]=new Color(i*6,i*6,84+i*9);
// Blue
colList[i+40]=new Color(84+i*9,i*5,i*5);
// Red
colList[i+60]=new Color(i*6,84+i*9,i*6);
// Green
colList[i+80]=new Color(84+i*9,84+i*9,i*6);
// Yellow
colList[i+100]=new Color(84+i*9,55+i*8,i*3);
// Orange
}
sideCols=new int[54];
for (i=0;i<54;i++)
sideCols[i]=i/9;
bgcolor=findBGColor();
resize(125,125);
repaint();
}
public Color findBGColor() // Convert hexadecimal RGB parameter to
color
{
int hex[];
String s,h="0123456789abcdef";
Color c;
hex=new int[6];
s=getParameter("bgcolor");
if ((s!=null)&&(s.length()==6))
{
for (i=0;i<6;i++)
for (j=0;j<16;j++)
```

```
if (s.charAt(i)==h.charAt(j))
hex[i]=j;
c=new Color(hex[0]*16+hex[1],hex[2]*16+hex[3],hex[4]*16+hex[5]);
}
else
c=Color.lightGray; // Default
return c;
}
// Various vector manipulation functions
public double scalProd(double v1[],int ix1,double v2[],int ix2)
{
return v1[ix1]*v2[ix2]+v1[ix1+1]*v2[ix2+1]+v1[ix1+2]*v2[ix2+2];
}
public double vNorm(double v[],int ix)
{
return m.sqrt(v[ix]*v[ix]+v[ix+1]*v[ix+1]+v[ix+2]*v[ix+2]);
}
public double cosAng(double v1[],int ix1,double v2[],int ix2)
{
return scalProd(v1,ix1,v2,ix2)/(vNorm(v1,ix1)*vNorm(v2,ix2));
}
public void normalize(double v[], int ix)
{
double t=vNorm(v,ix);
v[ix]=v[ix]/t;
v[ix+1]=v[ix+1]/t;
v[ix+2]=v[ix+2]/t;
}
public void scalMult(double v[], int ix,double a)
{
v[ix]=v[ix]*a;
v[ix+1]=v[ix+1]*a;
v[ix+2]=v[ix+2]*a;
}
public void addVec(double v1[], int ix1,double v2[],int ix2)
{
v2[ix2]+=v1[ix1];
v2[ix2+1]+=v1[ix1+1];
v2[ix2+2]+=v1[ix1+2];
}
public void subVec(double v1[], int ix1,double v2[],int ix2)
{
v2[ix2]-=v1[ix1];
v2[ix2+1]-=v1[ix1+1];
v2[ix2+2]-=v1[ix1+2];
}
public void copyVec(double v1[], int ix1,double v2[],int ix2)
{
```

```
v2[ix2]=v1[ix1];
v2[ix2+1]=v1[ix1+1];
v2[ix2+2]=v1[ix1+2];
}
public void vecProd(double v1[],int ix1,double v2[],int ix2,
double v3[],int ix3)
{
v3[ix3]=v1[ix1+1]*v2[ix2+2]-v1[ix1+2]*v2[ix2+1];
v3[ix3+1]=v1[ix1+2]*v2[ix2]-v1[ix1]*v2[ix2+2];
v3[ix3+2]=v1[ix1]*v2[ix2+1]-v1[ix1+1]*v2[ix2];
}
public void cutUpCube() // Produce large and small sub-cube for
twisting
{
boolean check;
for (i=0;i<24;i++) // Copy main coordinate data
{
topCorners[i]=corners[i];
botCorners[i]=corners[i];
}
copyVec(sideVec,3*twistSide,temp,0); // Start manipulating and build
new parts
copyVec(temp,0,temp2,0); // Fix new co-ordinates. Some need to be
altered.
scalMult(temp,0,1.3333);
scalMult(temp2,0,0.6667);
for (i=0;i<8;i++)
{
check=false;
for (j=0;j<4;j++)
if (i==sides[twistSide*4+j])
check=true;
if (check)
subVec(temp2,0,botCorners,i*3);
else
addVec(temp,0,topCorners,i*3);
}
// The sub-cubes need information about which colored fields belong
to them.
for (i=0;i<24;i++) // Fix the sub-cube blockings. First copy data
from main
{
topBlocks[i]=mainBlocks[i]; // Large sub-cube data
botBlocks[i]=mainBlocks[i]; // Small sub-cube data
}
for (i=0;i<6;i++)
{
if (i==twistSide)
```

```
{
botBlocks[i*4+1]=0; // Large sub-cube is blank on top
botBlocks[i*4+3]=0;
}
else
{
k=-1;
for (j=0;j<4;j++)
if (nextSide[i*4+j]==twistSide)
k=j;
switch (k) // Twisted side adjacent to...
{
case 0: // Up side?
{
topBlocks[i*4+3]=1;
botBlocks[i*4+2]=1;
break;
}
case 1: // Right side?
{
topBlocks[i*4]=2;
botBlocks[i*4+1]=2;
break;
}
case 2: // Down side?
{
topBlocks[i*4+2]=2;
botBlocks[i*4+3]=2;
break;
}
case 3: // Left side?
{
topBlocks[i*4+1]=1;
botBlocks[i*4]=1;
break;
}
case -1: // None
{
topBlocks[i*4+1]=0; // Small sub-cube is blank on bottom
topBlocks[i*4+3]=0;
break;
}
}
}
}
}
public boolean keyDown(java.awt.Event evt, int key)
{
```

```
if (key==114) // Restore
{
twisting=false;
naturalState=true;
for (i=0;i<54;i++)
sideCols[i]=i/9;
repaint();
}
else if (key==115) // Scramble
{
twisting=false;
naturalState=true;
for (i=0;i<20;i++)
colorTwist((int)(m.random()*6),(int)(m.random()*3+1));
repaint();
}
return false;
}
public boolean mouseDrag(java.awt.Event evt, int x, int y)
{
boolean check;
double x1,x2,y1,y2,alpha,beta;
if ((!twisting)&&(OKtoDrag))
{
OKtoDrag=false;
check=false;
for (i=0;i<dragReg;i++) // Check if inside a drag region
{
x1=dragCorn[i*8+1]-dragCorn[i*8];
x2=dragCorn[i*8+5]-dragCorn[i*8+4];
y1=dragCorn[i*8+3]-dragCorn[i*8];
y2=dragCorn[i*8+7]-dragCorn[i*8+4];
alpha=(y2*(lastX-dragCorn[i*8])-y1*(lastY-dragCorn[i*8+4]))/
(x1*y2-y1*x2);
beta=(-x2*(lastX-dragCorn[i*8])+x1*(lastY-dragCorn[i*8+4]))/
(x1*y2-y1*x2);
if ((alpha>0)&&(alpha<1)&&(beta>0)&&(beta<1)) // We're in
{
currDragDir[0]=dragDir[i*2];
currDragDir[1]=dragDir[i*2+1];
d=currDragDir[0]*(x-lastX)+currDragDir[1]*(y-lastY);
d=d*d/((currDragDir[0]*currDragDir[0]+currDragDir[1]*currDragDir[1])*
((x-lastX)*(x-lastX)+(y-lastY)*(y-lastY)));
if (d>0.6)
{
check=true;
twistSide=nearSide[i];
i=100;
```

```
}
}
}
if (check) // We're twisting
{
if (naturalState) // The cube still hasn't been split up
{
cutUpCube();
naturalState=false;
}
twisting=true;
phi=0.02*(currDragDir[0]*(x-lastX)+currDragDir[1]*(y-lastY))/
m.sqrt(currDragDir[0]*currDragDir[0]+currDragDir[1]*currDragDir[1]);
repaint();
return false;
}
}
OKtoDrag=false;
if (!twisting) // Normal rotation
{
dx=lastX-x; // Vertical shift
copyVec(eX,0,temp,0);
scalMult(temp,0,((double)dx)*0.016);
addVec(temp,0,eye,0);
vecProd(eY,0,eye,0,eX,0);
normalize(eX,0);
normalize(eye,0);
dy=y-lastY; // Horizontal shift
copyVec(eY,0,temp,0);
scalMult(temp,0,((double)dy)*0.016);
addVec(temp,0,eye,0);
vecProd(eye,0,eX,0,eY,0);
normalize(eY,0);
normalize(eye,0);
lastX=x;
lastY=y;
repaint();
}
else // Twist, compute twisting angle phi
{
phi=0.02*(currDragDir[0]*(x-lastX)+currDragDir[1]*(y-lastY))/
m.sqrt(currDragDir[0]*currDragDir[0]+currDragDir[1]*currDragDir[1]);
repaint();
}
return false;
}
public boolean mouseDown(java.awt.Event evt, int x, int y)
{
```

```
lastX=x;
lastY=y;
OKtoDrag=true;
return false;
}
public boolean mouseUp(java.awt.Event evt, int x, int y)
{
int quads;
double qu;
if (twisting) // We have let go of the mouse when twisting
{
twisting=false;
phibase+=phi; // Save twist angle
phi=0;
qu=phibase;
while (qu<0)
qu+=125.662;
quads=((int)(qu*3.183));
if (((quads % 5)==0)||((quads % 5)==4)) // Close enough to a corner?
{
quads=((quads+1)/5) % 4;
if (colDir[twistSide]<0)
quads=(4-quads) % 4;
phibase=0;
naturalState=true; // Return the cube to its natural state
colorTwist(twistSide,quads); // and shift the colored fields
}
repaint();
}
return false;
}
public void colorTwist(int sideNum, int quads) // Shift colored
fields
{
int i,j,k,l=0;
k=quads*2; // quads = number of 90-degree multiples
for (i=0;i<8;i++)
{
buffer[k]=sideCols[sideNum*9+circleOrder[i]];
k=(k+1) % 8;
}
for (i=0;i<8;i++)
sideCols[sideNum*9+circleOrder[i]]=buffer[i];
k=quads*3;
for (i=0;i<4;i++)
{
for (j=0;j<4;j++)
if (nextSide[nextSide[sideNum*4+i]*4+j]==sideNum)
```

```
l=j;
for (j=0;j<3;j++)
{
switch(l)
{
case 0:
buffer[k]=sideCols[nextSide[sideNum*4+i]*9+j];
break;
case 1:
buffer[k]=sideCols[nextSide[sideNum*4+i]*9+2+3*j];
break;
case 2:
buffer[k]=sideCols[nextSide[sideNum*4+i]*9+8-j];
break;
case 3:
buffer[k]=sideCols[nextSide[sideNum*4+i]*9+6-3*j];
break;
default:
break;
}
k=(k+1) % 12;
}
}
k=0;
for (i=0;i<4;i++)
{
for (j=0;j<4;j++)
if (nextSide[nextSide[sideNum*4+i]*4+j]==sideNum)
l=j;
for (j=0;j<3;j++)
{
switch(l)
{
case 0:
sideCols[nextSide[sideNum*4+i]*9+j]=buffer[k];
break;
case 1:
sideCols[nextSide[sideNum*4+i]*9+2+3*j]=buffer[k];
break;
case 2:
sideCols[nextSide[sideNum*4+i]*9+8-j]=buffer[k];
break;
case 3:
sideCols[nextSide[sideNum*4+i]*9+6-3*j]=buffer[k];
break;
default:
break;
}
```

```
k++;
}
}
}

public void paint(Graphics g)
{
dragReg=0;
offGraphics.setColor(bgcolor); // Clear drawing buffer
offGraphics.fillRect(0,0,120,120);
if (naturalState)
fixBlock(eye,eX,eY,corners,mainBlocks,0); // Draw cube
else
{
copyVec(eye,0,Teye,0); // In twisted state? Compute top observer
copyVec(eX,0,TeX,0);
Cphi=m.cos(phi+phibase);
Sphi=-m.sin(phi+phibase);
switch(twistSide) // Twist around which axis?
{
case 0: // z
Teye[0]=Cphi*eye[0]+Sphi*eye[1];
TeX[0]=Cphi*eX[0]+Sphi*eX[1];
Teye[1]=-Sphi*eye[0]+Cphi*eye[1];
TeX[1]=-Sphi*eX[0]+Cphi*eX[1];
break;
case 1: // -z
Teye[0]=Cphi*eye[0]-Sphi*eye[1];
TeX[0]=Cphi*eX[0]-Sphi*eX[1];
Teye[1]=Sphi*eye[0]+Cphi*eye[1];
TeX[1]=Sphi*eX[0]+Cphi*eX[1];
break;
case 2: // -y
Teye[0]=Cphi*eye[0]-Sphi*eye[2];
TeX[0]=Cphi*eX[0]-Sphi*eX[2];
Teye[2]=Sphi*eye[0]+Cphi*eye[2];
TeX[2]=Sphi*eX[0]+Cphi*eX[2];
break;
case 3: // x
Teye[1]=Cphi*eye[1]+Sphi*eye[2];
TeX[1]=Cphi*eX[1]+Sphi*eX[2];
Teye[2]=-Sphi*eye[1]+Cphi*eye[2];
TeX[2]=-Sphi*eX[1]+Cphi*eX[2];
break;
case 4: // y
Teye[0]=Cphi*eye[0]+Sphi*eye[2];
TeX[0]=Cphi*eX[0]+Sphi*eX[2];
Teye[2]=-Sphi*eye[0]+Cphi*eye[2];
```

```
TeX[2]=-Sphi*eX[0]+Cphi*eX[2];
break;
case 5: // -x
Teye[1]=Cphi*eye[1]-Sphi*eye[2];
TeX[1]=Cphi*eX[1]-Sphi*eX[2];
Teye[2]=Sphi*eye[1]+Cphi*eye[2];
TeX[2]=Sphi*eX[1]+Cphi*eX[2];
break;
default:
break;
}
vecProd(Teye,0,TeX,0,TeY,0);
if (scalProd(eye,0,sideVec,twistSide*3)<0) // Top facing away? Draw
it first
{
fixBlock(Teye,TeX,TeY,topCorners,topBlocks,2);
fixBlock(eye,eX,eY,botCorners,botBlocks,1);
}
else
{
fixBlock(eye,eX,eY,botCorners,botBlocks,1);
fixBlock(Teye,TeX,TeY,topCorners,topBlocks,2);
}
}
g.drawImage(offImage,0,0,this);
}
public void update(Graphics g)
{
paint(g);
}
// Draw cube or sub-cube
public void fixBlock(double beye[],double beX[],double beY[],
double bcorners[],int bblocks[],int mode)
{
copyVec(beye,0,light,0);
scalMult(light,0,-3);
addVec(beX,0,light,0);
subVec(beY,0,light,0);
for (i=0;i<8;i++) // Project 3D co-ordinates into 2D screen ones
{
newCoord[i*2]=(60+35.1*scalProd(bcorners,i*3,beX,0));
newCoord[i*2+1]=(60-35.1*scalProd(bcorners,i*3,beY,0));
}
for (i=0;i<6;i++)
{
if (scalProd(beye,0,sideVec,3*i)>0.001) // Face towards us? Draw
it.
{
```

```
k=(int)(9.6*(1-cosAng(light,0,sideVec,3*i)));
offGraphics.setColor(Color.black);
for (j=0;j<4;j++) // Find corner co-ordinates
{
rectX[j]=(int)newCoord[2*sides[i*4+j]];
rectY[j]=(int)newCoord[2*sides[i*4+j]+1];
}
offGraphics.fillPolygon(rectX,rectY,4); // First draw black
sideW=bblocks[i*4+1]-bblocks[i*4];
sideH=bblocks[i*4+3]-bblocks[i*4+2];
if (sideW>0)
{
sx=newCoord[2*sides[i*4]];
sy=newCoord[2*sides[i*4]+1];
sdxh=(newCoord[2*sides[i*4+1]]-sx)/sideW;
sdxv=(newCoord[2*sides[i*4+3]]-sx)/sideH;
sdyh=(newCoord[2*sides[i*4+1]+1]-sy)/sideW;
sdyv=(newCoord[2*sides[i*4+3]+1]-sy)/sideH;
p=bblocks[i*4+2];
for (n=0;n<sideH;n++) // Then draw colored fields
{
q=bblocks[i*4];
for (o=0;o<sideW;o++)
{
rectX[0]=(int)(sx+(o+0.1)*sdxh+(n+0.1)*sdxv);
rectX[1]=(int)(sx+(o+0.9)*sdxh+(n+0.1)*sdxv);
rectX[2]=(int)(sx+(o+0.9)*sdxh+(n+0.9)*sdxv);
rectX[3]=(int)(sx+(o+0.1)*sdxh+(n+0.9)*sdxv);
rectY[0]=(int)(sy+(o+0.1)*sdyh+(n+0.1)*sdyv);
rectY[1]=(int)(sy+(o+0.9)*sdyh+(n+0.1)*sdyv);
rectY[2]=(int)(sy+(o+0.9)*sdyh+(n+0.9)*sdyv);
rectY[3]=(int)(sy+(o+0.1)*sdyh+(n+0.9)*sdyv);
offGraphics.setColor(colList[20*sideCols[i*9+p*3+q]+k]);
offGraphics.fillPolygon(rectX,rectY,4);
q++;
}
p++;
}
}
switch (mode) // Determine allowed drag regions and directions
{
case 0: // Just the normal cube
t1=sx;
t2=sy;
t3=sdxh;
t4=sdyh;
t5=sdxv;
t6=sdyv;
```

```
for (j=0;j<4;j++)
{
dragCorn[8*dragReg]=t1;
dragCorn[8*dragReg+4]=t2;
dragCorn[8*dragReg+3]=t1+t5;
dragCorn[8*dragReg+7]=t2+t6;
t1=t1+t3*3;
t2=t2+t4*3;
dragCorn[8*dragReg+1]=t1;
dragCorn[8*dragReg+5]=t2;
dragCorn[8*dragReg+2]=t1+t5;
dragCorn[8*dragReg+6]=t2+t6;
dragDir[dragReg*2]=t3*twistDir[i*4+j];
dragDir[dragReg*2+1]=t4*twistDir[i*4+j];
d=t3;
t3=t5;
t5=-d;
d=t4;
t4=t6;
t6=-d;
nearSide[dragReg]=nextSide[i*4+j];
dragReg++;
}
break;
case 1: // The large sub-cube
break;
case 2: // The small sub-cube (twistable part)
if ((i!=twistSide)&&(sideW>0))
{
if (sideW==3) // Determine positive drag direction
if (bblocks[i*4+2]==0)
{
dragDir[dragReg*2]=sdxh*twistDir[i*4];
dragDir[dragReg*2+1]=sdyh*twistDir[i*4];
}
else
{
dragDir[dragReg*2]=-sdxh*twistDir[i*4+2];
dragDir[dragReg*2+1]=-sdyh*twistDir[i*4+2];
}
else
if (bblocks[i*4]==0)
{
dragDir[dragReg*2]=-sdxv*twistDir[i*4+3];
dragDir[dragReg*2+1]=-sdyv*twistDir[i*4+3];
}
else
{
```

```
dragDir[dragReg*2]=sdxv*twistDir[i*4+1];
dragDir[dragReg*2+1]=sdyv*twistDir[i*4+1];
}
for (j=0;j<4;j++)
{
dragCorn[dragReg*8+j]=newCoord[2*sides[i*4+j]];
dragCorn[dragReg*8+4+j]=newCoord[2*sides[i*4+j]+1];
}
nearSide[dragReg]=twistSide;
dragReg++;
}
break;
default:
break;
}
}
}
}
}
```

Example of Animation Applet

Fig. 15.6

Example 15.8 Fireworks Applet

The byte code of the applet includes two modules: Firework.class, Rocket.class.

The soundtrack file: fire.au

The source code: Firework.java

The setting of the parameters:

AnimationSpeed: the speed of the firework animation (1~100)

RocketSoundtrack: the soundtrack to effect when each rocket is fired (*.au)

RocketStyleVariability: the style variability of the rockets (1~100)

MaxRocketNumber: the max number of the rockets in the viewport (>=1)

MaxRocketExplosionEnergy: the max explosion energy of the rockets (>=1)

MaxRocketPatchNumber: the max number of the patches generated from rocket explosion (>=1)

MaxRocketPatchLength: the max track length of the patches from rocket explosion (>=1)

Gravity: the gravity (>=1)

```
/* "Firework.java", 1996.4.4 by Sid */
import java.applet.*;
import java.awt.*;
import java.lang.*;
import java.util.*;
import java.net.*;

public class Firework extends Applet implements Runnable
{
public int AnimationSpeed,
RocketStyleVariability,
MaxRocketNumber,
MaxRocketExplosionEnergy,
MaxRocketPatchNumber,
MaxRocketPatchLength,
Gravity;
public String RocketSoundtrack;

private int mx,my;
private Thread thread=null;

private Rocket rocket[];

public void init()
{
int i;
String p;

p=getParameter("AnimationSpeed");
AnimationSpeed=(p==null)?100:Integer.valueOf(p).intValue();

RocketSoundtrack=getParameter("RocketSoundtrack");

p=getParameter("RocketStyleVariability");
RocketStyleVariability=(p==null)?20:Integer.valueOf(p).intValue();

p=getParameter("MaxRocketNumber");
MaxRocketNumber=(p==null)?5:Integer.valueOf(p).intValue();

p=getParameter("MaxRocketExplosionEnergy");
MaxRocketExplosionEnergy=(p==null)?500:Integer.valueOf(p).intValue();

p=getParameter("MaxRocketPatchNumber");
MaxRocketPatchNumber=(p==null)?50:Integer.valueOf(p).intValue();
```

```
p=getParameter("MaxRocketPatchLength");
MaxRocketPatchLength=(p==null)?100:Integer.valueOf(p).intValue();

p=getParameter("Gravity");
Gravity=(p==null)?20:Integer.valueOf(p).intValue();

mx=size().width-1;
my=size().height-1;

rocket=new Rocket[MaxRocketNumber];
for(i=0;i<MaxRocketNumber;i++)rocket[i]=new Rocket(mx,my,Gravity);
}
public void start()
{
if(thread==null)
{
thread=new Thread(this);
thread.start();
}
}
public void stop()
{
if(thread!=null)
{
thread.stop();
thread=null;
}
}
public void run()
{
int i,
e=(int)(Math.random()*MaxRocketExplosionEnergy*3/4)+
MaxRocketExplosionEnergy/4+1,
p=(int)(Math.random()*MaxRocketPatchNumber*3/4)+
MaxRocketPatchNumber/4+1,
l=(int)(Math.random()*MaxRocketPatchLength*3/4)+
MaxRocketPatchLength/4+1;
long s=(long)(Math.random()*10000);
boolean sleep;
Graphics g=getGraphics();
URL u=null;

while(true)
{
try {
thread.sleep(100/AnimationSpeed);
}
```

```
catch(InterruptedException x){}

sleep=true;
for(i=0;i<MaxRocketNumber;i++)
sleep=sleep&&rocket[i].sleep;
if(sleep&&Math.random()*100<RocketStyleVariability)
{
e=(int)(Math.random()*MaxRocketExplosionEnergy*3/4)+
MaxRocketExplosionEnergy/4+1;
p=(int)(Math.random()*MaxRocketPatchNumber*3/4)+
MaxRocketPatchNumber/4+1;
l=(int)(Math.random()*MaxRocketPatchLength*3/4)+
MaxRocketPatchLength/4+1;
s=(long)(Math.random()*10000);
}

for(i=0;i<MaxRocketNumber;i++)
{
if(rocket[i].sleep&&Math.random()*MaxRocketNumber*l<1)
{
try {
u=new URL(getDocumentBase(),RocketSoundtrack);
}
catch(MalformedURLException x){}
play(u);

rocket[i].init(e,p,l,s);
rocket[i].start();
}
rocket[i].show(g);
}
}
}
public void paint(Graphics g)
{
g.setColor(Color.black);
g.fillRect(0,0,mx+1,my+1);
}
}

class Rocket
{
public boolean sleep=true;

private int energy,patch,length,
mx,my,
gravity,
ox,oy,
```

```
vx[],vy[],
x,y,
red,blue,green,
t;
private Random random;

public Rocket(int a,int b,int g)
{
mx=a;
my=b;

gravity=g;
}
public void init(int e,int p,int l,long seed)
{
int i;
energy=e;
patch=p;
length=l;

random=new Random(seed);

vx=new int[patch];
vy=new int[patch];

red=(int)(random.nextDouble()*128)+128;
blue=(int)(random.nextDouble()*128)+128;
green=(int)(random.nextDouble()*128)+128;

ox=(int)(Math.random()*mx/2)+mx/4;
oy=(int)(Math.random()*my/2)+my/4;

for(i=0;i<patch;i++)
{
vx[i]=(int)(Math.random()*energy)-energy/2;
vy[i]=(int)(Math.random()*energy*7/8)-energy/8;
}
}
public void start()
{
t=0;
sleep=false;
}
public void show(Graphics g)
{
if(!sleep)
if(t<length)
{
```

```
int i,c;
double s;
Color color;

c=(int)(random.nextDouble()*64)-32+red;
if(c>=0&&c<256)red=c;
c=(int)(random.nextDouble()*64)-32+blue;
if(c>=0&&c<256)blue=c;
c=(int)(random.nextDouble()*64)-32+green;
if(c>=0&&c<256)green=c;
color=new Color(red,blue,green);

for(i=0;i<patch;i++)
{
s=(double)t/100;
x=(int)(vx[i]*s);
y=(int)(vy[i]*s-gravity*s*s);

g.setColor(color);
g.drawLine(ox+x,oy-y,ox+x,oy-y);

if(t>=length/2)
{
int j;
for(j=0;j<2;j++)
{
s=(double)((t-length/2)*2+j)/100;
x=(int)(vx[i]*s);
y=(int)(vy[i]*s-gravity*s*s);

g.setColor(Color.black);
g.drawLine(ox+x,oy-y,ox+x,oy-y);
}
}
}

t++;
}
else
{
sleep=true;
}
}
}
```

Frog application

```
import java.awt.*;
import java.awt.image.*;
```

```
import java.net.*;
public final class frog extends java.applet.Applet implements Runnable
{
int
i,j,k,counter=0,flyX[],flyY[],flyOldX[],flyOldY[],flyDx[],flyDy[];
int nearX,nearY,nearNum,eatDx,eatDy;
int eatState=0;
int
flyBaseX[],flyBaseY[],tongueX[]={18,22,0,0},tongueY[]={27,28,0,0};
double tongue;
boolean flyOn[]={false,false,false,false,false};
int currHead=0;
final int headList[]={0,1,2,3,2,1};
double headcount=0;
Image collection,offImage,frog,frogheads[],legs,flies[];
Graphics offGraphics;
MediaTracker tracker;
ImageFilter filter;
Thread updateThread;
Math m;

public void init()
{
offImage=createImage(96,60);
offGraphics=offImage.getGraphics();
tracker=new MediaTracker(this);
collection = getImage(getCodeBase(),"froggies.gif");
tracker.addImage(collection,0);
try
{
tracker.waitForID(0);
}
catch(InterruptedException e) {}

frogheads=new Image[8];
flies=new Image[3];
filter=new CropImageFilter(0,0,96,60);
frog=createImage(new
FilteredImageSource(collection.getSource(),filter));
tracker.addImage(frog,1);
for (i=0;i<4;i++)
for (j=0;j<2;j++)
{
filter=new CropImageFilter(j*48,60+i*40,48,40);
frogheads[i*2+j]=createImage(new FilteredImageSource(
collection.getSource(),filter));
tracker.addImage(frogheads[i*2+j],1);
}
```

```
filter=new CropImageFilter(48,40,48,20);
l e g s = c r e a t e I m a g e ( n e w
FilteredImageSource(collection.getSource(),filter));
tracker.addImage(legs,1);
for (j=0;j<3;j++)
{
filter=new CropImageFilter(j*13,220,13,8);
flies[j]=createImage(new FilteredImageSource(
collection.getSource(),filter));
tracker.addImage(flies[j],1);
}
flyX=new int[5];
flyY=new int[5];
flyOldX=new int[5];
flyOldY=new int[5];
flyDx=new int[5];
flyDy=new int[5];
flyBaseX=new int[5];
flyBaseY=new int[5];

try
{
tracker.waitForID(1);
}
catch(InterruptedException e) {}

resize(500,60);
}

public void run()
{
while (updateThread !=null)
{
try
{
updateThread.sleep(75);
} catch (InterruptedException e) {}
counter=(counter+1)% 30;
nearX=500;
nearY=0;
nearNum=-1;
for (j=0;j<5;j++)
{
if (flyOn[j]) // Fly active?
{
flyOldX[j]=flyX[j];
flyOldY[j]=flyY[j];
if (counter==j)          // Pick new homing target
```

```
flyBaseX[j]=(int)(100+m.random()*400);
if (counter==(j+10))
flyBaseY[j]=(int)(16+m.random()*19);

if ((flyX[j]<flyBaseX[j])&&(flyDx[j]<11)) // Accelerate
flyDx[j]+=2;
else if ((flyX[j]>flyBaseX[j])&&(flyDx[j]>-11))
flyDx[j]-=2;
if ((flyY[j]<flyBaseY[j])&&(flyDy[j]<7))
flyDy[j]+=2;
else if ((flyY[j]>flyBaseY[j])&&(flyDy[j]>-7))
flyDy[j]-=2;
flyX[j]+=flyDx[j]; // Update location
flyY[j]+=flyDy[j];
if (flyX[j]<nearX) // See if this one is nearest to frog
{
nearX=flyX[j];
nearY=flyY[j];
nearNum=j;
}
}
else // Fly inactive?
{
if (m.random()<0.01) // Start new one?
{
flyX[j]=500;
flyY[j]=25;
flyBaseY[j]=25;
flyDx[j]=0;
flyDy[j]=0;
flyOn[j]=true;
}
}
}
switch (eatState)
{
case 0: // Normal
headcount+=0.003*(700-nearX); // Breathe faster when fly is close
if (headcount>12)
headcount-=6;
currHead=headList[((int)headcount)% 6];

if ((nearX>96)&&(nearX<130)&&(nearY<40)&&(nearY>6)) // Catch?
{
eatState=1;
eatDx=nearX-59;
eatDy=nearY-22;
tongue=1;
```

```
flyOn[nearNum]=false;
currHead=4;
}
break;
case 1: // Tongue out
tongue=tongue-0.3;
if (tongue<0)
{
eatState=2;
headcount=0;
currHead=5;
}
break;
case 2: // Swallowing
headcount+=0.1;
if (headcount<0.6)
currHead=5;
else if (headcount<3.3)
currHead=6+(((int)(headcount*2))&1);
else if (headcount<4.4)
currHead=5;
else
eatState=0;
break;
default:
break;
}
repaint();
}
}

public void start()
{
if (updateThread==null)
{
updateThread=new Thread(this,"Flies");
updateThread.start();
}
}

public void stop()
{
if ((updateThread!=null)&&(updateThread.isAlive()))
{
updateThread.stop();
}
updateThread=null;
}
```

```
public void paint(Graphics g)
{
g.drawImage(frog,0,0,this);
}

public void update(Graphics g)
{
offGraphics.setColor(Color.lightGray);
offGraphics.fillRect(0,0,96,60);
offGraphics.drawImage(legs,0,40,this);
offGraphics.drawImage(frogheads[currHead],0,0,this);
if (eatState==1) // Draw tongue and fly at the end of it
{
offGraphics.setColor(Color.gray);
tongueX[2]=(int)(18+tongue*eatDx);
tongueY[2]=(int)(30+tongue*eatDy);
tongueX[3]=tongueX[2];
tongueY[3]=(int)(28+tongue*eatDy);
offGraphics.fillPolygon(tongueX,tongueY,4);
offGraphics.drawPolygon(tongueX,tongueY,4);
offGraphics.drawImage(flies[2],(int)(11+tongue*eatDx),(int)(25+tongue*eatDy),this);
}
g.setColor(Color.lightGray); // Clear rest of background
g.fillRect(144,0,356,60);
g.drawImage(offImage,48,0,this);
for (k=0;k<5;k++) // Draw flies
if (flyOn[k])
g.drawImage(flies[counter & 1],flyX[k],flyY[k],this);
}
}
```

15.11 Color

Color is a class in the AWT. Individual colors like red or mauve are instances of this class, java.awt.Color. Be sure to import it if you want to use other than the default colors. You create new colors using the same RGB triples that you use to set background colors on web pages. However you use decimal numbers instead of the hex values used by the bgcolor tag. For example medium gray is Color(127, 127, 127). Pure white is Color(255, 255, 255). Pure red is (255, 0, 0) and so on. As with any variable you should give your colors descriptive names. For instance

```
Color medGray = new Color(127, 127, 127);
Color cream = new Color(255, 231, 187);
Color lightGreen = new Color(0, 55, 0);
```

A few of the most common colors are available by name. These are

```
Color.black
Color.blue
Color.cyan
Color.darkGray
```

```
Color.gray
Color.green
Color.lightGray
Color.magenta
Color.orange
Color.pink
Color.red
Color.white
Color.yellow
```

15.11.1 System Colors

In Java 1.1, the java.awt.SystemColor class is a subclass of java.awt.Color which provides color constants that match native component colors. For example, if you wanted to make the background color of your applet, the same as the background color of a window, you might use this init() method:

```
public void init {
this.setBackGround(SystemColor.window);
}
```

These are the available system colors:

```
SystemColor.desktop // Background color of desktop
SystemColor.activeCaption // Background color for captions
SystemColor.activeCaptionText // Text color for captions
SystemColor.activeCaptionBorder // Border color for caption text
SystemColor.inactiveCaption // Background color for inactive cap-
tions
SystemColor.inactiveCaptionText // Text color for inactive captions
SystemColor.inactiveCaptionBorder // Border color for inactive cap-
tions
SystemColor.window // Background for windows
SystemColor.windowBorder // Color of window border frame
SystemColor.windowText // Text color inside windows
SystemColor.menu // Background for menus
SystemColor.menuText // Text color for menus
SystemColor.text // background color for text
SystemColor.textText // text color for text
SystemColor.textHighlight // background color for highlighted text
SystemColor.textHighlightText // text color for highlighted text
SystemColor.control // Background color for controls
SystemColor.controlText // Text color for controls
SystemColor.controlLtHighlight // Light highlight color for con-
trols
SystemColor.controlHighlight // Highlight color for controls
SystemColor.controlShadow // Shadow color for controls
SystemColor.controlDkShadow // Dark shadow color for controls
SystemColor.inactiveControlText // Text color for inactive controls
SystemColor.scrollbar // Background color for scrollbars
SystemColor.info // Background color for spot-help text
SystemColor.infoText // Text color for spot-help text
```

15.12 Fonts

You've already seen one example of drawing text in the HelloWorldApplet program of the last chapter. You call the drawString() method of the Graphics object. This method is passed the String you want to draw as well as an x and y coordinate. If g is a Graphics object, then the syntax is

g.drawString(String s, int x, int y)

The String is simply the text you want to draw. The two integers are the x and y coordinates of the lower left-hand corner of the String. The String will be drawn above and to the right of this point. However letters with descenders like y and p may have their descenders drawn below the line.

Until now all the applets have used the default font, probably some variation of Helvetica though this is platform dependent. However unlike HTML Java does allow you to choose your fonts. Java implementations are guaranteed to have a serif font like Times that can be accessed with the name "Serif", a monospaced font like courier that can be accessed with the name "Mono", and a sans serif font like Helvetica that can be accessed with the name "SansSerif".

The following applet lists the fonts available on the system it's running on. It does this by using the getFontList() method from java.awt.Toolkit. This method returns an array of Strings containing the names of the available fonts. These may or may not be the same as the fonts installed on your system. It's implementation dependent whether or not all the fonts a system has are available to the applet.

```
import java.awt.*;
import java.applet.*;
public class FontList extends Applet
{
String[] availableFonts;
public void init () {
Toolkit t = Toolkit.getDefaultToolkit();
availableFonts = t.getFontList();
}
public void paint(Graphics g) {
for (int i = 0; i < availableFonts.length; i++) {
g.drawString(availableFonts[i], 5, 15*(i+1));
}
}
}
```

15.12.1 Choosing Font Faces and Sizes

Choosing a font face is easy. First you create a new Font object. Then you call g.setFont(Font f). To instantiate a Font object use this constructor:

public Font(String name, int style, int size)

name is the name of the font family, e.g. "Serif", "SansSerif", or "Mono".

size is the size of the font in points. In computer graphics a point is considered to be equal to one pixel. 12 points is a normal size font. 14 points is probably better on most computer displays. Smaller point sizes look good on paper printed with a high resolution printer, but not in the lower resolutions of a computer monitor.

style is an mnemonic constant from java.awt.Font that tells whether the text will be bold, italic or plain. The three constants are Font.PLAIN, Font.BOLD, and Font.ITALIC. The program below prints each font in its own face and 14 point bold.

```
import java.applet.*;
import java.awt.*;
public class FancyFontList extends Applet {
String[] availableFonts;
public void init () {
Toolkit t = Toolkit.getDefaultToolkit();
availableFonts = t.getFontList();
}
public void paint(Graphics g) {
for (int i = 0; i < availableFonts.length; i++) {
Font f = new Font(availableFonts[i], Font.BOLD, 14);
g.setFont(f);
g.drawString(availableFonts[i], 5, 15*i + 15);
}
}
}
```

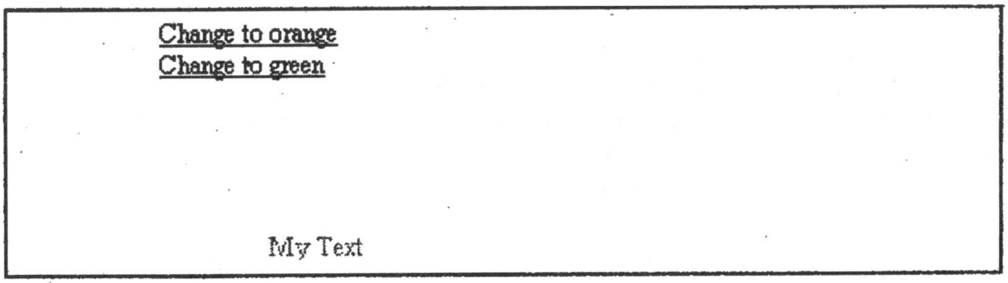

Fig. 15.7

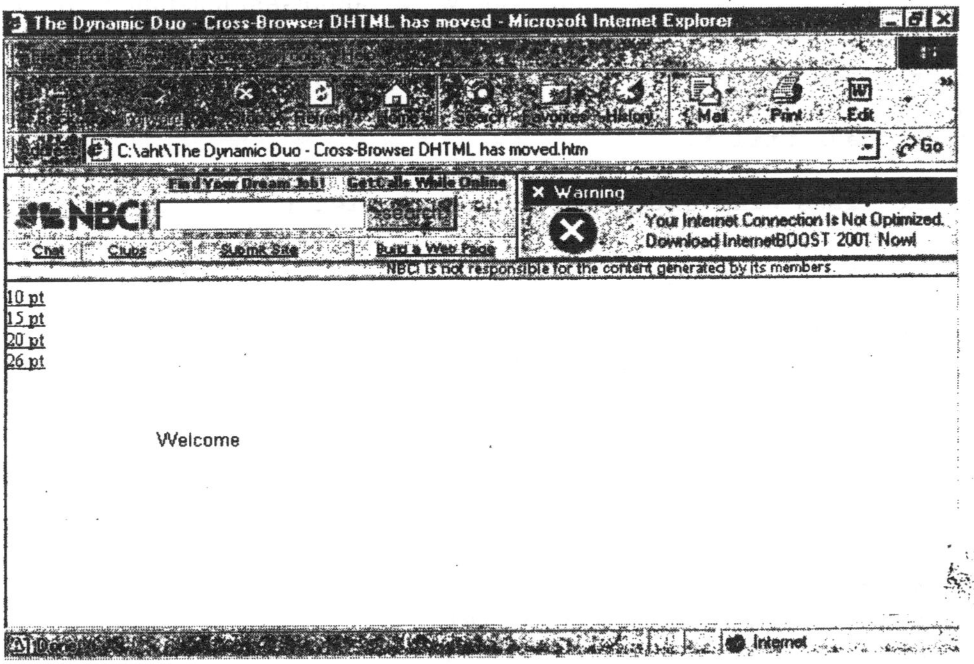

Fig. 15.8

15.12.2 Font Metrics

No word wrapping is done when you draw a string in an applet, even if you embed newlines in the string with \n. If you expect that a string may not fit in the applet, you should probably use a TextArea Component instead. You'll learn about text areas and other AWT Components next class. However there are times when you will need to concern yourself with how much space a particular string will occupy. You find this out with a FontMetrics object. FontMetrics allow you to determine the height, width or other useful characteristics of a particular string, character, or array of characters in a particular font.

As an example the following program expands on the DrawString applet. Previously text would run off the side of the page if the string was too long to fit in the applet. Now the string will wrap around if necessary.

In order to tell where and whether to wrap the String, you need to measure the string, not its length in characters which can be variable but rather its width and height in pixels. Measurements of this sort on strings clearly depend on the font that's used to draw the string. All other things being equal a 14 point string will be wider than the same string in 12 or 10 point type.

To measure character and string sizes you need to look at the FontMetrics of the current font. To get a FontMetrics object for the current Graphics object you use the java.awt.Graphics.getFontMetrics() method. From java.awt.FontMetrics you'll need fm.stringWidth(String s) to return the width of a string in a particular font, and fm.getLeading() to get the appropriate line spacing for the font. There are many more methods in java.awt.FontMetrics that let you measure the heights and widths of specific characters as well as ascenders, descenders and more, but these three methods will be sufficient for this program.

Finally you'll need the StringTokenizer class from java.util to split up the String into individual words. However you do need to be careful lest some annoying beta tester (or, worse yet, end user) tries to see what happens when they feed the word antidisestablishmentarianism or supercalifragilisticexpialidocious into an applet that's 50 pixels across.

```
import java.applet.*;
import java.awt.*;
import java.util.*;

public class WrapTextApplet extends Applet {

String inputFromPage;

public void init() {
this.inputFromPage = this.getParameter("Text");
}

public void paint(Graphics g) {

int i = 0;
int linewidth = 0;
int margin = 5;
StringBuffer sb = new StringBuffer();
FontMetrics fm = g.getFontMetrics();
```

```
StringTokenizer st = new StringTokenizer(inputFromPage);

while (st.hasMoreTokens()) {
String nextword = st.nextToken();
if (fm.stringWidth(sb.toString() + nextword) + margin <
this.getSize().width) {
sb.append(nextword);
sb.append(' ');
}
else if (sb.length() == 0) {
g.drawString(nextword, margin, ++i*fm.getHeight());
}
else {
g.drawString(sb.toString(), margin, ++i*fm.getHeight());
sb = new StringBuffer(nextword + " ");
}
}
if (sb.length() > 0) {
g.drawString(sb.toString(), margin, ++i*fm.getHeight());
}
}
}
```

15.13 Java 1.1 UI APIs

Java 1.1 has also added some important new functionality, including focus traversal, desktop color access, printing "inside the sandbox," and the beginnings of clipboard support.

Focus traversal is quite easy, since it's transparently present in the AWT library components and you don't have to do anything to make it work. If you make your own components and want them to handle focus traversal, you override isFocusTraversable( ) to return true. If you want to capture the keyboard focus on a mouse click, you catch the mouse down event and call requestFocus( ).

Desktop colors

The desktop colors provide a way for you to know what the various color choices are on the current user's desktop. This way, you can use those colors in your program if you desire. The colors are automatically initialized and placed in static members of class SystemColor, so all you need to do is read the member you're interested in. The names are intentionally self-explanatory: desktop, activeCaption, activeCaptionText, activeCaptionBorder, inactiveCaption, inactiveCaptionText, inactiveCaptionBorder, window, windowBorder, windowText, menu, menuText, text, textText, textHighlight, textHighlightText, textInactiveText, control, controlText, controlHighlight, controlLtHighlight, controlShadow, controlDkShadow, scrollbar, info (for help), and infoText (for help text).

EXERCISES

1. *Write a simple class called Message with a single public method that brings up a modal dialog with a user specified string message. The box should have a single button with the label "OK". When the button is pressed, the box is dismissed. This class should have a single static, public method with this signature:*

   public static void alert(String message, Frame parent)

   Use a layout manager of your choice to give the dialog a pleasing appearance.

2. *Revise the payroll applet from Class 6 so that an alert is displayed if the user enters a pay rate less than the minimum wage ($5.25 an hour).*

   To the Message class add an okCancel method similar to the last exercise with this signature:

   public static boolean alert(String message, Frame parent)

   This method should return true if the user presses the OK Button and false if they press the Cancel button. To the extent possible, there should be no other public methods in this class. (Methods you override from superclasses may have to be declared public.) Use a layout manager of your choice to give the dialog a pleasing appearance.

3. *Revise the payroll applet from Class 6 so that an alert is displayed if the user enters a pay rate less than the minimum wage ($5.25 an hour). If the user presses OK, the applet will calculate the total pay. Otherwise, it won't.*

   To the same message class add a third method that brings up a query dialog that has a TextField to allow the user to enter a single line of text, then returns the line of text. The method should have the following signature:

   public static String query(String question, Frame parent)

   The method should return whatever the user types in the box. To the extent possible, there should be no other public methods in this class. Use a layout manager of your choice to give the dialog a pleasing appearance.

4. *Revise the payroll applet from Class 6 so that if the user enters a pay rate less than the minimum wage ($5.25 an hour) or an incorrect pay rate (e.g. "Five dollars and 25 cents") the applet puts up a dialog asking for a new rate.*

All three exercises must be handed in. You should hand in a cover sheet with your name, ID#, URLs where the three applets can be found, and source code for each class. You should also provide screen shots of the applet running just in case the grader has trouble connecting to your web site.

16

Using AWT Controls, Layout Managers and Menus

16.1 Windowed Applications

It's possible to see that for safety's sake you can have only limited behavior within an applet. In a real sense, the applet is a temporary extension to the Web browser so its functionality must be limited along with its knowledge and control. There are times, however, when you'd like to make a windowed program do something else than sit on a Web page, and perhaps you'd like it to do some of the things a "regular" application can do and yet have the vaunted instant portability provided by Java. In previous chapters in this book we've made command-line applications, but in some operating environments (the Macintosh, for example) there isn't a command line. So for any number of reasons you'd like to build a windowed, non-applet program using Java. This is certainly a reasonable desire.

A Java windowed application can have menus and dialog boxes (impossible or difficult with an applet), and yet if you're using an older version of Java you sacrifice the native operating environment's look and feel. The JFC/Swing library allows you to make an application that preserves the look and feel of the underlying operating environment. If you want to build windowed applications, it makes sense to do so only if you can use the latest version of Java and associated tools so you can deliver applications that won't confound your users. If for some reason you're forced to use an older version of Java, think hard before committing to building a significant windowed application.

16.2 What is a Menu

Menus are composed of three hierarchical pieces. The menu bar contains the various menus. The menu bar is at the top of the screen on a Macintosh and in the top of the window in Windows and Motif.

Each menu bar contains one or more menus. Menus are organized topically. File would be one menu. Edit would be another.

Each menu contains one or more menu items. The menu items are the individual actions such as Open, Print, Cut or Copy. They are not shown except when the menu is active. No more than one menu will be active at a time.

This Edit menu has a disabled Undo menu item followed by a separator, followed by enabled Cut, Copy, paste and Clear menu items, followed by another separator, followed by an enabled Select All menu item.

16.3 The Menu Classes

The AWT contains four main classes to handle menus:

```
java.awt.Menu
```

```
java.awt.MenuBar
java.awt.MenuItem
java.awt.PopupMenu
```

To use menus in your application you need to add instances of all three classes, one MenuBar with one or more Menus, each with several MenuItems.

The java.awt.MenuComponent class is the ultimate superclass of all these classes. MenuComponent extends java.lang.Object. Thus menus, menu bars, and menu items are not components and cannot be added to containers in the usual fashion.

java.lang.Object

```
|
+—java.awt.MenuComponent
|
+—java.awt.MenuBar
|
+—java.awt.MenuItem
|
+—java.awt.Menu
|
+—java.awt.PopupMenu
```

Both MenuBar and MenuItem extend MenuComponent. Menu extends MenuItem. (This sounds a little strange, but if you think about it a menu is an item in a menu bar.) Furthermore, MenuBar implements the java.awt.MenuContainer interface.

16.4 Creating Menus

It's easiest to build the Menus before you display them. The typical order is

- ❑ Create a new MenuBar.
- ❑ Create a new Menu.
- ❑ Add items to the Menu.
- ❑ If necessary repeat steps 2 and 3.
- ❑ Add the MenuBar to the Frame.

The constructors you need are all simple. To create a new MenuBar object:

MenuBar myMenubar = new MenuBar();

To create a new Menu use the Menu(String title) constructor. Pass it the title of the menu you want. For example, to create File and Edit menus,

Menu fileMenu = new Menu("File");
Menu editMenu = new Menu("Edit");

MenuItems are created similarly with the MenuItem(String menutext) constructor. Pass it the title of the menu you want like this

MenuItem Cut = new MenuItem("Cut");

You can create MenuItems inside the Menus they belong to, just like you created widgets inside their layouts. Menu's have add methods that take an instance of MenuItem. Here's how you'd build an Edit Menu complete with Undo, Cut, Copy, Paste, Clear and Select All MenuItems:

```
Menu editMenu = new Menu("Edit");
```

```
editMenu.add(new MenuItem("Undo"));
editMenu.addSeparator();
editMenu.add(new MenuItem("Cut"));
editMenu.add(new MenuItem("Copy"));
editMenu.add(new MenuItem("Paste"));
editMenu.add(new MenuItem("Clear"));
editMenu.addSeparator();
editMenu.add(new MenuItem("Select All"));
```

The addSeparator() method adds a horizontal line across the menu. It's used to separate logically separate functions in one menu.

Once you've created the Menus, you add them to the MenuBar using the MenuBar's add(Menu m) method like this:

myMenubar.add(fileMenu);
myMenubar.add(editMenu);

Finally when the MenuBar is fully loaded, you add the Menu to a Frame using the frame's setMenuBar(MenuBar mb) method. Given a Frame f this is how you would do it:

f.setMenuBar(myMenuBar);

16.5 Creating Menus

There's an alternative add() method in java.awt.Menu that accepts a string> as an argument. This string is just the label of the menu item. This method still creates new MenuItem objects. It just does it behind your back. Here's how it would be used

```
Menu editMenu = new Menu("Edit");
editMenu.add("Undo");
editMenu.addSeparator();
editMenu.add("Cut");
editMenu.add("Copy");
editMenu.add("Paste");
editMenu.add("Clear");
editMenu.addSeparator();
editMenu.add("Select All");
```

Example 16.1 A Menu Example

An application may have dozens, even hundreds of menu items. Cramming these all into the init() method gets confusing. It's customary to create separate methods that create each individual menu and add it to the MenuBar. This program creates two fairly standard menus, File and Edit.

```
import java.applet.*;
import java.awt.*;
public class MenuTester extends Applet {
public void init () {
Frame f = new Frame("Simple Window");
f.add("Center", new Label("Look at the Menus", Label.CENTER));
f.setSize(this.getSize().width, this.getSize().height);
f.setLocation(320,240);
MenuBar myMenuBar = new MenuBar();
this.makeFileMenu(myMenuBar);
```

```
this.makeEditMenu(myMenuBar);
f.setMenuBar(myMenuBar);
f.setVisible(true);
}
void makeEditMenu(MenuBar mb) {
Menu editMenu = new Menu("Edit");
editMenu.add("Undo");
editMenu.addSeparator();
editMenu.add("Cut");
editMenu.add("Copy");
editMenu.add("Paste");
editMenu.add("Clear");
mb.add(editMenu);
}
void makeFileMenu(MenuBar mb) {
Menu fileMenu = new Menu("File");
fileMenu.add("New");
fileMenu.add("Open...");
fileMenu.addSeparator();
fileMenu.add("Close");
fileMenu.add("Save");
fileMenu.add("Save As...");
fileMenu.addSeparator();
fileMenu.add("Page Setup...");
fileMenu.add("Print");
fileMenu.addSeparator();
fileMenu.add("Quit");
mb.add(fileMenu);
}
}
```

16.6 Menu Events

When the user selects a menu item, the menu item fires an ActionEvent. This will be picked up by any action listeners registered on the menul item. The action command is set to the text of the menu item selected.

For example, the following applet puts the text of each menu item selected in the TextField.

```
import java.applet.*;
import java.awt.*;
import java.awt.event.*;
public class ActiveMenuTester extends Applet implements ActionListener {
TextField theChoice = new TextField(20);
public void init () {
Frame f = new Frame("Simple Window");
f.add("North", new Label("Look at the Menus", Label.CENTER));
f.add("South", theChoice);
f.setSize(300,100);
```

```
f.setLocation(220,240);
MenuBar myMenuBar = new MenuBar();
this.makeFileMenu(myMenuBar);
this.makeEditMenu(myMenuBar);
f.setMenuBar(myMenuBar);
f.setVisible(true);
}
protected addItem(Menu m, String s) {
MenuItem mi = new MenuItem(s);
mi.addActionListener(this);
m.add(mi);
}
void makeEditMenu(MenuBar mb) {
Menu editMenu = new Menu("Edit");
addItem(editMenu, "Undo");
editMenu.addSeparator();
addItem(editMenu, "Cut");
addItem(editMenu, "Copy");
addItem(editMenu, "Paste");
addItem(editMenu, "Clear");
mb.add(editMenu);
}
void makeFileMenu(MenuBar mb) {
Menu fileMenu = new Menu("File");
addItem(fileMenu, "New");
addItem(fileMenu, "Open...");
fileMenu.addSeparator();
addItem(fileMenu, "Close");
addItem(fileMenu, "Save");
addItem(fileMenu, "Save As...");
fileMenu.addSeparator();
addItem(fileMenu, "Page Setup...");
addItem(fileMenu, "Print");
fileMenu.addSeparator();
addItem(fileMenu, "Quit");
mb.add(fileMenu);
}
public void actionPerformed(ActionEvent e) {
theChoice.setText(e.getActionCommand());
}
}
```

16.7 Menu Shortcuts

Menu shortcuts, also known as menu accelerators and command key equivalents, rarely accelerate anything. Nonetheless users often mistakenly think they do, and so a salable application needs them.

The java.awt.MenuShortcut class represents such a keyboard accelerator. This class has two constructors:

```
public MenuShortcut(int key)
public MenuShortcut(int key, boolean useShiftModifier)
```

In both cases the key argument is the raw keycode that will be used to invoke this menu item.

If useShiftModifier is true, then the shift key must be held down for this shortcut to be activated. useShiftModifier is false by default.

To add an accelerator key to a menu item, pass a MenuShortcut to the item's setShortcut() method. For example,

```
MenuShortcut pShortcut = KeyEvent.VK_P;
MenuItem mi = new MenuItem("Print...");
mi.setShortcut(pShortcut);
```

You can also just pass the shortcut to the MenuItem() constructor like this:

MenuShortcut pShortcut = KeyEvent.VK_P;

MenuItem mi = new MenuItem("Print...", pShortcut);

To remove a shortcut, the MenuItem's deleteShortcut() method; for example:

mi.deleteShortcut();

16.8 Popup Menus

You've already encountered the Choice class that implements a popup menu component. Choices are fixed in a particular location.

The PopupMenu class, on the other hand, is activated when the user holds the right mouse button or otherwise indicates that they want to pop up a menu. Typically this is used for context sensitive menus.

java.awt.PopupMenu is a subclass of of java.awt.Menu. For the most part you use it just like you use a regular menu. Items are added to it with the add(MenuItem mi) method, and user selections are responded to by installing an ActionListener on the MenuItem. For example, to build a popup menu with a number of URLs you might do this:

```
PopupMenu pm = new PopupMenu();
MenuItem mi = new MenuItem("http://www.javasoft.com/");
mi.addActionListener(URLActionListener);
pm.add(mi);
mi = new MenuItem("http://home.netscape.com/");
mi.addActionListener(URLActionListener);
pm.add(mi);
mi = new MenuItem("http://sunsite.unc.edu/javafaq");
mi.addActionListener(URLActionListener);
pm.add(mi);
MenuItem mi = new MenuItem("http://www.roaster.com/news/");
mi.addActionListener(URLActionListener);
pm.add(mi);
```

However PopupMenus don't belong to any particular MenuBar. Instead they're added to a component. For example, given a Frame f, you would install the PopupMenu pm in the frame by passing it to the frame's add() method, like so:

```
f.add(pm);
```

(Is this the same add() method used to add components to a frame?)

The exact trigger for popping up the menu is platform dependent. For example, on Windows a PopupMenu is triggered on right mouse button up. However, in Motif a PopupMenu is triggered on right mouse button down. Regardless of the exact sequence of events leading to a menu popping up, when the user makes a selection, when a MenuItem is selected an ActionEvent is fired to any listeners registered for that item.

A PopupMenu can be deinstalled from a component by passing it to the component's remove() method like this:

```
f.remove(pm);
```

No more than one PopupMenu can be installed in any given component. If a PopupMenu is installed in a container, then triggers over the container's components will also trigger the popup, provided the contained component has no popup of its own.

16.9 Menu Components

It's impossible to put a menu directly on an applet (in Java 1.0 and Java 1.1; the Swing library does allow it), so they're for applications. Go ahead, try it if you don't believe me and you're sure that it would make sense to have menus on applets. There's no setMenuBar( ) method in Applet and that's the way a menu is attached. (You'll see later that it's possible to spawn a Frame from within an Applet, and the Frame can contain menus.)

There are four different types of MenuComponent, all derived from that abstract class: MenuBar (you can have one MenuBar only on a particular Frame), Menu to hold one individual drop-down menu or submenu, MenuItem to represent one single element on a menu, and CheckboxMenuItem, which is derived from MenuItem and produces a checkmark to indicate whether that menu item is selected.

Unlike a system that uses resources, with Java and the AWT you must hand assemble all the menus in source code. Here are the ice cream flavors again, used to create menus:

```
//: Menu1.java
// Menus work only with Frames.
// Shows submenus, checkbox menu items
// and swapping menus.
import java.awt.*;

public class Menu1 extends Frame {
String[] flavors = { "Chocolate", "Strawberry",
"Vanilla Fudge Swirl", "Mint Chip",
"Mocha Almond Fudge", "Rum Raisin",
"Praline Cream", "Mud Pie" };
TextField t = new TextField("No flavor", 30);
MenuBar mb1 = new MenuBar();
Menu f = new Menu()File");
Menu m = new Menu("Flavors");
Menu s = new Menu("Safety");
// Alternative approach:
```

```
CheckboxMenuItem[] safety = {
new CheckboxMenuItem("Guard"),
new CheckboxMenuItem("Hide")
};
MenuItem[] file = {
new MenuItem("Open"),
new MenuItem("Exit")
};
// A second menu bar to swap to:
MenuBar mb2 = new MenuBar();
Menu fooBar = new Menu("fooBar");
MenuItem[] other = {
new MenuItem("Foo"),
new MenuItem("Bar"),
new MenuItem("Baz"),
};
Button b = new Button("Swap Menus");
public Menu1() {
for(int i = 0; i < flavors.length; i++) {
m.add(new MenuItem(flavors[i]));
// Add separators at intervals:
if((i+1) % 3 == 0)
m.addSeparator();
}
for(int i = 0; i < safety.length; i++)
s.add(safety[i]);
f.add(s);
for(int i = 0; i < file.length; i++)
f.add(file[i]);
mb1.add(f);
mb1.add(m);
setMenuBar(mb1);
t.setEditable(false);
add("Center", t);
// Set up the system for swapping menus:
add("North", b);
for(int i = 0; i < other.length; i++)
fooBar.add(other[i]);
mb2.add(fooBar);
}
public boolean handleEvent(Event evt) {
if(evt.id == Event.WINDOW_DESTROY)
System.exit(0);
else
return super.handleEvent(evt);
return true;
}
public boolean action(Event evt, Object arg) {
```

```
if(evt.target.equals(b)) {
MenuBar m = getMenuBar();
if(m == mb1) setMenuBar(mb2);
else if (m == mb2) setMenuBar(mb1);
}
else if(evt.target instanceof MenuItem) {
if(arg.equals("Open")) {
String s = t.getText();
boolean chosen = false;
for(int i = 0; i < flavors.length; i++)
if(s.equals(flavors[i])) chosen = true;
if(!chosen)
t.setText("Choose a flavor first!");
else
t.setText("Opening "+ s +". Mmm, mm!");
}
else if(evt.target.equals(file[1]))
System.exit(0);
// CheckboxMenuItems cannot use String
// matching; you must match the target:
else if(evt.target.equals(safety[0]))
t.setText("Guard the Ice Cream! " +
"Guarding is " + safety[0].getState());
else if(evt.target.equals(safety[1]))
t.setText("Hide the Ice Cream! " +
"Is it cold? " + safety[1].getState());
else
t.setText(arg.toString());
}
else
return super.action(evt, arg);
return true;
}
public static void main(String[] args) {
Menu1 f = new Menu1();
f.resize(300,200);
f.show();
}
} ///:~
```

In this program I avoided the typical long lists of add( ) calls for each menu because that seemed like a lot of unnecessary typing. Instead, I placed the menu items into arrays and then simply stepped through each array calling add( ) in a for loop. This makes adding or subtracting a menu item less tedious.

As an alternative approach (which I find less desirable since it requires more typing), the CheckboxMenuItems are created in an array of handles called safety; this is true for the arrays file and other as well.

This program creates not one but two MenuBars to demonstrate that menu bars can be actively swapped while the program is running. You can see how a MenuBar is made up of Menus, and each Menu is made up of MenuItems, CheckboxMenuItems, or even other Menus (which produce submenus). When a MenuBar is assembled it can be installed into the current program with the setMenuBar( ) method. Note that when the button is pressed, it checks to see which menu is currently installed using getMenuBar( ), then puts the other menu bar in its place.

When testing for "Open," notice that spelling and capitalization are critical, but Java signals no error if there is no match with "Open." This kind of string comparison is a clear source of programming errors.

The checking and un-checking of the menu items is taken care of automatically, but dealing with CheckboxMenuItems can be a bit surprising since for some reason they don't allow string matching. (Although string matching isn't a good approach, this seems inconsistent.) So you can match only the target object and not its label. As shown, the getState( ) method can be used to reveal the state. You can also change the state of a CheckboxMenuItem with setState( ).

You might think that one menu could reasonably reside on more than one menu bar. This does seem to make sense because all you're passing to the MenuBar add( ) method is a handle. However, if you try this, the behavior will be strange and not what you expect. (It's difficult to know if this is a bug or if they intended it to work this way.)

This example also shows what you need to do to create an application instead of an applet. (Again, because an application can support menus and an applet cannot directly have a menu.) Instead of inheriting from Applet, you inherit from Frame. Instead of init( ) to set things up, you make a constructor for your class. Finally, you create a main( ) and in that you build an object of your new type, resize it, and then call show( ). It's different from an applet in only a few small places, but it's now a standalone windowed application and you've got menus.

16.10 Dialog Boxes

A dialog box is a window that pops up out of another window. Its purpose is to deal with some specific issue without cluttering the original window with those details. Dialog boxes are heavily used in windowed programming environments, but as mentioned previously, rarely used in applets.

To create a dialog box, you inherit from Dialog, which is just another kind of Window, like a Frame. Unlike a Frame, a Dialog cannot have a menu bar or change the cursor, but other than that they're quite similar. A dialog has a layout manager (which defaults to BorderLayout) and you override action( ) etc., or handleEvent( ) to deal with events. One significant difference you'll want to note in handleEvent( ): when the WINDOW_DESTROY event occurs, you don't want to shut down the application! Instead, you release the resources used by the dialog's window by calling dispose( ).

In the following example, the dialog box is made up of a grid (using GridLayout) of a special kind of button that is defined here as class ToeButton. This button draws a frame around itself and, depending on its state, a blank, an "x," or an "o" in the middle. It starts out blank, and then depending on whose turn it is, changes to an "x" or an "o." However, it will also flip back and forth between "x" and "o" when you click on the button. (This makes the tic-tac-toe concept only slightly more annoying than it already is.) In addition, the dialog box can be set up for any number of rows and columns by changing numbers in the main application window.

```
//: ToeTest.java
// Demonstration of dialog boxes
// and creating your own components
import java.awt.*;
```

```
class ToeButton extends Canvas {
int state = ToeDialog.BLANK;
ToeDialog parent;
ToeButton(ToeDialog parent) {
this.parent = parent;
}
public void paint(Graphics  g) {
int x1 = 0;
int y1 = 0;
int x2 = size().width - 1;
int y2 = size().height - 1;
g.drawRect(x1, y1, x2, y2);
x1 = x2/4;
y1 = y2/4;
int wide = x2/2;
int high = y2/2;
if(state == ToeDialog.XX) {
g.drawLine(x1, y1, x1 + wide, y1 + high);
g.drawLine(x1, y1 + high, x1 + wide, y1);
}
if(state == ToeDialog.OO) {
g.drawOval(x1, y1, x1+wide/2, y1+high/2);
}
}
public boolean
mouseDown(Event evt, int x, int y) {
if(state == ToeDialog.BLANK) {
state = parent.turn;
parent.turn= (parent.turn == ToeDialog.XX ?
ToeDialog.OO : ToeDialog.XX);
}
else
state = (state == ToeDialog.XX ?
ToeDialog.OO : ToeDialog.XX);
repaint();
return true;
}
}

class ToeDialog extends Dialog {
// w = number of cells wide
// h = number of cells high
static final int BLANK = 0;
static final int XX = 1;
static final int OO = 2;
int turn = XX; // Start with x's turn
public ToeDialog(Frame parent, int w, int h) {
```

```
super(parent, "The game itself", false);
setLayout(new GridLayout(w, h));
for(int i = 0; i < w * h; i++)
add(new ToeButton(this));
resize(w * 50, h * 50);
}
public boolean handleEvent(Event evt) {
if(evt.id == Event.WINDOW_DESTROY)
dispose();
else
return super.handleEvent(evt);
return true;
}
}
public class ToeTest extends Frame {
TextField rows = new TextField("3");
TextField cols = new TextField("3");
public ToeTest() {
setTitle("Toe Test");
Panel p = new Panel();
p.setLayout(new GridLayout(2,2));
p.add(new Label("Rows", Label.CENTER));
p.add(rows);
p.add(new Label("Columns", Label.CENTER));
p.add(cols);
add("North", p);
add("South", new Button("go"));
}
public boolean handleEvent(Event evt) {
if(evt.id == Event.WINDOW_DESTROY)
System.exit(0);
else
return super.handleEvent(evt);
return true;
}
public boolean action(Event evt, Object arg) {
if(arg.equals("go")) {
Dialog d = new ToeDialog(
this,
Integer.parseInt(rows.getText()),
Integer.parseInt(cols.getText()));
d.show();
}
else
return super.action(evt, arg);
return true;
}
public static void main(String[] args) {
```

```
Frame f = new ToeTest();
f.resize(200,100);
f.show();
}
} ///:~
```

The ToeButton class keeps a handle to its parent, which must be of type ToeDialog. As before, this introduces high coupling because a ToeButton can be used only with a ToeDialog, but it solves a number of problems, and in truth it doesn't seem like such a bad solution because there's no other kind of dialog that's keeping track of whose turn it is. Of course, you can take another approach, which is to make ToeDialog.turn a static member of ToeButton. This eliminates the coupling, but prevents you from having more than one ToeDialog at a time. (More than one that works properly, anyway.)

The paint( ) method is concerned with the graphics: drawing the square around the button and drawing the "x" or the "o." This is full of tedious calculations, but it's straightforward.

A mouse click is captured by the overridden mouseDown( ) method, which first checks to see if the button has anything written on it. If not, the parent window is queried to find out whose turn it is and that is used to establish the state of the button. Note that the button then reaches back into the parent and changes the turn. If the button is already displaying an "x" or an "o" then that is flopped. You can see in these calculations the convenient use of the ternary if-else described in Chapter 3. After a button state change, the button is repainted.

The constructor for ToeDialog is quite simple: it adds into a GridLayout as many buttons as you request, then resizes it for 50 pixels on a side for each button. (If you don't resize a Window, it won't show up!) Note that handleEvent( ) just calls dispose( ) for a WINDOW_DESTROY so the whole application doesn't go away.

ToeTest sets up the whole application by creating the TextFields (for inputting the rows and columns of the button grid) and the "go" button. You'll see in action( ) that this program uses the less-desirable "string match" technique for detecting the button press (make sure you get spelling and capitalization right!). When the button is pressed, the data in the TextFields must be fetched, and, since they are in String form, turned into ints using the static Integer.parseInt( ) method. Once the Dialog is created, the show( ) method must be called to display and activate it.

You'll notice that the ToeDialog object is assigned to a Dialog handle d. This is an example of upcasting, although it really doesn't make much difference here since all that's happening is the show( ) method is called. However, if you wanted to call some method that existed only in ToeDialog you would want to assign to a ToeDialog handle and not lose the information in an upcast.

16.11 File Dialogs

Some operating systems have a number of special built-in dialog boxes to handle the selection of things such as fonts, colors, printers, and the like. Virtually all graphical operating systems support the opening and saving of files, however, and so Java's FileDialog encapsulates these for easy use. This, of course, makes no sense at all to use from an applet since an applet can neither read nor write files on the local disk. (This will change for trusted applets in newer browsers.)

The following application exercises the two forms of file dialogs, one for opening and one for saving. Most of the code should by now be familiar, and all the interesting activities happen in action( ) for the two different button clicks:

```
//: FileDialogTest.java
```

```
// Demonstration of File dialog boxes
import java.awt.*;
public class FileDialogTest extends Frame {
TextField filename = new TextField();
TextField directory = new TextField();
Button open = new Button("Open");
Button save = new Button("Save");
public FileDialogTest() {
setTitle("File Dialog Test");
Panel p = new Panel();
p.setLayout(new FlowLayout());
p.add(open);
p.add(save);
add("South", p);
directory.setEditable(false);
filename.setEditable(false);
p = new Panel();
p.setLayout(new GridLayout(2,1));
p.add(filename);
p.add(directory);
add("North", p);
}
public boolean handleEvent(Event evt) {
if(evt.id == Event.WINDOW_DESTROY)
System.exit(0);
else
return super.handleEvent(evt);
return true;
}
public boolean action(Event evt, Object arg) {
if(evt.target.equals(open)) {
// Two arguments, defaults to open file:
FileDialog d = new FileDialog(this,
"What file do you want to open?");
d.setFile("*.java"); // Filename filter
d.setDirectory("."); // Current directory
d.show();
String openFile;
if((openFile = d.getFile()) != null) {
filename.setText(openFile);
directory.setText(d.getDirectory());
} else {
filename.setText("You pressed cancel");
directory.setText("");
}
}
else if(evt.target.equals(save)) {
FileDialog d = new FileDialog(this,
```

```
"What file do you want to save?",
FileDialog.SAVE);
d.setFile("*.java");
d.setDirectory(".");
d.show();
String saveFile;
if((saveFile = d.getFile()) != null) {
filename.setText(saveFile);
directory.setText(d.getDirectory());
} else {
filename.setText("You pressed cancel");
directory.setText("");
}
}
else
return super.action(evt, arg);
return true;
}
public static void main(String[] args) {
Frame f = new FileDialogTest();
f.resize(250,110);
f.show();
}
} ///:~
```

For an "open file" dialog, you use the constructor that takes two arguments; the first is the parent window handle and the second is the title for the title bar of the FileDialog. The method setFile( ) provides an initial file name - presumably the native OS supports wildcards, so in this example all the .java files will initially be displayed. The setDirectory( ) method chooses the directory where the file selection will begin. (In general, the OS allows the user to change directories.)

The show( ) command doesn't return until the dialog is closed. The FileDialog object still exists, so you can read data from it. If you call getFile( ) and it returns null it means the user canceled out of the dialog. Both the file name and the results of getDirectory( ) are displayed in the TextFields.

The button for saving works the same way, except that it uses a different constructor for the FileDialog. This constructor takes three arguments and the third argument must be either FileDialog.SAVE or FileDialog.OPEN.

16.12 Layout Managers

The LayoutManager class lets you control the locations of individual widgets in Java applets. Since you're never sure how big an area you'll have to work with or how it will be shaped, most of the controls are relative in nature. That is you say this widget should be above that one or left aligned with the other one; but you don't say that this widget's upper left hand corner is at pixel (42, 65).

16.12.1 What is a Layout Manager?

When you add a component to an applet or a container, the container uses its layout manager to decide where to put the component. Different LayoutManager classes use different rules to place components.

java.awt.LayoutManager is an interface. Five classes in the java packages implement it:

- FlowLayout
- BorderLayout
- CardLayout
- GridLayout
- GridBagLayout

A FlowLayout arranges widgets from left to right until there's no more space left. Then it begins a row lower and moves from left to right again. Each component in a FlowLayout gets as much space as it needs and no more. A FlowLayout is useful for laying out buttons but not for much else. This is the default LayoutManager for applets and Panels (special Containers to aid with layouts about which you'll learn more very shortly).

A BorderLayout organizes an applet into North, South, East, West and Center sections. North, South, East and West are the rectangular edges of the applet. They're continually resized to fit the sizes of the widgets included in them. Center is whatever's left over in the middle.

A CardLayout breaks the applet into a deck of cards, each of which has its own LayoutManager. Only one card appears on the screen at a time. The user flips between cards, each of which shows a different set of Components. The common analogy is with HyperCard on the Mac and Toolbook on Windows. In Java this might be used for a series of data input screens, where more input is needed than can comfortably be fit on one screen.

A GridLayout divides an applet into a specified number of rows and columns which form a grid of cells, each equally sized and spaced. As Components are added to the layout they are placed in the cells, starting at the upper left hand corner and moving to the right and down the page. Each component is sized to fit into its cell. This tends to squeeze and stretch components unnecessarily. However the GridLayout is great for arranging Panels.

GridBagLayout is the most precise of the five AWT LayoutManagers. It's similar to the GridLayout, but components do not need to be the same size. Each component can occupy one or more cells of the layout. Furthermore components are not necessarily placed in the cells beginning at the upper left-hand corner and moving to the right and down.

In simple applets with just a few components you often need only one layout manager. In more complicated applets, however, you'll often split your applet into panels, lay out the panels according to a layout manager, and give each panel its own layout manager that arranges the components inside it.

16.12.2 Flow Layout

A FlowLayout arranges widgets from left to right until there's no more space left. Then it begins a row lower and moves from left to right again. Each component in a FlowLayout gets as much space as it needs and no more. A FlowLayout is useful for laying out buttons but not for much else.

FlowLayout is the default layout for java.awt.Panel which java.applet.Applet subclasses. Therefore you don't need to do anything special to create a FlowLayout in an applet. However you do need to use the following constructors if you want to use a FlowLayout in a Window.

LayoutManagers have constructors like any other class. The constructor for a FlowLayout is

```
public FlowLayout()
Thus to create a new FlowLayout object you write
FlowLayout fl;
fl = new FlowLayout();
```

```
As usual this can be shortened to
FlowLayout fl = new FlowLayout();
```

You tell an applet to use a particular LayoutManager instance by passing the object to the applet's setLayout() method like this:

this.setLayout(fl);

Most of the time setLayout() is called in the init() method. You normally just create the LayoutManager right inside the call to setLayout() like this

this.setLayout(new FlowLayout());

The following applet uses a FlowLayout to position a series of buttons that mimic the buttons on a tape deck.

```
import java.applet.*;
import java.awt.*;
public class TapeDeck extends Applet {
public void init() {
this.setLayout(new FlowLayout());
this.add( new Button("Play"));
this.add( new Button("Rewind"));
this.add( new Button("Fast Forward"));
this.add( new Button("Pause"));
this.add( new Button("Stop"));
}
}
```

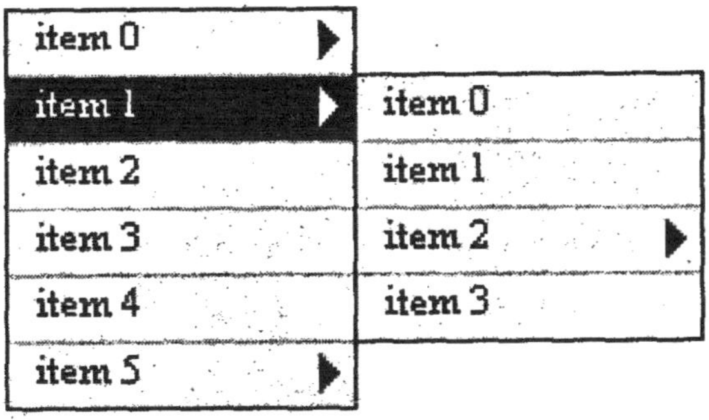

Fig. 16.1

FlowLayout

A LayoutManager rearranges the components in the container based on their size relative to the size of the container.

Consider the window that just popped up. It's got five buttons of varying sizes. Resize the window and watch how the buttons move. In particular try making it just wide enough so that all the buttons fit on one line. Then try making it narrow and tall so that there's only one button on line. See if you can manage to cover up some of the buttons. Then uncover them. Note that whatever you try to do, the order of the buttons is maintained in a logical way. Button 1 is always before button 2 which is always before button 3 and so on.

It's harder to show, but imagine if the components changed sizes, as they might if you viewed this page in different browsers or on different platforms with different fonts. The layout manager handles all these different cases for you to the greatest extent possible. If you'd used absolute positioning and the window were smaller than expected or the components larger than you expected, some components would likely be truncated or completely hidden. In essence a layout manager defers decisions about positioning until runtime.

16.12.3 Setting Flow Layout Alignment

You can change the alignment of a FlowLayout in the constructor. Components are normally centered in an applet. You can make them left or right justified instead. To do this just pass one of the defined constants FlowLayout.LEFT, FlowLayout.RIGHT or FlowLayout.CENTER to the constructor, e.g.

```
this.setLayout(new FlowLayout(FlowLayout.LEFT));
this.setLayout(new ElowLayout(FlowLayout.RIGHT));
this.setLayout(new FlowLayout(FlowLayout.CENTER));
Below you see all three variants:
```

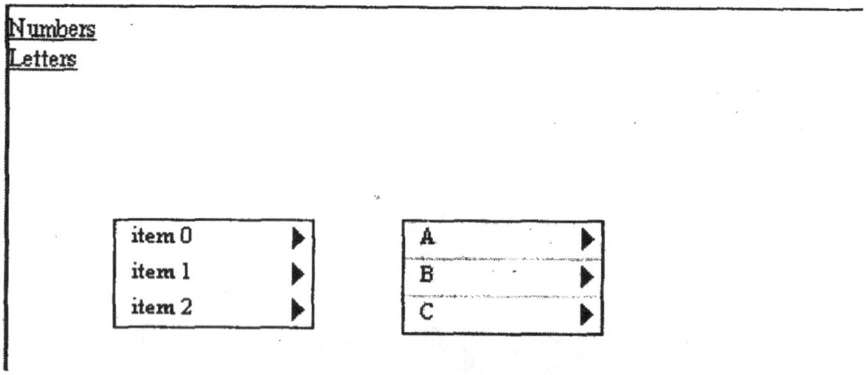

Fig. 16.2

A LayoutManager rearranges the components in the container based on their size relative to the size of the container.

Consider the window that just popped up. It's got five buttons of varying sizes. Resize the window and watch how the buttons move. In particular try making it just wide enough so that all the buttons fit on one line. Then try making it narrow and tall so that there's only one button on line. See if you can manage to cover up some of the buttons. Then uncover them. Note that whatever you try to do, the order of the buttons is maintained in a logical way. Button 1 is always before button 2 which is always before button 3 and so on.

It's harder to show, but imagine if the components changed sizes, as they might if you viewed this page in different browsers or on different platforms with different fonts. The layout manager handles all these different cases for you to the greatest extent possible. If you'd used absolute positioning and the window were smaller than expected or the components larger than you expected, some components would likely be truncated or completely hidden. In essence a layout manager defers decisions about positioning until runtime.

16.12.4 Separating Components with Space in a FlowLayout

Most LayoutManagers allow you to control the minimum amount of vertical and horizontal space between different components. To do this in a FlowLayout, you pass the horizontal and vertical space you want, in pixels, to the constructor immediately after the alignment argument.

```
public FlowLayout(int alignment, int hspace, int vspace);
```

For instance to set up a FlowLayout with a ten pixel horizontal gap and a twenty pixel vertical gap, aligned with the left edge of the panel, you would use the constructor

```
FlowLayout fl =  new FlowLayout(FlowLayout.LEFT, 20, 10);
```

Buttons arranged according to a center-aligned FlowLayout with a 20 pixel horizontal spacing and a 10 pixel vertical spacing

```
import java.applet.*;
import java.awt.*;
public class SpaceTapeDeck extends Applet {
public void init() {
this.setLayout( new FlowLayout(FlowLayout.LEFT, 20, 10));
this.add( new Button("Play"));
this.add( new Button("Rewind"));
this.add( new Button("Fast Forward"));
this.add( new Button("Pause"));
this.add( new Button("Stop"));
}
}
```

16.12.5 BorderLayout

A BorderLayout places objects in the North, South, East, West and center of an applet. You create a new BorderLayout object much like a FlowLayout object, in the init() method inside a call to setLayout like this:

```
this.setLayout(new BorderLayout());
```

There's no centering, left alignment, or right alignment in a BorderLayout. However, you can add horizontal and vertical gaps between the areas. Here's how you'd add a five pixel horizontal gap and a ten pixel vertical gap to a BorderLayout:

```
this.setLayout(new BorderLayout(5, 10));
```

To add components to a BorderLayout include the name of the section you wish to add them to like this

```
this.add("South", new Button("Start"));
A BorderLayout.
```

The rectangles were drawn deliberately so you could see the boundaries between sections and are not a feature of a generic BorderLayout.

As you can see from the above picture, the North and South sections extend across the applet from left to right. The East and West sections do not extend from the top of the applet to the bottom, but only from the bottom of the North section to the top of South section. The North, South, East and West sections will be made large enough for whatever components they hold. The center gets whatever is left over. The exact size is unpredictable. Similarly the exact packing of components inside a section is unpredictable as well.

Fig. 16.3

Example 17.1 BorderLayout

```
import java.applet.*;
import java.awt.*;
public class BorderButtons extends Applet {
public void init() {
this.setLayout(new BorderLayout(20, 10));
```

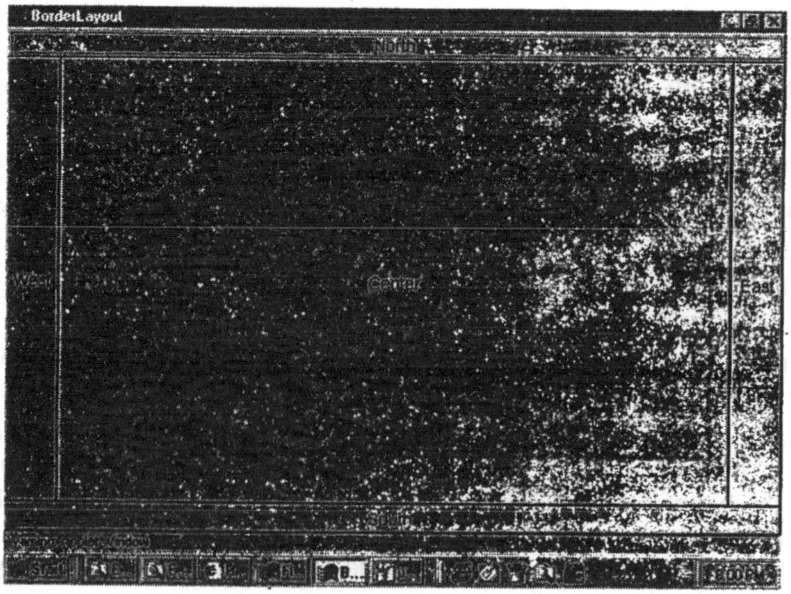

Fig. 16.4

```
this.add("North", new Button("North"));
this.add("South", new Button("South"));
```

```
this.add("Center", new Button("Center"));
this.add("East", new Button("East"));
this.add("West", new Button("West"));
}
}
```

16.12.6 Card Layout

The CardLayout is unusual. It breaks the applet into a deck of cards, each of which will normally have a panel with its own LayoutManager. Only one card appears on the screen at a time. You then flip between cards, each of which shows a different set of components. The common analogy is with HyperCard on the Mac and Toolbook on Windows. In Java this might be used for a series of data input screens, where more input is needed than can comfortably be fit on one screen. Conversely, you can use a CardLayout for a slide show, where there's more data to be presented than will fit on one screen.

For example, this CardTest applet, one of Sun's standard demo applets, uses a CardLayout to flip between different layouts for the same five buttons.

16.12.7 Using Card Layouts

You create a CardLayout with the CardLayout() constructor.

this.setLayout(new CardLayout());

As usual you can create a CardLayout with a specified gap between components like this.

this.setLayout(new CardLayout(3, 4));

In this example there will be a three pixel horizontal gap and a four pixel vertical gap between components.

Each card has a name. A new card is created when you add a component to the card. Add components to cards by passing the name of the card and the component to add to the add() method like this

```
this.setLayout(new CardLayout());
this.add("Pizza", new Label("How do you like your pizza?"));
this.add("Pizza", new Button("OK"));
this.add("Payment", new Label("How would you like to pay?"));
this.add("Payment", new Button("OK"));
this.add("Address", new Label("Delivery Instructions"));
this.add("Address", new Button("Order"));
One common technique is to name each card after a number.
this.setLayout(new CardLayout());
this.add("1", new Label("First Card"));
this.add("2", new Label("Second Card"));
this.add("3", new Label("Third Card"));
this.add("4", new Label("Fourth Card"));
this.add("5", new Label("Fifth Card"));
this.add("6", new Label("Sixth Card"));
```

Internally the list of cards and their names is stored in a java.util.Hashtable. This means that there's no guaranteed or built-in order to the cards. You need to keep track of this yourself.

Normally you add a panel with its own layout manager to each card. Each card should have some means for navigating between cards. The AWT does not provide one. Finally note that you can add the same component to more than one card. This is useful, for example, for creating a Choice menu with the names of all the cards as a navigation aid.

16.13 Grid Layout

A GridLayout specifies the number of rows and columns into which components will be placed. The applet is broken up into a table of equal sized cells.

GridLayout is useful when you want to place a number of similarly sized objects. It's great for putting together lists of checkboxes and radio buttons as you did in the Ingredients applet. Below is a modified version that sets aside eight rows and one column. This gives one row for each Checkbox. Compare the applet below to the one from Week 6 <../week6/19.html> to see how much nicer everything looks with proper use of a GridLayout.

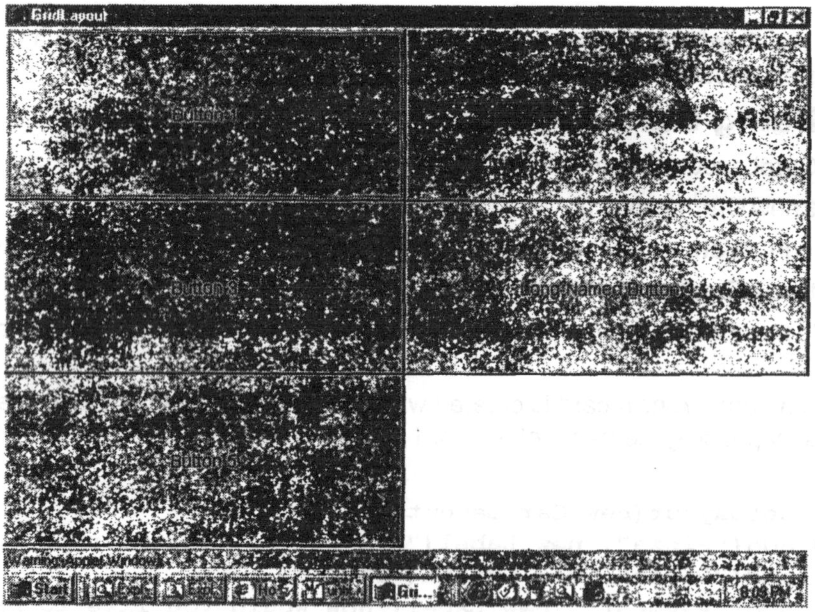

Fig. 16.5

GridLayout

Example 17.2

Here's the source code:

```
import java.applet.*;
import java.awt.*;
public class Ingredients2 extends Applet {
TextField t;
double price = 7.00;
public void init() {
this.setLayout(new GridLayout(11,1));
this.add(new Label("What do you want on your pizza?", Label.CENTER));
this.add(new Checkbox("Pepperoni"));
```

```
this.add(new Checkbox("Olives"));
this.add(new Checkbox("Onions"));
this.add(new Checkbox("Sausage"));
this.add(new Checkbox("Peppers"));
this.add(new Checkbox("Extra Cheese"));
this.add(new Checkbox("Ham"));
this.add(new Checkbox("Pineapple"));
this.add(new Checkbox("Anchovies"));
this.t = new TextField("$" + String.valueOf(price));
// so people can't change the price of the pizza
this.t.setEditable(false);
this.add(this.t);
}
/* I've removed the code to handle events
since it isn't relevant to this example, and since I haven't
had time to port it to 1.1 */
}
```

Grid layouts are very easy to use. This applet is just three lines different from the previous version and one of those is a change in the name of the class that wasn't really necessary.

16.13.1 Grid Bag Layout

The GridBagLayout provides a grid for components like GridLayout, but allows a single component element to occupy multiple cells of the grid. Each GridBagLayout uses a rectangular grid of cells, just like a GridLayout. However the cells are determined and shaped by the components placed in them rather than the components being shaped to fit the cells.

According to Peter van der Linden:

GridBagLayout was contributed to Javasoft by a programmer who wanted to support the Java effort. It was intended as a proof that the AWT offered enough features for programmers to write their own layout managers. It wasn't designed with human factors and ease of use in mind. If it bothers you (it bothers me) then just don't use it. Create your GUI on several panels and use the other layout managers as appropriate to get the exact effect you want. JavaSoft's AWT team project leader has said that eventually another layout manager will be added that does similar things to GBL, but is more intuitive. Bottom line: nobody has to waste any effort on GBL, there are better alternatives available.

16.13.2 Grid Bag Constraints

A GridBagConstraints object specifies the location and area of the component's display area within the container (normally the applet panel) and how the component is laid out inside its display area. The GridBagConstraints, in conjunction with the component's minimum size and the preferred size of the component's container, determines where the display area is placed within the applet.

The GridBagConstraints() constructor is trivial
GridBagConstraints gbc = new GridBagConstraints();

Your interaction with a GridBagConstraints object takes place through its eleven fields and fifteen mnemonic constants.

I'll demonstrate by showing you how to lay out this calculator. Notice that it has a TextField and 18 buttons of varying sizes, and naturally lends itself to a description as a grid.

The discussion assumes that you have imported all the necessary classes, particularly java.awt.GridBagLayout, java.awt.GridBagConstraints, java.awt.Button and java.awt.TextField. It also assumes you have created a GridBagConstraints object GBC_display like this

GridBagConstraints GBC_display = new GridBagConstraints();

16.13.3 A Grid for the Calculator

Here's a grid you can use to layout the calculator applet. Notice that there are more cells than there are components in the calculator. Some of the components in the calculator occupy more than one cell of the grid. For example, the TextField occupies the four cells (0, 0), (1, 0), (2, 0), and (3, 0).

```
(0, 0)  (1, 0)   (2, 0)   (3, 0)
(0, 1)  (1, 1)   (2, 1)   (3. 1)
(0, 2)  (1, 2)   (2, 2)   (3, 2)
(0, 3)  (1, 3)   (2, 3)   (3, 3)
(0, 4)  (1, 4)   (2, 4)   (3, 4)
(0, 5)  (1, 5)   (2, 5)   (3, 5)
```

16.13.4 Gridx and Gridy

The gridx and gridy fields specify the x and y coordinates of the cell at the upper left of the Component's display area. The upper-left-most cell has coordinates (0, 0). The mnemonic constant GridBagConstraints.RELATIVE specifies that the Component is placed immediately to the right of (gridx) or immediately below (gridy) the previous Component added to this container.

The calculator's display starts at the upper left hand corner of the applet. Thus its gridx and gridy members are set like this

GBC_display.gridx = 0;
GBC_display.gridy = 0;

The zero key would have

GBC_display.gridx = 0;
GBC_display.gridy = 5;

16.13.5 Gridwidth and Gridheight

The gridwidth and gridheight fields specify the number of cells in a row (gridwidth) or column (gridheight) in the Component's display area. The mnemonic constant GridBagConstraints.REMAINDER specifies that the Component should use all remaining cells in its row (for gridwidth) or column (for gridheight). The mnemonic constant GridBagConstraints.RELATIVE specifies that the Component should fill all but the last cell in its row (gridwidth) or column (gridheight).

The calculator's display is four cells wide and one cell high so it's set like this

GBC_display.gridwidth = 4;
GBC_display.gridheight = 1;

The equals key is two cells high and one wide so it's set like this

GBC_display.gridwidth = 1;
GBC_display.gridheight = 2;

16.13.6 Fill

The GridBagConstraints fill field determines whether and how a component is resized if the component's display area is larger than the component itself. The mnemonic constants you use to set this variable are

GridBagConstraints.NONE: Don't resize the component

GridBagConstraints.HORIZONTAL: Make the component wide enough to fill the display area, but don't change its height.

GridBagConstraints.VERTICAL: Make the component tall enough to fill its display area, but don't change its width.

GridBagConstraints.BOTH: Resize the component enough to completely fill its display area both vertically and horizontally.

For the display area of the calculator screen use

GBC_display.fill = GridBagConstraints.HORIZONTAL;

because you'd like the screen to show as many digits as it can.

16.13.7 Ipadx and Ipady

Each component has a minimum width and a minimum height, smaller than which it will not be. If the component's minimum size is smaller than the component's display area, then only part of the component will be shown.

The ipadx and ipady fields let you increase this minimum size by padding the edges of the component with extra pixels. For instance setting ipadx to two will guarantee that the component is at least four pixels wider than its normal minimum. (ipadx adds two pixels to each side.) This is not needed for the Calculator applet.

16.13.8 Insets

The insets field is an instance of the java.awt.Insets class. It specifies the padding between the component and the edges of its display area. For all the keys in the calculator applet the insets are set like this:

GBC_equals.insets = new Insets(3, 3, 3, 3);

which provides six pixels of space between each adjacent pair of keys (three from each key).

16.13.9 Anchor

When a component is smaller than its display area, the anchor field specifies where to place it in the grid cell. The mnemonic constants you use for this purpose are similar to those used in a BorderLayout but a little more specific. They are

```
GridBagConstraints.CENTER
GridBagConstraints.NORTH
GridBagConstraints.NORTHEAST
GridBagConstraints.EAST
GridBagConstraints.SOUTHEAST
GridBagConstraints.SOUTH
GridBagConstraints.SOUTHWEST
GridBagConstraints.WEST
GridBagConstraints.NORTHWEST
```

The default is GridBagConstraints.CENTER. This is not explicitly set in the calculator applet, because the components are large enough, relative to their display areas, that it really doesn't matter where they go and the default of center is fine.

16.13.10 Weightx and Weighty

The weightx and weighty fields determine how the cells are distributed in the container when the total size of the cells is less than the size of the container. With weights of zero (the default) the cells all have the minimum size they need, and everything clumps together in the center. All the extra space is pushed to the edges of the container.

Example 17.3 A GridBagLayout Example

Here's the init() method that lays out the calculator applet.

```
void init () {
GridBagLayout gbl = new GridBagLayout();
this.setLayout(gbl);
// Add the display to the top four cells
GridBagConstraints GBC_display = new GridBagConstraints();
GBC_display.gridx = 0;
GBC_display.gridy = 0;
GBC_display.gridwidth = 4;
GBC_display.gridheight = 1;
GBC_display.fill = GridBagConstraints.HORIZONTAL;

// add the text field
TextField display = new TextField(12);
gbl.setConstraints(display, GBC_display);
this.add(display);

// Add the clear button
GridBagConstraints GBC_clear = new GridBagConstraints();
GBC_clear.gridx = 0;
GBC_clear.gridy = 1;
GBC_clear.gridwidth = 1;
GBC_clear.gridheight = 1;
GBC_clear.fill = GridBagConstraints.BOTH;
GBC_clear.insets = new Insets(3, 3, 3, 3);

// add the button
Button clear = new Button("C");
gbl.setConstraints(clear, GBC_clear);
this.add(clear);

// Add the equals button
GridBagConstraints GBC_equals = new GridBagConstraints();
GBC_equals.gridx = 1;
GBC_equals.gridy = 1;
GBC_equals.gridwidth = 1;
GBC_equals.gridheight = 1;
GBC_equals.fill = GridBagConstraints.BOTH;
GBC_equals.insets = new Insets(3, 3, 3, 3);
```

```
// add the = button
Button equals = new Button("=");
gbl.setConstraints(equals, GBC_equals);
this.add(equals);

// Add the / button
GridBagConstraints GBC_slash = new GridBagConstraints();
GBC_slash.gridx = 2;
GBC_slash.gridy = 1;
GBC_slash.gridwidth = 1;
GBC_slash.gridheight = 1;
GBC_slash.fill = GridBagConstraints.BOTH;
GBC_slash.insets = new Insets(3, 3, 3, 3);

// add the button
Button slash = new Button("/");
gbl.setConstraints(slash, GBC_slash);
this.add(slash);

// Add the * button
GridBagConstraints GBC_times = new GridBagConstraints();
GBC_times.gridx = 3;
GBC_times.gridy = 1;
GBC_times.gridwidth = 1;
GBC_times.gridheight = 1;
GBC_times.fill = GridBagConstraints.BOTH;
GBC_times.insets = new Insets(3, 3, 3, 3);

// add the button
Button star = new Button("*");
gbl.setConstraints(star, GBC_times);
this.add(star);

// Add the 7 key
GridBagConstraints GBC_7 = new GridBagConstraints();
GBC_7.gridx = 0;
GBC_7.gridy = 2;
GBC_7.gridwidth = 1;
GBC_7.gridheight = 1;
GBC_7.fill = GridBagConstraints.BOTH;
GBC_7.insets = new Insets(3, 3, 3, 3);

// add the button
Button b7 = new Button("7");
gbl.setConstraints(b7, GBC_7);
this.add(b7);

// Add the 8 key
```

```
GridBagConstraints GBC_8 = new GridBagConstraints();
GBC_8.gridx = 1;
GBC_8.gridy = 2;
GBC_8.gridwidth = 1;
GBC_8.gridheight = 1;
GBC_8.fill = GridBagConstraints.BOTH;
GBC_8.insets = new Insets(3, 3, 3, 3);

// add the button
Button b8 = new Button("8");
gbl.setConstraints(b8, GBC_8);
this.add(b8);

// Add the 9 key
GridBagConstraints GBC_9 = new GridBagConstraints();
GBC_9.gridx = 2;
GBC_9.gridy = 2;
GBC_9.gridwidth = 1;
GBC_9.gridheight = 1;
GBC_9.fill = GridBagConstraints.BOTH;
GBC_9.insets = new Insets(3, 3, 3, 3);

// add the button
Button b9 = new Button("9");
gbl.setConstraints(b9, GBC_9);
this.add(b9);

// Add the - key
GridBagConstraints GBC_minus = new GridBagConstraints();
GBC_minus.gridx = 3;
GBC_minus.gridy = 2;
GBC_minus.gridwidth = 1;
GBC_minus.gridheight = 1;
GBC_minus.fill = GridBagConstraints.BOTH;
GBC_minus.insets = new Insets(3, 3, 3, 3);
// add the button
Button minus = new Button("-");
gbl.setConstraints(minus, GBC_minus);
this.add(minus);

// Add the 4 key
GridBagConstraints GBC_4 = new GridBagConstraints();
GBC_4.gridx = 0;
GBC_4.gridy = 3;
GBC_4.gridwidth = 1;
GBC_4.gridheight = 1;
GBC_4.fill = GridBagConstraints.BOTH;
GBC_4.insets = new Insets(3, 3, 3, 3);
```

```
// add the button
Button b4 = new Button("4");
gbl.setConstraints(b4, GBC_4);
this.add(b4);

// Add the 5 key
GridBagConstraints GBC_5 = new GridBagConstraints();
GBC_5.gridx = 1;
GBC_5.gridy = 3;
GBC_5.gridwidth = 1;
GBC_5.gridheight = 1;
GBC_5.fill = GridBagConstraints.BOTH;
GBC_5.insets = new Insets(3, 3, 3, 3);

// add the button
Button b5 = new Button("5");
gbl.setConstraints(b5, GBC_5);
this.add(b5);

// Add the 6 key
GridBagConstraints GBC_6 = new GridBagConstraints();
GBC_6.gridx = 2;
GBC_6.gridy = 3;
GBC_6.gridwidth = 1;
GBC_6.gridheight = 1;
GBC_6.fill = GridBagConstraints.BOTH;
GBC_6.insets = new Insets(3, 3, 3, 3);

// add the button
Button b6 = new Button("6");
gbl.setConstraints(b6, GBC_6);
this.add(b6);

// Add the + key
GridBagConstraints GBC_plus = new GridBagConstraints();
GBC_plus.gridx = 3;
GBC_plus.gridy = 3;
GBC_plus.gridwidth = 1;
GBC_plus.gridheight = 1;
GBC_plus.fill = GridBagConstraints.BOTH;
GBC_plus.insets = new Insets(3, 3, 3, 3);

// add the button
Button plus = new Button("+");
gbl.setConstraints(plus, GBC_plus);
this.add(plus);
```

```
// Add the 1 key
GridBagConstraints GBC_1 = new GridBagConstraints();
GBC_1.gridx = 0;
GBC_1.gridy = 4;
GBC_1.gridwidth = 1;
GBC_1.gridheight = 1;
GBC_1.fill = GridBagConstraints.BOTH;
GBC_1.insets = new Insets(3, 3, 3, 3);

// add the button
Button b1 = new Button("1");
gbl.setConstraints(b1, GBC_1);
this.add(b1);

// Add the 2 key
GridBagConstraints GBC_2 = new GridBagConstraints();
GBC_2.gridx = 1;
GBC_2.gridy = 4;
GBC_2.gridwidth = 1;
GBC_2.gridheight = 1;
GBC_2.fill = GridBagConstraints.BOTH;
GBC_2.insets = new Insets(3, 3, 3, 3);

// add the button
Button b2 = new Button("2");
gbl.setConstraints(b2, GBC_2);
add(b2);

// Add the 3 key
GridBagConstraints GBC_3 = new GridBagConstraints();
GBC_3.gridx = 2;
GBC_3.gridy = 4;
GBC_3.gridwidth = 1;
GBC_3.gridheight = 1;
GBC_3.fill = GridBagConstraints.BOTH;
GBC_3.insets = new Insets(3, 3, 3, 3);

// add the button
Button b3 = new Button("3");
gbl.setConstraints(b3, GBC_3);
this.add(b3);

// Add the = key
GridBagConstraints GBC_bigequals = new GridBagConstraints();
GBC_bigequals.gridx = 3;
GBC_bigequals.gridy = 4;
GBC_bigequals.gridwidth = 1;
GBC_bigequals.gridheight = 2;
```

```
GBC_bigequals.fill = GridBagConstraints.BOTH;
GBC_bigequals.insets = new Insets(3, 3, 3, 3);

// add the button
Button bigequals = new Button("=");
gbl.setConstraints(bigequals, GBC_bigequals);
this.add(bigequals);

// Add the 0 key
GridBagConstraints GBC_0 = new GridBagConstraints();
GBC_0.gridx = 0;
GBC_0.gridy = 5;
GBC_0.gridwidth = 2;
GBC_0.gridheight = 1;
GBC_0.fill = GridBagConstraints.BOTH;
GBC_0.insets = new Insets(3, 3, 3, 3);

// add the button
Button b0 = new Button("0");
gbl.setConstraints(b0, GBC_0);
this.add(b0);

// Add the . key
GridBagConstraints GBC_decimal = new GridBagConstraints();
GBC_decimal.gridx = 2;
GBC_decimal.gridy = 5;
GBC_decimal.gridwidth = 1;
GBC_decimal.gridheight = 1;
GBC_decimal.fill = GridBagConstraints.BOTH;
GBC_decimal.insets = new Insets(3, 3, 3, 3);

// add the button
Button bdecimal = new Button(".");
gbl.setConstraints(bdecimal, GBC_decimal);
this.add(bdecimal);
}
```

The full source code <GridBagCalculator.java> just contains a few additional methods to handle the window.

16.13.11 Manually Positioning Components

It is possible to precisely position widgets on the screen using x and y pixel coordinates that are relative to the applet's panel. Before you get the details you should hear why this is a bad idea:

Not every instance of your applet will have the same size panel to work with. You should only do this when the applet will only run on your web pages so you can control the applet's size. Free-standing windows may even be resized by the user on the fly. If you've used a layout manager to position your components, they'll be adjusted immediately to fit the new window size. This behavior is extremely hard to duplicate if you don't use a layout manager.

Components use varying amounts of space on different platforms. You should probably only use these techniques when you are writing a single-platform, compiled Java application. You should not use them for applets.

Laying out components manually is a lot of work, especially given the lack of Visual Basic like interface drawing environments. Don't you have better things to do with your time than moving widgets one pixel to the left, recompiling and running the applet only to discover the widget was probably better off where it started out?

The GridBagLayout and/or nested panels can probably do everything you want to do with manual layout anyway.

16.13.12 How to Manually Position Components

If none of those things convince you that you really shouldn't use absolute positioning, I'll let you in on the secret: pass null to setLayout(), that is call

setLayout(null);

Then move and resize each of your components to their desired locations and sizes in the paint() method using setLocation() and setSize():

public void setLocation(int x, int y)
public void setSize(int width, int height)

where x and y are the coordinates of the upper left hand corner of the bounding box of your component and width and height are the width and height in pixels of the bounding box of your component.

This applet that puts a button precisely 30 pixels wide by 40 pixels high at the point (25, 50):

```
import java.applet.*;
import java.awt.*;
public class ManualLayout extends Applet {
private boolean laidOut = false;
private Button myButton;
public void init() {
this.setLayout(null);
this.myButton = new Button("OK");
this.add(this.myButton);
}
public void paint(Graphics g) {
if (!this.laidOut) {
this.myButton.setLocation(25, 50);
this.myButton.setSize(30, 40);
this.laidOut = true;
}
}
}
```

16.14 Images

Java images are bitmapped GIF or JPEG files that can contain pictures of just about anything. You can use any program at all to create them as long as that program can save in GIF or JPEG format.

Once loaded into Java, images, whether GIF or JPEG, become instances of the abstract java.awt.Image class. The Image class has these eight methods:

```
public Image()
public abstract int getWidth(ImageObserver observer)
public abstract int getHeight(ImageObserver observer)
public abstract ImageProducer getSource()
public abstract Graphics getGraphics()
public abstract Object getProperty(String name, ImageObserver ob-
server)
public Image getScaledInstance(int width, int height, int hints)
public abstract void flush()
```

However, most of the work with images takes place in other classes, particularly java.awt.Graphics, java.awt.Component, and java.awt.Toolkit. You pass to an Image object to methods in these classes to load and display the image.

16.14.1 Where to Put Images

Images displayed by Java applets are retrieved from the web via a URL that points to the image file. An applet that displays a picture must have a URL to the image its going to display. Images can be stored on a web server, a local hard drive or anywhere else the applet can point to via a URL. Make sure you put your images somewhere the person viewing the applet can access them. A file URL that points to your local hard drive may work while you're developing an applet, but it won't be of much use to someone who comes in over the web.

Typically you put images in the same directory as either the applet or the HTML file. Though it doesn't absolutely have to be in one of these two locations, storing it there will probably be more convenient. Put the image with the applet .class file if the image will be used for all instances of the applet. Put the applet with the HTML file if different instances of the applet will use different images. A third alternative is to put all the images in a common location and use PARAMs in the HTML file to tell Java where the images are.

16.14.2 Loading Images

If you know the exact URL for the image you wish to load, you can load it like this:

URL imageURL = new URL("http://www.prenhall.com/logo.gif");
Image img = getImage(imageURL);

You can compress this into one line as follows

Image img = getImage(new URL("http://www.prenhall.com/logo.gif"));

The getImage() method is provided by java.applet.Applet so this works inside applets. Outside of applets you can use the getImage method from the default toolkit instead, like this:

URL imageURL = new URL("http://www.prenhall.com/logo.gif");
Image img = Toolkit.getDefaultToolkit.getImage(imageURL);

If you don't know the exact URL of the Image but you do know its name and that it's in the same directory as the applet, you can use an alternate form of getImage that takes a URL and a filename. Use the applet's getCodeBase() method to return the URL to the applet directory like this:

Image img = getImage(getCodeBase(), "test.gif");

The getCodeBase() method returns a URL that points to the directory where the applet came from.

Finally if the image file is stored in the same directory as the HTML file, use the same getImage method but pass it getDocumentBase() instead. This returns a URL that points at the directory which contains the HTML page in which the applet is embedded.

Image img = getImage(getDocumentBase(), "test.gif");

If an image is loaded from the Internet, it may take some time for it to be fully downloaded. Most of the time you don't need to worry about this. You can draw the image as soon as you've connected it to a URL. Java will update it as more data becomes available without any further intervention on your part.

Load all the images your applet needs in the init() method. In particular you do not want to load them in the paint() method. If you do they will be reloaded every time your applet repaints itself, and applet performance will be abysmal.

16.14.3 Drawing Images

Once you've downloaded an image from a URL, it's quite simple to draw it. Once the image is loaded draw it in the paint() method using the drawImage() method of the Graphics class public boolean drawImage(Image img, int x, int y, ImageObserver io) img is a member of the Image class which you should have already loaded. x and y are the coordinates of the point where the upper left hand corner of the Image will be drawn. io is an instance of a class which implements the ImageObserver interface.

The ImageObserver interface is how Java handles the asynchronous updating of an Image. java.awt.Component implements ImageObserver so for now just pass the keyword this to drawImage to indicate that the current applet is the ImageObserver that should be used.

A paint() method that does nothing more than draw an Image starting at the upper left hand corner of the applet might look like this

```
public void paint(Graphics g) {
g.drawImage(img, 0, 0, this);
}
```

Presumably, img is a field of the object which was initialized elsewhere.

Example 16.9 : *Drawing Images*

This image was loaded with this <APPLET> tag: <applet code="DisplayImage" width=158 height=189> <PARAM name=imagefile value=lightbulb.gif> <img src=lightbulb.gif width=158 height=189> </applet> Here's the code that produced it:

```
import java.awt.*;
import java.applet.*;
public class DisplayImage extends Applet {
Image theImage;
public void init() {
String filename=this.getParameter("imagefile");
theImage = this.getImage(this.getDocumentBase(), filename);
}
public void paint (Graphics g) {
g.drawImage(theImage, 0, 0, this);
}
}
```

16.14.4 Using the Return Value of DrawImage()

The drawImage() methods returns a boolean. Many people don't realize this, since the return value of drawImage() is often ignored. However, that boolean tells you whether or not the image was drawn successfully. If it was, drawImage() returns true. Otherwise drawImage() returns false.

For example, the following applet loads an image from the net. Until the image is finished loading, the applet displays the words "Loading Picture. Please hang on." Once the image has fully loaded, the applet displays it.

```
import java.awt.*;
import java.applet.*;
import java.awt.image.*;

public class showImage extends Applet {

Image thePicture;

public void init() {

thePicture = getImage(getDocumentBase(), "sun.gif");
}
public void paint(Graphics g) {

if(!g.drawImage(thePicture, 0, 0, this)) {
g.drawString("Loading Picture. Please hang on", 25, 50);
}
}
}
```

16.14.5 Resizing Images

You're not restricted to drawing an image at its natural width and height. The following variation on the paint() method let's you specify the width and height with which the image will be drawn:

public boolean drawImage(Image img, int x, int y,
int width, int height, ImageObserver io)

Here width and height are the width and height at which the image will be drawn in pixels. All other arguments are the same as before.

This image was loaded with this <APPLET> tag: <applet code="FillWithImage" width=100 height=200> <PARAM name=imagefile value=lightbulb.gif> <img src=lightbulb.gif width=100 height=200> </applet>
Here's the code that produced it:

```
import java.awt.*;
import java.applet.Applet;
public class FillWithImage extends Applet {
Image theImage;
public void init() {
String filename= this.getParameter("imagefile");
theImage = this.getImage(this.getDocumentBase(), filename);
}
public void paint (Graphics g) {
g.drawImage(theImage, 0, 0, getSize().height, getSize().width, this);
}
}
```

16.14.6 Determining the Size of an Image

If the rectangle you draw an image in is not proportional to the size of the image drawn, then the image may appear squashed or distorted.

To avoid disproportionate scaling you can use the Image's getHeight(ImageObserver observer) and getWidth(ImageObserver observer) methods to determine the actual size. Then scale appropriately. For instance this is how you would draw an Image scaled by one quarter in each dimension:

g.drawImage(img, 0, 0, img.getWidth(this)/4, img.getHeight(this)/4, this);

This applet reads an image file in the same directory as the HTML file and displays it at a specified magnification. The name of the image file and the magnification factor are specified via PARAMs. For example here's an applet tag that displays the image at half size:

This image was loaded with this <APPLET> tag:

```
<applet code="MagnifyImage" width=80 height=95> <PARAM name=imagefile
value=lightbulb.gif> <img src=lightbulb.gif width=80 height=95> </
applet>
```

```
import java.awt.*;
import java.applet.Applet;
public class MagnifyImage extends Applet {

Image theImage;
double scalefactor;

public void init() {

String filename=this.getParameter("imagefile");
theImage = this.getImage(getDocumentBase(), filename);
try {
scalefactor = Double.valueOf(
this.getParameter("scalefactor")).doubleValue();
}
catch (Exception e) {
scalefactor = 1.0;
}
}

public void paint (Graphics g) {
int x = theImage.getWidth(this);
int y = theImage.getHeight(this);
int scaleWidth = (int) (x * scalefactor);
int scaleHeight = (int) (y * scalefactor);
g.drawImage(theImage, 0, 0, scaleWidth, scaleHeight, this);
}
}
```

16.14.7 The java.awt.image Package

The java.awt.image package contains classes and interfaces that allow you to create new images from scratch rather than loading them from a file and to modify images that already exist.

```
Interfaces
ImageConsumer
ImageObserver
ImageProducer
Classes
AreaAveragingScaleFilter
ColorModel
CropImageFilter
DirectColorModel
FilteredImageSource
ImageFilter
IndexColorModel
MemoryImageSource
PixelGrabber
RGBImageFilter
ReplicateScaleFilter
```

16.14.8 Image Producers, Image Observers, and Image Consumers

An image does not magically appear, fully formed, the first time you call getImage(). It takes a finite amount of time for the image to be read. The larger the image the longer it takes. If the image is loaded from the Internet instead of a local file, it can take even longer.

Instead of waiting for the image to finish loading getImage() returns immediately, possibly before it's even connected to the remote site. It does return an Image object, but that Image object may not initially contain any data. All the different methods in the AWT that use images understand this and behave accordingly. For example, if only the top half of an image is available when drawImage() is called, then only the top half is drawn.

Meanwhile, in the background, in a separate thread, an ImageProducer object, that is a instance of a class which implements java.awt.ImageProducer, is filling the image with pixels as fast as it can. When more pixels become available, at least a scanline's worth, the ImageProducer notifies all ImageObserver objects that have registered an interest in this image.

How does an ImageObserver register its interest in an image? By being passed to a method that does something with the image. For example recall that both drawImage(), getWidth(), and getHeight() take ImageObservers as arguments.

java.awt.Component implements the ImageObserver interface so all its subclasses do too. This means buttons, TextAreas, check boxes, panels, applets, and more can all be used as ImageObservers. However in general you'll use the component that's actually trying to draw the image.

The ImageObserver interface declares a single method, imageUpdate():

```
public abstract boolean imageUpdate(Image img, int infoflags,
int x, int y, int width, int height)
```

An ImageProducer uses this method to tell the ImageObserver that more data is available for the image, so it should be redrawn.

16.14.9 Image Consumers

The ImageConsumer interface is less common. Whereas an ImageProducer only tells an ImageObserver that more of the image is ready, an ImageProducer gives an interested

ImageConsumer the actual image data. ImageConsumer defines these methods:

```
public abstract void setDimensions(int width, int height)
public abstract void setProperties(Hashtable props)
public abstract void setColorModel(ColorModel model)
public abstract void setHints(int hintflags)
public abstract void setPixels(int x, int y, int width, int  height,
ColorModel model, byte[] pixels, int off, int scansize)
public abstract void setPixels(int x, int y, int width, int height,
ColorModel model, int[] pixels, int off, int scansize)
public abstract void imageComplete(int status)
```

16.14.10 Waiting for an Image to Load

The java.awt.image.ImageObserver interface allows you to monitor the loading process so that you can keep the user informed, and use the image as quickly as possible once it does load.

When an ImageProducer receives additional data from an image, it calls the imageUpdate() method in each registered client. The default imageUpdate() method in java.awt.Component repaints the component when the image has changed.

However, variables that are set using a method like getWidth() or getHeight() are not updated automatically when imageUpdate() is called. It's your job to update them when the image changes.

Exactly how much data an ImageProducer receives before it calls imageUpdate() is unpredictable. Some texts (Graphic Java and my own Java Network Programming to mention two) incorrectly state that imageUpdate() is called for each scanline. This is not necessarily true.

16.14.11 Overriding Image Update()

The default imageUpdate() method in java.awt.Component repaints the component when the image has changed. However, you can override it to make it do something different. For example, the following applet prints a message in the status bar of the browser as the image loads.

```
import java.awt.*;
import java.applet.*;
import java.awt.image.*;
public class statusImage extends Applet implements ImageObserver {
Image thePicture;
public void init() {
thePicture = getImage(getDocumentBase(), getParameter("imagefile"));
}
public void paint(Graphics g) {
g.drawImage(thePicture, 0, 0, this)
}
public boolean imageUpdate(Image img, int infoflags, int x, int y,
int width, int height) {
if ((infoflags & ImageObserver.ALLBITS) != 0) {
showStatus("Image Complete");
repaint();
return false;
}
else {
```

```
showStatus("x: " + x + " y: " + y + " width: " + width
+ " height: " + height);
repaint();
}
return true;
}
}
```

16.15 What is an Image?

An image is a rectangular grid of pixels. It has a definite height and a definite width counted in pixels. Each pixel is square and has a fixed size on a given display. however different computer monitors may use different sized pixels.

Each pixel has a color. The color is a 32-bit integer. The first eight bits determine the redness of the pixel, the next eight bits the greenness, the next eight bits the blueness, and the remaining eight bits the transparency of the pixel.

```
1  1  1  1  1  1  1  1
1  1  1  1  1  1  1  1  1  1  1  1  1
1  1  1  1  1  1  1  1  1  1  1
```

Transparency

- Red
- Green
- Blue

Each of these values can be interpreted as an unsigned byte between 0 and 255. Within the color higher numbers are brighter. Thus a red of 0 is no red at all while a red of 255 is a very bright red.

Currently Java only supports two levels of transparency: Completely opaque (255) and completely transparent (0). Values of 1 through 254 are treated as completely transparent.

Different colors are made by mixing different levels of the three primary colors. For example, medium gray is 127 red, 127 green, and 127 blue.

255   127   127   127

Medium Grey

```
Pure white is 255 red, 255 green, 255 blue.

255 255   255   255
```

Bright White

```
Pure red is 255 red, 0 green, 0 blue.

255 255   0     0
```

Pure Red

```
A light cream is 255 red, 231 green, and 187 blue.

255 255   231   187
```

Light Cream

```
The << operator
The << operator moves the bits in an int to the left without sign
extension.
```

```
255 127  127  127
```

Medium Grey

The table above shows a color that is 50% gray. The alpha channel is 255 (11111111), that is fully opaque while each of the red, green, and blue channels is set to 127 (01111111). This means the color is equal to the integer 11111111011111110111111101111111 or -8,421,505. However the integer value has little meaning here. It's the individual bytes that matter.

So how do you create these colors? It's simple really. Just initialize ints to the values you want for each of the four channels, use << to shift them into place, and combine them with the bitwise or operator, |. This operator sets the bits in the result that are set in any of its operands. (A set bit is a 1 bit as opposed to a 0 bit.) For example, to create a pure blue,

```
int alpha = 255 << 24;
int red = 0 << 16;
int blue = 255 << 8;
int green = 0;
```

int pureblue = alpha | red | green | blue;
If you prefer, you can combine these on one line. For example, to create the 50% gray
int halfgray = (255 << 24) | (127 << 16) | (127 << 8) | 127;

16.15.1 Creating Images

Now that you know an image is just a grid of integers, it's not too difficult to create them. Of course you're not going to programmatically draw the Mona Lisa, but you might draw the Mandelbrot set or other pictures that can be created algorithmically.

There are a number of different ways to create an Image object from raw bytes. The easiest is with the java.awt.image.MemoryImageSource class. This class implements the java.awt.image.ImageProducer interface as will all classes that create images.

```
public MemoryImageSource(int w, int h, int pixels[], int offset, int
scan)
public MemoryImageSource(int w, int h, ColorModel cm, byte pixels[],
int offset, int scan)
public MemoryImageSource(int w, int h, ColorModel cm, byte pixels[],
int offset, int scan, Hashtable props)
public MemoryImageSource(int w, int h, ColorModel cm, int pixels[],
int offset, int scan)
public MemoryImageSource(int w, int h, ColorModel cm, int pixels[],
int offset, int scan, Hashtable props)
```

There are five different constructors in the MemoryImageSource class. for now let's concentrate on the first:

public MemoryImageSource(int w, int h, int pixels[], int offset, int scan)

w is the width of the image in pixels. h is the height of the image in pixels. pixels is an array that contains the actual image data. offset is the index in the array where the image data starts. scan is the number of pixels in each line of the array. Most of the time this is the same as h.

To create an image you first fill an array with the data for the image, then use that array to construct a new MemoryImageSource. Then you pass the MemoryImageSource to the createImage() method of the Component class to actually produce an Image object.

Example 16.9 : *An Example of Creating Images*

Let's suppose you want a 100 pixel wide, 50 pixel high image that's pure purple. A very nice purple shade is composed of 217 red, 10 green, 186 blue. (I used Adobe Photoshop to get these numbers, but there are many other ways.)

The integer value of this purple is formed like this:

```
int red = 217;
int green = 10;
int blue = 186;
int opaque = 255;
int purple = (opaque << 24 ) | (red << 16 ) | (green << 8 ) | blue;
```

The image we mant is 100 pixels wide by 50 pixels high so the array has to have 100 * 50 = 5000 elements. Thus,

```
int[] pixels = new int[5000];
```

Next, you fill the array with the purple value. A simple for loop suffices:

```
for (int i=0; i < pixels.length; i++) pixels[i] = purple;
```

Now that the array is created you can create the MemoryImageSource.

MemoryImageSource purpleMIS = new MemoryImageSource(100, 50, pixels, 0, 50));

Assuming you're inside an applet or other subclass of java.awt.Component, you can do the following. If you're not, you'll need to prefix the call to createImage() with a reference variable.

Image purplebox = createImage(purpleMIS);

You can now draw this image just like one you loaded from the network with getImage().

You can use one ImageProducer to create multiple images, and you can use one array of pixels to create multiple MemoryImageSources. However, if you do this you should not change the array after it's initially created.

Example 16.10 *make a purple box here*

The getRGB() method

It's not absolutely necessary to do the bit manipulation yourself. You can instead construct a new java.awt.Color object and use its getRGB() method to return the int value. For example,

```
Color purple = new Color(217, 10, 186)
int p = purple.getRGB();
int[] pixels = new int[5000];
for (int i=0; i < pixels.length; i++) pixels[i] = p;
MemoryImageSource purpleMIS = new MemoryImageSource(100, 50, pixels,
0, 50);
theImage = createImage(purpleMIS);
```

Blending Red and Green

A purple box is a pretty boring image, and they're several easier and more efficient ways to draw it. However some images are much easier to draw with an algorithmic approach. The following applet creates a 256 by 256 pixel image that blends from pure black to bright red on the lower left hand corner, bright green on the upper right hand corner, and various mixtures in between with yellow appearing in the bottom right corner.

(How good this applet looks depends heavily on the number of colors your monitor can display without dithering.)

```
import java.applet.*;
import java.awt.*;
import java.awt.image.*; // Don't forget this!
public class RGBlend extends Applet {
Image theImage;
public void init() {
int opaque = 255 << 24;
int[] pixels = new int[256*256];
for (int i=0; i < 256; i++) {
int red = i << 16;
for (int j = 0; j < 256; j++) {
int green = j << 8;
pixels[i*256 + j] = opaque | red | green;
}
}
MemoryImageSource RGBlendMIS =
new MemoryImageSource(256, 256, pixels, 0, 256);
theImage = this.createImage(RGBlendMIS);
}
public void paint(Graphics g) {
g.drawImage(theImage, 0, 0, this);
}
}
```

16.15.2 Filtering Images

Java provides support for image filters, chunks of code which transform an image in a predictable fashion. For example, an image filter might remove the green and blue components of an image, leaving only the red. Or a filter might sharpen lines, or blur an image. The study of image transformations and filters is an active field, and I am not going to attempt to summarize it here. However, I will demonstrate how you can write some simple filters. More complicated filters are written similarly except that they use more complicated algorithms to filter the data.

In Java an image filter requires a subclass of java.awt.image.ImageFilter and a subclass of java.awt.FilteredImageSource. The FilteredImageSource implements the java.awt.ImageProducer interface. Is starts with an existing Image, but passes it through the ImageFilter before sending the pixels to an ImageObserver or ImageConsumer.

Example 16.11 The Blue Filter Example

Here's a simple filter that extracts only the blue parts of an image.

```
import java.awt.image.*;
public class BlueFilter extends RGBImageFilter {
protected boolean canFilterIndexColorModel = true;
public int filterRGB(int x, int y, int rgb) {
return rgb & 0xFF0000FF;
}
}
```

canFilterIndexColorModel is set to true because the filtering is independent of position. The bitwise and operator, &, is used to select only the first eight bits and last eight bits of the rgb value. The transparency level is stored in the first eight bits. Thu blue component of the pixel is stored in the last eight bits. FF is 11111111 so all blue and transparency bits are retained. The remaining bits vanish.

Example 16.12 The Blue Filter Example

To use the blue image filter, you create a FilteredImageSource object.

For example,

Image src = getImage(getDocumentBase(), filename);

theImage = createImage(new FilteredImageSource(src.getSource(), new BlueFilter()));

The getSource() method returns a reference to the ImageProducer which produced this Image.

Here's a simple applet that loads an image specified in a PARAM tag, and uses the blue filter on it.

Note: Netscape 3.0.1 for the Mac and possibly other versions has trouble with this applet.

```
import java.awt.*;
import java.awt.image.*;
import java.applet.*;
public class BlueImage extends Applet {
Image theImage;
public void init() {
String filename=getParameter("imagefile");
Image src = getImage(getDocumentBase(), filename);
theImage = createImage(new FilteredImageSource(src.getSource(), new
BlueFilter()));
}
public void paint (Graphics g) {
g.drawImage(theImage, 0, 0, this);
}
}
```

Example 16.13 *The Blue Filter Example*

To use the blue image filter, you create a FilteredImageSource object.

For example,

```
Image src = getImage(getDocumentBase(), filename);
```

theImage = createImage(new FilteredImageSource(src.getSource(), new BlueFilter()));

The getSource() method returns a reference to the ImageProducer which produced this Image.

Here's a simple applet that loads an image specified in a PARAM tag, and uses the blue filter on it.

Note: Netscape 3.0.1 for the Mac and possibly other versions has trouble with this applet.

```
import java.awt.*;
import java.awt.image.*;
import java.applet.*;
public class BlueImage extends Applet {
Image theImage;
public void init() {
String filename=getParameter("imagefile");
Image src = getImage(getDocumentBase(), filename);
theImage = createImage(new FilteredImageSource(src.getSource(), new
BlueFilter()));
```

```
}
public void paint (Graphics g) {
g.drawImage(theImage, 0, 0, this);
}
}
```

Example 16.14 *The Greyscale Filter Example*

The following filter converts an image to greyscale. The red, green, and blue colors in each pixel are averaged. Then the resulting color is set to a grey scale with that average intensity.

```
import java.awt.image.*;
public class GreyFilter extends RGBImageFilter {
protected boolean canFilterIndexColorModel = true;
public int filterRGB(int x, int y, int rgb) {
int red =   rgb & 0x00FF0000;
red >>>= 16;
int green =   rgb & 0x0000FF00;
green >>>= 8;
int blue =   rgb & 0x0000FF;
int grey = (red + green + blue)/3;
return (0x000000FF << 24) | (grey << 16) | (grey << 8) | grey;
}
}
```

Notice that before averaging you have to shift the red and green components to the right 16 and 8 bits respectively. This forces them into the range 0 to 255. The >>> operator shifts right without sign extension.

```
import java.awt.*;
import java.awt.image.*;
import java.applet.Applet;
public class GreyImage extends Applet {
Image theImage;
public void init() {
String filename=getParameter("imagefile");
Image src = getImage(getDocumentBase(), filename);
theImage = createImage(new FilteredImageSource(src.getSource(), new
GreyFilter()));
}
public void paint (Graphics g) {
g.drawImage(theImage, 0, 0, this);
}
}
```

16.15.3 Filters that Depend on Position

It's not hard to write a filter where the filtering depends on the position of the pixel. For example, the following filter darkens the image the further away it is from the upper left hand corner of the applet.

```
import java.awt.*;
import java.awt.image.*;
import java.applet.*;
```

```
public class ShadowImage extends Applet {
Image theImage;
public void init() {
String filename = this.getParameter("imagefile");
Image src = this.getImage(getDocumentBase(), filename);
theImage = this.createImage(new FilteredImageSource(src.getSource(),
new ShadowFilter(this.getSize().width, this.getSize().height)));
}
public void paint (Graphics g) {
g.drawImage(theImage, 0, 0, this);
}
}
```

Notice here that I no longer set canFilterIndexColorModel to true. Each pixel must be treated individually. Also notice that this filter has a constructor. Although I'm not required provide a constructor for this subclass, I can if it's useful.

```
import java.awt.image.*;
public class ShadowFilter extends RGBImageFilter {
double edge;
public ShadowFilter(int width, int height) {
edge = Math.sqrt(width*width + height*height);
}
public int filterRGB(int x, int y, int rgb) {
double fraction = 1.0 - Math.sqrt(x*x + y*y)/edge;
if (fraction <= 0) return 0xFF000000;
int red =   rgb & 0x00FF0000;
red >>>= 16;
int green =   rgb & 0x0000FF00;
green >>>= 8;
int blue =   rgb & 0x0000FF;
int r = (int) (red * fraction);
int g = (int) (green * fraction);
int b = (int) (blue * fraction);
return (0x000000FF << 24) | (r << 16) | (g << 8) | b;
}
}
```

16.15.4 Filters that Depend on Adjacent Pixels

So far I've made the simplifying assumption that each pixel can be filtered independently of its neighbors. This isn't alawys true. For example a Gaussian blur or a sharpen or unspeckle filter, requires a substantial amount of information about other parts of the image.

When a filter must take into account the values of pixels other than the ones being filtered, it's no longer possible to use the simple RGBFilter class. Instead you have to work directly with java.awt.image.ImageFilter. You must override the two setPixels() methods to implement your filter.

```
public void setPixels(int x, int y, int w, int h, ColorModel model,
byte pixels[], int offset, int scan)
public void setPixels(int x, int y, int w, int h, ColorModel model
int pixels[], int offset, int scan)
```

16.16 Audio

Java allows you to play audio files that are encoded in a particular format. Sound files must be 8-bit, mono, mu-law encoded, .au files. This is fairly restrictive and does not even cover all .au files.

Furthermore, Java only allows sound to be played by applets. The java classes do not currently provide a means for playing sounds in non-applets.

These restrictions are likely to be relaxed in the future through the Java Media Framework and API. However for now Java's audio support is quite limited.

16.16.1 Playing Sounds

In the Java Applet package (java.applet), the Applet class and AudioClip interface provide basic support for playing sounds. Currently, the Java API supports only one sound format: 8 bit, flaw, 8000 Hz, one-channel, Sun ".au" files. You can create these on a Sun workstation using the audiotool application. You can convert files from other sound formats using an audio format conversion program.

16.16.2 Sound-Related Methods

Below are the sound-related Applet methods. The two-argument form of each method takes a base URL, which is usually returned by either getDocumentBase or getCodeBase, and the location of the sound file relative to the base URL. You should use the code base for sounds that are integral to the applet. The document base is used for sounds specified by the applet user, such as through applet parameters.

```
getAudioClip(URL), getAudioClip(URL, String)
Return an object that implements the AudioClip interface.
play(URL), play(URL, String)
Play the AudioClip corresponding to the specified URL.
The AudioClip interface defines the following methods:
```

- loop

Starts playing the clip repeatedly.

- play

Plays the clip once.

- stop

Stops the clip. Works with both looping and one-time sounds.

An Exampie

Here is an applet called SoundExample that illustrates a few things about sound. Note that, for instructional purposes, the applet adds up to 10 seconds to the load time for each sound. If the sounds were larger or the user's connection slower than ours, these delays might be realistic.

Fig. 16.6

Note: Because some old browsers don't support 1.1, the above applet is a 1.0 version (here is the

1.0 code; here's the 1.1 code). To run the 1.1 version of the applet, go to example-1dot1/SoundExample.html. For more information about running applets, refer to About Our Examples.

The SoundExample applet provides an architecture for loading and playing multiple sounds in an applet. For this reason, it is more complex than necessary. Essentially, the sound loading and playing code boils down to this:

```
AudioClip onceClip, loopClip;
onceClip = applet.getAudioClip(getCodeBase(), "bark.au");
loopClip = applet.getAudioClip(getCodeBase(), "train.au");
onceClip.play();       //Play it once.
loopClip.loop();       //Start the sound loop.
loopClip.stop();       //Stop the sound loop.
```

Since there's nothing more annoying than an applet that continues to make noise after you've left its page, the SoundExample applet stops playing the continuously looping sound when the user leaves the page, and resumes playing it when the user comes back. It does this by implementing its stop and start methods as follows:

```
public void stop() {
//If one-time sound were long, we'd stop it here, too.
//looping is a boolean instance variable that's initially
//false. It's set to true when the "Start sound loop" button
//is clicked and to false when the "Stop sound loop" or "Reload
//sounds" button is clicked.
if (looping) {
loopClip.stop();      //Stop the sound loop.
}
}

public void start() {
if (looping) {
loopClip.loop();      //Restart the sound loop.
}
}
```

The SoundExample applet features three classes:

- An Applet subclass, SoundExample, that controls the applet's execution.
- A Hashtable subclass, SoundList, that holds AudioClips. This is overkill for this applet, but if you were to write an applet that used lots of sound files, a class like this would be useful.
- A Thread subclass, SoundLoader, each instance of which loads an AudioClip in the background. During the applet's initialization, the applet preloads each sound by creating a SoundLoader for it.

Preloading the sounds in a background thread (with SoundLoader) improves the perceived performance by reducing the amount of time the user has to wait to be able to interact with the applet. It does this by reducing the amount of time spent in the init method. If you simply called getAudioClip in the applet's init method, it could take quite a while before getAudioClip returned, meaning that the applet couldn't perform the other statements in its init method, and that the applet's start wouldn't get called. (For this SoundExample applet, a delay in calling the start method doesn't matter.)

Another advantage of loading the sounds in a background thread is that it enables the applet to respond appropriately (and immediately) to user input that would normally cause a sound to play, even if that sound hasn't been loaded yet. If you simply use the Applet play methods, for example, then the first time the user does something to make the applet play a particular sound, the applet's drawing and event handling are frozen while the sound is loaded. Instead, this applet detects that the sound hasn't been loaded yet and responds appropriately.

16.16.3 The play() Methods

The java.applet.Applet class contains two methods which download a sound file from a particular URL and play it.

public void play(URL url)
public void play(URL url, String name)

Normally these are used relative to the code base or the document base for maximum portability. Alternately, the URLs can be specified in one of the applet's PARAM tags.

For example, the music you're hearing about now is produced by the following applet:

```
import java.applet.Applet;
public class SoundApplet extends Applet {
public void init() {
String soundfile = getParameter("soundfile");
if (soundfile != null) play(getDocumentBase(), soundfile);
}
}
```

16.16.4 Filters that Depend on Adjacent Pixels

So far I've made the simplifying assumption that each pixel can be filtered independently of its neighbors. This isn't alawys true. For example a Gaussian blur or a sharpen or unspeckle filter, requires a substantial amount of information about other parts of the image.

When a filter must take into account the values of pixels other than the ones being filtered, it's no longer possible to use the simple RGBFilter class. Instead you have to work directly with java.awt.image.ImageFilter. You must override the two setPixels() methods to implement your filter.

```
public void setPixels(int x, int y, int w, int h, ColorModel model,
byte pixels[], int offset, int scan)
public void setPixels(int x, int y, int w, int h, ColorModel model,
int pixels[], int offset, int scan)
```

16.16.5 Continuous Play

Instead of just playing a sound once, you can load it into a java.applet.AudioClip object and play it continously with that interface's loop() method. First you have to download the sound into an AudioClip like this:

```
AudioClip ac  = getAudioClip(new URL(
"http://sunsite.unc.edu/javafaq/course/week9/spacemusic.au"));
Then, once you have the AudioClip object, merely invoke it's loop()
method:
ac.loop();
When you're ready to stop playing the clip, invoke its stop() method
like this
```

```
ac.stop();
Here's the applet that's playing the music you're hearing now:
import java.applet.*;  // java.applet.Applet isn't enough

public class LoopApplet extends Applet {

AudioClip theSound;

public void init() {

String soundfile = getParameter("soundfile");
if (soundfile != null) {
theSound=getAudioClip(getDocumentBase(), soundfile);
}

}

public void start() {
if (theSound != null) theSound.loop();
}

public void stop() {
if (theSound != null) theSound.stop();
}
}
```

Notice in the applet above, that I take care to stop playing the music when the user leaves the page and the stop() method is invoked. Otherwise this could continue indefinitely until the user quit the web browser.

16.17 Control Fundamentals

16.17.1 Making a Button

Making a button is quite simple: you just call the Button constructor with the label you want on the button. (You can also use the default constructor if you want a button with no label, but this is not very useful.) Usually you'll want to create a handle for the button so you can refer to it later.

The Button is a component, like its own little window, that will automatically get repainted as part of an update. This means that you don't explicitly paint a button or any other kind of control; you simply place them on the form and let them automatically take care of painting themselves. So to place a button on a form you override init( ) instead of overriding paint( ):

```
//: Button1.java
// Putting buttons on an applet
import java.awt.*;
import java.applet.*;

public class Button1 extends Applet {
Button
```

```
b1 = new Button("Button 1"),
b2 = new Button("Button 2");
public void init() {
add(b1);
add(b2);
}
} ///:~
```

It's not enough to create the Button (or any other control). You must also call the Applet add( ) method to cause the button to be placed on the applet's form. This seems a lot simpler than it is, because the call to add( ) actually decides, implicitly, where to place the control on the form. Controlling the layout of a form is examined shortly.

16.17.2 Capturing an Event

You'll notice that if you compile and run the applet above, nothing happens when you press the buttons. This is where you must step in and write some code to determine what will happen. The basis of event-driven programming, which comprises a lot of what a GUI is about, is tying events to code that responds to those events.

After working your way this far through the book and grasping some of the fundamentals of object-oriented programming, you might think that of course there will be some sort of object-oriented approach to handling events. For example, you might have to inherit each button and override some "button pressed" method (this, it turns out, is too tedious and restrictive). You might also think there's some master "event" class that contains a method for each event you want to respond to.

Before objects, the typical approach to handling events was the "giant switch statement." Each event would have a unique integer value and inside the master event handling method you'd write a switch on that value.

The AWT in Java 1.0 doesn't use any object-oriented approach. Neither does it use a giant switch statement that relies on the assignment of numbers to events. Instead, you must create a cascaded set of if statements. What you're trying to do with the if statements is detect the object that was the target of the event. That is, if you click on a button, then that particular button is the target. Normally, that's all you care about - if a button is the target of an event, then it was most certainly a mouse click and you can continue based on that assumption. However, events can contain other information as well. For example, if you want to find out the pixel location where a mouse click occurred so you can draw a line to that location, the Event object will contain the location. (You should also be aware that Java 1.0 components can be limited in the kinds of events they generate, while Java 1.1 and Swing/JFC components produce a full set of events.)

The Java 1.0 AWT method where your cascaded if statement resides is called action( ). Although the whole Java 1.0 Event model has been deprecated in Java 1.1, it is still widely used for simple applets and in systems that do not yet support Java 1.1, so I recommend you become comfortable with it, including the use of the following action() method approach.

action( ) has two arguments: the first is of type Event and contains all the information about the event that triggered this call to action( ). For example, it could be a mouse click, a normal keyboard press or release, a special key press or release, the fact that the component got or lost the focus, mouse movements, or drags, etc. The second argument is usually the target of the event, which you'll often ignore. The second argument is also encapsulated in the Event object so it is redundant as an argument.

The situations in which action( ) gets called are extremely limited: When you place controls on a form, some types of controls (buttons, check boxes, drop-down lists, menus) have a "standard action" that occurs, which causes the call to action( ) with the appropriate Event object. For example, with a button the action( ) method is called when the button is pressed and at no other time. Usually this is just fine, since that's what you ordinarily look for with a button. However, it's possible to deal with many other types of events via the handleEvent( ) method as we will see later in this chapter.

The previous example can be extended to handle button clicks as follows:

```
//: Button2.java
// Capturing button presses
import java.awt.*;
import java.applet.*;

public class Button2 extends Applet
{
Button
b1 = new Button("Button 1"),
b2 = new Button("Button 2");
public void init() {
add(b1);
add(b2);
}
public boolean action(Event evt, Object arg)
{
if(evt.target.equals(b1))
getAppletContext().showStatus("Button 1");
else if(evt.target.equals(b2))
getAppletContext().showStatus("Button 2");
// Let the base class handle it:
else
return super.action(evt, arg);
return true; // We've handled it here
}
} ///:~
```

To see what the target is, ask the Event object what its target member is and then use the equals( ) method to see if it matches the target object handle you're interested in. When you've written handlers for all the objects you're interested in you must call super.action(evt, arg) in the else statement at the end, as shown above. Remember from Chapter 7 (polymorphism) that your overridden method is called instead of the base class version. However, the base-class version contains code to handle all of the cases that you're not interested in, and it won't get called unless you call it explicitly. The return value indicates whether you've handled it or not, so if you do match an event you should return true, otherwise return whatever the base-class event( ) returns.

For this example, the simplest action is to print what button is pressed. Some systems allow you to pop up a little window with a message in it, but applets discourage this. However, you can put a message at the bottom of the Web browser window on its status line by calling the Applet method getAppletContext( ) to get access to the browser and then showStatus( ) to put a string on the status line. [56] You can print out a complete description of an event the same way, with getAppletContext().showStatus(evt + ""). (The empty String forces the compiler to convert evt to a

String.) Both of these reports are really useful only for testing and debugging since the browser might overwrite your message.

Strange as it might seem, you can also match an event to the text that's on a button through the second argument in event( ). Using this technique, the example above becomes:

```
//: Button3.java
// Matching events on button text
import java.awt.*;
import java.applet.*;

public class Button3 extends Applet {
Button
b1 = new Button("Button 1"),
b2 = new Button("Button 2");
public void init() {
add(b1);
add(b2);
}
public boolean action (Event evt, Object arg) {
if(arg.equals("Button 1"))
getAppletContext().showStatus("Button 1");
else if(arg.equals("Button 2"))
getAppletContext().showStatus("Button 2");
// Let the base class handle it:
else
return super.action(evt, arg);
return true; // We've handled it here
}
} ///:~
```

It's difficult to know exactly what the equals( ) method is doing here. The biggest problem with this approach is that most new Java programmers who start with this technique spend at least one frustrating session discovering that they've gotten the capitalization or spelling wrong when comparing to the text on a button. (I had this experience.) Also, if you change the text of the button, the code will no longer work (but you won't get any compile-time or run-time error messages). You should avoid this approach if possible.

16.17.3 Text Fields

A TextField is a one line area that allows the user to enter and edit text. TextField is inherited from TextComponent, which lets you select text, get the selected text as a String, get or set the text, and set whether the TextField is editable, along with other associated methods that you can find in your online reference. The following example demonstrates some of the functionality of a TextField; you can see that the method names are fairly obvious:

```
//: TextField1.java
// Using the text field control
import java.awt.*;
import java.applet.*;

public class TextField1 extends Applet {
```

```
Button
b1 = new Button("Get Text"),
b2 = new Button("Set Text");
TextField
t = new TextField("Starting text", 30);
String s = new String();
public void init() {
add(b1);
add(b2);
add(t);
}
public boolean action (Event evt, Object arg) {
if(evt.target.equals(b1)) {
getAppletContext().showStatus(t.getText());
s = t.getSelectedText();
if(s.length() == 0) s = t.getText();
t.setEditable(true);
}
else if(evt.target.equals(b2)) {
t.setText("Inserted by Button 2: " + s);
t.setEditable(false);
}
// Let the base class handle it:
else
return super.action(evt, arg);
return true; // We've handled it here
}
} ///:~
```

There are several ways to construct a TextField; the one shown here provides an initial string and sets the size of the field in characters.

Pressing button 1 either gets the text you've selected with the mouse or it gets all the text in the field and places the result in String s . It also allows the field to be edited. Pressing button 2 puts a message and s into the text field and prevents the field from being edited (although you can still select the text). The editability of the text is controlled by passing setEditable( ) a true or false.

16.17.4 Text Areas

A TextArea is like a TextField except that it can have multiple lines and has significantly more functionality. In addition to what you can do with a TextField, you can append text and insert or replace text at a given location. It seems like this functionality could be useful for TextField as well, so it's a little confusing to try to detect how the distinction is made. You might think that if you want TextArea functionality everywhere you can simply use a one line TextArea in places where you would otherwise use a TextField. In Java 1.0, you also got scroll bars with a TextArea even when they weren't appropriate; that is, you got both vertical and horizontal scroll bars for a one line TextArea. In Java 1.1 this was remedied with an extra constructor that allows you to select which scroll bars (if any) are present. The following example shows only the Java 1.0 behavior, in which the scrollbars are always on. Later in the chapter you'll see an example that demonstrates Java 1.1 TextAreas.

```
//: TextArea1.java
```

```
// Using the text area control
import java.awt.*;
import java.applet.*;

public class TextArea1 extends Applet {
Button b1 = new Button("Text Area 1");
Button b2 = new Button("Text Area 2");
Button b3 = new Button("Replace Text");
Button b4 = new Button("Insert Text");
TextArea t1 = new TextArea("t1", 1, 30);
TextArea t2 = new TextArea("t2", 4, 30);
public void init() {
add(b1);
add(t1);
add(b2);
add(t2);
add(b3);
add(b4);
}
public boolean action (Event evt, Object arg) {
if(evt.target.equals(b1))
getAppletContext().showStatus(t1.getText());
else if(evt.target.equals(b2)) {
t2.setText("Inserted by Button 2");
t2.appendText(": " + t1.getText());
getAppletContext().showStatus(t2.getText());
}
else if(evt.target.equals(b3)) {
String s = " Replacement ";
t2.replaceText(s, 3, 3 + s.length());
}
else if(evt.target.equals(b4))
t2.insertText(" Inserted ", 10);
// Let the base class handle it:
else
return super.action(evt, arg);
return true; // We've handled it here
}
} ///:~
```

There are several different TextArea constructors, but the one shown here gives a starting string and the number of rows and columns. The different buttons show getting, appending, replacing, and inserting text.

16.17.5 Labels

A Label does exactly what it sounds like it should: places a label on the form. This is particularly important for text fields and text areas that don't have labels of their own, and can also be useful if you simply want to place textual information on a form. You can, as shown in the first example in this chapter, use drawString( ) inside paint( ) to place text in an exact location. When you use a Label it allows you to (approximately) associate the text with some other component via the layout manager (which will be discussed later in this chapter).

With the constructor you can create a blank label, a label with initial text in it (which is what you'll typically do), and a label with an alignment of CENTER, LEFT, or RIGHT (static final int s defined in class Label). You can also change the label and its alignment with setText( ) and setAlignment( ), and if you've forgotten what you've set these to you can read the values with getText( ) and getAlignment( ). This example shows what you can do with labels:

```
//: Label1.java
// Using labels
import java.awt.*;
import java.applet.*;

public class Label1 extends Applet {
TextField t1 = new TextField("t1", 10);
Label labl1 = new Label("TextField t1");
Label labl2 = new Label("                              ");
Label labl3 = new Label("                               ",
Label.RIGHT);
Button b1 = new Button("Test 1");
Button b2 = new Button("Test 2");
public void init() {
add(labl1); add(t1);
add(b1); add(labl2);
add(b2); add(labl3);
}
public boolean action (Event evt, Object arg) {
if(evt.target.equals(b1))
labl2.setText("Text set into Label");
else if(evt.target.equals(b2)) {
if(labl3.getText().trim().length() == 0)
labl3.setText("labl3");
if(labl3.getAlignment() == Label.LEFT)
labl3.setAlignment(Label.CENTER);
else if(labl3.getAlignment()==Label.CENTER)
labl3.setAlignment(Label.RIGHT);
else if(labl3.getAlignment() == Label.RIGHT)
labl3.setAlignment(Label.LEFT);
}
else
return super.action(evt, arg);
return true;
}
} ///:~
```

The first use of the label is the most typical: labeling a TextField or TextArea. In the second part of the example, a bunch of empty spaces are reserved and when you press the "Test 1" button setText( ) is used to insert text into the field. Because a number of blank spaces do not equal the same number of characters (in a proportionally-spaced font) you'll see that the text gets truncated when inserted into the label.

The third part of the example reserves empty space, then the first time you press the "Test 2" button it sees that there are no characters in the label (since trim( ) removes all of the blank spaces at each end of a String) and inserts a short label, which is initially left-aligned. The rest of the times you press the button it changes the alignment so you can see the effect.

You might think that you could create an empty label and then later put text in it with setText( ). However, you cannot put text into an empty label - presumably because it has zero width - so creating a label with no text seems to be a useless thing to do. In the example above, the "blank" label is filled with empty spaces so it has enough width to hold text that's placed inside later.

Similarly, setAlignment( ) has no effect on a label that you'd typically create with text in the constructor. The label width is the width of the text, so changing the alignment doesn't do anything. However, if you start with a long label and then change it to a shorter one you can see the effect of the alignment.

These behaviors occur because of the default layout manager that's used for applets, which causes things to be squished together to their smallest size. Layout managers will be covered later in this chapter, when you'll see that other layouts don't have the same effect.

16.17.6 Check Boxes

A check box provides a way to make a single on-off choice; it consists of a tiny box and a label. The box typically holds a little 'x' (or some other indication that it is set) or is empty depending on whether that item was selected.

You'll normally create a Checkbox using a constructor that takes the label as an argument. You can get and set the state, and also get and set the label if you want to read or change it after the Checkbox has been created. Note that the capitalization of Checkbox is inconsistent with the other controls, which could catch you by surprise since you might expect it to be "CheckBox."

Whenever a Checkbox is set or cleared an event occurs, which you can capture the same way you do a button. The following example uses a TextArea to enumerate all the check boxes that have been checked:

```
//: CheckBox1.java
// Using check boxes
import java.awt.*;
import java.applet.*;

public class CheckBox1 extends Applet {
TextArea t = new TextArea(6, 20);
Checkbox cb1 = new Checkbox("Check Box 1");
Checkbox cb2 = new Checkbox("Check Box 2");
Checkbox cb3 = new Checkbox("Check Box 3");
public void init() {
add(t); add(cb1); add(cb2); add(cb3);
}
public boolean action (Event evt, Object arg) {
if(evt.target.equals(cb1))
trace("1", cb1.getState());
else if(evt.target.equals(cb2))
trace("2", cb2.getState());
```

```
else if(evt.target.equals(cb3))
trace("3", cb3.getState());
else
return super.action(evt, arg);
return true;
}
void trace(String b, boolean state) {
if(state)
t.appendText("Box " + b + " Set\n");
else
t.appendText("Box " + b + " Cleared\n");
}
} ///:~
```

The trace( ) method sends the name of the selected Checkbox and its current state to the TextArea using appendText( ) so you'll see a cumulative list of the checkboxes that were selected and what their state is.

16.17.7 Radio Buttons

The concept of a radio button in GUI programming comes from pre-electronic car radios with mechanical buttons: when you push one in, any other button that was pressed pops out. Thus it allows you to force a single choice among many.

The AWT does not have a separate class to represent the radio button; instead it reuses the Checkbox. However, to put the Checkbox in a radio button group (and to change its shape so it's visually different from an ordinary Checkbox) you must use a special constructor that takes a CheckboxGroup object as an argument. (You can also call setCheckboxGroup( ) after the Checkbox has been created.)

A CheckboxGroup has no constructor argument; its sole reason for existence is to collect some Checkboxes into a group of radio buttons. One of the Checkbox objects must have its state set to true before you try to display the group of radio buttons; otherwise you'll get an exception at run time. If you try to set more than one radio button to true then only the final one set will be true.

Here's a simple example of the use of radio buttons. Note that you capture radio button events like all others:

```
//: RadioButton1.java
// Using radio buttons
import java.awt.*;
import java.applet.*;
public class RadioButton1 extends Applet {
TextField t =
new TextField("Radio button 2", 30);
CheckboxGroup g = new CheckboxGroup();
Checkbox
cb1 = new Checkbox("one", g, false),
cb2 = new Checkbox("two", g, true),
cb3 = new Checkbox("three", g, false);
public void init() {
t.setEditable(false);
```

```
add(t);
add(cb1); add(cb2); add(cb3);
}
public boolean action (Event evt, Object arg) {
if(evt.target.equals(cb1))
t.setText("Radio button 1");
else if(evt.target.equals(cb2))
t.setText("Radio button 2");
else if(evt.target.equals(cb3))
t.setText("Radio button 3");
else
return super.action(evt, arg);
return true;
}
} ///:~
```

To display the state, an text field is used. This field is set to non-editable because it's used only to display data, not to collect it. This is shown as an alternative to using a Label. Notice the text in the field is initialized to "Radio button 2" since that's the initial selected radio button.

You can have any number of CheckboxGroups on a form.

16.17.8 Drop-Down Lists

Like a group of radio buttons, a drop-down list is a way to force the user to select only one element from a group of possibilities. However, it's a much more compact way to accomplish this, and it's easier to change the elements of the list without surprising the user. (You can change radio buttons dynamically, but that tends to be visibly jarring).

Java's Choice box is not like the combo box in Windows, which lets you select from a list or type in your own selection. With a Choice box you choose one and only one element from the list. In the following example, the Choice box starts with a certain number of entries and then new entries are added to the box when a button is pressed. This allows you to see some interesting behaviors in Choice boxes:

```
//: Choice1.java
// Using drop-down lists
import java.awt.*;
import java.applet.*;

public class Choice1 extends Applet {
String[] description = { "Ebullient", "Obtuse",
"Recalcitrant", "Brilliant", "Somnescent",
"Timorous", "Florid", "Putrescent" };
TextField t = new TextField(30);
Choice c = new Choice();
Button b = new Button("Add items");
int count = 0;
public void init() {
t.setEditable(false);
for(int i = 0; i < 4; i++)
```

```
c.addItem(description[count++]);
add(t);
add(c);
add(b);
}
public boolean action (Event evt, Object arg) {
if(evt.target.equals(c))
t.setText("index: " +  c.getSelectedIndex()
+ "    " + (String)arg);
else if(evt.target.equals(b)) {
if(count < description.length)
c.addItem(description[count++]);
}
else
return super.action(evt, arg);
return true;
}
} ///:~
```

The TextField displays the "selected index," which is the sequence number of the currently selected element, as well as the String representation of the second argument of action( ), which is in this case the string that was selected.

When you run this applet, pay attention to the determination of the size of the Choice box: in Windows, the size is fixed from the first time you drop down the list. This means that if you drop down the list, then add more elements to the list, the elements will be there but the drop-down list won't get any longer [57] (you can scroll through the elements). However, if you add all the elements before the first time the list is dropped down, then it will be sized correctly. Of course, the user will expect to see the whole list when it's dropped down, so this behavior puts some significant limitations on adding elements to Choice boxes.

This behavior is apparently a bug and will be fixed in a later version of Java.

16.17.9 List Boxes

List boxes are significantly different from Choice boxes, and not just in appearance. While a Choice box drops down when you activate it, a List occupies some fixed number of lines on a screen all the time and doesn't change. In addition, a List allows multiple selection: if you click on more than one item the original item stays highlighted and you can select as many as you want. If you want to see the items in a list, you simply call getSelectedItems( ), which produces an array of String of the items that have been selected. To remove an item from a group you have to click it again.

A problem with a List is that the default action is double clicking, not single clicking. A single click adds or removes elements from the selected group and a double click calls action( ). One way around this is to re-educate your user, which is the assumption made in the following program:

```
//: List1.java
// Using lists with action()
import java.awt.*;
import java.applet.*;

public class List1 extends Applet {
```

```
String[] flavors = { "Chocolate", "Strawberry",
"Vanilla Fudge Swirl", "Mint Chip",
"Mocha Almond Fudge", "Rum Raisin",
"Praline Cream", "Mud Pie" };
// Show 6 items, allow multiple selection:
List lst = new List(6, true);
TextArea t = new TextArea(flavors.length, 30);
Button b = new Button("test");
int count = 0;
public void init() {
t.setEditable(false);
for(int i = 0; i < 4; i++)
lst.addItem(flavors[count++]);
add(t);
add(lst);
add(b);
}
public boolean action (Event evt, Object arg) {
if(evt.target.equals(lst)) {
t.setText("");
String[] items = lst.getSelectedItems();
for(int i = 0; i < items.length; i++)
t.appendText(items[i] + "\n");
}
else if(evt.target.equals(b)) {
if(count < flavors.length)
lst.addItem(flavors[count++], 0);
}
else
return super.action(evt, arg);
return true;
}
} ///:~
```

When you press the button it adds items to the top of the list (because of the second argument 0 to addItem( )). Adding elements to a List is more reasonable than the Choice box because users expect to scroll a list box (for one thing, it has a built-in scroll bar) but they don't expect to have to figure out how to get a drop-down list to scroll, as in the previous example.

However, the only way for action( ) to be called is through a double-click. If you need to monitor other activities that the user is doing on your List (in particular, single clicks) you must take an alternative approach.

❑ handleEvent( )

So far we've been using action( ), but there's another method that gets first crack at everything: handleEvent( ). Any time an event happens, it happens "over" or "to" a particular object. The handleEvent( ) method for that object is automatically called and an Event object is created and passed to handleEvent( ). The default handleEvent( ) (which is defined in Component, the base class for virtually all the "controls" in the AWT) will call either action( ), as we've been using, or other similar methods to indicate mouse activity, keyboard activity, or to indicate that the focus has moved. We'll look at those later in this chapter.

What if these other methods - action( ) in particular - don't satisfy your needs? In the case of List, for example, what if you want to catch single mouse clicks but action( ) responds to only double clicks? The solution is to override handleEvent( ) for your applet, which after all is derived from Applet and can therefore override any non- final methods. When you override handleEvent( ) for the applet you're getting all the applet events before they are routed, so you cannot just assume "This has to do with my button so I can assume it's been pressed," since that's true only for action( ). Inside handleEvent( ) it's possible that the button has the focus and someone is typing to it. Whether it makes sense or not, those are events that you can detect and act upon in handleEvent( ).

To modify the List example so that it will react to single mouse clicks, the button detection will be left in action( ) but the code to handle the List will be moved into handleEvent( ) as follows:

```
//: List2.java
// Using lists with handleEvent()
import java.awt.*;
import java.applet.*;
public class List2 extends Applet {
String[] flavors = { "Chocolate", "Strawberry",
"Vanilla Fudge Swirl", "Mint Chip",
"Mocha Almond Fudge", "Rum Raisin",
"Praline Cream", "Mud Pie" };
// Show 6 items, allow multiple selection:
List lst = new List(6, true);
TextArea t = new TextArea(flavors.length, 30);
Button b = new Button("test");
int count = 0;
public void init() {
t.setEditable(false);
for(int i = 0; i < 4; i++)
lst.addItem(flavors[count++]);
add(t);
add(lst);
add(b);
}
public boolean handleEvent(Event evt) {
if(evt.id == Event.LIST_SELECT ||
evt.id == Event.LIST_DESELECT) {
if(evt.target.equals(lst)) {
t.setText("");
String[] items = lst.getSelectedItems();
for(int i = 0; i < items.length; i++)
t.appendText(items[i] + "\n");
}
else
return super.handleEvent(evt);
}
```

```
else
return super.handleEvent(evt);
return true;
}
public boolean action(Event evt, Object arg) {
if(evt.target.equals(b)) {
if(count < flavors.length)
lst.addItem(flavors[count++], 0);
}
else
return super.action(evt, arg);
return true;
}
} ///:~
```

The example is the same as before except for the addition of handleEvent( ). Inside, a check is made to see whether a list selection or deselection has occurred. Now remember, handleEvent( ) is being overridden for the applet, so this occurrence could be anywhere on the form and it could be happening to another list. Thus, you must also check to see what the target is. (Although in this case there's only one list on the applet so we could have made the assumption that all list events must be about that list. This is bad practice since it's going to be a problem as soon as another list is added.) If the list matches the one we're interested in, the same code as before will do the trick.

Note that the form for handleEvent( ) is similar to action( ): if you deal with a particular event you return true, but if you're not interested in any of the other events via handleEvent( ) you must return super.handleEvent(evt). This is vital because if you don't do this, none of the other event-handling code will get called. For example, try commenting out the return super.handleEvent(evt) in the code above. You'll discover that action( ) never gets called, certainly not what you want. For both action( ) and handleEvent( ) it's important to follow the format above and always return the base-class version of the method when you do not handle the event yourself (in which case you should return true). (Fortunately, these kinds of bug-prone details are relegated to Java 1.0. The new design in Java 1.1 that you will see later in the chapter eliminates these kinds of issues.)

In Windows, a list box automatically allows multiple selections if you hold down the shift key. This is nice because it allows the user to choose a single or multiple selection rather than fixing it during programming. You might think you'll be clever and implement this yourself by checking to see if the shift key is held down when a mouse click was made by testing for evt.shiftDown( ). Alas, the design of the AWT stymies you - you'd have to be able to know which item was clicked on if the shift key wasn't pressed so you could deselect all the rest and select only that one. However, you cannot figure that out in Java 1.0. (Java 1.1 sends all mouse, keyboard, and focus events to a List, so you'll be able to accomplish this.)

16.18 Controlling Layout

The way that you place components on a form in Java is probably different from any other GUI system you've used. First, it's all code; there are no "resources" that control placement of components. Second, the way components are placed on a form is controlled by a "layout manager" that decides how the components lie based on the order that you add( ) them. The size, shape, and placement of components will be remarkably different from one layout manager to another. In addition, the layout managers adapt to the dimensions of your applet or application window, so if that window dimension is changed (for example, in the HTML page's applet specification) the size, shape, and placement of the components could change.

Both the Applet and Frame classes are derived from Container, whose job it is to contain and display Components. (The Container is a Component so it can also react to events.) In Container, there's a method called setLayout( ) that allows you to choose a different layout manager.

In this section we'll explore the various layout managers by placing buttons in them (since that's the simplest thing to do). There won't be any capturing of button events since this is just intended to show how the buttons are laid out.

16.18.1 Flow Layout

So far, all the applets that have been created seem to have laid out their components using some mysterious internal logic. That's because the applet uses a default layout scheme: the FlowLayout. This simply "flows" the components onto the form, from left to right until the top space is full, then moves down a row and continues flowing the components.

Here's an example that explicitly (redundantly) sets the layout manager in an applet to FlowLayout and then places buttons on the form. You'll notice that with FlowLayout the components take on their "natural" size. A Button, for example, will be the size of its string.

```
//: FlowLayout1.java
// Demonstrating the FlowLayout
import java.awt.*;
import java.applet.*;
public class FlowLayout1 extends Applet {
public void init() {
setLayout(new FlowLayout());
for(int i = 0; i < 20; i++)
add(new Button("Button " + i));
}
} ///:~
```

All components will be compacted to their smallest size in a FlowLayout, so you might get a little bit of surprising behavior. For example, a label will be the size of its string, so right-justifying it yields an unchanged display.

16.18.2 BorderLayout

This layout manager has the concept of four border regions and a center area. When you add something to a panel that's using a BorderLayout you must use an add( ) method that takes a String object as its first argument, and that string must specify (with proper capitalization) "North" (top), "South" (bottom), "East" (right), "West" (left), or "Center." If you misspell or mis-capitalize, you won't get a compile-time error, but the applet simply won't do what you expect. Fortunately, as you will see shortly, there's a much-improved approach in Java 1.1.

Here's a simple example:

```
//: BorderLayout1.java
// Demonstrating the BorderLayout
import java.awt.*;
import java.applet.*;

public class BorderLayout1 extends Applet {
public void init() {
```

```
int i = 0;
setLayout(new BorderLayout());
add("North", new Button("Button " + i++));
add("South", new Button("Button " + i++));
add("East", new Button("Button " + i++));
add("West", new Button("Button " + i++));
add("Center", new Button("Button " + i++));
}
} ///:~
```

For every placement but "Center," the element that you add is compressed to fit in the smallest amount of space along one dimension while it is stretched to the maximum along the other dimension. "Center," however, spreads out along both dimensions to occupy the middle.

The BorderLayout is the default layout manager for applications and dialogs.

16.18.3 Grid Layout

A GridLayout allows you to build a table of components, and as you add them they are placed left-to-right and top-to-bottom in the grid. In the constructor you specify the number of rows and columns that you need and these are laid out in equal proportions.

```
//: GridLayout1.java
// Demonstrating the FlowLayout
import java.awt.*;
import java.applet.*;

public class GridLayout1 extends Applet {
public void init() {
setLayout(new GridLayout(7,3));
for(int i = 0; i < 20; i++)
add(new Button("Button " + i));
}
} ///:~
```

In this case there are 21 slots but only 20 buttons. The last slot is left empty; no "balancing" goes on with a GridLayout.

16.18.4 CardLayout

The CardLayout allows you to create the rough equivalent of a "tabbed dialog," which in more sophisticated environments has actual file-folder tabs running across one edge, and all you have to do is press a tab to bring forward a different dialog. Not so in the AWT: The CardLayout is simply a blank space and you're responsible for bringing forward new cards. (The JFC/Swing library contains tabbed panes that look much better and take care of all the details for you.)

16.18.5 Combining Layouts

This example will combine more than one layout type, which seems rather difficult at first since only one layout manager can be operating for an applet or application. This is true, but if you create more Panel objects, each one of those Panels can have its own layout manager and then be integrated into the applet or application as simply another component, using the applet or application's layout manager. This gives you much greater flexibility as seen in the following example:

```
//: CardLayout1.java
```

```
// Demonstrating the CardLayout
import java.awt.*;
import java.applet.Applet;
class ButtonPanel extends Panel {
ButtonPanel(String id) {
setLayout(new BorderLayout());
add("Center", new Button(id));
}
}
public class CardLayout1 extends Applet {
Button
first = new Button("First"),
second = new Button("Second"),
third = new Button("Third");
Panel cards = new Panel();
CardLayout cl = new CardLayout();
public void init() {
setLayout(new BorderLayout());
Panel p = new Panel();
p.setLayout(new FlowLayout());
p.add(first);
p.add(second);
p.add(third);
add("North", p);
cards.setLayout(cl);
cards.add("First card",
new ButtonPanel("The first one"));
cards.add("Second card",
new ButtonPanel("The second one"));
cards.add("Third card",
new ButtonPanel("The third one"));
add("Center", cards);
}
public boolean action(Event evt, Object arg)
{
if (evt.target.equals(first)) {
cl.first(cards);
}
else if (evt.target.equals(second)) {
cl.first(cards);
cl.next(cards);
}
else if (evt.target.equals(third)) {
cl.last(cards);
}
else
return super.action(evt, arg);
return true;
```

```
    }
} ///:~
```

This example begins by creating a new kind of Panel: a ButtonPanel. This contains a single button, placed at the center of a BorderLayout, which means that it will expand to fill the entire panel. The label on the button will let you know which panel you're on in the CardLayout.

In the applet, both the Panel cards where the cards will live and the layout manager cl for the CardLayout must be members of the class because you need to have access to those handles when you want to manipulate the cards.

The applet is changed to use a BorderLayout instead of its default FlowLayout, a Panel is created to hold three buttons (using a FlowLayout), and this panel is placed at the "North" end of the applet. The cards panel is added to the "Center" of the applet, effectively occupying the rest of the real estate.

When you add the ButtonPanels (or whatever other components you want) to the panel of cards, the add( ) method's first argument is not "North," "South," etc. Instead, it's a string that describes the card. Although this string doesn't show up anywhere on the card, you can use it if you want to flip that card using the string. This approach is not used in action( ); instead the first( ), next( ), and last( ) methods are used. Check your documentation for the other approach.

In Java, the use of some sort of "tabbed panel" mechanism is quite important because (as you'll see later) in applet programming the use of pop-up dialogs is heavily discouraged. For Java 1.0 applets, the CardLayout is the only viable way for the applet to have a number of different forms that "pop up" on command.

16.18.6 Grid Bag Layout

Some time ago, it was believed that all the stars, planets, the sun, and the moon revolved around the earth. It seemed intuitive from observation. But then astronomers became more sophisticated and started tracking the motion of individual objects, some of which seemed at times to go backward in their paths. Since it was known that everything revolved around the earth, those astronomers spent large amounts of time coming up with equations and theories to explain the motion of the stellar objects.

When trying to work with GridBagLayout, you can consider yourself the analog of one of those early astronomers. The basic precept (decreed, interestingly enough, by the designers at "Sun") is that everything should be done in code. The Copernican revolution (again dripping with irony, the discovery that the planets in the solar system revolve around the sun) is the use of resources to determine the layout and make the programmer's job easy. Until these are added to Java, you're stuck (to continue the metaphor) in the Spanish Inquisition of GridBagLayout and GridBagConstraints.

My recommendation is to avoid GridBagLayout. Instead, use the other layout managers and especially the technique of combining several panels using different layout managers within a single program. Your applets won't look that different; at least not enough to justify the trouble that GridBagLayout entails. For my part, it's just too painful to come up with an example for this (and I wouldn't want to encourage this kind of library design). Instead, I'll refer you to Core Java by Cornell & Horstmann (2 nd ed., Prentice-Hall, 1997) to get started.

There's another light on the horizon: in the JFC/Swing library there is a new layout manager that uses Smalltalk's popular "Springs and Struts," and this could significantly reduce the need for GridBagLayout.

16.18.7 Alternatives to Action

As noted previously, action( ) isn't the only method that's automatically called by handleEvent( ) once it sorts everything out for you. There are three other sets of methods that are called, and if you want to capture certain types of events (keyboard, mouse, and focus events) all you have to do is override the provided method. These methods are defined in the base class Component, so they're available in virtually all the controls that you might place on a form. However, you should be aware that this approach is deprecated in Java 1.1, so although you might see legacy code using this technique you should use the Java 1.1 approaches instead.

16.19 Component Method

When it's called

- action (Event evt, Object what)

When the "typical" event occurs for this component (for example, when a button is pushed or a drop-down list item is selected)

- keyDown (Event evt, int key)

A key is pressed when this component has the focus. The second argument is the key that was pressed and is redundantly copied from evt.key.

keyUp(Event evt, int key)

A key is released when this component has the focus.

lostFocus(Event evt, Object what)

The focus has moved away from the target. Normally, what is redundantly copied from evt.arg.

```
gotFocus(Event evt, Object what)
The focus has moved into the target.
mouseDown(Event evt,
int x, int y)
A mouse down has occurred over the component, at the coordinates x,
y.
mouseUp(Event evt, int x, int y)
A mouse up has occurred over the component.
mouseMove(Event evt, int x, int y)
The mouse has moved while it's over the component.
mouseDrag(Event evt, int x, int y)
```

The mouse is being dragged after a mouseDown occurred over the component. All drag events are reported to the component in which the mouseDown occurred until there is a mouseUp.

```
mouseEnter(Event evt, int x, int y)
The mouse wasn't over the component before, but now it is.
mouseExit(Event evt, int x, int y)
The mouse used to be over the component, but now it isn't.
```

You can see that each method receives an Event object along with some information that you'll typically need when you're handling that particular situation - with a mouse event, for example, it's likely that you'll want to know the coordinates where the mouse event occurred. It's interesting to note that when Component's handleEvent( ) calls any of these methods (the typical case), the extra arguments are always redundant as they are contained within the Event object. In fact, if you look at the source code for Component.handleEvent( ) you can see that it explicitly plucks the additional arguments out of the Event object. (This might be considered inefficient coding in some languages, but remember that Java's focus is on safety, not necessarily speed.)

To prove to yourself that these events are in fact being called and as an interesting experiment, it's worth creating an applet that overrides each of the methods above (except for action( ), which is overridden in many other places in this chapter) and displays data about each of the events as they happen.

This example also shows you how to make your own button object because that's what is used as the target of all the events of interest. You might first (naturally) assume that to make a new button, you'd inherit from Button. But this doesn't work. Instead, you inherit from Canvas (a much more generic component) and paint your button on that canvas by overriding the paint( ) method. As you'll see, it's really too bad that overriding Button doesn't work, since there's a bit of code involved to paint the button. (If you don't believe me, try exchanging Button for Canvas in this example, and remember to call the base-class constructor super(label). You'll see that the button doesn't get painted and the events don't get handled.)

The myButton class is specific: it works only with an AutoEvent "parent window" (not a base class, but the window in which this button is created and lives). With this knowledge, myButton can reach into the parent window and manipulate its text fields, which is what's necessary to be able to write the status information into the fields of the parent. Of course this is a much more limited solution, since myButton can be used only in conjunction with AutoEvent. This kind of code is sometimes called "highly coupled." However, to make myButton more generic requires a lot more effort that isn't warranted for this example (and possibly for many of the applets that you will write). Again, keep in mind that the following code uses APIs that are deprecated in Java 1.1.

```
//: AutoEvent.java
// Alternatives to action()
import java.awt.*;
import java.applet.*;
import java.util.*;

class MyButton extends Canvas {
AutoEvent parent;
Color color;
String label;
MyButton(AutoEvent parent,
Color color, String label) {
this.label = label;
this.parent = parent;
this.color = color;
}
public void paint(Graphics  g) {
g.setColor(color);
int rnd = 30;
g.fillRoundRect(0, 0, size().width,
size().height, rnd, rnd);
g.setColor(Color.black);
g.drawRoundRect(0, 0, size().width,
size().height, rnd, rnd);
FontMetrics fm = g.getFontMetrics();
int width = fm.stringWidth(label);
int height = fm.getHeight();
int ascent = fm.getAscent();
```

```
int leading = fm.getLeading();
int horizMargin = (size().width - width)/2;
int verMargin = (size().height - height)/2;
g.setColor(Color.white);
g.drawString(label, horizMargin,
verMargin + ascent + leading);
}
public boolean keyDown(Event evt, int key) {
TextField t =
(TextField)parent.h.get("keyDown");
t.setText(evt.toString());
return true;
}
public boolean keyUp(Event evt, int key) {
TextField t =
(TextField)parent.h.get("keyUp");
t.setText(evt.toString());
return true;
}
public boolean lostFocus(Event evt, Object w) {
TextField t =
(TextField)parent.h.get("lostFocus");
t.setText(evt.toString());
return true;
}
public boolean gotFocus(Event evt, Object w) {
TextField t =
(TextField)parent.h.get("gotFocus");
t.setText(evt.toString());
return true;
}
public boolean
mouseDown(Event evt,int x,int y) {
TextField t =
(TextField)parent.h.get("mouseDown");
t.setText(evt.toString());
return true;
}
public boolean
mouseDrag(Event evt,int x,int y) {
TextField t =
(TextField)parent.h.get("mouseDrag");
t.setText(evt.toString());
return true;
}
public boolean
mouseEnter(Event evt,int x,int y) {
TextField t =
```

```
(TextField)parent.h.get("mouseEnter");
t.setText(evt.toString());
return true;
}
public boolean
mouseExit(Event evt,int x,int y) {
TextField t =
(TextField)parent.h.get("mouseExit");
t.setText(evt.toString());
return true;
}
public boolean
mouseMove(Event evt,int x,int y) {
TextField t =
(TextField)parent.h.get("mouseMove");
t.setText(evt.toString());
return true;
}
public boolean mouseUp(Event evt,int x,int y) {
TextField t =
(TextField)parent.h.get("mouseUp");
t.setText(evt.toString());
return true;
}
}

public class AutoEvent extends Applet {
Hashtable h = new Hashtable();
String[] event = {
"keyDown", "keyUp", "lostFocus",
"gotFocus", "mouseDown", "mouseUp",
"mouseMove", "mouseDrag", "mouseEnter",
"mouseExit"
};
MyButton
b1 = new MyButton(this, Color.blue, "test1"),
b2 = new MyButton(this, Color.red, "test2");
public void init() {
setLayout(new GridLayout(event.length+1,2));
for(int i = 0; i < event.length; i++) {
TextField t = new TextField();
t.setEditable(false);
add(new Label(event[i], Label.CENTER));
add(t);
h.put(event[i], t);
}
add(b1);
add(b2);
}
```

```
} ///:~
```

You can see the constructor uses the technique of using the same name for the argument as what it's assigned to, and differentiating between the two using this:

this.label = label;

The paint( ) method starts out simple: it fills a "round rectangle" with the button's color, and then draws a black line around it. Notice the use of size( ) to determine the width and height of the component (in pixels, of course). After this, paint( ) seems quite complicated because there's a lot of calculation going on to figure out how to center the button's label inside the button using the "font metrics." You can get a pretty good idea of what's going on by looking at the method call, and it turns out that this is pretty stock code, so you can just cut and paste it when you want to center a label inside any component.

You can't understand exactly how the keyDown( ), keyUp( ), etc. methods work until you look down at the AutoEvent class. This contains a Hashtable to hold the strings representing the type of event and the TextField where information about that event is held. Of course, these could have been created statically rather than putting them in a Hashtable, but I think you'll agree that it's a lot easier to use and change. In particular, if you need to add or remove a new type of event in AutoEvent, you simply add or remove a string in the event array - everything else happens automatically.

The place where you look up the strings is in the keyDown( ), keyUp( ), etc. methods back in MyButton. Each of these methods uses the parent handle to reach back to the parent window. Since that parent is an AutoEvent it contains the Hashtable h , and the get( ) method, when provided with the appropriate String, will produce a handle to an Object that we happen to know is a TextField - so it is cast to that. Then the Event object is converted to its String representation, which is displayed in the TextField.

It turns out this example is rather fun to play with since you can really see what's going on with the events in your program.

EXERCISES

1. *Write a stand-alone application which allows the user to edit some text in multiple windows. (You'll probably want to use a TextArea and a BorderLayout in each Frame.) Include standard File and Edit menus as discussed in class. At a minimum the File menu should have New, Open, Close, Save, Save As..., Print, and Quit menu items. The Edit menu should have Cut, Copy, Paste, Clear, Select All, and Undo menu items. The New menu item should bring up a new text editing window. The Close menu item should close the current window. The Quit menu item should exit the application. All other menu items should be disabled for now. Include the standard shortcuts for those menu items that have them, (e.g. N for New, C for Copy, and so on)*

2. *Write an image filter that produces a negative of an image. The basic algorithm here is to subtract the value of each color from 255. For example a red value of 200 would be transformed into a red value of 255 - 200 = 55.*

   ***Note:** I'm not 100% sure this will actually produce a photographic negative. Consider this an experiment.*

3. *Write a simple class called Message with a single public method that brings up a modal dialog with a user specified string message. The box should have a single button with the label "OK". When the button is pressed, the box is dismissed. This class should have a single static, public method with this signature:*

   public static void alert(String message, Frame parent)

   Use a layout manager of your choice to give the dialog a pleasing appearance.

4. *Revise the payroll applet from Class 6 so that an alert is displayed if the user enters a pay rate less than the minimum wage ($5.25 an hour).*

To the Message class add an okCancel method similar to the last exercise with this signature:

public static boolean alert(String message, Frame parent)

This method should return true if the user presses the OK Button and false if they press the Cancel button. To the extent possible, there should be no other public methods in this class. (Methods you override from superclasses may have to be declared public.) Use a layout manager of your choice to give the dialog a pleasing appearance.

5. *Revise the payroll applet from Class 6 so that an alert is displayed if the user enters a pay rate less than the minimum wage ($5.25 an hour). If the user presses OK, the applet will calculate the total pay. Otherwise, it won't.*

   To the same message class add a third method that brings up a query dialog that has a TextField to allow the user to enter a single line of text, then returns the line of text. The method should have the following signature:

   public static String query(String question, Frame parent)

   The method should return whatever the user types in the box. To the extent possible, there should be no other public methods in this class. Use a layout manager of your choice to give the dialog a pleasing appearance.

6. *Revise the payroll applet from Class 6 so that if the user enters a pay rate less than the minimum wage ($5.25 an hour) or an incorrect pay rate (e.g. "Five dollars and 25 cents") the applet puts up a dialog asking for a new rate.*

17

Introduction to Java Beans

In this section, you will learn about:

- The JavaBeans architecture
- The Beans Event Model
- Introspection to query Beans about their contents
- Bean component creation
- Customization of Beans
- Persistence to store and retrieve Beans
- The development of applications comprised of Bean components
- The creation of simple builder application

17.1 Introduction to Java Beans

JavaBeans takes Java's "Write Once, Run AnywhereTM" capability and extends it to include "reuse everywhere". "JavaBeans is a portable, platform-independent component model, written in Java." With it, you create small, reusable, software components. A visual "builder" program combines components from disparate sources to create applications quickly and easily.

17.1.1 What's a Bean?

A Bean is a JavaBeans component. Beans are independent, reusable software modules. Beans may be visible objects, like AWT components, or invisible objects, like queues and stacks. A builder/integration tool manipulates Beans to create applets and applications.

17.2 Beans Architecture

Beans consist of three things:

- Events
- Properties
- Methods

Also, since Beans rely on their state, they need to be able to be persistent over time.

17.3 Events

Events are for notifying others when something is happening. The delegation-event model of AWT, introduced with Java 1.1, demonstrates the Beans event model. It has three parts:

- EventObjects
- AWT Event in the AWT world.

EventListeners ActionListener, ItemListener, ...

and

- ❑ Event Sources (Beans)

17.4 The different AWT Components.

Anyone can register an EventListener with a Component, provided the Component understands the event set. (For instance, you cannot register an ActionListener with a TextArea, but you can with a TextField). When something happens within the Component, it notifies any listener(s) by sending each an EventObject, through the appropriate method of the listener.

17.4.1 Properties

Properties define the characteristics of the Bean. For instance, when examining an AWT TextField for its properties, you will see properties for the caret position, current text, and the echo character, among others. In the simplest case, a method or methods in the following design pattern defines a property:

public void setPropertyName(PropertyType value);
public PropertyType getPropertyName();

Where PropertyName is the name of the property, and PropertyType is its datatype. If only one method is present, the property is read-only (set missing) or write-only (get missing).

Methods

Bean methods are available for anyone to call by just making each public. However, you can restrict which methods are visible to the Bean builder/integration tool by providing a getMethodDescriptors method along with your Bean's BeanInfo. Every Bean can provide a supporting BeanInfo class to customize a Bean's appearance to an integration tool. More on BeanInfo later.

17.4.2 Persistence

Persistence is the ability of an object to store its state, for recreation later. Beans use Java's object serialization capabilities for persistence. The ObjectInput and ObjectOutput interfaces are the basis for serialization within Java. The ObjectInputStream and ObjectOutputStream classes, respectively, implement the interfaces. Serialization saves all non-static and non-transient instance variables of an object. If one of those is a reference to another object, that object is recursively saved, too, until everything saved is primitive datatypes. If one object is referred to by multiple references, Java serializes it only once. This ensures the creation of an identical object network when reading the primary object back. To demonstrate, use a fictitious TreeNode class to create the network:

```
TreeNode top = new TreeNode("top");
top.addChild(new TreeNode("left child"));
top.addChild(new TreeNode("right child"));
```

and then to save:

```
FileOutputStream fOut =
new FileOutputStream("test.out");
ObjectOutput out = new ObjectOutputStream(fOut);
out.writeObject(top);
out.flush();
out.close();
```

Now, your program can exit, knowing that when it restarts it can recreate the tree from the test.out file.

```
FileInputStream fIn = new FileInputStream("test.out");
```

```
ObjectInputStream in = new ObjectInputStream(fIn);
TreeNode n = (TreeNode)in.readObject();
```

17.5 Technology Comparison to ActiveX/COM

JavaBeans is a framework for building applications out of Java components (Beans).

ActiveX is a framework for building compound documents with ActiveX controls.

A Bean is very similar to an ActiveX control. However, a Bean is written in Java, so has Java's security and cross platform nature.

ActiveX controls written in Java is possible, however they require a port of Microsoft's Common Object Model (COM) to be used outside of Microsoft Windows.

More frequently, programmers create ActiveX controls in Visual Basic or Visual C++ and compile them into native libraries.

17.6 JavaBeans Benefit Analysis

- Write Once, Run AnywhereTM java.beans package part of Core API
- Component Reusability Reuse Everywhere — across platforms/tools/solutions
- Example: 3D Charting Bean - drop into any container, regardless of platform tool
- Interoperability Communicate with other component architectures
- Beans-ActiveX Bridge now beta, Beans-OpenDoc under development

17.7 Writing Bean Components

To create a Bean, you need to determine what it should do and then define the events, properties, and methods to get it there. Actually, most of the method definitions fall out of the definition of events and properties for the Bean.

17.8 Events

An event allows your Beans to communicate when something interesting happens. There are three parts to this communication:

- EventObject
- EventListener - (the sink)
- An Event Source (the Bean)

17.8.1 EventObject

The java.util.EventObject class is the basis of all Beans events.

```
public class java.util.EventObject
extends Object implements java.io.Serializable {
public java.util.EventObject (Object source);
public Object getSource();
public String toString();
}
```

Although you can create EventObject instances directly for your Bean events, design pattern guidelines require you to subclass EventObject so you have a specific event type. For example, to define an event for an employee's hire date, you could create a HireEvent class.

```
public class HireEvent extends EventObject {
private long hireDate;
```

```
public HireEvent (Object source) {
super (source);
hireDate = System.currentTimeMillis();
}
public HireEvent (Object source, long hired) {
super (source);
hireDate = hired;
}
public long getHireDate () {
return hireDate;
}
}
```

17.8.2 Event Listener

The EventListener interface is empty, but serves as a tagging interface that all event listeners must extend; that way, Beans integration tools can work. A listener is something that desires notification when an event happens. The listener receives the specific EventObject subclass as a parameter. The name of the new listener interface is EventTypeListener. For the new HireEvent, the listener name would be HireListener. The actual method names within the interface have no specific design pattern to follow, but, should describe the event that is happening.

```
public interface HireListener
extends java.util.EventListener {
public abstract void hired (HireEvent e);
}
```

17.8.3 Event Source

Without an event source, the HireEvent and HireListener are virtually useless. The event source defines when and where an event will happen. Classes register themselves as interested in the event, and they receive notification when the event happens. A series of methods patterns represents the registration process:

public synchronized void addListenerType(ListenerType l);

public synchronized void removeListenerType(

ListenerType l);

The event source needs to maintain the list itself, so the entire code to do this is:

```
private Vector hireListeners = new Vector();
public synchronized void addHireListener (
HireListener l) {
hireListeners.addElement (l);
}
public synchronized void removeHireListener (HireListener l) {
hireListeners.removeElement (l);
}
```

If you are using AWT components, AWT events already have this behavior. Maintaining listeners is only necessary for new event types, or adding listeners where they previously were not (ActionEvent within a Canvas).

If you want to permit only one listener (unicast), you have the addListenerType method throw the java.util.TooManyListenersException exception when adding a second listener (and you do not need a Vector). Also, remember to synchronize the add/remove methods to avoid a race condition.

Once the event happens, it is necessary for the event source to notify all the listeners. For the hiring example, this would translate into a method like the following:

```
protected void notifyHired () {
Vector l;
// Create Event
HireEvent h = new HireEvent (this);
// Copy listener vector so it won't
// change while firing
synchronized (this) {
l = (Vector)hireListeners.clone();
}
for (int i=0;i<l.size();i++) {
HireListener hl = (HireListener)l.elementAt (i);
hl.hired(h);
}
}
```

You have to call the method directly when the triggering event happens.

17.8.4 Properties

A property is a public attribute of the Bean, usually represented by a non-public instance variable. It can be read-write, read-only, or write-only. There are four different types of properties:

- Simple
- Indexed
- Bound
- Constrained

(1) Simple Properties

As the name implies, simple properties represent the simplest of the four. To create a property, define a pair of set/get routines. Whatever name used in the pair of routines, becomes the property name (no matter what instance variable name you use). Normally, the instance variable name matches the property name. However, there is nothing that requires this. For instance, to define a property salary for an Employee Bean:

```
float salary;
public void setSalary (float newSalary) {
salary = newSalary;
}
public float getSalary () {
return salary;
}
```

If you need a read-only property, only define a getPropertyName routine. If you want a write-only property, only define a setPropertyName routine. Boolean properties can change their get routine to an isPropertyName routine:

boolean trained;

```
public void setTrained (boolean trained) {
```

```
this.trained = trained;
}
public boolean isTrained () {
return trained;
}
```

(2) Indexed Properties

An indexed property is for when a single property can hold an array of values. The design pattern for these properties is:

```
public void setPropertyName (PropertyType[] list)
public void setPropertyName (
PropertyType element, int position)
public PropertyType[] getPropertyName ()
public PropertyType getPropertyName (int position)
```

For instance, if you were to complete the item indexed property for the AWT List component, it might look something like this:

```
public class ListBean extends List {
public String[] getItem () {
return getItems ();
}
public synchronized void setItem (String item[]) {
removeAll();
for (int i=0;i<item.length;i++)
addItem (item[i]);
}
public void setItem (String item, int position) {
replaceItem (item, position)
}
}
```

The String getItem (int position) routine already exists for List.

The AWT List class is still a Bean without these methods. However, item is not fully defined to be an indexed property.

(3) Bound Properties

Revisit the Employee Bean, and make salary a bound property. That way, if two people were using an employee Bean (say a manager and a spouse), and one (the manager) changes an employee's salary, the other (the spouse) would like to know about said change. In order for the notification to happen, you need to maintain a watch list for PropertyChangeEvents via the PropertyChangeSupport class. First, you have to create a list of listeners to maintain:

```
private PropertyChangeSupport changes =
new PropertyChangeSupport (this);
```

And then, you have to maintain the list:

```
public void addPropertyChangeListener (
PropertyChangeListener p) {
changes.addPropertyChangeListener (p);
}
```

```
public void removePropertyChangeListener (
PropertyChangeListener p) {
changes.removePropertyChangeListener (p);
}
```

Finally, when the change happens (setSalary in this case), you check to see if the property value changed, and if so, notify all the listeners.

```
public void setSalary (float salary) {
Float oldSalary = new Float (this.salary);
this.salary = salary;
changes.firePropertyChange (
"salary", oldSalary, new Float (this.salary));
}
```

On the receiving end, you then need a propertyChange method.

public void propertyChange(PropertyChangeEvent e);

Since Java reports PropertyChangeEvents at the class (Bean) level (versus the property level), you need to check the property name via getPropertyName to see if you received a PropertyChangeEvent you were expecting, or something else. Also, if the property datatype is primitive, you need to wrap it into the appropriate object when firing.

(4) Constrained Properties

Constrained properties are similar to bound properties. In addition to maintaining a list of PropertyChangeListeners, the Bean maintains a list of VetoableChangeListeners. Then, prior to the Bean changing a property value, it asks the VetoableChangeListeners if its okay. If it isn't, the listener throws a PropertyVetoException, which you declare the set routine to throw.

Changing salary to be a constrained property (so a spouse can veto salary decreases), results in the following additions:

```
private VetoableChangeSupport vetoes =
new VetoableChangeSupport (this);
public void addVetoableChangeListener (
VetoableChangeListener v) {
vetoes.addVetoableChangeListener (v);
}
public void removeVetoableChangeListener (
VetoableChangeListener v) {
vetoes.removeVetoableChangeListener (v);
}

And changes:
public void setSalary (float salary)
throws PropertyVetoException {
Float oldSalary = new Float (this.salary);
vetoes.fireVetoableChange (
"salary", oldSalary, new Float (salary));
this.salary = salary;
changes.firePropertyChange (
"salary", oldSalary, new Float (this.salary));
}
```

On the receiving end, your VetoableChangeListener needs a vetoableChange method.

public void vetoableChange(PropertyChangeEvent e)

throws PropertyVetoException;

Instead of providing one listener for all property change events, and another for all vetoable change events, you can elect to maintain separate lists of listeners for each property. The design pattern for this is:

```
public void addPropertyNameListener (
PropertyChangeListener p);
public void removePropertyNameListener (
PropertyChangeListener p);
and
public void addPropertyNameListener (
VetoableChangeListener v);
public void removePropertyNameListener (
VetoableChangeListener v);
```

17.9 Methods

Methods are operations for others to interact with a Bean. Basically, anything can call any public method of a Bean. Beans receive notification of events by having the appropriate method called on them by the event source.

Besides all the methods required for each property and event of a Bean, you usually create support methods which accept no arguments or an argument of an event you listen for. That way, a builder application can inspect a class quickly for a list of the appropriate methods it can connect to. Non-public support methods may also be available. However, public methods with other parameter patterns are usually the result of a bad design pattern, and not easily connectable from a builder application. For instance, if you always pass along a time-stamp with an event, you should probably subclass the event, add a time-stamp attribute, and pass the subclass around. This results in a simplified design and easier maintainability.

17.10 Intro to Customization

Customization of Beans allows you as the Beans developer to control what a Bean-integrator will see when they use a builder tool. By default, a builder tool uses reflection to determine what to display when designing programs with Beans. In most cases, this is sufficient. However, there are times when you want to provide different functionality. For instance, if you want to provide your own customization interface, instead of using the default property sheet, you can implement the Customizer interface and provide a custom Panel. The OurButton Bean in the Beans Development Kit (BDK) provides a Customizer.

On the other hand, if you want to provide an alternative input mechanism for one property (like an enumerated list of valid choices), you can extend the PropertyEditorSupport class. The Molecule Bean in the BDK uses a property editor to provide a list of molecules it can display.

Using either of these mechanisms requires your Bean to provide a supporting class, along with the Bean itself. This second class implements the BeanInfo interface.

17.11 BeanInfo

The BeanInfo interface allows you to describe your Bean in greater detail then reflection alone can do. You usually want to do this to provide your Bean integrator with less options, or more restrictive options, so the Bean is easier to work with. In order for the system to locate the BeanInfo for a Bean, you must name it after the Bean, with BeanInfo at the end of the Bean's classname. For instance, if your Bean was called Foo, the BeanInfo for the Foo Bean would be called FooBeanInfo. It isn't necessary to implement the entire BeanInfo yourself. The SimpleBeanInfo class provides a basis, then you just selectively override methods.

Beans must be able to operate in a running application as well as inside a builder. At design-time, Beans must provide the design information necessary to edit properties and customize behavior. Also it has to expose methods and events so a builder tool can create code that interacts with the Bean at run-time. The Beans.isDesignTime method allows you to check for the current mode.

17.12 Introspection

Introspection is the process of determining the supported properties, methods, and events of a Bean. It can be done with the help of the Introspector class, or directly through the use of the Reflection API. The Introspector provides access to the BeanInfo for the Bean component via its getBeanInfo method, which requires an instance of Class as its parameter:

TextField tf = new TextField ();
BeanInfo bi =
Introspector.getBeanInfo (tf.getClass());

If you don't provide BeanInfo for a Bean, the Reflection API is used to determine the different pieces for you.

17.12.1 Events

The getEventSetDescriptors method reports all the events that this Bean fires. For every pair of add/removeListenerTypeListener methods (that return void), an event set is defined for the Bean.

```
EventSetDescriptor[] esd =
bi.getEventSetDescriptors();
for (int i=0;i<esd.length;i++)
System.out.print (esd[i].getName() + " ");
System.out.println ();
```

For a TextField, this would print:

text mouse key component action focus mouseMotion

17.12.2 Properties

The getPropertyDescriptors method reports all the properties of a Bean. A property is defined by one or more routines with the following pattern:

```
public void setPropertyName(PropertyType value);
public PropertyType getPropertyName();
public boolean isPropertyName();
PropertyDescriptor pd[] =
bi.getPropertyDescriptors();
for (int i=0;i<pd.length;i++)
System.out.print (pd[i].getName() + " ");
System.out.println ();
```

For a TextField, this would print:

selectionStart enabled text preferredSize
foreground visible background selectedText
echoCharacter font columns echoChar name
caretPosition selectionEnd minimumSize editable

17.12.3 Methods

The getMethodDescriptors method reports all the methods of a Bean. This is an all-inclusive list of public methods, which enable you to call any one of them without knowing their name before hand. For each method descriptor, you can discover the parameter types through the getParameterDescriptors method.

```
MethodDescriptor md[] = bi.getMethodDescriptors();
for (int i=0;i<md.length;i++)
System.out.print (md[i].getName() + " ");
System.out.println ();
```

For a TextField, this would print the names of all 155 methods available, most of which are inherited from Component. This includes the add/remove event listener methods, as they are methods like the others.

17.12.4 BeanInfo

Although the examples have been using the Introspector so far, when a custom BeanInfo isn't provided for a Bean, the Introspector uses the Reflection API to determine the events, properties, and methods of the Bean. If you want to restrict a builder tool to display less choices, you can override the default behavior and implement your own BeanInfo. The BeanInfo interface is not implemented by the Bean itself, but by a secondary class. If we've created a SizedTextField Bean, the SizedTextFieldBeanInfo class would provide the Bean's BeanInfo. If you only wanted to display one property, length, you could define that class as such:

```
import java.beans.*;
public class SizedTextFieldBeanInfo
extends SimpleBeanInfo {
private final static Class beanClass =
SizedTextField.class;
public PropertyDescriptor[]
getPropertyDescriptors() {
try {
PropertyDescriptor length =
new PropertyDescriptor("length", beanClass);
PropertyDescriptor rv[] = {length};
return rv;
} catch (IntrospectionException e) {
throw new Error(e.toString());
}
}
}
```

Then, instead of the 17 properties of TextField, the only property displayed by the tool, would be the new length property. The SizedTextField class still needs to implement the set/getLength methods. Also, creating a custom BeanInfo does not prevent someone from calling the methods of the now hidden properties. The property accessor methods are still public. So, by using the Reflection API (or just knowing the method names), you can still invoke all the public methods.

Also, if you wanted to have the Bean have a space delimited name, instead of being all crunched together, you could add the following to the SizedTextFieldBeanInfo definition:

```
public BeanDescriptor getBeanDescriptor() {
BeanDescriptor bd = new BeanDescriptor(beanClass);
bd.setDisplayName("Sized Text Field");
return bd;
}
```

And, to wrap things up, you could even supply an icon for your Bean with the help of an image file and the following added to your BeanInfo definition:

```
public Image getIcon (int iconKind) {
if (iconKind == BeanInfo.ICON_COLOR_16x16) {
Image img = loadImage("sized.gif");
return img;
}
return null;
}
```

17.13 Customizers

Using Customizers allow YOU, the Bean builder, to control how your Bean user is going to configure visually your Bean at design time. Instead of relying on the builder tool's property sheet to setup the properties of a Bean, you can provide either a full-screen customization option or an alternative to the datatype's default property sheet option.

17.13.1 Writing Customizers

If the Employee Bean only had a salary property, you could create a customizer like the following. It would only permit numeric characters in the input field. Customizers are much more powerful than this implies. However, they result in rather lengthy examples and this should provide a sufficient framework to get you started.

```
package employee;
import java.awt.*;
import java.awt.event.*;
import java.beans.*;

public class EmployeeCustomizer extends Panel
implements Customizer, KeyListener {
private Employee target;
private TextField salaryField;
private PropertyChangeSupport support =
new PropertyChangeSupport(this);
public void setObject(Object obj) {
target = (Employee) obj;
Label t1 = new Label("Salary :");
add(t1);
salaryField = new TextField(
String.valueOf(target.getSalary()), 20);
add(salaryField);
salaryField.addKeyListener(this);
```

```
}
public Dimension getPreferredSize() {
return new Dimension(225,50);
}
public void keyPressed(KeyEvent e) {}
public void keyTyped(KeyEvent e) {}
public void keyReleased(KeyEvent e) {
Object source = e.getSource();
if (source==salaryField) {
String txt = salaryField.getText();
try {
target.setSalary(
(new Float(txt)).floatValue());
} catch (NumberFormatException ex) {
salaryField.setText(
String.valueOf(target.getSalary()));
}
support.firePropertyChange("", null, null);
}
}
public void addPropertyChangeListener(
PropertyChangeListener l) {
support.addPropertyChangeListener(l);
}
public void removePropertyChangeListener(
PropertyChangeListener l) {
support.removePropertyChangeListener(l);
}
}
```

All of this work results in the following screen being displayed when the developer chooses to customize your Bean.

This also assumes that the following EmployeeBeanInfo class is defined:

```
package employee;
import java.beans.*;
public class EmployeeBeanInfo extends SimpleBeanInfo {
public BeanDescriptor getBeanDescriptor() {
return new BeanDescriptor(
beanClass, customizerClass);
}
private final static Class beanClass =
Employee.class;
private final static Class customizerClass =
EmployeeCustomizer.class;
}
```

17.13.2 Writing Property Customizers

If you think providing a custom screen for all the properties is not necessary, but want to have some control over what is displayed in the property sheet for a specific property, implementing PropertyEditor may be in store for you. You can implement the class yourself or use the framework in the PropertyEditorSupport class as your basis.

If you add a position property to the Employee, you can provide a list of positions by creating a EmployeePositionEditor class (that subclasses PropertyEditorSupport).

```
import java.beans.*;
public class EmployeePositionEditor
extends PropertyEditorSupport {
public String[] getTags() {
String values[] = {
"President",
"Technical Support",
"Window Washer",
"Janitor"};
return values;
}
}
```

When using a tag list with a property, the property must be initialized to one of the tags. If you forget, when a Bean user goes to use the property editor, a mysterious IllegalArgumentException will be thrown.

```
Then you add a few things to the EmployeeBeanInfo:
public PropertyDescriptor[] getPropertyDescriptors() {
try {
PropertyDescriptor pd =
new PropertyDescriptor("position", beanClass);
pd.setPropertyEditorClass(positionEditorClass);
PropertyDescriptor result[] = { pd };
return result;
} catch (Exception e) {
System.err.println("Unexpected exception: " + e);
return null;
}
}
```

And, the property sheet for the Employee Bean might look like this:

If there are multiple PropertyDescriptors, the order in the array determines the display order. If you do not call setPropertyEditorClass for a particular PropertyDescriptor, the PropertyEditorManager locates a suitable/default PropertyEditor.

17.14 Using System Property Editors

The JDK comes with a handful of suitable property editors available for your use. You should expect similar editors available with other tools:

- Datatype Editor
- Boolean BoolEditor

- Byte ByteEditor
- Color ColorEditor
- Double DoubleEditor
- Float FloatEditor
- Font FontEditor
- Int IntEditor
- Long LongEditor
- Number NumberEditor
- Short ShortEditor
- String StringEditor

All of these are part of the sun.beans.editors package. You do not have to do anything special to use them. The BDK's BeanBox tool is smart enough to know that if you have a float or Float property, to use the FloatEditor, similarly for the other datatypes. If you are not using the BeanBox, you can try to use them in your own environment.

17.15 Persistence

Persistence is the ability of an object to store its state. Beans use Java's object Serialization API to provide a great medium-weight solution for persistence. In the simplest case, the way to enable the serialization of any object is to implement the Serializable interface. The Serializable interface has no methods that must be implemented; however, any data fields of a class that implements this interface must also be serializable.

17.16 Bean Serialization

A Serializable object is serialized by calling the ObjectOutput.writeObject method, with the object as its parameter. To deserialize, the ObjectInput.readObject method is called. You, as a Bean creator, do NOT call these methods. What you do need to do is ensure your Bean is serializable.

- Is your class Serializable?
- Are all instance variables Serializable?
- Do you want everything that isn't transient or static to be saved?
- Should you serialize the object in its current structure?
- How do I initialize transient and static variables upon deserialization?
- Do you want to add a validator to the serialization process?

If you're Serializable and want the default behavior for everything else, you're set and don't have to do anything extra. However, if not, you have something to do.

The first is easy, does your class implement the Serializable interface (directly or indirectly)? If it doesn't, make it. (Note, there is also an Externalizable interface for when you need to control all aspect of Serialization, usually for security purposes.)

For the second, check to see if all each instance variable is Serializable. Primitive datatypes are, by default. The rest you have to check manually, until you learn which aren't. (Image isn't). If one isn't, you need to figure out what to do about it. (For instance, image files can be kept separate and re-read when a Bean is deserialized.) Do you initialize it to a default value, make it transient, or provide some other means to initialize?

The third is easy. Is it okay to save everything?

Fourth, is it more efficient to save the data in a different format? For instance, it is more efficient to serialize a Hashtable's pieces, and recreate the structure, then to save the mostly empty hashtable. Also, should you encrypt the information?

Fifth, is it okay to use default values for non-persistent variables? If not, you have to add code to handle this.

Finally, do you want to validate the deserialized object network? Like, is your graph consistent? If yes, you need to register a validation method.

For instance, if you wanted to have a Date instance variable of a class, but wanted it to be the 'last-created' date vs. a 'first-created' date, you could have a transient variable that is reset when deserialized:

```
public class TreeNode implements Serializable {
Vector children;
TreeNode parent;
String name;
transient Date date;
public TreeNode(String s) {
children = new Vector(5);
name = s;
initClass();
}
private void initClass () {
date = new Date();
}
...
private void writeObject(ObjectOutputStream s)
throws IOException {
s.defaultWriteObject();
}
private void readObject(ObjectInputStream s)
throws ClassNotFoundException, IOException {
s.defaultReadObject();
initClass();
}
}
```

Although the writeObject does the default functionality, whenever a readObject method is provided, a writeObject method is necessary.

17.17 Bean Reconstitution

Normally, you call new when you want to create an instance of a class. With Beans, you can still do that, however, there is another way. The Beans.instantiate method is normally used by builder tools to recreate a Bean from a serialized Bean source. The reason being, tool vendors do not want to restrict what Beans you could use to only those it knew about when the tool was created. For instance, to create a TextField, without new, just call:

```
Component c =
(Component)Beans.instantiate(
null, "java.awt.TextField");
```

By itself, this is identical to Component c = new TextField(); However, before you get too excited, build on this a bit. First, create your own TextField class, by subclassing TextField.

```
public class MyTextField extends java.awt.TextField
```

```
{
}
```

Nothing fancy yet. But, create a little program to save a serialized MyTextField, with a couple of properties set:

```
import java.awt.*;
import java.io.*;

public class TfSaver {
public static void main(String args[]) {
MyTextField mtf = new MyTextField();

// set the properties
Font ft = new Font("Serif", Font.ITALIC, 36);
mtf.setFont(ft);
mtf.setText("Hello World");

// serialize
try {
FileOutputStream f = new FileOutputStream(
"MyTextField.ser");
ObjectOutputStream s =
new ObjectOutputStream(f);
s.writeObject(mtf);
s.flush();
} catch (Exception e) {
System.out.println(e);
}
System.exit(0);
}
}
```

Now, if you create an application that uses a MyTextField instance, it can start with the font and text properties already set (to 36-point italic Serif font and "Hello World" text).

Component c =
(Component)Beans.instantiate(null, "MyTextField");

If a filename of the form Classname.ser exists (MyTextField.ser in this case), then the class is deserialized. Otherwise, the Bean will be created by using the default no-arg constructor of the class.

With MyTextField.ser

Without MyTextField.ser

17.18 Bean Versioning

Changes made to a Bean that change the persistence structure flag the new version as incompatible with the old, and prevents reconstitution. While this sounds good in theory, in practice it has its shortcomings. Adding any new method to a Bean makes the new class definition incompatible (for deserialization), resulting in a java.io.InvalidClassException being thrown. However, since a method does not add (or remove) any state information (behavior is not serialized), the two classes should be compatible. In order to ensure the new version can be reconstituted from the original, you need to add a Stream Unique Identifier (SUID) variable to your class definition.

```
private static final long serialVersionUID = -2966288784432217853L;
```

Then, when the versions are truly incompatible, you change the SUID variable. When this does happen, you should keep track of all the old values so you can properly handle the differences (e.g., default setting for new instance variable). If you forget to save the old setting, it is necessary to revert back to an old version, regenerating the value, and moving forward again.

The values are generated from a hash algorithm, not randomly picked out of the air nor even a one-up numbering scheme. Since static variables are not serialized, the value is regenerated during deserialization and compared against the current class definition. The program to generate the values is serialver and has one argument of the classname. If you run the program with the -show argument instead, serialver displays a graphical interface, which allows you to cut and paste the results into your editor.

18

Java Database Connectivity

18.1 JDBC Database Access

Java Database Connectivity (JDBC) is Sun Microsystems' standard SQL database access interface, providing uniform access to a wide range of relational databases. It consists of a set of classes and interfaces written in the Java programming language. The diagram below shows components of the SCO JDBC model. See below the diagram for an explanation of each component.

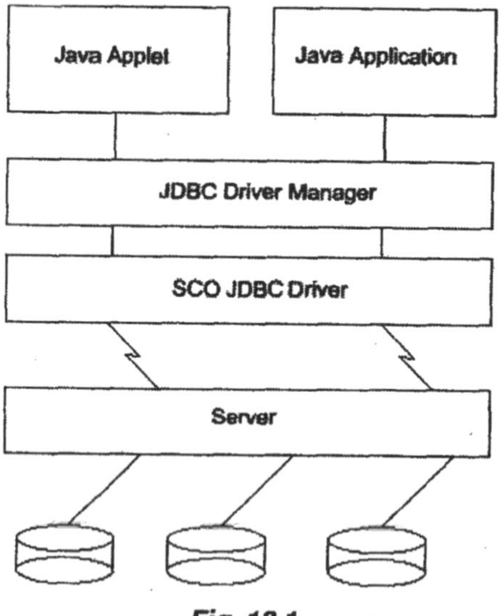

Fig. 18.1

JDBC-Aware Java applet. A Java applet that uses the JDBC API can manipulate a database. This will typically be downloaded over the Internet.

JDBC-Aware Java application. A Java application that uses the JDBC API can manipulate a database. This will be installed on the client device.

JDBC driver manager. The JDBC API defines Java classes to represent database connections, SQL statements, result sets, database metadata, and so on. The JDBC API is implemented via a driver manager that can support multiple drivers connecting to different databases. This must be installed on the client device. The driver manager is provided by Sun Microsystems.

SCO JDBC driver. The driver is a set of Java classes that processes JDBC calls and returns results to the applet or application. The SCO JDBC driver is a JDBC-Net pure Java driver. This will typically be downloaded over the Internet. The driver is provided by SCO.

Server module. The SCO JDBC driver has a component based on the client device and a server module that are connected through a RPC mechanism built into the driver.

JDBCTM was designed to keep simple things simple. This means that the JDBC API makes everyday database tasks, like simple SELECT statements, very easy. This trail will walk you through examples of using JDBC to execute common SQL statements, letting you see for yourself how easy it is to use the basic JDBC API.

Leading database, middleware and tool vendors have been building support for JDBC technology into many new products. This ensures that customers can build portable Java applications while choosing from a wide range of competitive products for the solution best suited to their needs. The following list is a partial listing of companies that are shipping products with support for JDBC technology (please see the Java Software web site for the most recent list):

- Vendor DBMS Supported
- Borland InterBase 4.0
- Caribou Lake Software Ingres, Oracle
- IBM IBM DB2
- IDS Software Oracle, Sybase, MS SQL Server, MS Access, Informix, * Watcom, and others via ODBC
- Imaginary mSQL
- Information Builders over 70 databases
- Informix Informix
- Merant DB2, Ingres, Informix, Oracle, Microsoft SQL Server, Sybase
- OpenLink Oracle, Informix, Sybase, MS SQL Server, CA-Ingres, Progress, Unify, and Postgress95
- Oracle Oracle
- Software AG ADABAS D
- Sybase, Inc Sybase SQL Server, SQL Anywhere, Sybase IQ,Replication Server and more than 25 enterprise and Legacy database servers via Sybase

18.1.1 The JDBC API: Universal Data Access for the Enterprise

The "Write Once, Run Anywhere" Java 2 Platform is a safe, flexible, and complete cross-platform solution for developing robust Java applications for the Internet and corporate intranets. The open and extensible Java Platform APIs are a set of essential interfaces that enable developers to build their Java applications and applets. The Java 2 Platform provides uniform, industry-standard, seamless connectivity and interoperability with enterprise information assets.

The JDBCTM API is the industry standard for database-independent connectivity between the Java programming language and a wide range of databases. The JDBC API provides a call-level API for SQL-based database access. JDBC technology allows developers using the Java programming language to exploit "Write Once, Run Anywhere" capabilities for applications that require access to enterprise data.

The JDBC API makes it possible to do three things:

- Establish a connection with a database or access any tabular data source
- Send SQL statements
- Process the results

18.1.2 JDBC Architecture

The JDBC API contains two major sets of interfaces: the first is the JDBC API for application writers, and the second is the lower-level JDBC driver API for driver writers. JDBC technology drivers fit into one of four categories. Applications and applets can access databases via the JDBC API using pure Java JDBC technology-based drivers, as shown in the following figure:

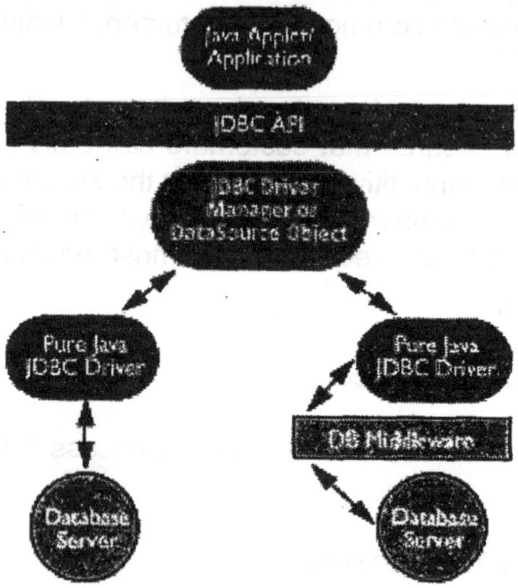

Fig. 18.2

Type 4. Direct-to-Database Pure Java Driver: This style of driver converts JDBC calls into the network protocol used directly by DBMSs, allowing a direct call from the client machine to the DBMS server and providing a practical solution for intranet access.

Type 3. Pure Java Driver for Database Middleware: This style of driver translates JDBC calls into the middleware vendor's protocol, which is then translated to a DBMS protocol by a middleware server. The middleware provides connectivity to many different databases.

The graphic below illustrates JDBC connectivity using ODBC drivers and existing database client libraries.

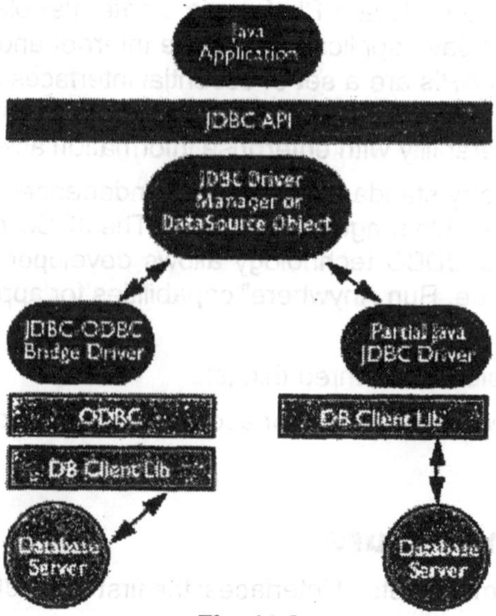

Fig. 18.3

Type 1. JDBC-ODBC Bridge plus ODBC Driver: This combination provides JDBC access via ODBC drivers. ODBC binary code—and in many cases, database client code— must be loaded on each client machine that uses a JDBC-ODBC Bridge. Sun provides a JDBC-ODBC Bridge driver, which is appropriate for experimental use and for situations in which no other driver is available.

Type 2. A native-API partly Java technology-enabled driver: This type of driver converts JDBC calls into calls on the client API for Oracle, Sybase, Informix, DB2, or other DBMS. Note that, like the bridge driver, this style of driver requires that some binary code be loaded on each client machine.

18.1.3 Advantages of JDBC Technology

With JDBC technology, businesses are not locked in any proprietary architecture, and can continue to use their installed databases and access information easily - even if it is stored on different database management systems.

(1) Simplified Enterprise Development

The combination of the Java API and the JDBC API makes application development easy and economical. JDBC hides the complexity of many data access tasks, doing most of the "heavy lifting"for the programmer behind the scenes. The JDBC API is simple to learn, easy to deploy, and inexpensive to maintain.

(2) Zero Configuration for Network Computers

With the JDBC API, no configuration is required on the client side. With a driver written in the Java programming language, all the information needed to make a connection is completely defined by the JDBC URL or by a DataSource object registered with a Java Naming and Directory InterfaceTM (JNDI) naming service. Zero configuration for clients supports the network computing paradigm and centralizes software maintenance.

(3) Full Access to Metadata

The JDBC API provides metadata access that enables the development of sophisticated applications that need to understand the underlying facilities and capabilities of a specific database connection.

(4) No Installation

A Pure JDBC technology-based driver does not require special installation; it is automatically downloaded as part of the applet that makes the JDBC calls.

(5) Database Connection Identified by URL

JDBC technology exploits the advantages of Internet-standard URLs to identify database connections. The new JDBC 2.0 API adds an even better way to identify and connect to a data source, using a DataSource object, that makes code even more portable and easier to maintain.

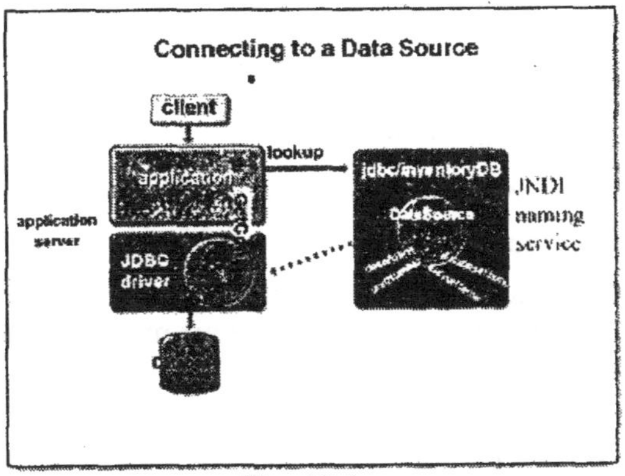

Fig. 18.4

In addition to this important advantage, DataSource objects can provide connection pooling and distributed transactions, essential for enterprise database computing. This functionality is provided transparently to the programmer.

(6) Included in the Java Platform.

As a core part of the Java 2 Platform, the JDBC 2.0 core API is available anywhere that the platform is. This means that Java applications can truly write database applications once and access data anywhere. The Java 2 Platform, Enterprise Edition (J2EETM), includes both the JDBC core API and the JDBC Optional Package API. The Optional Package API contains server-side functionality for industrial strength scalability. An example of a J2EE based architecture that includes a JDBC implementation:

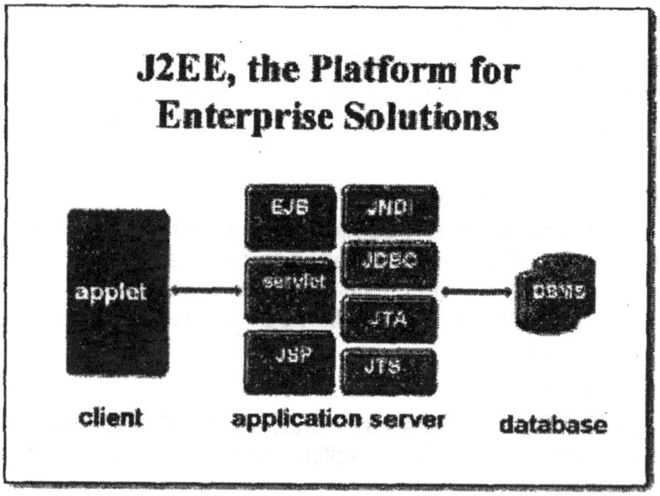

Fig. 18.5

18.2 JDBC Basics

The first thing you need to do is check that you are set up properly. This involves the following steps:

(1) Install Java and JDBC on your machine.

To install both the Java tm platform and the JDBC API, simply follow the instructions for downloading the latest release of the JDK tm (Java Development Kit tm). When you download the JDK, you will get JDBC as well. The sample code demonstrating the JDBC 1.0 API was written for JDK1.1 and will run on any version of the Java platform that is compatible with JDK1.1, including JDK1.2. Note that the sample code illustrating the JDBC 2.0 API requires JDK1.2 and will not run on JDK1.1.

You can find the latest release (JDK1.2 at the time of this writing) at the following URL:

http://java.sun.com/products/JDK/CurrentRelease

(2) Install a driver on your machine.

Your driver should include instructions for installing it. For JDBC drivers written for specific DBMSs, installation consists of just copying the driver onto your machine; there is no special configuration needed.

The JDBC-ODBC Bridge driver is not quite as easy to set up. If you download either the Solaris or Windows versions of JDK1.1, you will automatically get the JDBC-ODBC Bridge driver, which does not itself require any special configuration. ODBC, however, does. If you do not already have ODBC on your machine, you will need to see your ODBC driver vendor for information on installation and configuration.

(3) Install your DBMS if needed.

If you do not already have a DBMS installed, you will need to follow the vendor's instructions for installation. Most users will have a DBMS installed and will be working with an established database.

18.3 Setting Up a Database

We will assume that the database COFFEEBREAK already exists. (Creating a database is not at all difficult, but it requires special permissions and is normally done by a database administrator.) When you create the tables used as examples in this tutorial, they will be in the default database. We purposely kept the size and number of tables small to keep things manageable.

Suppose that our sample database is being used by the proprietor of a small coffee house called The Coffee Break, where coffee beans are sold by the pound and brewed coffee is sold by the cup. To keep things simple, also suppose that the proprietor needs only two tables, one for types of coffee and one for coffee suppliers.

First we will show you how to open a connection with your DBMS, and then, since what JDBC does is to send your SQL code to your DBMS, we will demonstrate some SQL code. After that, we will show you how easy it is to use JDBC to pass these SQL statements to your DBMS and process the results that are returned.

This code has been tested on most of the major DBMS products. However, you may encounter some compatibility problems using it with older ODBC drivers with the JDBC-ODBC Bridge.

18.4 Establishing a Connection

The first thing you need to do is establish a connection with the DBMS you want to use. This involves two steps: (1) loading the driver and (2) making the connection.

18.4.1 Loading Drivers

Loading the driver or drivers you want to use is very simple and involves just one line of code. If, for example, you want to use the JDBC-ODBC Bridge driver, the following code will load it:

```
Class.forName("sun.jdbc.odbc.JdbcOdbcDriver");
```

Your driver documentation will give you the class name to use. For instance, if the class name is jdbc.DriverXYZ , you would load the driver with the following line of code:

```
Class.forName("jdbc.DriverXYZ");
```

You do not need to create an instance of a driver and register it with the DriverManager because calling Class.forName will do that for you automatically. If you were to create your own instance, you would be creating an unnecessary duplicate, but it would do no harm.

When you have loaded a driver, it is available for making a connection with a DBMS.

18.4.2 Making the Connection

The second step in establishing a connection is to have the appropriate driver connect to the DBMS. The following line of code illustrates the general idea:

```
Connection con = DriverManager.getConnection(url,
"myLogin", "myPassword");
```

This step is also simple, with the hardest thing being what to supply for url . If you are using the JDBC-ODBC Bridge driver, the JDBC URL will start with jdbc:odbc: . The rest of the URL is generally your data source name or database system. So, if you are using ODBC to access an ODBC data source called " Fred, " for example, your JDBC URL could be jdbc:odbc:Fred . In place of " myLogin " you put the name you use to log in to the DBMS; in place of " myPassword " you put your password for the DBMS. So if you log in to your DBMS with a login name of " Fernanda " and a password of " J8, " just these two lines of code will establish a connection:

```
String url = "jdbc:odbc:Fred";
Connection con = DriverManager.getConnection(url, "Fernanda",   "J8");
```

If you are using a JDBC driver developed by a third party, the documentation will tell you what subprotocol to use, that is, what to put after jdbc: in the JDBC URL. For example, if the driver developer has registered the name acme as the subprotocol, the first and second parts of the JDBC URL will be jdbc:acme: . The driver documentation will also give you guidelines for the rest of the JDBC URL. This last part of the JDBC URL supplies information for identifying the data source.

If one of the drivers you loaded recognizes the JDBC URL supplied to the method DriverManager.getConnection , that driver will establish a connection to the DBMS specified in the JDBC URL. The DriverManager class, true to its name, manages all of the details of establishing the connection for you behind the scenes. Unless you are writing a driver, you will probably never use any of the methods in the interface Driver , and the only DriverManager method you really need to know is DriverManager.getConnection .

The connection returned by the method DriverManager.getConnection is an open connection you can use to create JDBC statements that pass your SQL statements to the DBMS. In the previous example, con is an open connection, and we will use it in the examples that follow.

18.5 Setting Up Tables

18.5.1 Creating a Table

First, we will create one of the tables in our example database. This table, COFFEES , contains the essential information about the coffees sold at The Coffee Break, including the coffee names, their prices, the number of pounds sold the current week, and the number of pounds sold to date. The table COFFEES , which we describe in more detail later, is shown here:

Request Object Variables	Collections in Which They Are Found
CGI Variables	Server Variables collection
Query string parameters	QueryString collection
Form parameters	Form collection
Client cookies	Cookies collection
Client certificates	Certificate collection

Fig. 18.6

The column storing the coffee name is COF_NAME, and it holds values with an SQL type of VARCHAR and a maximum length of 32 characters. Since we will use different names for each type of coffee sold, the name will uniquely identify a particular coffee and can therefore serve as the primary key.

The second column, named SUP_ID , will hold a number that identifies the coffee supplier; this number will be of SQL type INTEGER . The third column, called PRICE, stores values with an SQL type of FLOAT because it needs to hold values with decimal points. (Note that money values would normally be stored in an SQL type DECIMAL or NUMERIC , but because of differences among DBMSs and to avoid incompatibility with older versions of JDBC, we are using the more standard type FLOAT for this tutorial.) The column named SALES stores values of SQL type INTEGER and indicates the number of pounds of coffee sold during the current week. The final column, TOTAL , contains an SQL INTEGER which gives the total number of pounds of coffee sold to date.

SUPPLIERS , the second table in our database, gives information about each of the suppliers:

Response.Write	Most frequently used method.
Response.Redirect	Redirects browser to another URL.
Response.ContentType	Specifies a content type other than the default (text/html).
Response.Cookies	Sets cookies in the user's browser.
Response.Buffer	Turns buffering on or off, delaying transmission of output until script processing in the current ASP file has completed.

Fig. 18.7

The tables COFFEES and SUPPLIERS both contain the column SUP_ID , which means that these two tables can be used in SELECT statements to get data based on the information in both tables. The column SUP_ID is the primary key in the table SUPPLIERS , and as such, it uniquely identifies each of the coffee suppliers. In the table COFFEES , SUP_ID is called a foreign key. (You can think of a foreign key as being foreign in the sense that it is imported from another table.) Note that each SUP_ID number appears only once in the SUPPLIERS table; this is required for it to be a primary key. In the COFFEES table, where it is a foreign key, however, it is perfectly all right for there to be duplicate SUP_ID numbers because one supplier may sell many types of coffee. Later in this chapter, you will see an example of how to use primary and foreign keys in a SELECT statement.

The following SQL statement creates the table COFFEES . The entries within the outer pair of parentheses consist of the name of a column followed by a space and the SQL type to be stored in that column. A comma separates the entry for one column (consisting of column name and SQL type) from the next one. The type VARCHAR is created with a maximum length, so it takes a parameter indicating that maximum length. The parameter must be in parentheses following the type. The SQL statement shown here, for example, specifies that the name in column COF_NAME may be up to 32 characters long:

```
CREATE TABLE COFFEES
(COF_NAME VARCHAR(32),
SUP_ID INTEGER,
PRICE FLOAT,
SALES INTEGER,
TOTAL INTEGER)
```

This code does not end with a DBMS statement terminator, which can vary from DBMS to DBMS. For example, Oracle uses a semicolon (;) to indicate the end of a statement, and Sybase uses the word go . The driver you are using will automatically supply the appropriate statement terminator, and you will not need to include it in your JDBC code.

Another thing we should point out about SQL statements is their form. In the CREATE TABLE statement, key words are printed in all capital letters, and each item is on a separate line. SQL does not require either; these conventions simply make statements easier to read. The standard in SQL is that keywords are not case sensitive, so, for example, the following SELECT statement can be written various ways. As an example, these two versions below are equivalent as far as SQL is concerned:

```
SELECT First_Name, Last_Name
FROM Employees
WHERE Last_Name LIKE "Washington"
select First_Name, Last_Name from Employees where
Last_Name like "Washington"
```

Quoted material, however, is case sensitive: in the name " Washington, " " W " must be capitalized, and the rest of the letters must be lowercase.

Requirements can vary from one DBMS to another when it comes to identifier names. For example, some DBMSs require that column and table names be given exactly as they were created in the CREATE TABLE statement, while others do not. To be safe, we will use all uppercase for identifiers such as COFFEES and SUPPLIERS because that is how we defined them.

So far we have written the SQL statement that creates the table COFFEES . Now let's put quotation marks around it (making it a string) and assign that string to the variable createTableCoffees so that we can use the variable in our JDBC code later. As just shown, the DBMS does not care about where lines are divided, but in the Java programming language, a String object that extends beyond one line will not compile. Consequently, when you are giving strings, you need to enclose each line in quotation marks and use a plus sign (+) to concatenate them:

```
String createTableCoffees = "CREATE TABLE COFFEES " +
"(COF_NAME VARCHAR(32), SUP_ID INTEGER, PRICE FLOAT, " +
"SALES INTEGER, TOTAL INTEGER)";
```

The data types we used in our CREATE TABLE statement are the generic SQL types (also called JDBC types) that are defined in the class java.sql.Types . DBMSs generally use these standard types, so when the time comes to try out some JDBC applications, you can just use the application CreateCoffees.java , which uses the CREATE TABLE statement. If your DBMS uses its own local type names, we supply another application for you, which we will explain fully later.

Before running any applications, however, we are going to walk you through the basics of JDBC.

18.5.2 Creating JDBC Statements

A Statement object is what sends your SQL statement to the DBMS. You simply create a Statement object and then execute it, supplying the appropriate execute method with the SQL statement you want to send. For a SELECT statement, the method to use is executeQuery . For statements that create or modify tables, the method to use is executeUpdate .

It takes an instance of an active connection to create a Statement object. In the following example, we use our Connection object con to create the Statement object stmt :

Statement stmt = con.createStatement();

At this point stmt exists, but it does not have an SQL statement to pass on to the DBMS. We need to supply that to the method we use to execute stmt . For example, in the following code fragment, we supply executeUpdate with the SQL statement from the example above:

```
stmt.executeUpdate("CREATE TABLE COFFEES " +
"(COF_NAME VARCHAR(32), SUP_ID INTEGER, PRICE FLOAT, " +
"SALES INTEGER, TOTAL INTEGER)");
```

Since we made a string out of the SQL statement and assigned it to the variable createTableCoffees , we could have written the code in this alternate form:

stmt.executeUpdate(createTableCoffees);

18.5.3 Executing Statements

We used the method executeUpdate because the SQL statement contained in createTableCoffees is a DDL (data definition language) statement. Statements that create a table, alter a table, or drop a table are all examples of DDL statements and are executed with the method executeUpdate . As you might expect from its name, the method executeUpdate is also used to execute SQL statements that update a table. In practice, executeUpdate is used far more often to update tables than it is to create them because a table is created once but may be updated many times.

The method used most often for executing SQL statements is executeQuery . This method is used to execute SELECT statements, which comprise the vast majority of SQL statements. You will see how to use this method shortly.

18.5.4 Entering Data into a Table

We have shown how to create the table COFFEES by specifying the names of the columns and the data types to be stored in those columns, but this only sets up the structure of the table. The table does not yet contain any data. We will enter our data into the table one row at a time, supplying the information to be stored in each column of that row. Note that the values to be inserted into the columns are listed in the same order that the columns were declared when the table was created, which is the default order.

The following code inserts one row of data, with Colombian in the column COF_NAME , 101 in SUP_ID , 7.99 in PRICE , 0 in SALES , and 0 in TOTAL . (Since The Coffee Break has just started out, the amount sold during the week and the total to date are zero for all the coffees to start with.) Just as we did in the code that created the table COFFEES , we will create a Statement object and then execute it using the method executeUpdate .

Since the SQL statement will not quite fit on one line on the page, we have split it into two strings concatenated by a plus sign (+) so that it will compile. Pay special attention to the need for a space between COFFEES and VALUES . This space must be within the quotation marks and may be after COFFEES or before VALUES ; without a space, the SQL statement will erroneously be read as " INSERT INTO COFFEESVALUES . . ." and the DBMS will look for the table COFFEESVALUES . Also note that we use single quotation marks around the coffee name because it is nested within double quotation marks. For most DBMSs, the general rule is to alternate double quotation marks and single quotation marks to indicate nesting.

```
Statement stmt = con.createStatement();
stmt.executeUpdate(
"INSERT INTO COFFEES " +
"VALUES ('Colombian', 101, 7.99, 0, 0)");
```

The code that follows inserts a second row into the table COFFEES . Note that we can just reuse the Statement object stmt rather than having to create a new one for each execution.

```
stmt.executeUpdate("INSERT INTO COFFEES " +
"VALUES ('French_Roast', 49, 8.99, 0, 0)");
```

Values for the remaining rows can be inserted as follows:

```
stmt.executeUpdate("INSERT INTO COFFEES " +
"VALUES ('Espresso", 150, 9.99, 0, 0)");
stmt.executeUpdate("INSERT INTO COFFEES " +
"VALUES ('Colombian_Decaf', 101, 8.99,0, 0)");
stmt.executeUpdate("INSERT INTO COFFEES " +
"VALUES ('French_Roast_Decaf', 49, 9.99, 0, 0)");
```

18.5.5 Getting Data from a Table

Now that the table COFFEES has values in it, we can write a SELECT statement to access those values. The star (*) in the following SQL statement indicates that all columns should be selected. Since there is no WHERE clause to narrow down the rows from which to select, the following SQL statement selects the whole table:

SELECT * FROM COFFEES

The result, which is the entire table, will look similar to the following:

COF_NAME	SUP_ID	PRICE	SALES	TOTAL
Colombian	101	7.99	0	0
French_Roast	49	8.99	0	0
Espresso	150	9.99	0	0
Colombian_Decaf	101	8.99	0	0
French_Roast_Decaf	49	9.99	0	0

The result above is what you would see on your terminal if you entered the SQL query directly to the database system. When we access a database through a Java application, as we will be doing shortly, we will need to retrieve the results so that we can use them. You will see how to do this in the next section.

Here is another example of a SELECT statement; this one will get a list of coffees and their respective prices per pound:

SELECT COF_NAME, PRICE FROM COFFEES

The results of this query will look something like this:

COF_NAME	PRICE
Colombian	7.99
French_Roast	8.99
Espresso	9.99
Colombian_Decaf	8.99
French_Roast_Decaf	9.99

The SELECT statement above generates the names and prices of all of the coffees in the table. The following SQL statement limits the coffees selected to just those that cost less than $9.00 per pound:

SELECT COF_NAME, PRICE

FROM COFFEES

WHERE PRICE < 9.00

The results would look similar to this:

COF_NAME	PRICE
Colombian	7.99
French_Roast	8.99
Colombian Decaf	8.99

18.6 Retrieving Values from Result Sets

We now show how you send the above SELECT statements from a program written in the Java programming language and how you get the results we showed.

JDBC returns results in a ResultSet object, so we need to declare an instance of the class ResultSet to hold our results. The following code demonstrates declaring the ResultSet object rs and assigning the results of our earlier query to it:

ResultSet rs = stmt.executeQuery(
"SELECT COF_NAME, PRICE FROM COFFEES");

18.6.1 Using the Method next

The variable rs , which is an instance of ResultSet , contains the rows of coffees and prices shown in the result set example above. In order to access the names and prices, we will go to each row and retrieve the values according to their types. The method next moves what is called a cursor to the next row and makes that row (called the current row) the one upon which we can operate. Since the cursor is initially positioned just above the first row of a ResultSet object, the first call to the method next moves the cursor to the first row and makes it the current row. Successive invocations of the method next move the cursor down one row at a time from top to bottom. Note that with the JDBC 2.0 API, covered in the next section, you can move the cursor backwards, to specific positions, and to positions relative to the current row in addition to moving the curs or forward.

18.6.2 Using the getXXX Methods

We use the getXXX method of the appropriate type to retrieve the value in each column. For example, the first column in each row of rs is COF_NAME , which stores a value of SQL type VARCHAR . The method for retrieving a value of SQL type VARCHAR is getString . The second column in each row stores a value of SQL type FLOAT , and the method for retrieving values of that type is getFloat . The following code accesses the values stored in the current row of rs and prints a line with the name followed by three spaces and the price. Each time the method next is invoked, the next row becomes the current row, and the loop continues until there are no more rows in rs .

```
String query = "SELECT COF_NAME, PRICE FROM COFFEES";
ResultSet rs = stmt.executeQuery(query);
while (rs.next()) {
String s = rs.getString("COF_NAME");
float n = rs.getFloat("PRICE");
System.out.println(s + "   " + n);
}
```

The output will look something like this:

```
Colombian   7.99
French_Roast   8.99
Espresso   9.99
```

```
Colombian_Decaf    8.99
French_Roast_Decaf    9.99
```

Note that we use a curved arrow to identify output from JDBC code; it is not part of the output. The arrow is not used for results in a result set, so its use distinguishes between what is contained in a result set and what is printed as the output of an application.

Let's look a little more closely at how the getXXX methods work by examining the two getXXX statements in this code. First let's examine getString .

```
String s = rs.getString("COF_NAME");
```

The method getString is invoked on the ResultSet object rs , so getString will retrieve (get) the value stored in the column COF_NAME in the current row of rs . The value that getString retrieves has been converted from an SQL VARCHAR to a String in the Java programming language, and it is assigned to the String object s . Note that we used the variable s in the println expression shown above, that is, println(s + " " + n) .

The situation is similar with the method getFloat except that it retrieves the value stored in the column PRICE , which is an SQL FLOAT , and converts it to a Java float before assigning it to the variable n .

JDBC offers two ways to identify the column from which a getXXX method gets a value. One way is to give the column name, as was done in the example above. The second way is to give the column index (number of the column), with 1 signifying the first column, 2 , the second, and so on. Using the column number instead of the column name looks like this:

```
String s = rs.getString(1);

float n = rs.getFloat(2);
```

The first line of code gets the value in the first column of the current row of rs (column COF_NAME), converts it to a Java String object, and assigns it to s . The second line of code gets the value stored in the second column of the current row of rs , converts it to a Java float , and assigns it to n . Note that the column number refers to the column number in the result set, not in the original table.

In summary, JDBC allows you to use either the column name or the column number as the argument to a getXXX method. Using the column number is slightly more efficient, and there are some cases where the column number is required. In general, though, supplying the column name is essentially equivalent to supplying the column number.

JDBC allows a lot of latitude as far as which getXXX methods you can use to retrieve the different SQL types. For example, the method getInt can be used to retrieve any of the numeric or character types. The data it retrieves will be converted to an int; that is, if the SQL type is VARCHAR , JDBC will attempt to parse an integer out of the VARCHAR. The method getInt is recommended for retrieving only SQL INTEGER types, however, and it cannot be used for the SQL types BINARY, VARBINARY, LONGVARBINARY, DATE, TIME, or TIMESTAMP.

Table 24, Methods for Retrieving SQL Types shows which methods can legally be used to retrieve SQL types and, more important, which methods are recommended for retrieving the various SQL types. Note that this table uses the term "JDBC type" in place of "SQL type." Both terms refer to the generic SQL types defined in java.sql.Types , and they are interchangeable.

18.6.3 Using the Method getString

Although the method getString is recommended for retrieving the SQL types CHAR and VARCHAR , it is possible to retrieve any of the basic SQL types with it. (You cannot, however, retrieve the new SQL3 datatypes with it. We will discuss SQL3 types later in this tutorial.) Getting all values with getString can be very useful, but it also has its limitations. For instance, if it is used to retrieve a numeric type, getString will convert the numeric value to a Java String object, and the value will have to be converted back to a numeric type before it can be operated on as a number. In cases where the value will be treated as a string anyway, there is no drawback. Further, if you want an application to retrieve values of any standard SQL type other than SQL3 types, use the getString method.

18.6.4 Use of ResultSet.getXXX Methods to Retrieve JDBC Types

table3a.bmp + table3a.bmp + table3a.bmp

An "x" indicates that the getXXX method may legally be used to retrieve the given JDBC type.

An " X " indicates that the getXXX method is recommended for retrieving the given JDBC type.

18.6.5 Updating Tables

Suppose that after a successful first week, the proprietor of The Coffee Break wants to update the SALES column in the table COFFEES by entering the number of pounds sold for each type of coffee. The SQL statement to update one row might look like this:

```
String updateString = "UPDATE COFFEES " +
"SET SALES = 75 " +
"WHERE COF_NAME LIKE 'Colombian'";
```

Using the Statement object stmt , this JDBC code executes the SQL statement contained in updateString :

stmt.executeUpdate(updateString);

The table COFFEES will now look like this:

COF_NAME	SUP_ID	PRICE	SALES	TOTAL
Colombian	101	7.99	75	0
French_Roast	49	8.99	0	0
Espresso	150	9.99	0	0
Colombian_Decaf	101	8.99	0	0
French_Roast_Decaf	49	9.99	0	0

Note that we have not yet updated the column TOTAL , so it still has the value 0 .

Now let's select the row we updated, retrieve the values in the columns COF_NAME and SALES , and print out those values:

```
String query = "SELECT COF_NAME, SALES FROM COFFEES " +
"WHERE COF_NAME LIKE 'Colombian'";
ResultSet rs = stmt.executeQuery(query);
while (rs.next()) {
String s = rs.getString("COF_NAME");
int n = rs.getInt("SALES");
System.out.println(n + " pounds of " + s +
} sold this week.");
}
```

This will print the following:

75 pounds of Colombian sold this week.

Since the WHERE clause limited the selection to only one row, there was just one row in the ResultSet rs and one line printed as output. Accordingly, it is possible to write the code without a while loop:

```
rs.next();
String s = rs.getString(1);
int n = rs.getInt(2);
System.out.println(n + " pounds of " + s + " sold this week.");
```

Even when there is only one row in a result set, you need to use the method next to access it. A ResultSet object is created with a cursor pointing above the first row. The first call to the next method positions the cursor on the first (and in this case, only) row of rs . In this code, next is called only once, so if there happened to be another row, it would never be accessed.

Now let's update the TOTAL column by adding the weekly amount sold to the existing total, and then let's print out the number of pounds sold to date:

```
String updateString = "UPDATE COFFEES " +
"SET TOTAL = TOTAL + 75 " +
"WHERE COF_NAME LIKE 'Colombian'";
stmt.executeUpdate(updateString);
String query = "SELECT COF_NAME, TOTAL FROM COFFEES " +
"WHERE COF_NAME LIKE 'Colombian'";
ResultSet rs = stmt.executeQuery(query);
while (rs.next()) {
String s = rs.getString(1);
int n = rs.getInt(2);
System.out.println(n + " pounds of " + s + " sold to date.");
}
```

Note that in this example, we used the column index instead of the column name, supplying the index 1 to getString (the first column of the result set is COF_NAME), and the index 2 to getInt (the second column of the result set is TOTAL). It is important to distinguish between a column's index in the database table as opposed to its index in the result set table. For example, TOTAL is the fifth column in the table COFFEES but the second column in the result set generated by the query in the example above.

18.7 JDBC-ODBC Bridge with ODBC Driver

Open DataBase Connectivity (ODBC) is Microsoft's programming interface for accessing a large number of relational databases on numerous platforms. The JDBC-ODBC bridge is built into the Solaris and Windows versions of the Java platform so you can do two things:

1. Use ODBC from a Java program
2. Load ODBC drivers as JDBC drivers. This example uses the JDBC-ODBC bridge to load an ODBC driver to connect to the database. The applet has no ODBC code, however.

The DriverManager uses environment settings to locate and load the database driver. For this example, the driver file does not need to be locally accessible.

Start the Applet: Here is the DbaOdb.html file for running the DbaOdbAppl applet:

```
<HTML>
<BODY>
<APPLET CODE=DbaOdbAppl.class
WIDTH=200
HEIGHT=100>
```

```
</APPLET>
</BODY>
</HTML>
```

And here is how to start the applet:

appletviewer DbaOdb.html

Reading a Stack Trace: If the DbaOdbAppl.java applet is launched without a policy file, the following stack trace is generated when the end user clicks the Click Me button.

java.security.AccessControlException: access denied

```
(java.lang.RuntimePermission
accessClassInPackage.sun.jdbc.odbc )
```

The first line in the above stack trace tells you access is denied. This means this stack trace was generated because the applet tried to access a system resource without the proper permission. The second line means you need a RuntimePermission that gives the applet access to the sun.jdbc.odbc package. This package provides the JDBC-ODBC bridge functionality to the Java1 virtual machine (VM).

You can use Policy tool to create the policy file you need, or you can create it with an ASCII editor. Here is the policy file with the permission indicated by the stack trace:

```
grant {
permission java.lang.RuntimePermission
"accessClassInPackage.sun.jdbc.odbc";
};
```

Run the applet again, this time with a policy file named DbaOdbPol that has the above permission in it:

```
appletviewer -J-Djava.security.policy=DbaOdbPol
DbaOdb.html
```

You get a stack trace again, but this time it is a different error condition.

```
java.security.AccessControlException:
access denied (java.lang.RuntimePermission
file.encoding read)
```

The stack trace means the applet needs read permission to the encoded (binary) file. Here is the DbaOdbPol policy file with the permission indicated by the stack trace added to it:

```
grant {
permission java.lang.RuntimePermission
"accessClassInPackage.sun.jdbc.odbc";
permission java.util.PropertyPermission
"file.encoding", "read";
};
```

Run the applet again. If you use the above policy file with the Runtime and Property permissions indicated, it works just fine.

```
appletviewer -J-Djava.security.policy=DbaOdbPol
DbaOdb.html
```

18.8 Database Access by Servlets

Servlets are under the security policy in force for the web server under which they run. When the database read and write code is added to the FileIOServlet ,the DbaServlet.java servlet executes without restriction under Java WebServerTM 1.1.1.

The web server has to be configured to locate the database. Consult your web server documentation or database administrator for help. With Java WebServer 1.1.1, the configuration setup involves editing the startup scripts with such things as environment settings for loading the ODBC driver, and locating and connecting to the database.

```
<Picture>
dba11.gif
<Picture>
dba2.gif
import java.io.*;
import javax.servlet.*;
import javax.servlet.http.*;

import java.sql.*;
import java.net.*;
import java.io.*;

public class DbaServlet extends HttpServlet {

private Connection c;
final static private String _driver =
"sun.jdbc.odbc.JdbcOdbcDriver";
final static private String _user = "username";
final static private String _pass = "password";
final static private String
_url = "jdbc:odbc:jdc";

public void doPost(HttpServletRequest request,
HttpServletResponse response)
throws ServletException, IOException{
response.setContentType("text/html");
PrintWriter out = response.getWriter();
out.println("<title>Example<title>" +
"<body bgcolor=FFFFFF>");

out.println("<h2>Button Clicked</h2>");

String DATA = request.getParameter("DATA");

if(DATA != null){
out.println("<STRONG>Text from
form:</STRONG>");
out.println(DATA);
```

```
} else {
out.println("No text entered.");
}

//Establish database connection
try{
Class.forName (_driver);
c = DriverManager.getConnection(_url,
_user,
_pass);
} catch (Exception e) {
e.printStackTrace();
System.exit(1);
}

try{
//Code to write to database
Statement stmt = c.createStatement();
String updateString = "INSERT INTO dba " +
"VALUES (" + DATA + "')";
int count = stmt.executeUpdate(updateString);

//Code to read from database
ResultSet results = stmt.executeQuery(
"SELECT TEXT FROM dba ");
while(results.next()){
String s = results.getString("TEXT");
out.println("<BR>
<STRONG>Text from database:</STRONG>");
out.println(s);
}
stmt.close();
}catch(java.sql.SQLException e){
System.out.println(e.toString());
}

out.println("<P>Return to
<A HREF="../dbaHTML.html">Form</A>");
out.close();
}
}
```

18.9 Using the Connection Manager

The term data servers is a convenient shorthand for referring to many different data sources, including:

- Relational databases such as DB2, Oracle, Informix, and Sybase
- Other types of products, whose special services for managing and accessing data vary by

product

- Typically, the data server is part of a "three tier" application in which several machines are networked:
- The first tier is the user's machine, providing the visual interface to the application. The interface is often a Web browser.
- The second tier machine contains the business logic of the application, which often runs in conjunction with a Web server, such as the Lotus Domino Go Webserver.
- The third tier machine runs the data server, which manages the data that is used by the application.

Technical documentation on the three tier architecture usually describes significant advantages in managing and scaling three tier applications compared to other application architectures. The advantages of the three tier architecture will not be further discussed here. The connection manager runs under the Application Server and, if you are using the three tier architecture, both the Application Server and the connection manager run on the second tier machine.

Web-based applications and traditional, non-Web applications interact similarly with data servers. Typically, an application connects to the data server, spending server resources to create the connection. The application uses the connection to interact with the data server - retrieving data, updating data, and so on. The application disconnects from the data server, using further resources.

For a non-Web application, the overhead required to make and break connections is small compared to the resources required for the entire interaction. For example, consider intra-company applications. These typically have a small, predictable number of users with relatively long user interaction times. The length of interactions drives resource usage, as relatively little time is spent connecting and disconnecting.

In contrast, Web-based applications accessing data servers incur higher and less predictable overhead, because users connect and disconnect more frequently. Often, more resources are spent connecting and disconnecting than are spent during the interactions themselves. Users interactions are typically shorter, due to the "surfing" nature of the Internet. Users are often from outside the company (Internet, rather than intranet) making usage volumes larger, and harder to predict.

For example, consider a Web-based application that interacts with three users for one minute each. At the same time, a cash machine (running on a non-Web application) outside a bank performs one transaction that lasts three minutes. If it takes the same amount of time for each application to make and break a connection, the Web application clearly incurs higher overhead per unit of interaction time. Both applications might spend the same amount of time establishing a single connection, but the Web-based application spends less time using the connection - it lacks the same "return on investment."

The connection manager lets you control and reduce the resources used by your Web-based applications. The connection manager spreads the connection overhead across several user requests by establishing a pool of connections, which user servlets can use. Put another way, each user request incurs the overhead of only a fraction of the cost of a connect/disconnect. After the initial resources are spent to produce the connections in the pool, additional connect/disconnect overhead is insignificant because the existing connections are reused repeatedly.

The servlets use the connection pool as follows: When a user makes a request over the Web to a servlet, the servlet uses an existing connection from the pool, meaning the user request does not incur the overhead of a data server connect. When the request is satisfied, the servlet returns the connection to the connection manager pool for use by other servlets. The user request therefore does not incur the overhead of a data server disconnect.

The connection manager also lets you control the number of concurrent connections to a data server product. This is particularly useful if the data server license agreement limits you to a certain number of users - create a pool for the data server and set the Maximum Connections parameter for the connection manager pool equal to the maximum number of users permitted by the data server product. Note that this does not guarantee compliance if you connect to the data server with other programs, bypassing the connection manager.

18.9.1 Connection Manager Architecture

The connection manager maintains a pool of open data server connections to specific data server products. Each data server can have one or more identical or non-identical pools. Multiple data servers can be supported by one running instance of the connection manager.

Figure Connection manager architecture

Above figure illustrates the typical interactions between the connection manager and a servlet seeking to use a connection from the connection manager's connection pool. The following list traces the sequence followed when a connection is available when requested. As you will see later, the sequence changes if a connection is not available when the servlet requests one.

The connection manager, which runs under the Application Server, is loaded by the Application Server when the first servlet tries to communicate with the connection manager. The connection manager stays loaded as long as the Application Server is running.

1. The Application Server passes a user request to a servlet.
2. The servlet uses methods of the connection manager to request a connection from the pool.
3. The pool gives the servlet a connection.
4. The servlet uses the connection to talk directly to the data server, using the standard APIs for the specific data server.
5. The data server returns data through the connection to the servlet.
6. When the servlet ends communications with the data server, the servlet returns the connection to the pool for use by another user request.
7. The servlet sends the response back through the Application Server to the user.
8. A connection is not always available from the pool when the servlet requests it (in above Figure , see the action labeled 3). In this case, the connection manager communicates directly with the data server. It:

- ❑ requests a new connection (9)
- ❑ adds the connection to the pool (10)
- ❑ gives the new connection to the servlet (4)

(The numbers refer to above figure.)

Note that the connection manager will not add a new connection to the pool if the specified limit for the number of connections in the pool has been reached.

Creating a new connection for the pool is a high overhead task and the new connection will use resources on the data server machine. For this reason, the connection manager seeks to maximize the probability that a servlet can get an existing connection from the pool. At the same time, the connection manager must minimize the idle connections in the pool, as they are a significant waste of resources.

The connection manager works with the servlet to perform these minimizing and maximizing tasks. For optimal performance, choose the proper settings for the connection manager parameters. See the Application Server Manager online help for a detailed discussion of these parameters.

The connection manager maintains the verify timestamp, last-used timestamp, and in-use flag of each connection. When a servlet first gets a connection, the connection's verify timestamp and last-used timestamp are set to the current time and the connection's in-use flag is set to true.

If the servlet is going to use the connection to communicate with the data server multiple times over an extended period, you may want to add code to the servlet to verify that it still owns the connection just before each use of the connection. (This is because the connection manager can be configured to take a connection away from a servlet that has not used the connection for a length of time specified by the connection manager Maximum Age parameter.) To verify that it still owns a connection, the servlet invokes the verifyIBMConnection() method that in turn gets the connection manager to check the verify timestamp of the connection. If the servlet still owns the connection, the last-used timestamp is automatically updated to the current time, as part of invoking the verifyIBMConnection() method. The servlet then uses the connection to communicate with the data server, confident that the connection will work. When the servlet finishes with the connection, it releases it back to the connection pool. The connection manager sets the in-use flag to false, and sets the verify and last-used timestamps to the current time.

The connection manager removes idle connections from the pool because they are wasting the significant resources. To decide which connections are idle, the connection manager checks the connection flags and timestamps in a periodic reap of the connection pool:

The connection manager looks at the last-used timestamp of the in-use connections. If the time between the last-used and current time exceeds the Maximum Age configuration parameter, the connection is assumed to be an orphan connection, meaning the owning servlet has died or is otherwise unresponsive. The orphan connection is returned to the pool for use by another servlet, its in-use flag is set to false, and its verify and last-used timestamps are set to the current time.

The connection manager examines connections not in use by any servlet - those connections whose in-use flags are false. If the time between the last-used and current time exceeds the Maximum Idle Time configuration parameter, the connection is assumed idle. Idle connections are removed from the pool, down to the lower limit specified by Minimum Connections configuration parameter.

Additional parameters, discussed in the Application Server Manager online help, complete the picture of how the connection manager does its work.

18.9.2 Servlet-connection Manager Interaction and Related APIs

The sample servlet code (Sample connection manager servlet) assumes you can write servlets and are familiar with JDBC APIs. Currently, the only underlying data servers supported by the connection manager are relational database products that support JDBC, or relational database products that can be reached using the JDBC-ODBC bridge. The sample servlet code assumes that the underlying server is one of these.

18.9.2 How Servlets use the Connection Manager

All servlets using the connection manager will follow these steps (the steps are marked in the sample servlet, which you might also want to look at now):

1. Create the Connection Specification:

The servlet prepares a specification object identifying information necessary for connecting to the underlying data server. Some of the information is unique to the specific data server, while some is general, applying to any underlying data server. The servlet either prepares the specification only once and uses it for all user requests, or it prepares a new specification for each user request. If a new specification is prepared for each user request, it must be done before step 3, which uses the specification.

It is worth noting that different specifications can be used to get connections with different properties. For example, a data server may allow access to certain critical data only if the connection was created with a specific user ID. Therefore, the specification must properly identify the user ID in order to get the suitable connection to the data server.

2. Connect to the connection manager:

The servlet gets a reference to the connection manager in order to communicate with the connection manager. This needs to be done only once in the lifetime of the servlet.

3. Get a connection manager connection:

The servlet asks the connection manager for a connection to a specific data server using the connection specification prepared in step 1. The connection object returned is from a connection manager pool, and is an instance of a class defined in the connection manager APIs - it is not an object from a class in the API set of the underlying data server. Call this first connection a connection manager connection, or a CM connection for short. Usually, your servlet gets a CM connection for every user request.

4. Use the CM connection to access a pre-established data server connection:

The servlet invokes a method on the CM connection returned in step 3, retrieving an object defined in the API set of the underlying data server. Call this object a data server connection (or a data connection for short) to distinguish it from the CM connection.

The data connection, unlike the CM connection, is from the underlying data server API set. The data connection is not created for the servlet - the servlet instead uses the pre-established data connection by virtue of owning a CM connection pool from the pool.

The data connection will be used for the actual interactions with the data server, using the methods from the underlying data server API set. For example, in the sample servlet code the underlying data server will be a JDBC database and the data connection object will be from the Connection class in the JDBC APIs. The JDBC APIs are found in the java.sql package.

Interact with the data server:

The servlet interacts with the data server - retrieving data, updating data, and so on - using methods of the data connection object. These methods will be specific to the underlying data server, because the data connection will actually be from the API set of the underlying data server. The data connection for a different underlying data server will have different methods.

Full documentation for the methods will be found with the API documentation for the specific data server product. For example, for a JDBC data connection, you will need to look at the documentation for the java.sql package and at any documentation that comes with the JDBC-enabled relational database you are using. Note: If you use the data connection for more than one data server interaction within the same user request, you may want to verify before the additional interactions that your servlet still owns the associated CM connection. The connection manager periodically checks a last-used timestamp to see if your servlet has been using the CM connection, and if not, the connection manager assumes that your servlet has failed or has otherwise become unresponsive. It takes the CM connection away. Verifying the CM connection (using the verifyIBMConnection() method) also updates the last-used timestamp.

Release the connection:

The servlet returns the CM connection to the connection manager pool, freeing the connection for use by another servlet or by another request to the same servlet.

Prepare and send the response:

The servlet prepares and returns the response to the user request. In this step you will probably not be using any connection manager APIs.

18.9.3 Connection Manager APIs

Some of the connection manager APIs will now be discussed, to illustrate how they relate to the steps discussed above. The APIs will be covered in the approximate order that they are used in the sample servlet (Sample connection manager servlet). The complete APIs are covered in the connection manager Javadoc. You can find links to the connection manager Javadoc in the documentation on your Application Server machine. Use your browser to:

- For Windows NT, open the file applicationserver_root\doc\ index.html
- For AIX, open the file applicationserver_root/doc/index.html
- For Sun Solaris, open the file applicationserver_root/doc/ index.html

18.9.4 IBMJ dbc Conn Spec class

Create a specification object of this class to record the specifications for the connection to the desired data server. This is typically done in step 1. Note that the specification object does not actually set the specifications, but is used as an argument by another method, the method that sets the specifications (see the getIBMConnection() method in the IBMConnMgr class below). Currently, the connection manager supports connections only to JDBC compliant data servers, so only a JDBC specification class is available. When other data servers become supported, additional specification classes will be made available. After constructing the specification object, its possible to use get and set methods to specify the connection requirements, but you will usually specify all the requirements during the initial construction of the specification object. The constructor details are:

```
public IBMJdbcConnSpec(String poolName, boolean waitRetry, String
dbDriver, String url, String user, String password)
```

Parameters:

The first two parameters are common to all data servers.

- **poolName**

The connection manager pool containing the connection type you want. See the Webmaster for the pool name.

- **waitRetry**

Whether to wait for a connection to free up if the pool does not currently have an available connection. (To wait, specify true). The Webmaster uses the Connection Time Out parameter to set the length of the wait for the entire pool, so if a connection cannot be made available by that time, your request will fail. Specify false for an immediate failure if a connection from the pool is not available. The remaining parameters are specific to JDBC data servers.

- **dbDriver**

The driver class provided with a specific JDBC product, or the name of the driver providing the

JDBC-ODBC bridge. See the Webmaster or database administrator for the driver name. See the Driver class in the java.sql package for more information.

- **url**

A database URL. See the getConnection() method in the DriverManager class in the java.sql package for more information.

- **user**

The database user on whose behalf the connection is being made. See the getConnection() method in the DriverManager class in the java.sql package for more information.

- **password**

The user password. See the getConnection() method in the DriverManager class in the java.sql package for more information.

See the Javadoc for the Application Server APIs for information about the get and set methods for the IBMJdbcConnSpec class.

18.9.5 IBM Conn MgrUtil Class

Use a method of this class to get a reference to the connection manager. This is typically done in step 6. You will use the reference to communicate with the connection manager and use its services. Only one class or static method is of interest:

```
public static IBMConnMgr getIBMConnMgr()
```

Returns:

A reference to the connection manager

18.9.6 IBM Conn Mgr class

The running instance of the connection manager is an instance of this class. You will get a reference to the connection manager in step 6. Your servlet never creates an instance of the connection manager, but instead uses a reference to the existing instance. For details, see the getIBMConnMgr() method of the IBMConnMgrUtil class, discussed above.

Only one method of this class is of interest - the getIBMConnection() method to get a CM connection from the pool (used in step 3).

18.9.7 get IBM Connection()

```
public IBMConnection getIBMConnection(IBMConnSpec connSpec)
throws IBMConnMgrException
```

This method gets a CM connection from the pool for use by your servlet, if such a connection is available. Note, the only parameter passed is a specification object (created in step 1) for the connection. If a CM connection is not immediately available, and if waitRetry in the specification object is set to true, the servlet can wait for a CM connection to become available. The length of the wait is set by the Webmaster using the Connection Time Out parameter. The Webmaster can also disable the wait or extend the wait indefinitely. If a CM connection does not become available after the wait period, the getIBMConnection() method will throw an IBMConnMgrException exception. If waitRetry is false, failure to get a CM connection causes the getIBMConnection() method to throw the exception right away.

Note the returned IBMConnection object is a "general" connection object and must be cast to a connection object specific to the underlying data server you need to access. For example, in the sample servlet, the returned IBMConnection object is cast to an IBMJdbcConn object. Without the appropriate cast, the connection object cannot use its methods to get to the underlying data server in step 5.

Parameters:

- **connSpec**

An extension of the IBMConnSpec class, containing detailed connection requirements for a specific underlying data server. This will be an IBMJdbcConnSpec object (created in step 1) in the sample servlet.

Returns:

An IBMConnection object from the connection manager pool

18.9.8 IBM Jdbc Conn class

The IBMConnection object retrieved in step 3 needs to be cast to a connection object with respect to the underlying data server to be accessed. Otherwise, there is no access to the APIs associated with the underlying data server. Currently, only one such specialized connection class is available - the IBMJdbcConn class for JDBC data server access. Access to the APIs of the JDBC server through a IBMJdbcConn object is typically established in step 4.

The IBMJdbcConn class has one method of interest:

```
public Connection getJdbcConnection()
```

Returns:

A Connection object to the underlying JDBC data server

The connection class is from the JDBC API and is documented with the java.sql package. Methods of the Connection class let you interact with the JDBC data server. Elsewhere in this chapter the Connection class is referred to more generically as the data connection, to distinguish it from the CM connection. Recall that the CM connection is not part of the API set of the underlying data server.

18.9.9 IBM Connection Class

The IBMJdbcConn class is an extension of the IBMConnection class. Thus, many of the methods in the IBMConnection class are also in instances of the IBMJdbcConn class. Two methods of the IBMConnection class (also in IBMJdbcConn) are of interest - the verifyIBMConnection() method to verify that the CM connection is still valid (optionally used in step 5), and the releaseIBMConnection() method to return the CM connection to the pool (used in step 6).

```
verifyIBMConnection()
public boolean verifyIBMConnection()
throws IBMConnMgrException
```

The connection manager might take a CM connection away from a servlet if the CM connection has been inactive for a specified length of time. (Check with the Webmaster to determine the behavior configured for the connection manager). If you use your data connection for several interactions within one user request, you may want to invoke the verifyIBMConnection() method before each interaction to check whether your servlet still owns the associated CM connection from the pool. If the servlet still owns the connection, invoking the method will also reset a last-used timestamp.

If you anticipate that all your servlet interactions with the data server (from one user request) will complete within a few seconds, and if the Maximum Age parameter for the connection manager pool is at least several minutes long, then there is probably no need to use the verifyIBMConnection()

method — the request will complete long before there is any chance that the connection manager will take away the connection.

Returns:

True if the servlet still owns the CM connection, otherwise false

```
releaseIBMConnection()
public void releaseIBMConnection()
throws IBMConnMgrException
```

When a servlet no longer needs the CM connection object, the servlet uses this method to release the connection back to the pool. This should be done at the end of each user request.

18.10 Sample Connection Manager Servlet

The sample servlet should be easy to follow, based on the previous discussions, comments in the code, and the choice of variable names. The sample below follows the steps outlined in the How servlets use the connection manager.

```
// * IBMConnMgrTest.java - test the connection manager import
java.io.*;
import javax.servlet.*;
import javax.servlet.http.*;
import java.sql.*;
import java.util.*;
import com.ibm.servlet.connmgr.*;

public class IBMConnMgrTest extends HttpServlet
{
// Variables
// Use to communicate with connection manager.
static IBMConnMgr connMgr = null;

// Use later in init() to create JDBC connection specification.
static IBMConnSpec spec      = null;      // the spec
static String DbName         = null;      // database name
static String Db             = "db2";     // JDBC subprotocol for DB2
static String poolName       = "JdbcDb2"; // from Webmaster
static String jdbcDriver     = "COM.ibm.db6.jdbc.app.DB2Driver";
static String url            = null;      // constructed later
static String user           = null;   // user and password could
static String password       = null;      // come from HTML form
static String owner          = null;      // table owner

// Name of property file used to complete the user, password,
// DbName, and table owner information at runtime. ".properties"
// extension assumed.
static final String CONFIG_BUNDLE_NAME = "login";

// Initialize servlet when it is first loaded public void
```

```
init(ServletConfig config)
throws ServletException
{
super.init(config);
try
{
//  Get information at runtime (from an external property file
// identified by CONFIG_BUNDLE_NAME) about the database name
//  and the associated database user and password. This
// information could be provided in other ways.  It could be
//  hardcoded within this application, for example.
PropertyResourceBundle configBundle =
(PropertyResourceBundle)PropertyResourceBundle.
getBundle(CONFIG_BUNDLE_NAME);
DbName   = configBundle.getString("JDBCServlet.dbName");
url      = "jdbc:" + Db + ":" + DbName;
user = configBundle.getString("JDBCServlet.dbUserid");
password = configBundle.getString("JDBCServlet.dbPassword");
owner    = configBundle.getString("JDBCServlet.dbOwner");
}
catch(Exception e)
{
System.out.println("read properties file: " + e.getMessage());
}
try
{
//  STEP 1
// Create JDBC connection specification.
spec = new IBMJdbcConnSpec
(poolName,    // pool name from Webmaster
true,        // waitRetry
jdbcDriver,  // Remaining four
url,         // parameters are
user,        // specific for a
password);   // JDBC connection.
//  STEP 2
// Get a reference to the connection manager.
connMgr = IBMConnMgrUtil.getIBMConnMgr();
}
catch(Exception e)
{
System.out.println("set connection spec,
get connection manager: " + e.getMessage());
}
}

// Respond to user GET request public void doGet(HttpServletRequest
req, HttpServletResponse res)
```

```
{
IBMJdbcConn cmConn    = null;
Connection dataConn   = null;
Vector firstNameList = new Vector();
try
{
//  STEP 3
// Get an IBMJdbcConn object (cmConn) meeting JDBC
// connection specs, from the connection manager pool.
cmConn = (IBMJdbcConn)connMgr.getIBMConnection(spec);
//  STEP 4
// Get a Connection object (dataConn).  This is
// an object from the java.sql package and it is used
// for JDBC access.
dataConn = cmConn.getJdbcConnection();
//  STEP 5
// Run DB query - create a Vector of first names of all people
// whose last name is 'PARKER'.
// Standard JDBC coding follows.  Change the query for your
// specific situation.
Statement stmt = dataConn.createStatement();
String query   = "Select FirstNme " +
"from " + owner + ".Employee " +
"where LASTNAME = 'PARKER'";
ResultSet rs   = stmt.executeQuery(query);
while(rs.next())
{
firstNameList.addElement(rs.getString(1));
}
// Invoke close() on stmt, which also closes rs, freeing
// resources and completing the interaction.  You must
// not, however, close the dataConn object.  It must
// remain open and under the control of connection manager
// for possible use by other requests to this servlet or
// to other servlets.
stmt.close();
// If you now want to use the dataConn object again for
// another interaction, you may want to make sure that you
// still own the associated cmConn object.  Use the
// verifyIBMConnection() method to do this, which also
// updates a last-used timestamp.  If the
// verifyIBMConnection() method fails, you will need
// to get new instances of the cmConn and dataConn objects
// before you can use them.  The actual need to use
// the verifyIBMConnection() method depends on the
// Maximum Age parameter set for the connection manager
// and the length of time that you anticipate your
// servlet will need to use the cmConn and dataConn
```

```
// objects.
}
catch(Exception e)
{
System.out.println ("get connection, process statement: "+
e.getMessage());
}
//  STEP 6
// Release the connection back to the pool.
finally
{
if(cmConn != null)
{
try
{
cmConn.releaseIBMConnection();
}
catch(IBMConnMgrException e)
{
System.out.println("release connection: "+ e.getMessage());
}
}
}
//  STEP 7
// Prepare and return HTML response - say Hello to everyone
// whose last name is 'Parker' and address them with their first
// and last name.
res.setContentType("text/html");
// Next three lines prevent dynamic content from being cached
// on browsers.
res.setHeader("Pragma", "no-cache");
res.setHeader("Cache-Control", "no-cache");
res.setDateHeader("Expires", 0);
try
{
ServletOutputStream out = res.getOutputStream();
out.println("<HTML>");
out.println("<HEAD><TITLE>Hello DBWorld</TITLE><HEAD>");
out.println("<BODY>");
if(firstNameList.isEmpty())
{
out.println("<H1>Nobody named Parker</H1>");
}
else
{
for(int i = 0; i < firstNameList.size(); i++)
{
out.println("<H1>Hello " +
```

```
firstNameList.elementAt(i) +
"Parker</H1>");
}
}
out.println("</BODY></HTML>");
out.close();
}
catch(IOException e)
{
System.out.println("HTML response: "+ e.getMessage());
}
}
}
```

18.10.1 How the Sample Servlet Uses the Connection Man ager

The sample servlet performs the following steps during its interactions with the connection manager. The steps correspond to the sequence of servlet-connection manager interactions introduced in How servlets use the connection manager.

18.10.2 Create the Connection Specification

The connection specification named spec is created in the init() method when the servlet is first loaded. In the sample servlet, information needed to create the spec object is read into the servlet earlier in the init() method. This information comes from an external Java properties file named login.properties. Alternatively, you could hardcode the information into your servlet — the user, password, and other related information.

It is also possible to create a new specification for each user request. This would normally be done just before step 3 in the sample servlet. In this way, the spec object could be created based on information submitted with the user request.

18.10.3 Connect to the Connection Manager

The servlet establishes communications with the connection manager just once in the servlet's lifecycle - when the servlet is loaded. This is conveniently done in the servlet's init() method, which is provided for such initialization tasks. Use the static method getIBMConnMgr() of the IBMConnMgrUtil class to establish the communications. Note that the single instance of the connection manager, namely connMgr, is used by all user requests to the sample servlet.

18.10.4 Get a Connection Manager Connection

Use the connection manager connMgr to get the CM connection cmConn from the pool. Note that cmConn is declared within the doGet() method, so that every user request gets its own CM connection. Also note that cmConn is cast to the IBMJdbcConn class so that cmConn will have methods available to it to get at the APIs of the underlying data server.

18.10.5 Get a Data Server Connection

Use the CM connection cmConn to get the data connection dataConn. Note that dataConn is a Connection object from the API set of the underlying data server. You will be using APIs of the underlying data server, rather than connection manager APIs, for interactions with the data server.

Note: cmConn and dataConn are declared within the doGet() method, giving each user request its own copies of the variables. If instead cmConn and dataConn had been declared outside of all the methods of the servlet, all user requests would use the same copy of each connection. In the latter case, concurrent user requests would mix their data server interactions on the same data connection, with unpredictable results.

18.10.6 Interact with The Data Server

Use the dataConn object from the Connection class in the JDBC APIs to communicate with DB6. The Statement object stmt and ResultSet object rs also belong to the JDBC APIs, documented in the Javadoc for the java.sql package. It is worthwhile to reiterate that access to the underlying data server is achieved using the APIs provided with that data server. Data servers may differ in their API sets. Regardless, the data server API sets are not part of the connection manager APIs.

Note also that no dataConn.close() statement appears anywhere in the servlet. Management of the connection, such as connecting to and disconnecting from the underlying data server, must be handled by the connection manager.

18.10.7 Release the Connection

Release the connection as soon as your servlet is through interacting with the data server. The connection will return to the pool where it can be used again. The connection manager is probably configured to take a connection away from a servlet if the connection has been idle for a period of time, thus reclaiming unreleased connections. Until that time period expires, however, the connection resource is unavailable for use.

Notice how releasing the connection is done in a finally block. This ensures that the connection is released if the previous try block completes normally, or if the previous try block fails for any reason.

18.10.8 Prepare and Send the Response

Prepare and send the response to the user, based on information retrieved in step 5.

18.10.9 Running the Sample Servlet

The Application Server includes the source file and the compiled class file for the IBMConnMgrTest servlet. See Running sample servlets and applications for details on where to find the source file and how to run the compiled servlet. If you want to make changes to the source file and test the resulting compiled servlet, be sure to follow the guidelines in Placing servlets on your Application Server. Since you will be compiling a servlet that accesses IBM DB2, you need to have a proper reference to the DB2 Java APIs (db2java.zip) in your CLASSPATH. The Application Server Java Classpath must also be set to properly reference the DB2 Java APIs (db2java.zip) in order to run the compiled servlet. See the Webmaster to ensure the proper setup of the Application Server Java Classpath.

18.11 Coding Considerations

*** Custom pools**

Review with the Webmaster the needs of your servlet and the connection manager configuration options. Even if there is only one underlying data server, consider creating several connection pools for the data server in order to meet the performance and resource access needs of several classes of servlets.

*** Custom error handling**

You may find it useful to modify the error handing code of your servlet — you can design the error messages to assist you and the Webmaster in tuning a connection manager pool for a specific class of servlets. Assume, for example, that due to many requests coming in over the Internet, a connection manager pool contains the maximum number of connections set by its Maximum Connections parameter.

If your servlet waitRetry parameter is set to true, your servlet request for a connection from the pool will fail if the servlet waits for a free connection for a time that exceeds the Connection Time Out parameter set in the connection manager pool. This behavior was discussed earlier in this chapter. If your servlet waitRetry parameter is set to false, your servlet request for a connection from the pool will fail right away. This behavior was also discussed earlier in this chapter.

You can modify your servlet to more clearly identify that these events are happening, and this can help in tuning the connection manager pool to minimize the failures. Initially, a catch block in your servlet might look something like:

```
catch(Exception e)
{
System.out.println(e.getMessage());
}
```

You would begin by modifying the catch block to invoke the errorHandler() method:

```
catch(Exception e)
{
System.out.println(errorHandler(e));
}
```

The errorHandler() method is a new method that you add to your servlet. The errorHandler() method in turn calls the connMgrExceptionHandler() method, which you also add to your servlet. The two methods are shown in the code below, which you can modify to meet your specific needs:

```
protected String errorHandler(Exception e)
{
String retString = null;
String className = e.getClass().getName();
if(className.equals(IBMConnMgrConstants.ExceptionClassName))
{
retString = connMgrExceptionHandler((IBMConnMgrException)e);
}
else
{
retString = e.getMessage();
}
return retString;
}
protected String connMgrExceptionHandler(IBMConnMgrException e)
{
StringBuffer retString = new StringBuffer(e.getMessage());
String reason = e.getReason();
if(reason.equals(IBMConnMgrConstants.ConnectionTimeOut))
{
retString.append(" The Connection wait timed out. Consult ");
retString.append("with your Webmaster to tune the ");
retString.append("Connection Time Out pool parameter.");
}
```

```
else if(reason.equals(IBMConnMgrConstants.MaxConnsExceeded))
{
retString.append(" The maximum number of connections in the ");
retString.append("pool has been reached.  Consult with your ");
retString.append("Webmaster to tune the Maximum ");
retString.append("Connections pool parameter.");
}
return retString.toString();
}
```

Look at the IBMConnMgrConstants class in the connection manager Javadoc to get an idea of other exceptions you can write special code for to assist in debugging a servlet or tuning a connection manager pool for a servlet.

You may also want to look at the Javadoc for the IBMConnMgr class — the class has methods that you may want to use to monitor the behavior of a connection pool, but the methods will not be discussed further here.

18.12 Security

In the sample servlet, note that the connection specification information is read from data hardcoded in a login.properties file, and that the same connection specification is used for all user requests. It is also possible for a new connection specification to be created for each user request, based on information passed in with the user request. This might involve, for example, passing user and password information over the Internet, with obvious security issues. Hardcoding user and password information into files located on the Web server machine is clearly more secure.

Alternatively, you can specify initialization parameters to be read in by the servlet when the servlet is loaded. See Using the Application Server Manager. The initialization parameters can be read in the servlet's init() method using the getInitParameterNames() and getInitParameter() methods. This information can then be used to create a connection specification, allowing servlets to be more generic. User, password, database name information, as well as other information, is specified only when the servlet is loaded, without the need to recompile the servlet for each change.

18.13 Using the verify IBM Connection() method

If your servlet uses a connection for multiple interactions with the data server, for each user request, taking place over a period of time, you may want to use the verifyIBMConnection() method before each additional interaction to make sure that your servlet still owns the connection. The reasons for this were discussed earlier in this chapter.

As an example of how this might be coded, consider step 5 of the sample servlet (Sample connection manager servlet). Just after the interaction completed with stmt.close(), you want to begin another interaction with the data server. The code fragment below (to be added after stmt.close() in step 5 of the sample servlet) shows how you might do this.

```
try
{
if(!cmConn.verifyIBMConnection())
{
// Get valid cmConn and dataConn objects if cmConn
// has "timed-out".
```

```
cmConn = (IBMJdbcConn)connMgr.getIBMConection(spec);
dataConn = cmConn.getJdbcConnection();
}
}
catch(IBMConnMgrException e)
{
System.out.println(e.getMessage());
}
// Now use dataConn for another query, update, etc, using
// cmConn and dataConn objects known to be good because of
// the verify.
// INSERT INTERACTION CODE HERE
// Complete the interaction.
stmt.close();
```

Remember that using the verifyIBMConnection() method is warranted only if your servlet has multiple interactions with the data server and if it is likely to take a length of time to respond to the request that is comparable to the Maximum Age parameter of the connnection pool.

18.14 Monitoring the Connection Manager

The Application Server Manager provides a monitor for the connection manager — it is named "DB Pool Connections" in the monitor list in the Application Server Manager. See Using the Application Server Manager for information on how to start the Application Server Manager and on how to display the connection manager monitor. The connection manager monitor online help gives full details on what information the monitor provides. You can use the information to see how connection pools are performing and to suggest possible changes in the connection pool parameters. You can monitor a pool after you change the parameters in order to see the change in pool behavior and to assist you in further tuning of the pool.

You can pick the specific pool you want to monitor from a selection list. The resulting monitor display consists of two parts:

- The top part lists each connection in the pool that you have selected.
- The bottom part lists summary information about the pool as a whole.

Information provided by the connection list (top part of the monitor) includes:

- Whether the connection is in use by a servlet.
- The servlet class that currently owns the connection (or the servlet class that last released the connection if it is free).
- The verify and last used timestamps for the connection.
- Additional information, some of which may depend on the type of data server.

Information provided by the pool summary (bottom part of the monitor) includes:

*** Pool Name:**

This is the unique name of a pool, used by the servlet programmer to access the pool and used within the monitor to identify a pool and the statistics associated with it.

*** Total connections:**

This is a cumulative total of only the successful requests forconnections made to the pool.

*** Requests:**

This is a cumulative total of both the successful and the unsuccessful requests for connections made to the pool.

*** Waiting:**

This is the number of connection requests currently waiting for a connection from the specified pool. When a servlet's waitRetry parameter is set to true, the servlet can wait for a short time for a connection if the pool does not have one immediately available. Requests waiting for a connection will fail if the connection is not made available within the time specified by the Connection Time Out parameter. See the Rejected statistic below for the number of requests that actually fail. If the servlets using this pool are important, you may want to increase the Maximum Connections parameter for the pool to reduce the chances that a connection request will have to wait.

*** Rejected:**

This is the number of connection requests that were refused a connection. It is the cumulative total of the Waiting requests that failed to get a connection, plus failed requests from servlets whose waitRetry parameter was set to false and thus failed right away when a connection was not available. Generally, you will want Rejected to be a small compared to Total connections, particularly if important servlets are using the pool. Look at increasing the Maximum Connections and the Connection Time Out parameters of the connection pool to keep Rejected a small percentage of Total connections.

*** Orphaned:**

This is the number of connections taken away from servlets that have died or otherwise become unresponsive, or taken away from servlets that may have been coded improperly. The connections are taken away from the servlets in the periodic reap process and are returned to the pool so that other servlets can use them. Something is probably wrong if the Orphaned statistic is other than zero, and you should look at making servlet coding changes. If the value is other than zero, it may mean that connections are not being used and yet the connections are not available to be used by a new request. This can happen if a servlet fails without explicitly releasing connections that it owns, or if the servlet performs normally but the programmer neglects to explicitly release the connection after sending the response back to the user — the servlet should probably should be changed to use the releaseIBMConnection() method in case of a servlet failure and at the the end of a successful response. The Orphaned statistic can also be other than zero if a servlet neglects to periodically verify with the connection manager that it still needs to hold a connection over an extended period of time (see the discussion earlier in this chapter on using the verifyIBMConnection() method).

*** Idled:**

This is the cumulative number of connections that the periodic reap process has removed from the pool (and disconnected from the data server). The connections may be removed after they remain idle (unassigned to any servlets) beyond a certain time. If the Inactive statistic is high compared to Total connections, it may mean that there is a lot of connect/disconnect overhead compared to the number of requests actually serviced. This in turn might be due to excessive fluctuations in the number of user requests — connections are created to satisfy a temporary peak, and then discarded during a temporary lull. You might want to make the pool less sensitive to such fluctuations by increasing the Reap Time or Maximum Idle Time pool parameters.

Review the connection manager monitor online help for other statistics that may be of use in managing and tuning the connection pools and the servlets that use the pools.

18.15 File Access by Servlets

Although servlets are invoked from a browser, they are under the security policy in force for the web server under which they run. When file input and output code is added to ExampServlet.java from Lesson 5, FileIOServlet for this lesson executes without restriction under Java WebServerTM 1.1.1.

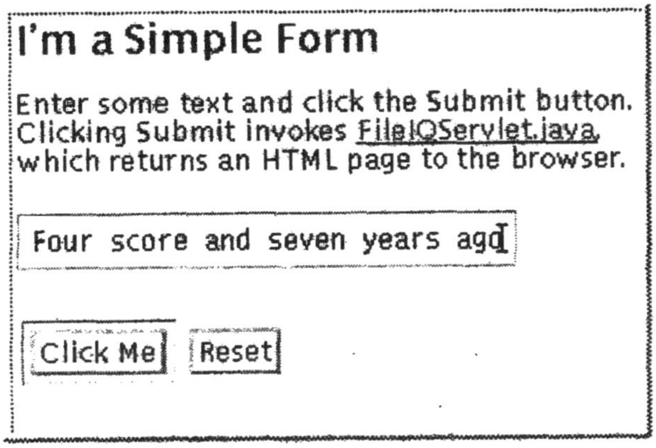

Fig. 18.8

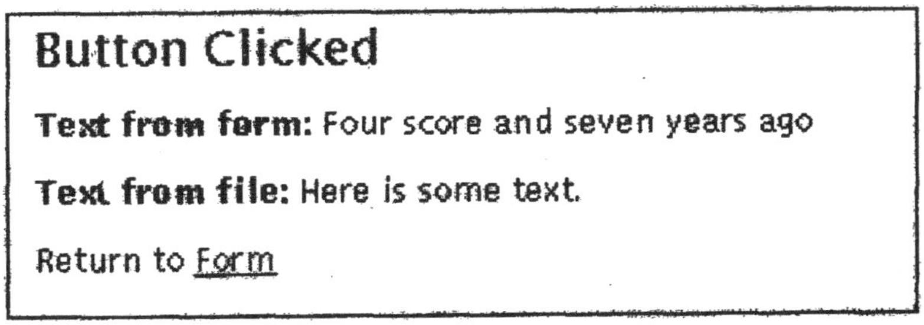

Fig. 18.9

```
import java.io.*;
import javax.servlet.*;
import javax.servlet.http.*;

public class FileIOServlet extends HttpServlet {

public void doPost(HttpServletRequest request,
HttpServletResponse response)
throws ServletException, IOException
{
response.setContentType("text/html");
PrintWriter out = response.getWriter();
out.println("<title>Example<title>" +
"<body bgcolor=FFFFFF>");

out.println("<h2>Button Clicked</h2>");
```

```
String DATA = request.getParameter("DATA");

if(DATA != null){
out.println("<STRONG>Text from
form:</STRONG>");
out.println(DATA);
} else {
out.println("No text entered.");
}
try{
//Code to write to file
String outputFileName=
System.getProperty("user.home",
File.separatorChar + "home" +
File.separatorChar + "monicap") +
File.separatorChar + "text.txt";
File outputFile = new File(outputFileName);
FileWriter fout = new FileWriter(outputFile);
fout.write(DATA);
fout.close();
//Code to read from file
String inputFileName =
System.getProperty("user.home",
File.separatorChar + "home" +
File.separatorChar + "monicap") +
File.separatorChar + "text.txt";
File inputFile = new File(inputFileName);
FileReader fin = new
FileReader(inputFile);
char c[] = new
char[(char)inputFile.length()];
int i;
i = fin.read(c);
String s = new String(c);
out.println("<P>
<STRONG>Text from file:</STRONG>");
out.println(s);
fin.close();
}catch(java.io.IOException e){
System.out.println("Cannot access text.txt");
}

out.println("<P>Return to
<A HREF="../simpleHTML.html">Form</A>");
out.close();
}
}
```

QUESTIONS AND ANSWERS FOR ADDITIONAL LEARNING

Q.1. *What's the JDBC 2.0 API?*

Ans. The JDBC 2.0 API is the latest update of the JDBC API. It contains many new features, including scrollable result sets and the new SQL:1999 (formerly SQL 3) data types. There are two parts to the JDBC 2.0 API:

- *JDBC 2.0 core API (the java.sql package), which is included in the JavaTM 2 SDK, Standard Edition*
- *JDBC 2.0 Optional Package API (the javax.sql package), which is available separately or as part of the Java 2 SDK, Enterprise Edition*

Q.2. *Does the JDBC-ODBC Bridge support the new features in the JDBC 2.0 API?*

Ans. No, the JDBC-ODBC Bridge that is included in the Java 2 Platform initial release does not support the new features in the JDBC 2.0 API. However, Sun and Merant are working to produce a new version of the Bridge that does support the new features. Note that we do not recommend using the Bridge except for experimental purposes or when you have no other driver available.

Q.3. *Can the JDBC-ODBC Bridge be used with applets?*

Ans. Use of the JDBC-ODBC bridge from an untrusted applet running in a browser, such as Netscape Navigator, isn't allowed. The JDBC-ODBC bridge doesn't allow untrusted code to call it for security reasons. This is good because it means that an untrusted applet that is downloaded by the browser can't circumvent Java security by calling ODBC. Remember that ODBC is native code, so once ODBC is called, the Java programming language can't guarantee that a security violation won't occur. On the other hand, Pure Java JDBC drivers work well with applets. They are fully downloadable and do not require any client-side configuration.

It is possible to use the JDBC-ODBC bridge with applets that will be run in appletviewer since appletviewer assumes that applets are trusted. It is also possible to use the JDBC-ODBC bridge with applets that are run in the HotJavaTM browser (available from Java Software), since HotJava provides an option to turn off applet security. In general, it is dangerous to turn applet security off, but it may be appropriate in certain controlled situations, such as for applets that will only be used in a secure intranet environment. Remember to exercise caution if you choose this option, and use an all-Java JDBC driver whenever possible to avoid security problems.

Q.4. *How do I start debugging problems related to the JDBC API?*

Ans. A good way to find out what JDBC calls are doing is to enable JDBC tracing. The JDBC trace contains a detailed listing of the activity occurring in the system that is related to JDBC operations.

If you use the DriverManager facility to establish your database connection, you use the DriverManager.setLogWriter method to enable tracing of JDBC operations. If you use a DataSource object to get a connection, you use the DataSource.setLogWriter method to enable tracing. (For pooled connections, you use the ConnectionPoolDataSource.setLogWriter method, and for connections that can participate in distributed transactions, you use the XADataSource.setLogWriter method.)

Q.5. *How can I use the JDBC API to access a desktop database like Microsoft Access over the network?*

Ans. Most desktop databases currently require a JDBC solution that uses ODBC underneath. This is because the vendors of these database products haven't implemented all-Java JDBC drivers.

The best approach is to use a commercial JDBC driver that supports ODBC and the database you want to use. See the JDBC drivers page for a list of available JDBC drivers.

The JDBC-ODBC bridge from Sun's Java Software does not provide network access to desktop databases by itself. The JDBC-ODBC bridge loads ODBC as a local DLL, and typical ODBC drivers for desktop databases like Access aren't networked. The JDBC-ODBC bridge can be used together with the RMI-JDBC bridge , however, to access a desktop database like Access over the net. This RMI-JDBC-ODBC solution is free.

Q.6. Does the JDK include the JDBC API and the JDBC-ODBC Bridge?

Ans. Yes, the JDK 1.1 and the Java 2 SDK, Standard Edition (formerly known as the JDK 1.2), contain both the JDBC API and the JDBC-ODBC Bridge. The Java 2 SDK, Standard Edition, contains the JDBC 2.0 core API, which is the latest version. It does not include the JDBC 2.0 Optional Package, which is part of the Java 2 SDK, Enterprise Edition, or which you can download separately.

Note that the version of the JDBC API and the JDBC-ODBC Bridge provided for separate download on the JDBC download page are only for use with the JDK 1.0.2.

Q.7. Are there any ODBC drivers that do not work with the JDBC-ODBC Bridge?

Ans. Most ODBC 2.0 drivers should work with the Bridge. Since there is some variation in functionality between ODBC drivers, the functionality of the bridge may be affected. The bridge works with popular PC databases, such as Microsoft Access and FoxPro.

Q.8. Does the JDBC-ODBC Bridge work with Microsoft J++?

Ans. No, J++ does not support the JDBC-ODBC bridge since it doesn't implement the Java Native Interface (JNI). Any all-Java JDBC driver should work with J++, however.

Q.9. Why do the java.sql and java.math packages fail to download java. packages? Is there a workaround?*

Ans. For security reasons, browsers will not download java.* packages. In order to use the JDBC API with browsers that have not been upgraded to JDK1.1 or beyond, we recommend that the java.sql and java.math packages be renamed jdbc.sql and jdbc.math. Most vendors supplying JDBC technology-enabled drivers that are written purely in the Java programming language already provide versions of these renamed packages. When JDK 1.1 support has been added to your browser, you should convert your applets back to the java.* package names.

Q.10. Can the JDBC API be added to JDK 1.0.2?

Ans. Yes. Download the JDBC 1.22 API from the JDBC download page and follow the installation instructions in the release notes. If you are using any version of the JDK from 1.1 on, the JDBC API is already included, and you should not download the JDBC 1.22 API.

Q.11. How do I retrieve a whole row of data at once, instead of calling an individual ResultSet.getXXX method for each column?

Ans. The ResultSet.getXXX methods are the only way to retrieve data from a ResultSet object, which means that you have to make a method call for each column of a row. It is unlikely that this is the cause of a performance problem, however, because it is difficult to see how a column could be fetched without at least the cost of a function call in any scenario. We welcome input from developers on this issue.

Q.12. Are all the required JDBC drivers to establish connectivity to user's database part of the JDK?

Ans. No. There aren't any JDBC technology-enabled drivers bundled with the JDK 1.1.x or Java 2 Platform releases other than the JDBC-ODBC Bridge. So, developers need to get a driver and install it before they can connect to a database. We are considering bundling JDBC technology- enabled drivers in the future.

Q.13 Is the JDBC-ODBC Bridge multi-threaded?

Ans. No. The JDBC-ODBC Bridge does not support concurrent access from different threads. The JDBC-ODBC Bridge uses synchronized methods to serialize all of the calls that it makes to ODBC. Multi-threaded Java programs may use the Bridge, but they won't get the advantages of multi-threading. In addition, deadlocks can occur between locks held in the database and the semaphore used by the Bridge. We are thinking about removing the synchronized methods in the future. They were added originally to make things simple for folks writing Java programs that use a single-threaded ODBC driver.